COLOR PLUS DESIGN

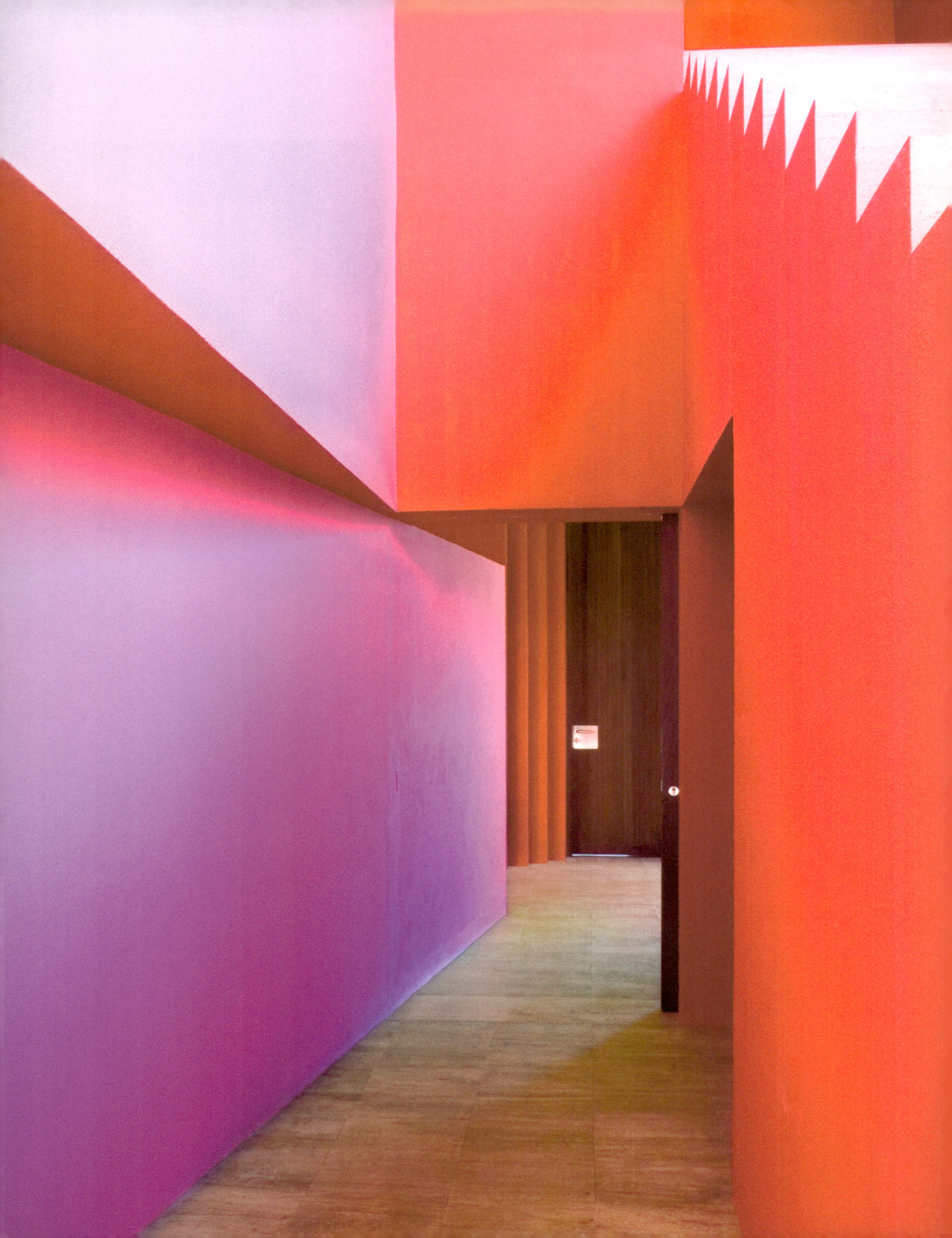

COLOR PLUS DESIGN

Transforming Interior Space

Third Edition

RON REED

MS, RID, NCIDQ Certified, IIDA, IDEC

FAIRCHILD BOOKS

NEW YORK • LONDON • OXFORD • NEW DELHI • SYDNEY

FAIRCHILD BOOKS
Bloomsbury Publishing Inc
1385 Broadway, New York, NY 10018, USA
50 Bedford Square, London, WC1B 3DP, UK
29 Earlsfort Terrace, Dublin 2, Ireland

BLOOMSBURY, FAIRCHILD BOOKS and the Fairchild Books
logo are trademarks of Bloomsbury Publishing Plc

First edition published 2010
Second edition published 2017
This edition published 2021
Reprinted 2022, 2024 (twice)

For legal purposes the Acknowledgments on p. xiii constitute
an extension of this copyright page.

Cover design: Eleanor Rose
Cover image: Rafael Perez Cuellar / EyeEm / Getty images

Library of Congress Cataloging-in-Publication Data
Names: Reed, Ron, author.
Title: Color plus design : transforming interior space / Ron Reed, MS, RID, IIDA.
Other titles: Color + design
Description: Third edition. | New York : Fairchild Books, 2021. | Includes
bibliographical references and index.
Identifiers: LCCN 2020025207 | ISBN 9781501362729 (paperback) | ISBN
9781501362682 (pdf)
Subjects: LCSH: Color in interior decoration.
Classification: LCC NK2115.5.C6 R44 2021 | DDC 701/.85--dc23
LC record available at https://lccn.loc.gov/2020025207

ISBN: 978-1-5013-6272-9

Typeset by Lachina Creative, Inc
Printed and bound in Great Britain

CONTENTS

Extended Table of Contents **vii**
Preface **x**
Acknowledgments **xiii**
Introduction **xiv**

PART I COLOR FUNDAMENTALS **1**

1 color + culture **3**
2 color + theory **25**
3 color association + perception **49**
4 color + health **73**

PART II COLOR AND DESIGN THEORY **91**

5 color + balance **93**
6 color + rhythm **109**
7 color + emphasis **125**
8 color + proportion + scale **139**
9 color + unity + harmony **157**
10 color + variety + design elements **173**

Afterword **191**
Appendix: Color Theory History, adapted from Connie B. D'Imperio **193**
Glossary **198**
Bibliography **202**
Credits **207**
Index **210**

EXTENDED CONTENTS

Preface x
Acknowledgments xiii
Introduction xiv

PART I
COLOR FUNDAMENTALS 1

1 color + culture 3

Native America 4
Mexico 7
Italy 10
Pakistan 12
Morocco 13
South Africa 15
Japan 17
Thailand 20
Becoming Culturally Literate 21
Review Questions 23
Vocabulary 23
Exercises 23

2 color + theory 25

What Is Color Theory? 26
Let There Be Light 26
Properties of Light 29
- Additive Color 31
- Subtractive Color 31
- The Many Faces of Color 32
- Effects of Natural and Artificial Light on Color Perception 36
- Light Reflectance 37

Color Systems 37
- Isaac Newton 37
- Albert H. Munsell 39
- Josef Albers 39
- Johannes Itten 40
- Faber Birren 41
- Natural Color System® (NCS®) 41
- Pantone® 42
- Color-Aid® 42
- Digital Color Media 42

Color Language 43
Review Questions 47
Vocabulary 47
Exercises 47

3 color association + perception 49

Color Design Process 50
Color Associations and Perceptions 51
Color Responses 52
Color Myths and Biases 53
Color and Space 56
Color Contrasts and Other Phenomena 61
Bezold Effect 62
Color Perception Tips and Techniques 63
The Influence of Color 63
Color History 63
Color Trends and Forecasting 66
Color Consumerism 68
Review Questions 69
Vocabulary 69
Exercises 69

4 color + health 73

Color and Health and Healing 74
Mental Health and Well-Being 74
Anxiety and Depression 77
Attention Deficit Hyperactivity Disorder (ADHD) 80
Autism Spectrum Disorder (ASD) 80
International WELL Building Institute (IWBI) 81
Color and Light Therapy 82
Seasonal Affective Disorder (SAD) 82
Color and Vision 82
Color Blindness 83
Color for Special Populations 85
Color for Aging 85
The Aging Eye 85
Color Guidelines for Older Adults 85
Color and Design for Access 86
ADA—Americans with Disabilities Act 87
Universal Design 87
Summary 88
Review Questions 89
Vocabulary 89
Exercises 89

PART II COLOR AND DESIGN THEORY 91

5 color + balance 93

What Is Balance? 94
What Is Color Balance? 96
Types of Color Balance 96
Value Contrast (Light/Dark) 96
Hue Balance (Complements) 98
Intensity Contrast (Bright/Dull) 99
Size of Color Area (Large/Small) 100
Location of a Color Palette within the 3D Environment 101
Illusion of Vertical and Horizontal Space 101
Chroma/Value Factor 104
Single-Color Overload 104
Multiple-Color Overload 105
Review Questions 107
Vocabulary 107
Exercises 107

6 color + rhythm 109

Color and Music 111
Nature and Rhythm 112
Types of Rhythm 115
Repetition 116
Alternation 117
Progression 119
Continuation or Transition 120
Radiation 121
Color and Line as Rhythm 121
Final Thoughts on Rhythm and Hue 122
Review Questions 123
Vocabulary 123
Exercises 123

7 color + emphasis 125

Emphasis with Contrast 126
- Color Emphasis through Location and Isolation 127
- Contrast of Hue and Value 129
- Contrast of Design Feature (Shape and Form) 131
- Contrast of Texture 131
- Emphasis with Color Dominance (Focal Point) 132
- Contrast of Anomaly 134
- Color Contrast for Safety and Welfare 134

Design Tips 135
Review Questions 136
Vocabulary 137
Exercises 137

8 color + proportion + scale 139

Color and Proportion 140
Color and Scale 145
- Practical Applications with Color and Perception of Scale 145

Additional Methods for Establishing Proportional Relationships 146
- The Golden Section 149
- Fibonacci Sequence 150
- Le Modulor 151
- Nature's Proportions 152

Review Questions 155
Vocabulary 155
Exercises 155

9 color + unity + harmony 157

Six Elements of Color Harmony 158
- Harmonies of Analogy 159
- Harmonies of Contrast 159

The Seven Color Harmonies 159
- Monochromatic 160
- Complementary 161
- Complementary neutralization 162
- Split Complementary and Double Complementary 163
- Analogous 163
- Triadic and Tetradic 164
- Multi-hue 165
- Achromatic 166
- Color, Space, Harmony 168

Review Questions 170
Vocabulary 171
Exercises 171

10 color + variety + design elements 173

Variety and Interest 175
Color and the Design Elements 179
- Color and Line 179
- Color and Shape 181
- Color and Form 182
- Color and Pattern and Texture 184
- Color and Time 189

Review Questions 190
Vocabulary 190
Exercises 190

Afterword 191
Appendix: Color Theory History, adapted from Connie B. D'Imperio 193
Glossary 198
Bibliography 202
Credits 207
Index 210

PREFACE

The third edition of *color + design* has added a new focus and expansion of color concepts with updated content to provide design students, design professionals, and color enthusiasts with a firm foundation from which to build their skills in color planning. The addition of a new chapter on color and health provides an expanded emphasis on how color may influence people, space, and place in our built environment. Illustrations in the third edition have been added and revised, figures have been expanded and updated, and additional before-and-after color manipulations of interior spaces have been included.

This book is about color—not color science or color art, but rather a design process for using color confidently: a visual training tool for seeing the spatial transformations that occur with successful and not-so-successful color applications. The book focuses specifically on the visual aspect of the process by which color is realized in an interior, and it is organized to present color theory side by side with the principles of design.

The information presented will assist the reader with photos of projects that illustrate how a space takes on different spatial characteristics through color manipulation. Each example will show alternative color solutions, with a picture illustrating less successful uses of color. Each chapter will provide a series of study problems to be used in the instruction of color. Each study problem will include the study purpose, the design process, the intended outcomes, and the supplies needed for execution where applicable. The third edition provides learning objectives at the beginning of each chapter and a list of review questions and color vocabulary at the conclusion of each chapter.

Organization of the Text

In Chapter 1 on color and culture, we peer into eight cultures across the globe and compare the differences in color meanings, symbolism, and social customs that shape each culture's perceptions of colors. This chapter begins our journey on color and design to generate a deeper appreciation of our differences and establishes a global context for studying color before progressing to the next chapter in the book.

Chapter 2 is an introduction to basic color theory and systems for color management commonly used within the design industry. Color systems and properties of light and color are discussed. It is very difficult to systemize or create a "magic formula" for using color. The complexity of color has been studied by many theorists. This chapter presents the works of Newton, Munsell, Albers, Itten, and Birren. In the third edition, information on the National Color System® and Pantone® have been expanded

Chapter 3 examines the color associations and perceptions that shape the way we interact with color in the built environment. Imagine for one moment a world without color, a black and white land void of blue skies and green grasslands. As a communication tool, color is imperative to our daily activities. We use color to convey messages to each other, whether it is a red light that signals a driver to stop, a yellow and black sign that warns of potential danger, or a bouquet of red roses that expresses our love. Color has the power to change our feelings, to express our personalities, to convey excitement, a sense of professionalism, or melancholy. In this chapter we will also explore color vision, physiological processes of how we see color, and impairments to color vision. A trip through history will unveil how color trends are formed and the forecasting of colors. Color is an experience; we are greatly affected by the color choices of others, and color is a personal choice that reflects who we are, information about ourselves that we share with those with whom we come into contact.

In the third edition, the information on Programming has moved to this chapter to introduce the concepts behind color planning sooner in the text. Sections on color history, trends, and consumerism have also been revised and updated.

New to this edition, Chapter 4 discusses the relationship and influence of color to health, healing, and well-being. Information on Color and Light Therapy, previously in Chapter 3, has been relocated to this chapter and expanded to include seasonal affective disorder. Previously in Chapter 3, sections on color and vision, color blindness, and color for special populations, are expanded and are now supporting this new chapter and focus on health.

Color and health discusses the effects of environmental color on anxiety and depression, attention deficit hyperactivity disorder, and autism spectrum disorder. The International WELL Building Institute and standards that address color and health are presented in this chapter. Lastly, the section on color and design for access discusses the importance of color use for special populations, including the Americans with Disabilities Act and universal design.

Chapter 5 introduces the first principle of design: balance. Balance typically refers to a balance of proportion, but color balance also affects the interior. Chapter 4 discusses the four types of balance achieved with color: value contrast (light/dark), hue balance (complements), intensity contrast (bright/dull), and size of color area (large/small). This chapter also presents methods to visually manipulate perceived spatial size by balancing the volume of the interior with color.

Chapter 6 deals with color and rhythm. Five types of rhythm are discussed in this chapter: repetition, alternation, progression, continuation, and radiation. This chapter examines natural forms as inspiration for natural color rhythm.

Chapter 7 examines color and emphasis and how contrast is critical for effective points of visual interest. Color is one of the first elements that attracts attention and begins the initial experience of a place. This chapter presents contrast of hue and value, contrast of design feature (shape and form), contrast of texture, emphasis with color dominance, and contrast of anomaly to generate points of interest within the interior.

Chapter 8 discusses color proportion and scale by introducing practical applications of color to change perception of spatial size. This chapter is a preface to Chapter 9, which is concerned with establishing harmonious spatial proportions with color.

Chapter 9 presents the seven color harmonies commonly used for interior color palettes: monochromatic, complementary, split complementary and double complementary, analogous, triadic and tetradic, multi-hue, and achromatic. Illustrations of each harmony will be presented and discussed, along with interior examples to reinforce the harmonic color concepts. The third edition includes the addition of information on complementary neutralization to expand the understanding of how neutral color can be formed with complementary hues.

Chapter 10 examines color and variety as key principles to stimulate our visual experiences. This chapter discusses color and the elements of line, shape, form, pattern, texture, and time to add interest and excitement that can enhance and modify the interior space. For the third edition, texture has been expanded to discuss surface quality and characteristics which influence color perception and the appearance of designed spaces.

This research, ever important to understanding the presence of color in our lives, yields practical methods for working quickly and efficiently. Color should be studied holistically, as a part of the larger contexts of design, and within the totality of design theory. Exploring the various faces of color as they relate to the principles of design, balance, rhythm, emphasis, proportion and scale, harmony and unity, and variety provides an enriched way of learning about color and design.

Instructor and Student Resources

color + design STUDIO

The book is accompanied by an online multimedia resource, color + design STUDIO. The online STUDIO is specially developed to complement this book with rich media ancillaries that students can adapt to their visual learning styles to better master concepts and improve grades. Within the STUDIO, students will be able to:

- Study smarter with self-quizzes featuring scored results and personalized study tips
- Review concepts with flashcards of essential vocabulary
- Download interactive exercises and their solutions, to test your knowledge of color

STUDIO access cards are offered free with new book purchases and also sold separately through Bloomsbury Fashion Central (www.BloomsburyFashionCentral.com).

Instructor Resources

- The Instructor's Guide provides suggestions for planning the course and using the text in the classroom, supplemental assignments, grading rubrics, and a CIDA Professional Standards Matrix mapped to the chapters in the book. Black and white versions of the interior room illustrations used throughout the book are also available for experimenting with color manipulations through either hand drawing or computer rendering to demonstrate comprehension of chapter topics.
- The Test Bank includes sample test questions for each chapter
- PowerPoint® presentations include images from the book and provide a framework for lecture and discussion

Instructor's Resources may be accessed through Bloomsbury Fashion Central (www.BloomsburyFashionCentral.com).

ACKNOWLEDGMENTS

I am truly blessed and grateful for the opportunity to share with you the third edition of *Color Plus Design*. This would have never happened without the many people whose professional guidance and contributing ideas shaped an idea into the soul of this book and continue to inspire my joy of color and design. I am so grateful to the authors before me whose writings on color have provided me with a wealth of knowledge, and I hope this inspires future authors to continue to add to the literature on color.

I thank the many students whose work is contained within. And to the students beginning to learn about color, I hope the pages unfold and enlighten you all to the wonder color can bring to your design projects and careers. I also wish to acknowledge with pride my former students whose careers have now flourished over the decades since I began teaching. While our time in the classroom is a distant memory, you continue to inspire me in your career successes. I am hopeful this work carries forward to inspire you in your design practice.

I am so thankful and filled with gratitude to the publishing team at Fairchild Books and Bloomsbury who have supported and guided the third edition: To Academic Publishing Director Kevin Ohe, thank you for this opportunity and for continuing to invest in my work. The good fortune to produce a third edition with Bloomsbury is humbling. Emily Samulksi, acquisition editor, thank you for your guidance, communication, and encouragement of the project. I appreciate your kind spirit and have enjoyed working with you and developing the vision for the third edition. To Edie Weinberg, art development editor, you are an absolute delight to work with. I cannot express more my sincere appreciation for your patience, talent, and support in the art revision of this edition. I would especially like to thank Development Editor Corey Kahn. I am fortunate that we have worked on several projects now, and it's a pleasure to team with you again. Thank you for your expertise, advice, proofreading, and most of all patience on deadlines to make the third edition of *Color Plus Design* the best edition to date.

I would also like to thank the many artists, interior and graphic designers, and architects who contributed their work, and for their generosity in support of the project. Without the professional experience and support of many, this work would not have been possible. To the reviewers of the third edition—Jonathan Barnes, St. Petersburg College; Yikui Gu, College of Southern Maryland; Melissa Halvorson, Marist College; Tammy Powell, Cape Fear Community College; Sandra Reicis, Villa Maria College—your suggestions and recommendations for the revision were very helpful; thank you.

And finally, I would thank to thank my friends and family who have supported me through this journey.

The publisher wishes to gratefully acknowledge and thank the editorial team involved in the publication of this book:

Acquisitions Editor: Emily Samulski
Senior Development Editor: Corey Kahn
Editorial Assistant: Jenna Lefkowitz
Art Development Editor: Edie Weinberg
In-House Designer: Lachina Creative, Inc.
Production Manager: Ken Bruce
Project Manager: Molly Montanaro

INTRODUCTION

At the root of design are the theoretical principles and elements of design that describe the visual information about space and objects. The principles and elements, like wood and nails, help to create a building. And a building, like color, needs a foundation to keep it from falling down. Just as interior space is influenced by the building, color is influenced by its surroundings. A designer cannot use color without taking other variables into consideration that can significantly impact its use. Interior spaces are created with all or part of the principles and elements of design and variations of their applications. It is the use of these theoretical approaches that informs your design practice and color planning. The eight principles of design are balance (radial, symmetrical, asymmetrical), rhythm (repetition of size, shape, or color), emphasis, proportion, scale, unity, harmony, and variety. The eight elements of design are color, space, line, shape, form, pattern, texture, and time (see Table I.1). For the purpose of this book, the elements of design are considered aspects within the design principle *variety* and therefore will be discussed in the final chapter. The process whereby designers decide how color is to be used in conjunction with the principles of design, discussed in this book as the *color design process*, is intended to make your use of color more successful. Color and light help users connect to the space more than any other design element. This connection should satisfy the personal needs, both physical and psychological, of the user of the interior space without compromising the integrity of the design. The process of designing follows a set of guiding principles and theories for evaluating the success of new concepts and ideas. By following the color design process, you will discover your own palettes to explore and use. Absent the strong pull of color trends, any imaginable color can be used without a preconceived notion of what is and is not appropriate. The examples presented in this book are less focused on trends, or quick fads, in color as these are short-lived and fade over time. Rather, the focus is on methods, techniques, and concepts of color theory that are timeless.

Beginning design students are introduced to a core of design values referred to as the elements and principles. These two categories hold the basic concepts for communication within all design professions and are the tools for creativity and execution of design ideas. Color in conjunction with the design principles can be used to help organize interior space. The principles of design are the core of any successful design project. Whether you're a novice designer or an experienced professional, understanding how to use the principles of design well is critical. These are our tools for achieving any successful design solution, for producing an aesthetic effect, or for protecting the health, safety, and welfare of our clients.

Pentti Routio (2004) identifies specific goals that all designs should achieve: usability—utility and function; beauty—aesthetics (principles and elements of design); meaning—messages sent; ecology—impact on the environment; economy—value and price; and safety. Our relationship to art, architecture, and interior design is a personal one based on the way we perceive our surroundings and our natural environment via our senses.

Beginning design students must understand how to use the elements of design (color, in this case) in coordination with the principles of design for the outcomes to be effective, appropriate, and creative.

Just as we use color to code and organize our office files, color can be applied with the principle of balance to bring order to our surroundings and communicate the identity of the space. Color provides an additional stimulus to help us decipher and decode the overwhelming amount of visual information we encounter on a daily basis. Too much color can oversaturate our visual field, and too much of the same color can create monotony, too much blending, and the loss of important visual cues within our environment.

The principles and elements of design have often been referred to by designers as the basic theory and concepts for describing and creating interior space. Their importance should be considered as integral to understanding the complexity of color. Funneling design properties with color facilitates an approachable and accessible method for working through complexity to confidently use color in personal and professional applications.

The color design process presented in this book refers to the way designers use the principles of design to solve color design problems. Combining design principles with smart use of color is necessary to realize a final design that has quality, long-lasting functional value, and aesthetic appeal. The principles should not be regarded as definite rules in the design process, but rather as tools that can help the process.

Beginning design students are anxious to work with color and choose color for fabrics, finishes, and building materials. Interior design is a visual profession. Students of any design discipline are visual learners. The more visual aids available, the more we increase a student's awareness of the process and application of color. Applying color in any space is part science, part intuition, and part luck. We have learned through trial and error that choosing and applying color is more complicated than it seems. Color must be carefully understood to ensure it is used well; however, many new designers learn on the job, making critical mistakes in order to learn what works and what doesn't work. Color is crucial to the overall quality of the finished design.

Now, where to begin? A common dilemma experienced when searching through trade publications, books, and magazines is the wide range of interior photos available. In many respects, these photos may not illustrate a significant use of color, relying instead on schemes composed of neutral palettes occasionally accented with color. This void leaves a lack of access to good visuals in teaching color palettes for interior design. Second, what if we could go back in time and change these interiors, to "reassign" the color palette? In addition to positive changes in color within a space, demonstrations of poor color usage could help students see both successful and unsuccessful approaches to using color. This is an invaluable visual tool for helping design students see how to avoid making color errors. Design students are rarely able to see the full color transformations that can take place by including all design elements (finishes/materials) that compose our living environments.

A designer might find balance and rhythm to be the key factors in the creation of a room and proportion and emphasis to be less prominent in the final design. Depending on your goal, these tools can be used at your discretion. The point to be made is they cannot be ignored altogether. They are essential to the arguable terms "good design" or "bad design." Design is a personal experience for each individual. What one person finds ugly, a second person may find beautiful. Elevating design beyond everyday experiences can be achieved by understanding the principles of design well and utilizing them creatively and logically to execute a vision, concept, or idea.

Anyone wishing to study color must work independently to discover the nuances of color. The skill of an interior designer is what clients rely on when they choose colors that support a healthy, stimulating, and comfortable environment to live or work in. However, the majority of people have either never worked with a designer or have attempted to make color choices for themselves without the aid of a designer or color consultant. More and more, paint companies are making it easier for the general public to learn about color by providing educational tools and interactive software available on the Web and through apps, preselected color palettes within their lines, and publications on color basics. Intuition and a sense of "good taste" tend to drive more color design decisions than a prescriptive, scientific method of choosing the right palette. In this text, we seek new ways to simplify the color evaluation process and make it more enjoyable.

TABLE I.1 PRINCIPLES AND ELEMENTS OF DESIGN

Principle	Definition
Balance	Refers to the relationship of colored elements as they occupy an applied axis within a space perceived to be equal in visual weight. **Symmetrical** (Formal balance) Elements on either side of an implied axis are equally balanced and of the same shape and form (mirror image). **Asymmetrical** (Informal balance) Elements on either side of an implied axis are equal weight but vary in shape and size. Often more visually interesting and can be achieved through value and/or hue contrast. **Radial** Balance achieved by the equal rotation of design elements around a central axis.
Rhythm	Movement or path created by related visual elements, resulting in a constant pattern. Repetition A continued, even sequence of the same design element within a space. Alternation The alternation between two different design elements by pattern, shape, or color where the eye follows in a rhythmic motion. Progression The progression of a design element from large to small or small to large.
Emphasis	Also called focal point, indicates attention drawn between colored elements within a space through one of the seven types of color contrast.
Proportion	Refers to the relationship of the individual parts of a composition to the whole.
Scale	Represents the actual size of an object relative to its surroundings.
Unity	Opposite of variety, focuses on the whole rather than the individual parts within a composition or space, using colors that create a balanced relationship.
Harmony	The agreement or compatibility of colored components in a composition or space.
Variety	The continual change and variation of design elements (shape, size, color, pattern, and texture) through subtle changes in contrast.
Element	**Definition**
Color	The natural quality of an object that when reflected by light produces the visible spectrum.
Space	The combination of the elements and principles of design used to create a three-dimensional inhabitable environment.
Line	The connection between two points (vertical, horizontal, curved, diagonal, or free form).
Shape	Two-dimensional shapes, including square, rectangle, circle, and triangle.
Form	Three-dimensional volume and mass of shapes.
Pattern	The repetition and arrangement of shapes and forms.
Texture	The perceptual or physical qualities of material that result in a visual and/or tactile experience such as rough or smooth.
Time	The physical qualities of color and materials that change in appearance over the course of time.

Predetermined color palettes available in retail stores are necessary in some cases for those wary of beginning color selection on their own. For the consumer, paint manufacturers have done an excellent job of eliminating the sometimes torturous task of deciding what color to use and then choosing two to three other hues that work well with the color. However, predetermined color palettes do not aid the novice designer in knowing *where* the color placement and distribution should be within the space and to what interior elements the colors should be assigned. Without some knowledge of where and how to apply these, color becomes almost impossible to grasp. It is not my intent to prescribe a perfect set of color palettes—color is a personal choice based on your own preferences and perceptions. In Chapter 9 we discuss the common color harmonies and ways to select color palettes that are harmonious. With these skills, you will be able to work virtually any color combination into your projects.

Personal choice should be at the forefront of color decisions, guided by research to make the choices rational. This book is but one journey you'll make in studying color. It will provide invaluable illustrations for learning and understanding color and design.

With effective color usage, a designer can manipulate our experiences in the built environment. Knowing this tremendous power and developing the skill to use it give the designer the ability to orchestrate the reactions of the inhabitants of an interior space. This book presents a different approach to thinking about color and design that will enable you to become more informed and successful in your use of color.

Color is a boundless subject that is studied across many disciplines including art, architecture, interior design, art history, and graphic design to name a few. There are many great resources and writings available to extend your understanding of color theory. The intent of this book is to focus on color specific to the built environment. It is the author's recommendation that you will continue to read and explore color amid other disciplines to broaden your scope and understanding of how to use color in your own work. And while the interior environment is composed with many colored elements, the broader intent of the book is an overview and survey of color theory and design to permit the reader to form their own personal understanding and exploration of color in their professional pursuits.

Color shapes behavior, behavior shapes culture, and culture shapes design. Our world is constantly changing, technology is constantly changing, color is constantly changing, and approaches to design will forever evolve. Learning to apply color theory in your creative work is being unafraid to experiment—and being willing to fail in the process.

– Be Color Minded!

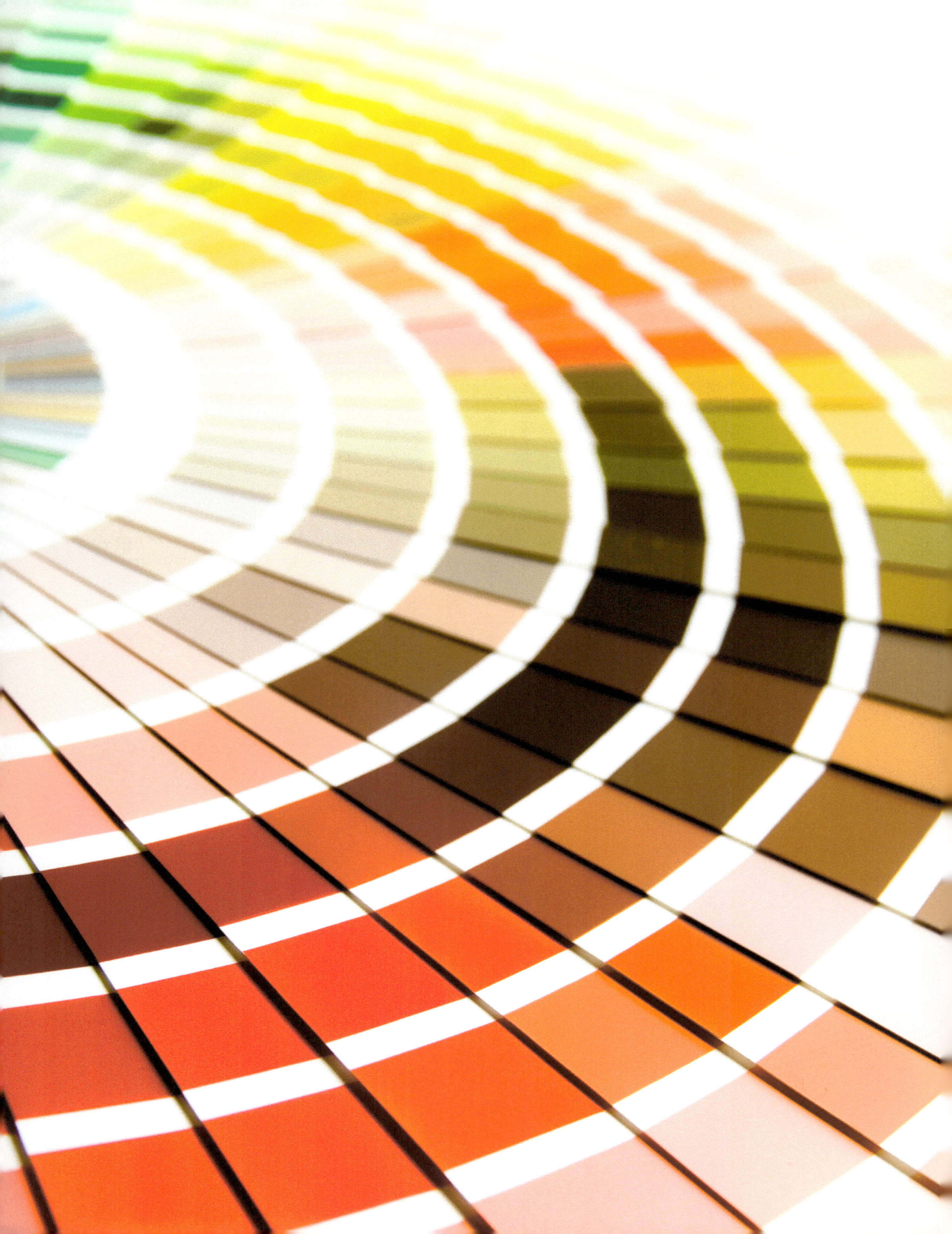

PART I

Color Fundamentals

Forming a basic knowledge of color and light establishes a foundation for applying color in the built environment. In Part I we will consider how our personal cultural traditions and differences shape our understanding, expression, and use of color. Our associations and meanings assigned to color are uniquely shaped by our personal experiences across the globe. Next, we will explore the basic science behind color and the theories that shape how we organize and use color. We'll also cover fundamental color terminology, how we see and perceive color, light, and the various color systems that aid in communicating color relationships and guide planning for interior design.

Exploring why certain individuals prefer a specific color over another, or association and perceptions of colors and response to those colors vary based on our learned biases and environmental influences. We'll explore these myths along with the color phenomena that alter people's color perception. Color psychology examines how color has the potential to influence color preferences including history, trends, and consumer behavior.

And lastly; we will explore how color can influences health and behavior. What is known about color for mood disorders that may aid a designer when planning spaces for a person known to have a mental, behavioral, or cognitive health condition?

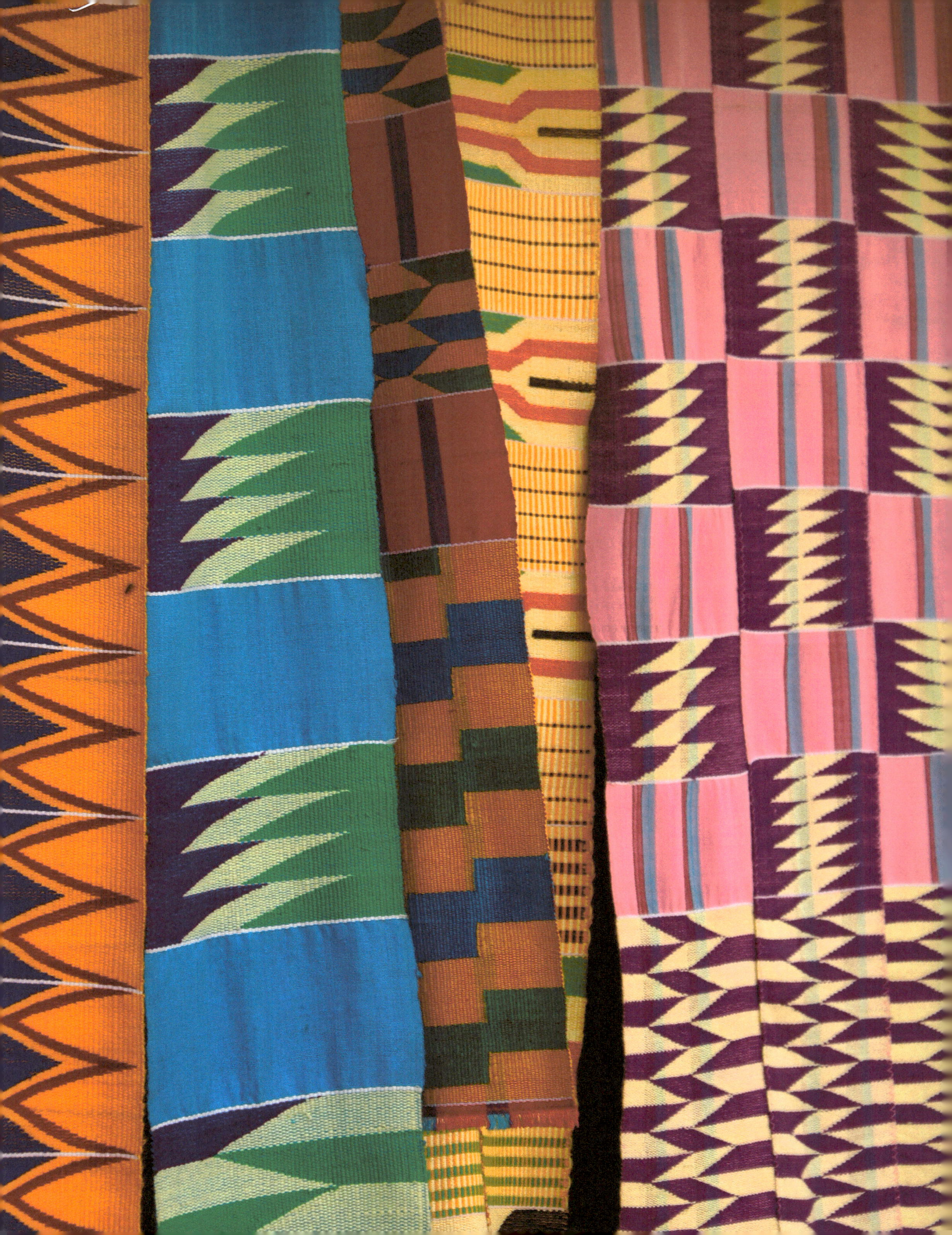

1

color + culture

Learning Outcomes

After studying this chapter, you will be able to:

- **Compare and contrast how color plays an important role in the traditions and history of cultures around the world.**
- **Describe the historical, cultural, and symbolic meanings of color.**
- **Discuss how religious, political, and social values shape differences in color symbolism and meaning within different cultures.**
- **Recognize cross-cultural color as an excellent inroad to exploring our unique differences in color meanings and symbolism.**
- **Execute color planning that respects our cultural differences.**

In the United States, color symbolism abounds: red for stop or hot, green for go or nature, yellow for caution or cowardice, white for purity and virginity, or white lie, blue for water and the skies above, brown for the richness of soil, black for death and mourning, and so on.

Appreciation and respect for cultural differences are important during the color design process. We cannot assume that for every client our own color meanings and symbolism reach across individual and cultural differences. The influences of Asia, Latin America, and the Middle East require us to understand differing interpretations of color among diverse cultures, and in doing so, we enrich our own lives and the lives of people we design for.

Many design firms are crossing oceans and contracting work with other countries, setting up satellite offices, and embarking in design that embraces cultural differences. It is easy to view color through a narrow lens, never once considering that color meaning and cultural traditions influence color, and therefore differences among individuals will vary and depart from those of Western traditions or our own personal associations. A cultural sensitivity should be taken into consideration during the planning of design projects, especially in public spaces where there are opportunities for various cultures to experience these spaces.

A bride in America is expected to dress in white as a symbol of purity, whereas this color represents death and mourning or respect in several Asian cultures. Are these meanings shared across a large population? Are they unique to a specific region or group within a particular country? Many factors, including geography, religion, tradition, and shifting political power, can contribute to a wide cultural difference in color meaning, preference, and symbolism. No one source is the authority on color diversity because it changes as each new generation embarks on making its own mark in the historical timeline. Wars, revolutions, disasters, and change in leadership can bring about a new era of color meanings. Social media, a person's age, and technological advancement that connect us more than ever are influencing our perceptions and meanings of color and culture. Whatever the future may hold, understanding the past is critical to understanding the future.

Variations exist among sources, and generalizations have been drawn to indicate the common color meanings among the cultures explored in this chapter. An infinite number of color meanings are possible, and aside from surveying the population of these cultures, no book of this size would scratch the surface of the many to be explored. Just as color is vast, so are the preferences and perceptions of the people in each nation. Whether color is influenced by fashion trends or politics, a study of color meanings can shed light on the ideological differences that exist in this world.

It is important to note that I have chosen to focus primarily on the positive associations, with the exceptions of those colors that represent death and mourning. I encourage you in your color research to seek the duality of meanings to avoid design solutions that may impart negative reactions or memories of tragic events to certain individuals. References to color meanings and symbolism of specific flags of countries are presented in this chapter as a source for exploring political and social differences one must consider. Individual responses to flags as political images do not necessarily reflect a collective mindset that represent everyone equally. Images of these flags, and many more, can be found at the following URL: https://www.countries-ofthe-world.com/flags-of-the-world.html. With so many wonderful countries and cultures to highlight, I've included those that represent a cross section of our globe. It is my hope that you will be inspired by the cultures presented to research others in your color studies.

Native America

Different tribes occupied different areas of what is now the United States, and according to the National Congress of American Indians, there are 562 federally recognized tribes. The largest of these tribes are the Navajo, Cherokee, and Sioux (U.S. Census, 2010). Native American beliefs are rooted in traditions that respect and hold sacred the land and every living thing on the planet. Color meanings illustrate how Native Americans honor nature through their rituals.

The **medicine wheel**, or sacred hoop, is a symbol used to represent health and healing. The wheel is traditionally a large monument of stones constructed on land (Laframboise & Sherbina, 2008). The most well-known wheel is the Bighorn Medicine Wheel in Wyoming (Figure 1.1). Over time, the wheel has taken on other forms,

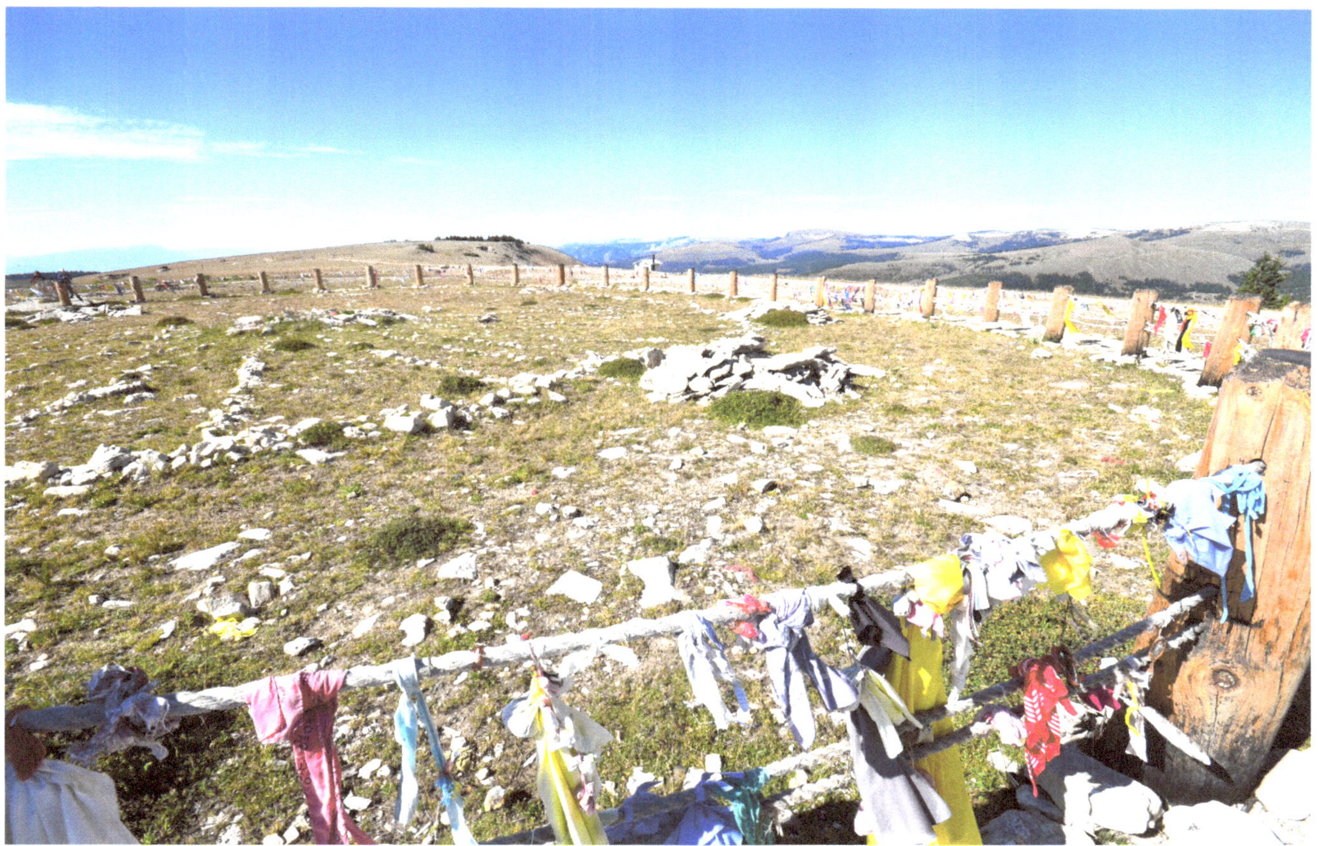

Figure 1.1 Medicine wheel in Wyoming. Located at nearly 10,000 feet, the wheel is a sacred stone circle with significant meanings in Native American culture.

including paintings and handmade symbols in Native American artwork and ritual crafts. The divisions of the medicine wheel are directed toward each of the cardinal points on the compass (Native American Designs and Colors, 2011). Each point was given a color—yellow, red, black, or white—that varied in its location around the wheel depending on the tribe (Figure 1.2). Other colors seen in the medicine wheel included blue, purple, and green. These sacred colors were used for costumes, rituals, and tribal meetings.

Color meanings and symbolism can vary between tribes. The cardinal points may represent stages of one's life, seasons of the year, nature, or spirit animals. For instance, the White Mountain Apache represent north with white, which means snow, south with green, east with yellow and the rising sun, and west with black or the setting sun. The Cherokee represent north with blue, meaning cold, defeat, or trouble; south with white, meaning warmth, peace, and happiness; east with red,

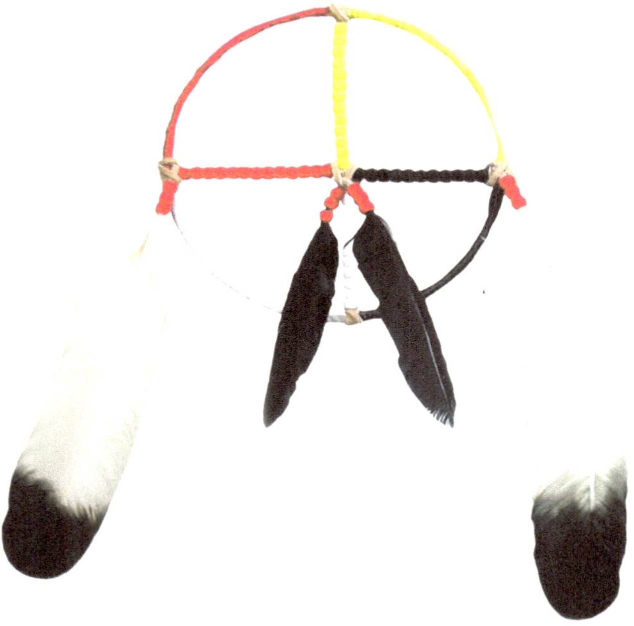

Figure 1.2 A hand-crafted Native American medicine wheel.

meaning fire, power, and blood; and west with black, meaning problems and death. Black among Native Americans is also seen as the color of balance (Krause, 2015).

During council meetings and storytelling, the **talking stick** or talking feather was held to indicate who could speak at one time (Talking Sticks, 2011). When the person speaking was finished, the talking stick was passed to the next person. The talking stick provided an opportunity for everyone to listen and to be heard. These sticks were elaborately decorated and adorned with beads, feathers, and leather (Figure 1.3). The types of wood, feathers, and colors all had individual meanings and importance in the rituals. The colors adorning the stick often represented the cardinal points or the natural elements: white for spirit and air, red for fire and life, yellow for knowledge, and black for clarity and focus. Other colors may have included green for earth; orange for kinship; and blue for prayer, wisdom, and water.

Intricate beadwork, pottery, clothing, and woven textiles were additional artifacts that expressed the individual tribal cultures. Ritual clothes, moccasins, and blankets were patterned with colorful beads and decorated with feathers and leather in a rainbow of hues that included blue, pink, white, red, yellow, green, and black (Figure 1.4). Clay pottery that was created for utilitarian purposes had little decoration, but later clay pots made for rituals were etched and painted with blacks, terra-cotta, and blues: colors made with vegetable dyes and ground minerals (Dockstader, 1961). The pots are valued for their detailed geometric shapes symbolizing the sun, rain, and wisdom and for their stylized animal designs.

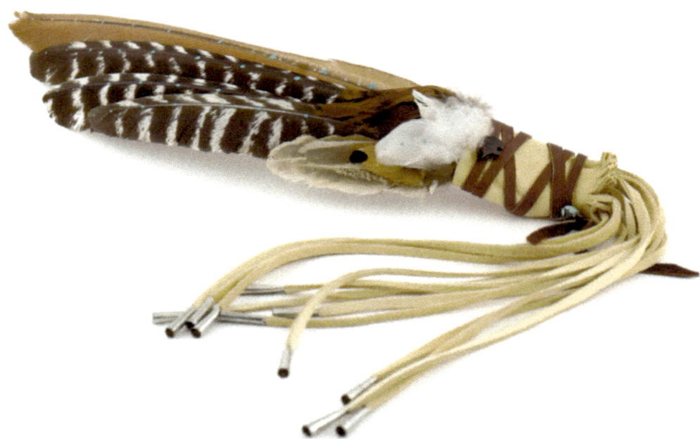

Figure 1.3 Native American talking feathers with turquoise decoration wrapped in leather with leather tassels and tin ends.

Whatever meanings these symbols have are known only to the potters and weavers. The recognizable diamonds and triangles in Navajo blankets have been known to represent the cardinal points and make use of red, black, and white colorations (Figure 1.5). Patterns in Navajo rugs also symbolize the mountains and luck.

The symbols in Native American ritual artifacts were also important for documenting and recording events. Dreamcatchers adorned with natural and found objects were designed to catch and hold on to the good things in life and release the negative through their open design. Totem poles were carved with animal spirits and guides as symbols connected to loved ones who had passed away and to record the history and events of a particular tribe (Native American Culture, n.d., para. 3). Natural red clays, black soot, copper, turquoise, and other natural pigments were painted onto these totems. Colors and symbols played a vital role in telling the story of a particular tribe or family.

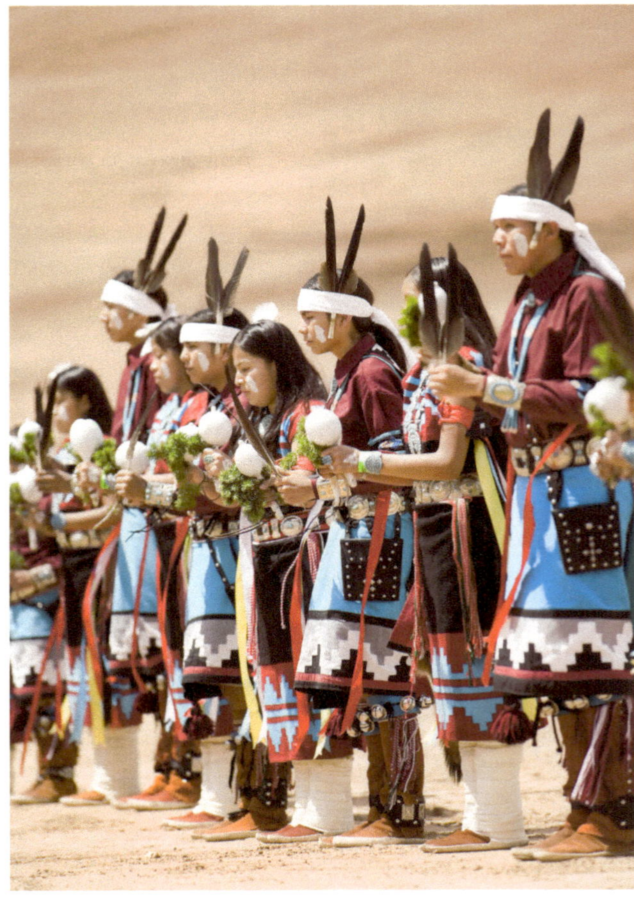

Figure 1.4 Men and women participate in a Navajo Indian Gourd Dance, Gallup, New Mexico.

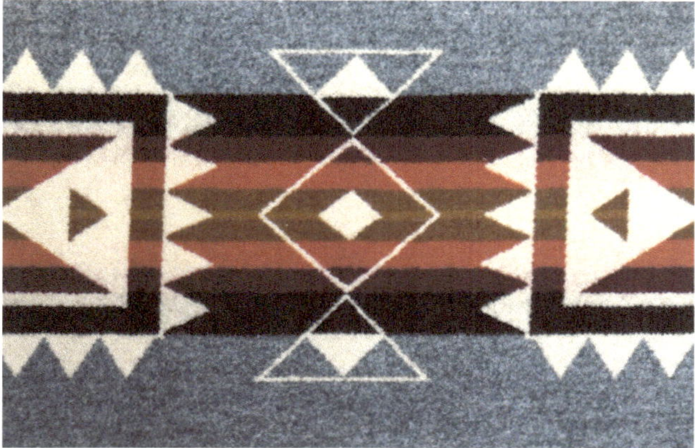

Figure 1.5 Grey, black and white Navajo blanket with traditional banded horizontal stripes incorporating a favored color, red, created from vegetable dyes.

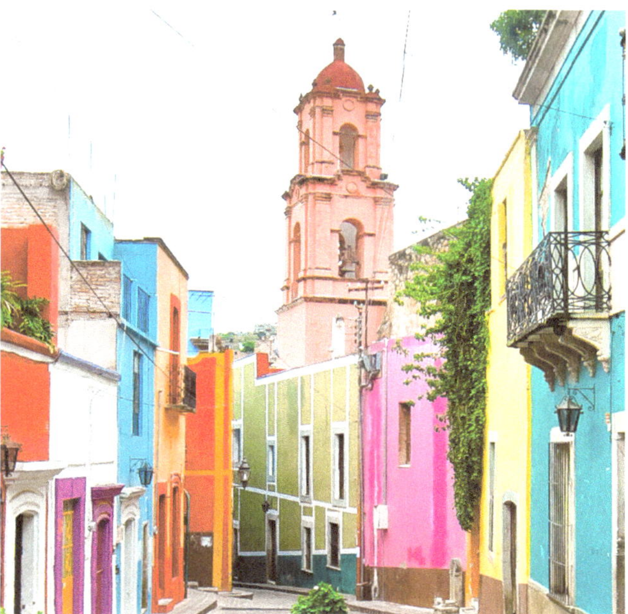

Figure 1.6 Colorful explosion of Latin color in the city center of Guanajuato.

Mexico

When you think of Latin America, a culture of vivid and bright colors comes to mind. A spectrum of color is common in Mexican architecture and interiors (Figure 1.6). Mexican color in architecture and design draws upon its Aztec heritage. Temples of ancient Mayan and Aztec cities used color to represent cardinal directions. Rooms facing east were decorated in gold, west in turquoise blue, south in white, and north in red. Spanish influence in Mexico brought about the use of natural materials to create colored dyes in rich reds, blues, and yellow. These included cochineal, indigo, and sea snails. Dark blue to purple is commonly worn to symbolize mourning and death. Cemeteries in Mexico use vibrant colors to celebrate the passing on of their kin. Mexican textiles and decorative tiles are further examples of the prolific use of vibrant colors (Figure 1.7). Traditional Mexican clothing is vibrant and colorful. Intricate patterns and embroidery adorned clothing; including the Huipil, a type of tunic worn by indigenous women (Figure 1.8). The patterns and colors hold unique meanings depending on the region and spoke to one's social status with the more detailed and intricate designs worn during ceremonial events. Colorful blankets based on Mayan textiles are key decorative elements in Mexican homes. Red and blue colors are used in attracting the gods, with blue relating to the heavens, sky, and tranquility.

The conquest of the Aztecs by the Spaniards brought about a cultural shift in which people were demoted to a lower class and not permitted to have or use gold. Gold

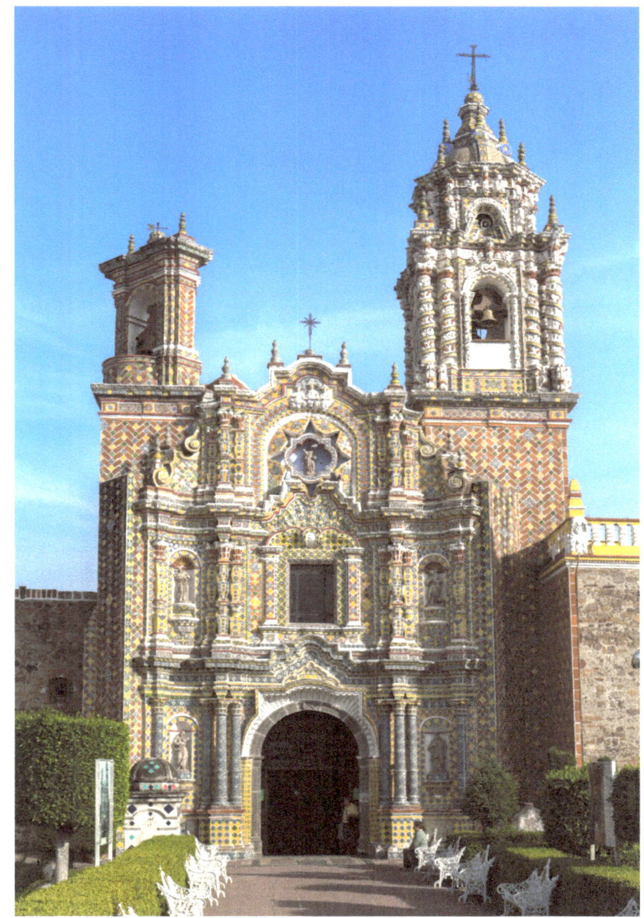

Figure 1.7 Multicolored Talavera tiles cover the exceptionally ornate facade of this church, making it resemble a temple of porcelain. Church of San Francisco, Acatepec, Cholula, Mexico.

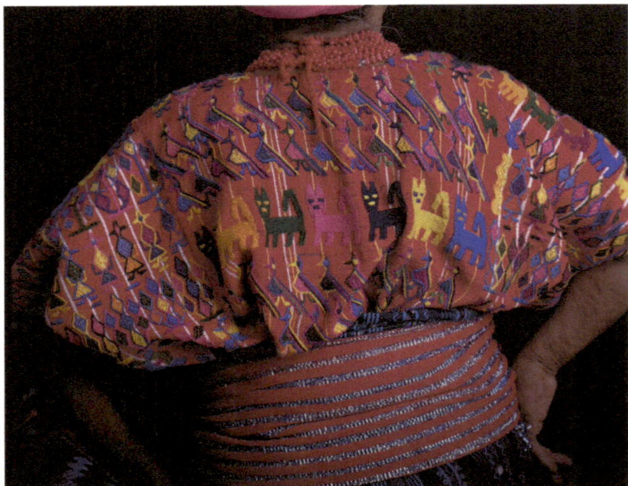

Figure 1.8 The traditional costume of the Mayan Indians of Guatemala consists of a huipil, a linen blouse or tunic with its own unique patterns and colors designated to symbolize the women of a particular village. The geometric patterns of birds, animals, flowers, and trees symbolize the earth, the sky or natural elements.

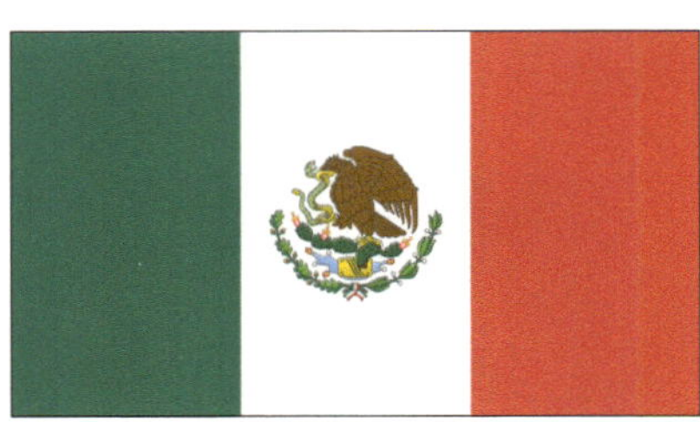

Figure 1.9 National flag of Mexico.

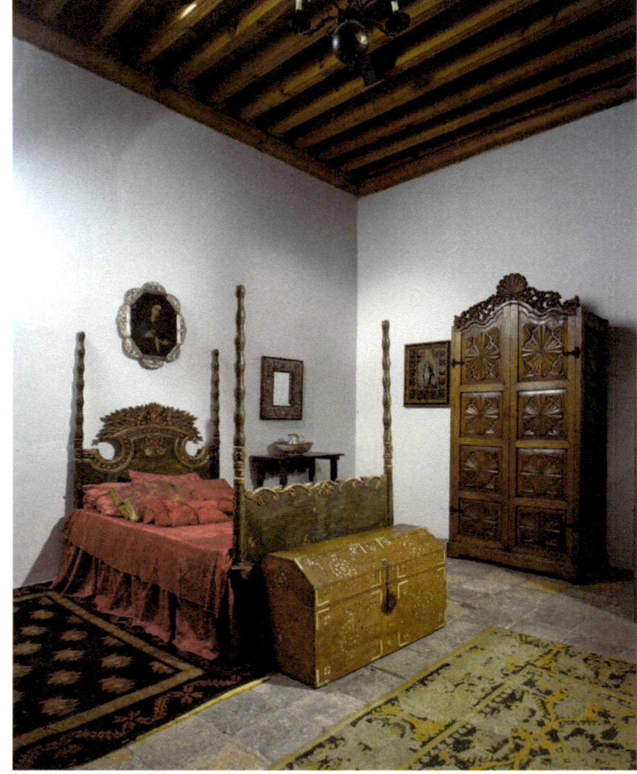

Figure 1.10 Reconstruction of a bedroom furnished with bed, bedside table, wardrobe, and chest. Colonial period, Mexico, eighteenth century.

was used extensively in cathedrals and other public buildings. The poor began to use tin as a replacement for gold, and it continues to be a predominant material in Mexican arts and design.

The Mexican flag (Figure 1.9) consists of green, white, and red, with the center coat of arms symbolizing Aztec heritage. Green signifies hope, white stands for unity, and red stands for heroes who shed blood in the efforts for independence (Xerox, 2008, p. 1). The interior in Figure 1.10 is predominately white, which is common in **Spanish colonial** interiors, with accents of red in the rugs and textiles representative of the national flag. The Spanish colonial style consisted of hand-carved wood furnishings, heavy wooden ceiling beams, stucco walls, and **Saltillo** tiled floors.

Bright blue was used in Mexican homes to defend against evil spirits. Yellow represents the sun and fire, with blue symbolizing wisdom, peace, truth, and the heavens above and sea below. Rich terracotta red and burnt sienna taken from the pigment and soil of the landscape are commonplace in Mexican interiors (Figure 1.11a and b). The work of architect Luis Barragán has brought a modernist sensitivity to the ancient Aztec architects while using the bright, bold hues of contemporary Mexican culture to weave the thread of history and emotion associated with Mexico's past. Barragán's work had greatly influenced Mexican architect Ricardo Legorreta whose use of bold color was his trademark (Figure 1.12). The landscape of Mexico influences the palette used in Mexican architecture, design, and arts. Tropical plants; cacti; the alamanda flower with its hues of pink, peach, and yellow; bougainvillea; and sunflowers have all been sources of color and meaning for the Mexican people. Places of worship are often highly decorated in tiles of many colors and patterns. The Church of San Francisco of Acatepec is an example of the Baroque influence in Mexico. The façade and interior are adorned in blue, black, orange, green, yellow, and brown Talavera tiles. Talavera is a Mexican pottery that originated in the region of Talavera in the province of Toledo, Spain (Figure 1.13a and b).

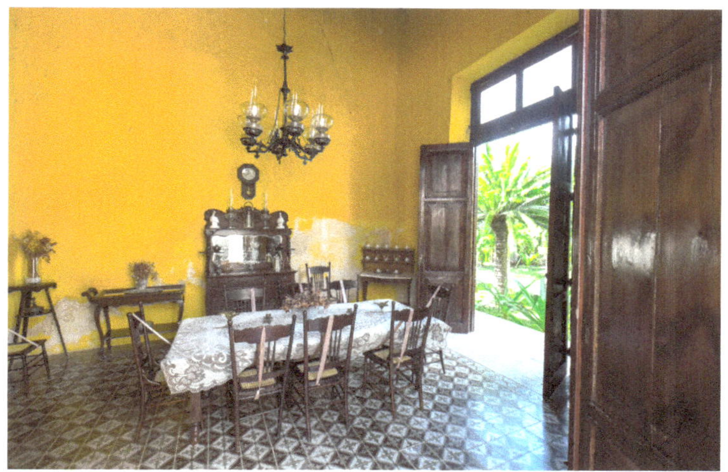

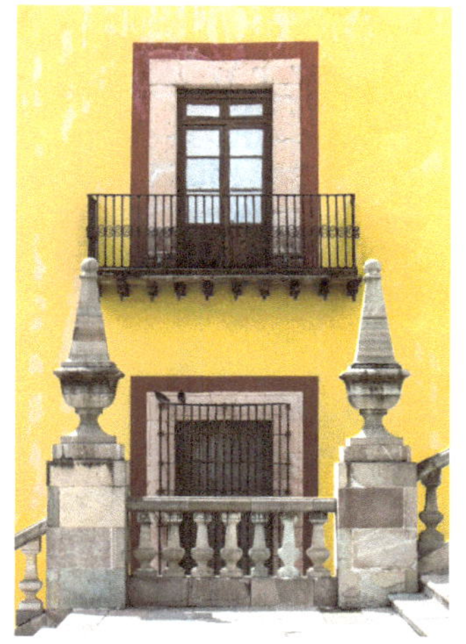

Figure 1.11a (left) Hacienda Yaxcopoil dating back to the seventeenth century in Merida, Yucatan, Mexico.

Figure 1.11b (right) The architecture of the historical city of Guanauiato is known for its bright colors.

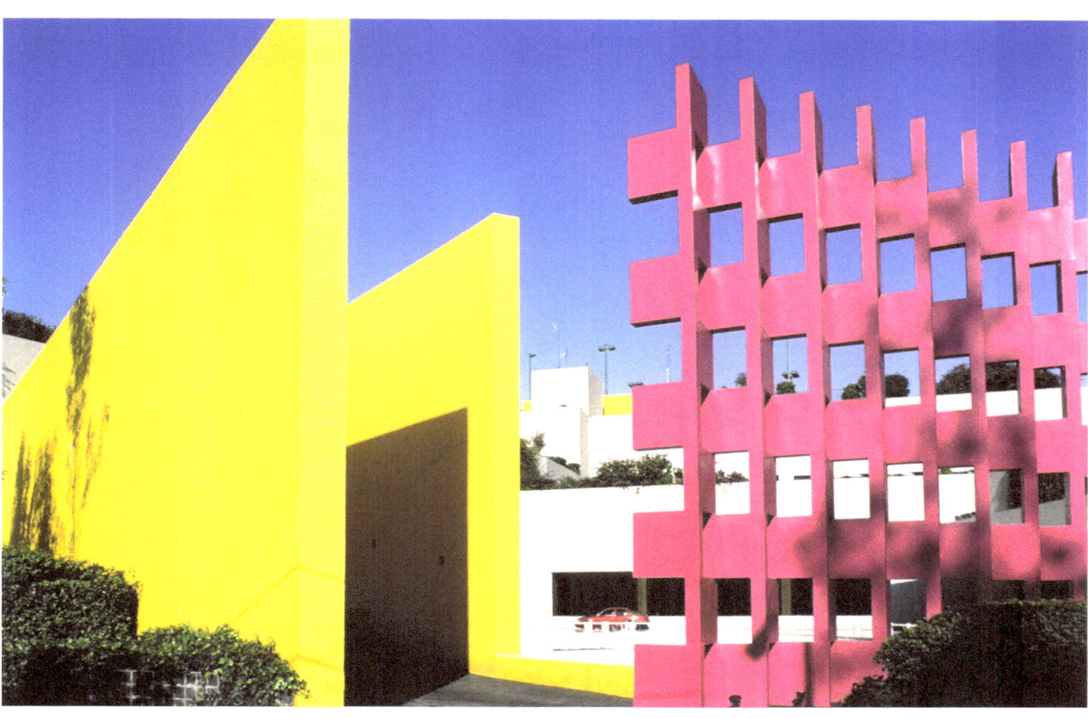

Figure 1.12 Camino Real Hotel, Mexico City, by Legorreta Architects.

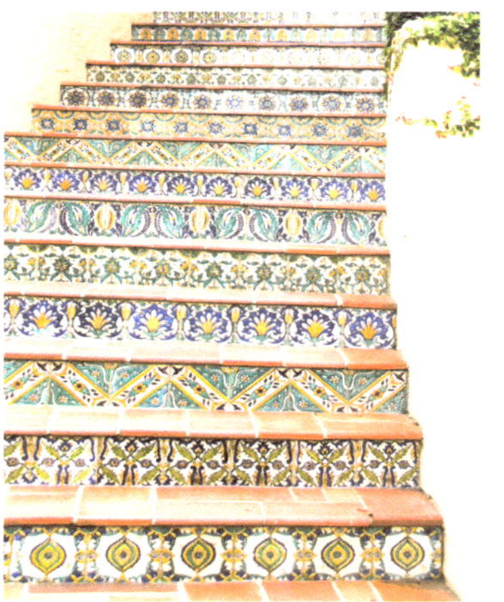

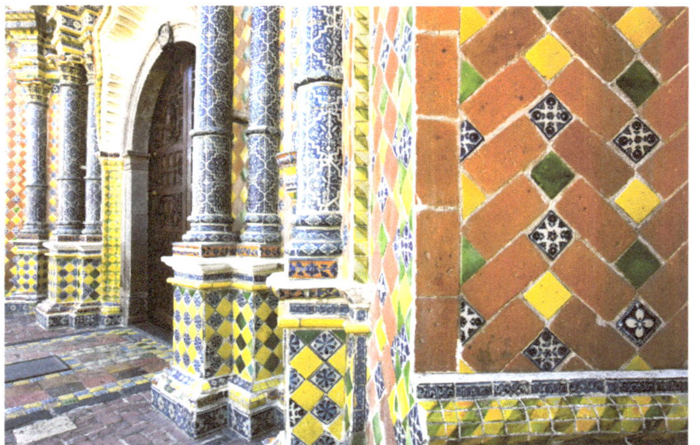

Figure 1.13a (left) Stairway adorned with Mexican Talavera tiles in bright, bold colors.

Figure 1.13b (right) Pillars of Church of San Francisco, Acatepec, Cholula, Mexico.

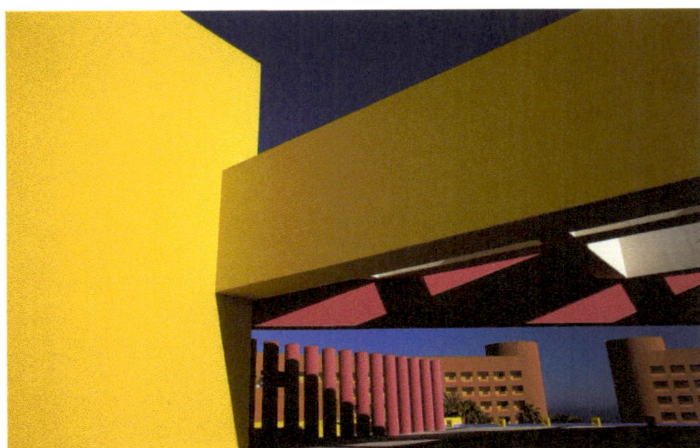

Figure 1.14 Westin Regina Resort, Cabo San Lucas, Mexico.

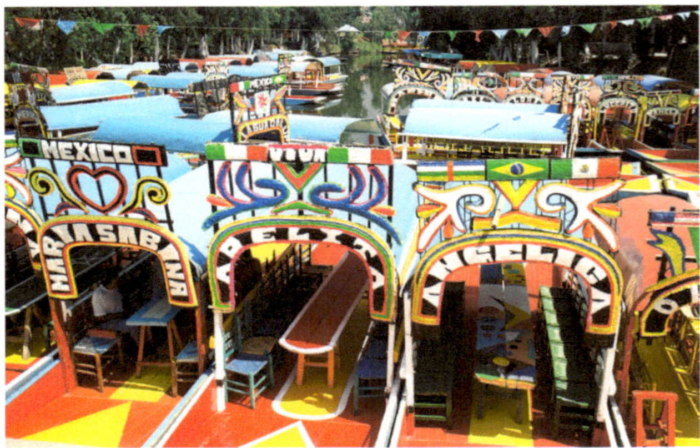

Figure 1.15 Colourful trajineras (gondolas), Mexico City, Mexico.

At the center of Mexican culture is the *Dia de los Muertos*, or **Day of the Dead**. This celebration, held yearly in October, honors those who have passed. Skeletons and colors of orange and pink are common among this celebration that represents the return of lost souls. Figure 1.14 illustrates a modern resort in Cabo San Lucas, Mexico, using the traditional pinks, oranges, and yellow colors. Xochimilco canals south of Mexico City are a popular attraction, where brightly colored trajineras (gondolas) are used for holidays and tourists (Figure 1.15).

Even as the landscape of Mexico becomes modernized, the traditional bright hues continue to reflect the cultural heritage evident in residential neighborhoods. The bright colors common in Aztec and Mexican culture are taken directly from their landscape, the skyline, and vivid green plant life. The *fiesta* is celebrated and recognized with the use of bright reds and yellows. The Mexican landscape reflects colonial, coastal, and modern approaches to living, but at the heart lies color, the essence of life for Mexican people, and a way to remember their past and celebrate their future.

Italy

The epicenter of Renaissance architecture and design, Italy's rich landscape and cobblestoned streets and canals offer the eye a kaleidoscope of colors. The work of Leonardo da Vinci, Raphael, and Michelangelo add to the rich culture and decadent lifestyle supported by the strong, vibrant colors of Italy. The color sienna, a reddish-brown hue, derived its name from the city of Sienna in Italy, where stucco façades are painted in this hue. The city of Magenta in the province of Milan is another example of color naming often associated with the color heritage of a particular culture. Naples yellow is a lead-based paint that was used in ceramics and painting as early as the 1500s. The pigment was originally made in Naples, Italy, where the natural pigment of the color came from the earth near Mount Vesuvius. (Lead is no longer used in the manufacturing of Naples yellow due to its harmful effects.) The color is commonly seen in Tuscan palettes alongside terracotta (brownish red) in tile flooring and wall mosaics, and leafy greens reminiscent of the Italian countryside (Figure 1.16).

The Italian flag, composed of green for hope, white for faith, and red for charity, was adopted in 1796 and became the symbol of freedom and unity (Figure 1.17). The Italian government has gone so far as to adopt

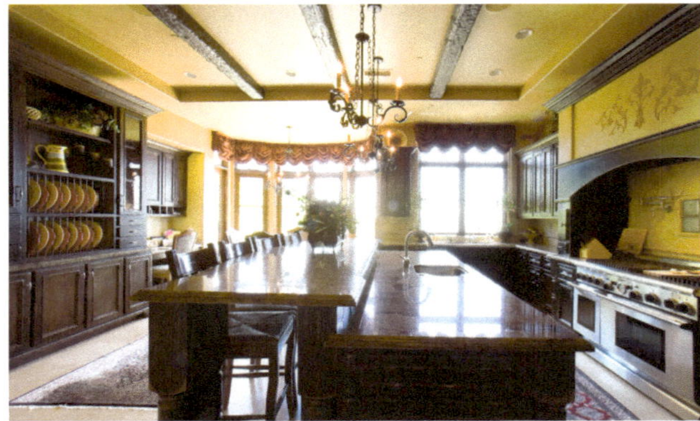

Figure 1.16 Italian kitchen interior colored in Naples yellow.

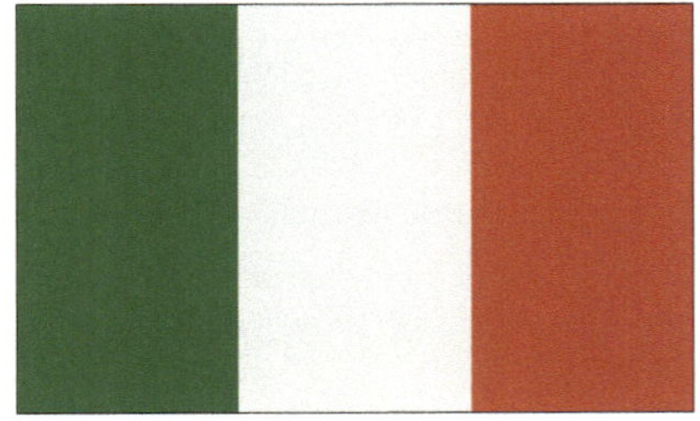

Figure 1.17 National flag of Italy.

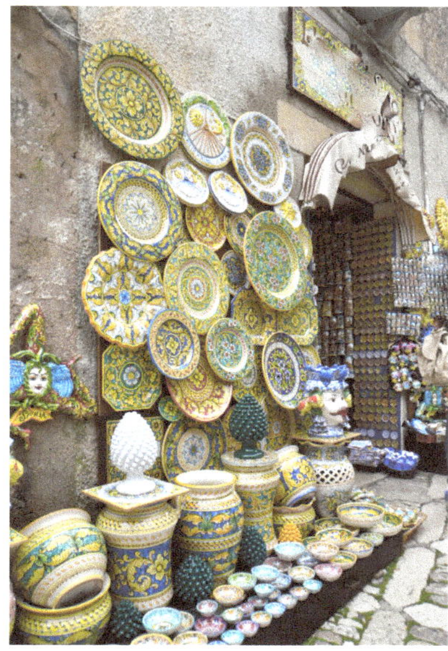

Figure 1.18 An assortment of traditional handmade Sicilian pottery in Italy.

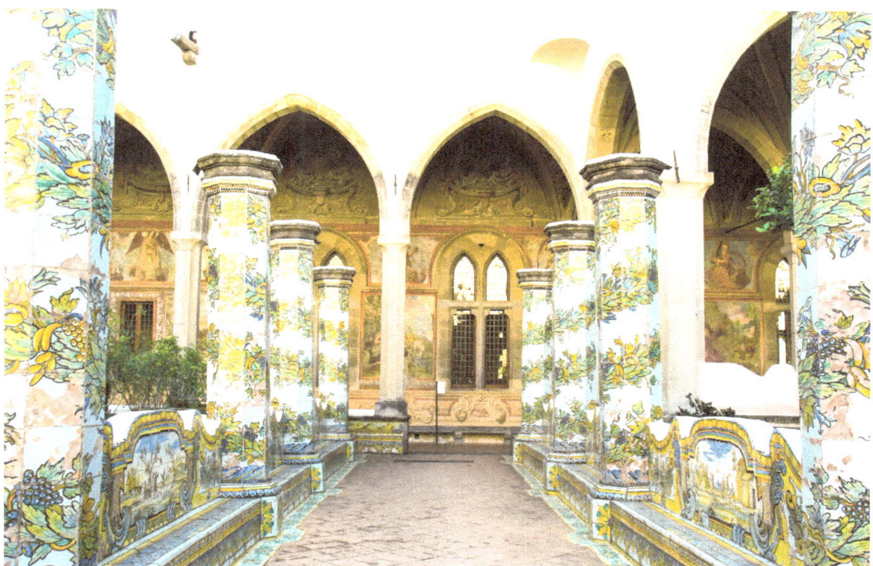

Figure 1.19 The Cloister of Santa Chiara, Naples, Italy. This church dates back to the fourteenth century and is known for its octagonal columns covered in brightly colored clay tiles.

descriptive terms for its flag in an attempt to express and reflect the culture of Italy: "meadow green, milk white, and tomato red" (http://www.flagspot.net). Red and green symbolize the Catholic faith in Italy, along with gold for divinity, as seen in churches of Rome. Red is worn for good luck in the New Year, and surprisingly, the giving of red underwear is common (Morton, 2004, p. 56). Green symbolizes the landscape of spring and youthfulness. Blue represents the heavens, and purple—a combination of blue and red—represents death and mourning. In addition to black being used to mark the death of a loved one, the death of a young child is mourned by the wearing of white.

Italian homes may be designed to include red tiled roofs, stucco walls, brightly painted walls, and a palette of colors expressing the foods and landscape of Italy. Brightly colored pottery adorns many historic homes in Italy (Figure 1.18). Decorative ceramic tiles are an important material used in Italian architecture. These tiles are highly detailed with arabesques, floras, herbs, and geometric patterns in hues of the surrounding landscape (Figure 1.19). The traditional home reflects a stronger direct use of color and pattern, whereas the modern Italian home represents a contemporary lifestyle among ancient Roman ruins. The love of history and design, both traditional and modern, has led to many interior interpretations of the colors, styling, and details of Italian interiors (Figure 1.20a and b).

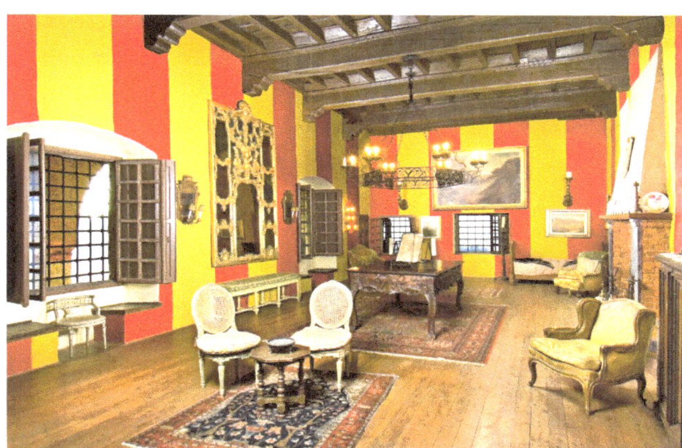

Figure 1.20a Traditional Italian interior.

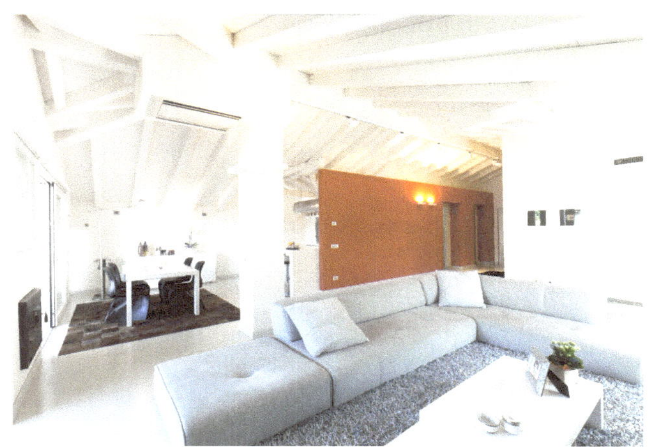

Figure 1.20b Modern Italian interior.

Pakistan

Pakistan is a relatively young country, having gained its independence from India in 1947. The country's primary religion is Islam, and it is one of the largest Muslim states in the world. Vivid colors of green, white, gold, red, and black are an important part of Pakistan culture. Emerald green is the color of the national flag and is the most popular color, symbolizing life and Islam (Figure 1.21). The flag of Pakistan marks its independence with a green and white field with the emblem of a five-pointed star and crescent. The crescent symbolizes progress, and the star represents light and knowledge. The larger field of green represents the majority Muslim population, and the white stripe the minority populations.

Green and white are also evident in Pakistan's architecture, most notably in its mosque tilework. Green is associated with the Islamic religion, nature, and life. Figure 1.22 illustrates a nineteenth-century mosaic of ceramic fragments predominantly in green and white. Marriage is a highly celebrated festival in Pakistan. Prior to the wedding, two events are hosted: **Mayoun** (celebration of the bride) and **Mehendi** (celebration of the groom). Yellow is the color worn by a bride in a simple **shalwar kameez** or loose pajama-like clothing that is worn during Mayoun. During Mehendi, an event hosted by the groom's family, shades of green and yellow are worn. In this ceremony the bride's hands and feet are decorated with henna. Red is strongly associated with women in Pakistan and is traditionally worn during wedding ceremonies (Figure 1.23), while the traditional white **sherwani**, a long coat-like garment embroidered in gold, is worn by men. It is customary for the bride to receive a package of garments from the groom's family, neatly wrapped and displayed a week before the wedding day. This package is called a **bari**. Women also wear bangles as a sign of marriage, in contrast to the wedding ring in America. Bangles come in a variety of red, green, and yellow colors.

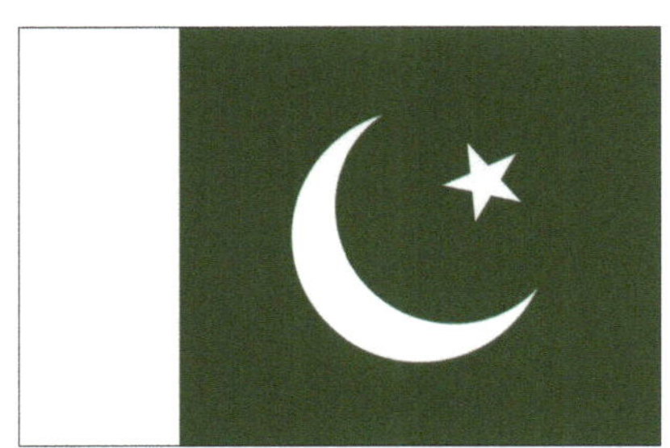

Figure 1.21 National flag of Pakistan.

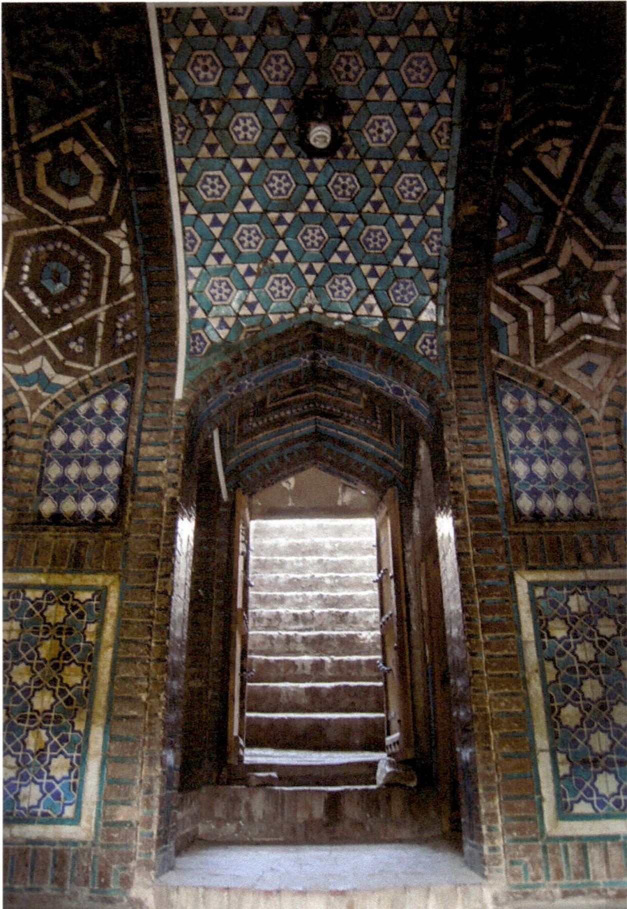

Figure 1.22 Entrance of Styun Jo Aastaan with Pakistani mosaic ceramic tile pattern of triangles and hexagons in green, white, and blue.

The national flower of Pakistan is the white jasmine, used in weddings, celebrations, and religious events and worn on Friday, a holiday. Blue is regarded as a protective color, and in periods of mourning, women wear black and men wear white. Purple is generally "disliked" by Pakistani men (Morton, pg. 68, 2004). Black represents divine truth or beauty and is commonly worn by Muslim women.

The Basant Festival of kites welcomes spring into Pakistan. Many spring colors, especially yellow, are worn to celebrate the seasonal change. The Baluch people of western Pakistan are known for their highly ornate and detailed textilework. Their textiles are often dyed with a spectrum of colorful, bright hues, embellished with floral and geometric patterns. The **kalamandi**, or "ink-pot," images common in Baluch rugs are large hexagons filled with stylized patterns including trees (Figure 1.24a and b).

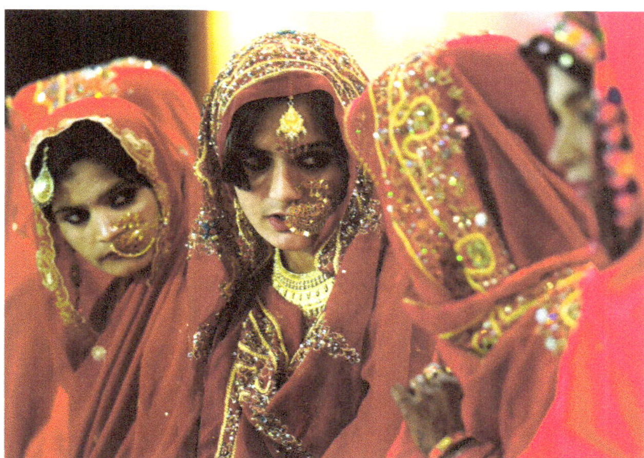

Figure 1.23 Pakistani brides talk as they attend a mass-wedding ceremony in Karachi on March 24, 2014. Some 115 couples participated in the mass-wedding ceremony organized by a local charity welfare trust.

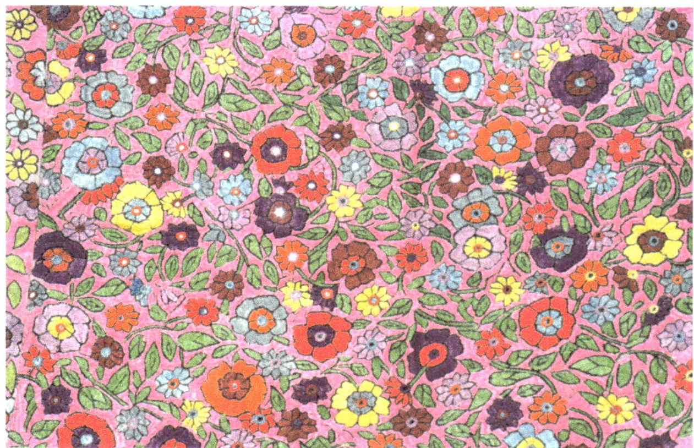

Figure 1.24a Pakistani handwoven and vegetable-dyed Baluch rug.

Morocco

Situated in the northwest region of Africa, Morocco is a country of diverse cultural influences. Since it lies close to Spain, Portugal, and France, these countries have done much to influence the Moroccan culture, which is considered the gateway to the Arab world. Moroccan carpets, carvings, ceramics, and weavings are common designed objects used in homes. The elaborate Mediterranean styling is largely sought after for home décor in the West and used extensively by U.S. retailers. Color in Moroccan design is bold, with bright blues, yellows, and muted oranges. Colors of natural foods are often sources for design inspiration, including eggplant, olives, and saffron spice. As in many countries, the flag is a national symbol of pride in which one can find color meanings for a particular culture. The Moroccan flag of red symbolizes the prophet Mohammed, and the green star symbolizes life, wisdom, and good health, in addition to the Islamic religion (Figure 1.25). Green and red are among the favorite colors of Morocco's people.

Walking through the streets of Morocco, a curious Western eye will ponder at the plethora of blue-painted doors, windows, and shutters. In a tradition dating back to early Egyptian times, blue is used to ward off evil and to protect from the "evil eye." Light blue is commonly painted on the front of Moroccan doors and window shutters (Figure 1.26). Red, royal blues, emerald greens, brilliant gold, and purple symbolize royalty and riches in

Figure 1.24b Baluch textilework from Pakistan.

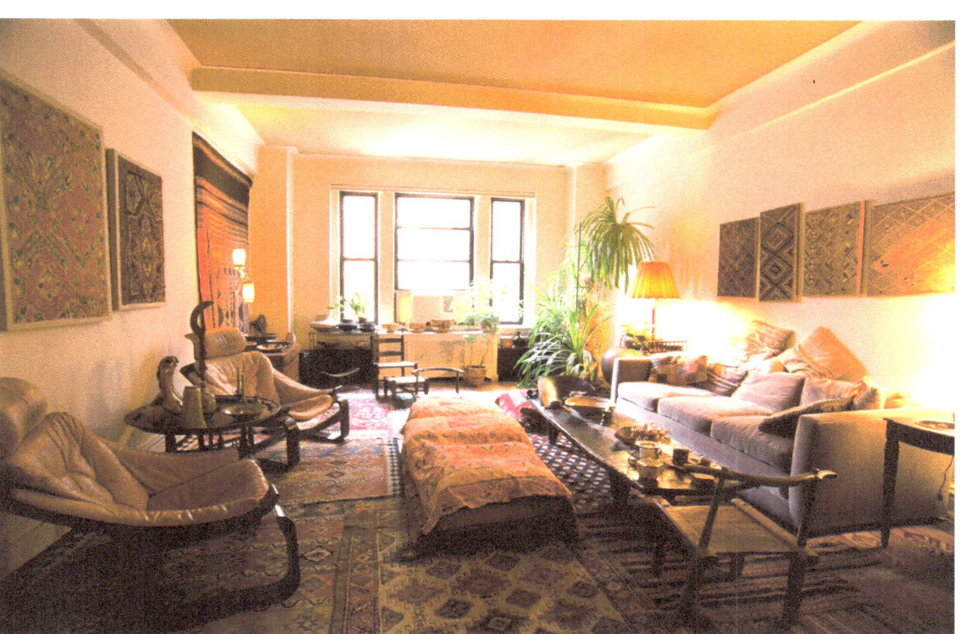

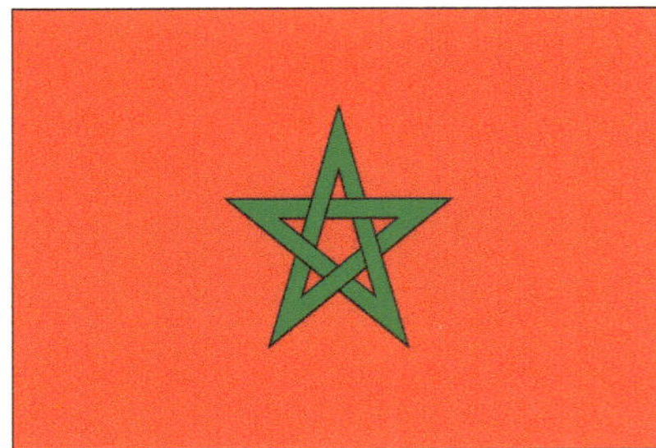

Figure 1.25 National Flag of Morocco.

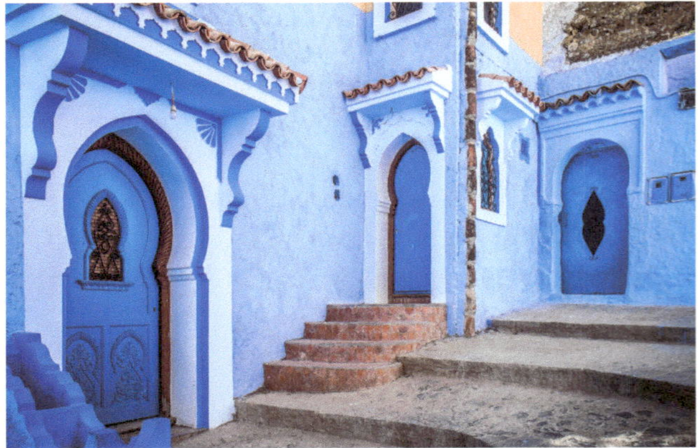

Figure 1.26 Traditional blue-painted doors in the Blue Village, Morocco.

Morocco. White is commonly worn on Fridays and special occasions and is frequently painted on the exterior of homes. The white illuminates the interior by reflecting the natural light surrounding the window and windowsill into the home and in turn deflecting unwanted heat, keeping the interior cool. Interiors are a kaleidoscope of colors using aquamarine and turquoise to reflect the beauty of the cool, aquatic Mediterranean coastline.

The Berbers, first inhabitants of northern Africa, created elaborate handspun carpets and rugs. The name is synonymous with the style—reflecting the colors of the landscape and natural materials that were used to make the colored dyes of beige, brown, saffron, terracotta, and cinnamon (Figure 1.27). These carpets were mainly used for the beddings and blankets of the nomadic Berber tribe. The carpet pile ranged from long and thick for colder climates to short and dense for warmer climates. Today, Berber carpets are known for their durability and speckled appearance, reflecting the natural characteristics of the original Berber tradition.

The blend of culture and tradition defines the color palettes of Moroccan culture. Whether terracotta

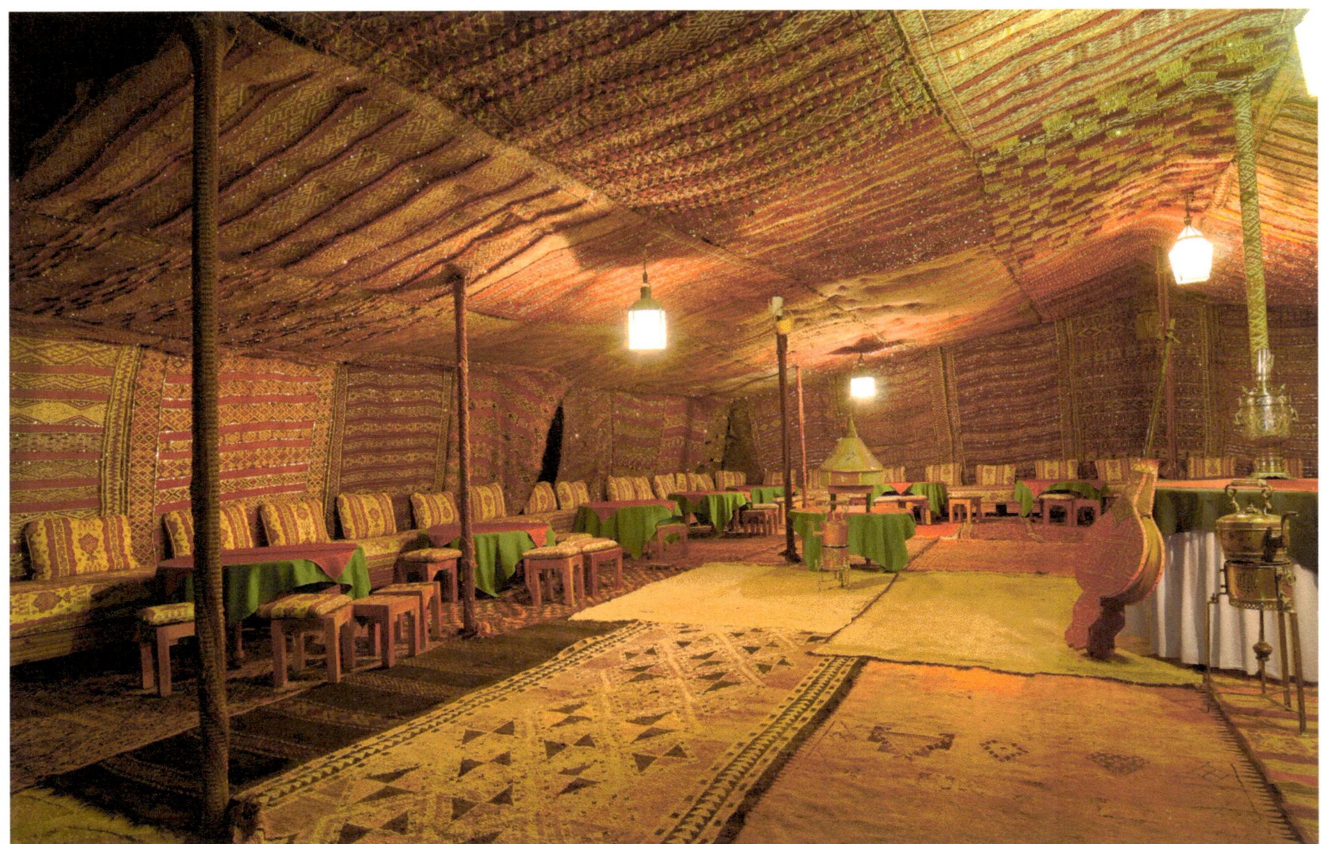

Figure 1.27 Traditional carpeted Berber tent Tinehir, Morocco.

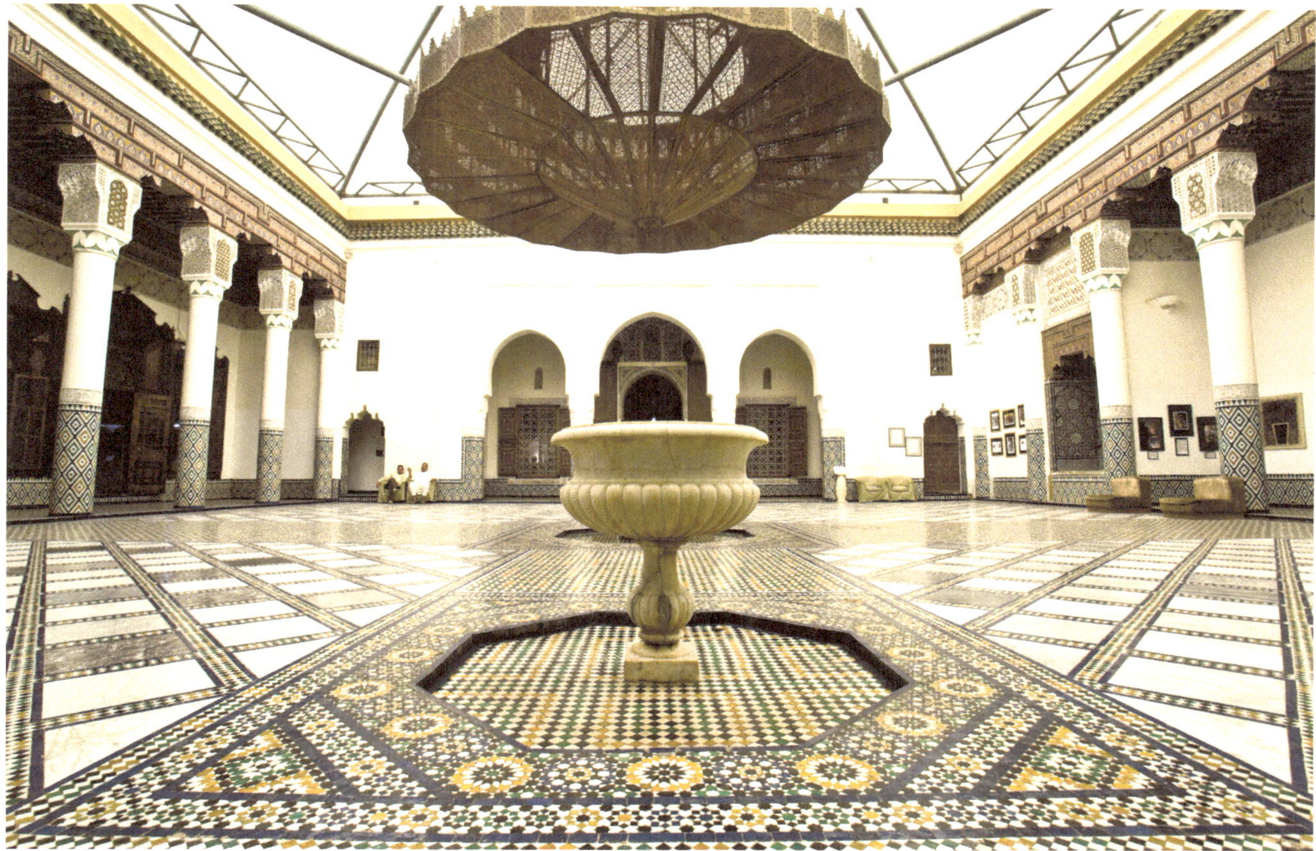

Figure 1.28 Intricate tilework in the Museum of Marrakech, Marrakesh, Morocco.

ceramics, aquamarine and turquoise textured walls, or the brilliant blues, purples, and crimsons of the tilework, the culture of Morocco is a sweet treat of color for the beholder. Moroccan interiors consist of thousands of tiny tiles arranged in complex mosaics in a variety of vibrant hues (Figure 1.28). Moroccan tiles can be seen covering every interior surface from floor, to wall, to ceiling.

South Africa

The continent of Africa is a visually rich landscape of deserts, mountain ranges, safaris, and wildlife preserves. Africa's diverse indigenous peoples are known for creating strong, colorful textiles, beadwork, and vibrant paintings that reflect their different cultures, including the Ghanaian culture in West Africa and the Ndebele and Zulu cultures of South Africa.

The flags of Africa are examples of the vivid colors used throughout the second largest and second most populated continent (Figure 1.29). The flag of the southernmost tip of the continent, South Africa (also referred to as the *Rainbow Nation*) consists of six colors (World Flags, n.d.). There are variations in the symbolic meanings of each color. Black, yellow, and green are known to represent the African National Congress. Black also symbolizes the native people, blue the sky, and red the blood shed in seeking independence. The strong influence of the African land creates double meanings, with green symbolizing the fertile land and the unique "Y" symbol created with green representing both the diversity and unity of the people. Lastly, yellow represents gold and mineral wealth, while white represents

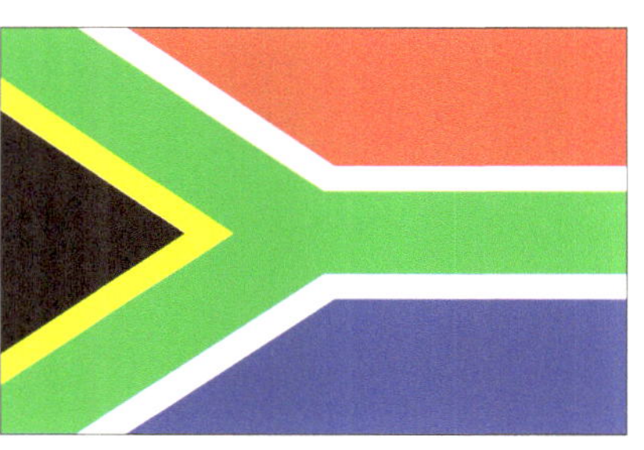

Figure 1.29 National flag of South Africa.

colonial Europeans and the peace between countries. The abundant use of bright, bold colors extends to other parts of African culture as well, including clothing and jewelry.

Beads are an important part of African culture, dating back as far as 12,000 B.C. During European travels into Africa and trade for gold, beads were used as a form of currency. Vast collections of unique, colorful glass beads evolved into an elaborate and decorative form of ceremonial communication, ornamentation in the form of necklaces, armbands, and anklets, and personal expression. For example, the colorful beadwork in Zulu ceremonial clothing conveys different meanings among the women (Zulu Beadwork Culture, n.d.). Zulu beadwork is used to represent a combination of social status, courtship, and marriage. Symbols such as the triangle signify the structure of the family, with the three points relating to the father, mother, and child (Biyela, 2013). When the triangle points upward, it symbolizes a girl, and pointed downward it symbolizes a boy. Two triangles combined into a diamond shape refer to a married woman, and two triangles reversed, forming an hourglass shape, symbolize a married man. Traditional Zulu beadwork includes a maximum of seven colors: white, blue, black, red, green, pink, and yellow. Each color has both positive and negative associations, with the exception of white, which means love and purity with no negative meaning assigned (Biyela, 2013). Modern beadwork that is being sold, rather than being used for personal and ritual use, may include additional colors, for instance, orange and light blue (Figure 1.30). African artists and craftspeople are highly regarded for their work.

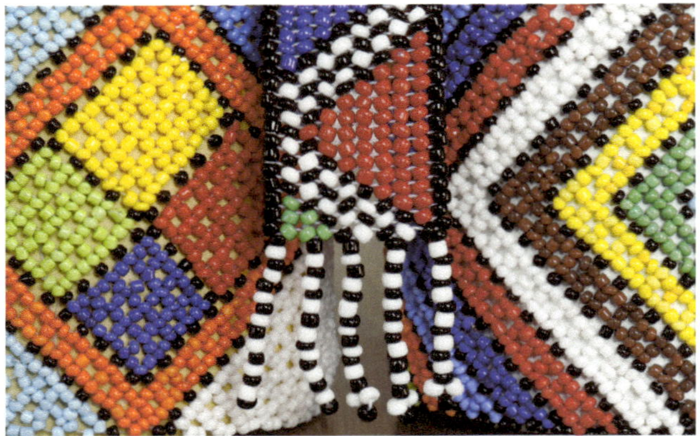

Figure 1.30 Authentic Zulu beadwork.

The Ndebele of southern Africa consist of four subtribes; one of these, the Ndzundza, are famous for their decorative and intricate house-painting. Abstract geometric designs using vivid hues are commonly painted on a white house (Mahlangu, 2014). The patterns are first outlined in black and then filled with color (Figure 1.31). The paint colors and symbols do not hold any particular meaning and are crafted as a form of personal expression. While men are mostly responsible for housebuilding and toolmaking, this domestic practice is common among the women of the home. Originally, the colors were made

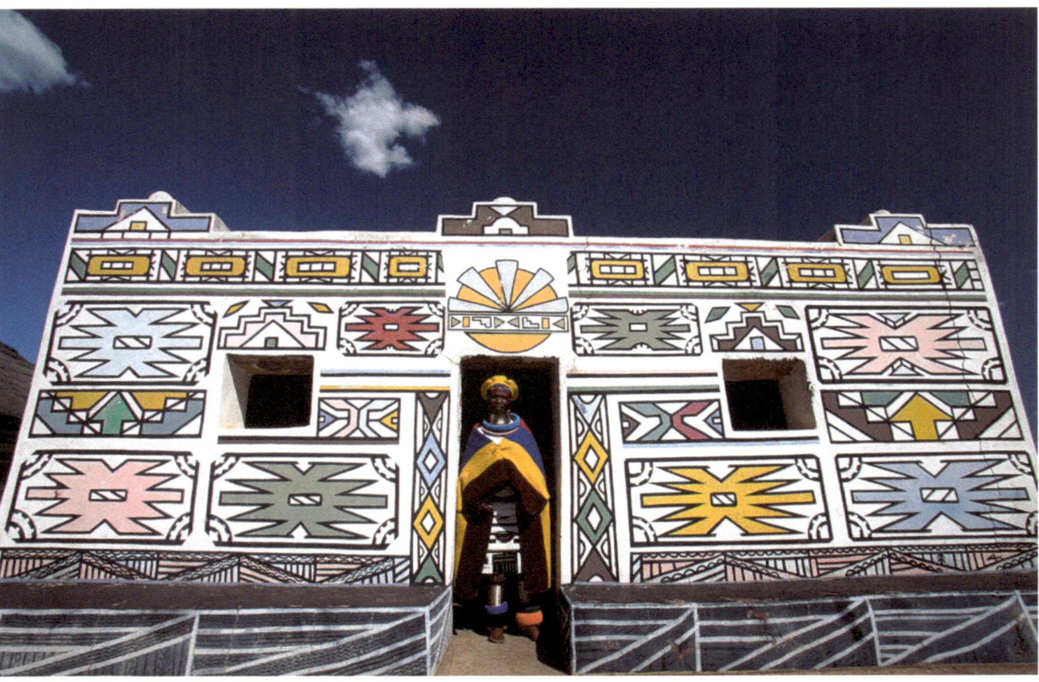

Figure 1.31 Painted Ndebele house.

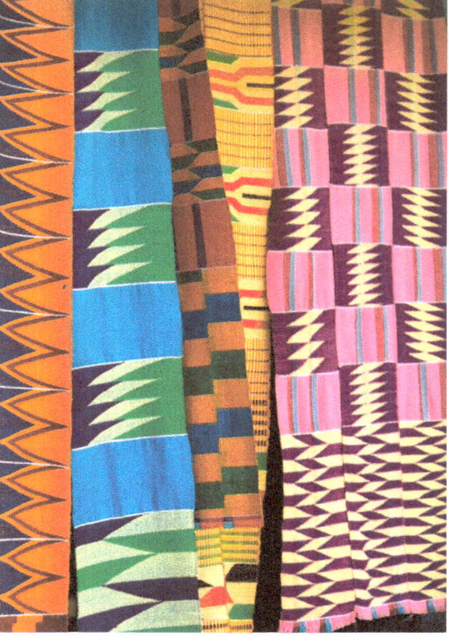

Figure 1.32 Colorful Kente cloth produced in the weaving craft of Adanwomanse in the shanti Region of Ghana, West Africa. Kente cloth is worn by Ghana royals and the nobility.

from local, natural materials such as limestone, ochre, clay ash, and black and red clays. Later, synthetic paints were used as access to these resources became available with urban sprawl.

Africa is a large continent with a wide variety of traditions, craft, and expressions of domestic living. While the focus has been primarily on the southern region of Africa, one cannot conclude a brief introduction to color in Africa without mentioning the Asante people of Ghana in West Africa and their well-known Kente cloth. The cloth is known for its multi-color and geometric patterns with yellow-orange and burgundy as the most commonly used colors. A few of the color meanings include purple for royalty and femininity, green for growth and renewal, and blue for spirituality, peace, and love. The cloth consists of individual cotton and silk strips, approximately four inches wide and several feet long, that are sewn together side-by-side (Figure 1.32). Traditionally a royal cloth and used for clothing, the Kente has become more widely used, including for wall art and furniture upholstery. Over three hundred patterns of Kente cloth have been documented that capture the traditions, culture, rituals, and daily life of the Ghanaian people.

Japan

Japan is a small island with approximately 127 million people. Religion plays a significant part in Japanese culture, with 94 percent practicing Buddhism. The Buddhist faith influences all aspects of Japanese life, evident in its architecture, art, and literature. Buddhist homes often have small altars ornately decorated with photographs of deceased family members. Dragons are a common symbol in Japan and represent power, strength, and wisdom. Often portrayed in vibrant hues of pink and violet, they are present during celebrations and adorn many gardens as water fountains. The ceiling of the Japanese temple in Figure 1.33 is elaborately adorned with gold dragons.

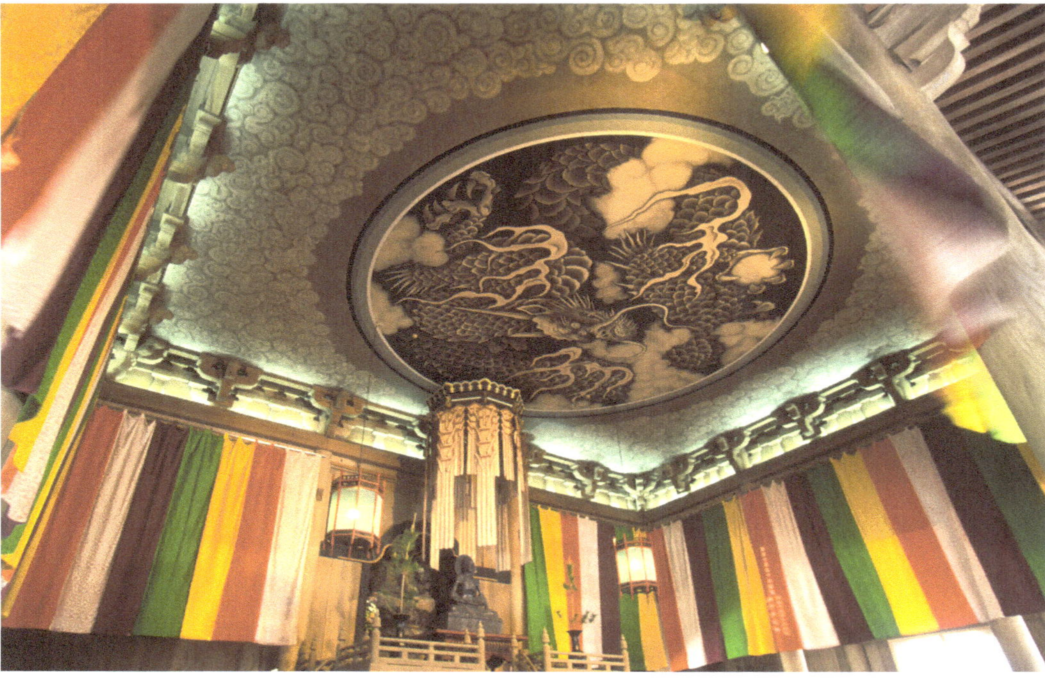

Figure 1.33 Interior of Hatto building containing statues of Buddha and ceiling decorated with dragon painting; in grounds of Kencho-ji temple.

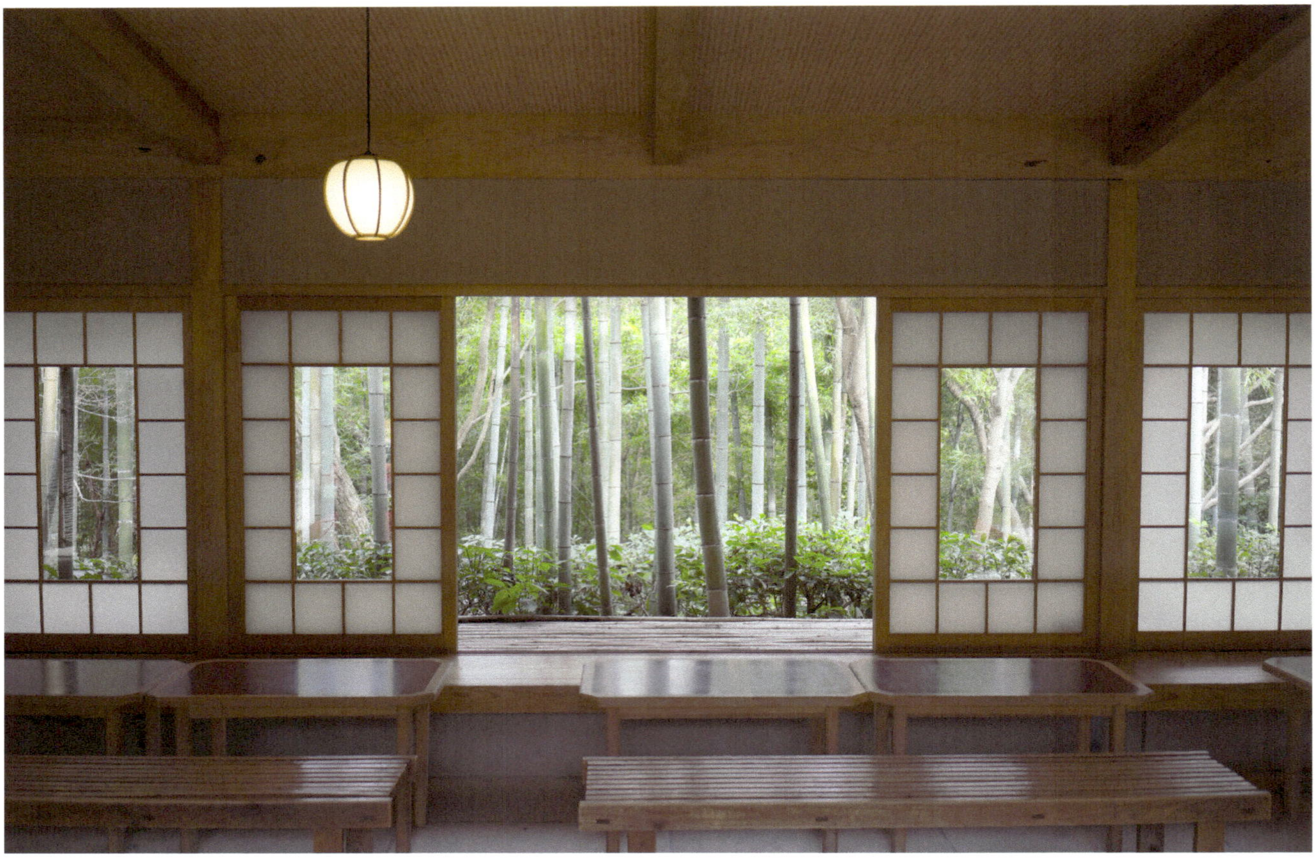

Figure 1.34 Japanese fusuma doors open this space and connect nature to the interior.

The interiors of Japanese homes are modest, refined, and elegant. Rooms serve multiple purposes as a family room, dining room, and bedroom. Traditional opaque sliding **fusuma** doors, or shoji panels, made of wood and paper, can screen for privacy to create a bedroom (Figure 1.34). These doors can be opened to create larger spaces or closed for intimate occasions. Geometry and proportioning of interior space are essential to the Japanese desire for order and the Eastern philosophy of simplicity.

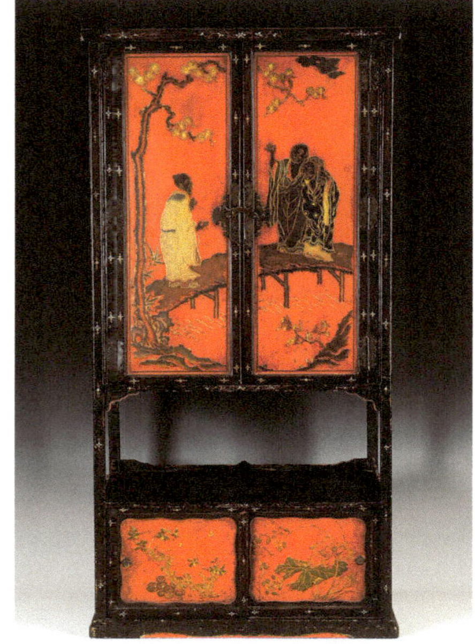

Figure 1.35 Eighteenth-century Butsudan family shrine decorated with figures of monks and floral motifs, in wood, lacquer, gold, mother of pearl and metal.

Brighter, bolder colors of red, yellow, blue, orange, and green are often reserved for shrines and sacred places of worship. The Butsudan is a small traditional household Buddhist altar that houses and protects religious icons that are used for family worship. It is commonly adorned in ebony black, gold, and deep reds (Figure 1.35). The altar can vary from ornate to simple with more contemporary styles that are plain wood with little decoration or gold (Nelson, 2008).

Orange, commonly seen in dishware and textiles, represents the knowledge and civilization of Japan. Colors are found in many building materials in Japanese homes, including stone, paper, bamboo, cane, and cedar and maple woods. When color is introduced into the home, it is usually in the form of a single hue used as a strong point of interest. Figure 1.36 shows a modern-day Japanese living room that uses natural, organic materials and neutral color to reinforce the connection with nature. There is a balance of space, form, textures, and natural materials in Japanese culture. The interior colors are an extension of the Japanese landscape used in the home interior to bring harmony between life and nature.

Wedding white in Western society symbolizes purity; in Japan, women wear the classical white kimono for purity, but more to symbolize their departure from their family or death (Figure 1.37). The Japanese flag is white with a red circle that symbolizes the sun (Figure 1.38). The combination of red and white on the flag is commonly used in the wedding ceremony and frequents dining spaces as a strong hue combined with black lacquer. Purple, a ceremonial color, represents royalty and nobility and is prohibited in weddings. Blue symbolizes youthfulness—unlike in North America, where green has this association. During times of war among dynasties, warriors were known to wear a yellow chrysanthemum as a symbol of courage in battle. The yellow chrysanthemum used in Japanese gardens may be the only color and/or flower used. The chrysanthemum flower is commonly displayed in Japanese porcelain along with other bold colors. While colors are ever present in the Japanese culture, the hues and textures of their native landscape provide balance and emotional harmony. Silver and gray are commonly used to represent maturity and old age. Japan is a land of rich history and balanced lifestyle.

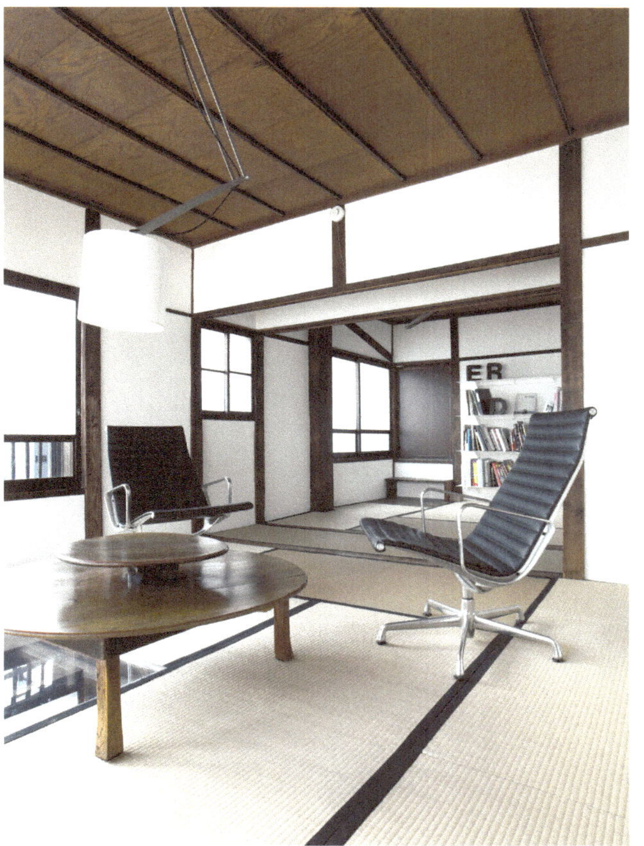

Figure 1.36 Contemporary tatami room in a Japanese living room. The use of natural colors and materials form a geometric order and provide a sense of peace.

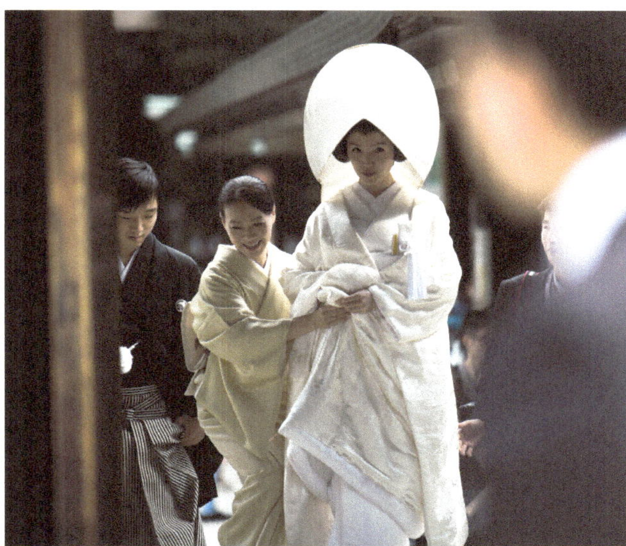

Figure 1.37 Japanese bride on her wedding day in a classical white kimono at the Meiji Shrine.

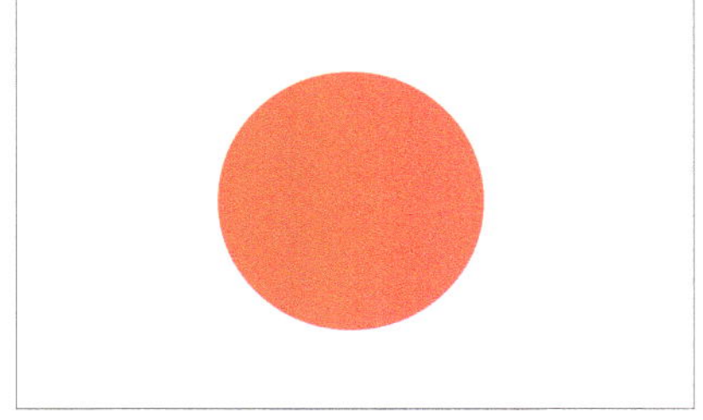

Figure 1.38 National flag of Japan.

Thailand

Thailand extends down the Malaysian peninsula in the center of Southeast Asia. It is a rich landscape of forested mountains, fertile plains, and beaches with tropical vegetation, rainforests, and abundant wildlife. This colorful landscape mirrors Thailand's culture, religion, and customs.

The national flag of Thailand is tricolored in red, white, and blue. It consists of five horizontal bands with the center blue band twice the size of the remaining four (World Flags, n.d.). The red symbolizes the blood shed by Thailand to maintain its independence; *Thai* means "free," with *Thailand* meaning "land of the free." The largest band of color, blue, is the national color of Thailand and represents the monarchy (Figure 1.39). White symbolizes purity and represents the Buddhist religion.

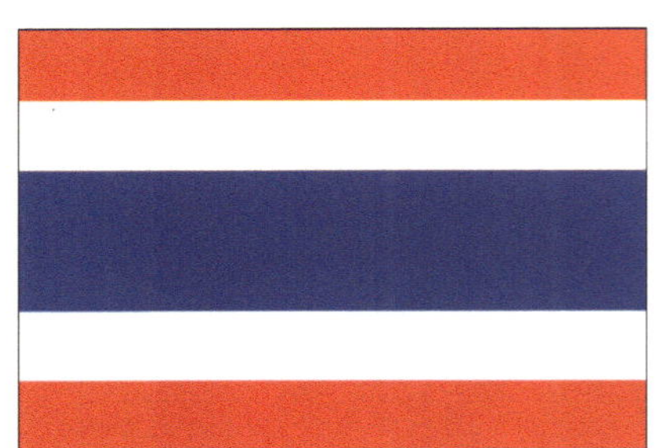

Figure 1.39 National flag of Thailand.

The prevailing religion in Thailand is **Theravada Buddhism**, the more conservative of the two Buddhist traditions. Approximately 95 percent of Thailand's population are Buddhist, with the remaining being Muslim and Christian. Bangkok, the largest city in Thailand, hosts some of the oldest Buddhist temples and shrines. The wat is a Buddhist monastery-temple and place for worship in Thailand. The elaborate architecture and details of the temples include multitiered, sloping roofs with stone tiles, colorful decorative glazed stone, and glass tiles with exaggerated, overhanging eaves. Wooden finials in the shape of mythical beasts and golden gilded beams, ridges, and pillars adorn the temples (Figure 1.40). Depictions of Buddha are concentrated in Thai fine art, paintings, murals, sculpture, and architecture.

Another example of Thailand color is the Grand Palace located in the heart of Bangkok. This was the primary residence of the kings of Siam (later Thailand), which began construction in 1782 (Kislenko, 2004). The palace is a massive complex, lavished in gold and colorful cut glass, that includes numerous buildings, temples, rooms, and courtyards. The palace today is used exclusively for ceremonies. Festivals and holidays are a frequent occurrence in Thailand and offer the viewer a colorful way to experience the bright costumes during these celebrations.

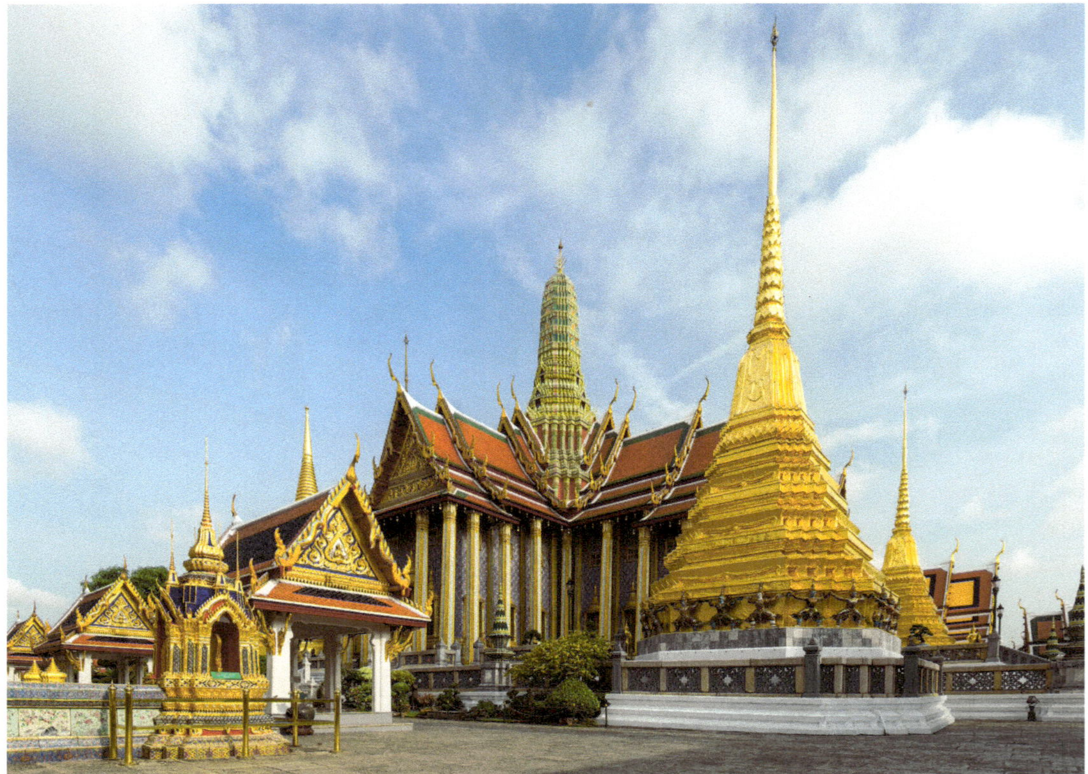

Figure 1.40 Inside of Wat Phra Kaew or the Temple of the Emerald Buddha, Grand Palace, Bangkok, Thailand. This temple is regarded as the most sacred temple of Thailand.

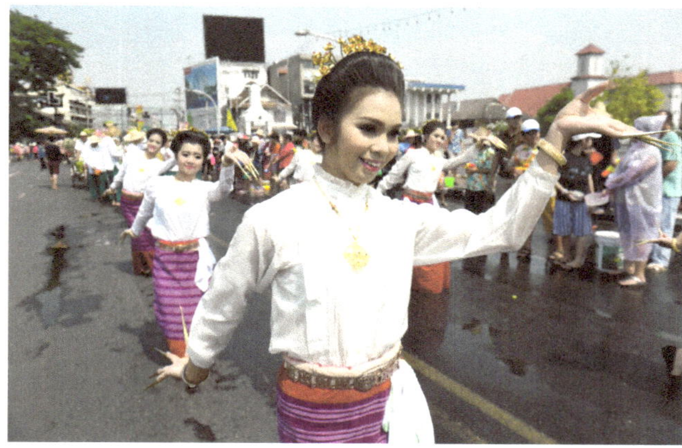

Figure 1.41 Thai women dressed in traditional costumes perform a traditional dance during the Songkran festival.

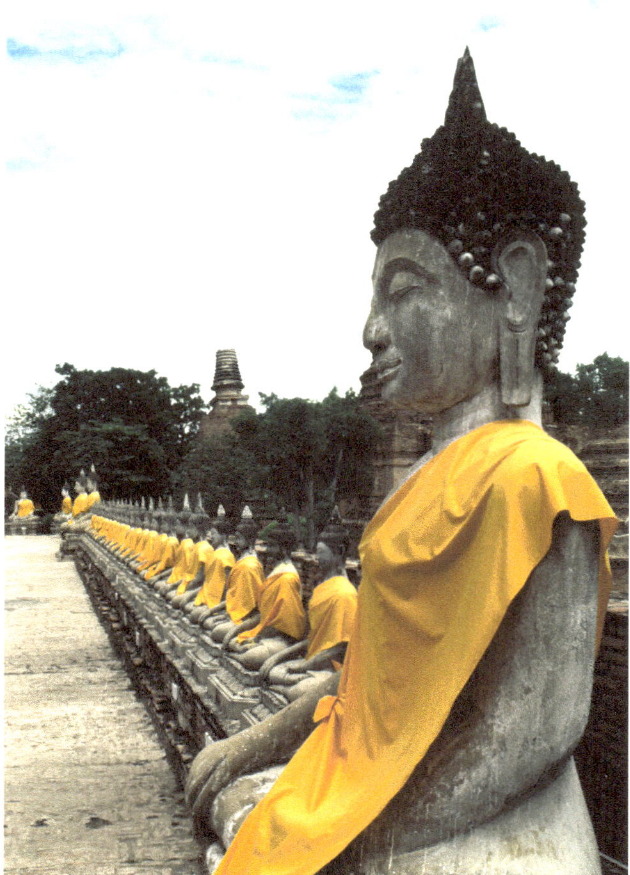

Figure 1.42 Buddha statues dressed in safron yellow robes.

Songkran, or *water festival*, the traditional Thai New Year is the longest holiday in Thailand and is celebrated over several days during the month of April prior to the hot, dry season. The water is a celebration of cleansing and purification to bring luck and prosperity in the coming year. Colorful, floral, and festive clothing is worn during the celebration, and women perform the **Fawn Lep**, a traditional Thai dance known as the *fingernail dance* (Figure 1.41). The dancers are dressed in high-quality, brightly colored, embroidered Thai silk with jewelry and other adornments in gold.

Color is deeply rooted in the traditions of Thailand. Different hues are associated with the days of the week, in the belief that when one wears a certain color on its particular day, it brings forth good luck (Pathak, 2012). Depending on the day you were born, your color of the week may be expressed by yellow for Monday, pink for Tuesday, green for Wednesday, orange for Thursday, blue for Friday, purple for Saturday, and red for Sunday. Many Thai people wear yellow on Monday in honor of the king of Thailand, who was born on Monday. Black means evil and bad luck and is also associated with funerals. Purple is often associated with the mourning of a widow. Gold is reserved for Buddhist temples and is considered a sacred color in Thailand. Yellow is associated with the Buddhist religion and the Thai national flower (Figure 1.42). Yellow also represents royalty and wealth, a contrast with the use of purple in the West.

Becoming Culturally Literate

Getting to know the character, history, traditions, and customs of a particular culture will bring sensibility to your design work. Selecting color for projects goes beyond the aesthetics and fashionable trends. Understanding the traditions and social graces of your clients will prepare you to make accurate and pleasing color choices.

As the divide among cultures shrinks, designers will be required to consider the cultural differences among clients when preparing color solutions for projects. Your success can be increased through careful color planning that engages you in researching these differences. You will benefit and appreciate the rich, colorful diversity on our planet. To expand on the cultures presented so far, a quick overview of color meanings and symbolism for China, Korea, Ireland, Egypt, and India is shown in Table 1.1.

Color plays a vital and important role in our lives. Deeply formed traditions and rituals are often associated with color which symbolize different meanings around the world. Color and design shape our behavior and attitudes, behavior shapes our culture and sense of

TABLE 1.1 CROSS-CULTURAL COLOR SYMBOLISM (CHINA, KOREA, IRELAND, EGYPT, AND INDIA)

Hue	China	Korea	Ireland	Egypt	India
RED	Good luck, happiness, success, and celebration	"Power and authority, high class and luxury"; some Koreans believe the color can prevent "misfortune," and as such, it is the color for the Korean soccer team	Red wool is believed to relieve sore throats	Death, historically, Egyptians associated themselves as "red people" and used natural materials to dye their skin red	Purity and is the common color for a bride's clothing. Fertility and prosperity.
BLUE	Represents the heavens, clouds, and immortality	Darker values associated with death	Peace and truth	Virtue, faith, wards off evil	Associated with Lord Krishna, it represents bravery, determination, and virtue
GREEN	Infidelity of women when worn in clothing; youthfulness	Life, youth, prosperity	Represent Catholicism (national flag), shamrock for luck	National color, commonly used on mosque and places of worship, symbolizes fertility and strength	Happiness, relation to nature, soil and plant life, growth, and faith, fertility
YELLOW	Wealth, power, imperial color of the Qing dynasty, masculine	"Relates to the sun, energy and rich harvesting of the fall"	Favorite color among people	Prosperity, mourning, eternity	Knowledge, learning, meditation, happiness
PURPLE	Not popular among residents	Wealth, inner peace	Rosaries of the Catholic faith are commonly amethyst and represents cardinal direction east	Favored color of Cleopatra, used Purpura snails for dye, faith	Sorrow and mourning
ORANGE	Happiness and good health	Result of yellow (energy) and red (power and love), orange represents cheerfulness and often is associated with youth because of its "casual" nature	Represents Protestants (national flag) because of William of Orange, the Protestant English king	Not used in ancient times; however, iron oxides and coppers were used with other minerals to produce red and green paints	Referred to as Saffron, it symbolizes fire, courage, sacrifice, and the rejection of materialism
BLACK	Water	Color of trigrams in their national flag, representing the elements of fire, water, earth, wood, and metal	Represents the devil and cardinal direction north	Dignity, luck, rebirth	Evil, anger, and darkness and associated with the absence of energy
WHITE	Death and mourning	Innocence, purity	Unity of two faiths (Catholic and Protestant) and represents cardinal direction south	Sacred, holy, used in ceremonial activities, joy	Peace, truth and purity. Also the color of death, mourning, and unhappiness

Contributions for Korea: Jin Gyu, Phillip Park, Associate Professor, College of Visual Arts and Design, University of North Texas

collective and individual identity, and culture ultimately shapes how we design. Our world is ever changing, and design is ever evolving. As author Galen Cranz stated, "what is true of the chair is true of all the artifacts we create . . . we design them; but once built, they shape us" (2000, p. 15).

REVIEW QUESTIONS

1. Why is it important for the designer to study color in different cultures?
2. List three aspects that shape color symbolism and meaning across cultures.
3. List two cultures that associate blue with warding off evil spirits.
4. Which two colors symbolize the Catholic faith in Italy? Explain why.
5. What color is sacred among Muslims and represents life and Islam?
6. Explain the association of gold and yellow with Buddhism in Thailand.
7. In what culture does the traditional interior often connect to nature with naturalistic materials and color?
8. Symbols are an important communicative tool; describe and explain how symbols and color are used in African culture.
9. Which culture used purpura snails, and what were they used for?

Vocabulary

Medicine wheel
talking stick
Spanish colonial
Saltillo
Day of the Dead
Mayoun
Mehendi
shalwar kameez
sherwani
bari
kalamandi
fusuma
Theravada Buddhism
Songkran
Fawn-Lep

EXERCISES

1. You are taking on the role of a designer or design team preparing conceptual ideas and imagery for a presentation to a local museum for an upcoming exhibit on Culture, Color, and Design. Select a country or culture and prepare a conceptual board (11 by 17 inches or 18 by 24 inches) to include textiles, magazine clippings of interiors, objects, symbols, and decorative items (pottery, art, sculpture) that reflect the selected country's culture and use of color.
2. Prepare a brief two- to three-page report of differences in color meanings between two cultures or countries. This project can be done individually or in a group. Select from the following cultures: African, Native American, Indian, German, Russian, Romanian, Swedish, Thai, Australian, Hawaiian, Guatemalan, Indonesian, Jamaican, and Dutch.
3. Historical color palettes represent preferences for color schemes that were predominately used by certain cultures or individuals or that were popular during a specific time period. These palettes are often representative of the social climate during their time of development and offer a window into the design of a historical period. Historical color harmonies can provide a relief from the market saturation of color trends. Many paint manufacturers recognize this and have developed color palettes based on period color harmonies. Studying authentic historical examples of color harmonies will expand your skills in creating as well as recognizing classic combinations that have stood the test of time. How would you design a room if you were commissioned to represent a decade of the past? Choose a decade and create a concept board.
4. Research the history of your ancestors and create a collage that represents the color and heritage of your background. Provide a brief written statement of your research findings to support your collage design.

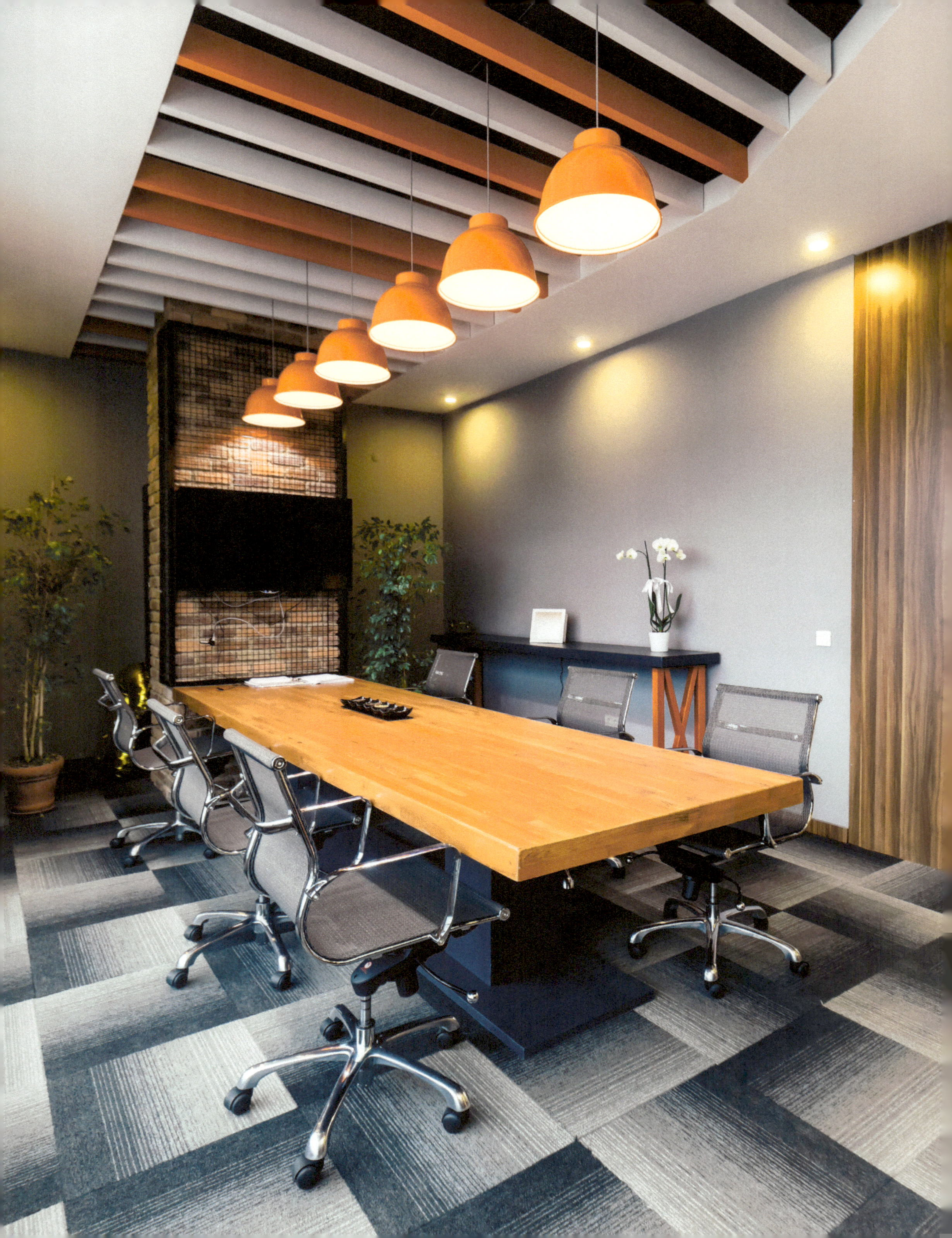

2

color + theory

Learning Outcomes

After studying this chapter, you will be able to:

- **Describe the three properties of light.**
- **Characterize the three dimensions of color.**
- **Discuss the characteristics of color that produce tint, tone, and shade.**
- **Explain the difference between additive and subtractive color.**
- **Compare and contrast a variety of color systems that are available to designers.**
- **Identify and produce the different color harmonies.**

Why do interior designers need to know about color? **Color** is an intangible, powerful sensation that has the ability to enhance our physical environment, influence our personal experiences of space, and provide a greater sense of health and well-being. Eighty percent of sensory experiences are visual. Color is unstable and constantly changing, which could exhaust a designer working with color matter. Our interaction with colored media—for instance, television, computer screens, and roadside billboards—can create an unexpected experience depending on the colors we are exposed to. We do not have control over these color sources, and the resulting emotional experiences are therefore uncertain. Unlike with these media sources, our direct interaction with printed and colored materials, including paint and fabrics, allows for our complete control and choice of selection.

Viewing colored media causes receptors in our eyes to transmit messages to our brain, which tries to give our experiences meaning. Color theorists have engaged in debates and discourses to explain the phenomena of color, from Newton's first studies in the 1660s to Albers's work some three hundred years later in the 1960s. Different professions require different approaches to interpret and express their ideas with color. A graphic designer works with printed color media, a theater lighting specialist works with colored light and light mixing, a painter brings a painting to life by mixing pigments, and an interior designer uses colored materials to intricately create spaces for his or her clients' desired outcomes. This complex process—color theory—has been studied for centuries.

Color resists any one schematic system, which is why so many color theorists have spent countless hours trying to fit a square peg into a round hole. Designers rely more on instinct and experience than on one theoretical color approach to guide them. Despite the many approaches, however, a basic understanding of color theory is fundamental to a well-rounded education in interior design.

Before we examine color theory more closely, let's first look at what is meant by *theory*. Theory explains the concepts and ideas involved in describing and rationalizing phenomena about a particular subject. Theories, for the most part, are unproven and continue to be studied to provide additional insight into the particular subject.

What Is Color Theory?

Color theory is the study and practice of a set of principles used to understand the logical relationships among color and light in our visual experiences of art and design. Color theory has been studied for decades, and new ideas and practices are continuously being unraveled. Understanding the role color plays in art, design, and other allied professions is important to using color successfully. A certain amount of knowledge of the scientific aspects of color is also necessary from a design perspective; we are engaged in the human interface involving the way people respond to color. Whether in our homes, offices, schools, or businesses, color transforms our surroundings.

Let There Be Light

Without light, there is no color. Color transforms as light is experienced. Light is the essence of color and is energy traveling through the air at 186,000 miles per second. Light and color together illuminate a space, guide focal point and attention, and set the mood and expression of the interior. Color materials and lighting types should be selected simultaneously to create harmony within the interior. If selected separately, the results can be problematic.

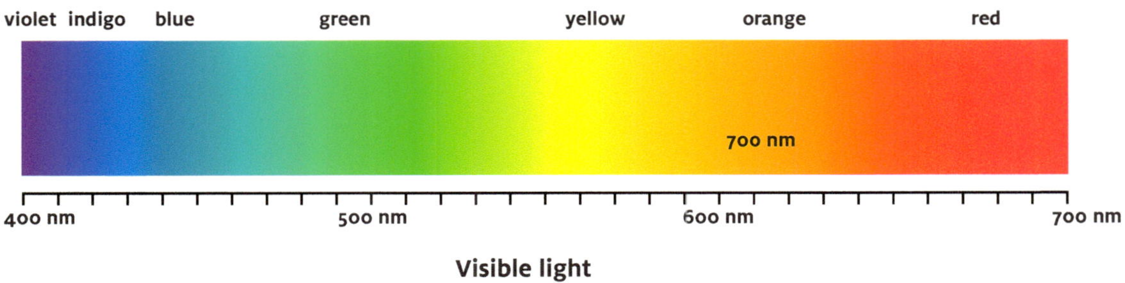

Figure 2.1 The visible spectrum of colored light

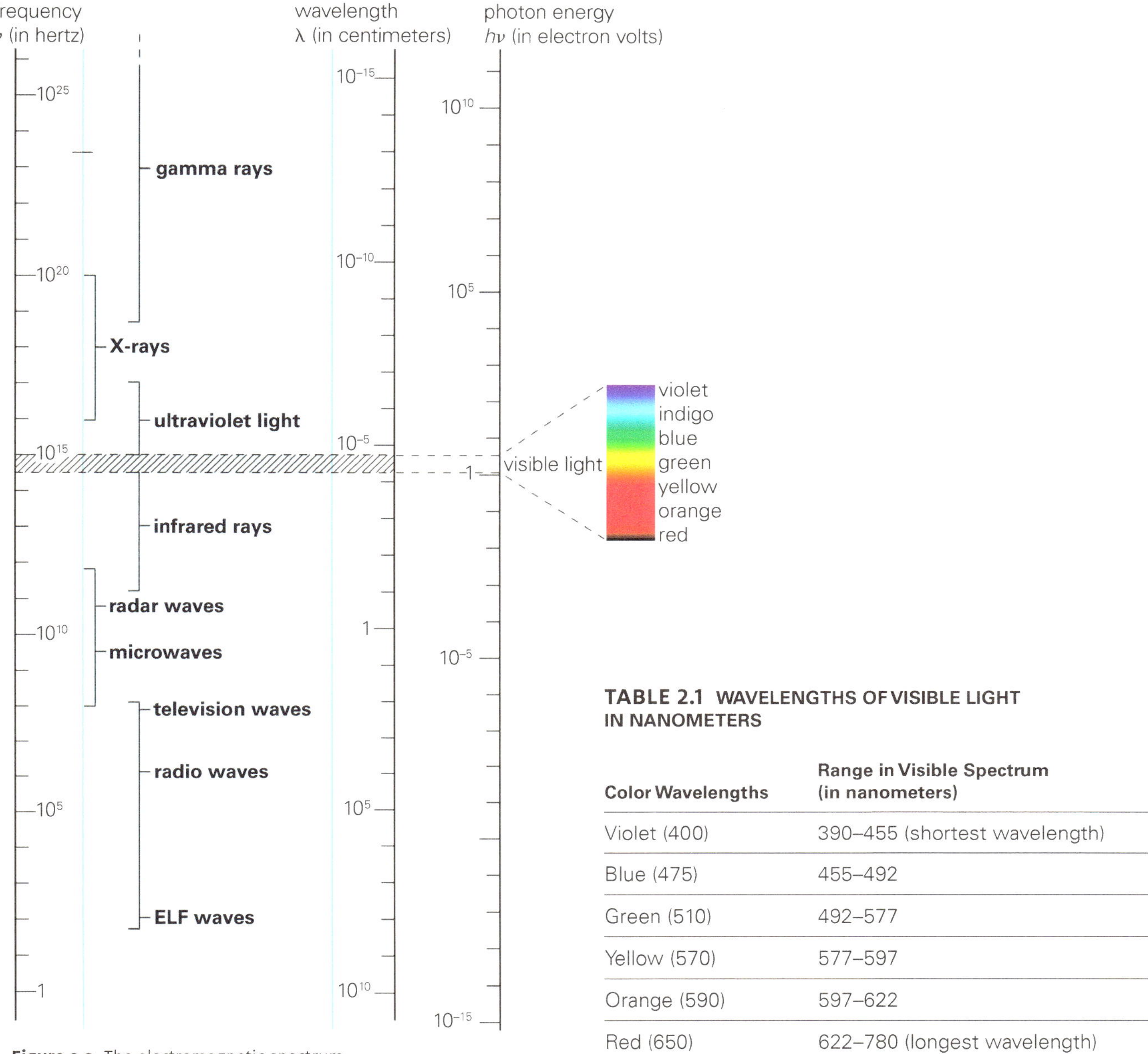

Figure 2.2 The electromagnetic spectrum.

TABLE 2.1 WAVELENGTHS OF VISIBLE LIGHT IN NANOMETERS

Color Wavelengths	Range in Visible Spectrum (in nanometers)
Violet (400)	390–455 (shortest wavelength)
Blue (475)	455–492
Green (510)	492–577
Yellow (570)	577–597
Orange (590)	597–622
Red (650)	622–780 (longest wavelength)

Colored light consists of a series of wavelengths, each varying in length and strength. This colored light we can see is called the **visible spectrum** (Figure 2.1). The human eye is capable of seeing a very small portion of the electromagnetic spectrum, which consists of gamma rays, X-rays, ultraviolet light, infrared rays, microwaves, and radio waves (Figure 2.2).

The visible portion of light we see is located between ultraviolet light and infrared light, approximately 390 to 780 **nanometers** (nm; 1 millimeter = 1 million nm), the unit used to describe and measure the wavelengths of visible light (see Table 2.1). Violet light has the shortest wavelength, and red has the longest. The longer the wavelength of light, the more effort the eye must make to see the object. Red light will focus behind the retina of the eye; green, the most pleasing color for the eye to view, on the retina; and violet slightly in front of the retina. The eye can have trouble focusing on violet, and it can have a "hazy" quality in large doses (Figure 2.3). Extensively red-colored space can be tiring and irritating if viewed for extended periods of time (Figure 2.4). It is recommended to use pure red in small doses, as an accent, or in locations where people visit for shorter periods. Tints and tones of this hue will not have the same effect.

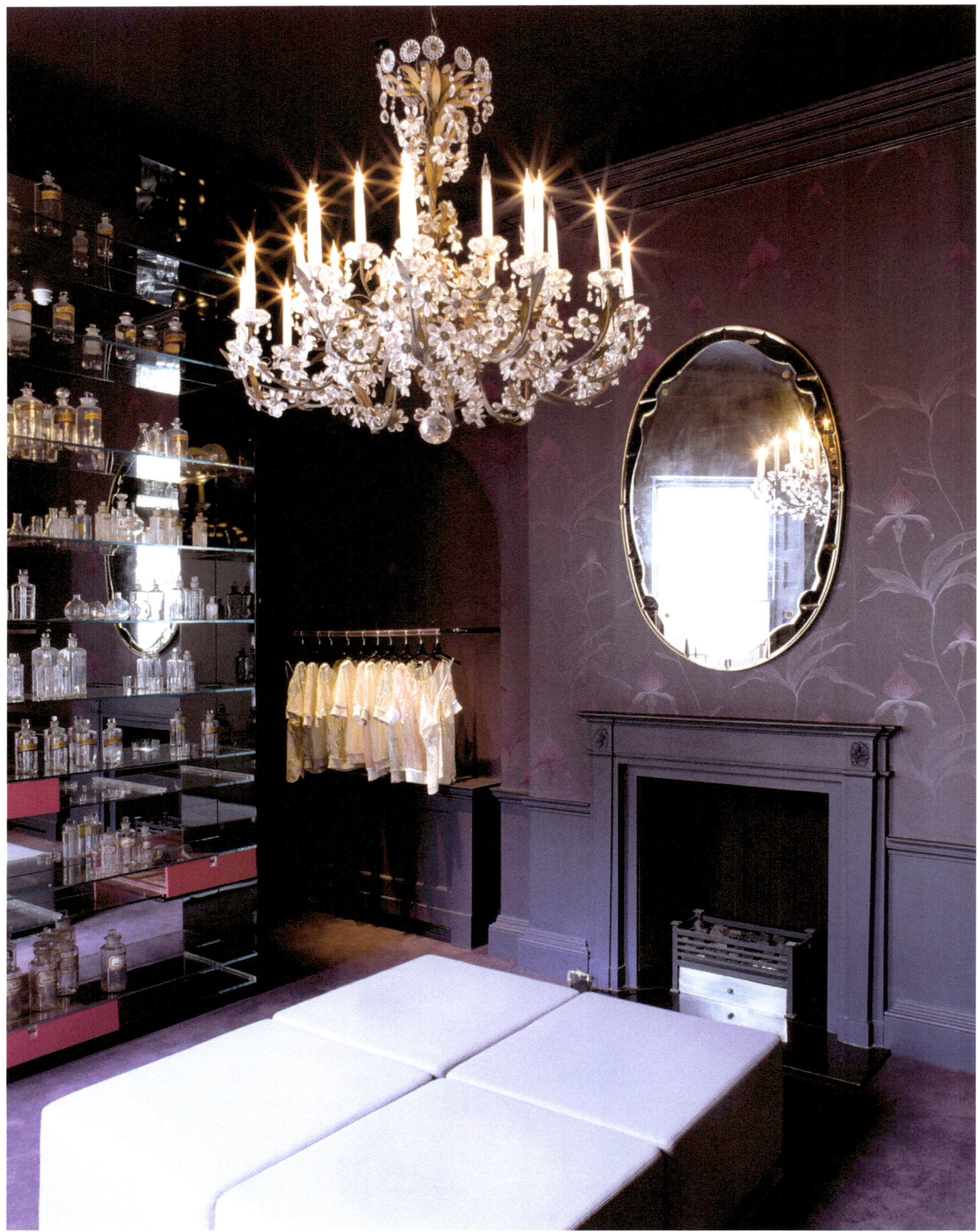

Figure 2.3 The Stella McCartney flagship store in London uses a combination of violet finishes and decorative lighting to create an ethereal, dreamlike quality.

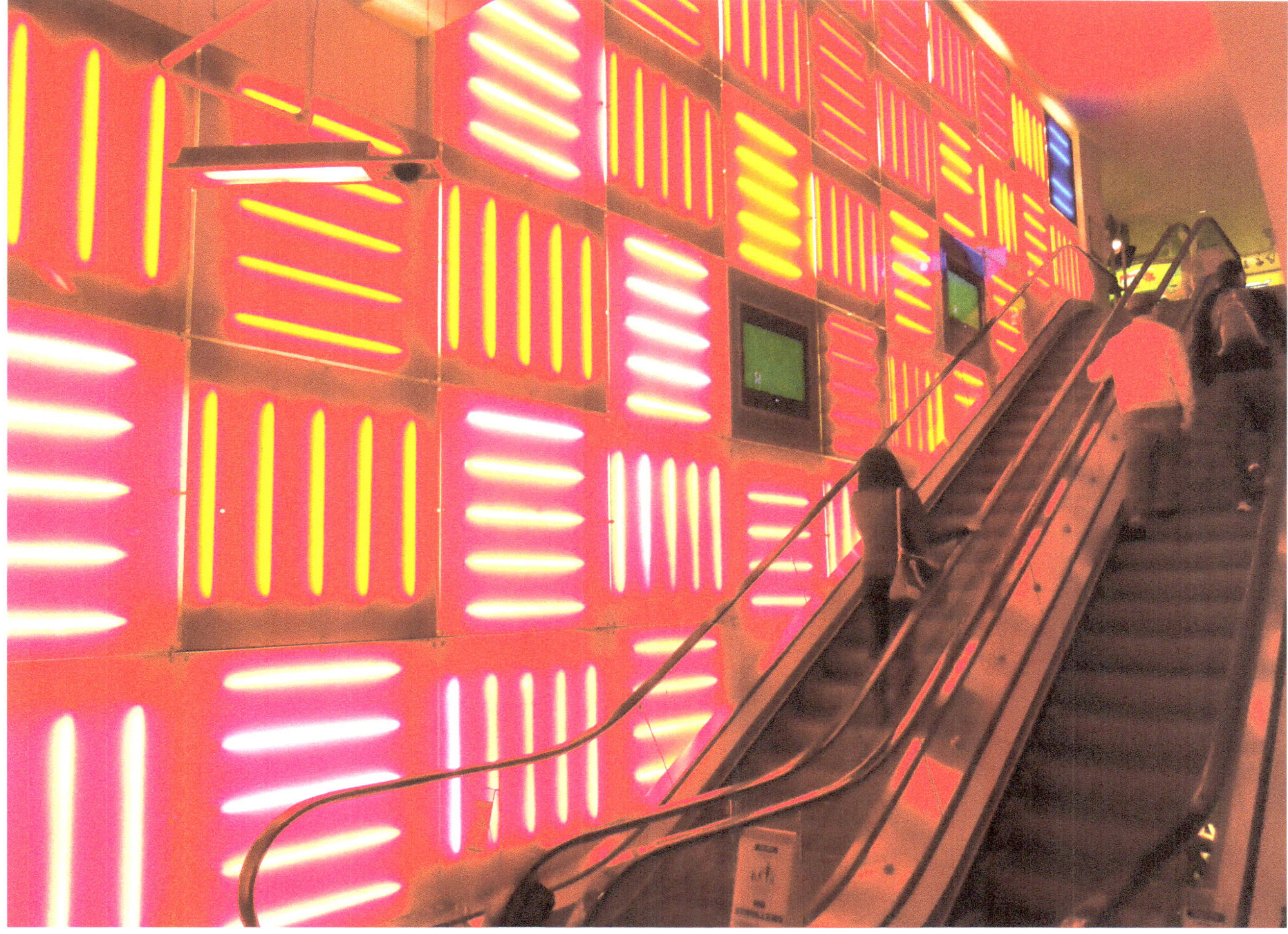

Figure 2.4 Variations of the red light create a dramatic but potentially straining visual experience in the Toys "R" Us store in New York.

Properties of Light

Three properties of light are commonly experienced in the design of the physical environment: reflection, diffraction, and refraction. **Reflection** occurs when light strikes an object, and in the case of seeing color, the light reflected back from an object results in the color we see. **Diffraction** occurs when light is partially obstructed by an object. This interference of the light bends the waves around the edges of the object or opening and spreads outward, producing light, dark, or colored bands. Lastly, **refraction** results when one or more light rays moves through a light medium to another, denser medium such as air to water or a prism, causing light to bend (Figure 2.5). Colored light results in a prism and rainbow when light is slowed due to the material it is passing through. This reduced speed allows for the spectral colors to be seen by the human eye.

Direct color results from viewing a color on a particular surface. **Indirect color** results from adjoining or opposite wall surfaces or objects reflecting their color. When light strikes one or more colored surfaces, it will bounce throughout the space, impacting colored objects nearby. The reflected color mixes with other colored surfaces it's reflected onto or, in the case of a white wall, tints the surface with the reflected colored light (Figures 2.6 and 2.7). A blue-colored wall whose light is reflected onto oak flooring—a yellow-gold—will mix with the floor color, resulting in the floor appearing to have a tinge of green. Additionally, the more colored light is reflected through the space, the less intense the colors become as the light is dispersed. It is because of this process that we will need to move away from the preconceived notion that you can "match" a color with other materials to look for the "acceptable match."

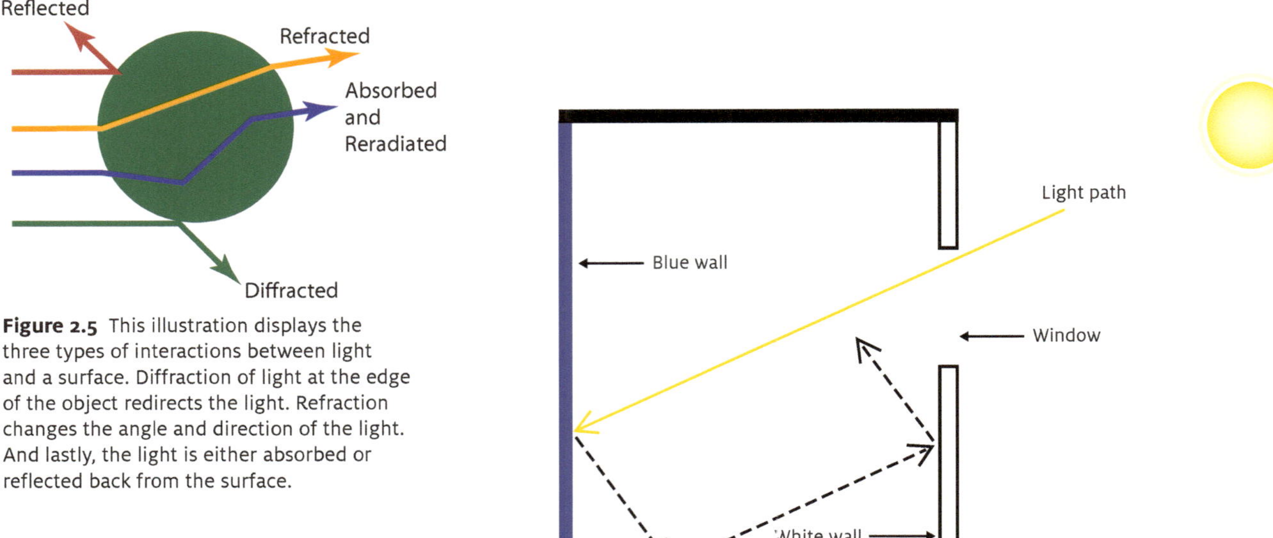

Figure 2.5 This illustration displays the three types of interactions between light and a surface. Diffraction of light at the edge of the object redirects the light. Refraction changes the angle and direction of the light. And lastly, the light is either absorbed or reflected back from the surface.

Figure 2.6 The ray of sunlight passes through the window and is reflected off the blue wall; the color is then reflected onto other surfaces, leaving a slight blue cast. This reduces as the strength of daylight diminishes.

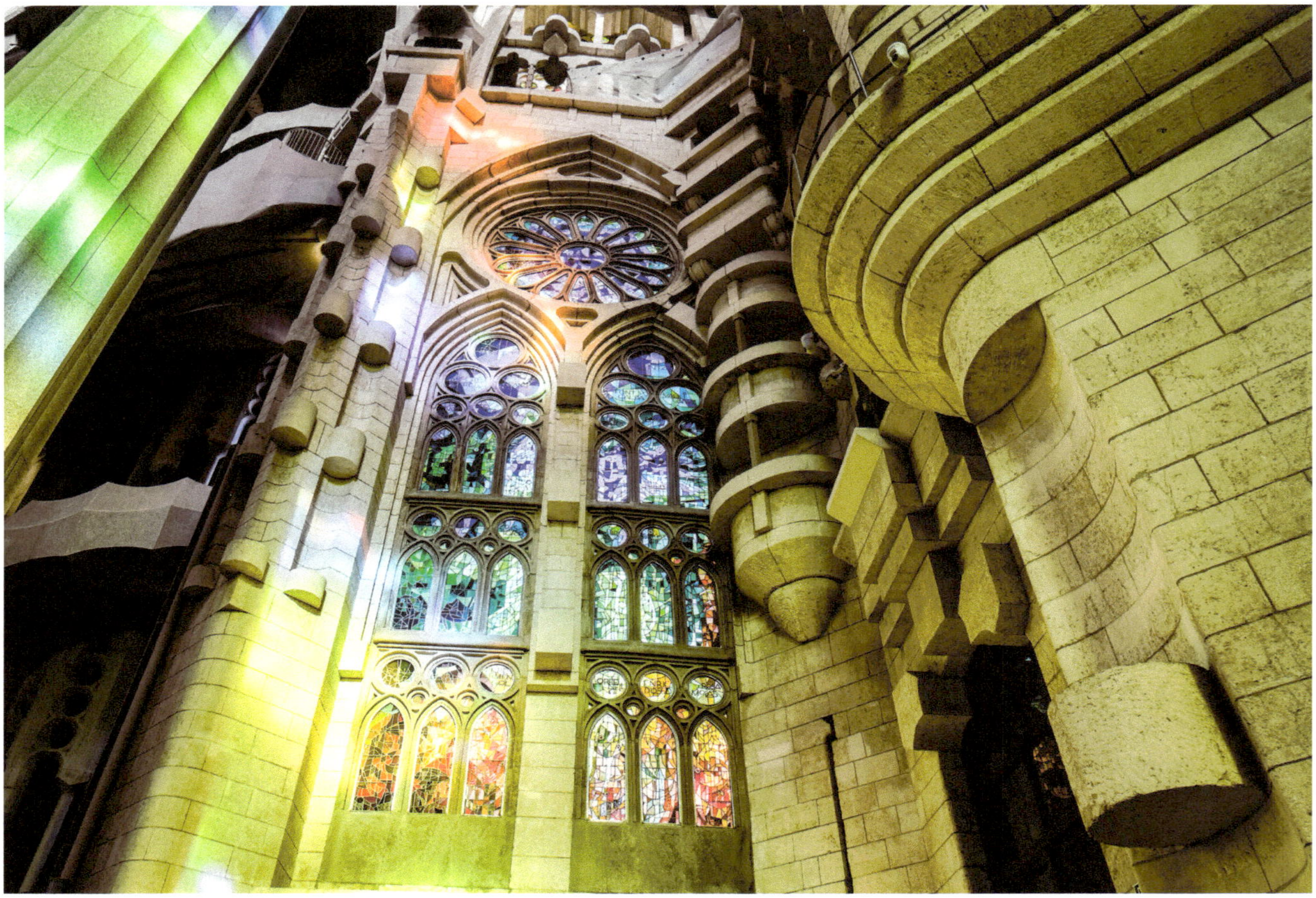

Figure 2.7 Interior view of the Sagrada Familia, Barcelona, Spain. The basilica is a largely unfinished Roman Catholic church, designed by Catalan architect Antoni Gaudi. The stained-glass windows cast indirect colored light onto the surrounding walls of the interior.

While you must understand the mechanics of this process to understand the physical manifestation of color, the most important aspect to remember is that not everyone sees color the same way despite this universal process. Whether the person is working with color for the first time or is a seasoned professional, he or she should be aware of the physical conditions that alter the visual perception of color. These include, but are not limited to, age, gender, aging health of the eye, personality, and forms of color blindness, which will be discussed in Chapter 3. Consider each of the three properties of light when using color in interiors. Each property offers its own unique spin to the way color can be perceived.

Additive Color

There are two basic types of color mixing: with light and pigment. Additive color involves mixing light, and subtractive color involves mixing pigment. In **additive color**, the primary-light colors red, green, and blue are mixed. When these three colors of light are mixed or "added" together, white light is the result, and rationally, the absence of all colored light is black. In addition, when varying intensities of these lights are generated, multiple color combinations are possible. For instance, when the primaries overlap one another, the additive secondary colors are produced: Red light overlapping with blue results in magenta (bluish red), red overlapping with green produces yellow light, and blue light overlapping with green light produces cyan—a greenish blue (Figure2.8).

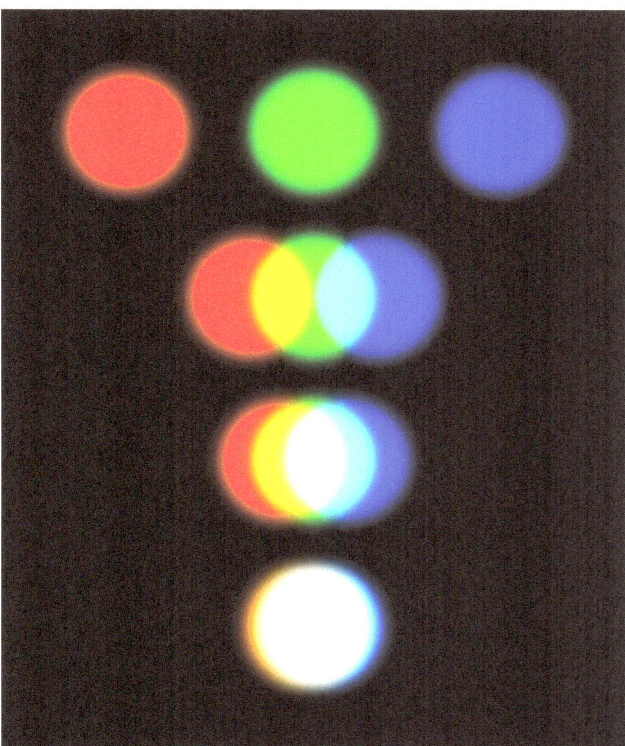

Figure 2.8 Additive color light mixing. RGB color model with three overlapping spotlights representing the additive color mixing model. As the colors are gradually mixed, yellow and cyan hues appear. In this example, blue and red are not overlapping to form magenta. The combination of the primary colors, red, green, and blue in equal intensities makes white light.

Subtractive Color

Subtractive color applies to paint, dyes, colorants, and inks, where blue, red, and yellow are identified as the primary colors. The use of RYB—red, yellow, and blue is referred to as the artist's color wheel and most commonly introduced to children when painting in school (Figure 2.9). In printing and photography they are cyan, magenta, and yellow (CMYK). The letter "K" stands for black. With subtractive mixing, the solid material we are viewing will absorb and reflect wavelengths of color. A red apple will absorb or "subtract out" all colored light and reflect the red wavelength of light back to the eye, resulting in the red apple we see. In reality, an apple isn't red, but rather all other colors of light. The combination

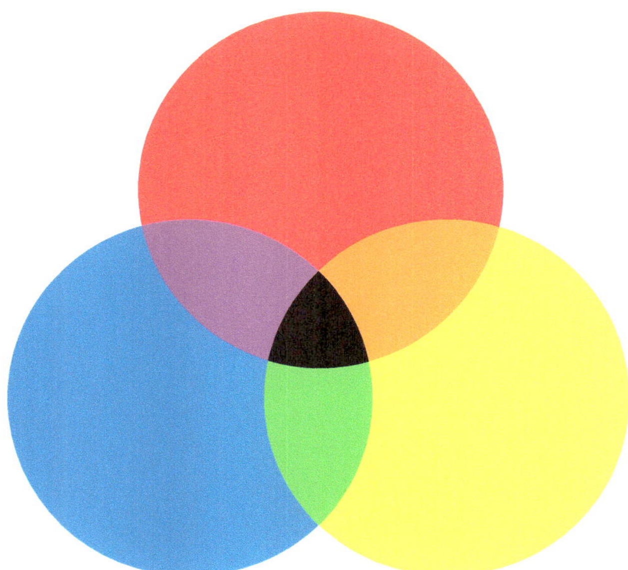

Figure 2.9 Subtractive color mixing with RYB, often referred to as the artist's color wheel. Primary colors red, blue, and yellow mix to create secondary colors violet, green, and orange.

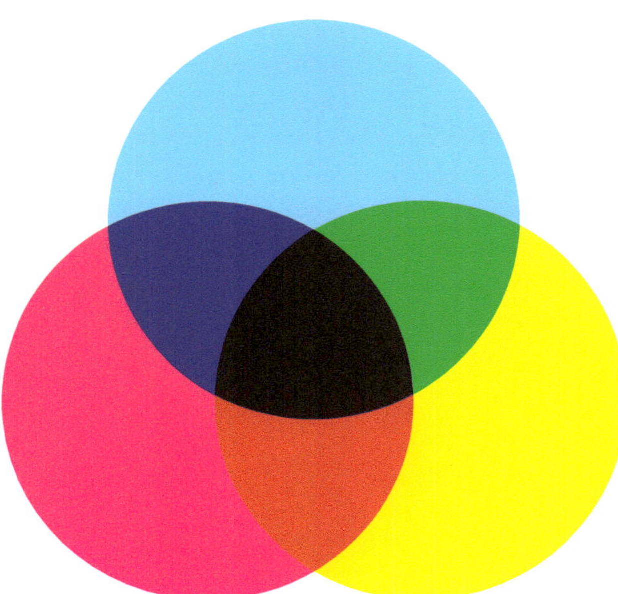

Figure 2.10 Subtractive color process mixing with CMYK.

of the subtractive primaries will result in the secondary colors violet, green, and orange. Further combination of varying degrees of secondary colors with each other and/or their respective primaries will result in a multitude of various color hues (Figure 2.10).

The Many Faces of Color

The key factor that determines a color characteristic in the interior environment is the light source—an often-forgotten design element that can determine whether working with color is stressful or stress-free. I often see students labor over trying to get or create the exact color they have in mind only to have it change in appearance in different lighting conditions. This phenomenon is referred to as **metamerism**. Avoid making color choices under one set of lighting conditions. Whether you're seeing the color during various times of the day, each resulting in different amounts of sunlight; under incandescent or lamp light, fluorescent light or **LED—light emitting diode**; or during different seasonal lighting conditions, each will have a different effect on the perceived color of the object. Because natural light is sunlight, and thus pure light, it consists of all visible colors of light, or white light. Any form of manmade light will vary in color rendition, from a small percentage to much greater, depending on the lighting type being used.

Let's look at an example. Suppose you are standing before hundreds of color choices in a showroom, and you think you've determined just the right colors for your project. You take the swatches home, and suddenly the blue no longer looks blue—it's now green. What happened? Did you pick up the wrong sample? This is an all-too-familiar incident for many people when selecting color swatches for upholstering new furnishings. We've become so accustomed to color, we don't even realize how complicated it can be, taking it for granted and assuming that it will always stay constant no matter how or where we decide to use it. Light is the key, since, after all, color *is* light, and many times we ignore light, not realizing it is more important than the color itself.

Color can be daunting to work with, offering a multitude of possibilities that often make you feel like you are playing a game of roulette trying to find the perfect color palette. Because of the importance of light in selecting color, it is crucial to examine the color source in different lighting conditions. Color choices are mistakenly made in showrooms without clients ever seeing the color at home. Showrooms are typically illuminated with multiple light sources, including fluorescent bulbs. Artificial light sources never render the true color characteristics of fabrics, trims, paint, or wood tones (Figure 2.11). Fluorescent lights generally emit reddish (warm) or bluish (cool) light that will alter the true color of materials, and once the materials are placed within our homes, they will appear noticeably different. The correlated color temperature, defined in degrees **Kelvin**, of various light sources will determine the proper color rendition of surface finishes and materials under various lighting conditions (Figure 2.12). The Kelvin temperature scale is based on a numerical system where natural sunlight is generally noted at around 5,500 K and candlelight is around 1,500 K (Figure 2.13). A 40-watt incandescent lamp is around 2,680 K, and most incandescent lamps range from 2,600 to 3,100 K. Fluorescent lamps will have a color temperature around 4,100 K. Kelvin represents the full color range in the visible spectrum. The higher the Kelvin number, the cooler the temperature, and the lower the number, the warmer the temperature, relative to the color wavelengths mentioned earlier. The first two numbers represent the range of 0 to 100, with the second number indicating the Kelvin temperature to the nearest hundred. LED lighting color temperature can range from warm (low Kelvin) to cool (high Kelvin) and be adjustable

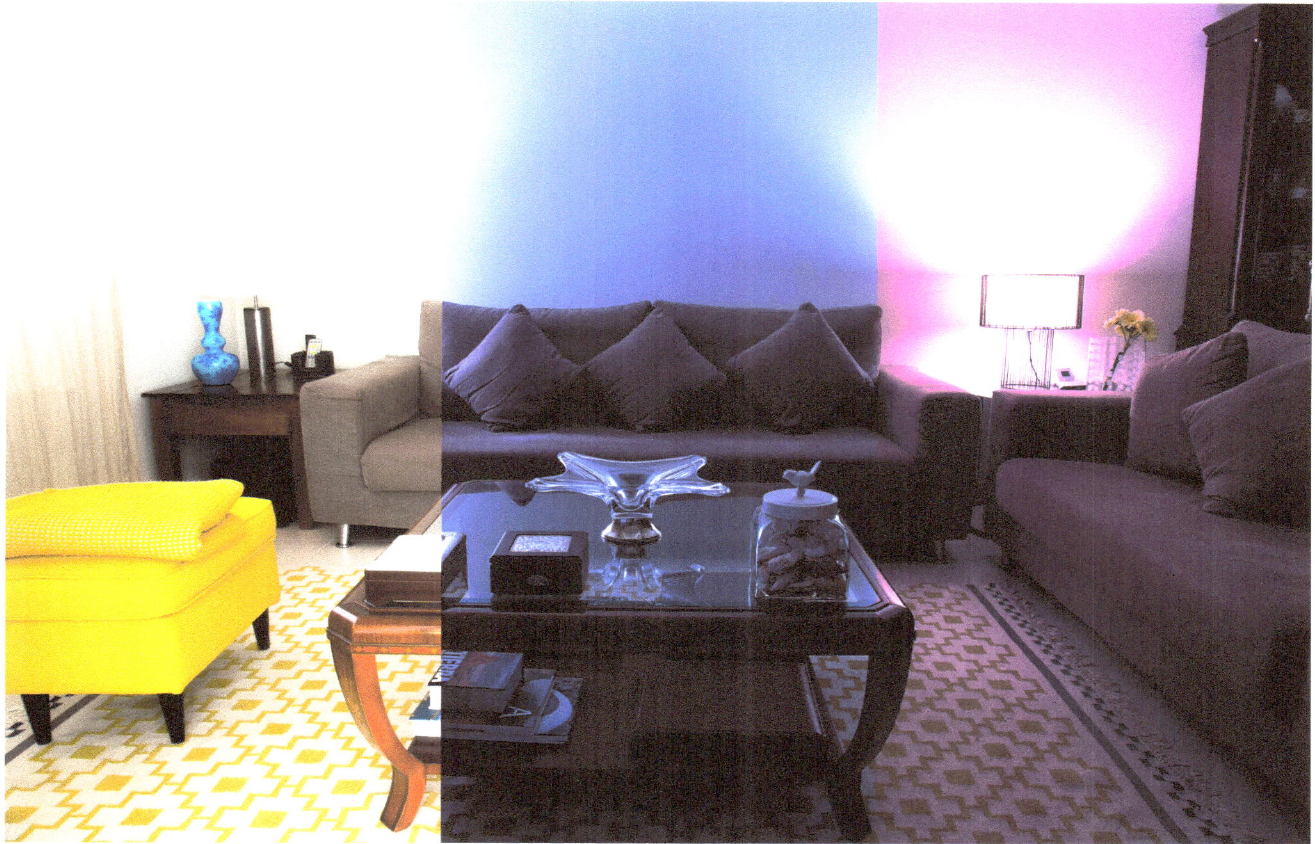

Figure 2.11 Influence of day, night, natural and artificial lighting on color perception.

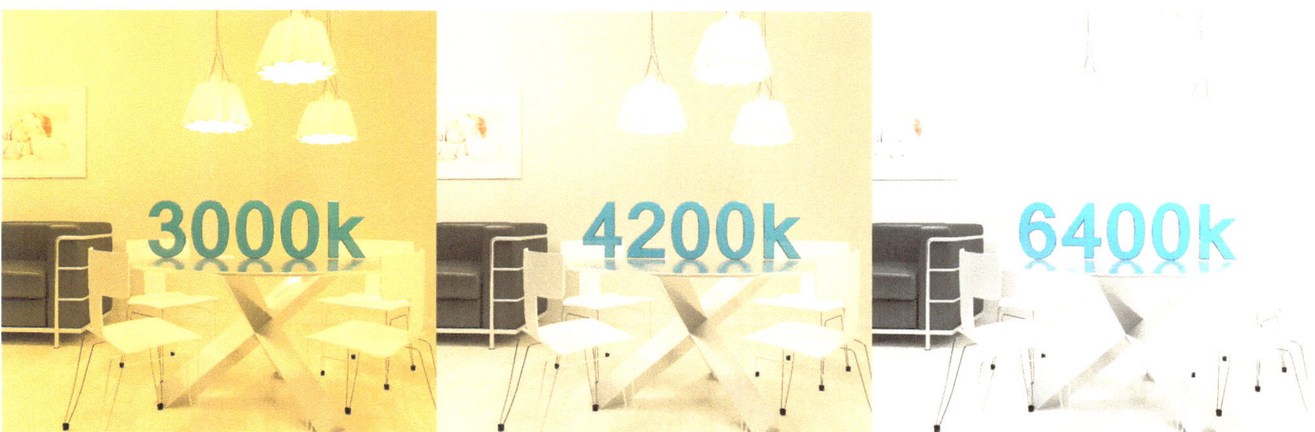

Figure 2.12 This 3D rendering illustrates how lighting color temperature change affects the overall character and mood of a space.

to the desired color temperature needed for a particular space. The color of light, room type and function, and the desired effect will influence the color temperature needed for your light sources. **The color rendering index** (CRI) indicates the light source's ability to render the true color of an object as it would appear in natural light using Kelvin to identify the color temperature. The higher the CRI index rating (80 or above), the less likely an individual color will vary in appearance from its appearance in sunlight.

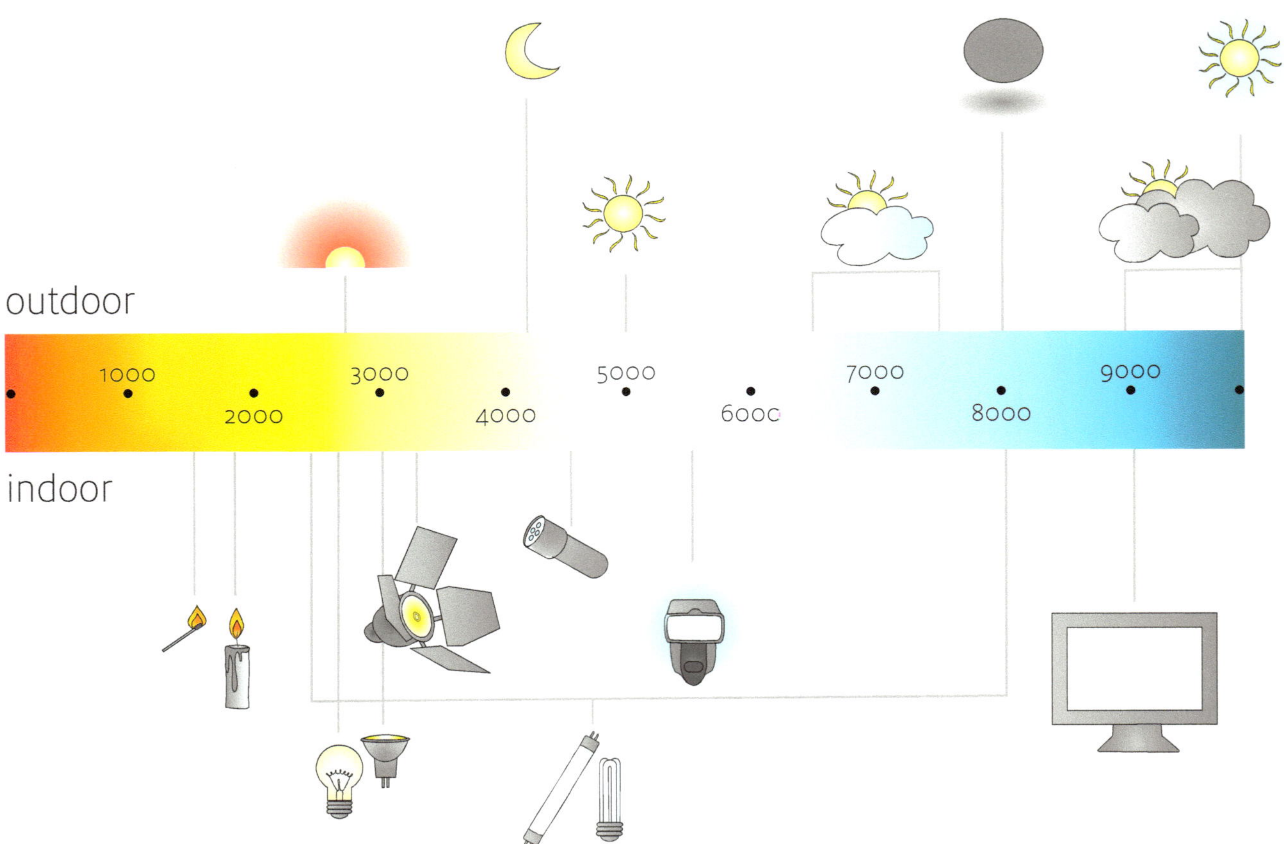

Figure 2.13 Kelvin scale with common indoor lighting types and outdoor lighting conditions indicated by color temperature.

Working with a knowledgeable lighting designer or lighting specialist will eliminate the guesswork concerning the characteristics of the many possible light sources. Following are a few tips to keep in mind:

- Showrooms typically provide **memo samples** of upholstery used in their furniture lines. These samples are large and show one or multiple repeats of the pattern design. Be sure not to work with small samples when making color decisions. The small samples are inadequate in representing the true color and pattern on furniture, drapery, walls, and so on. When possible, take the samples home and view the fabrics under the different light sources in the home. Examine the textile in morning, afternoon, and nighttime lighting conditions. The location in the room, time of day, and amount of natural sunlight reaching a particular area in your room, as well as the artificial lighting in the home, will all contribute to the many faces of the color. Generally speaking, neutrals and lighter tones will have a greater color change than darker tones. Neutral colors can have a remnant of other colors present that, when intensified by certain light sources, might result in a hint of the color coming through. For instance, perhaps you've had the experience where that lovely shade of antique-white paint you selected looked pink once applied to a wall.
- The surface characteristics of textiles, trims, and wood will also play a role in their perceived color. The color of highly textured surfaces will appear darker in value, and glossy surfaces will appear lighter. This is because of the amount of light that is reflected off the surface—the more light reflected, the brighter the color; the less light reflected, the darker the color. If

you are attempting to match a color, surface texture is a key factor to your success. It will be difficult to match two items of the same color with different textures. At most, you can coordinate.

- When you are examining the color source at different times of the day and under different light sources to see how dramatically the color changes, also examine the source in different positions. If you are selecting a textile, lay the textile flat on the seat of a chair or sofa as well as vertically to examine how its color changes. Light reflects off vertical and horizontal surfaces differently, and color will vary accordingly. It is best to view your color selections in the location where they are intended to be used; otherwise, you run the risk of improper color selection and balancing with other colors in the room. The same principles apply to paint. It is better to buy a quart and paint a large (about 5 feet by 5 feet) area on your walls in different locations within the rooms and examine how much the color changes under various light sources and at different times of day. If using this technique, paint the sample area with the same finish that will be used on the walls (flat, eggshell, gloss); otherwise, the reflective qualities will change the paint color. Some designers paint the color onto pieces of white foamboard or drywall to test the color before painting. Caution is needed if your walls are textured, since foam board is a smooth surface, which may cause the color to appear lighter.
- If you are a student at a school of design, check to see if you have a color-viewing light-box. This tool incorporates various lighting sources where colored materials and product samples can be viewed to witness these color changes (Figure 2.14).

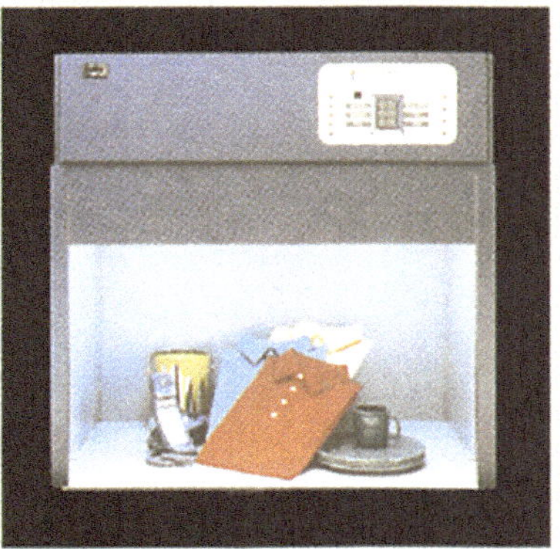

Daylight D75

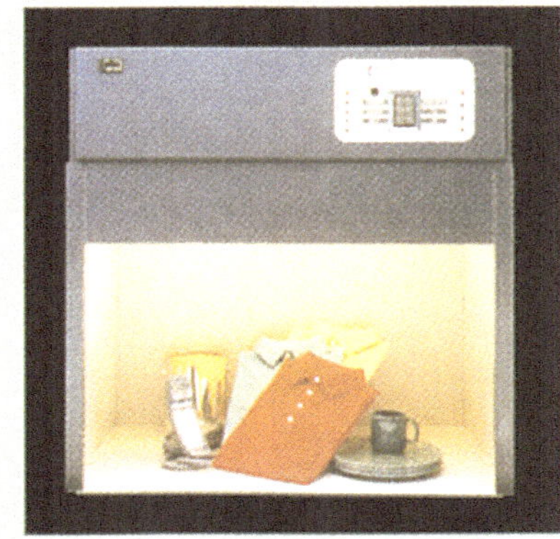

Horizon daylight

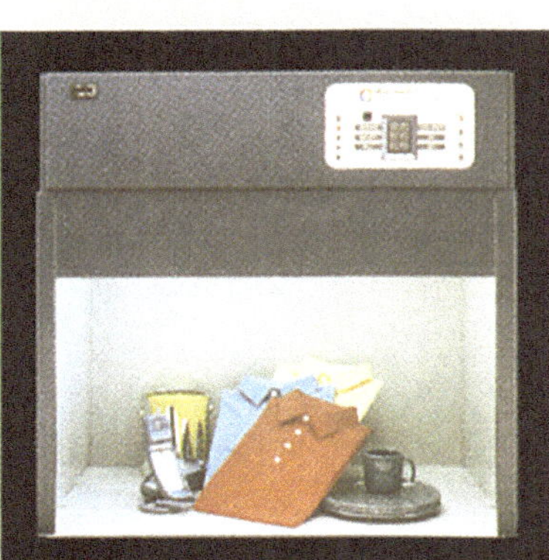

Cool white florescent

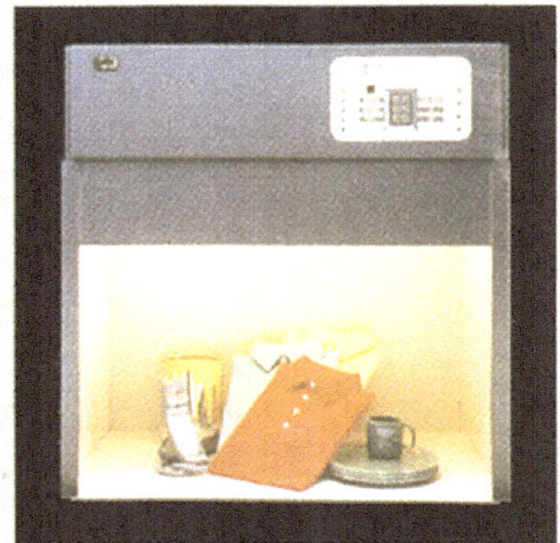

Illuminant A (incandescent)

Figure 2.14
Color changes under various simulated lighting conditions.

These tips will ensure that the color sources chosen do not change in such a way as to compromise the overall room design and will assist you in finding colors that are appealing to your sense of style. Color is complicated, but with some basic skills and a fearless attitude, you'll gain a greater sense of security to explore with color.

Effects of Natural and Artificial Light on Color Perception

Natural light produces an emotional and behavioral response to our environments that affects our perception of color, space, and material texture. Spaces flooded with low natural light levels, which occur early in the morning and late in the evening, tend to feel more intimate and quiet. Natural daylight during sunrise and sunset is around 3,500K producing warm, soft, red and yellow light. Brighter sunlight during midday, between 5,000–6,500K, is whiter: bluer light seen as more vivid and can produce the perception of excitement and energy. As sunlight moves through our day, surface color shifts and changes. Window placement and solar orientation to this light will influence our perception of color (Figure 2.15).

North-facing windows receive no direct sunlight. The light from this direction is cool, gray, and bluish throughout the day. Colors that are bright are generally effective in these spaces and warm colors will counter the cool northern exposure they receive. Southern light exposure is hot and provides the brightest light throughout the day; however, the intense direct light will often weaken and fade the appearance of color. As a result, darker, richer color will work well and can absorb some of the intense light and reduce glare and the use of cool colors will counter the warm southern exposure rooms. Additionally, muted hues and neutral and cooler palettes can be successful in offsetting the brightness and temperature

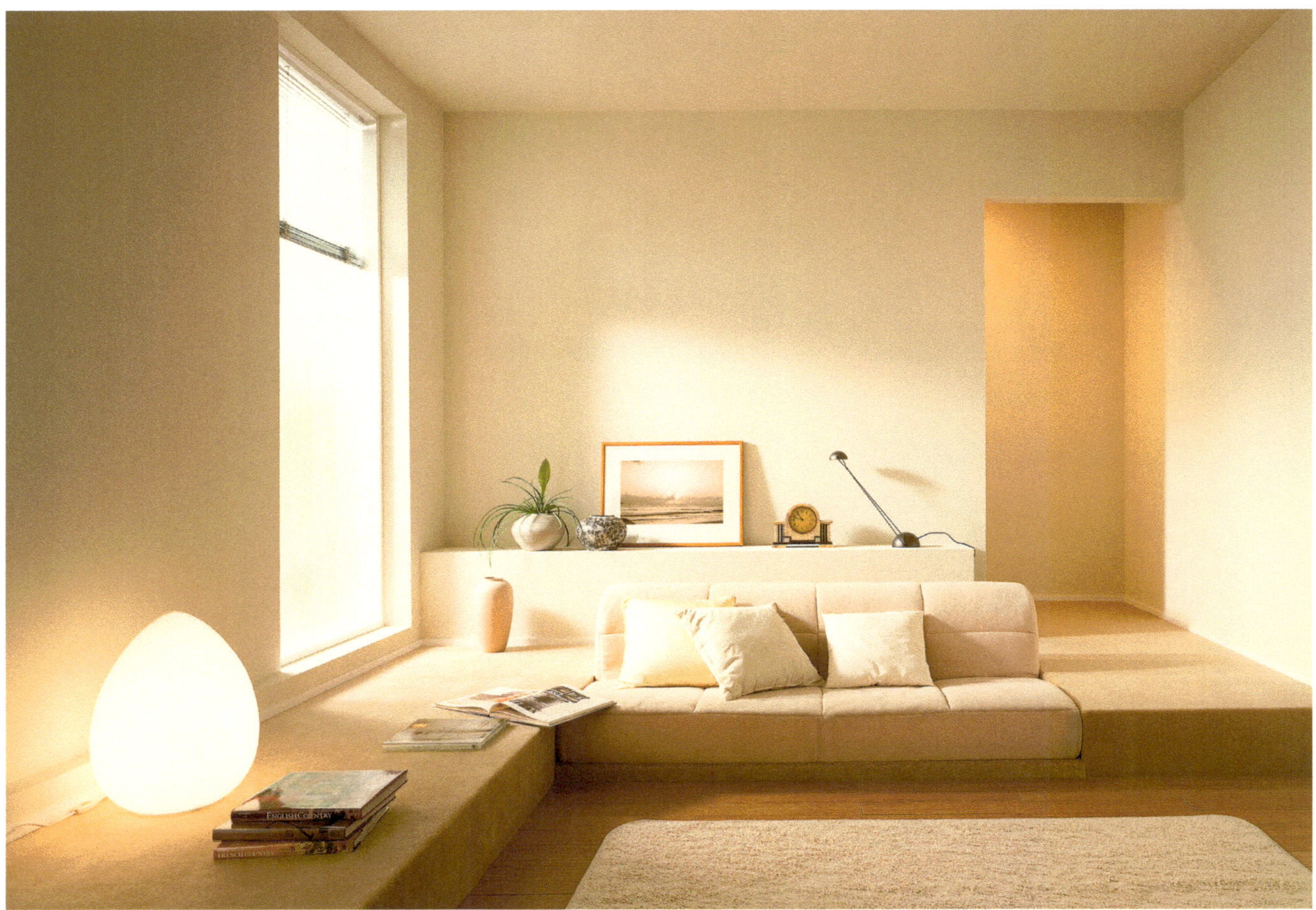

Figure 2.15 The color of the walls and surrounding areas in this living room change in appearance depending on whether these surfaces are illuminated by natural or artificial lighting.

one might experience, creating a comfortable space. East-facing windows tend to receive warm, yellow sunlight before noon. Spaces with warm color palettes work well in these areas, with the temperature cooler, creating inviting, cheerful spaces. West-facing spaces will receive warm sunlight starting at midday, although with less intensity than southern light. Most color reads well in these lit spaces. Warm colors will appear more intense.

Light Reflectance

Light reflectance value (LRV) refers to the percentage of light that is reflected from a colored surface back into the interior space. Paint manufacturers provide light reflectance values ranging in percentage from 0 to 100 for their products. Zero has no reflectance value (black), and 100 reflects the most light (white). Take caution to avoid high reflectance values, as the glare can cause discomfort and eye fatigue. Avoid in places of extensive or continuous use, such as surfaces in work environments. A good rule of thumb for residential spaces is that anything within 50 percent LRV is generally acceptable. The amount of reflectance from vertical and horizontal surfaces and the interior finishes within must be taken into consideration. Ceilings need a reflectance value between 60 and 90 percent, walls between 30 and 60 percent, and floors between 15 and 35 percent. In spaces where task lighting is needed versus ambient lighting, these numbers should increase approximately 10 percent in reflectance value.

Surface characteristics add to the visual perception of colored matter. Surfaces that are reflective weaken the apparent color, whereas textured surfaces strengthen the perceived darkness of color, particularly due to the shadows that are created in this process. There are varying degrees of reflected qualities of surfaces, and much like the value scale, the textural qualities of these surfaces will change the perceived lightness or darkness of a color (Figure 2.16). The most common time that interior designers consider properties of reflection is when working with paints—when the choice of flat, eggshell, satin, semigloss, and gloss sheens is available. If there is too much glare in the surface material, it will be difficult to see the color.

Color Systems

Color theorists study and explain the characteristics of color creations, interactions, and arrangements. Many theorists and authors have spent years researching color and providing systems to aid those interested in expanding their knowledge and increasing their confidence in using color. An entire book could be dedicated to delving into the historical developments of color systems. The complexities alone are addressed in a series of books. No single system has been identified as ideal for interior design. Over the last three centuries, there have been twelve books considered "crucial to the study of color" (Burchett, 2005, p. 91), starting as early as 1749 with the works of Goethe. A chronological history of these twelve works is presented in Table 2.2. For this book, we will look at those systems that are more commonly known and referred to today in design education and practice.

Isaac Newton

Several theoretical approaches and interpretations of the color wheel have been developed since Sir Isaac Newton's work was published in 1666. Between 1664 and 1666, Newton developed his theory of color and delivered his findings in a lecture series conducted between 1670 and 1672. His work on color theory was later produced in his book *Opticks*. Newton was more interested in the physics of color and is known for having discovered refracted colors—a phenomenon that results when light passes through a prism (Figure 2.17). He developed the first of what would later become many color wheels, which consisted of the visible colors of the spectrum (primary and secondary) constructed with their relative proportions, as seen when colored light is refracted (Figure 2.18).

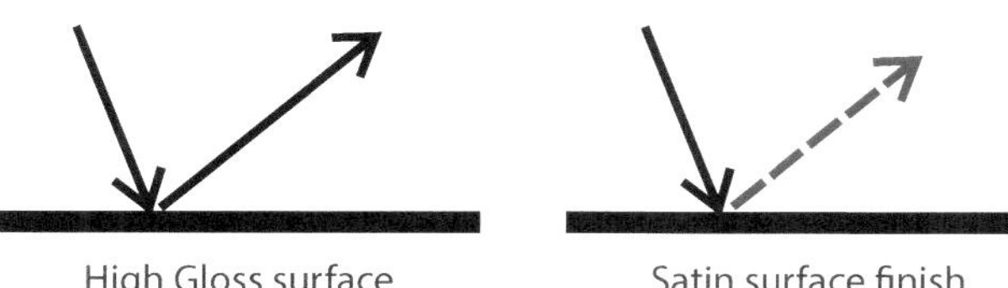

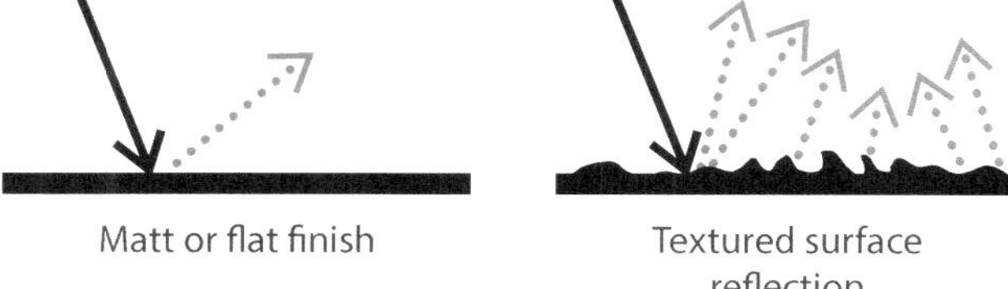

Figure 2.16 Surface texture reflection characteristics.

TABLE 2.2 CHRONOLOGICAL HISTORY OF TWELVE WORKS ON COLOR THEORY

Timeline scale: 1750 · 1775 · 1800 · 1825 · 1850 · 1875 · 1900 · 1925 · 1950 · 1975 · 2000

Name	Born	Work	Died
Goethe	1749	1810	1832
Chevreul	1786	1839	1889
Helmholtz	1821	1856–1866	1894
Munsell	1858	1905	1918
Katz	1884	1911	1953
Kandinsky	1866	1912	1944
Pope	1880	1929	1976
Wright	1906	1944	1997
Judd	1900	1952	1972
Arnheim	1904	1954	2007
Itten	1888	1961	1967
Albers	1888	1963	1976

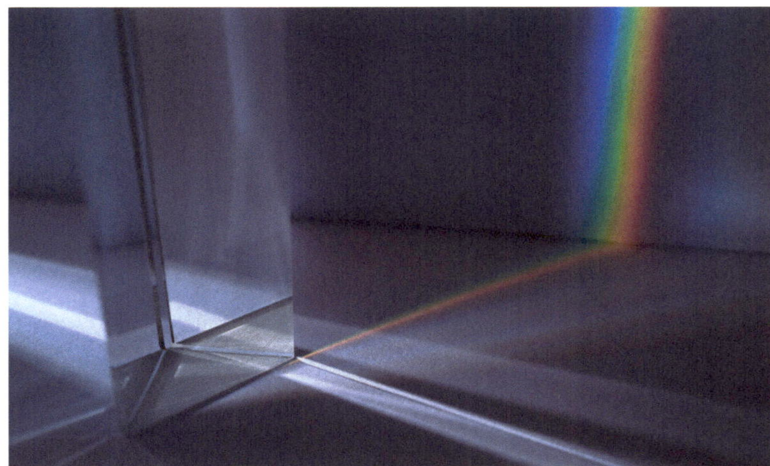

Figure 2.17 Colored light spectrum refracted through a prism.

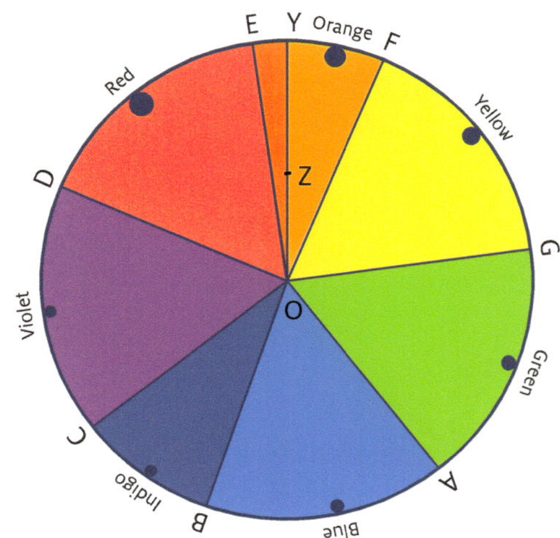

Figure 2.18 Newton color wheel.

Albert H. Munsell

American-born Munsell (1858–1918) developed the most widely used color system, known as the "color tree" (Figure 2.19). His book *A Color Notation* (1905) has become a must-read in art and design schools. Munsell was credited for developing the three dimensions of color: hue, value, and chroma (saturation). **Hue** (pure color) is the property of light by which the color of an object is classified as red, blue, green, or yellow in reference to the visible spectrum. Hue is expressed in the "branches" of the color tree. Munsell's color tree consists of ten hues. Each hue in the color trees is assigned a letter and numerical notation: 5R (red), 5YR (yellow-red), 5Y (yellow), 5GY (green-yellow), 5G (green), 5BG (bluegreen), 5B (blue), 5PB (purple-blue), 5P (purple), 5RP (red-purple). The number 5 represents the center of the color family, where each color is at its purest. **Value** refers to the lightness or darkness of a color. Munsell identifies value on a scale of 0 to 10, with pure white at the top for 0, gray in the middle for 5, and black at the bottom for 10. Value is expressed in the "trunk" of the tree. **Chroma** refers to the purity of a color, completely absent of any white, gray, or black that would lessen its intensity or saturation, two additional terms acceptable for describing the color strength. Chroma is represented by the horizontal scale on the color tree (Figure 2.20). As you move up the trunk and outward, the hues become lighter in value. As you move down the trunk and outward, the hues become darker. The closer you are to the trunk with any given hue, the less saturated the color; the farther out on the branches, the purer the color will be.

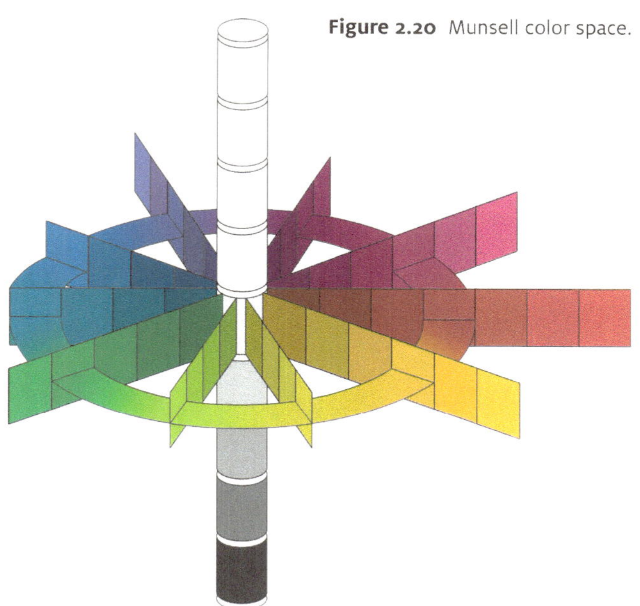

Figure 2.20 Munsell color space.

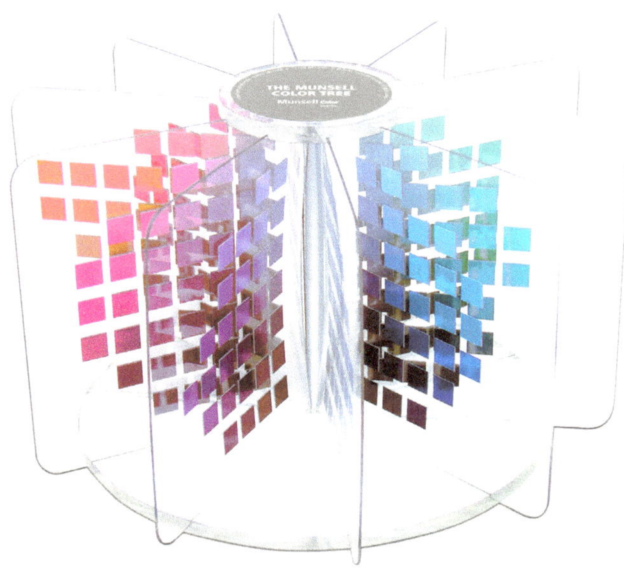

Figure 2.19 Munsell color tree system.

Josef Albers

Josef Albers (1888–1976) was a German-born artist who taught at the Bauhaus School of Art, which was founded by Walter Gropius and operated between 1919 and 1933. Albers is notably credited with his work in color relationships published in his book *Interaction of Color* in a series of well-known artworks (Figure 2.21). Albers's work investigates illusions of color using colored paper—a material that is easily available, inexpensive compared to electronic color media, and commonly used in design school today. After the closure of the Bauhaus school, Albers immigrated to the United States in 1933, where he taught color theory at Black Mountain College until 1949. Albers moved to Connecticut, and from 1950 to 1959 he was the chairman of the Department of Design at the Yale University School of Art (Droste, 2006, p. 242). Since designers are constantly working with color media, his work is of importance when you need to quickly investigate color manipulation and changes. Examples of his interactions are demonstrated in Chapter 3, Figure 3.11.

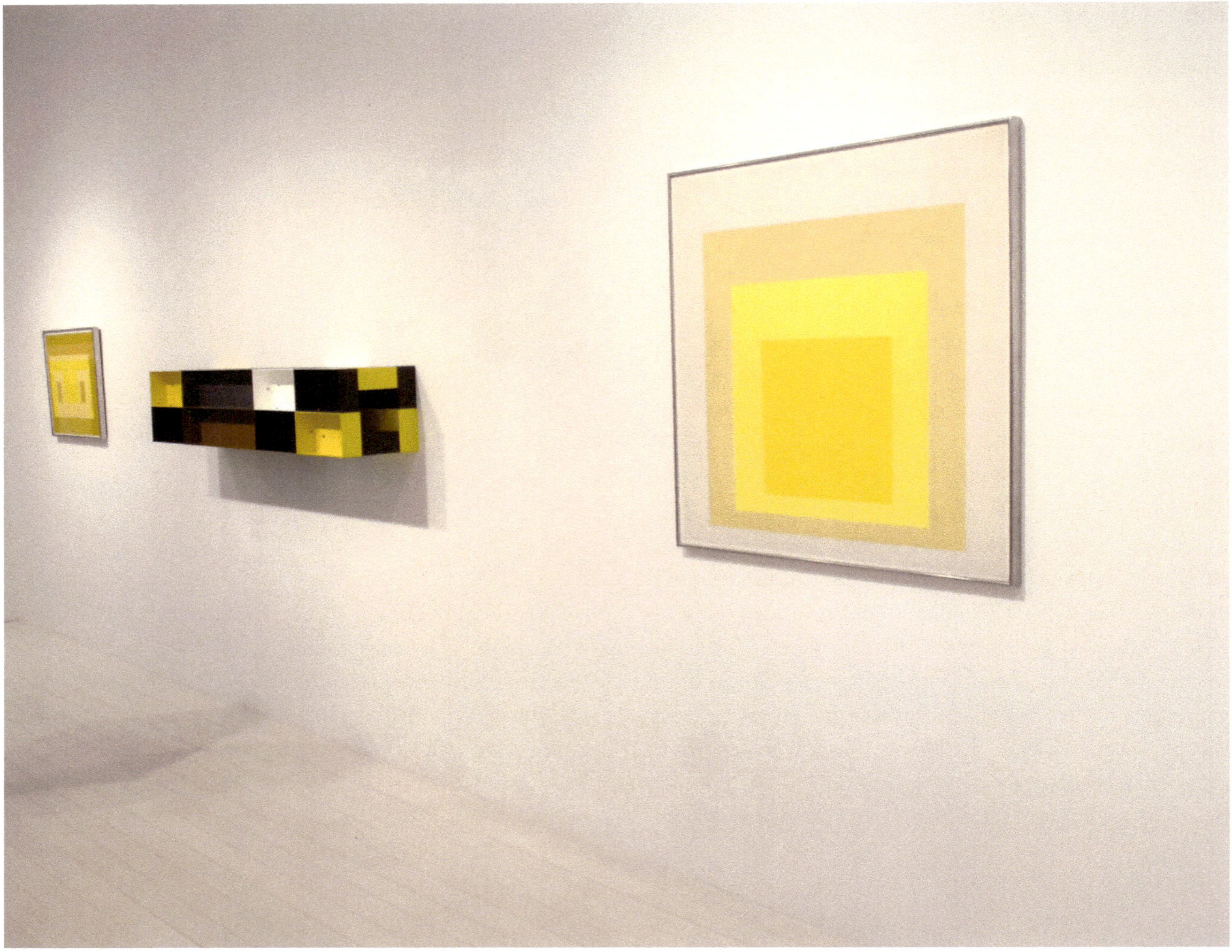

Figure 2.21 *Homage to Square* by Josef Albers.

Johannes Itten

Johannes Itten (1888–1967) was a Swiss-born painter, textile designer, and teacher of color theory. Itten began teaching at the Bauhaus in 1919 and left in 1923 due to conflicts with Walter Gropius over his teaching methods (Froebel Web, 2002, ¶7). Itten wrote several books on color theory, including *The Elements of Color* and *The Art of Color*. Itten developed the twelve-pointed color star (Figure 2.20) in which he primarily explored contrast, most notably cold-warm contrasts. Itten was the first to explore color expressed through shape and form using astrological, cultural traditions, and symbols that have greatly influenced our perception of color and shape. His theory is explained further in Chapter 3.

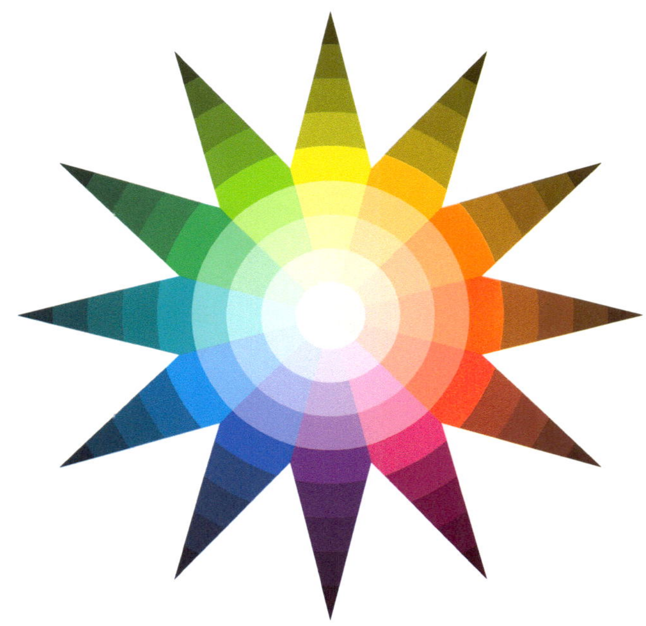

Figure 2.22 The Color Star by Johannes Itten.

Faber Birren

American-born Faber Birren (1900–1988) attended the University of Chicago from 1920 to 1921, where he studied color theory. At the age of thirty, Birren moved to New York to work as a color consultant. Birren is well known for publishing twenty-five books on color, beginning with *Color in Vision* in 1928. His most notable pieces of work—*Principles of Color, Color and Human Response*, and *Light, Color, and Environment*—are still used in art and design schools today. Birren was one of the first color theorists to recognize the human biological and psychological responses to color. His research focused on the changing physical environment and the emotional characteristics of its inhabitants.

Natural Color System® (NCS®)

The Natural Color System originated in Switzerland and is the country's national color standard. Originally founded in 1945 and later called the Color Institute, its current name was established in 1978. The original NCS color Atlas consisted of 1,412 standard colors. Since its inception, additional colors have been added with the current collection comprised of 1,950 colors. NCS is currently represented in twenty-two countries and is currently the national color standard in Norway, Spain, South Africa, and Sweden and is one of the most widely used international systems for color communication among designers and architects. The Natural Color System was developed based on the way we see and perceive color visually to describe and communicate color rather than how it is processed or made. The NCS system is used world-wide by architects, designers, and material manufacturers. For example, a manufacturer could use the NCS chromatic system to develop a line of porcelain tiles or architectural products. The most notable element is their forty-hue color circle which is a horizontal section of the three-dimensional color model located at fifty percent, or center, of the color model using red, blue, green, and yellow as its distinctive primaries, with nine intermediate steps between each (Figure 2.23a). In this figure, the color in bold-faced type, R90B, refers to the color red with ninety percent of blue. This is further subdivided into a three-dimensional color space (Figure 2.23b) and individual triangles (Figure 2.23c) representing a vertical section of the model for each hue with fifty-three individual color separations. The triangle shows

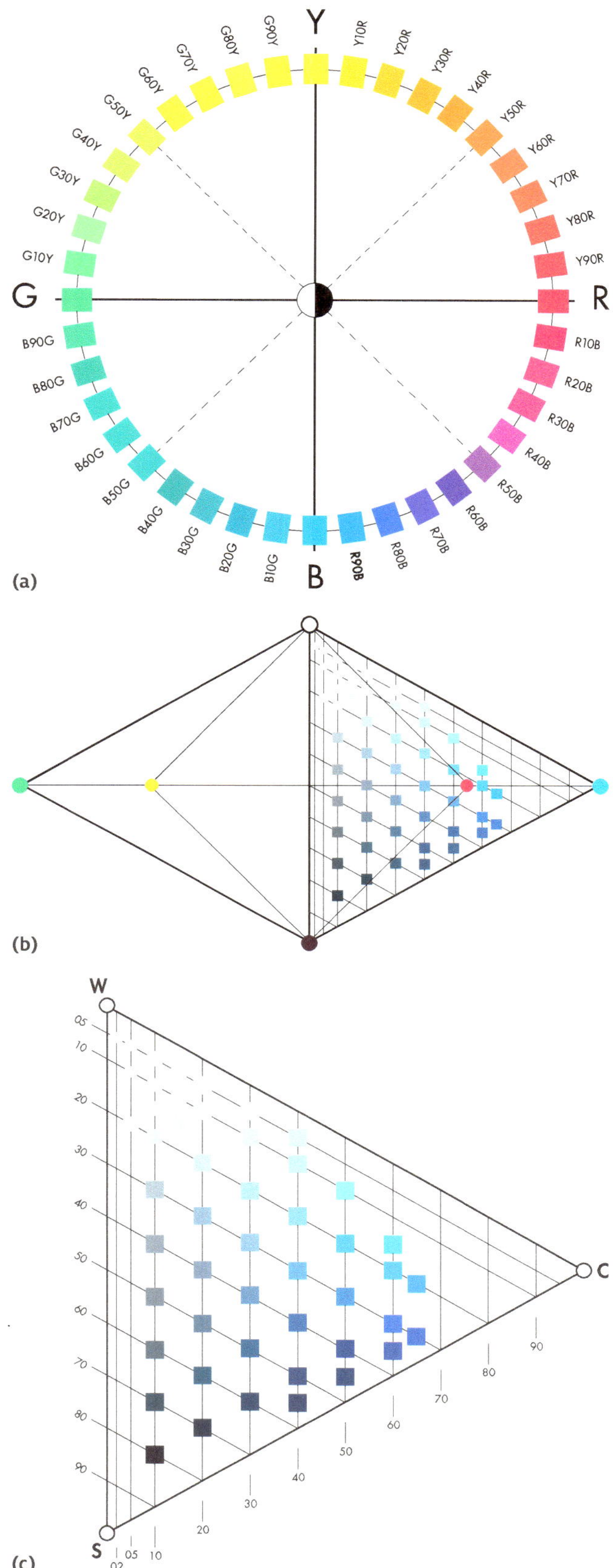

Figure 2.23 (a) NCS color circle—forty hues. (b) NCS Three-dimensional color space. (c) NCS color triangle showing the grey scale of a hue, in this case R90B.

the value nuance for each hue from white (W) to black (S) and the chroma (C) within each hue. In a complete color notation, S 1050-R50B, the S refers to the current standard color edition, the number 1050 refers to the value (ten-percent blackness) and chroma (fifty-percent color strength). And as we mentioned earlier; the letter R represents the color red with fifty-percent blue; this would be violet, halfway between pure red and pure blue. Locate this color on the chart in Figure 2.23a. To ensure consistency in color across products and materials, the NCS system is used globally from car manufacturers to furniture manufactures, including Volvo® and IKEA®.

The NCS offers a variety of educational tools for students and teachers of color theory. These educational tools provide students with a multitude of color samples to explore various visual manipulations of color. Several of the exercises represent the work of Albers and Itten. Information on purchasing these materials is available on the Web at www.ncscolour.com.

Pantone®

Pantone was introduced in 1963 and located in New York City as a color matching system for the commercial ink and print industry. Pantone formula guides provide a tool for color management, matching, identification, and communication of color to produce color more accurately. Pantone is currently used in retail, fashion, graphic arts, paint, interiors, and product development. It offers a variety of media to use for color specification and selection, including cotton swatch charts, color charts, colored plastics, and design books, to name a few. Pantone colors are organized into two systems, one that can be used for print and packaging with paper and plastics, and the second for product design, including textiles for fashion, apparel, home interiors, coatings and pigments, and plastics. The system began with 500 colors and has expanded to include additional colors depending on the media type. For example, there are presently 1,867 colors for printing on paper and 2,310 colors available on dyed cotton or nylon.

The proprietary numbering system corresponds to the specific media type. For example, the dye on cotton fabric color named grape kiss is identified by the number 18-3014 TCX. The two-digit number refers to the lightness or darkness of the color followed by a dash and a four-digit number which refers to the specific color. The letter C refers to the specific media, in this example, cotton. When a specific color is selected for a logo or brand color, home interiors, apparel and fashion, the PMS system is optimized for color management and consistency of the color across different materials.

The Pantone system of reference guides, samples, and software are used globally as a language of color. The Pantone Color Institute offers international color consulting conducting color psychology and consumer color preference research, color trend forecasting, and brand development, and identifies cultural influences on color and design. Additional information about Pantone® is available on the Web at www.pantone.com.

Color-aid®

The Color-aid system is an acid-free colored-paper system developed in 1948 and used extensively by Josef Albers in teaching color in art and design classes. The system consists of 314 colors with 34 vivid hues (saturated colors), 100 tints (clean, light colors), 47 shades (dark, deep colors), 114 pastels (muted or soft colors), and 17 grays from dark to light, plus black and white organized to reflect the Munsell system. The matte-finish samples are offered in sizes ranging from 2 by 3 inches to 6 by 9 inches. This system can be an invaluable tool for design students who will eventually work with color charts, color decks, and other color matching and management systems for color selection and specification.

Digital Color Media

A variety of printing techniques and computer applications that expand on these various systems are used in the communication design industry. In the visualization of interiors, these systems are limited in function and convenience. Computer screens and television technology use the additive theory RBG, or red, blue, and green, light for color mixing. CYMK is another system composed of cyan, yellow, magenta, and black. While these systems do have their place in working with color, the common problem is the difference that results between the colors viewed on a screen (light) and the printed paper (pigment); the designer must always keep in mind that pixels aren't the same as paint. This can be seen when students use various manufacturers' online sample programs for specifying materials and finishes. Students are often confused when they've selected a fabric, paint, or solid surface material for a project online only

Figure 2.24 The colored square on the far left is the pure hue for orange. In each of the subsequent squares, the original hue has been modified with white, then gray, then black to show the changes that occur in the purity of the orange color.

to receive the sample through the mail and realize that the color appearance is different than the screen sample. Since designers in practice commonly work with actual materials, color charts, samples, paints, dyed materials, and various colorants, the use of computers for color management has limited value for the designer. However, as computer technology continues to advance and use within design firms increases, this may very well change.

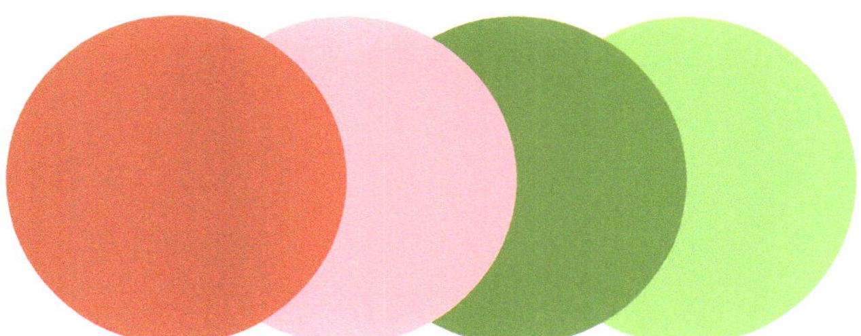

Figure 2.25a Complementary–red and green.

Color Language

In addition to hue, value, and chroma, there are several terms that are used to describe the various qualities of color. A clear understanding of each will ensure clarity among users of color. You can change color three ways: through tint, tone, and shade. Adding any amount of white to a color produces a **tint**, such as pink. Adding gray to a color (mixture of black and white) produces a **tone**, such as the color puce. Adding black to a color results in a **shade**, such as burgundy. A **pure hue** is a color void of any white, gray, or black and is at its highest intensity or brightness, such as red (Figure 2.24). **Chromatic** refers to all colors minus black, white, and gray. **Achromatic** refers to black, white, and gray, each of which is without color. **Primary hues** are red, blue, and yellow. Each of the primary hues cannot be produced by any combination of one another. **Secondary hues** are violet, green, and orange, each made from combining two primaries. **Tertiary hues** are red-violet, blue-violet, blue-green, yellow-green, yellow-orange, and red-orange, each made by combining a secondary hue with one of the primaries.

Complementary colors result from two colors opposite one another on the color wheel: red/green, blue/orange, and violet/yellow (Figure 2.25a–b). **Analogous**

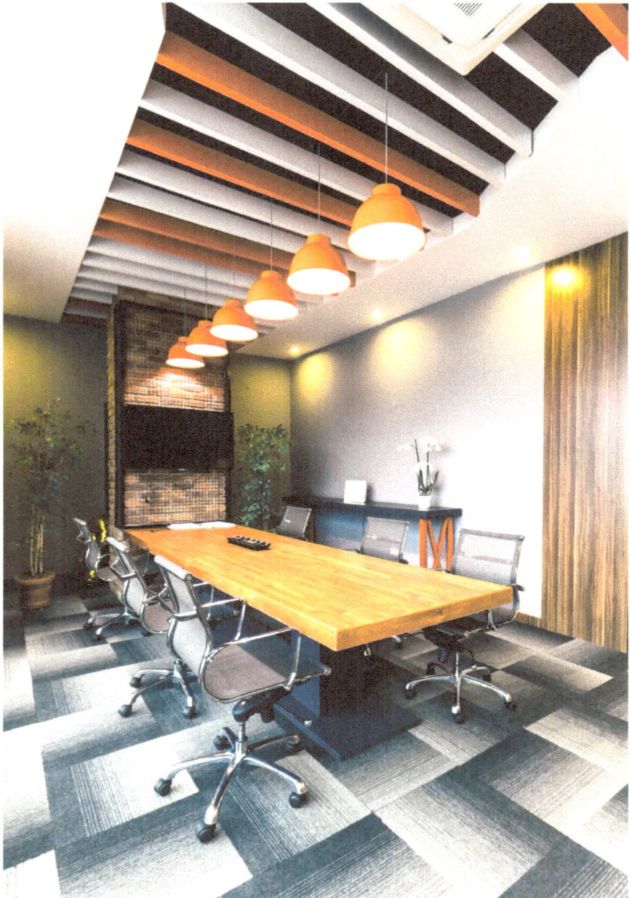

Figure 2.25b Example of a complementary color harmony–red-orange and blue-green. Contemporary office conference room.

color schemes result from two or more colors adjacent to one another on the color wheel: blue/blue-green/green. Commonly, three to four colors constitute a pleasing analogous scheme by allowing a wider range of colors to harmonize. Any less or any more color can be monotonous or overwhelming. A **split complementary** color scheme is similar to the complementary scheme; however, it's composed of three colors consisting of one main hue plus the two hues each adjacent to its complement—for example, blue, red-orange, and yellow-orange (Figure 2.26a–b). A **monochromatic** color scheme is based on variations of single hue, such as red or blue. **Triadic** color schemes are composed of three colors equally spaced along the color wheel (Figure 2.27a–b). **Tetradic** color schemes are composed of four colors equally spaced along the color wheel (Figure 2.28a–b). Cool colors are blues, greens, and blue-violets. Warm colors are red, red-violets, yellow, and oranges (Figure 2.29). Notice that brown has been left out of the discussion thus far. Brown is the only hue that is not part of the color wheel. Mixing orange, red, and small amounts of black results in a brownish, neutral hue and variations of this hue can be achieved by adding more black (dark brown) or white (tan). Another method for creating neutral hues is by mixing complementary colors: red and green, blue and orange, and yellow and violet. Digital mixing of complementary hues is shown in Figure 2.30.

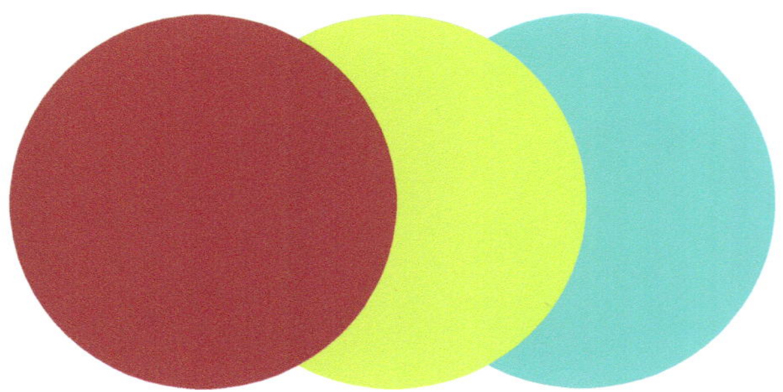

Figure 2.26a Split complementary–red, yellow-green, blue-green.

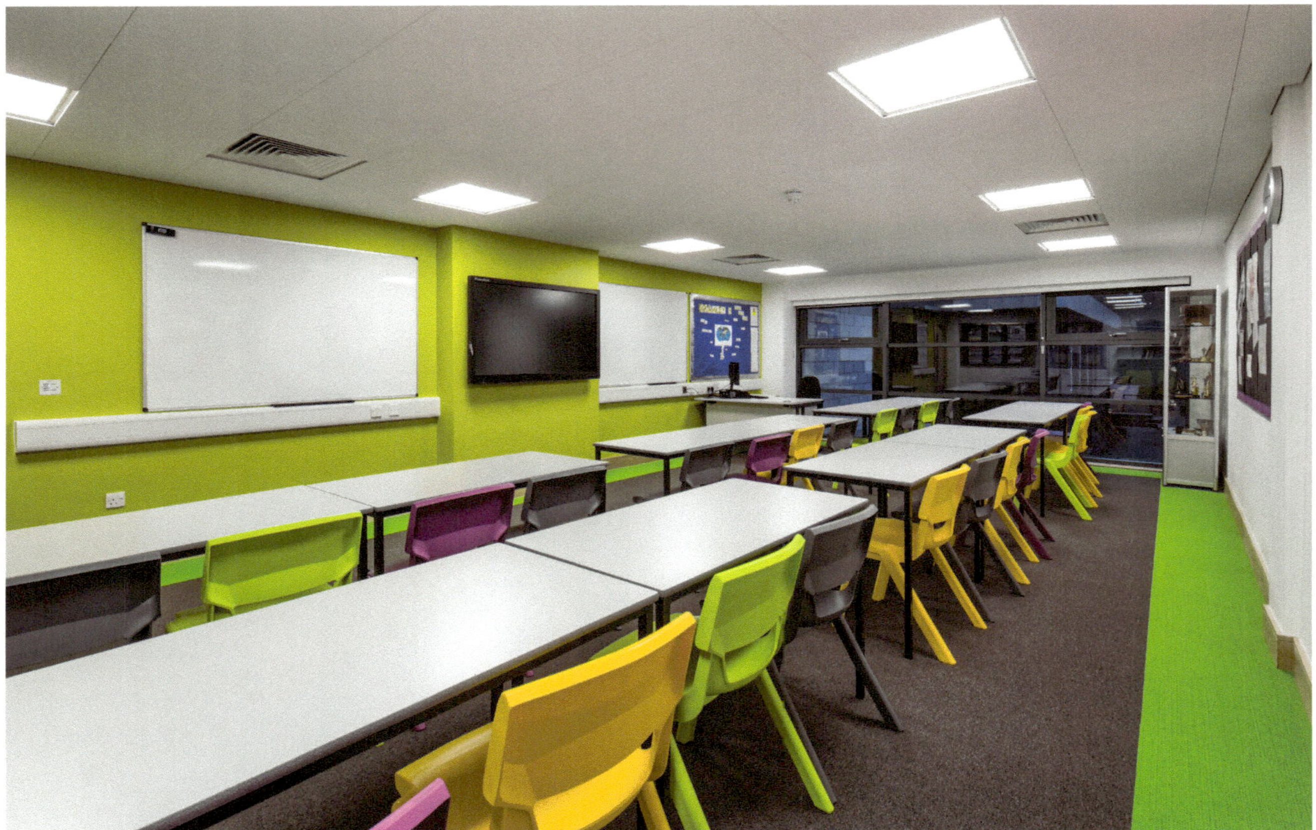

Figure 2.26b Example of a split complementary color harmony–violet, yellow-green, and yellow-orange. Colfe's School, a co-educational school located in London, United Kingdom designed by architectural firm Barnsley Hewett and Mallison.

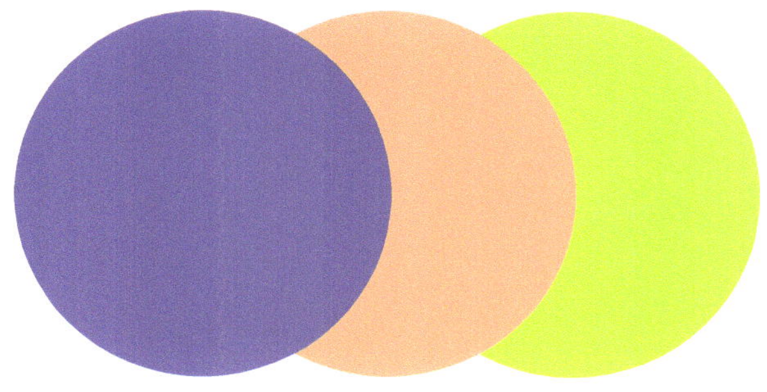

Figure 2.27a Triadic–violet, orange, and green.

Additional information and example of complementary mixing with pigments is discussed in Chapter 9.

In this chapter we've presented the systems most commonly referenced and used in the design industry and the foundations of color theory applicable to interior space. To expand your knowledge, you might want to research the following individuals: Wilhelm Ostwald, Frans Gerritsen, and Johann Wolfgang von Goethe. In addition, the appendix provides a historical timeline tracking the chronological evolution of color, colorants, and dyes.

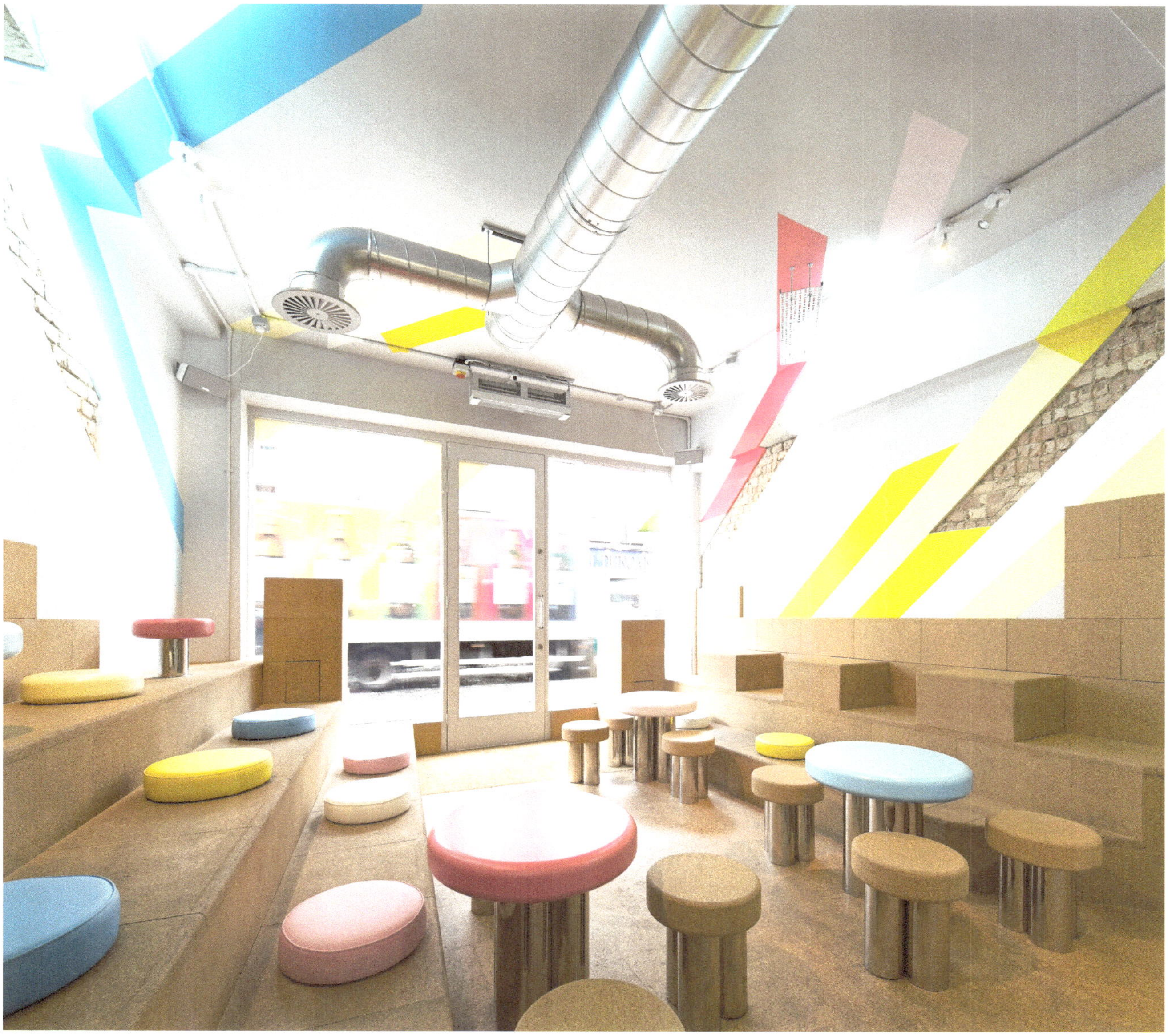

Figure 2.27b Example of a triadic color harmony–red, yellow, and blue. Biju Bubble Tea Room, London, UK designed by architectural firm Gundry and Ducker.

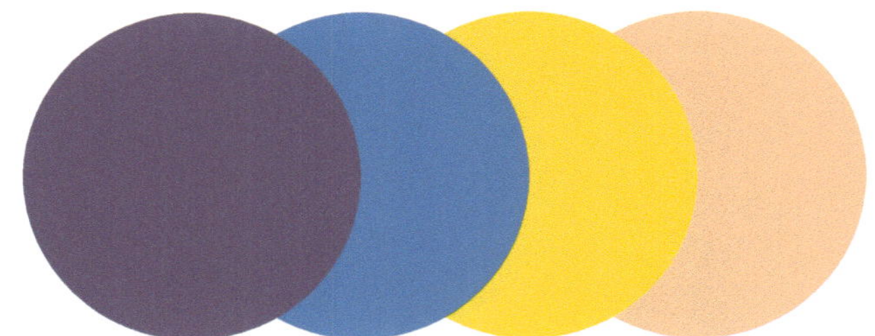

Figure 2.28a Tetradic–violet, blue, yellow, orange.

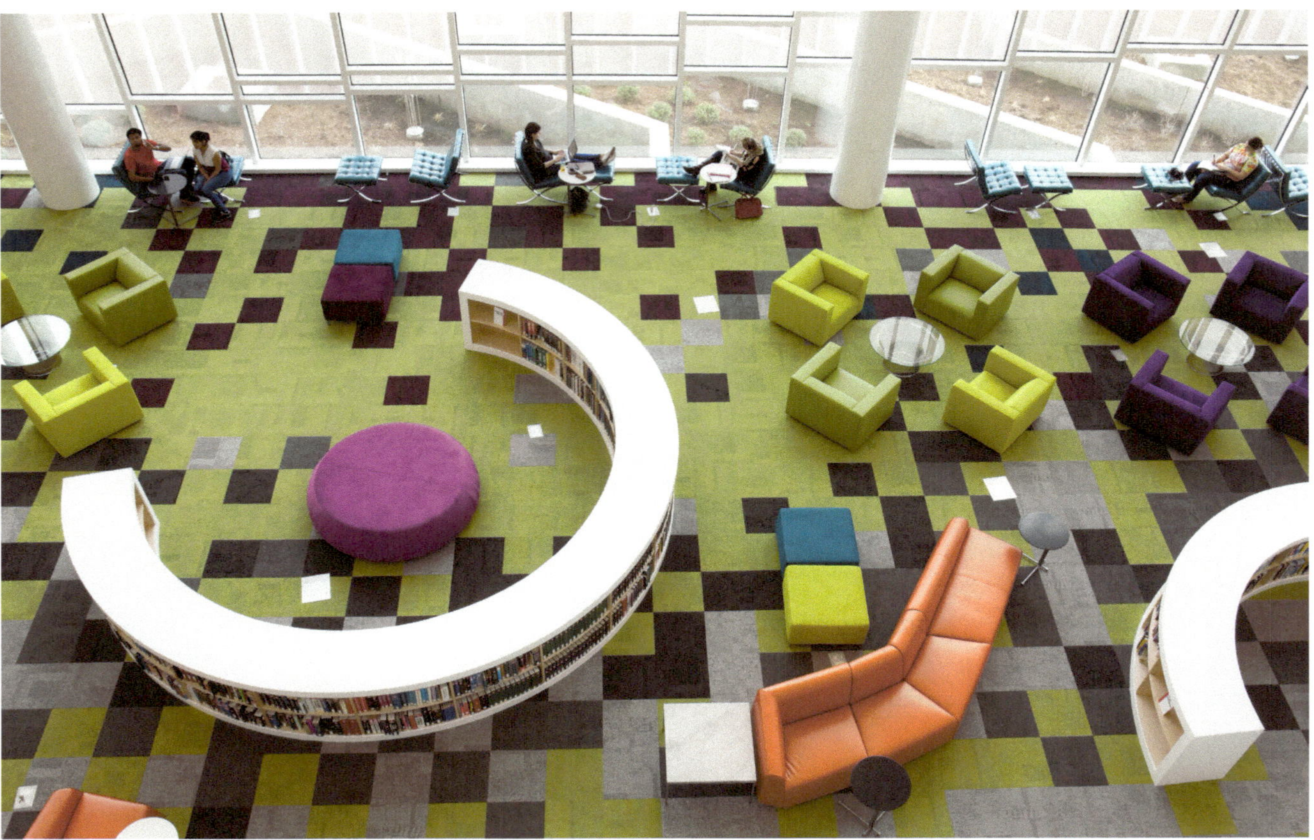

Figure 2.28b Example of a triadic color harmony–red-violet, blue-green, yellow-green, and red-orange. Students study in the new North Carolina State University James B. Hunt Jr. Library designed by Norwegian architectural practice SnAhetta.

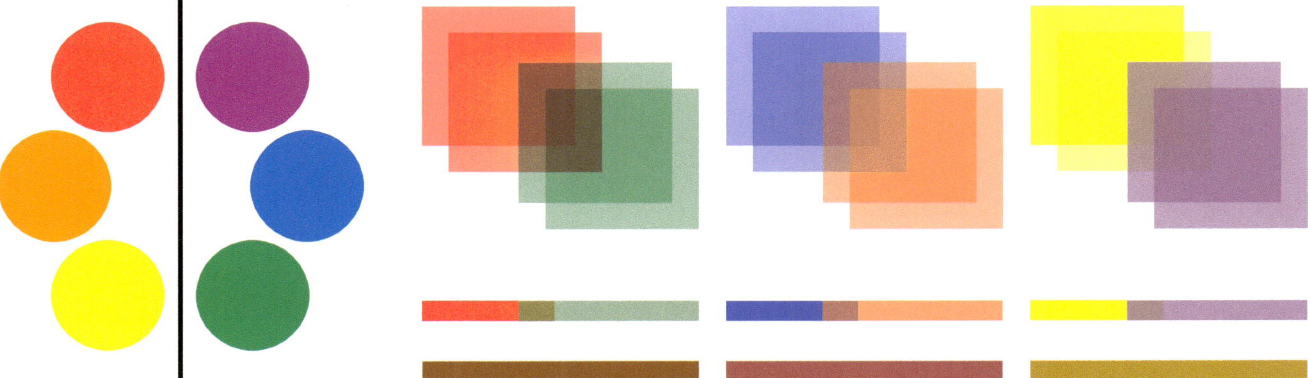

Figure 2.29 Primary and secondary hues showing the division of warm and cool colors.

Figure 2.30 Digital mixing of complementary colors (red and green; blue and orange; purple and yellow) using a transparent filter in the second colors to illustrate the resulting brownish hues created from the mixture.

REVIEW QUESTIONS

1. Describe the visible spectrum.
2. What are nanometers?
3. Explain the difference between reflection, diffraction, and refraction.
4. Compare and contrast color rendering index versus light reflectance value.
5. How does surface texture affect color perception?
6. Explain the concepts of additive versus subtractive color theory.
7. Provide an example of how metamerism could be experienced.
8. List and describe Munsell's three dimensions of color.
9. Explain the differences between tint, tone, and shade.
10. Achromatic color refers to what?
11. List or diagram examples of complementary, analogous, split-complementary, triadic, and tetradic color harmonies.

EXERCISES

1. Observe your surroundings and look for examples of the three qualities of light mentioned in the chapter (reflection, refraction, diffraction). Take several photographs of the phenomena and write brief descriptions of what you experience and see.
2. Using Color-aid paper or gouache paint, generate a ten-step incrementally distributed value scale similar to Munsell's.
3. Produce the 5R value scale for hue red and the six-step chroma scale for red using Munsell's color tree. Use Color-aid paper to produce the value and chroma, and create a separate value and chroma scale using red-dyed or printed textiles. Using the two different media will challenge you to find the color sequence with the added texture and light reflectance of the textile.
4. Practice subtractive color mixing using water-based gouache paints. Tools needed include tubes of red, yellow, blue, white, and black gouache paint, watercolor or other artist paper, suitable watercolor brushes medium round, cup of water to clean brushes, and second cup of water for dilute. For this exercise, it may be helpful to use a metal ruler and pencil to layout a grid of one-inch by two-inch rectangles to place your color mixtures. Next, prepare three separate color mixtures that result in each of the following secondary hues produced: violet, orange, and green. Next, using water to dilute primary and secondary colors; prepare a range of values—light to dark. Generate at least a five-step scale to practice creating equally distributed value steps; recommend ten-steps for better results. Lastly, using white and black gouache, prepare a value scale similar to the Munsell example from the chapter. Refer back to additional examples shown in this chapter as needed.

Vocabulary

color
color theory
visible spectrum
nanometers
reflection
diffraction
refraction
direct color
indirect color
additive color
subtractive color
metamerism
LED–light emitting diode
Kelvin
color rendering index
memo samples
light reflectance value (LRV)
hue
value
chroma
tint
tone
shade
pure hue
chromatic
achromatic
primary hues
secondary hues
tertiary hues
complementary
analogous
split complementary
monochromatic
triadic
tetradic

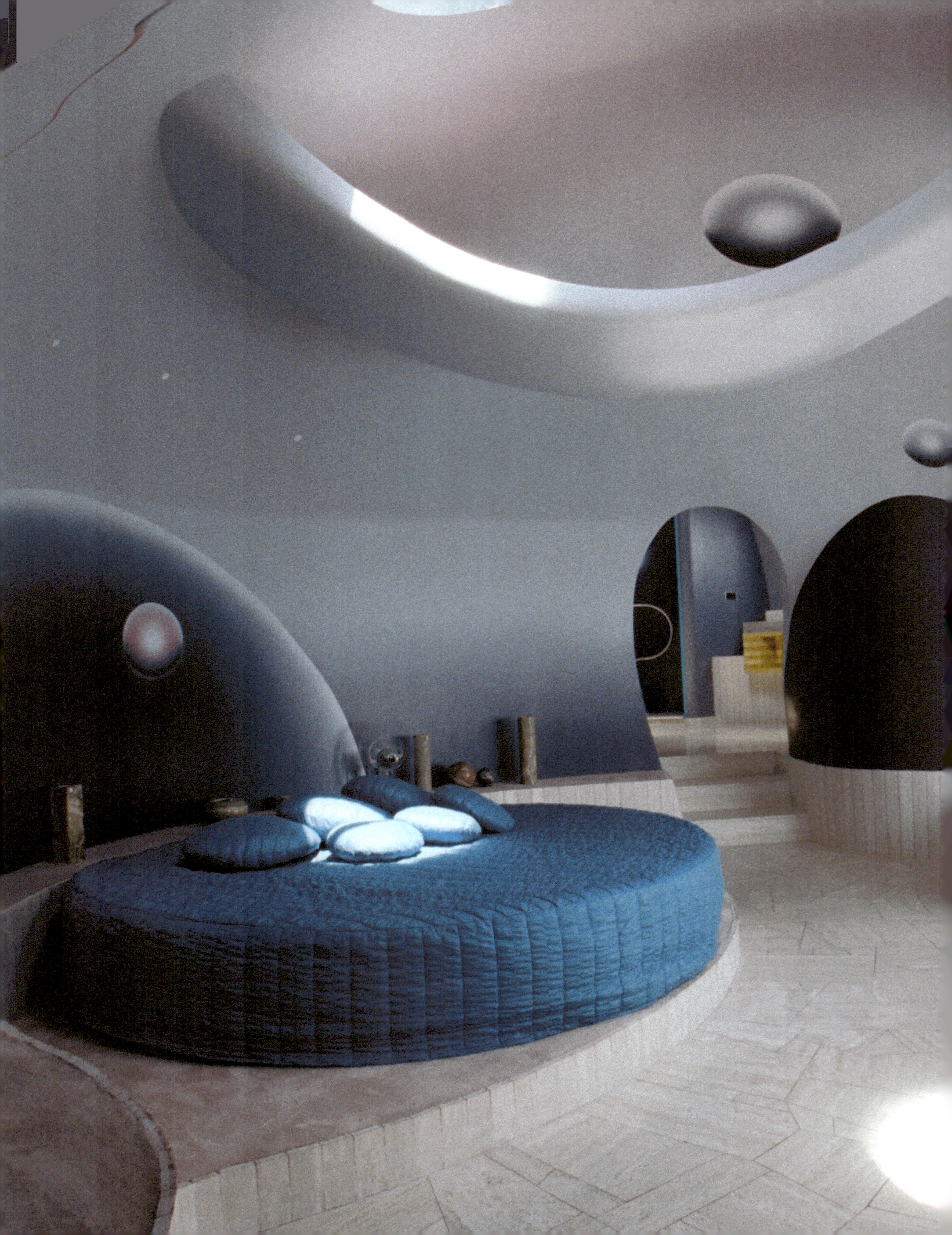

3

color association + perception

Learning Outcomes

After studying this chapter, you will be able to:

- **Implement the color design process in your work.**
- **Explain how color relates and changes under varying conditions in interior spaces.**
- **Explain the three key concepts of color perception.**
- **Develop the seven types of color contrasts in design projects.**
- **Understand the influences of history and culture on color trends and color forecasting.**

Just as water is necessary for life, color sustains our souls. Color is emotionally subjective. There are no universal rules or prescriptions that serve every instance or individual, but there is a common understanding that people have an associated response to color that one must be aware of when selecting color for others. Factors that drive artists and design professionals in color selection include trends, styles, and aesthetics; behavior and emotions; symbolic meaning based on age, gender, and cultural differences; pragmatic value—what the space needs to work well; and personal preference. We've become so preoccupied with color that we've lost sight of simply enjoying it for what it is. However one approaches the study of color, whether quantitatively or intuitively, success depends on one's positive response to choice and individual expression.

Color Design Process

Whether for residential or commercial spaces, color is a critical element and must be considered in the beginning of the design process. Color, as an element of design, is often studied separately and independently from the theories for design composition (principles and elements) due to its complexity. In a study on integrating color as part of the interior design process, Dianne Smith surveyed interior designers and architects on the need to be educated in color before entering design practice. Of those surveyed, 81 percent were educated in color and 88 percent integrated color as a design tool. The majority of color selections occurred during the early stages of the design process, with 44 percent occurring at concept generation and 56 percent during the schematic design phase (2003, p. 363).

Figure 3.1 diagrams the relationship between color, interior design, the principles and elements of design, and the design specialty. This model suggests examining color, at the center of all interior design decisions, along with the elements of design (shape, line, form, and texture) and the principles of design (balance, rhythm, emphasis, proportion and scale, unity and harmony, and variety). The design process as presented by Kilmer and Kilmer (2014) identifies the eight steps designers use during project implementation. These include committing to the design problem, stating the design problem to be solved, collecting data, analyzing data, creating ideas of potential design solutions, choosing a final solution, implementing the design, and evaluating the final results (pp. 156–157). During this process, color is recommended to be filtered through each design stage. Rather than being a last-minute design decision or for decorative purposes only, a research-driven, holistic approach to color can help you achieve greater success in your designs.

Our homes are private spaces where we make personal choices that ultimately affect our living environment. At the opposite end, you have commercial spaces (e.g., healthcare, work, retail, and hospitality) as public domains, which require more informed decisions about color use and application. Preparation and planning beforehand helps to identify the needs and goals of your project.

When working with a client to refine and solve their design problem(s); the interior designer should evaluate those individual needs that have the highest priority based on programming information and assign the appropriate combination of the elements and principles of design to achieve the desired solution. **Programming** is one of the stages within the design process where you begin the data collection for a particular project. At any stage in the process, client feedback and input should be sought. Following are general questions you can begin to use when gathering information during the programming phase of a design project.

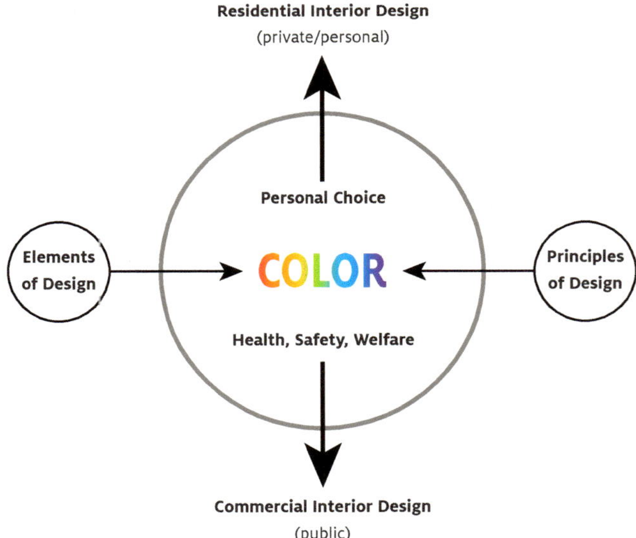

Figure 3.1 Color application to design practice model.

1. What type of space are you planning (waiting area, business office, living room, dining room)?
2. On average, how much time per day will you be spending in this space?
3. How many people will be using this space at any given time? You may need to consider age and gender ranges in this question.
4. What types of activities will be performed in this space (writing, reading, working at a computer, conversation, meetings, etc.)?
5. Does the space provide natural, artificial, or a combination of lighting types?
6. Are there preexisting aspects of the design that cannot be removed or altered? In this question, you may need to determine if the color can be changed even if the design feature cannot. For instance, if there is a wood floor, can it be refinished? If it is a marble or terrazzo floor, this will be an important point of consideration in determining and working a new color scheme. Cost in the later phases is a key aspect that will determine the final outcome. It is much easier to apply a color or finish to materials than to remove and replace with new. Always know your boundaries and constraints on a project. In the design industry, it is rarely carte blanche. A great designer knows how to work within these constraints and achieve the client's goals.
7. What colors appeal and do not appeal to you? (Ask every member involved in the use of the space.) If you are designing a space occupied by a small number of people, a question on color preferences for each individual is easy to collect. If it is a space to be used by a large number of people, you can take a color inventory of preferences and look for commonalities among the group that may lead to an appropriate color scheme that satisfies the users. If the space is significantly large or consists of multiple spaces or floors, here are two suggested approaches: (1) Select a palette that is appropriate for the activity of the space, and use accent colors in places of socialization or areas of frequent interaction that do not receive extended periods of use. This might be an accent wall in a corridor, entrance, or conference room. (2) Prepare two or three color palettes and have the client select from your choices. Be careful not to prepare too many alternatives or your client may find it difficult to decide.

You will learn to build on these questions and modify them as needed depending on the project type you are working on. Each of these questions will influence color decisions. The questionnaire can be used whether you are designing for commercial or residential spaces.

These color decisions have the ability to affect the health, safety, and welfare of our clients and the multiple users of these spaces. We will break down the color components that invoke perceptual, emotional, and symbolic associations in the remainder of the text. The psychological associations and perceptions we have of color space can be a fascinating genre of design to explore. The information presented represents general and the most common types of responses, but individual reactions to color stimuli vary from person to person.

Color Associations and Perceptions

Scientific experiments have shown that humans can discriminate between very subtle differences in color, and estimates of the number of colors we can see range as high as 7 to 10 million. Rudolph Arnheim describes our visual perception of color as a process where the eye doesn't "record each of the infinitely many shades of hue by a particular kind of message but limits itself to a few fundamental colors, or ranges of color, from which all the others are derived . . . a kind of abstraction by which, at the level of conscious perception, we see colors as variations and combinations of a few primaries" (1969, p. 21). He goes on to explain that the millions of colors we can potentially see would be "unmanageable" when distinguishing colored objects and our brain must process and screen the large amount of information into a simple "order" to be able to adequately respond to the visual stimulation we encounter daily (p. 22).

Color response is highly personal. What one person is attracted to, another may be repulsed by. Emotional response to color varies from person to person. There is no such thing as a bad color—color can be seen as negative, positive, or neutral—neither good nor bad. Of all the elements and principles of design; color is one of the strongest at affecting our emotions (Day, 2013). We use color to describe our emotions and feelings. Color meanings and usage will vary from culture to culture. Color associated with certain objects or shapes can produce a strong psychological response that is formed between the object and the user. For instance, a favorite toy as a child, a memorable birthday present, or a holiday symbol can have positive associations that you carry with you. A family heirloom that was handed down from generation to generation may create a positive connection with its color. The opposite can be true for colors you may not like; a traumatic event in your life may be associated with a particular color. When you consider the colors you like or dislike, think about why you feel this way versus accepting the emotional reaction. This is valuable when talking with clients about color for a specific project.

Some crayon color names have led to negative associations, such as flesh, Prussian blue, and Indian red. These color names were deemed offensive by civil rights groups and later changed to more appropriate names: peach, midnight blue, and chestnut (Crayola, 2008, ¶ 3–4). Tests conducted on color and emotions resulted in "yellow, blue, and orange as happy colors and red, black, and brown as sad colors" (Singh, 2006, p. 785). The basic colors (primary and secondary) trigger their own unique responses when viewed in isolation or in combination. These associations will vary depending on the context of their use within the built environment.

In March 2002 the Department of Homeland Security introduced a color-coded, threat-based advisory system to alert the public of potential safety threats. This five-step system used color to inform Americans of the country's current threat level. The colors advanced from green (low), blue (guarded), yellow (elevated), and orange (high), to red (severe). While this system was phased out of use in April 2011, we are exposed to many other color-coded systems in our daily lives (Figure 3.2).

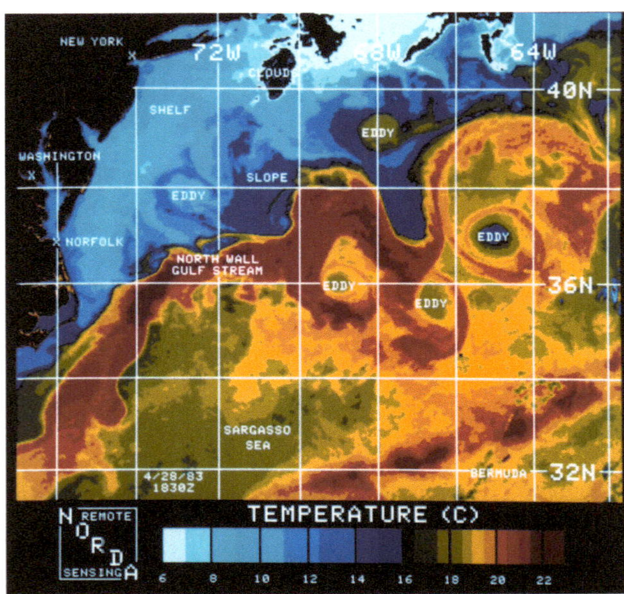

Figure 3.2 Weather satellite captures an infrared picture in the Gulf Stream of color temperature variations represented with pale blues for colder weather to dark red for warmer weather.

Color Responses

Emotional responses to color cannot be simply measured or limited to any one particular hue. Color's effect on mood is ever changing as perceptions of our environment change. Color isn't seen in isolation, and, therefore, most of our visual responses occur as a result of the combination of colors, color in context with the immediate surroundings, and the interplay of light and texture as well as shape. Color perception is affected by individual associations of color. This is affected by culture, society, politics, entertainment/media, fashion, and design trends.

Our experience of color can be categorized into four types: the luminosity or saturation of the hue (bright/dull, light/dark), the color as it relates to a particular object to which we've assigned emotional attachment, our emotional response to a particular color (like or dislike), and the character or mood a color expresses to a particular observer. The last is often the result of social and cultural biases that have imprinted these characteristics into our psyche, along with the media through television, the internet, and magazines.

Color preferences are generally listed in the order of blue, red, green, violet, orange, and yellow. Blue is the first choice of Western cultures. In Japan, red is ranked as the favorite color. Age and gender can have an impact on color perception. Newborns can only see contrast between light and dark—the first hue to be recognizable is yellow because it is the most luminous of colors. Children in grade school grow out of yellow and show a stronger preference in adolescence for red and blue. In older adults, a shift occurs toward blues and greens. With aging of the eye and yellowing of the lens of the eye, there is a stronger need for the color blue.

Preferences for color can be associated with geographical regions and historic traditions. Red is alluring and striking, drawing people into a positive selling environment; however, it can make people feel tense. Bright, warm colors tend to produce quick impulse-buying.

Dark, warm colors are often associated with luxury products. The perceived luxury of a retail space can increase a shopper's emotional response and enjoyment (Cho and Lee, 2016). Soft, cool colors tend to encourage deliberation and are best used on costly purchases where consumers are encouraged to stay longer before making a decision. Product packaging should catch the consumers' eye first. Research indicates that consumers scan each package on a supermarket shelf for only three-hundredths of a second (Machin, 2005, ¶ 17). Thus, the packaging must attract the customer to buy it, and the color should also help convey an image of the contents. If I were to ask you to walk down the supermarket isle and pick up a box of Cheerios® or Campbell's® soup, you would easily be able to find the product among the many options available simply by color recognition. Our perception of color influences our desire for a product. Bottled water manufacturers use clear or blue-tinted plastic to make the water appear more refreshing. If they suddenly decided to place water in brown bottles, the public perception might be that the water is dirty. Packaging of healthy or "diet" food products are often placed in white or lighter colored packaging adding to our perception of the food being low-calorie or "lite". Red, yellow, and orange draw attention most; purple is associated with luxury; blue suggests cleanliness and/or quietness; green suggests nature; and gold, silver, and black are effective in promoting high-quality merchandise.

Insects displaying yellow and black markings warn potential predators to stay away, including the Monarch butterfly, coral snake, and poison dart frog (Figure 3.3). Colors that are used on road signs to alert drivers, when used in interior spaces, may elicit negative responses, including tension, an increase in heart rate, nervousness, and fear.

Literature has indicated that men prefer cool colors, whereas women prefer warm colors. Other studies have shown that color preference is very similar between the sexes; the only difference is that men tend to favor orange over yellow and women favor yellow over orange (Khouw, 2007, ¶ 3).

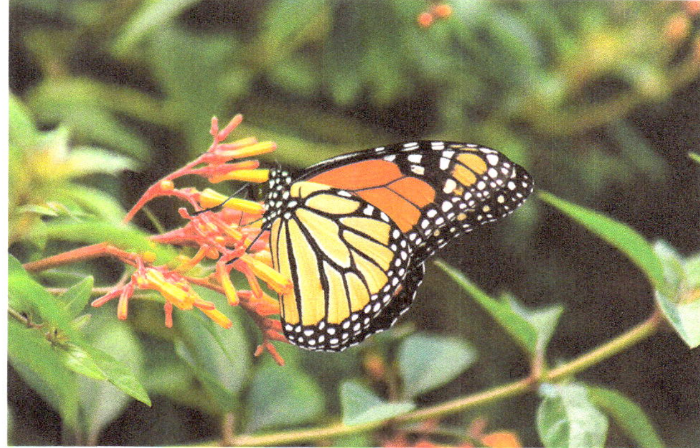

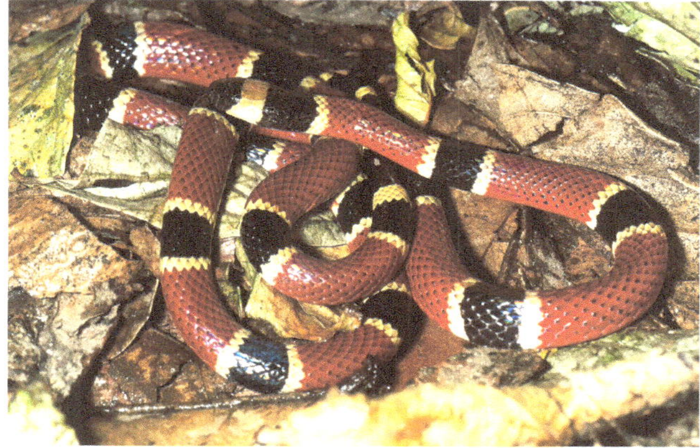

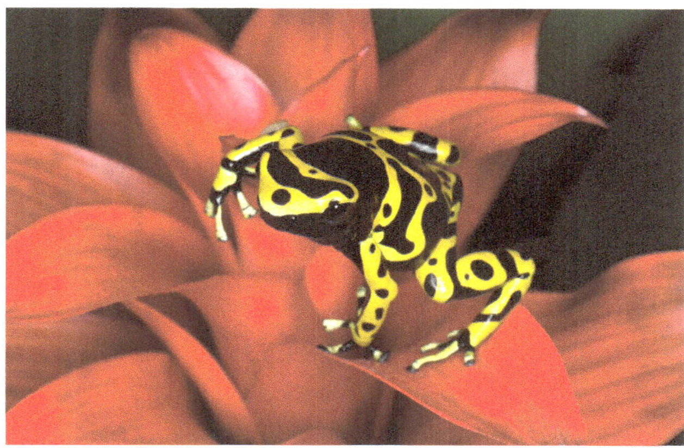

Figure 3.3 (top) Monarch butterfly colorations signal danger to predators. (middle) Striped coral snakes are protected by black, red, and yellow skin pigments that warn predators of potential danger. (bottom) The poison dart frog uses yellow and black coloring to warn potential predators to stay away.

Color Myths and Biases

In Western and European countries, it is more common to believe that infant boys wear blue and girls wear pink, and studies have shown that girls prefer pink and purple as their favorite color compared to boys who choose blue and green (Jonauskaite et al., 2018; Bonnardel et al., 2017). Preconceptions about color have led to several misconceptions about color. Gender bias for color didn't begin until the twentieth century and didn't acquire conformity until the 1950s. Historically, pink was favored and used for boys and blue for girls (Paoletti, 2013). Pink originates from red, which was and still is considered a powerful, strong color suit for young boys (colourlovers .com, 2007). Historically, babies wore white, and no color at all. In modern times, with the current discourse on gender and identity, the use of non-gendered color is something we might want to reconsider.

Color carries no inherent message, but we superimpose our ideas on it. Society, media, and social and political issues are all factors that inevitably endow us with biases; we don't question—they are automatic. The world is colored, and for the most part, people have little control over the color they encounter day to day. These decisions are made by others—often by interior designers—and we interact with our environment either positively or negatively based on our perceived notions of particular colors.

With their soft, blunt shape, and a size that is easy to grasp, a Crayola crayon is often the first writing tool for a child in the United States. Even in this instance the color names are taken from the U.S. Commerce Department's National Bureau of Standards book called *Color: Universal Language and Dictionary of Names* (Kelly & Judd, 1976). Many crayon names are also borrowed from traditional artists' paints, such as burnt sienna and raw umber. Americans' favorite Crayola crayon color is blue. As children, coloring is one of our first interactions with and control over a variety of hues.

Over time, our preferences for colors change. Research on gender preference and color has indicated that most men find red, then purple and pink as the most stimulating and blue as the most appealing when they are experiencing stress. "Men are more tolerant for neutral hues such as black, white and gray than women" (Singh, 2006, p. 785). "Pink is used to calm violent prisoners in jails. The color suppresses anger, antagonistic, and anxiety-ridden behavior among prisoners: Even if a person tries to be angry or aggressive in the presence of pink, he can't. The heart muscles can't race fast enough. It's a tranquilizing color that zaps your energy" (Color Matters, 2008, ¶ 2). However, a study conducted in 1979 concluded that when prisoners were left in pink-painted jail cells for extended periods of time, they became "violent and out of control" (Uribes, 2008, ¶ 14).

The question for designers to consider is: how does pink affect the mood of young girls or teens whose rooms are painted pink because social norms tell them that is what is appropriate? People are more productive in blue rooms, and studies show weightlifters are able to handle heavier weights in blue gyms.

Another popular color myth is the bias toward red vehicles. A common misconception among drivers is that red cars will receive more speeding tickets than cars of other colors. Red has been associated with sports cars and speed. "There's also the supposed optical illusion created by their color that makes the cars appear to be going faster than they really are" (Edmunds Inc., 2008, ¶ 7). In actuality, according to Carolyn Gorman, vice president of the Insurance Information Institute and Insurance Trade Association, "there is no data to support the assertion that red cars receive more traffic tickets than cars of any other color" (Edmunds Inc., 2008, ¶ 7).

This phenomenon with the color red has been used by interior designers to influence individuals' perception of the passage of time. Red has been shown to increase the perception of time, whereas blue decreases the perceived amount of time spent. Red is commonly used in fast-food restaurants to indicate quick, speedy service, and casinos use red in the interior to excite and trick patrons into believing they have not spent much time in the space. Darker reds used in restaurants are intended to make customers spend more time, and in doing so, they are likely to spend more money for a dessert, wine, and a full-course meal. Blue and purple, commonly used as appetite suppressants, could fare well for an "all-you-can-eat" buffet where limiting the amount of return trips of its customers can save the restaurant money (Singh, 2006, p. 785).

Design research has yielded statistical data that can be confidently used for evidence-based design decisions. Birren terms this "functional color," where the outcomes of color usage are based on the practical versus decorative uses of color (1992, p. 242). A color study examined the relationship of color to emotions associated with bodily movement without participants being made aware of any emotional expression or sound. Based on the body movements of actors expressing panic, fear, or elated joy, participants observing these movements indicated the colors in the red-yellow range expressed elated joy and cyan-blue colors expressed panic and fear (Dael et al., 2016).

Solid research findings support your design decisions and can be used to add value and truth to your work. Table 3.1 expands on the common myths and biases with additional perceptual properties of color, including common positive associations, negative associations, and consumer behaviors associated with particular hues.

TABLE 3.1 PERCEPTUAL PROPERTIES AND ASSOCIATION OF COMMON COLOR

Hue	Positive Associations	Negative Associations	Consumer Behavior
RED	Courage, excitement, love, passion, sexy, increases appetite, festivity (holidays)	Hatred, aggressive, rage, war, raises blood pressure, fear Financial debt—in the red Embarrassment—red in the face Associated with the erotic—red light district Associated with communism—red flag	Used to increase impulse buying, often used for fast-food restaurants indicating quick, fast service
PINK	Mostly positive: feminine, sweet, babyish, delicate, passion (when hue is closer to red)	Physically weakening—use in jail cells or clothing of prison inmates to calm tempers	Popular color for the cosmetic industry. Color name is often more lavish to increase appeal, such as "passion fruit" (Skorinko, Kemmer, et al., 2006, p. 979)
BLUE	Associated with water; cool, calm, comfortable, relaxing, clean; successful in bathrooms Vary shades to prevent boredom and depressive affect Royalty, coolness, truth, loyalty, success (first place), security, high-technology, nautical, comfort, wetness, cleanliness Has been known to reduce the appetite Light blue: Gentle, reflective Navy blue: Strength, authority (uniformed men and women)	Introversion, sadness, depression, cold, low-class, isolation, loneliness, gloominess Blue and bluish-purple are appetite suppressants	Fashion consultants recommend wearing blue to job interviews because it symbolizes loyalty. People are more productive in blue rooms. Studies show weightlifters are able to handle heavier weights in blue gyms Lighter shades have been used to symbolize luxury (Tiffany blue)
GREEN	Relaxed, growth, renewal, eternal life Green is the warmest of the cool colors Regarded as the most "natural" color Excellent color to bring the "outdoors indoors" Renewal, freshness, youthful, healthy, tranquility, peaceful, wealthy, may reduce allergic responses and negative reactions to food	Poison, envy, inexperience, immaturity, nausea, sourness, disease, guilt, rawness Careful to avoid yellow-green in large quantities—association to sickness, mold, and decay	People waiting to appear on TV sit in "green rooms" to relax Hospitals often use green because it relaxes patients Brides in the Middle Ages wore green to symbolize fertility Not a good color for business attire, means immaturity
YELLOW	Cheerful, sun, gold, happiness, wisdom, vitality, hope, optimism, and self-esteem Yellow toward blue: A yellow ribbon tied around a tree signifies hope and waiting for family members serving in the military to return home Yellow toward red: Intellect, reflection Gold: Physical, active, honor, loyal, wealth	Caution, sickness, nervousness "Can cause tempers to flare, children to cry, uncontrolled muscular movements in older adults" (Kopacz, 2004, p. 78)	Yellow enhances concentration, hence its use for legal pads and pencils 50th wedding anniversary

(continued on next page)

TABLE 3.1 ***(CONTINUED)***

Hue	Positive Associations	Negative Associations	Consumer Behavior
PURPLE	Bravery, mystery, royalty, sacred, aristocratic Lavender: Spiritual, soft, atmospheric	Conceit, mourning, death, rage, pompous, ostentatious, gloomy	Luxury, used to indicate indulgence or expensive items (fine chocolates, automobiles, specialty wines, and perfumes)
ORANGE	Warmth, fruitfulness, brightness, happiness, cheerfulness, jovial, strength, endurance, festivity (holidays) When hue is reduced in chroma can be associated with richness and sensuality	Brashness, danger, increases pulse rate, can seem intrusive, inexpensive/ cheap	Associated with inexpensive items and highlight sale items Often used as a color to attract teens to purchase products (music players, cell phones)
WHITE	Purity, birth, cleanliness, innocence/ virginity, empowerment	Surrender, cowardice, emptiness, clinical	Associated with "high-tech" products (Color Wheel Pro) Simplicity associated with modern design
BLACK	Sophistication and power	Death, emptiness, bad luck	In clothing, black can mean safety, security, privacy
BROWN	Relates to the comforts of home, wood, and farming Relationship to dirt and soil Best when combined with hues red, yellow, orange Comfort, security	Men are more likely to say brown is one of their favorite colors; gloom, melancholy, boredom, se f-centeredness, gloom, melancholy, boredom	Associations with chocolate, coffees, espresso; this color has become a color of luxury for merchandise
GRAY	Technology, intelligence (gray matter), wealth in association with silver and platinum	Confusion, lcss of distinction, depression, lack of confidence, old age	Known for being a stable color, often used for products to indicate it will have a long useful life (computers, televisions, handheld tech devices, cars)
SILVER	Elegance, sophistication	No known negative associations	25th wedding anniversary With the new millennia, silver and platinum overtook gold and brass as the trendier, more popular colors in the home

Color and Space

Color interactions in three-dimensional spaces have the ability to affect the size, shape, mass, and volume of interiors. Color is a key component in forming our first impressions of space and place. Color as a component of all materials of the environment—furniture, accessories, lighting, structure, plants, and more—can be used to communicate and express boundaries of **space**, visually connect architectural elements, and create the properties of the mood or atmosphere desired. Like time, we do not stand still; we are constantly moving through space, and therefore our experience is multifaceted and multisensory. Color speaks to us, helping us navigate and understand the visually complex world around us. The shape of an object conveys little without color to clarify its meaning. Color is not an "extra to an environmental situation but instead has an active role in the . . . relationship between a person and the surrounding environment" (Smith, 2008, p. 316).

Color and shape change as our locations and positions within interior spaces change. The interplay between color and space, lighting, and materials is experienced through all our senses. Because color is one of the first properties of our space we experience, its power and propensity to inform our environment are limitless. We simultaneously begin to make associations and emotional judgments on the space we have just encountered. These emotional judgments are reactions based on our visual perceptions. Our immediate responses to our environment include, but are not limited to, recognizing the space type through design cues such as a bright-colored retail storefront to indicate point of access, or a seating group organized around a reception station indicating a public space (waiting room or lobby). How we may perceive different space types will determine first impressions (like or dislike), which are greatly influenced by the color palette and materials chosen. For instance, when you enter a retail establishment, color is often the first cue to indicate what type of clothing section you are in. The children's clothing section may be indicated with pale, pastel colors of yellow, pink and blue, the women's with light hues of violet, green, and turquoise, and the men's clothing section with darker hues of blue, gray, and black (Figure 3.4). Color cues make it easier to locate where you need to be with very little effort. If all sections within a retail environment were the same color, how quickly would you be able to locate items in the space?

In this chapter, as part of our discussion of the psychology of color perception, we will briefly touch upon how factors of color influence our perception of space and place. Further illustration of each concept within each of the chapters will then connect color and each of the principles of design.

Our visual perception of color can be influenced by (1) the color surrounding the object, (2) the size of the color area (a smaller area of color appears darker, whereas a large area of color appears lighter), (3) the surface characteristics that affect the intensity of a color (rough or smooth texture, gloss and metallic reflection properties), and (4) warm versus cool hues.

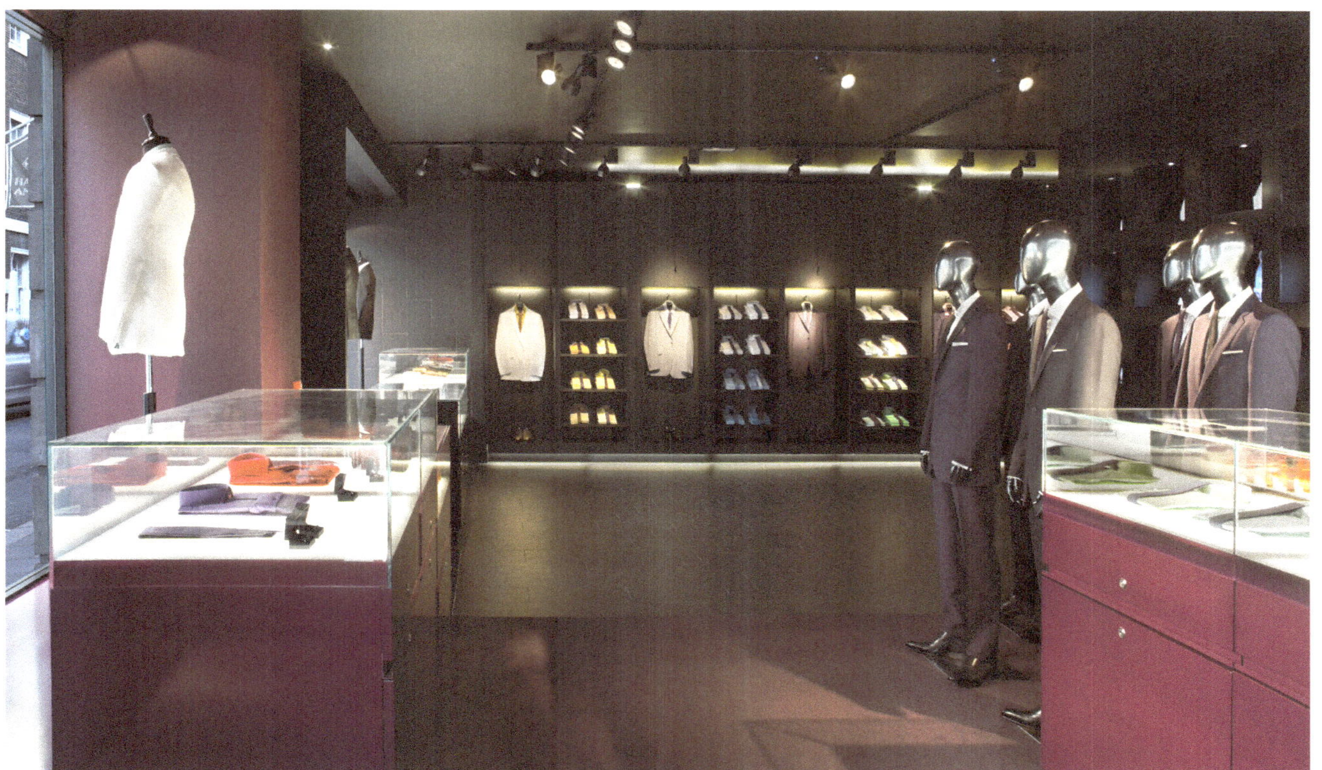

Figure 3.4 Fashion Designer Ozwald Boateng Flagship Men's Clothing Store, Savile Row, London, W1, United Kingdom. Architect: Adjaye Associates. Saturation, value, and color choice in this retail space convey luxury and help to communicate the fashion brand and image to the consumer.

Dark colors absorb light and generally make spaces appear smaller. Light colors reflect light and generally make spaces appear larger. Warm colors advance toward the viewer and therefore have the tendency to make spaces seem smaller, whereas cool colors recede visually and therefore expand and make spaces seem larger. Figure 3.5 illustrates this concept. Student Kelly Geister has selected an original image on the left-hand side, color-keyed the three main hues within the interior space and identified the color scheme. On the right, she has selected three corresponding hues equal in intensity and color-rendered a new **recoloration** of the space to examine this effect. If there is too much contrast between visual elements, the eye has a difficult time adapting to the changes. This particular exercise is a great tool for refining and improving your illustration, drawing, perspective, and rendering skills.

Yellow is perceived as the brightest of all colors, even over white. Due to this perception, yellow can be an excellent choice for interior spaces where sunlight is at a minimum or in spaces, such as basements, where natural light may be absent.

A dark-colored piece of furniture against a light background will have more visual weight and sense of stability than a light piece of furniture against a dark background. Rule of thumb: Light objects advance and appear larger; darker objects recede and appear smaller.

The use of values in your color **palette** will add dimension to the space, create visual interest, and elicit positive emotions. The use of pure color without value change or contrast can be overpowering, and in these cases, the color overwhelms the space, resulting in the design elements and details of the space going unnoticed (see Figure 3.6a). This can be successful with enough contrasts of color and pattern, as shown in the salon in Figure 3.6b. Figure 3.6c illustrates acceptable levels of single-hue contrast.

Johannes Itten proposed that perceptions of particular hues can be reinforced abstractly by combining meaning, shape, and form with a particular hue. The formation of all interior design begins with the basic shapes of the square, triangle, and circle, along with their variations—rectangle, rounded triangle, and oval. Itten proposed that the color red, symbolizing power, strength, and stimulation, relates to the square, which, with its horizontal and vertical lines, is associated with the same characteristics. Red, as a powerful color, and the stability of a square combine to increase the perception of "structural planes and sharp angles" (Birren, 1992, p. 171). A triangle relates to yellow, with the

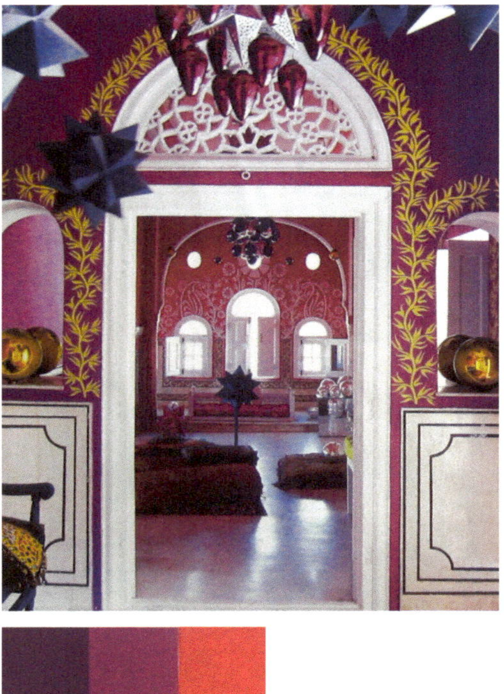

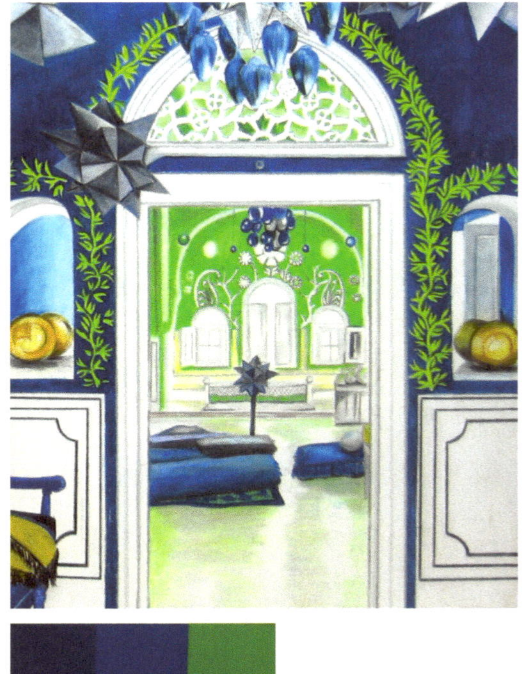

Figure 3.5 Recoloration using colored pencil and Color-aid papers for an interior space to investigate the perceptual changes between warm and cool colors.

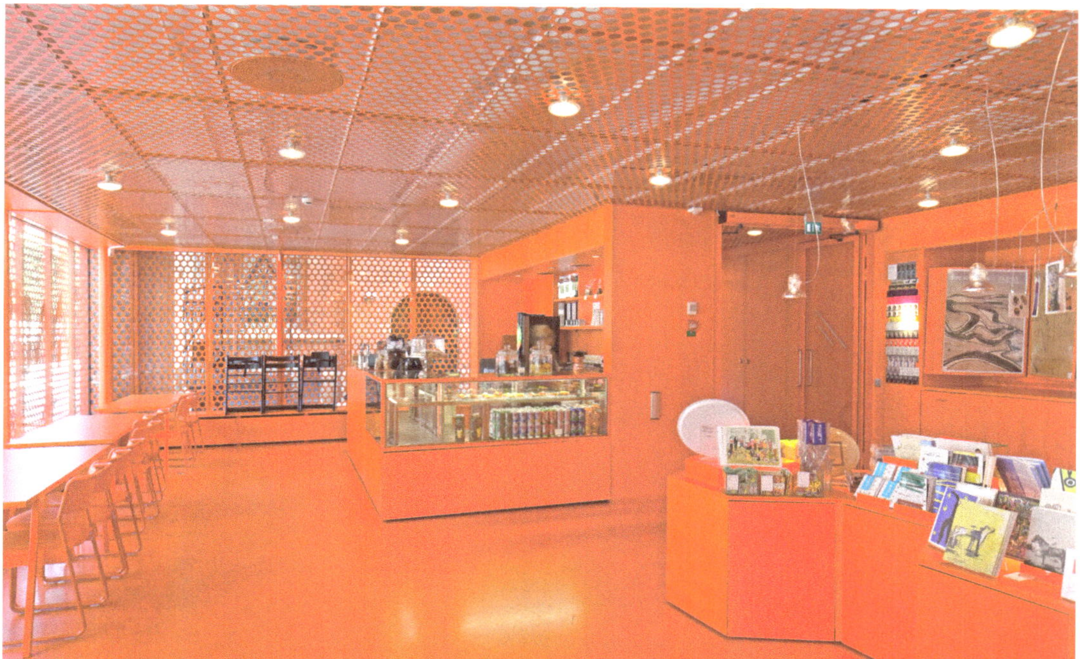

Figure 3.6
(a) Use of a single color overwhelms space, losing focus on the important details.

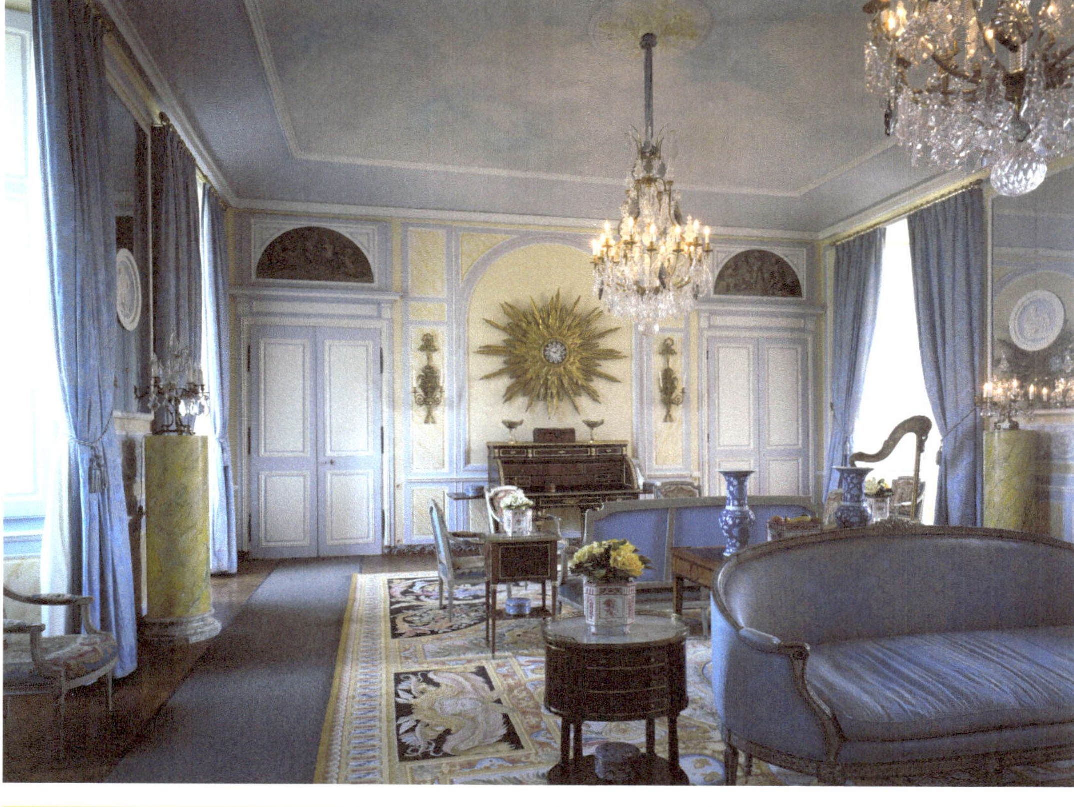

(b) Single hue of vivid blue is successfully balanced with pattern, scale, and contrast.

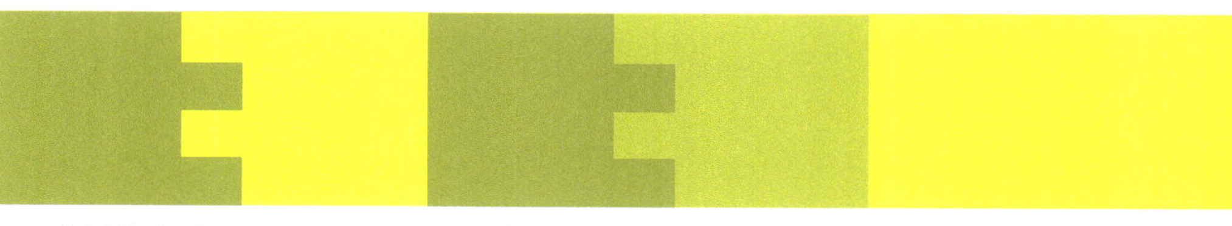

light/dark—Strong contrast | dark/light—Subtle contrast | light/light—Weak contrast

(c) Acceptable levels of color contrast.

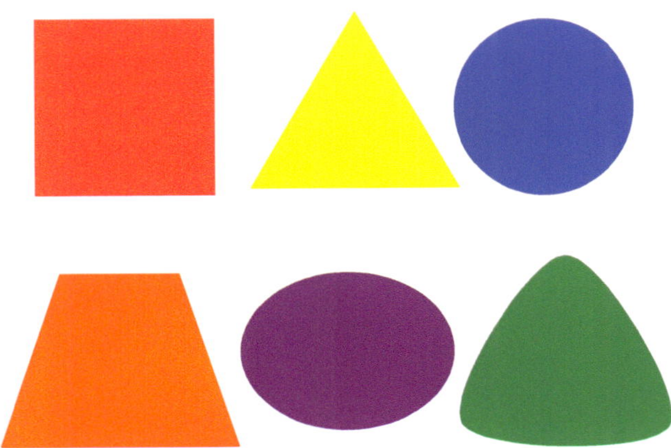

Figure 3.7 Color and shape associations.

angularity of the shape symbolizing a sense of weightlessness; yellow is also the color symbol for thought. The color yellow represents the heavens and the sun and is supported by the sides of a triangle slanting upward from the base. Blue relates to the circle for relaxation, motion, and "celestial" qualities (Birren, 1992, p. 171). Orange is for knowledge, creativity, and trust and is supported by variations of the square—a trapezoid or rectangle. Orange is closely related to red and therefore suggests the same rigid qualities of "angles and details" (Birren, 1992, p. 171). Violet relates to the oval, supporting spirituality, wisdom, mystery, purity, and intuition. And, finally, green relates to the rounded triangle, symbolizing nature, growth, life, and renewal, which one might associate with a tree (Figure 3.7).

In each of these cases, you can make associations with particular elements in your environment. In doing so, you can begin to relate these meanings and characteristics to the interior space. For example, red is known for being aggressive; therefore, strong lines and hard edges would serve to reinforce this concept (Figure 3.8). The same would apply with its application within the interior space by using vertical support columns colored in red or applying the color to a particular strong visual element in your design to suggest strength, importance, or a key design feature. Orange and yellow would follow red with a similar perceived character. The cool colors blue, violet, and green, associated with calm and restfulness, would therefore be supported by applying curvilinear and organic lines (see Figure 3.9). In a spa or space of healing and meditation, blues and greens used with free-form, organic lines support the concept of restfulness. Doubly reinforcing color meanings with design elements and principles strengthens the final design, encouraging meaningful connections between the user and the space.

Colors interact with one another and therefore create visual illusions. In some instances, we may not even realize it is happening. A basic understanding of these perceptual constructs will provide you with the strategies needed to ensure proper color selection for your design projects.

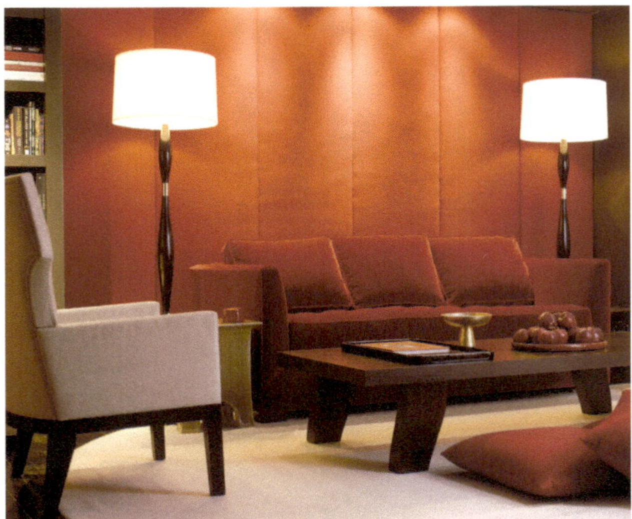

Figure 3.8 Luxury living room in New York City apartment uses strong vertical lines supported by a combination with red hue.

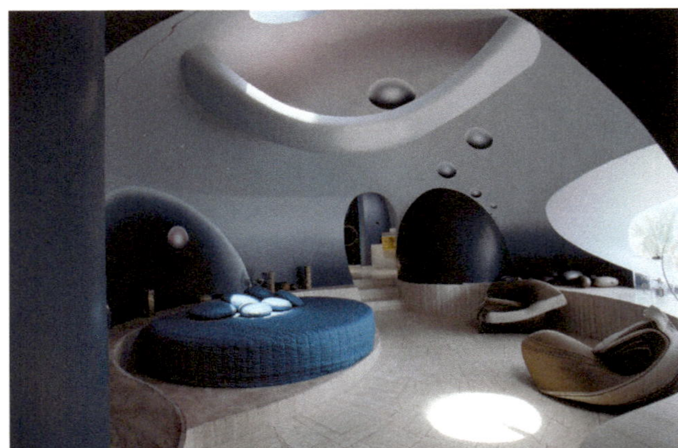

Figure 3.9 A futuristic bedroom in the Bubble Palace, or Le Palais Bulles, is decorated by a contemporary artist in soft blues. It sits on a hillside in Théoule-sur-Mer in the French Riviera, overlooking the Mediterranean Sea. The futuristic mansion, composed of rounded rooms with rotating floors, was designed by Pierre Cardin and architect Antti Lovag.

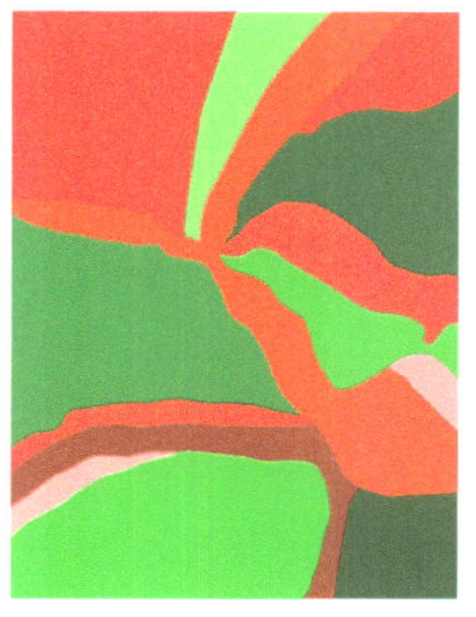

(a) Simultaneous contrast.

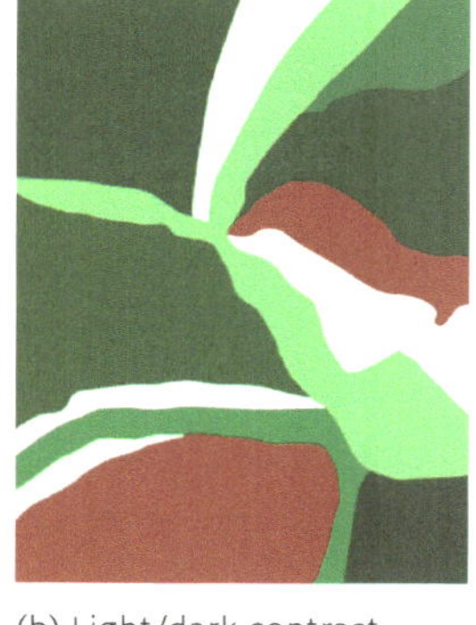

(b) Light/dark contrast.

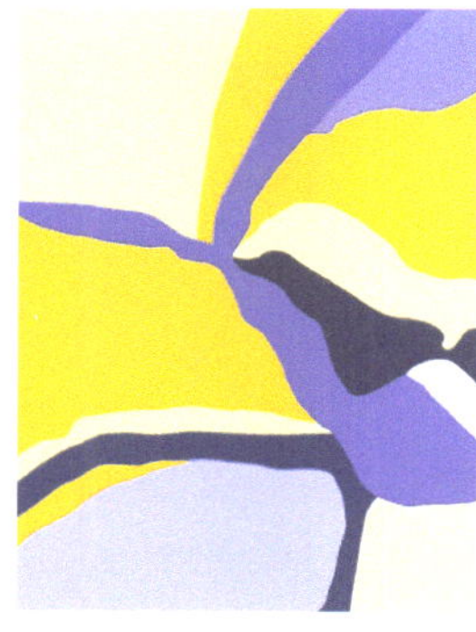

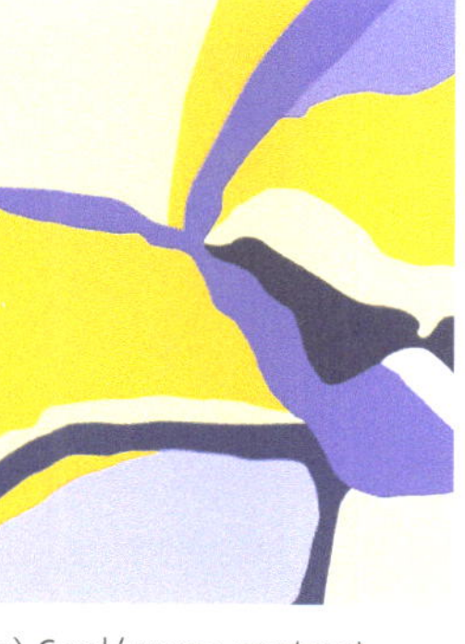

(c) Cool/warm contrast.

Figure 3.10 Seven types of color contrast identified by Itten.

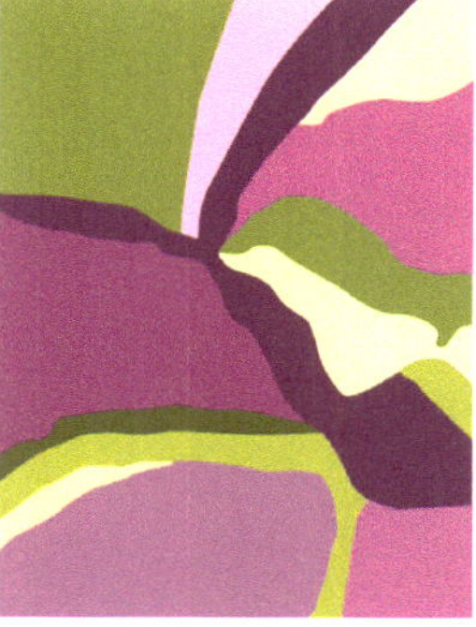

(d) Complementary contrast.

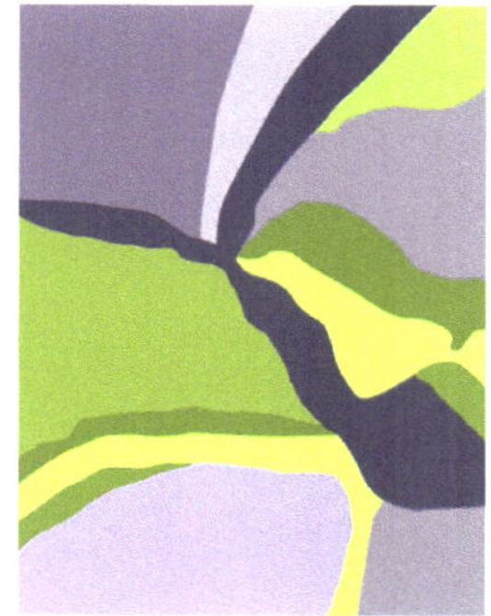

(e) Contrast of hue.

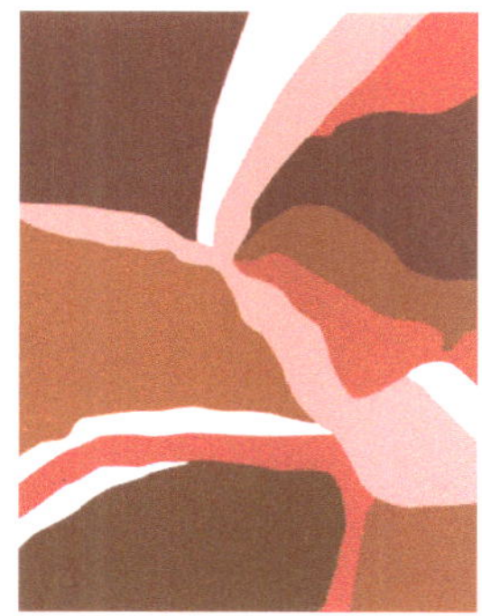

(f) Contrast of saturation or intensity.

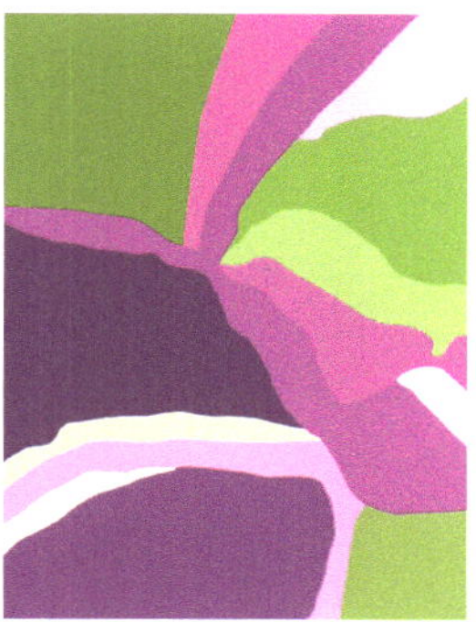

(g) Contrast of extension.

Color Contrasts and Other Phenomena

Itten identified seven distinct types of color contrast, which designers can use to manipulate the interior space: **simultaneous contrast** (Figure 3.10a), contrast of light/dark (Figure 3.10b), cool/warm contrast (Figure 3.10c), complementary contrast (Figure 3.10d), contrast of hue (Figure 3.10e), contrast of saturation or intensity (Figure 3.10f), and contrast of extension (Figure 3.10g) or the relative quantity or proportion of color. Simultaneous contrast occurs when there is a shift in color from two adjacent hues that have reduced or increased each other's intensity, resulting in a perceived third color. This concept can be seen across the value range illustrated in Figure 3.11. The thin gray bar is the same color; however, as it moves across lighter values, it appears darker, and conversely, when it moves over the darker values, it appears lighter.

Simultaneous contrast results when two equal values create a "vibrancy" effect or strong contrast that occurs

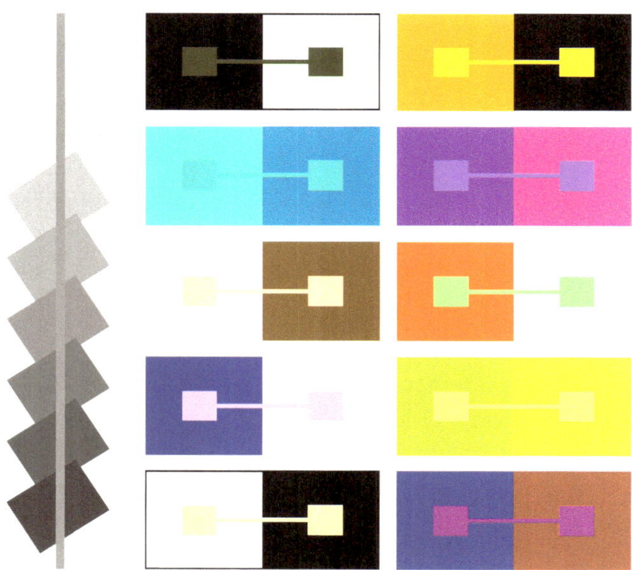

Figure 3.11 (a) In this value scale, the thin gray bar is one value; however, as it moves across light to dark values, it is reduced or increased in apparent lightness or darkness, creating a value shift. (b) Examples of Josef Albers's color interactions where no single color is seen in isolation from one another. The different background colors produce a perceived difference in the single hue of the smaller portion of color.

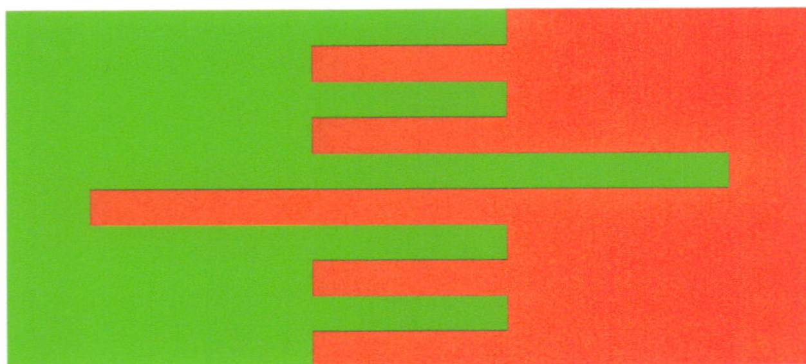

Figure 3.12 Two colors close in saturation levels can create an afterimage, or vibrancy effect, when placed close to one another. These color combinations are hard to read and are visually overstimulating.

Figure 3.13 Yellow is the only color that, as black is added, shifts to a green shade.

around the edges where the two colors meet. This is rarely used in design, and in commercial spaces, it can be a disturbing visual effect. Certain hues will create a more intense vibrancy than others (Figure 3.12). When layering visual elements in a space, be aware of this phenomenon. Most hues maintain their original key, shifting only lighter and darker as they move from white to black. Oddly, yellow is the one color that makes a slight chameleon change to green as it moves closer to black. The black neutralizes the red light waves reflected from the yellow object, leaving green to mix with the yellow hue as it draws closer to black (see Figure 3.13).

Bezold Effect

The **Bezold effect** is the common phenomenon a designer encounters when working with color patterns common with textiles, wall coverings, carpet, or other patterned materials that are available in more than one color palette. Developed by rug maker Wilhelm von Bezold during the nineteenth century, the effect occurs when the largest color area is replaced by a new color, creating a color interaction that changes the overall impression of the design (see Figure 3.14). The same effect can be successful if you choose the smaller color field, as long as the contrast and intensity of the newly introduced color are greater than the remaining surrounding hues.

Along the same lines as the Bezold effect, colored patterns seen from afar will optically mix, generating a new hue. For instance, a blue and yellow pattern will mix and produce green. Our eyes are not able to discriminate the individual colors, resulting in the mixture. Complementary colors such as blue and orange will mix and create a muddy tone (Figure 3.15). It is a common error to assume that you can create a color palette from the individual hues within a smaller pattern when the overall colors in the design blend together and create a new color. During the material selection process involving colored patterns, look at the coloration from afar and in the context in which they will be experienced, such as vertically on a wall or horizontally across a piece of furniture, for an accurate representation of the final outcome.

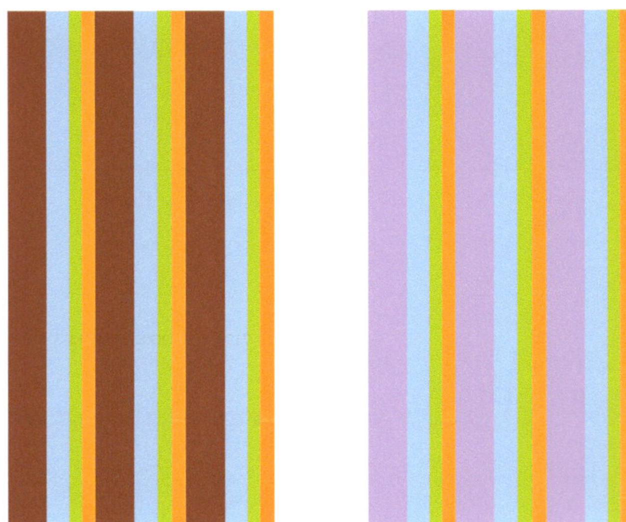

Figure 3.14 Bezold effect—change of large color field.

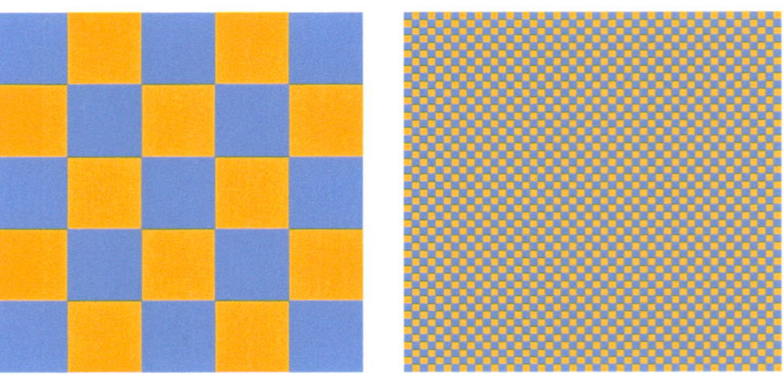

Figure 3.15 When the scale of the squares in the two complementary colors blue and orange are reduced, the eye has difficulty discerning between each hue. In this instance, optical mixing occurs, and complementary neutralization results with a gray tone being produced as a result of the blue and orange hues combining in our visual system. Optical mixing takes place when a combination of colors and pattern reduce in scale or when the distance of the viewer from color source increases. Stand a few feet away from the two images and look at how the color changes in the image on the right.

Color Perception Tips and Techniques

The following tips and techniques of color application can be applied to your interior design projects. Experiment with these concepts using study models, manual techniques, or computer rendering to see how the effects may be perceived. Google SketchUp and Adobe Illustrator are excellent computer programs for generating multiple color studies that you can quickly manipulate in order to analyze possible solutions.

- Color has a direct relationship to the physical temperature we perceive and experience in a room. When people are placed into temperature-controlled rooms, one painted a warm hue and the other cool, and are asked to indicate their perceived temperature of the space, participants will indicate the temperature to be slightly higher in the warm-colored space and colder in the cool-colored space (Stone and English, 1998, p. 181). A room that is painted dark colors and receives an adequate amount of natural sunlight has the potential for elevated room temperatures. The dark surfaces will absorb the light energy and then radiate small amounts of heat into the space. This phenomenon can be beneficial to clients by offsetting perceived coolness in colder regions such as Alaska, Minnesota, and Michigan and in arid regions such as New Mexico, Nevada, or Arizona, where the accumulated warmth from daylight harnesses some warmth for cold nights.
- In spaces that are predominately monochromatic (single-hue scheme), applying small amounts of the hue's complement can decrease the monotony and visual boredom.
- Avoid color schemes that use an equal amount of each hue. This can create some confusion, especially when the palette contains more than two colors. The lack of proportion can prevent contrast and emphasis of certain architectural design elements in the space.

The Influence of Color

Earlier I stated how color is both an art and a science; it is a vast, historical, complex field of study that has many beginnings and influences and a wide variety of contributors. Ancient civilizations used natural materials ground into powders to produce pigments. From cave paintings in black and reds in France and Spain to Italian frescos—paintings made directly on the surface of plaster walls—the availability of local minerals dictated the color palette of the period. Eventually, advances in technology and the start of the Industrial Revolution brought forth manufacturing processes in the eighteenth and nineteenth centuries that gave artists, designers, and industrialists an expanded palette of brilliant chemically produced synthetic pigments. Many facets of daily living affected the historical roots and range of color palettes, including religion, art, fashion, architecture, culture, and technology.

Color History

Our brief trip through color popularity in history will focus primarily on the twentieth century. Colors used in a period of time mirrored the personalities of the people, social customs, and events occurring at that particular time in history. The 1920s were a time of glamor following World War I and a surge in economic growth. The Art Deco style fashionable at the time was identified with white and black interiors, lacquered furniture, and ornamental metalwork in silver, gold, and metallic finishes with accent colors in bright reds, oranges, and greens.

During the early part of the 1930s, and following the Great Depression, neutral color schemes continued as white, ivory, cream, flesh tones, and beige—made popular by Chanel—were seen throughout the home (Figure 3.16). Color palettes in the 1930s included gardenia, tea rose, raspberry, and deep browns, gray, and yellow. Film and the *Golden Age of Hollywood* influenced color popularity. The latter half of the thirties saw richer color coming into popularity with hyacinth blue, turquoise, and shocking pink. With the beginning of the *machine age*, chrome and tubular furniture was gaining in popularity, including works by architects Marcel Breuer, Mies van der Rohe, and Le Corbusier.

The architecture of Frank Lloyd Wright, Alvar Aalto, and Le Corbusier continued to grace the landscape into the next decade with beautiful modern structures and colors inherent in the various natural materials they were each known for using: concrete, brick, steel, glass, limestone, and wood. Despite these earthy tones, colors in the home continued to be vibrant in the 1940s, even as the world entered into war for the second time. Patriotism was celebrated with red, blue, and white. Other colors commonly seen during this decade include navy, dusty

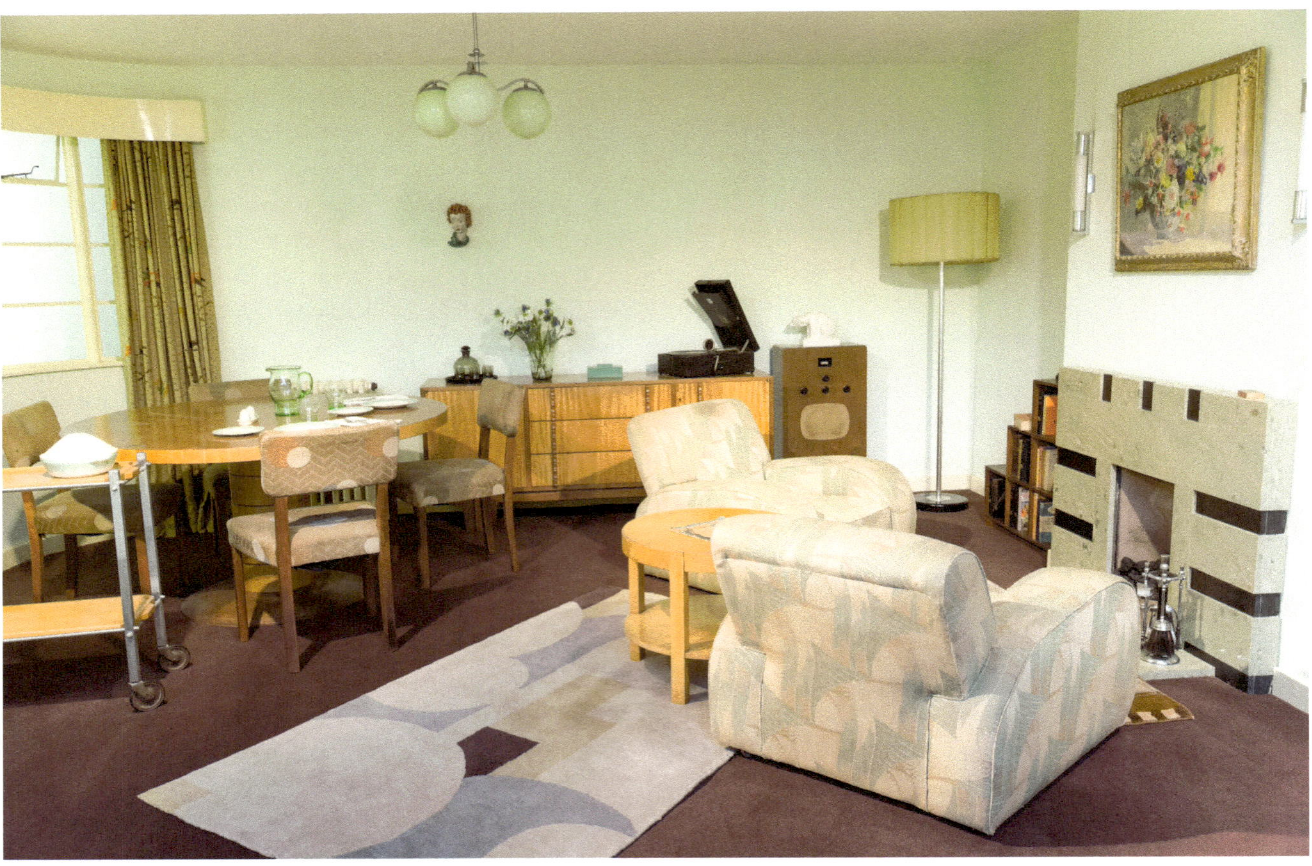

Figure 3.16 1930s period room in the Museum of the Home, formerly the Geffrye Museum, London, England, UK.

coral, honey yellow, mauve, powder blue, and earthy browns seen in fashion and the home.

Mid-century modern design continued to influence the 1950s and 60s with clean, simple lines, organic materials. (Figure 3.17). Colors during this time were both earthly, warm, brown hues as well as vivid, energetic color. Coincidently, the names given to colors often hint of the specific time and social attitudes that each influenced the color names and popularity. Abstract art, television, and rock-n-roll music of the 1950s saw the colors "Hot pink, Ice blue, Summer gold, and Pistachio." Muscle cars, the Beatles, and space exploration of the 1960s saw the colors "Hot rod, Mellow yellow, Magic dragon and Kozmic blue" (Varley, 1980, pp. 134–135).

New social trends and changing times marked the 1970s. The modern style leading up to the seventies was giving way to a more playful, hippie, and individualistic form of expression. Bold abstract graphics with avocado green, harvest gold, bright orange, brown, rust, and earthy colors synonymous with environmentalism of the seventies were fashionable (Figure 3.18). Floral motifs, shag carpet, bean-bag chairs, lava lamps, teak, and tubular steel furniture also marked the interior of a seventies home.

Eventually, the overabundance of earthy color in the 1970s began to wane and gave way to a softer palette in the 1980s and later to a brighter decade of color to follow.

The 1980s were a time of a global economic boom. This decade was celebrated with an explosive and wide range of color trends and unconventional color mixes. The eighties began with a response to the seventies' bold color choices by introducing softer, pastel colors. Mauve, pink, light blue, peach, and teal dominated the home. Fashion gave way to neon, fluorescent hues, and primary colors paired with black and white. This bold color trend was further expressed in the furniture of the Italian designers known as the Memphis Group popular from 1981 to 1987. A time of self-expression countered by conservative attitudes, the 1980s were the brightest and most diverse decade of color to be seen so far.

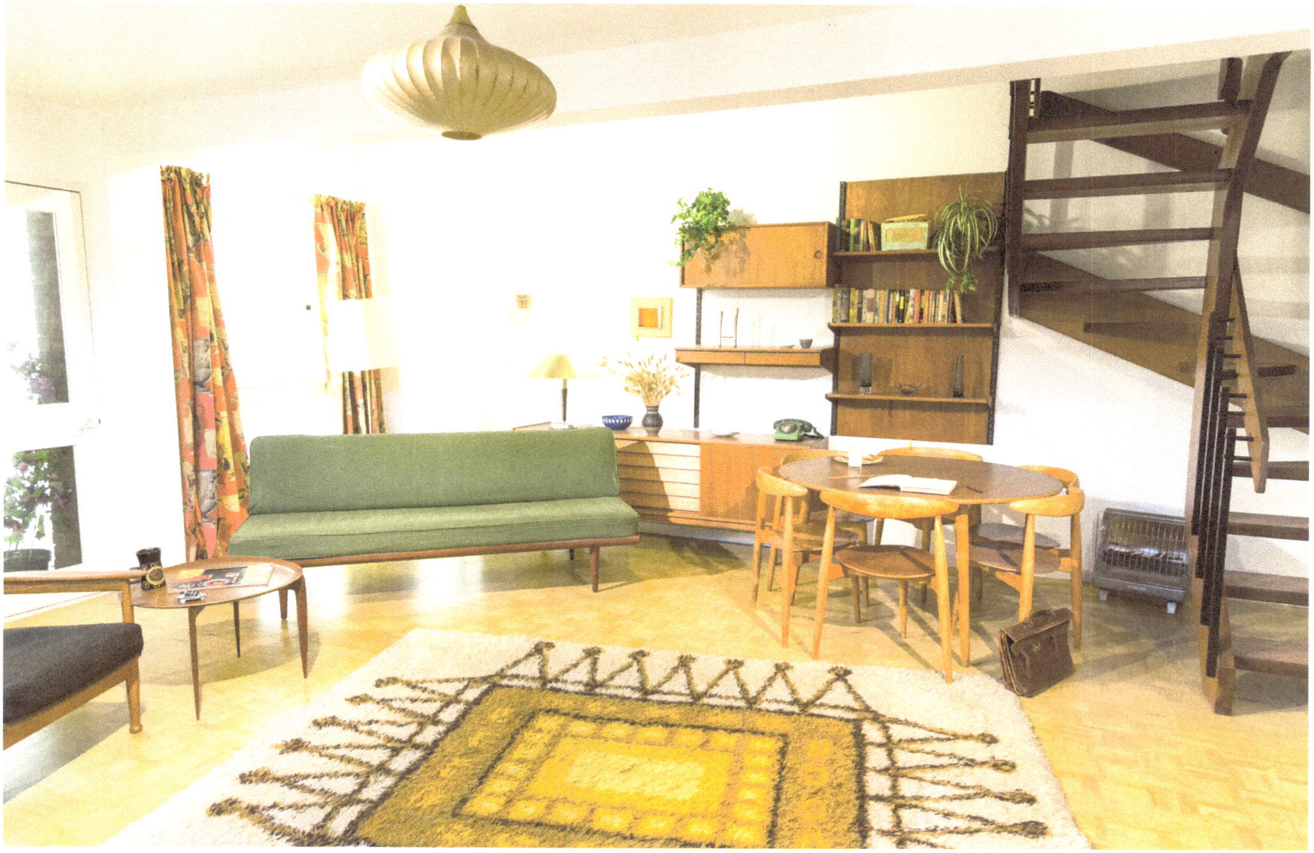

Figure 3.17 1955–65 mid-century period room Museum of the Home, formerly the Geffrye Museum, London, England, UK.

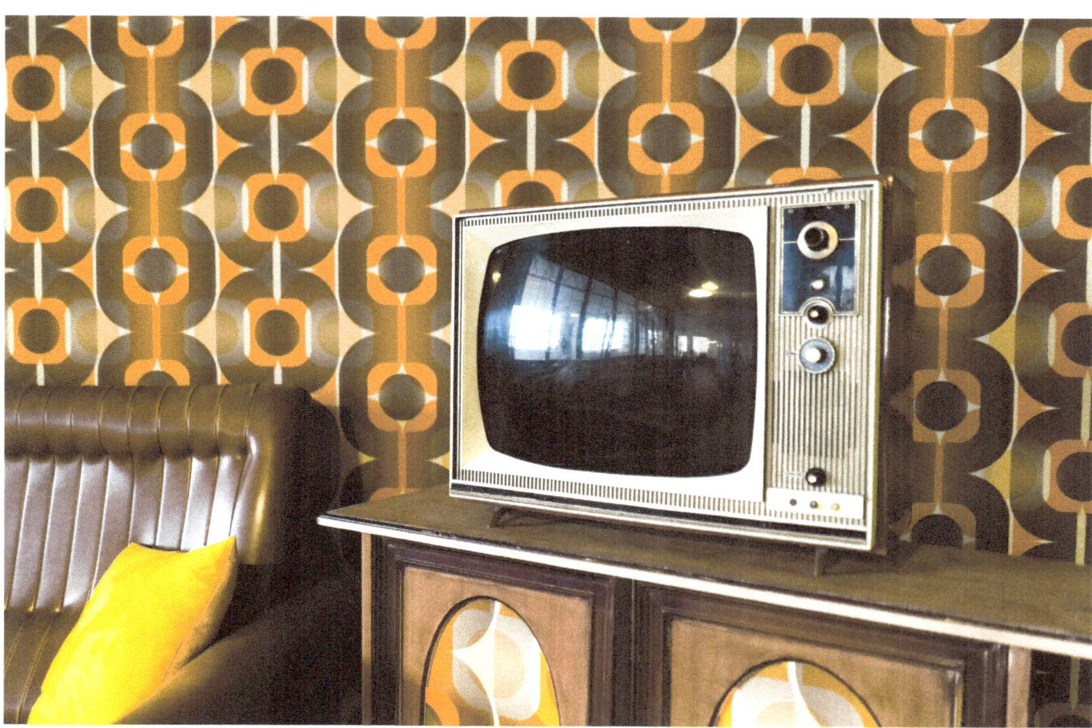

Figure 3.18 Vintage living room with popular brown, yellow, and orange colors during the 1970s.

Bold colors from the eighties carried over into the early parts of the 1990s. By the mid-nineties, trends consisting of white kitchens with living spaces in burgundy and hunter green color palettes were common in home décor. Design styles began to emerge with more minimalist, cleaner lines, and green became common as the decade showed signs of nature and environmentalism. Technology became more commonplace as the decade came to a close with cell phones and personal computers connecting the globe and influencing our transition into the new millennium.

In the start of the new millennium—2000–2009—technology dominates, and so do the colors that reflect this new decade and the future. Silver, gray, cerulean blue, and metallic finishes were seen in fashion, technology, and home décor at the onset of the new decade. The 2000s gave rise to increased concern for the environment, and colors giving a nod to nature emerged, including subdued oranges, sky blues, reds, turquoise, and warm neutrals. Future influences in color trends will reflect our global connectedness, networking, new technology, and fashion. The interior spaces of our homes are scaling down in size; multi-use space that serves more than one purpose has become commonplace in neutral colors; and quieter color schemes counter the fast-paced, busy lifestyle.

These themes continue to influence the years 2010–2019. The internet has impacted design with unlimited consumer access to products, shopping, design, and social media and influencers on home, fashion and style. Trends, while present, gave way to more individual pursuits of expression and identity. Modern and minimalist became trendy and softer colors led by neutral warm grays took over our spaces. The resurgence of satin-brass, coppers, and vintage metals arose in our homes and public spaces. Comfort, simplicity, peace and meditative spaces for work and life balance drew greater emphasis.

Looking from 2020 and beyond, colors that reflect optimism, hope, spirituality, and personal growth will influence the years ahead. Pantone's selection of the *Color of the Year* greatly influences product development and a review of past colors provide a window into our past. Each year, Pantone along with many other organizations, including the **Color Marketing Group**—a nonprofit international association of color design professionals founded in 1962 that identifies global color trends in the marketplace—will announce the leading colors that will shape our future trends and influence consumer culture.

Color Trends and Forecasting

Color forecasting helps to identify patterns in the tastes of consumers and gives projections of preferences that affect many industries, including fashion design, interior design, home goods including small appliances, technology such as your smart phone, and even automobiles. The goal of identifying color and design trends is to increase and create excitement in the retail realm. Color trends affect product development, purchasing habits, and the placement of products in the marketplace that are in fashion to ultimately drive greater sales and increase customer attraction and market opportunities (Tantanatewin and Inkarojrit, 2016). The tastes and preferences are unique and based on economies, pop culture, politics, and cultural differences. A global examination of common color patterns often leads to a broader understanding of color's impact on products that will be of interest to the consumer.

Trends in color often begin and are led by the fashion industry, and they set the tone for other industries. These trends often originate in Europe and begin to make their way westward. Trends typically follow a seven-year curve, and in the first one to two years color trends can be seen in fashion, followed by interiors. The markets for home décor, furniture, and upholstery textiles will take cues from the color leaders. Their success and general consumer interests, along with market research, will determine whether electronics and small appliances for the home follow suit. Lastly, we see the color trends refined down to colors that the auto industry wishes to make available to consumers. Because tech and auto industries risk losing a large amount of money when committing to colors that may or may not be received well, they often wait until the middle or later end of the trend curve to see what's most popular.

An easy way to peer into the future of color trends is to make a quick trip to your local high-end department store and peruse the color of women's fashion. The colors you see here will soon be seen in other retail areas. Overexposure of a color will soon result in its demise, and it will slowly shift or go away. Individual trend colors often evolve rather than disappear entirely. A red that is more toward red-orange may shift into a new trend where it is more red-violet.

We cannot speak of trends without clarifying a **fad**. Trends have a longer effect on consumer culture and result from a myriad of influences, as previously explained. A fad is usually temporary, lasting from a few months to maybe a year, and is often generated by an individual or group of people for the purpose of quick sales that is driven by mass popularity. The life of color trends, in contrast, permeates culture and consumer tastes more deeply and can be more difficult to predict.

Figure 3.19 illustrates a collection of past color trends in the design and fashion industry. Color in the retail industry changes swiftly, and period palettes and those associated with particular design movements may inspire your interior color schemes. When working in period styles, research the colors for accuracy—referencing images of historic buildings and interiors is an additional source for color inspiration and harmonious palettes that are timeless. The *Color Compendium* by Hope and Walch (1990) is an excellent source for historical and cultural color harmonies. In Figures 3.20a to 3.20c, students generate a series of color studies using color palettes shaped into various motifs representing each of the historical periods.

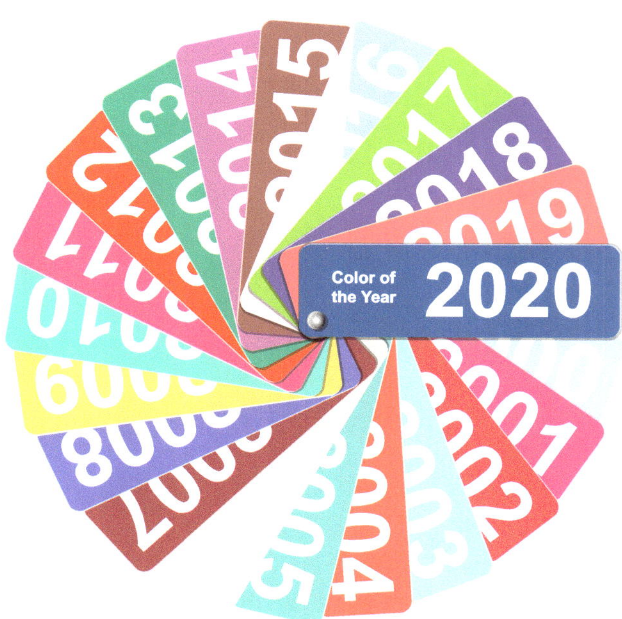

Figure 3.19 Example of Pantone's color of the year over the last twenty-years. These color trends are driven by social, cultural, environmental, and political changes; color trends are identified by multiple influences from around the world.

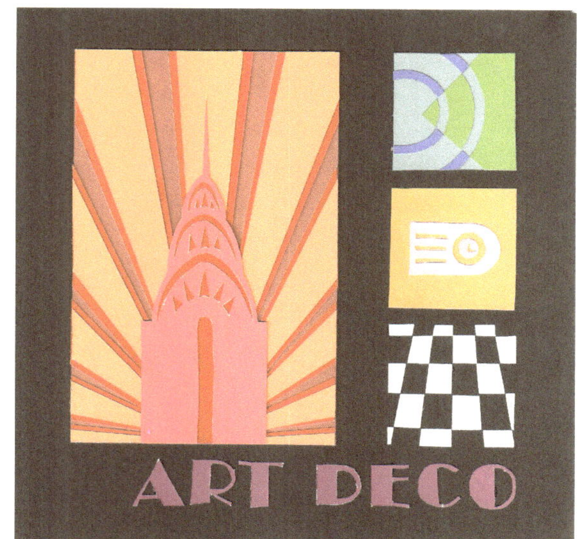

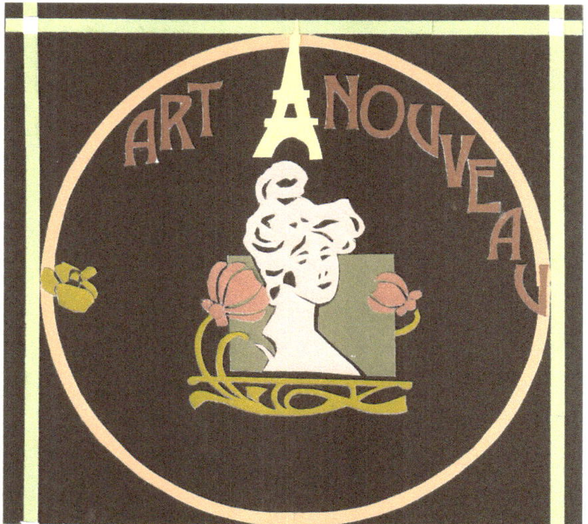

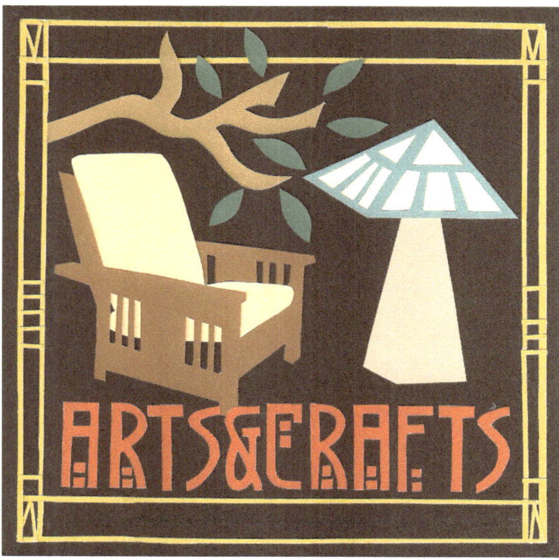

Figure 3.20 Historical color palettes. (a) Art Deco. (b) Art nouveau. (c) Arts & Crafts.

Color Consumerism

Color and shape are characteristics of objects designed to attract and retain our attention. Color can be considered one of the most powerful elements for expressing personality, creating visual appeal, and generating interest in consumer products. Branding and product recognition result from color that communicates information to the consumer—such as price, quality, taste, and value—affecting perceptions and preferences, and, ultimately, product sales. Ownership of the product communicates personalization, individuality, identity, meaning, and memories. According to the Color Marketing Group, color has the potential to increase a brand's retail sales as much as 80 percent and can be as much as 85 percent of the reason consumers buy a particular product (Color Marketing Group, 2008). Color is important for brand recognition and for eliciting both positive and negative associations with the product. Consumers are no longer content with black and white color choices when purchasing goods. This has influenced manufacturers to create an array of color choices for their products to attract buyers and provide flexibility and personalization. Take for instance the KitchenAid® stand mixer. This mixer is available in thirty colors and can be engraved and customized to reflect you as a home baker. Color influences profits and brand recognition. Consider orange for Amazon.com® or blue for Facebook®. According to Think Marketing, 85 percent of consumers indicate that color is a primary reason for selecting a particular product, 66 percent will not buy certain home appliance if it is not available in their favorite color, and 80 percent of manufacturers products are more likely to be recognized by color (2014).

These statistics are the direct result of color trends and buying patterns of consumers. Color trends are an excellent way to stay abreast of what consumers are demanding and what is available or to become available in interior design-related products. As some of you will recall, in earlier days, cell phones were first available only in black or gray—which are associated with the image of technology and corporate America. In order to attract a larger market, colors were introduced at a later stage. Today, personal technology devices are available in a wide range of colors and patterns and can be customized to personal preference. Observing the retail industry, where many of the products we use for interiors are presented, including custom designs, is an insightful way of staying informed and prepared to select successful colors. Prior to the year 2000, most home interior products were produced in black, white, beige, rusty browns, and faux finishes. In vogue with the idea of the millennium, the future, and advancing technology, silver began to make its way into the home. Now you can hardly walk into a design showroom without seeing metallic finishes abundantly displayed. While often overlooked, identifying the particular consumer products your client likes will enlighten you to potential color preferences. At the least, a good conversation into why the color was chosen and the meaning it may have to the individual is a springboard for ideas.

Finding and selecting colors for a design project can be an overwhelming task. With so many options available in the market, along with influences from TV, magazines, and popular culture tempting you to use current color trends, finding the perfect color might seem all but impossible. Color is a personal choice that should reflect the user. Put simply, if you don't like it, don't use it. If you do not prefer changing colors every one to two years, consider selecting classic color choices and avoid trends.

The flexibility of choice and need for personalization with color is now being seen in design and building products that can change color. These products have **thermochromatic** properties that utilize heat sensitive papers, inks, and pigments that change with touch or environment, such as warm water or radiant heated flooring systems. These products with papers, inks, and pigments. Examples include the temperature sensitive Northern Lights™ heat sensitive, color changing tiles; smart textiles such as E-ink, a paper-thin smart electronic display material that changes in color with controlled electronic data; and Nanoleaf™ light panels, available in a variety of shapes operates with touch and motion detection for color changing capabilities. Technology will continue to trickle down into the home furnishings market, and the future of color will include textiles woven with fiber-optics, allowing you to change the color of your furnishings with the flip of switch. The Phillips Lighting® luminous textile, Kvadrat Soft Cells, is an example of a large luminous surface that can be applied to walls and ceilings. This product allows you to change the atmosphere of any designed space with color.

Color changes as fashions and trends change, and a color that is widely received today could be shunned tomorrow. Cultural movements produce changes in color preferences, which also influence color decisions; however, we must be careful not to be too prescriptive about color harmony, lest we forget that it depends partly on theory and partly on personal preference. It is important to remember that colors do not change, only our acceptance of them over time.

REVIEW QUESTIONS

1. What is programming?
2. Give an example of a color myth or a color bias.
3. List two to three colors and a positive and negative association with each.
4. List the four qualities that affect our visual perception of color.
5. Explain how the size of an interior can be made to appear smaller or larger with the use of color and light.
6. Describe the color phenomenon called simultaneous contrast.
7. List the seven types of color contrasts identified by color theorist Johannes Itten.
8. Describe the Bezold effect.
9. Explain how a color trend is formed and what influences these trends.
10. Describe the difference between a trend and a fad.

Vocabulary

Programming
space
recoloration
palette
simultaneous contrast
Bezold effect
color forecasting
trend
fad
Color Marketing Group
thermochromatic

EXERCISES

The following tools may be used for the following exercises: Color-aid paper, paint samples, or colored artist papers available at your local art supply store, X-acto knife, metal rule, rubber cement, and neutral-colored (gray works best) matboard or illustration board for presentation.

1. Select ten to fifteen images from various media and/or photograph a particular scene that provides you with emotional responses such as warm/hot, cool/cold, like/dislike, soft/hard, excitement/boredom. If taking photographs, be sure to consider the scene at different times of the day, as light can alter the emotional response. Arrange your images into two organized collages, one for positive emotional response and the other for negative. Analyze why each image elicited your responses. This is a great tool for beginning discussions of color with potential clients in your design projects.
2. Visit a local retail establishment. Locate several examples of how color is used to market and increase consumers' potential to buy its products. Analyze the way the colors are used and explain how the design and color may entice the consumer to buy. Pay attention to the age group or type of person the product is targeting and why.
3. The following is an exercise in recoloration:
   a. Select a full-page color photo of an interior space from a design publication.
   b. Using the photograph of an interior space, analyze the color usage and document the major and minor hues used.
   c. Locate these colors within a Color-aid® packet or paint chips from a local paint retailer.
   d. Redraw (tracing/outlining, etc.) the interior using a black pen (felt tip works best). Use drafting equipment when necessary to draw straight vertical/horizontal/diagonal lines.
   e. Rework the room interior with a contrast warm/cool palette by using a different color scheme with balance in chroma and values from the original photo.

TABLE 3.2 COLOR PREFERENCES REVEALED

STEP 1	1. Think of a color, any color that immediately pops into your head. It does not have to be your favorite or least favorite, just the first color that comes to mind. 2. If you could move to any location in the world, where would it be? List two to four colors you associate with this place. 3. As a child, we all have favorite rooms, whether our own or places we've played. When you were between the ages of five and nine, what was your favorite room in the home? Now list the colors you remember seeing in this space. How did they make you feel? Were the colors chosen and the rooms designed to make you feel a certain way? 4. Think of a favorite vacation you've taken in the past. List two to three colors you see in this place. Write about their special properties and how they made the place memorable and enjoyable. 5. Think of a person who has had a significant impact in your life. What color(s) do you associate with that person? Why? 6. Now, open your bedroom closet door and peer inside. Do certain colors dominate your wardrobe? If so, list three of them. 7. Gifts or cherished memorabilia often leave us with positive feelings, remind us of a loved one, a place visited, or a time of joy in our life. Think of the most cherished object in your home, the one thing you would grab if your house were about to disappear. What color is it? 8. Consider an event in your life that might have made you sad or angry. Do you see one or two colors that reflect that memory?
STEP 2	Look at the colors you have written and list the top two to three that occur most often. These are the colors you're most likely to feel comfortable around. Examine those colors listed from question 8. These are possibly colors you may feel uncomfortable around.

(Adapted from McCleary, 2002, p. 7)

TABLE 3.3 COLOR PERCEPTIONS QUIZ

Match the concept in the left-hand column with the correct color and description in the right-hand column.

Which color relaxes the nervous system?	**RED** Red spaces will make someone feel anxious, but rooms with red accents make people lose track of time. Bars and casinos often use this color to get people to "stick around."
Which color makes people feel anxious?	**PINK** If you are in a pink room, you just don't have enough energy to get angry! Pink has been used for criminal uniforms and wall surfaces of penitentiaries to eliminate conflict among cellmates.
Which color has the potential to make people angry?	**ORANGE** There is a preference toward this color for food due to the pleasant flavors associated with oranges, mangoes, apricots, pumpkins, and other yellow and yellow-orange vegetables.
Which color can cause fatigue and lack of energy?	**BLUE** Blue causes your body to produce chemicals that calm the nervous system.
Which color is known to make people nervous or tense?	**BLACK** Black creates a sense of endlessness and is a "color" that does not get brighter during the day. Also associated with night, witchcraft, and death. Bad luck for a black cat to cross your path.
Which color is considered one of the most appetizing?	**YELLOW** Highly luminescent, pure yellow can hurt the eyes and causes people to lose their tempers more easily.

f. Mount the original photograph and the recoloration with your color samples from your Color-aid® packet or paint samples onto a sheet of illustration board. Place your color samples below each photograph.

g. Label both drawings with their respective color scheme, and provide a comparative analysis of the color transformation to the interior.

4. See Table 3.2 for an exercise to find your color preferences. This is a great tool to use for your future design projects when you need to determine a client's preference for colors.
5. See Table 3.3 for a color perception quiz.
6. Using color artists' papers or digital drawing tools, generate a composition using the Bezold effect. Next, recreate the same design replacing one of the key colors from the original with a new color that results in the Bezold effect.

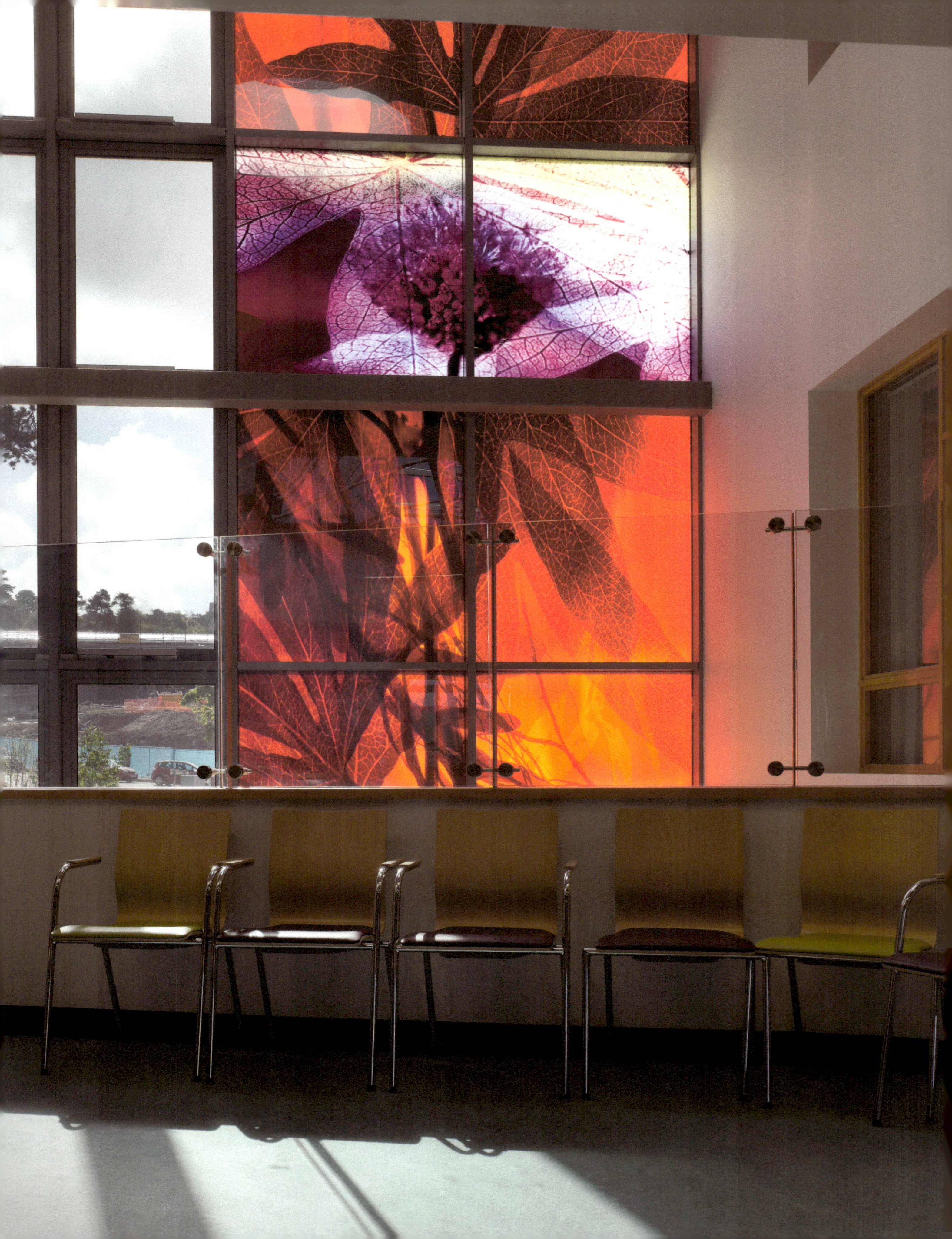

4

color + health

Learning Outcomes

After studying this chapter, you will be able to:

- **Explain how color may influence a person's health and well-being.**
- **Consider how color, and certain attributes of color and light, may affect a person's mood and behavior.**
- **Discuss the anatomy of the eyes and how we see and perceive color.**
- **Identify the different types of color blindness and describe how color is actually seen with each color deficiency.**
- **Describe what occurs to the aging eye and how color can be used to support the needs of older adults.**
- **Illustrate how color, contrast, and light can be applied to assist all individuals with easier access and use of interior spaces.**

As discussed in Chapter 3, there are commonalities and broad views on association and our sensory perception of color with information suggesting both positive and negative emotional and psychological and physiological responses that may occur. Factors including age, gender, health, culture and beliefs, are a few factors that contribute to influencing these perceptions (Tofle et al., 2004; Elliot, 2015). The interior space may affect our sense of positive health and well-being, considering that we spend most of our time indoors.

In this chapter, discussion of research and understanding of the influence of color and light in the built environment to health, will be discussed. Health and well-being care occurs in a broad spectrum of spaces and settings. Information pertaining to the influence of color to provide guidance on the importance of color in supporting positive health and well-being will be the focus. Individual response to color varies, and no one solution is predictable at supporting positive health outcomes with specific colors.

The information presented in this chapter is not intended to substitute established guidelines for the design of mental health, prescribed medical treatment, or to use in place of any developed health guides. Rather, the information presented is intended to create a dialogue on the potential influence color has on our well-being. Within a health setting, environmental conditions which may influence behavior include color contrast, color saturation and brightness, visual patterns, and quality of lighting. Continued practice of **evidence-based design**—a process resulting in decisions about the built environment based on credible research to achieve optimal outcomes—is needed to provide more conclusive evidence to support specific color for health and well-being. Mindfulness of the current research and the effects of light, color lightness, brightness, and color temperature—warm and cool, for example—may lead to more informed color solutions for health-specific design projects. Supportive evidence and recent research regarding the effects of color on behavioral health and its effects in interior space presented in this chapter are building blocks for this effort.

Color and Health and Healing

Vision impairments, aging of the eye, behavioral and mood disorders are just some health-related concerns. Color selection may aid in supporting a person's health and sense of well-being (Ghamari & Amor, 2016). It is understandable with the complexity of color and light that seeking to simplify and create an easy rule book to work from, or to state that a particular color may excite or reduce a mood, should be done with caution rather than be assumed. Best practices may include testing these theories on a case-by-case basis with the individuals or groups where the color is experienced and may lend to positive outcomes.

Isolating ourselves from color in our environment is rather difficult. Therefore, certain colors we are exposed to may contribute to our mood, mental health, stress, anxiety, depression which indicates that the qualities of the space we design can influence positive or negative human behavior (Platt et al., 2017; Gray et al., 2012).

Please note that no single color is responsible for a specific outcome; with many variations of a single hue, including value and saturation, which have potential influences on health. Table 4.1 summarizes proposed relationship and associations between color and health reported in research. The table represents generalities of common hues' effect on health and healing. In the next section, we will explore a few examples of common behavioral health concerns and how color and light can play an active role in addressing responses to this stimuli.

Mental Health and Well-Being

Positive health and well-being are central to daily functioning. According to the National Alliance on Mental Illness, 1 in 5 U.S. adults experience mental illness, 19 percent are anxiety related, and 17 percent of youth ages 6–17 experience some form of mental health disorder (2020). The National Alliance on Mental Illness (NAMI) lists several of the most prevalent mental health conditions, which include anxiety, depression, and **attention deficit hyperactivity disorder** (ADHD), a disorder identified with symptoms of inattention, hyperactivity,

TABLE 4.1 RELATIONSHIP AND ASSOCIATION OF COLOR TO MOODS AND HEALTH CONDITIONS

Hue	Health
RED	Under red lighting, our body secretes more adrenalin, increasing our blood pressure and our rate of breathing while raising our body temperature just slightly. Sensitivity towards red is supported by those in states of anger and hostility (Fetterman et al., 2015).
PINK	Pink to soothe upset stomach—Pepto Bismol Has been known to heal headaches
BLUE	Physiological research shows that blue light will slow your heartbeat, decrease your temperature, and relax your muscles Assists with balance and equilibrium Its calming nature has been known to "lower blood pressure, slow pulse rate, or decrease body temperature" (Kopacz, 2004, p. 79)
GREEN	Assists with balance and equilibrium Can ease tremors, twitching, and muscle spasms Association of health and well-being
YELLOW	Speeds up the human metabolism; was documented by Arab physician Avicenna as an indicator of liver disorder based on yellowing of skin color (Hope & Walch, 1990, pp. 161–162)
PURPLE	Violet—the color closer to blue than red—has been known to calm anxiety
ORANGE	Has been known to increase the amount of oxygen supply to the brain
WHITE	Was documented by Arab Physician Avicenna as an indicator of spleen disorder based on whitening of skin color (Hope & Walch, 1990, pp. 161–162)
BLACK	In color therapy it is associated with the kidney and bladder; can induce sadness, fear, and despair
BROWN	Has been known to be negatively received by those identified with depression and anxiety (Caruthers et al., 2010).
GRAY	If overly used, may cause depression and loneliness. Also associated with high levels of anxiety (Korkmaz et al., 2016)
SILVER	Healing of hormonal imbalances

and impulsivity. **Autism spectrum disorder** (ASD), like ADHD, is an additional developmental condition; however, ASD impairs a person's ability to socialize and communicate with others.

Health is defined as "the condition of being sound in body, mind, or spirt" and **well-being** is the "state of being happy, healthy, or prosperous" (Merriam-Webster, 2020). The World Health Organization indicates that one's mental health and well-being is attributed to a person's ability to manage the daily stresses of one's life, to enjoy a healthy lifestyle, and be productive and contribute to one's community. Considering that the average person spends approximately 90 percent of their lives indoors, how we apply design to our surroundings, and in particular with color, may affect our health and well-being.

According to the *Mental Health Facilities Design Guide* developed by the Department of Veterans Affairs–Office of Construction & Facilities Management, it is recommended that environmental solutions that incorporate natural lighting and provide views to natural surroundings, have been "shown to advance healing and recovery" (MHFDG, p. 2-3, 2010). Using "natural materials, a soothing color palette and residential character" in the design of care settings reduces patient stress (MHFDG, p. 2-11, 2010). Research on design and behavioral health suggest that views of nature and access to daylight or depictions of nature and landscapes are supportive of positive health and well-being (Card et al., 2018; HMC Architects, 2018; Thorsen, 2018; Hoisington, 2017; Stroupe, 2014). Incorporating color palettes that remind

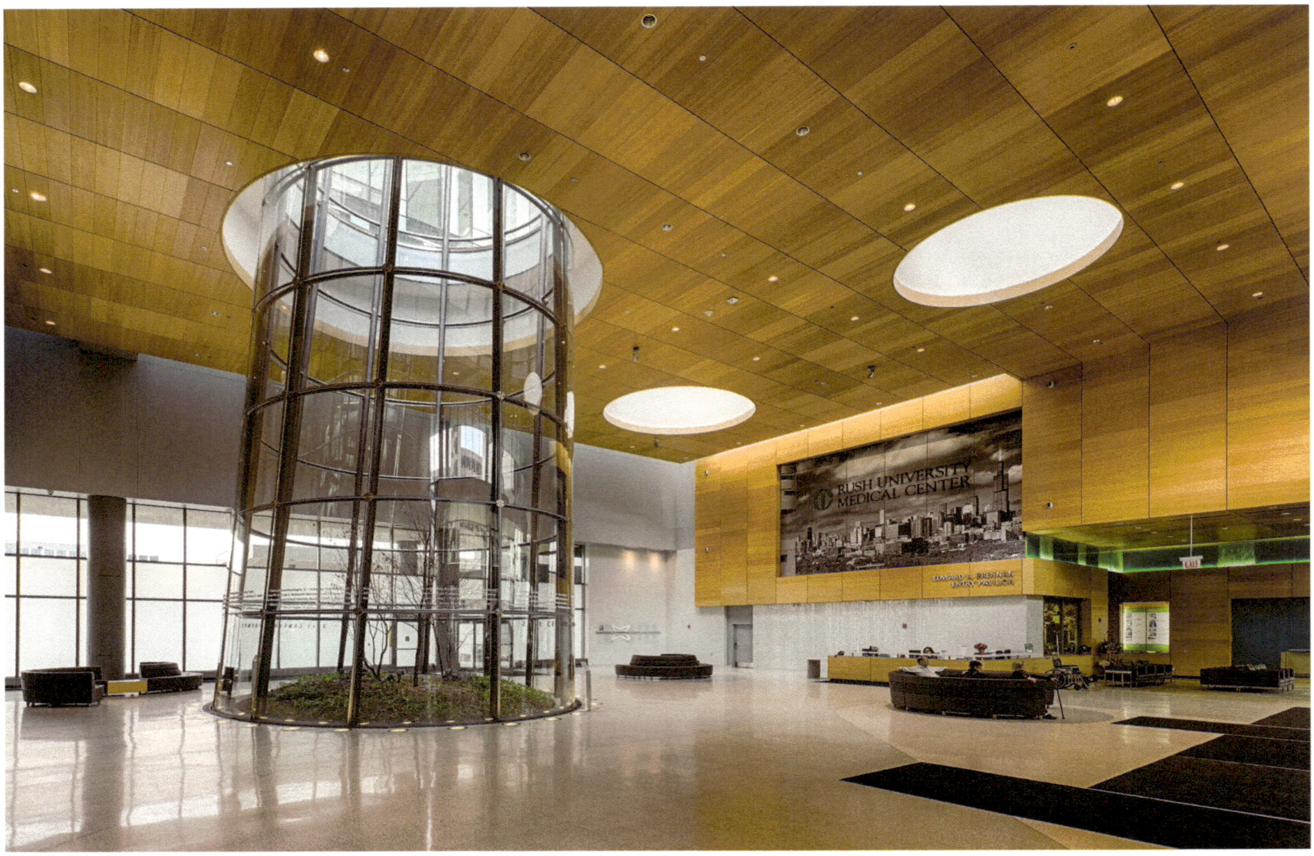

Figure 4.1 This terrarium in the lobby of the Rush University Medical Center in Chicago, Illinois designed by Perkins+Will is clad in wood with abundant use of natural light. Choices of wood finishes and green accents helps to provide a calming environment.

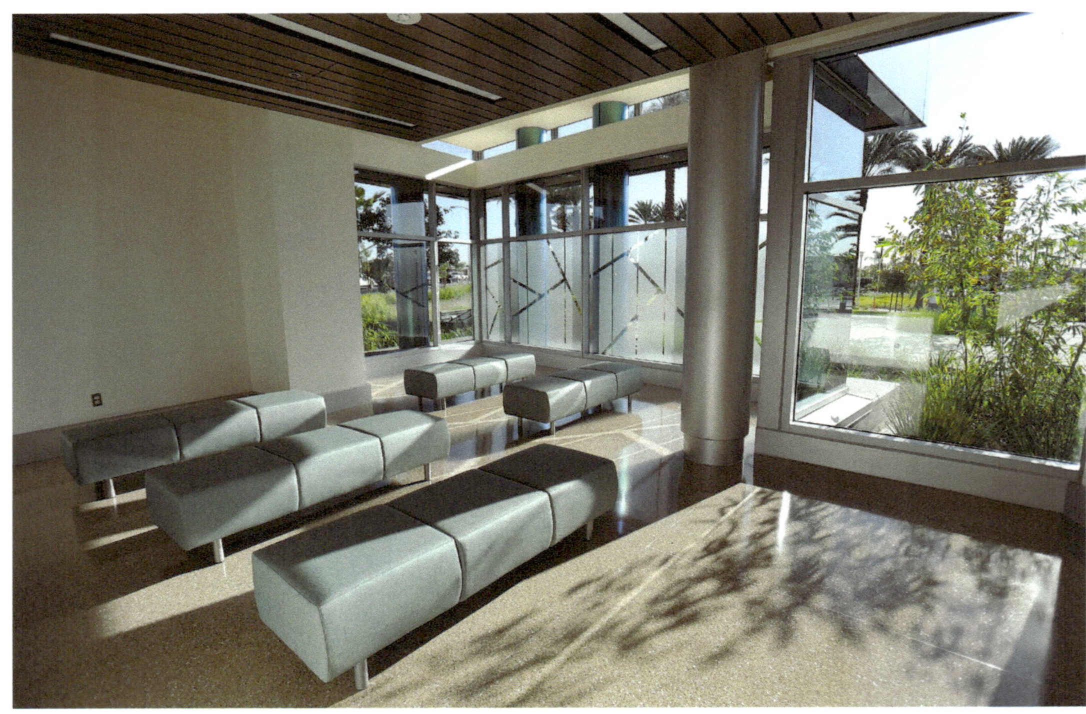

Figure 4.2 Meditation area of Miller's Children Hospital in Long Beach, CA. Providing access to natural views, water, landscaping, and daylight has the potential to reduce stress and anxiety. The soft color palette and low contrast help to create a calming space.

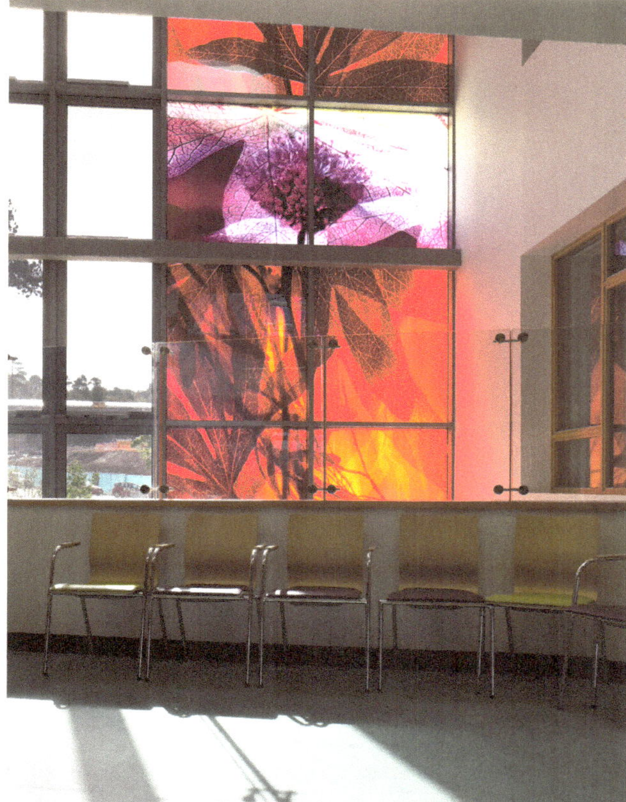

Figure 4.3 Knockbreda Community Care and Treatment CentreBelfast, Antrim, United Kingdom by Architect Penoyre and Prasad. Large scale for impact; this art installation incorporates daylight and filtered colored light for healing potential.

someone of nature, and incorporating natural materials, such as wood, and access to daylight in your design, may be helpful in producing a healthy sense of well-being (Figures 4.1 and 4.2).

Figure 4.3 depicts the use of natural forms through artwork that integrates color and daylight. The use of art can create a more familiar homelike setting in health spaces. This is an easier way to integrate color into a design since it isn't permanent and can be changed as needed with little interruption to the space. However, be mindful of black and white photography or images that may be seen as negative for individuals with depression (Hoisington, 2017).

Anxiety and Depression

In the information age with access to technology, the constant flow of information, frequency and speed of communication, and constant distractions, sensory overload is inevitable. In addition, our environments can cause increased stress through our interaction in spaces that further influence our sense of well-being; this is heightened in health settings where stress occurs (Chamari and Amor, 2016).

Design research, health and design guides, and available literature on color and healing propose recommendations for color selections for health and well-being. However, recommendations that are provided refer to a subjective description of color, such as soothing, warm, or inviting, versus specific recommendations for color selections to aid in mental health care or treatment (Hunt et al., 2019; Department of Veterans Affairs, 2010). Recommendations for colors to avoid in mental health clinics are provided and include "harsh colors such as black, chartreuse, and orange" (Department of Veterans Affairs, 4–28, 2010). Others have supported the use of calm colors, and also suggest avoiding achromatic color—not white or gray—in patient rooms (Shepley & Pasha, 2013). There is agreement that incorporating color or accent color, rather than no color or monochromatic palettes, into interior spaces among other characteristics of the space—natural light, natural materials, subtle patterns, matte finishes—where patients received care considers psychological needs (Figure 4.4).

In several studies on well-being, color is often associated and identified by users through a described level of comfort that can be attained (Thorsen, 2018; Platt et al., 2017). Comfort can be achieved when the stressor is removed and a state of mental restoration can begin (Augustin, 2009). Rooms with an extended, prolonged exposure to color, or a complete lack of color, can have more lasting negative effects on patient comfort, recovery and modified behavior. During color planning and design for health, mindfulness of solutions that are too arousing, either in saturated, bold color and complex patterns, can overwhelm (Hoisington, 2017). Designing with restraint and moderation is recommended. Specifying colors that may be associated with trauma or negative images may also cause heightened negative mood and disruptive behavior (Hoisington, 2017). Assessment of these triggers can be hard to pinpoint and predict due to differences, personalities, cultural differences, biases and the extent of the health condition affecting a person or group.

The *Behavioral Health and Design Guide* published by the National Association of Psychiatric Health Systems suggests that patterns and color combinations that

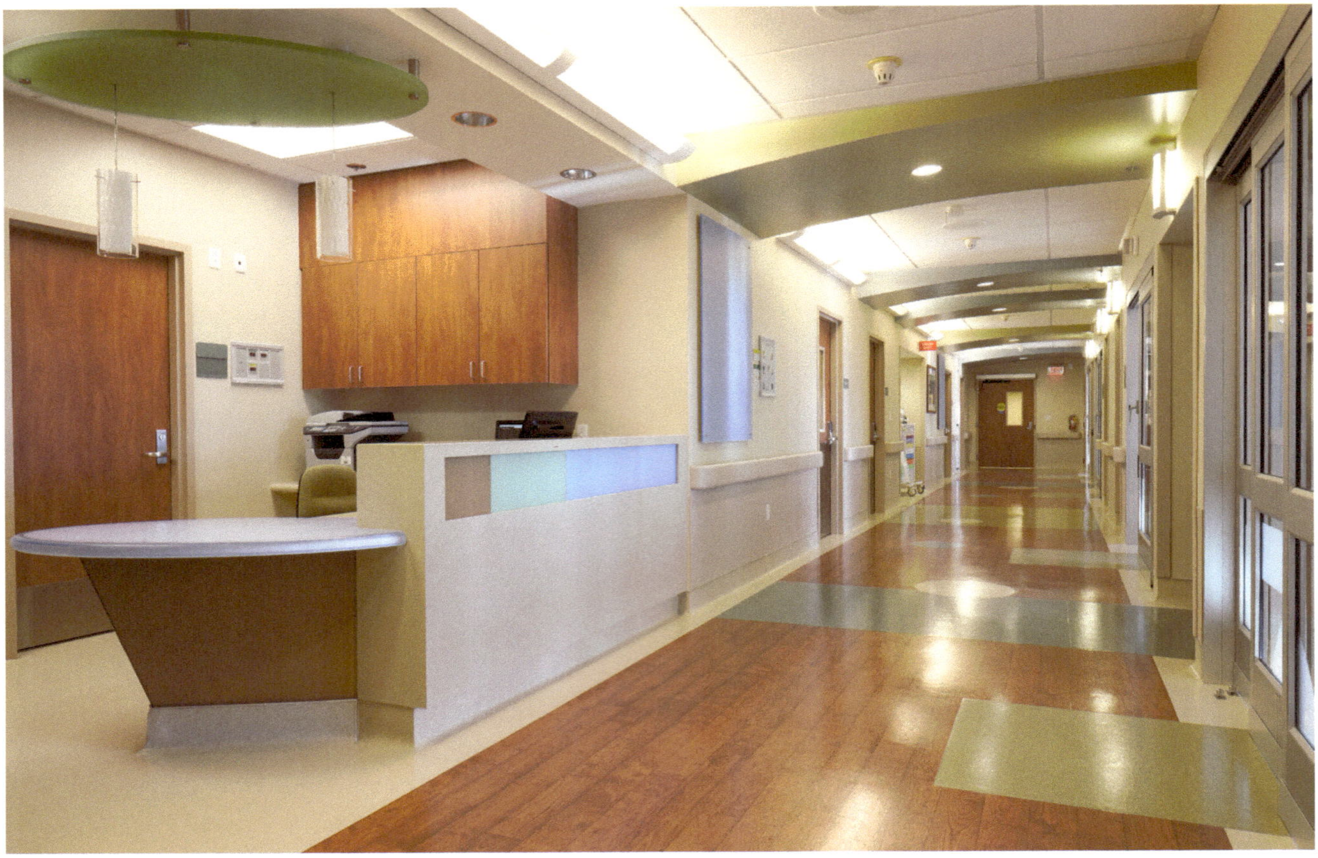

Figure 4.4 Red-orange wood tones, complimentary green hues, soft curves, and a balance of both natural and artificial lighting provide a warm and comfortable entrance and corridor to this medical space.

create movement or sudden changes in color contrast, in particular with flooring, could appear as barriers creating the need for a patient to step over or cause them to feel disoriented and should be avoided (Hunt et al., 2019). The guide also suggests "soothing" colors for less-stimulating spaces. This creates further subjectivity of color and light, adding difficulty in identifying clear solutions for supportive health spaces.

Additional research proposes that specific colors may be identified to validate a person's level of anxiety and depression (Carruthers et al., 2010). In a study on color association with anxiety and depression, individuals were presented with a series of thirty-eight colors within six easily identifiable color ranges—red, blue, green, yellow, orange, and purple—each color selected in relation to the Munsell color system. Identified as the Manchester Color Wheel (Figure 4.5); this wheel consists of four values for each hue presented for an added range of lightness and darkness, and also includes white, gray, and black neutrals along with pink and brown as they may relate to

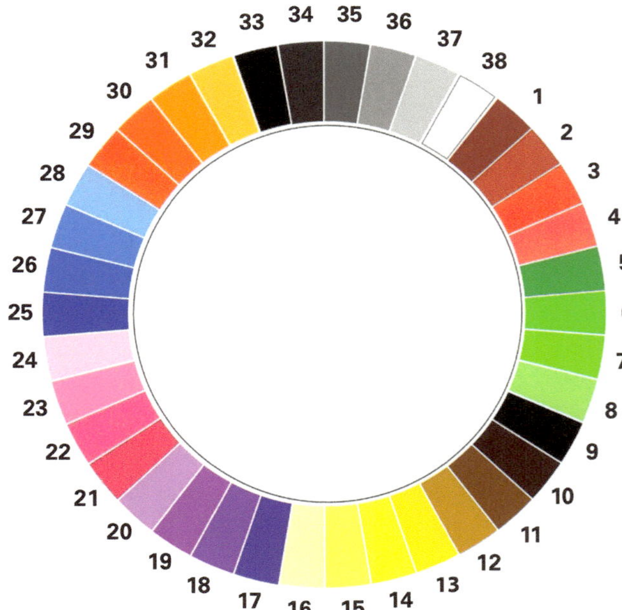

Figure 4.5 The Manchester Color Wheel was developed to help identify color and choice as a way for patients to describe their mood—healthy, anxious, or depressed.

"bodily tissues and functions" (2010, p. 2). Participants who self-identified as healthy, anxious, or depressed, were asked to select specific colors they associated as positive or liked, were most drawn to, and that they identified with their recent moods; as this would relate to their state of being healthy, depressed, or anxious.

Whether the participants identified as healthy or unhealthy, positive associations were given to the colors blue and yellow. The lightest of the four blue hues in the color wheel was selected as most favorable, and the second to lightest was most preferred amongst those identified with anxiety and depression. Only 39 percent of those in the study identified their mood with color, with yellow as the most preferred, and gray as the top choice for anxious and depressed.

Cool colors are considered low arousal and further supported with low chroma (Figure 4.6). As discussed in the previous chapter; the color blue has been associated with calming and relaxing and studies have indicated that when spaces use blue, the color can help reduce anxiety and stress (Bosch et al., 2012; Clark and Costall, 2008; Verhoeven et al., 2006). Green, another color associated with calm or coolness, has also been shown to be the preferred color by those suffering from PTSD–post-traumatic stress disorder (Korkmaz et al., 2016). While it's difficult to determine the level of a person's mood through conversation and verbal cues alone, using visual tools, such as the Manchester Color Wheel, may provide a less invasive way to determine a person's behavior in prescribing color for design and/or treatment.

It is also worth noting that a single color alone is not the sole factor in determining associative color and mood (O'Connor, 2011). The brightness of the color was associated with a positive mood as compared to a dark color that was associated with negative mood (Ghamari & Amor, 2016). This further suggests that specific hues alone are less a factor in positive versus negative reactions. Rather, it is the brightness and saturation of the color that has greater influence on individual perceptions, and colors that are too bright or vibrant can be stress-inducing (Silvis, 2012; Carruthers et al., 2010).

As we've discussed, learned biases, cultural norms, and associations that are often developed early during childhood may contribute to the mood and color association rather than actual physiological responses (Tofle et al., 2003). Isolating, and attempting to pinpoint color and

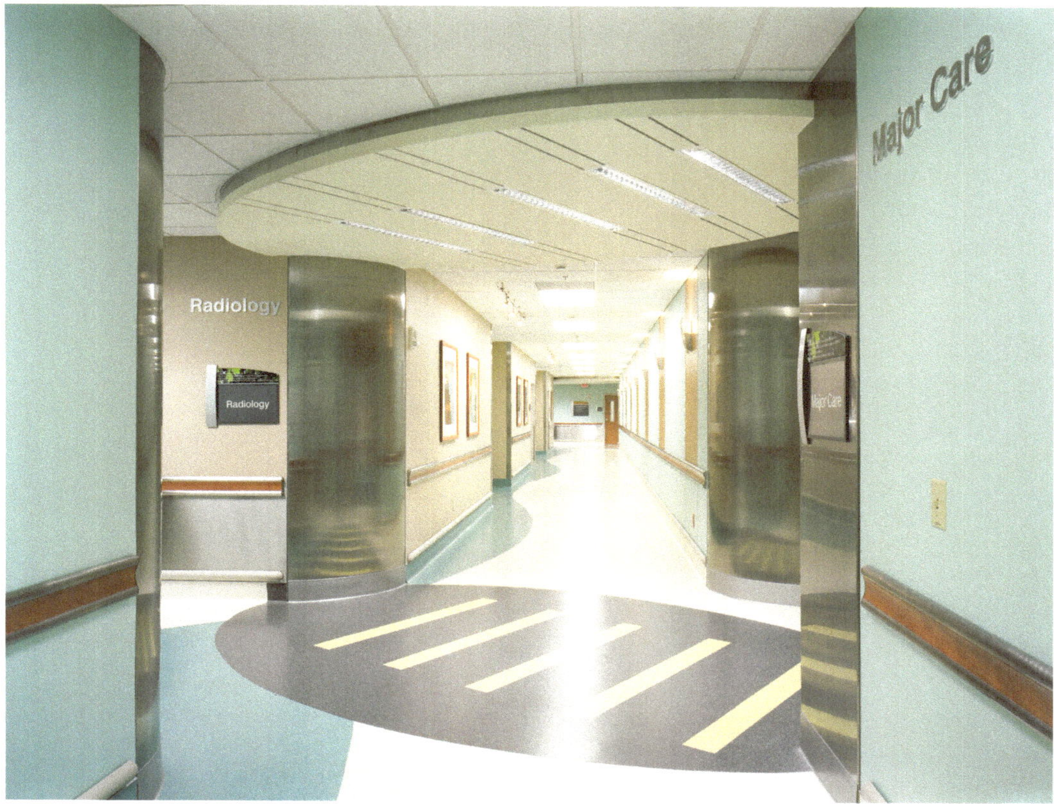

Figure 4.6 Soft colors, low contrast, organic natural lines represented in ceiling and floor design may help to reduce prolonged stay in medical spaces and speed the recovery process.

associative mood, has created a widespread one-color-fits all approach. In Chapter 3, we looked at myths and biases that have been learned over time. And while some of these associations may ring true, and provide a place to begin color planning efforts, much like a fingerprint, individual responses to color are personal.

Attention Deficit Hyperactivity Disorder (ADHD)

ADHD—attention deficit hyperactivity disorder—is a cognitive impairment that limits the individual's ability to process information or reduces mental focus and functioning for extended periods of time. Symptoms of ADHD include difficulty focusing, hyperactivity, and being easily distracted (Mayo Clinic, 2020).

The challenge establishing guidelines for specific color and placement in designing for ADHD is that the needs for each individual are unique and varied. When choosing color for residential and commercial spaces there are general criteria that can be considered to guide your color planning:

- High contrast between color and materials, which can be beneficial to designate changes in surface levels, can overwhelm someone that may suffer from anxiety or ADHD.
- Too much color variation, pattern, and texture can add to a space that is overstimulating (Augustin, 2009). This may require additional mental processing to generate a sense of predictability in our surrounding, which adds comfort and security.
- Use color to accent and emphasize architectural elements in the space to keep the person focused.
- Use color and value to reduce the vastness of space, creating a more intimate space.
- Avoid color phenomena such as vibrancy and after-images, or irritating color combinations that may increase activity.
- Reduce busy patterns to eliminate distractions.
- As you will later read on color and balance, the size of color area and quantity of a color not only affects perception of weight and scale; exposure to large surface areas of color may "overstimulate individuals no matter the color temperature or preference (Gaines & Curry, pp. 49, 2011). This could be important to consider for those individuals identified with ADHD or severe anxiety.

Autism Spectrum Disorder (ASD)

Individuals with ADHD cannot focus or concentrate while those with autism can become fixated on items they are drawn to. Unlike ADHD, those with autism will have an intense reaction to environmental stimulation (Paron-Wildes, 2013). Concentration and fixation on a single item, being unresponsive, withdrawn, and having impaired social interaction also occurs. As the term spectrum implies, individuals with ASD vary on a scale from mild to severe that make it difficult to establish singular approaches to prescribe color to reduce reactions to their surroundings. Additionally, individuals with autism can be sensitive to color, texture, pattern, and lighting (Kopec, 2018).

Certain colors are more stimulating than others and may appear brighter or more intense to someone with ASD (Paron-Wildes, 2013). Subtle colors, such as blue and green, are often more preferred than brighter colors like yellow, pink, and red (Grandgeorge and Masataka, 2016). According to Paron-Wildes, subdued color choices should be given priority in environments where a person will be more mentally engaged—classrooms, therapy spaces, bathing, sleeping, and eating areas. Here are a few general guidelines to help color planning:

- Reduce the use of bold, highly saturated colors; use subtle color choices.
- Avoid highly contrasting color and abrupt changes from one color to another; gradual contrast is acceptable.
- Limit color variations and complex patterns in the selection of material and textiles that may overstimulate a person with ASD.
- Minimize spaces that incorporate too many cool color choices. Warm colors are preferred.
- Provide options for different lighting types and control of light levels.
- Warmer light color, closest to natural sunlight or an incandescent light, produces a positive response.

Public spaces, with loud noises and many people, can overwhelm someone with autism (Gaines et al., 2016). Creating a sensory experience for those with intellectual disabilities can aid in relaxing an agitated person. Consider designing into spaces, where appropriate, a sensory wall. Interactive spaces for tactical sensitivity in autism to touch and feel provides a place to focus their attention which can help calm and comfort a person during high stress or in busy public environments (Figure 4.7).

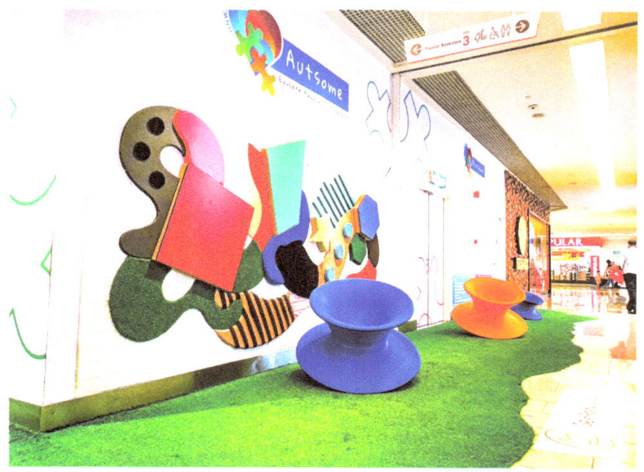

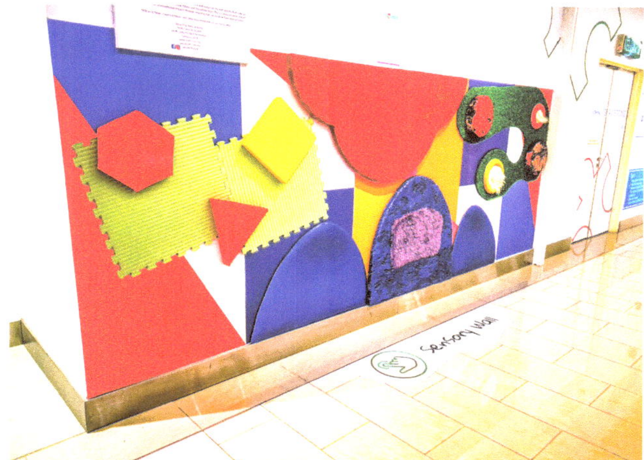

Figure 4.7 Sensory wall with tactile collages of textures and materials are displayed on the walls of this shopping center providing an Autism-friendly experience for families. Kuala Lumpur, Malaysia.

Our spaces serve and accommodate many people, and consideration of the research, along with the examples that have been presented, can be beneficial to guide and narrow the color and light solutions. Since each individual person and case is unique, approach with care to ensure the best solutions for health and well-being.

International WELL Building Institute (IWBI)

The IWBI developed the WELL Building standards, certification, and credentialing program in October 2014. The standards, which integrate both science and medical research on health outcomes in the built environment, promote improved comfort, health and wellness in workplace building design and interior spaces. Ten concepts form the standards for promoting health and wellness: air, water, nourishment, light, movement, thermal comfort, sounds, materials, mind, and community. Two of these standards, light and mind, provide specific guidelines for healthy solutions with color and light.

The WELL concept light consists of eight features for natural and artificial lighting design. Providing exposure to natural light is indicated to reduce symptoms of depression. Feature L03–*Circadian Lighting Design* specifically addresses circadian rhythm to ensure that the environment is supporting this natural cycle with appropriate exposure to light and light levels. As previously discussed, the color of the light will have an impact on the people using the space and should be factored into your lighting design. This standard expands to discuss glare control, increase exposure and access to daylight to mitigate potential depression and reduce stress.

Section L07–*Electric Light Quality* provides direction on the issue with color rendering and color quality of light, previously discussed in Chapter 2. This concept in the WELL standard suggest that a higher color rendering index (CRI > 90) similar to daylight that portrays environmental color more realistically has the potential to impact cognition and behavior, and may improve comfort and create a healthy space.

Last, the concept of *Mind* in the WELL standard, consists of fifteen features addressing the importance of promoting mental health in overall space design. Specifically, features M09–*Enhanced Access to Nature*, suggest that natural views and access to nearby nature helps to relieve stress. The concept states "Providing access to nature in built spaces can play a key role in supporting healthy environments by mitigating stressors and positively impacting cognitive and emotional health, focus, productivity and overall well-being" (WELL, 2020). The WELL feature for access to nature includes recommendations for these spaces identified as "green spaces" (park or forest) or "blue spaces" (ocean, lake, and rivers). When planning your design work, standard M07–*Restorative Spaces* requires "calming colors, textures, and forms." Explore options with natural materials, patterns and colors for reduced stress, anxiety, and positive emotional and mental support.

Color and Light Therapy

Color can affect our brainwaves, emotions, and biological systems. Colored surfaces and colored light have the ability to increase and decrease heart rate, blood pressure, respiratory rate, and body temperature, and can be used to treat cancer, depression, and bacterial infections. The full spectrum of daylight is needed to stimulate our endocrine systems properly.

Color therapy, or **chromotherapy**, is the "practice of using colored light and color in the environment to cure specific illness and in general to bring about beneficial health effect" (Hope & Walch, 1990, p. 75). Color therapy is a rather new science in the United States and is not well understood; however, within the past twenty years, its popularity has increased as we have moved from speculation to understanding because of positive results observed in patients. Ancient Egypt and certain Asian cultures commonly used color as a healing tool. Our bodies are like prisms; we absorb white light and, thus, all colors. Difficulty in breathing can be offset by natural light filtered through yellow glass. Migraine headaches can be treated with sunlight filtered through blue glass. Depression has been known to be treated with green light, red and red-violet light, and nervousness and irritability with blue light as opposed to yellow (Dearing & Singg, 1996; Oren, et al., 1991; Hope & Walsh 1990). A sore throat can be eased with the use of green light. Individuals who have lost their sight can have their mood affected by the transmission of colored light, which releases a hormone in the hypothalamus that controls mood (Hope & Walsh, 1990, p. 75).

The Behavioral Health and Design Guide recommends lighting color temperatures to support our **circadian rhythm**—a natural internal process that regulates our sleep cycle (Hunt et al., 2019). Consider limiting the exposure to blue light, in particular late in the evening and at night, to prevent disrupting this natural process (Oh et al., 2014). Lower light levels and less saturated warmer color temperatures or warm color tones may create a less stimulating environment and help with promoting positive health (Hunt et al., 2019, p. 71; Department of Veterans Affairs, 2010).

Seasonal Affective Disorder (SAD)

According to the National Institute of Mental Health, **seasonal affective disorder** is a type of depression associated with the seasons, usually occurring in the fall and winter, and subsides with the coming of spring and summer (NIMH, 2020). The cause of SAD remains unknown; however, our circadian rhythm and brain chemistry that affects mood and sleep patterns may play a role (Mayo Clinic, 2020). Symptoms of SAD include feeling depressed and having low energy and problems with sleep.

Reduced exposure to full spectrum daylighting may cause increased depression and providing light therapy may improve symptoms for those with seasonal affective disorder (Zauder & Ganzer, 2015). Exposure to fluorescent light, particularly cool, blue color, may increase stress hormones, hyperactivity, and irritability. Due to the diminished natural light during fall and winter months, daily exposure to light therapy that filters out ultraviolet light has been shown to ease the symptoms of SAD. Twenty to sixty minutes of exposure at 10,000 **lux**—the total amount of measured light falling onto a surface—of cool-white fluorescent light is recommended (NIMH, 2020; Zauderer & Ganzer, 2015).

Observation is the key to learning. Pay attention to your moods for a short period of time and notice the color of the environment and light sources present within the space. Fatigue can occur because of extended periods of visual exposure to saturated or high chroma colors, such as pure red or yellow, despite their properties of being colors that induce excitement and energy. Much like loud music from a concert, certain stimuli can have negative impacts on our body's energy level from overexposure. These colors will strain the eye, sending messages of confusion and discomfort to the brain. Let's explore the process of how light is processed in our visual system that leads to our experience of how we see color.

Color and Vision

The eye is an extension of the brain. The components of the eye send information—such as color, shape, and

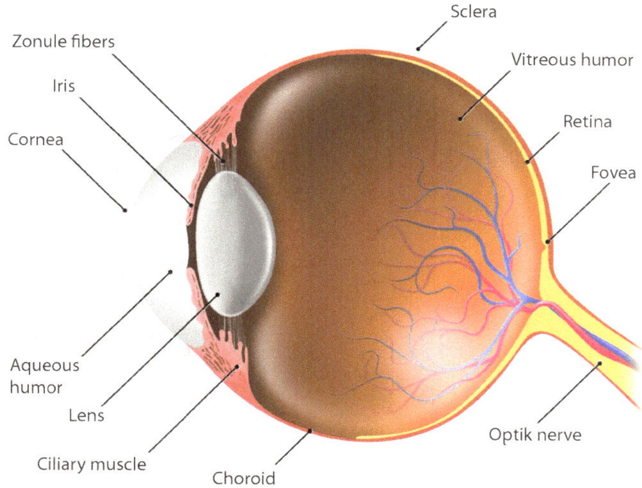

Figure 4.8 Cross section of the human eye. The retina contains light-sensitive nerve cells called cones and rods.

movement—via the optic nerve to the brain, where the electrical impulses of information are interpreted. Color is a complex process resulting from light entering the eye. Two types of light-sensitive nerve cells within the retina—**cones** (daylight/color receptors) and **rods** (dim light/value receptors)—transmit nerve impulses to the brain, resulting in color vision (Figure 4.8). There are three sets of cones sensitive to wavelengths of light: red, blue, and green.

Light reflects off surfaces, and, in fact, objects have no color of their own. The color of an object occurs from varying degrees of absorption of light energy, with the remaining light reflecting off the object into the eye, resulting in a vision of color (Figure 4.9). White-colored objects are absent of color, as they reflect all colored light. Black-colored objects contain all color and therefore will absorb all colored light. Since light is heat, the absorption of colored light by black objects or other dark-colored objects results in the absorption of this heat. White deflects the colored light and therefore is typically cool to the touch. An apple, for instance, is the result of all colored light being absorbed into the apple and only red light being reflected back into the eye. So, in a way, an apple isn't red, but every other color but red.

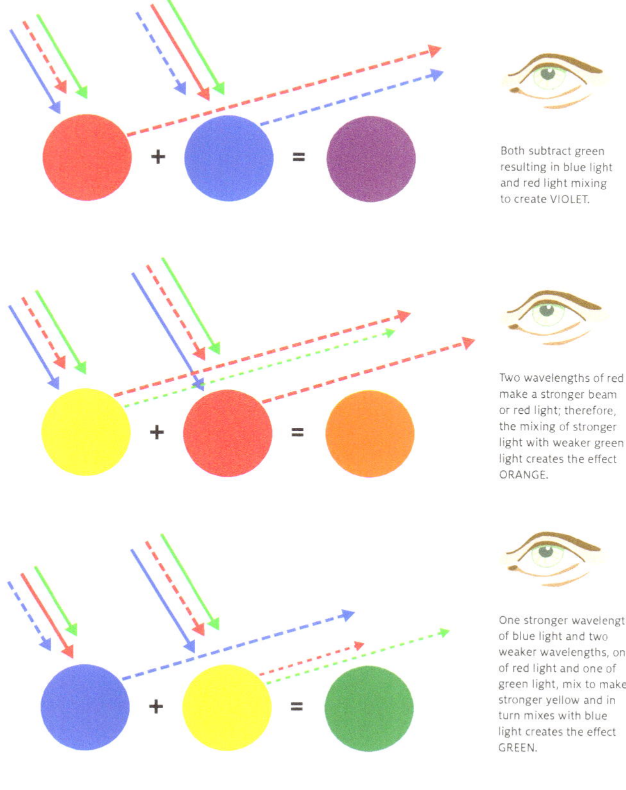

Figure 4.9 This illustrates how red, blue, and green primaries of light (additive color theory) are either absorbed, reflected, or partially reflected off of colored objects. These primaries of light will then mix—depending on each of their relative strengths—with one another when the reflected light bounces back into our eyes, resulting in the color we see.

Color Blindness

Color blindness is typically a genetic and inherited condition, or it can result from damage or diseases of the eye. Color blindness may also occur from the physiological effects of aging. The abnormality may affect one or both eyes and typically affects the color-sensitive cells for red, green, and blue or the cones (Bright & Cook, 2010; Zollinger, 1999). Color blindness does not mean that a person only sees in black and white, or grayscale. In fact, a person who is color blind can still see color; however, only a few hues within the visible spectrum can be distinguished. Think less blindness and more deficiency when seeing color.

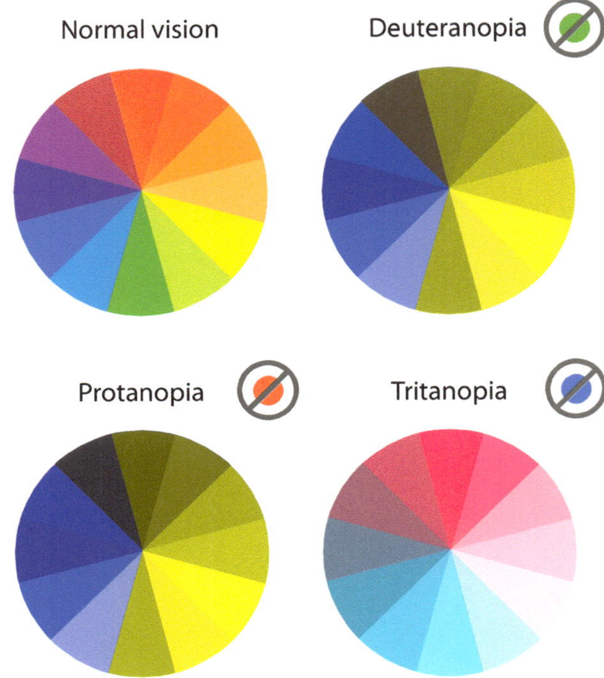

Figure 4.10 Illustration of color as they appear to individuals with normal color vision and with the three common forms of color blindness.

There are several forms of **color-blindness**. One or more of the cones in the eye's retina—red, green, or blue—is deficient, and color perception is altered from normal color vision because of this missing cone due to its limited function (Figure 4.10). The absence of red-green in color-blindness, called **Deuteranopia**, the most common form of color-blindness, results in vision where reds and green often appear yellow. Any color that would include red, including violet, would be difficult to distinguish very well. Individuals with **protanopia** are less able to distinguish reds, greens and some blue coloring. And last, **tritanopia**, results in an inability to distinguish blues from greens and yellow from violet.

Deficiencies resulting in genetic color blindness, which is the most common form, are present in the X chromosomes of our genes. Females receive two X chromosomes—one from their mother and one from their father—and males receive one X chromosome from their mother. As a result, if the single X chromosome in males contains abnormal genes for the photopigments needed for color vision, he will have color blindness. Both X chromosomes for females must be abnormal to impart color blindness; therefore, it is less common in females (Fairchild, 2005; Birren, 1961). Approximately 1 out of 12 males (8 percent) have some form of color blindness, whereas 1 out of 20 females (less than 5 percent) have color blindness (Morton, 2008; Fairchild, 2005; Zollinger, 1999).

In the most common type of color blindness, red and green are perceived as being the same. As you can see in Figure 4.11, within each circle is a number; if you have difficulty seeing the number or can't see it at all, you may have a form of color blindness. Color recognition is a vital part of our daily lives. When designing for individuals with color blindness, contrast, brightness, or saturation will be most valuable in the built environment. Labeling and noting color with supportive graphics for clarity while performing activities of daily living—reading magazines and interior signage, cooking, or selecting clothing to wear—may ease frustration.

Figure 4.11 Color blindness test plates. See if you can identify the following numbers from top to bottom, left to right: 7, 13, 16, and 8, 12, and 9. You can also take a more extensive online color vision deficiency test at the following URL: *https://www.color-blindness.com/ishihara-38-plates-cvd-test/#prettyPhoto*

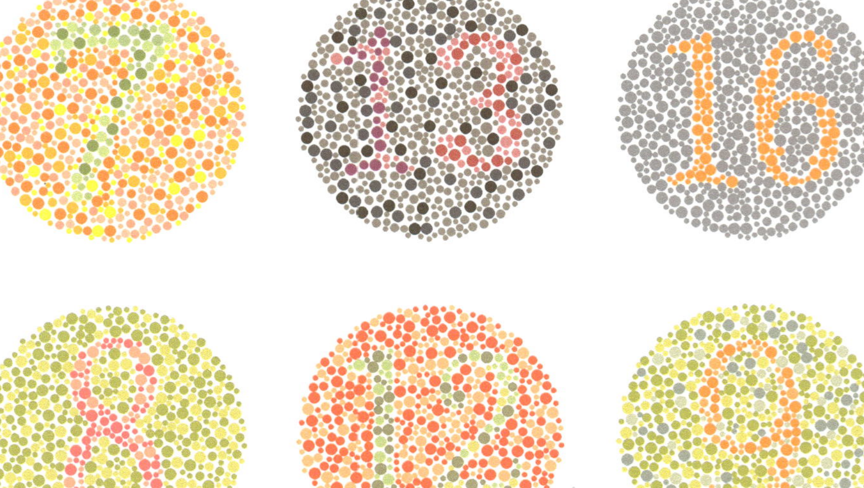

Vision and ability to see and discern color and light can alter our perceptions. Reduced and low vision should be considered for best color and contrast of visual elements (wall, floors, surfaces, changes in levels) for increased accessibility, safety, and functioning in the built environment. The particular choice of color, warm hue or cool hue, brightness, darkness, and saturation levels have all been shown to influence the perception of color in our immediate surroundings.

Color for Special Populations

Certain groups of people may require special consideration when selecting color and light for health, safety, and welfare. In this section, we will examine how color and light is selected and used to support the needs of those with visual impairments resulting from the aging process and other health and physical impairments. How color is selected and applied in interior design can help to provide easier access to buildings regardless of age or disability. In doing so, an opportunity to create a meaningful and positive experience of our designed spaces can occur, improving our well-being.

Color for Aging

According to the National Institute on Aging, many older adults want the choice to remain in their homes as they grow older and prefer **aging in place.** This is a term used to describe the ability to remain in one's home of choice as we grow older. The needs of older adults, which includes design to support for reduced vision, increased risk of falls because of decreased muscle strength and imbalance, and overall decrease in mobility can remove obstacles that impact the daily life of our older adults.

Aging in place provides a sense of safety and security to our aging adults (Wiles et al., 2011). Because of these physical changes, and in particular deterioration of vision as we age, how an older person sees color may affect their well-being and daily functioning. Designing a space to address vision and color that will help an older person with orientation within their home, clear visibility of surfaces and delineation in transitions between levels with color for example, will contribute to a more positive, secure, and healthy life experience. Let's discuss what occurs when our eye ages, along with steps to ensure safety for vision impairments.

The Aging Eye

When designing spaces for individuals with vision impairments and the effects of aging on the eyes, one needs to consider environmental conditions that support health, safety, and welfare. Color and light have the potential to significantly affect the well-being of those inhabiting designed spaces.

The most common type of physiological change with the aging eye is the yellowing of the lens, which is located just behind the pupil and iris. It is a flexible, clear structure that focuses the light entering the iris. The lenses tend to lose their flexibility and harden as we age. Along with hardening, the lens significantly increases the ability for short-wavelength light—blue and violet—to be absorbed and scattered (Fairchild, 2005; Boyce, 2003). These conditions cause reduced sensitivity to levels of contrast, or **cataracts**—a yellowing or clouding of the lens of the eye that affects vision. It becomes difficult to see and discriminate between blue and violet (National Eye Institute, 2015; Carter, 1982).

Color Guidelines for Older Adults

It is important to note that each individual will respond differently to supportive conditions designed into the physical space that assist in improving color recognition and vision. Research on this topic contains various recommendations for color, health, and aging; however, we can note some commonalities to begin the process of exploring potential effective solutions:

1. Increase the illumination level of the interior to increase color discrimination.
2. Consider using sources of light that have a high CRI (color rendering index) so that individual colors are much easier to discern.
3. Employ effective color contrast—light and dark colors—to assist seniors in navigating their space safely and sense of depth perception. Using color with higher intensity or saturation provides easier color discernment. Choose colors that are opposite one another on the color wheel to increase contrast, a key component to seeing level changes and discriminating between vertical and horizontal surfaces and objects (Figure 4.12). The greater the degree of contrast, or lightness versus darkness, the more discernible are the individual colors. For instance, violet and yellow will be more effective than blue and blue-green. Color

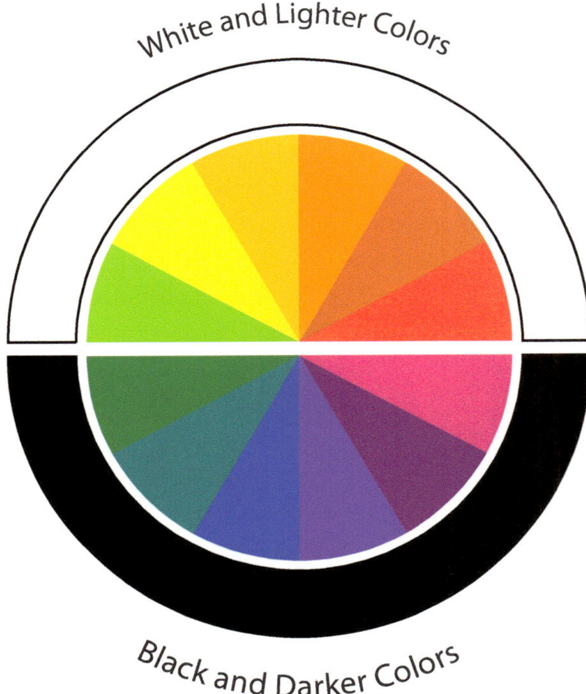

Figure 4.12 Effective contrast color wheel for visual impairments.

with low saturation should be limited or avoided. This will assist the older adult in seeing floor-to-wall changes, increased visibility of the edge change and transition between steps and stairs, contrast of the edge between a countertop and sink, and the edge of a seat and the floor, all providing a safer environment (Figure 4.13). Color and texture can be combined to assist with contrast and indicating changes between surface levels (NAHB, 2020). When specifying flooring products where color contrast is important to prevent slips and falls, select products that will not color fade over time due to exposure to UV light, moisture, or from frequent abrasion.

4. With the preceding suggestions you do want to be considerate of too much variation in color and over-use of high contrast between surfaces as this can lead to a sense of disorientation for those with low vision that may cause dizziness and the potential falls and injury.
5. Use multiple sources of light that provide an even distribution of light in the space. The light should be diffused rather than direct, which can cause eye strain and glare. Diffused light will also minimize shadows.
6. When designing with light, plan for even and gradual changes of illumination as a person moves through the space. A harsh change from a bright to dark space is difficult for the aging eye to adjust to quickly and can result in temporary blindness.
7. Last, select color while considering the physiological effects and perceptions of older adults that relate to their mental health and well-being (Hegde, 2011; Arditi, 2016; Boyce, 2001).

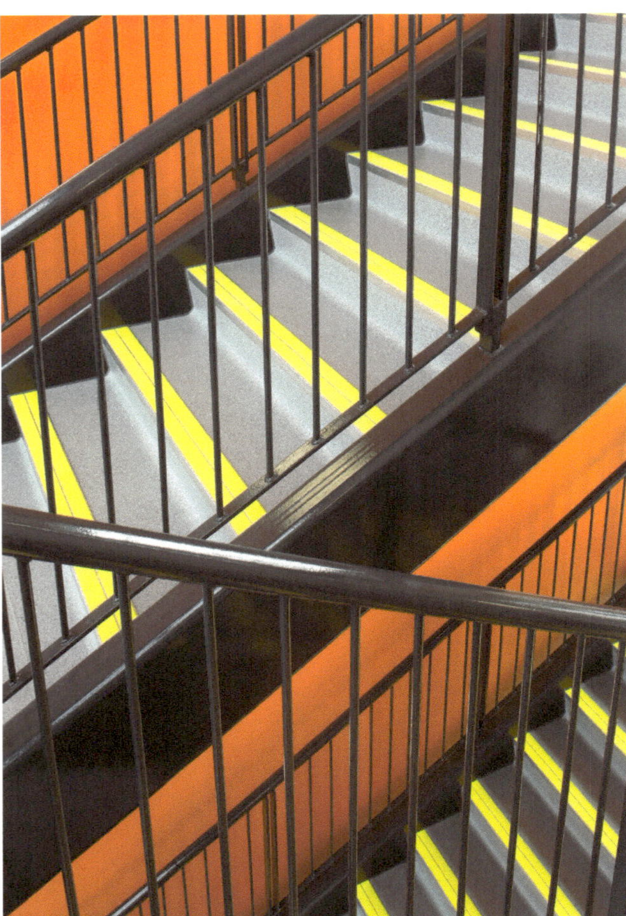
Figure 4.13 Color contrasting edge markings on these stairs are clearly visible to prevent falls and injuries.

Color and Design for Access

According to the National Association for Home Builders Research Center, there are four basic categories that encompass features to address accessibility and aging in place: (1) universal design, (2) accessible design, (3) adaptable design, and (4) visitability (NAHB, p. 27, 2002). **Adaptable design** refers to spaces that can be easily changed over time to accommodate the needs of an individual. This might include adding wood blocking in a bathroom to support grab bars for shower and toilet areas or designing closets in a two-story space where they are stacked over one another to accommodate an elevator in the future.

Visitability is design that permits users who may use a wheelchair full access to the first or ground level of a space. This provides a minimum level of access, removing steps and providing clear door widths of at least 32 inches, so that passage through the spaces is not prevented.

For our purposes, we will examine how color plays an important role in supporting equitable access through accessibility and universal design.

ADA—Americans with Disabilities Act

The **Americans with Disabilities Act** (ADA) became the United States' first civil rights law passed by Congress in 1990 that addressed the needs of people with disabilities, prohibiting any form of discrimination in employment, public service, public accommodations, and telecommunications. The ADA established guidelines for construction and renovation of buildings and enforces standards to protect and provide access to the built environment for people with disabilities.

The ADA does not set forth a comprehensive list of requirements that address the specific use of color. In the American with Disabilities Act Accessibility Guidelines, Chapter 7: *Communication Elements and Features*; section 703, *Signs*; a.703.5.1 *Finish and Contrast*, the requirements recommend that for persons with low vision, text and background color of signs should contrast as much as possible for added legibility (ADAAG, 2010).

Legibility of text with a dark background and light letters, or the reverse, creates the best visibility for public signage and graphics (Figure 4.14). The guidelines include information requiring non-glare finishes and cast shadows by lighting sources on signage. These may affect the ease in the legibility of text on signage in public spaces.

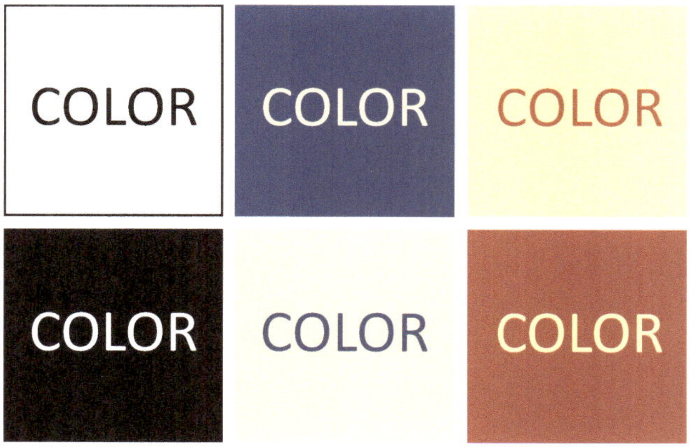

Figure 4.14 Examples of effective color contrast for text and background signage design.

Universal Design

Universal design, also known as inclusive design, is the practice of designing for all people, regardless of disabilities. Concern for universal, barrier-free, and inclusive design practice and principles helped to form federal legislation for disability rights began as far back as the 1960s. The term universal design was coined by architect Ronald Mace who stated that " universal design is the design of products and environment to be usable by all people, to the greatest extent possible, with no need for adaptation or specialized design" (The Center for Universal Design, 2008).

Color plays a critical role in universal design. As we move through our spaces, we use guideposts and signs to assist with knowing where we are, where we are going, and where we need to be for a sense of safety and security (Figure 4.15). **Wayfinding**—physical awareness of one's place or orientation in a space—can be enhanced with color as a tool to direct users regarding where to look first

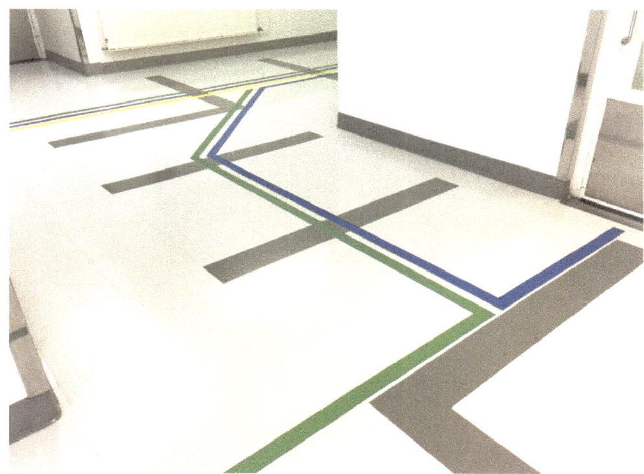

Figure 4.15 Wayfinding placed into the floor design using a color-guided pattern to orient and move visitors and patients through this medical space. Helsinki, Finland.

to orient their position in the space. Color has become a common element used for organizing environmental information in large spaces, including educational, office, retail, airports, and medical settings. In multi-story spaces, color coding by level can mitigate disorientation and reduce stress and anxiety. Color that is associated with common objects can assist with wayfinding. For instance, color coding blue for sky and green with grass, along with relatable symbols, patterns and shapes can be helpful to communicate a person's whereabouts in their immediate surroundings (Figure 4.16). Providing adequate contrast in hue to avoid elements looking the same will avoid unnecessary stress (Bosch et al., 2012).

Considering deficiency in color vision among certain individuals, providing a sufficient contrast between background and foreground elements in signage can draw attention and distinction to visual information, rather than using color alone. Color can be applied to distinguish spatial depth, increase object detection including furniture and architectural elements, and emphasize vertical and horizontal surfaces to aid in providing equitable access to the interior space.

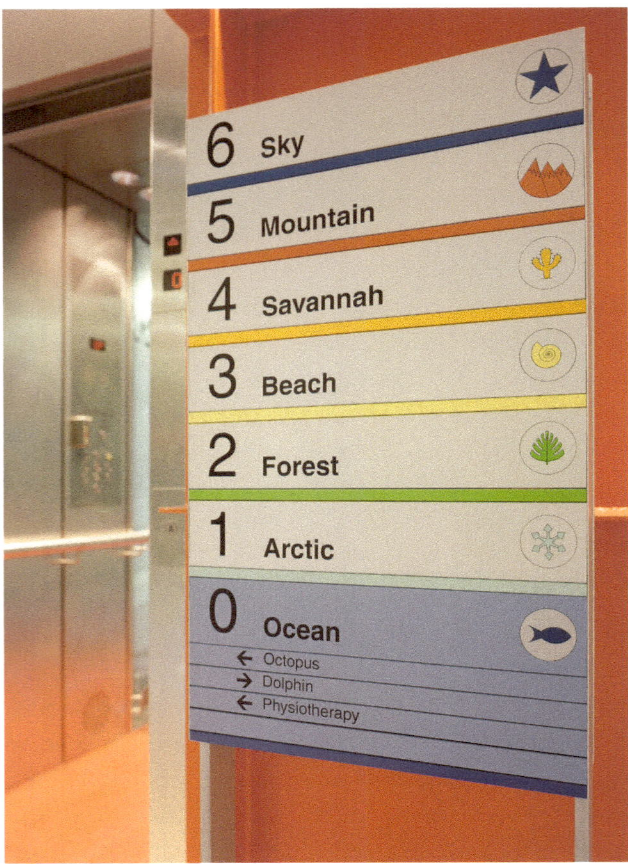

Figure 4.16 This signage in a children's medical center becomes symbolic for the colors green for grass and upward towards blue for sky.

Summary

This chapter explored the potential for color and light to affect health and well-being. Several guidelines, research, and recommendations were discussed; however, these are not intended to be wide-sweeping solutions or accepted as generalization intended to cover all people and instances in your color planning. An awareness and general understanding of color's influence on health can help direct your project specific needs towards appropriate and effective design solutions with color for health and well-being. There is not a definitive guide to selecting color to aid in a person's mental health or well-being; and whether a definitive guide is in the best interest of the design for health remains (Young, 2007; Tofle et al., 2004).

Confirmation of the effect color has on health is still inconclusive, and there is still much research to be done on color and specific colors that influence our well-being. Correlations may exist between positive health outcomes and color usage in the built environment. Color selection and decisions for spaces that do not yet exist create speculation on how the final design will be received by users. Design tools of the trade, including drawings, sketches, and color renderings, are heavily relied upon to predetermine how a person may respond to the designed conditions. Additionally, a design professional's education, training, certifications, and reliance upon existing research helps to navigate uncertainty for best practices. Simulations and vignettes of these spaces to create, as close as possible, the environment being designed, may produce better outcomes for testing behavioral response. With the continued advancement in technology, using virtual and augmented reality for simulations of color in the spatial condition to be experienced can help to bridge the speculative gap supporting claims of color influences on health, mood and emotion. Color planning and selection that is informed by research, rather than subjective influences including color trends or popularity and personal biases and assumptions, may prevent unhealthy and unsafe spaces supporting a person's positive well-being.

REVIEW QUESTIONS

1. Give examples of how color and light may affect stress, anxiety, and depression.
2. How may color and light be used to alleviate stress and depression?
3. Describe the difference between attention deficit hyperactivity disorder and autism spectrum disorder.
4. What is chromotherapy?
5. What is circadian rhythm and how does colored light affect this natural process?
6. What are the two types of light-sensitive nerve cells that allow for color vision?
7. Describe how the eye sees color.
8. Explain how color blindness occurs.
9. Summarize the three common types of color blindness and describe the specific color deficiencies resulting from each.
10. Explain the concept of aging-in-place.
11. Explain how color can be used to assist older adults with impaired vision.
12. List the design strategies with color and light for combating visual deficiencies of the aging eye.
13. Explain how color and contrast can be used for universal design and to assist those with vision impairments.
14. Describe the concept of wayfinding and how color can be used as a communication device and for safety.

Vocabulary

Evidenced-based design
attention deficit hyperactivity disorder (ADHD)
autism spectrum disorder (ASD)
health
well-being
chromotherapy
circadian rhythm
seasonal affective disorder (SAD)
lux
cones
rods
color blindness
deuteranopia
protanopia
tritanopia
age-in-place
cataracts
adaptable design
visitability
Americans with disabilities act (ADA)
universal design
wayfinding

EXERCISES

1. Form teams of two people. Place a blindfold on one team member. Select a random color sample or colored object that neither have seen until this point. Ask the sighted person to describe the color to the person who is blindfolded. You may not describe the color with its common color name—red, blue, green etc. Upon completion, reverse the exercise with the second partner. Have a discussion about the process, words used, challenges, etc. How would you describe this color to a person who has never seen it before?
2. Perform the Farnsworth Munsell Hue Test. This vision test helps to determine your level of hue discernment through order placement of eighty-eight individual hues arranged in four rows. You can access an online version of this test here: https://www.color-blindness.com/farnsworth-munsell-100-hue-color-vision-test/#prettyPhoto/2/

   Please note that a more accurate assessment of color vision should be conducted with the physical hue test. Information about this product can be found here: https://www.xrite.com/categories/visual-assessment-tools/fm-100-hue-test.
3. Select a variety of colored paper samples; create a collage arranged into a composition size of your choosing with hues individually selected based on your current mood. In a few brief sentences, describe your mood. Analyze your color selection; why are you drawn to these colors based on your mood? How does your mood relate to the colors selected and the composition you chose? If you are in a classroom setting, compare and contrast the compositions with your peers. If you do not have access to colored paper, you can use the Manchester Color Wheel in the chapter or you can print a version available online here: https://bmcmedresmethodol.biomedcentral.com/articles/10.1186/1471-2288-10-12/figures/2

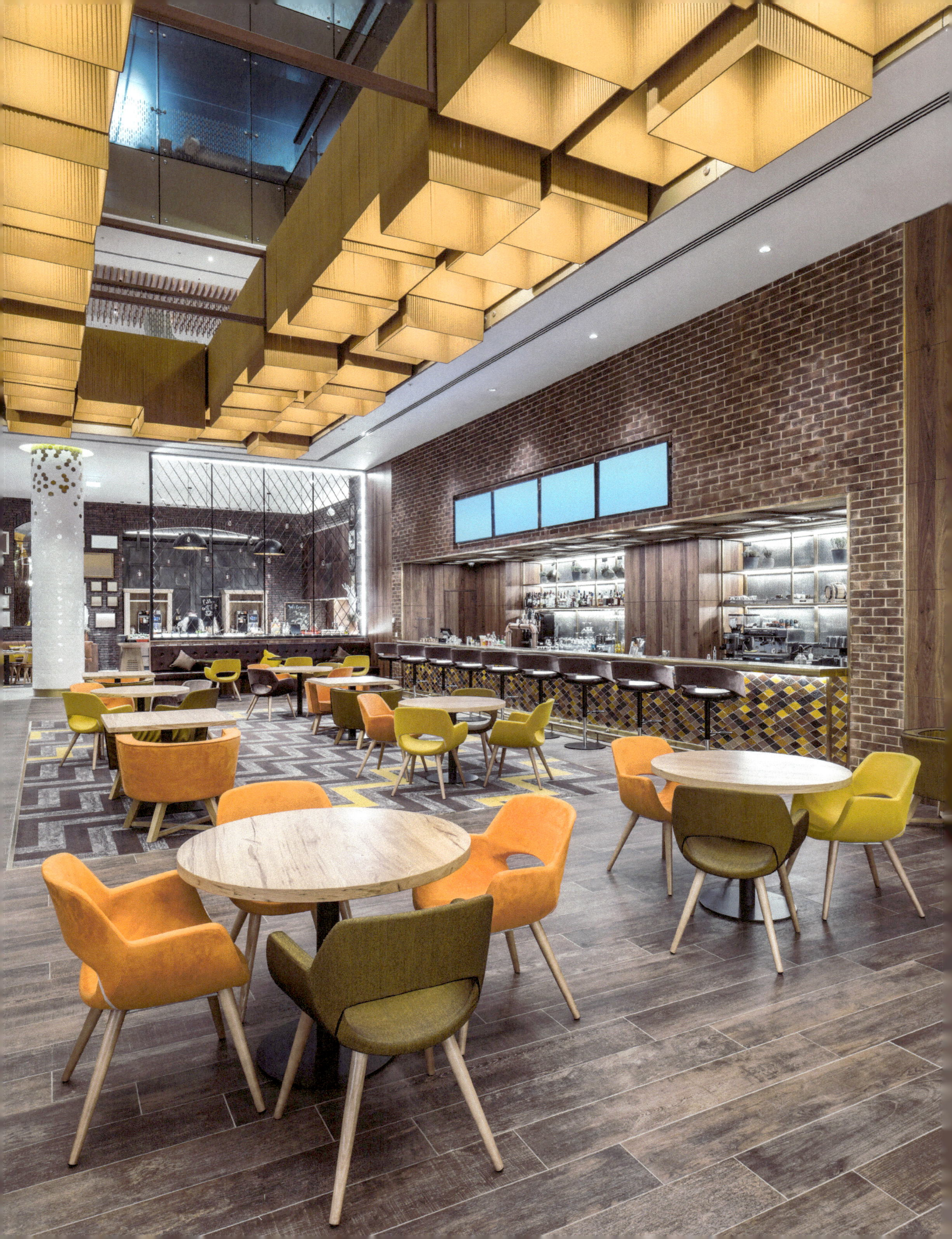

PART II

Color and Design Theory

Understanding the basic visual theories and rules which form the building blocks for organizing design, referred to as the principles and elements of design; can guide a designer's work toward solutions that will form two-dimensional and three-dimensional design solutions. In Part II, we will explore color alongside the principles of design—balance, rhythm, emphasis, proportion and scale, unity and harmony, and variety; and the design elements—line, shape, form, pattern, texture, and time.

Color, an element of design, is inherently present in all things that surround us. In exploring the principles of design with color, color becomes the lens through which we will focus our study to develop the knowledge of how color largely influences these principles, together, to transform our expression of designed objects.

The beginning designer will develop design thinking and an awareness of the impact color and design have on our built environment. With before and after images of designed spaces, this illustrated approach of what is and is not as effective will develop an informed and intentional use of color. Consideration of color's influence over the principles and elements of design, and their effects on shaping our experience of interior space, the aesthetic quality of our visual information, results in more purposeful and effective solutions to interior design problems.

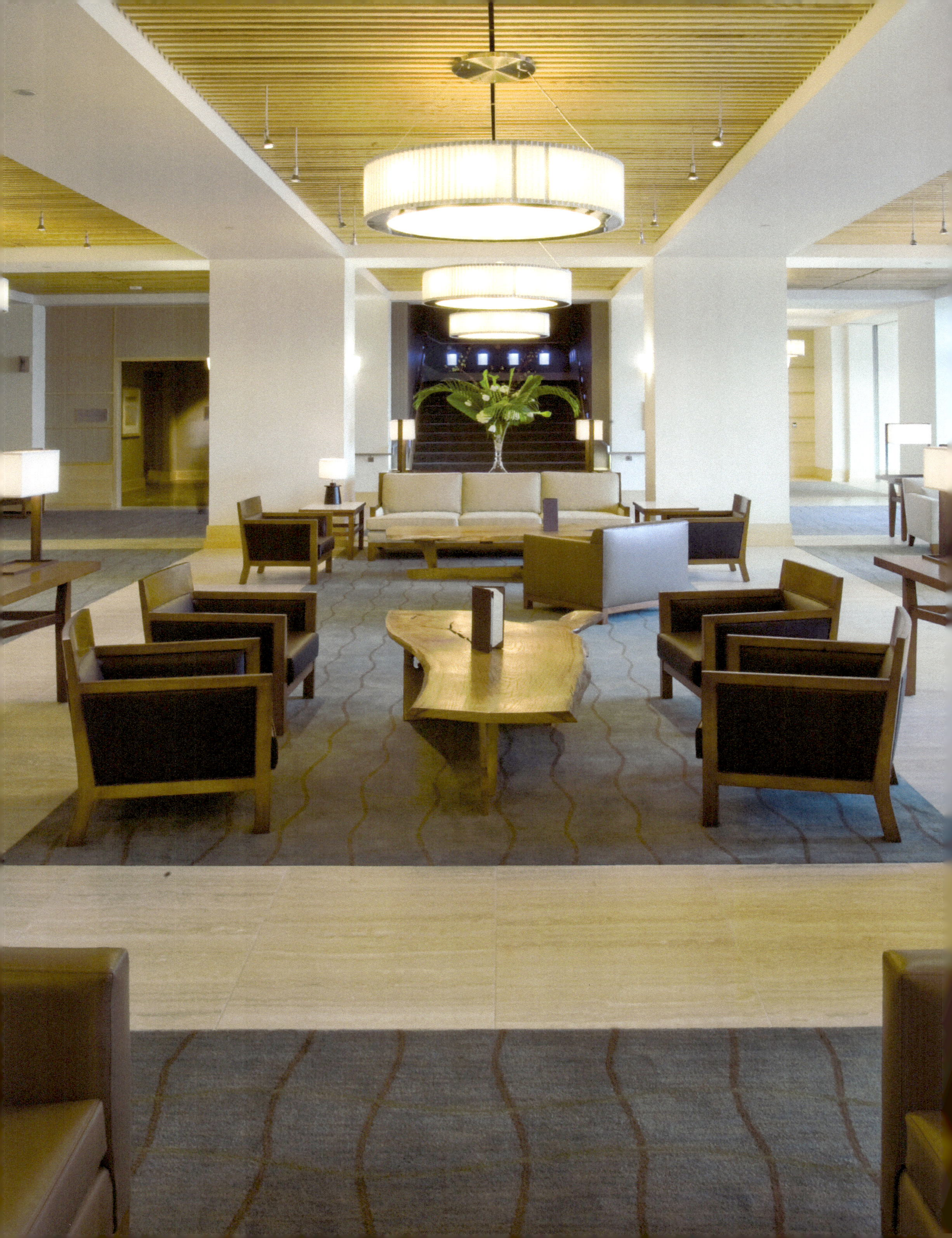

5

color + balance

Learning Outcomes

After studying this chapter, you will be able to:

- Explain how color can be used to create three types of balance: symmetric, asymmetric, and radial.
- Demonstrate color balance through value contrast, balance between hues, intensity contrast, and size of the color area.
- Recall that cool colors appear heavier in visual weight than do warm colors.
- Apply color to interior elements to visually alter the perception of space, and in turn, achieve necessary balance of space and volume.

Just as graphic designers manage visual information on a page, interior designers manage visual information within our immediate surroundings. We use balance to make sense of the world around us—to make our environments aesthetically pleasing. To achieve balance, we strive to create order among chaos for the purpose of organizing our living spaces. This order serves to communicate to others the design intent. When color is used with the design principles—for instance, balance—unity within a space can occur.

What Is Balance?

Balance refers to the relationship of different hues to one another when each is perceived to be equal in perceived visual weight. We have a natural attraction to beauty and images pleasing to the eye. Take the human body, for instance. Greek artisans have portrayed the beauty of the human body in art and sculpture for centuries. The symmetry of the human form represents pure aesthetic beauty that has been emulated in historical and contemporary architecture and interior design. Research indicates that people are more attracted to objects that contain symmetry—a perfect balance of parts (Lidwell, Holden, & Butler, 2003, pp. 190–191).

When speaking of balance and design, we must first make a distinction between physical balance and perceived or visual balance. Physical balance is the optimal measure of gravitational forces that keeps you from falling. Like a scale, it is the distribution of weight to achieve equilibrium. This type of balance is separate from the type of balance we manipulate in our visual fields to achieve an aesthetically pleasing painting, photograph, landscape, building, or interior. Perceptual balance involves the object itself (size, scale) and the visual weight of the color (appears heavy or light). The amount of color used, the number of different colors used, the visual weight of the colors, and the locations of the colors within the space are the four key factors in establishing good color balance.

Balance is a general term used to describe the physical or perceptual state of equality or order of objects within a larger composition. Balance is described by three types: symmetry (formal balance), asymmetry (informal balance), and radial balance (radiating from a central axis). Symmetry is the most common type of balance used in architecture and interior design. Symmetry ("measured together") comes from the Latin word *symmetria* and the Greek word *symmetros*. **Symmetry** (formal balance) is the arrangement of elements on either side of an implied axis that are equally balanced and of the same shape and form (i.e., mirror image). When symmetry is achieved, a state of beauty and balance occurs (Figure 5.1). Balance out of chaos creates order; order creates purpose and meaning within our physical environment. Chaos results when there is no relation to or consideration of the design elements that make up our physical environment. Symmetry is everywhere around us. Examine the petals of a flower, a seashell, an artichoke, a pinecone, a snowflake, the human body, and even animals.

Radial balance is achieved by the equal rotation of design elements around a central axis. This is the least of the three balance types to impact color planning and is more of an organizational concept; however the visual weight of color in this type of balance can visually influence the radial balance design solution. Radial balance could be applied to a situation where one color, a distinct pattern created with color, or a single colored shape is used as a focal point within a space. In this instance, the colored focal point would be centrally located and all other design elements would extend outward (see Figure 5.2).

Balance is an important part of the design process. Without balance, the remaining principles and elements get lost and a lack of cohesion in the finished design results. Balance is considered the most important principle and is often listed first among the principles of design. Without balance, chaos ensues and has the potential to elicit a negative reaction to interior spaces; it often compels users to "solve the problem" by fixing, in some cases, what they do not know to be wrong until balance is achieved. We have become so accustomed to living with balance that we sometimes take the phenomenon for granted. It is only when it is removed that we become aware that something is awry. Balance is the yin and yang of our visual experience. The contrast between order and chaos sends the message to our brain that something does not feel right. This can be a daunting task in the field of interior design, and more so for the inexperienced home or business owner or for a student studying design. To pair the property of balance with color, one must cultivate proper skills and a basic understanding of their underlying influences within our physical environments.

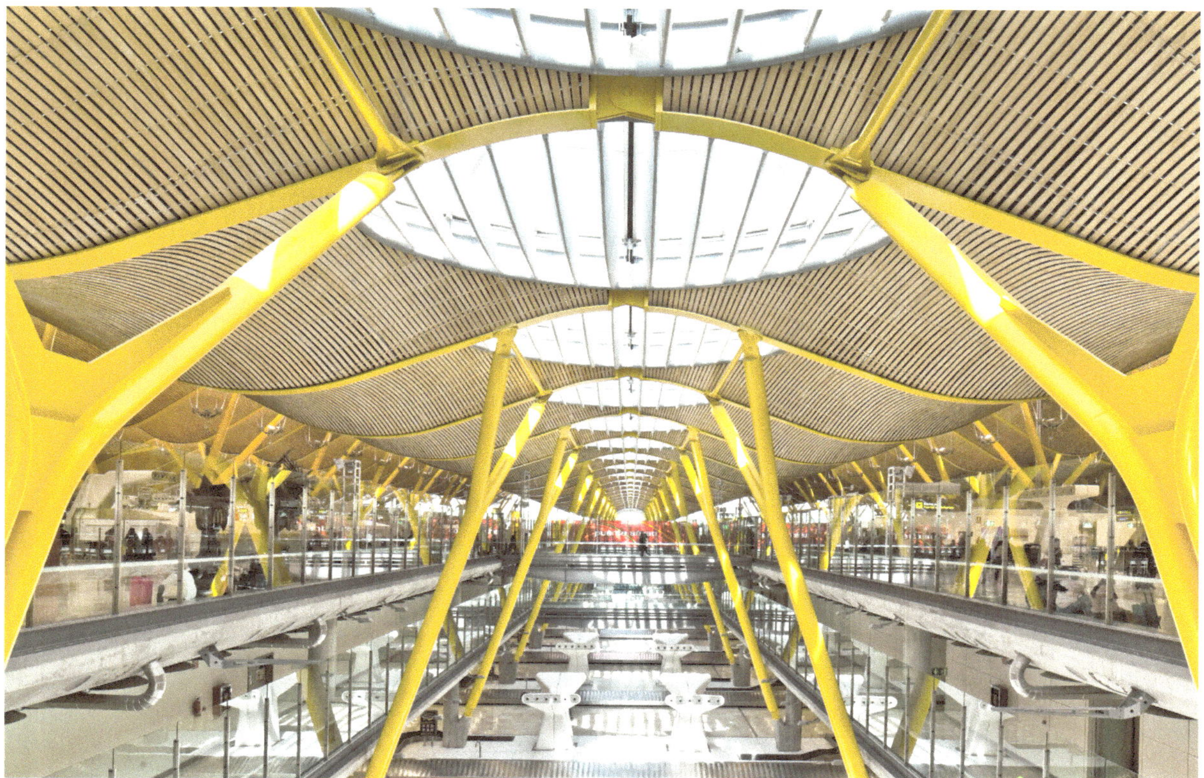

Figure 5.1 Barajas Airport Terminal 4 in Madrid, Spain. Architect: Richard Rogers, 2015.

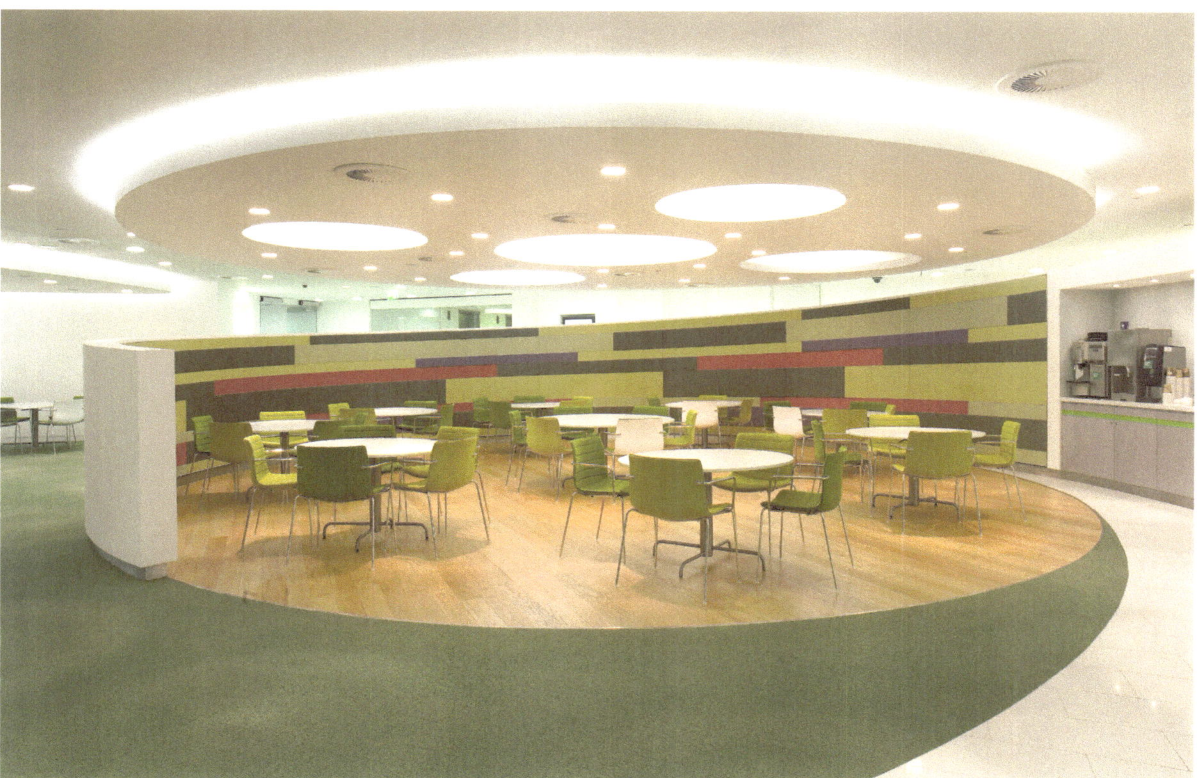

Figure 5.2 Dining space applying radial balance as a design tool through the dropped cloud ceiling feature, curved flooring material change, and sloping focal wall.

What Is Color Balance?

Balance is the striving to achieve the point of equilibrium between two or more forces. Balance is a means whereby harmony, peace, and connection can be made between the observer and that which is observed. This visual process is innately intuitive; however, a series of steps can be used to ensure a finished interior space that incorporates a balance of colors.

The spatial context of the color used can vary depending on the size of the space, lighting both natural and artificial, influences from and interaction with other colors, textures, and the physical orientation of the architectural space (vertical walls or horizontal floors, or angles and arcs in limitless combinations).

The addition or subtraction of color in the interior space will improve the impression or perception the designer intends. This balance does not represent a physical weight of color, but instead the perceptual attributes one assigns to each particular color: If you examine each of the primary and secondary colors in the next section, you can assign a numeric order from 1 to 6, 1 being the lightest and 6 being the heaviest for each of these primary and secondary hues. If this is expanded to include the tertiary colors, the balance scale extends further. Note that these colors are being represented in their purist sense, not influenced by adding white (tint) or black (value) to the color.

Interiors, at a minimum, should attempt to contain a three-value scheme. This allows a space to maintain depth and visual interest. Interiors that are too light appear delicate and almost unnatural, potentially lacking any interest. Middle tones can become too complacent and uninteresting, and an interior with the dark values only can be overwhelming and depressing. Too little or too much of any one color can lead to an interior that is disengaging, is lacking unity, and can be perceived as chaotic. Balance is most critical in establishing harmony and unity within an interior. We will discuss harmony and unity in a later chapter.

When clients ask "what colors should I use?" or "what colors are trendy?" my goal is to redirect them, establishing the rule that no one color is good or bad. Rather, it is how the color is used within the space that determines its success, along with the design style being established in the interior with direct relation to the architecture of the building. The first task is to determine what colors appeal to you. An interior that is designed with palettes chosen by the designer or by recommendation of the latest fashion magazine could end up feeling like a space that is disconnected from its inhabitants.

Our brains want to "connect the dots." When a space lacks good color balance, a disconnection of the space's components emerges. If only a portion of the "dots" are connected, then only a portion of the design will be aesthetically pleasing and enjoyable.

Types of Color Balance

"Balance enforces the demand for oppositional groups . . . and it achieves its objectives as soon as oppositional forces are clearly identified" (Ellinger, 1980, p. 28). In order to achieve this, we must have contrast of hues, values, and chroma. In this chapter we discuss four types of balance that can be achieved through color application: value contrast (light/dark), hue balance (complements), intensity contrast (bright/dull), and size of color area (large/small).

Value Contrast (Light/Dark)

Contrast is opposition in order to show or emphasize differences between two objects. When working with color, adequate contrast creates more stimulating results. The amounts of contrast desired depend on the space types and the design application needed. High contrast should be used for areas where safety is a concern, such as on edges to differentiate between changes in level to prevent falls, or low contrast, such as a medical waiting room, where limiting anxiety or tension is critical. In each of these examples, the contrast of light and dark surroundings is the key.

With regard to visual weight, the lightness or darkness of a color refers to the perceived color weight of an object. In this instance, we are not concerned about the physical weight or heaviness, rather the weight imparted by our perceptions of the color itself. White is perceived as lighter than black. A black object will appear to be visually heavier than white (Figure 5.3). The Munsell value scale illustrates a nine-step scale from pure black (1) to pure gray, which is an equal mixture of black and white (5), to pure white (9). See Figure 5.4. This illustrates a scale that proceeds from heavy to light. Now, let's utilize

Figure 5.3 Value and perception of weight.

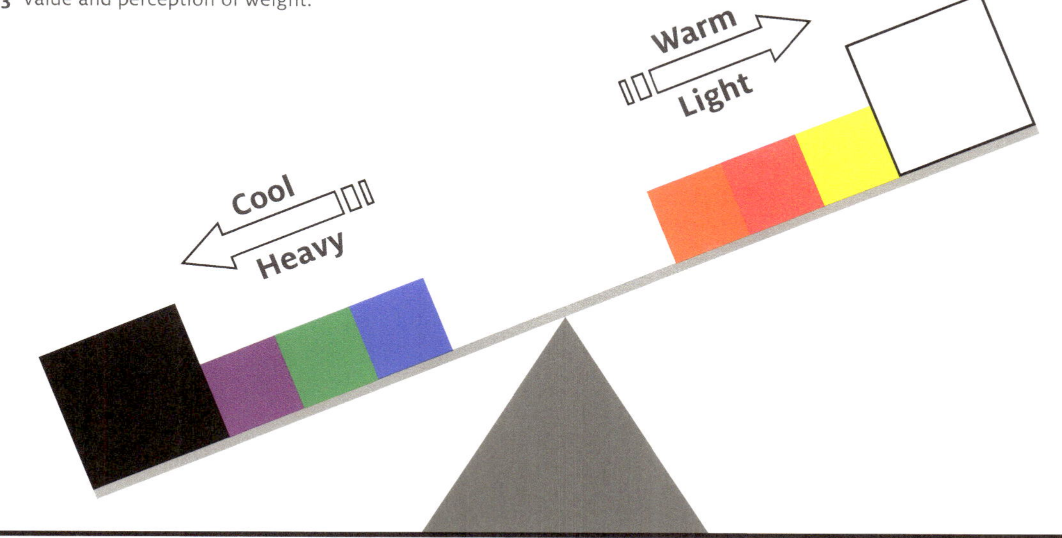

this same scale to organize our primary and secondary hues—red, blue, yellow and violet, green, orange. Yellow is perceived as being the brightest or lightest of the primary and secondary hues, whereas blue is perceived as the darkest. Based on the apparent lightness or darkness, we can assign a range from heavy to light with any hue. Note that when working with multiple colors, the physical comparison between those colors will result in the "weight scale" for that particular color palette. Let's take yellow for an example. Yellow can assume the role of the heaviest hue in your palette when grouped with lighter values of a darker color, such as a soft, pale pastel or a hue tinted or toned with white or gray (Figure 5.5). In this example we purposefully assign dominance to yellow in our color scheme by downplaying the lightness and chroma of the supporting hues. Since we typically work with samples of dyed material or paint swatches, you will want to practice recognizing when a physical material sample's hue represents a tint (adding white), tone (adding gray), or shade (adding black) of color. With value contrast, the relative lightness or darkness of any neutral (black, white, gray) or hue (red, blue, yellow) when compared to one another results in the "weight scale" for that particular project.

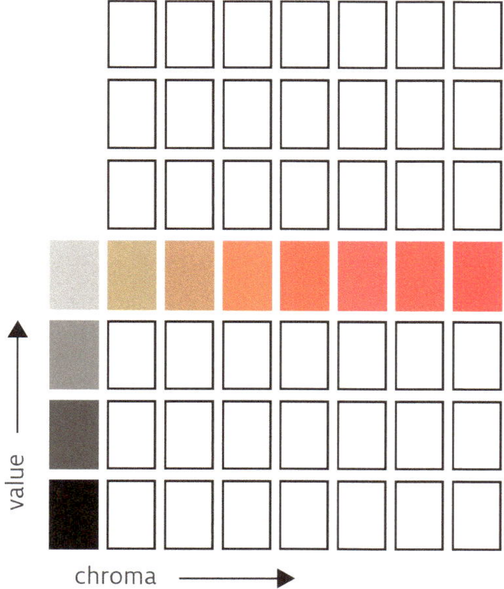

Figure 5.4 Munsell value and chroma scale.

Figure 5.5 Yellow, perceived as being the lightest in visual weight of the primary and secondary colors, can become the heaviest when balanced with lighter or pastel hues.

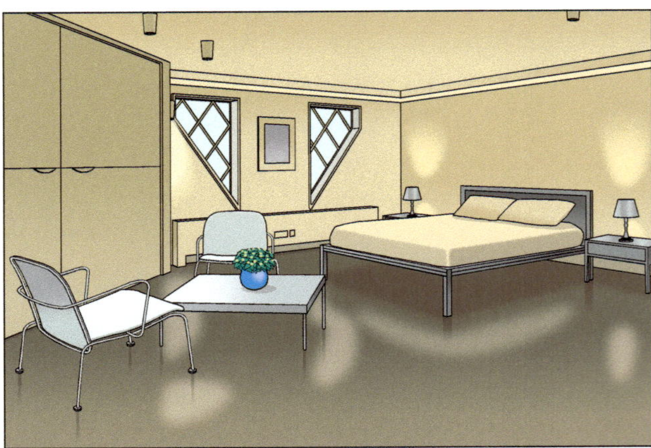

Figure 5.6a Modern bedroom space lacking visual color contrast and balance of design elements and surfaces.

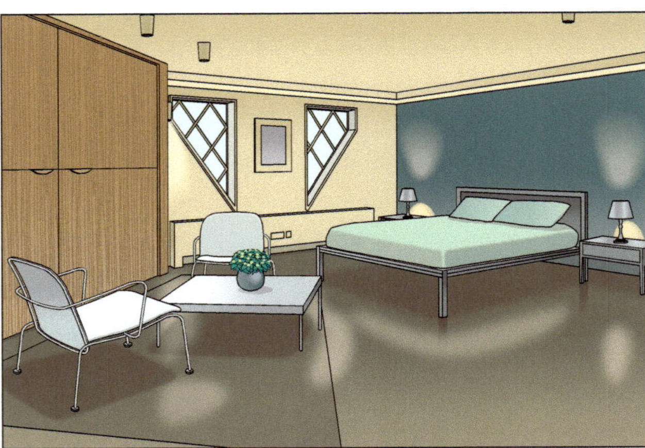

Figure 5.6b Introduction of color, texture, and value contrast adds visual interest and balance to the interior.

The second type of value contrast results not from comparing two individual colors side by side, but rather by comparing them when they share the same area or overlap within a visual field. Generally speaking, a dark color on a light background will appear to be much darker than it really is. Conversely, a light color on a dark background will appear lighter than it really is. This manipulation, discovered by Josef Albers, is explained further in his book *Interaction of Color* (1975). This principle, often referred to as "one color like two," illustrates the juxtaposition of colored elements in a space. Refer to Chapter 3 (Figure 3.14b). The vertical and horizontal planes of our living spaces (wall and floors) serve as backdrops to the objects we place within them. Being that these are the largest spans of surface within our spaces, they are likely to contain the largest color area. Therefore, depending on the color that is placed in relation to those areas, it can now appear lighter or darker. Color should be organized within the interior to draw a logical color order to the visual information.

Figure 5.6a illustrates a modern bedroom space. The interior is absent of color and contrast, with the exception of the floor and walls, to distinguish horizontal and vertical surfaces. Additionally, the left side of the space contains more visual weight (a cabinet, two chairs, and table that generate the perception of heaviness) than the right side, which appears lighter. In Figure 5.6b the addition of contrast, texture and visual interest balances the opposite side of the room. The color scheme's low intensity reduces possible overstimulation in a room designated for sleep and relaxation. Darker color can draw attention to information that is most important and balance opposing elements in space.

Hue Balance (Complements)

Complementary colors are those colors that when placed next to one another intensify the other hue, making each to appear brighter. These colors are directly opposite each other on a color wheel. See Figure 5.7. The phenomenon occurs due to the lack of relation between the two. This creates a very strong contrast and in turn creates asymmetrical balance of light/bright and dark/dull depending on the property of that particular color, as previously illustrated by the arrangement of primary and secondary hues by visual weight. **Asymmetry** (or informal balance) results when elements on either side of an

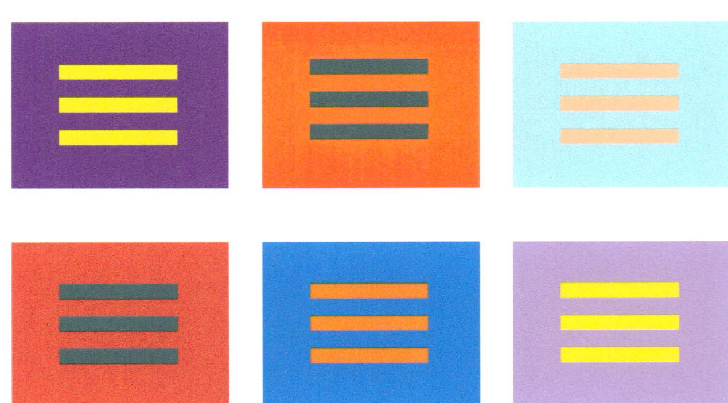

Figure 5.7 Asymmetrical balance through complementary contrast.

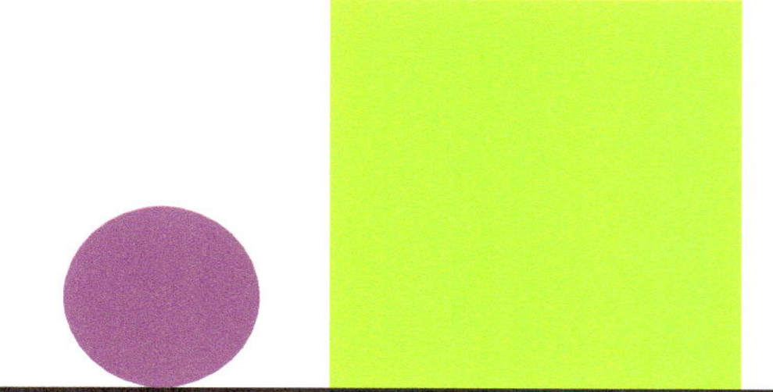

Figure 5.8 Asymmetrical balance. The two different shapes and sizes appear to have the same visual weight because the perceived lighter hue (green) is assigned to the larger square shape to balance the smaller darker circle in violet.

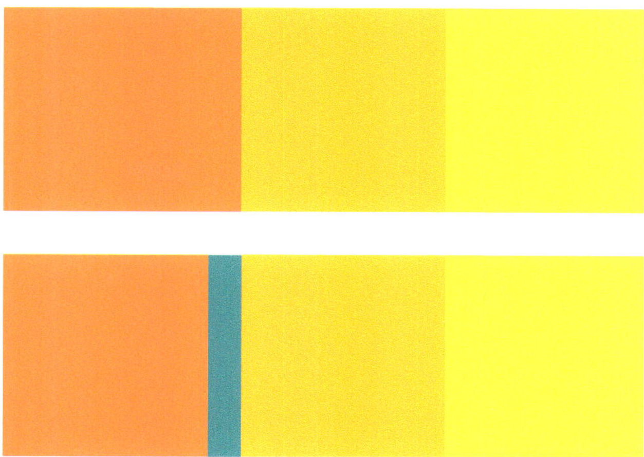

Figure 5.9 Palette of warm hues requires the addition of a cool hue (blue-green) to balance the intensity level.

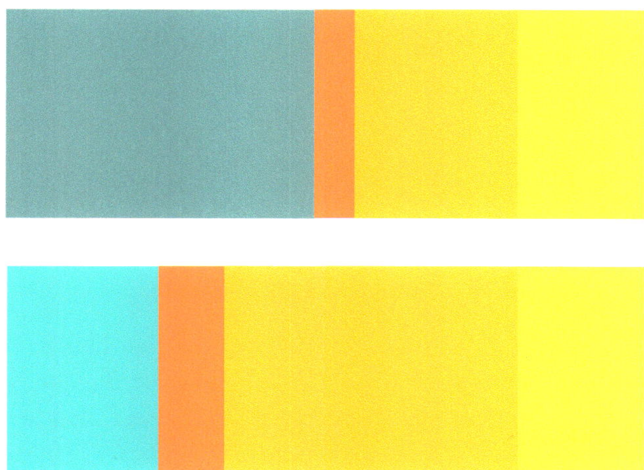

Figure 5.10 Color balance improved with addition of contrasting hue in two intensity levels.

implied axis are equal in visual or color weight but may vary in shape and size. This type of balance is often more visually interesting and can be achieved through value and/or hue contrast (Figure 5.8).

The colors provide to each other what they lack in themselves. Green complements red, since red contains no traces of the hue green. Orange complements blue, and yellow complements violet for the same reasons. By bringing the two contrasting colors together, a harmonic order of color is achieved and balance ensues.

The palette in Figure 5.9 is composed of the warm hues of red-orange and yellow-orange; yellow can be balanced with the introduction of a cool hue (blue-green) to add visual contrast and balance the bright and dull hues. When used in different proportions, this color combination will balance the palette, resulting in a more pleasing aesthetic, as shown in Figure 5.10. Introducing the blue cools the warm palette, making it more palatable for an interior space.

Intensity Contrast (Bright/Dull)

The relative brightness or dullness of color is established by adding the complementary color to a particular hue or adding gray. Color intensity does not refer to *lightness* or *darkness*—that occurs from adding white (light) or black (dark) to a color.

Purity of hue, or chroma, results when a color is not influenced by other colors. Red in its purest form contains no traces of white, black, gray, or other color. However, once gray is added to the pure hue red, the intensity or brightness of the color begins to decrease. A brighter color will advance, whereas a duller color will recede. Adding pure white produces a tint (pink), and adding pure black produces a shade (burgundy). The same perceptual properties of weight will apply with light colors and dark colors, known as value. Light colors will appear to advance toward the viewer, and dark colors will tend to recede. Intensity changes in color become more apparent as the color strays from its original hue more toward gray. The property of advancing and receding correlates to the apparent visual weight of the colors as well. Light colors will appear closer and visually light; darker colors will appear farther away and visually heavier.

Figure 5.11 illustrates the differences between light, dark, and dull colors. Notice which colors appear closer and farther away in addition to the perception of visual weight where the colors appear lighter and heavier.

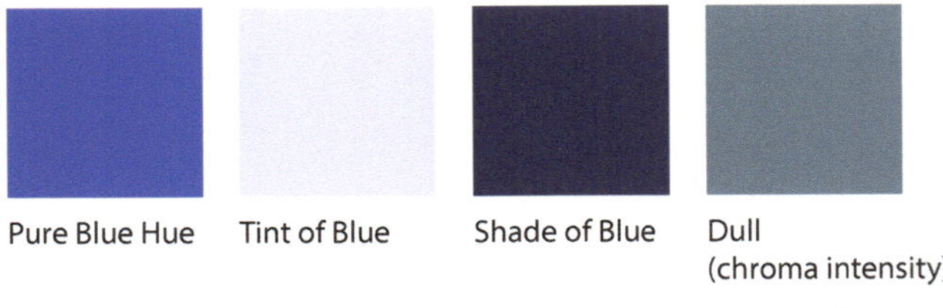

Figure 5.11 Perceptual weight shifts with changes in value and intensity in this example of a blue hue.

Interior spaces are generally more accepted and pleasing to the user when small amounts of intense color are balanced by larger amounts of duller color. Variations in intensity do not change the original hue. Assign darker, heavier colors toward the bottom one-third of space and work upward to the light values of your palette. Reversing this order is unsettling and is contrary to the natural gravitational pull. However, this technique can be reversed in spaces to visually lower ceiling height. Using a darker color on the ceiling and floors will lessen the apparent vertical height, compressing the perceived volume (Figure 5.12).

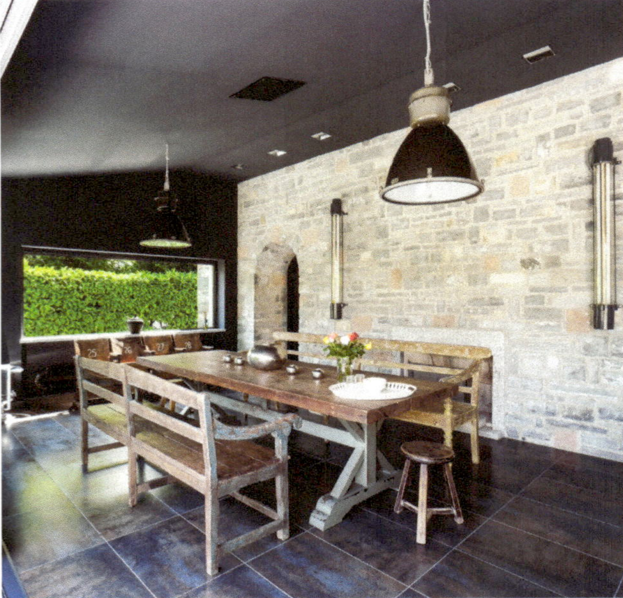

Figure 5.12 Residential dining space in which the dark ceiling and floor visually compress the spatial volume.

Size of Color Area (Large/Small)

The larger the amount of color used, the lighter it appears; the smaller the amount of color used, the darker it appears. This effect is intensified in colors that are placed against a secondary color of opposite lightness or darkness. **Color interaction** involves the contrast of light and dark values; when one value is placed next to or surrounded by the other, the visual weight of the smaller of the two color areas is intensified. When using this contrast, you must consider not only the weight of the color that is changing but also the hue itself, depending on the background color. In Figure 5.13 the two larger squares, with equally weighted background colors, are used in the top example, one belonging closer to the blue family and one to the red. At the center of each square is a smaller square of hue consisting of a combination of the two background colors—in this case a red-violet. The background color of each square is visually subtracted from the smaller square, and the result is the appearance of two completely different hues, resulting in value shift or "weight" change. The smaller square appears redder on the left side, whereas the smaller square on the right side appears bluer. The remaining two images represent additional shifts in color balance relative to the

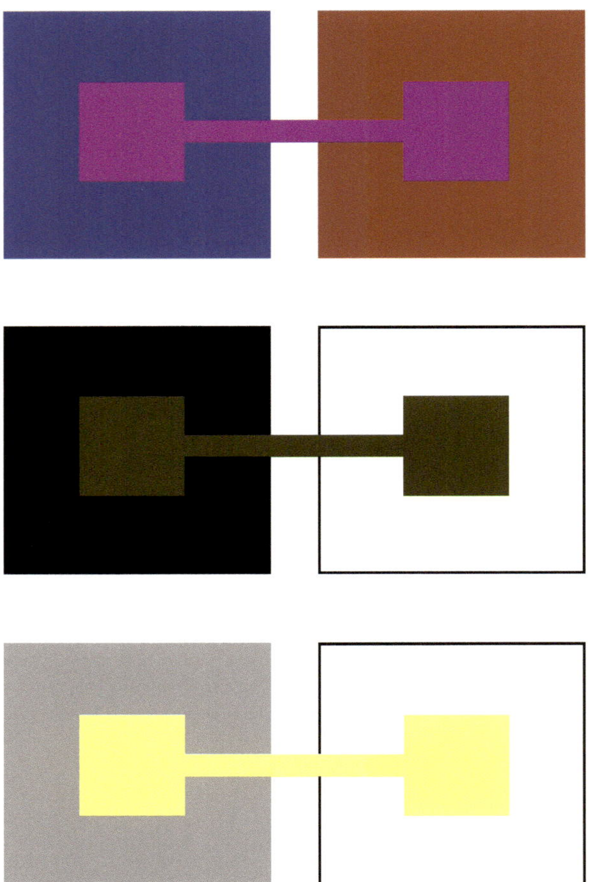

Figure 5.13 In each row the smaller squares are identical, but the balance and perceived color shift because of the variations in the background hues.

background colors' influence on their perceived weight. This phenomenon in balance shift, known as simultaneous contrast, was discussed in Chapter 3.

During your color selection process, determine which of your hues, based on the information presented, is likely to consume more of the visual space. Organize your colors by weight and assign their location to maximize your effect of increased or decreased volume. You do not want all your hues to appear equally balanced in light/dark or bright/dull. This will lead to a drab, lifeless interior. Later in the text we will discuss proportion. Accomplished color schemes are the result of the color balance techniques and proper portioning of each hue.

Location of a Color Palette within the 3D Environment

The location of colors within the physical environment is just as important to a balanced composition as the selection of color itself. The shape of interior space is divided into specific surface planes: vertical surfaces (walls) and horizontal surfaces (wall, floors, and ceiling). Our eyes would otherwise move around a space randomly, but color acts as a carrier, focusing our attention on specific design features and elements and repeating the color to guide your observation throughout the space. Color can connect the design elements and create a sense of harmony within the space. A lack of "color connection" leaves the viewer attempting to "connect the dots," trying to find a logical sense in the visual arrangement of elements.

In the retail space in Figure 5.14a, the color palette can be perceived as hot and uncomfortable. This imbalance can be offset by reducing the intensity of the red or introducing a cooler hue, green (Figure 5.14b). Be careful to avoid having a color palette that is "a combination of half warm and half cool," as this will only send an "unclear message" to the users of the intended experience—warm or cool (Eiseman, 1998, p. 154). Chapter 8 presents proportional strategies to avoid such an occurrence.

Illusion of Vertical and Horizontal Space

We can define our living spaces as two general experiences, the vertical and horizontal experience. Our floor and ceiling serve as our horizontal planes and the walls our vertical planes. Balance can be achieved and maintained by the location of the color choices on these planes. Isolating color on one plane alone can visually slice the spaces into segments and thus create visual imbalance. Contrasting lines of color can be an effective way to create illusions that reduce over- and underexaggerated spatial size, balancing the user experience.

Contrast of light and dark surfaces, striped floor patterns, and ceiling details of an interior can be used interchangeably to increase the apparent depth, width, and scale of a space (Figures 5.15a and b). Application of wood moldings and trims paired with color contrast may also divide vertical space, increase or decrease the perceived height, and add interest and balance to larger volumes (Figure 5.16). Spatial extremes can be

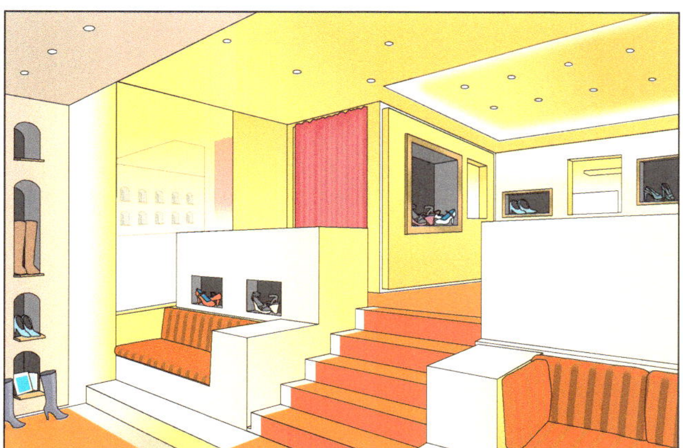

Figure 5.14a The color balance is shifted more toward the warm side of the color wheel, potentially creating a perceived uncomfortable, hot, retail experience.

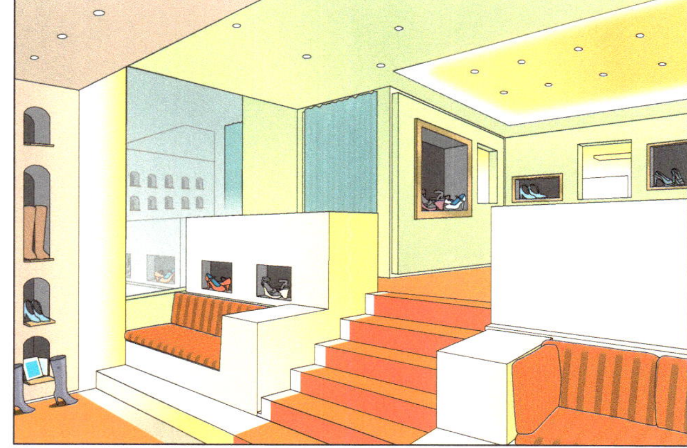

Figure 5.14b Introduction of cool hues softens the warm palette, providing complementary contrast between surfaces and a more palatable experience.

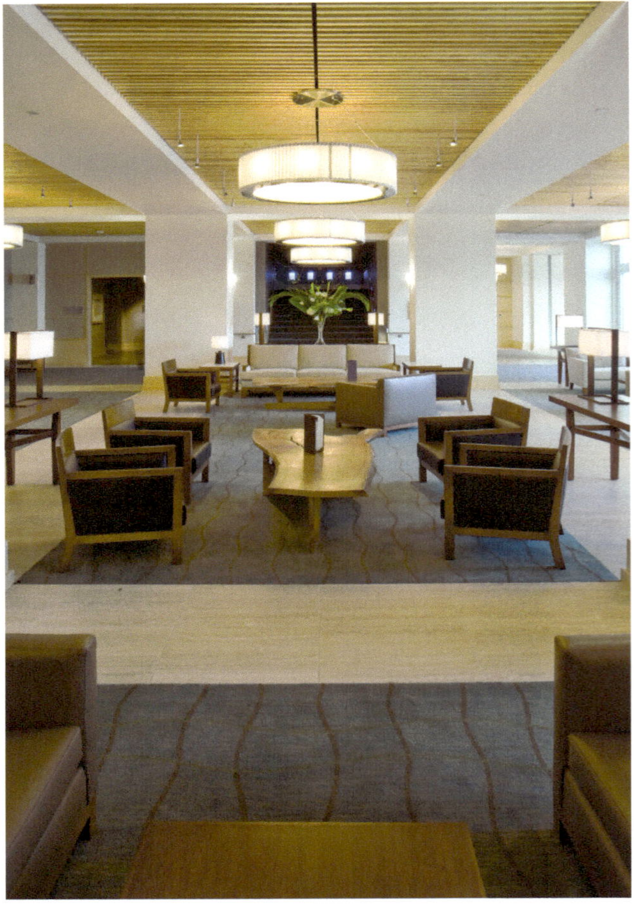

Figure 5.15a Organic lines in the carpet insets paired with contrasting light and dark ceiling details and darker furnishings balance the spatial volume of this hotel lounge.

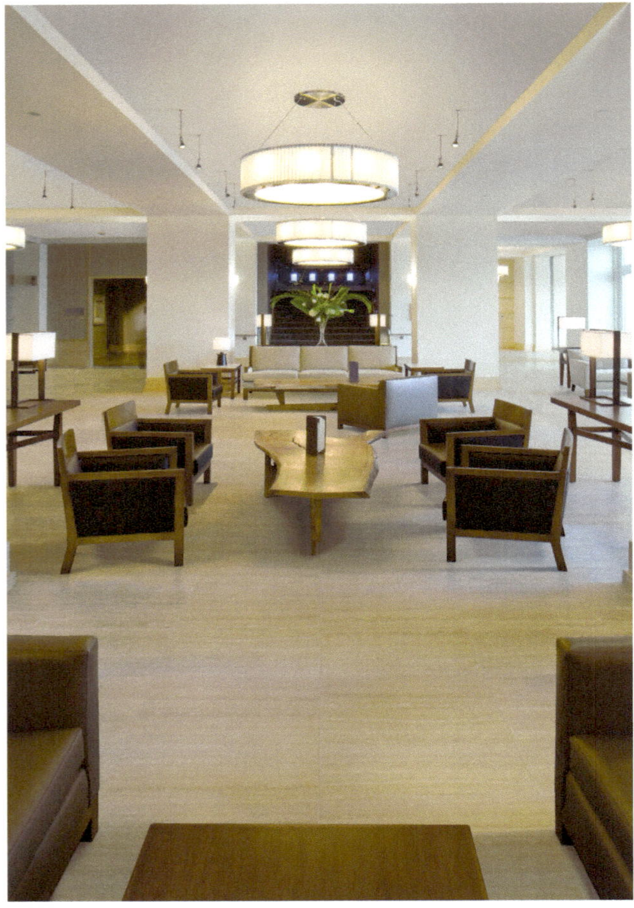

Figure 5.15b Removal of design details reduces balance, and the seating groups are no longer grounded in the space.

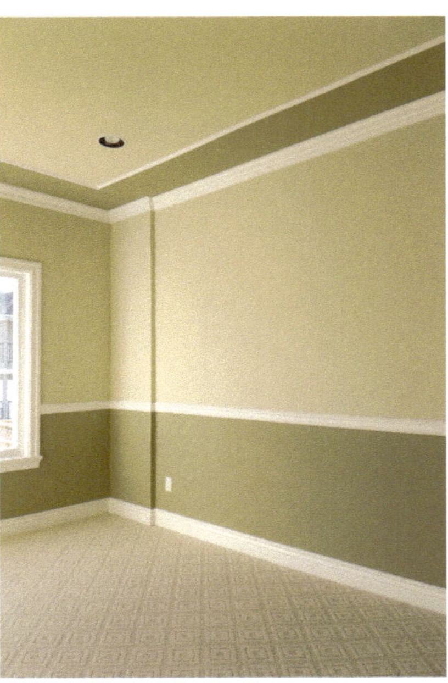

Figure 5.16 White-painted wood moldings at the ceiling, wall, and floor contrast with the two-toned wall colors, each contributing to the illusion of decreased ceiling height and a more intimate interior.

modified in this manner to adjust visually unbalanced interiors. Positioning design elements or bands of lines in a slight diagonal to a vertical plane in a space can create the illusion of more depth. In Figure 5.17 the smaller, tighter space, which has a high contrast of black and white, employs lines of text and type carried from the wall to the floor that is effective in creating the appearance of a larger space. This tool is successful in smaller confined areas and adds more interest to simple interiors. In large-volume spaces, high contrast of color can be used vertically to balance the volume and bring space to a more comfortable human scale (Figure 5.18). In Figure 5.19 adding black to the structural columns blends them into the surrounding interior, lessening their large scale, which could overwhelm the space. The darker color on the wall reduces the spatial depth, balancing the overall interior.

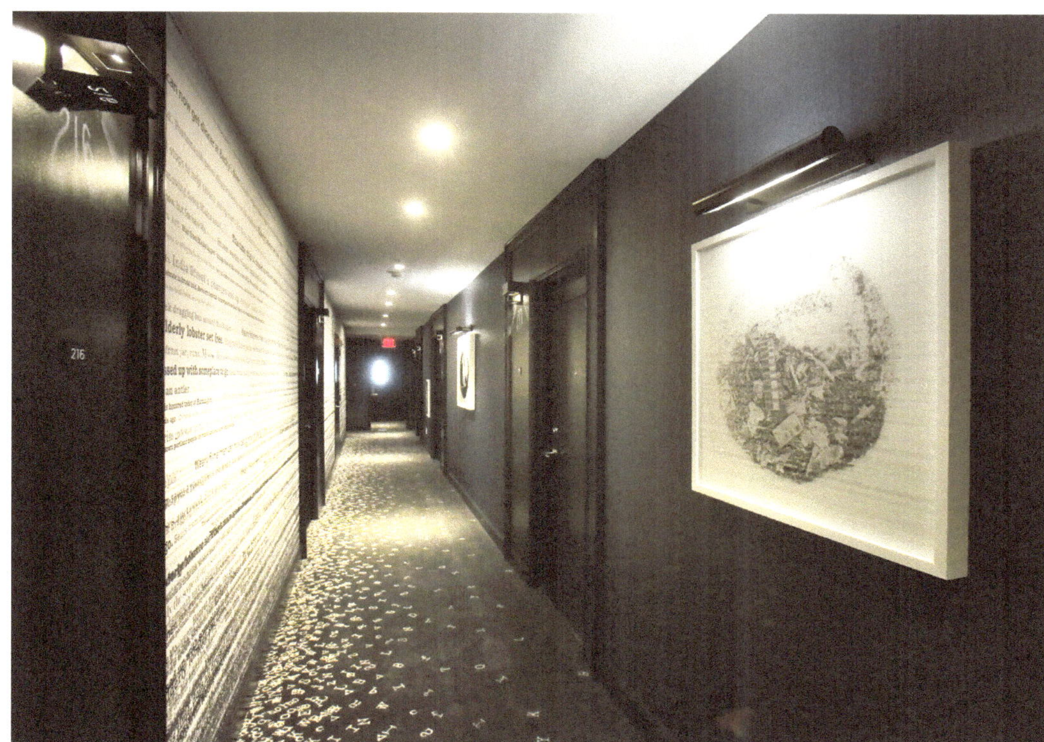

Figure 5.17 The hallway for guest rooms on the second floor at the Press Hotel in Portland, Maine, where the newsroom for the Portland Press Herald was located, resembles the pages of a newspaper with its white walls and black type.

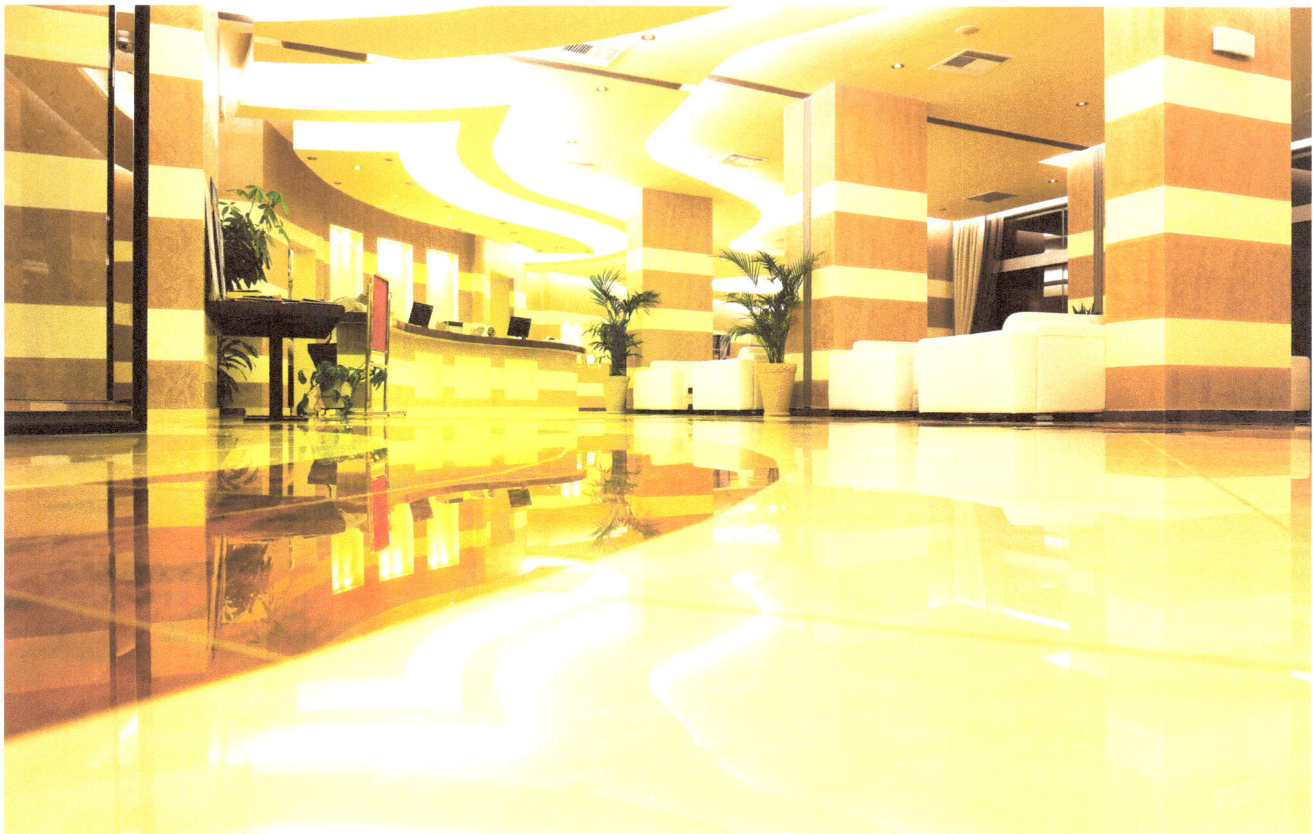

Figure 5.18 Hotel entrance in marble and stone.

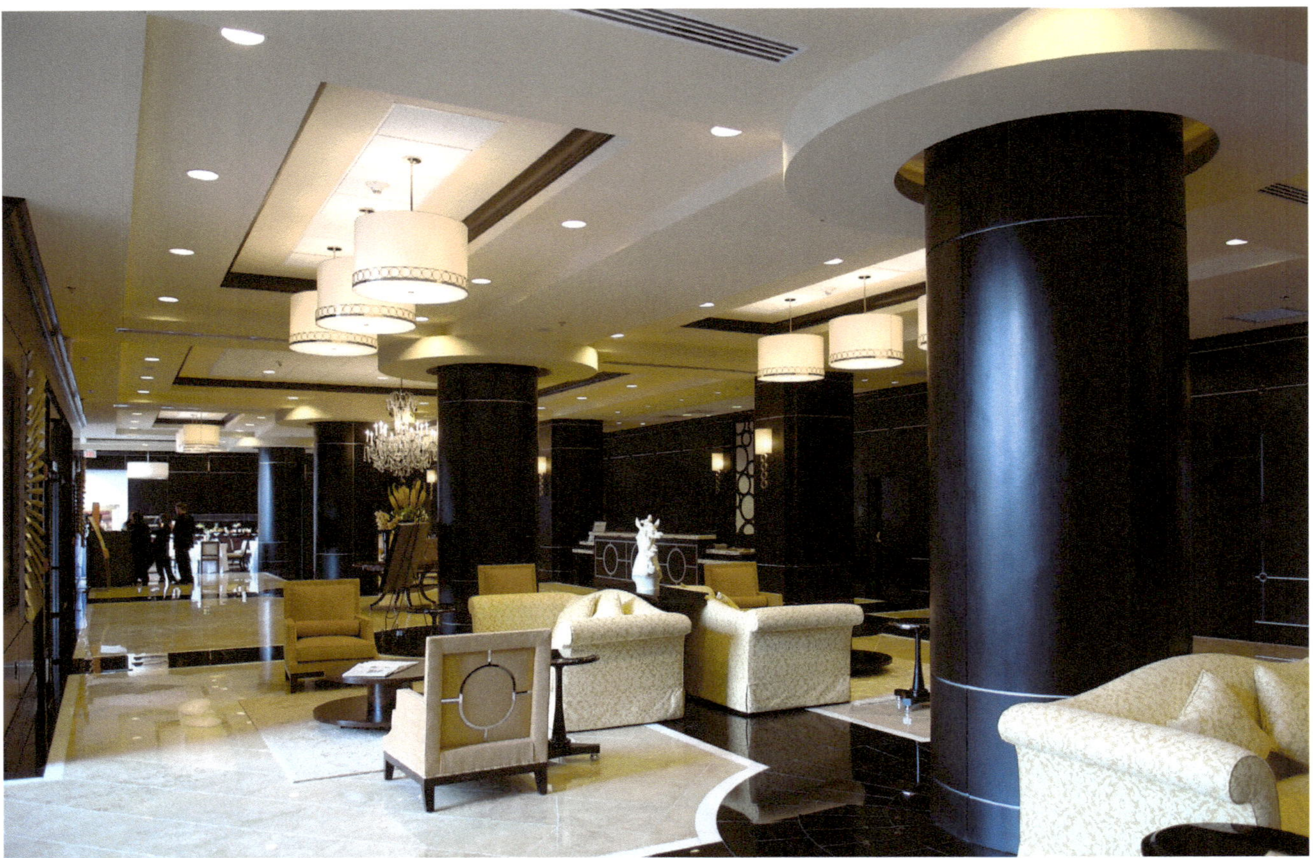

Figure 5.19 Interior of a luxury hotel in which the space is divided into more comfortable groupings of furniture with carpeted floors separated by black marble leading to the columns. This balances the overall interior and creates a comfortable, inviting space.

Chroma/Value Factor

Another common error in color usage relates to the application and variation of value and chroma within an interior space. Too much variation of chroma (high intensity not balanced with dull) or value (light not balanced with dark) creates little contrast, an element essential to an interior that provides a visually pleasing space through balance of opposing forces. A level of contrast must be present. See Figure 5.18 for examples of poor color contrasts (too light, too dark); the bottom palette successfully balances both. A certain amount of dark is needed for the eyes to rest. Without the darker areas, eyestrain could occur from the intense lighter and brighter hues that will reflect more natural light into the eyes—similar to the experience of walking from inside a building to the bright outdoors. Consider this especially in spaces with a large percentage of intense color. Intense color should always be balanced with dull color or neutral white, black, or gray to avoid eyestrain from constant shifts in values.

This error typically occurs in conjunction with a lack of relation between the brightness and dullness of a color. For example, the colors shown in Figure 5.21a illustrate two complementary colors, red and green, whose intensity has been grayed to a duller version of their original selves. In stark contrast, the same colors red and green are shown in Figure 5.21b, although there is an obvious lack of balance due to the intensity level. The green is too intense and appears unrelated to the red despite their being complementary colors. Figure 5.21c illustrates the green adjusted by muting the hue to balance the red.

Single-Color Overload

A color palette is not confined to any number of required hues within one space. As a general rule of thumb, rooms can contain as little as one color and should contain no more than five colors. With color schemes consisting of more than five colors, the first three might be of different

Palette balance is weak, not stimulating.

Palette balance is too dark, not stimulating.

Palette balances light and dark value, adding interest.

Figure 5.20 Color palettes with weak contrast and improved palette integrating both lights and darks.

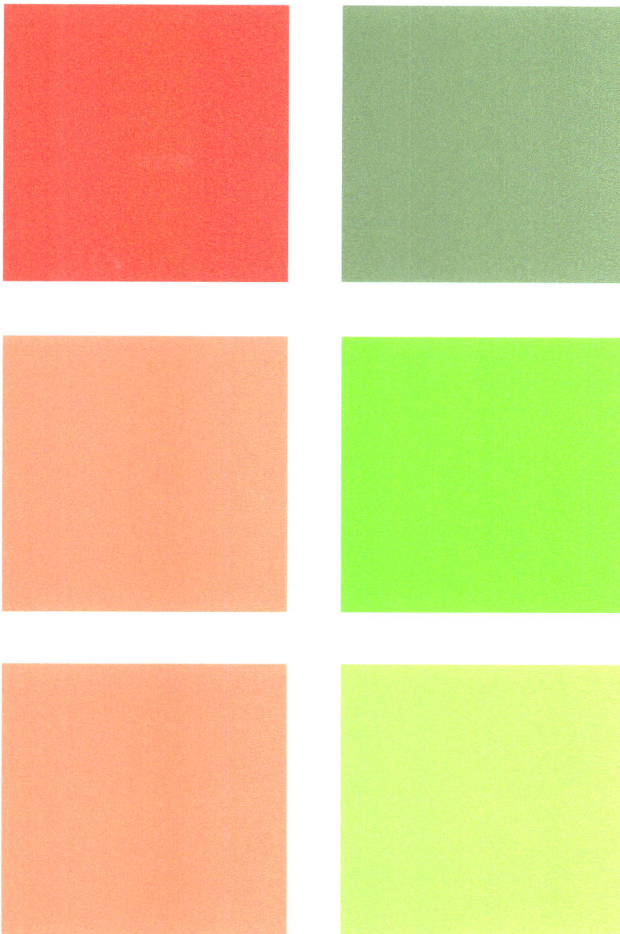

Figure 5.21a–c (a) Top. Balanced value and intensity of complimentary red and green hues. (b) Middle. Balance altered when the previous red and green hue saturation levels are reduced. (c) Bottom. Improved intensity balance of the hues with previously reduced saturation levels adjusted.

hues, with the remaining two a tint or shade of the one or more of the other three. A space that contains only one hue has the potential to become monotonous and boring. To address this problem, incorporate a variety of contrasts to add visual stimulation within the interior space. One color needs to play the dominant role in your color scheme, with lighter and mid tones balancing the palette. Figure 5.22 illustrates two color palettes, each involving the single hue, violet. The top example illustrates too much monotony and no balance of light and dark. The second palette addresses this problem with added value contrast to provide visual stimulation. Notice that the darker value is now less dominant and the lighter/brighter values balance the darker values for added contrast. In summary, light colors need to be balanced with dark colors, highly saturated colors need to be balanced with dull colors, and the intensities of colors must relate to one another to create a harmonious palette.

Multiple-Color Overload

When considering four or more colors within an interior space, care has to be taken to ensure that the colors relate to one another. Remember, to create balance within any space, pleasing relationships must be present. Apparent relationships help the person living in or using the space to make personal and functional connections, promoting

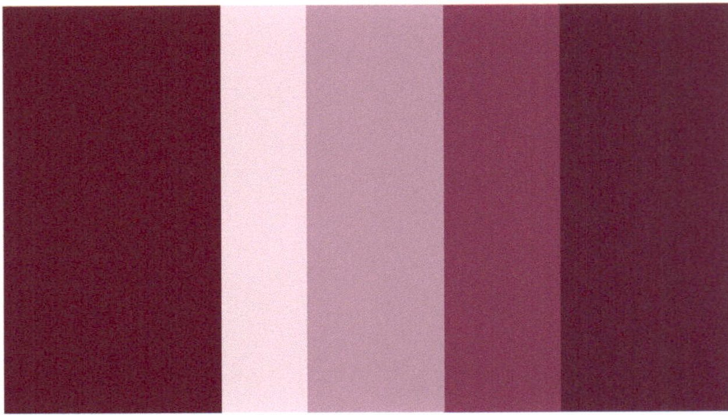

Figure 5.22 Monochromatic palette with weak balance of light and dark values. The addition of lighter values improves the color balance in the bottom image.

comprehension of what is being viewed. Otherwise, disorientation may result when the user first experiences a place. When you consider large commercial spaces, such as hospitals, retail establishments, or large office buildings, color chaos could make wayfinding almost impossible. If too many separate colors are chosen, the space will appear unbalanced, with little connection among the elements.

The way we decide to dress directly relates to balancing and making sound color choices. Imagine for a moment that you decide to dress yourself in blue pants, a green jacket, orange scarf, purple belt, and, for fun, yellow shoes. Would you be comfortable stepping out in public in this color combination? The same rules apply to design; too much color is an overload and creates disorder (Figure 5.23). To bring order to chaos, apply the same color or similar colors to unrelated design elements—creating a relationship—that will aid in limiting the perceived confusion.

The following checklist can be used to ensure that the key components of color balance are incorporated into your design projects.

- How many different colors are going to be used?
- Have I organized my palette colors according to their respective visual weights?

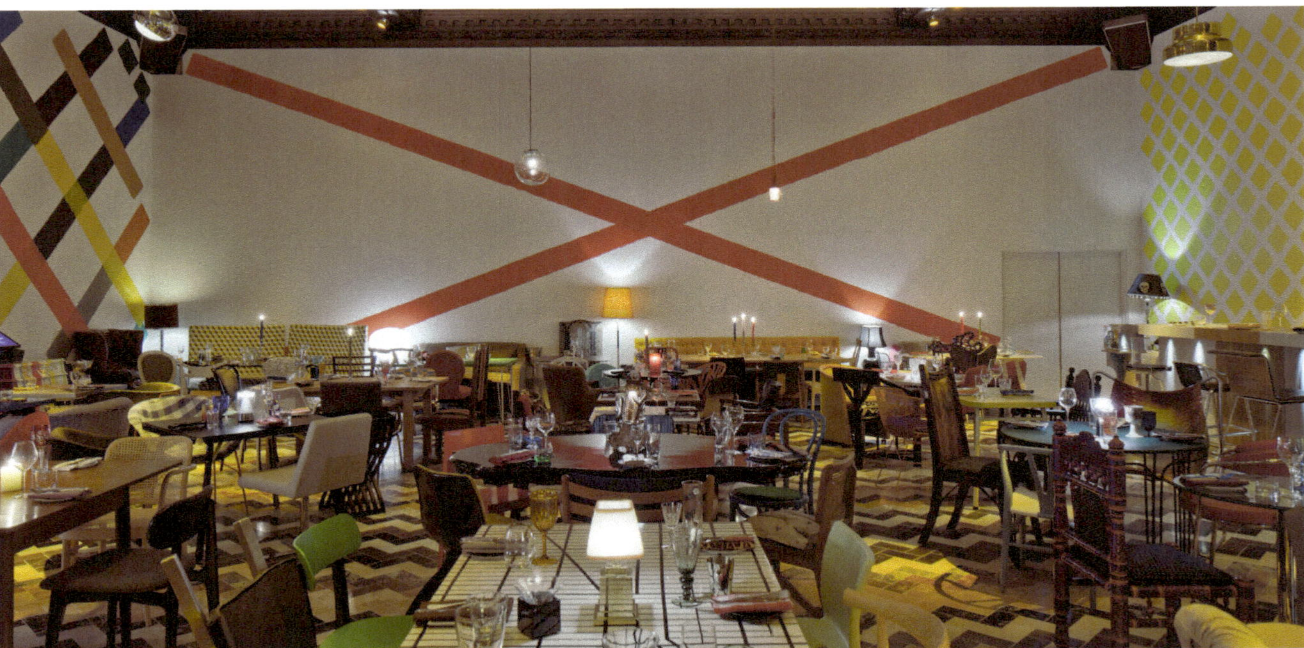

Figure 5.23 A restaurant with an eclectic mix of mismatched chairs, tables, glassware, and bold graphics. Sketch Gallery Restaurant, Europe, United Kingdom, designed by artist Martin Creed.

- Have I established a balance of light and dark color in my palette? If not, then readjusting the lightness/darkness of the corresponding colors will be needed.
- Have I assigned the color selections throughout the space, establishing good color balance?
- Have I selected a dominant color for my palette?

REVIEW QUESTIONS

1. List and describe the three types of balance.
2. Describe the use of contrast for achieving color balance with each of the three types of balance.
3. Explain how bright or dull color can be used to simulate advancing or receding perception of size.
4. Compare and contrast symmetrical versus asymmetrical balance with the use of color.
5. Explain how the size of the color area affects balance.
6. Provide two examples of creating the illusion of vertical space with color and balance.
7. Explain the concepts of single-color and multiple-color overload and how these two affect balance.

Vocabulary

Balance
symmetry
radial balance
contrast
asymmetry
color interaction

EXERCISES

1. Work with the following exercises in color weight.
   a. Construct a value scale and chroma scale using colored paper—that is, the Color-aid® system of colored paper. The exercise will help you learn the subtle changes in value and the color terminology (tint, tone, and shade), in addition to recognizing visual color weight.
   b. Select thirty different-colored papers—ten tints, ten shades, and ten hues—with less saturated chroma. Organize these hues into three weight scales from lightest to heaviest. This exercise reinforces analyzing color for visual weight while learning to recognize and select color based on these three properties.
2. Create balanced compositions that explore visual weight changes by using background hues of simultaneous contrasts to make "one color like two" and two colors like one. Focus these exercises using single hues of light and dark values rather than additional hues that are formed by color mixing. Provide a written analysis of your processes (both successful and not successful attempts) and why the final solution was chosen.

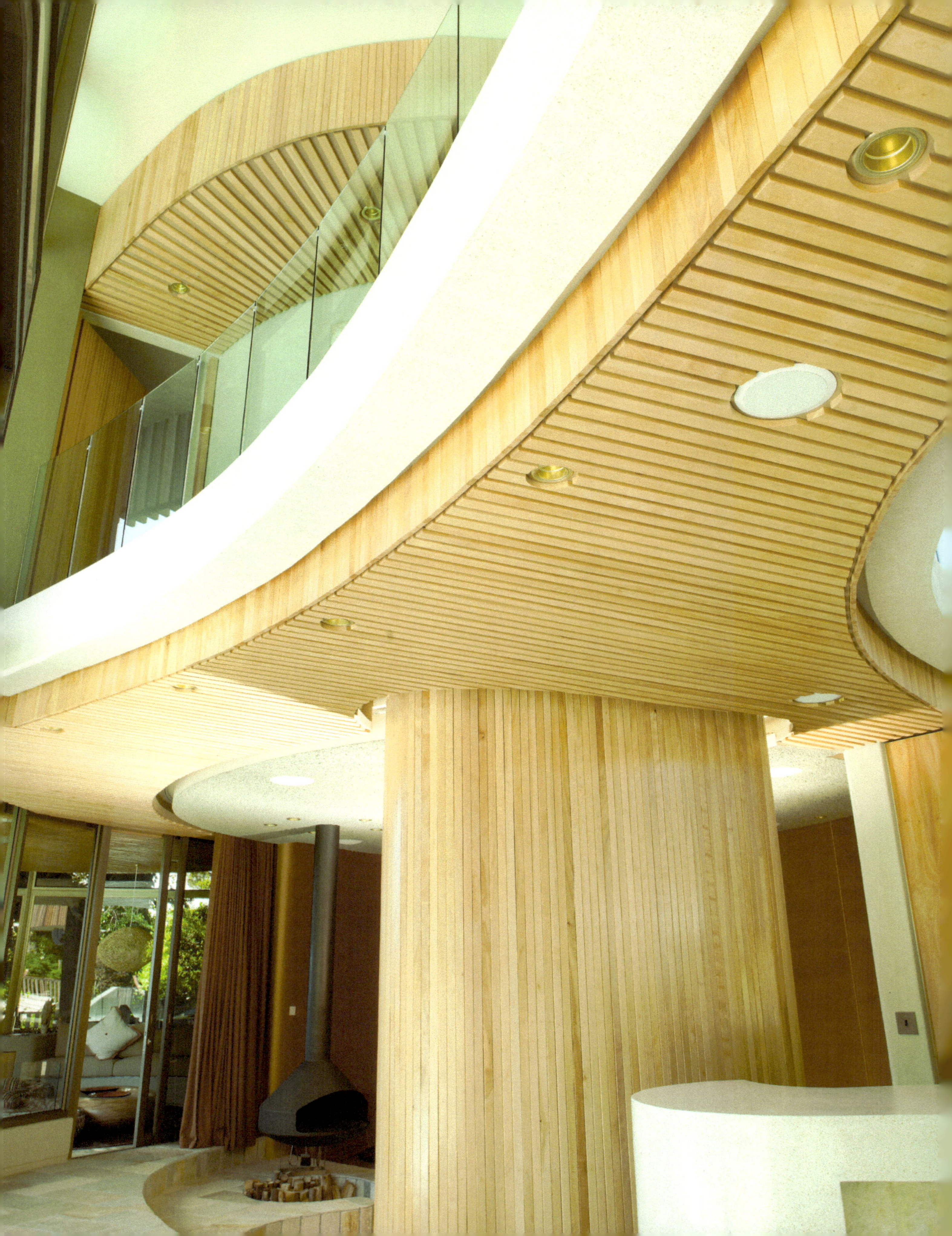

6

color + rhythm

Learning Outcomes

After studying this chapter, you will be able to:

- **Explain how rhythm and color can be used to create five types of visual effect: repetition, alternation, progression, continuation, and radiation.**
- **Explain how an interior space absent of visual movement can be supported with multiple color shifts in hue, value, and intensity to create a desired rhythmic order.**
- **Demonstrate outlining with color as a way to add visual movement with minimal effort to impact the overall design.**
- **Recall that the stronger the contrast of color, the stronger the color rhythm.**
- **Recall that the weaker the contrast of color, the weaker the color rhythm.**
- **Explain why a color rhythm of more than three hues should be limited due to visual clutter. The exception would be a gradual succession of light to dark values.**
- **Describe how lighting levels are considered in addition to color to achieve the desired rhythmic pattern.**
- **Show how a series of similarly shaped objects with color contrasts between the repeating elements will create a regular color rhythm.**
- **Repeat a series of progressively larger elements with more dramatic contrasts between each design element for a progressive, dynamic color rhythm.**
- **Repeat a color hue with a repeating shape to create a calming, even pattern of movement.**
- **Repeat the same element in the same position on wall, floor, and ceiling surfaces in a space to unify the composition.**

Rhythm is movement through space that guides and leads the eye connecting and organizing pieces of visual information into patterns. **Rhythm** is a natural evolutionary trait in nature that can be transferred to interior spaces and can be further emphasized with color (Figure 6.1). Alternating hues, progressive values, and contrasts of saturation are methods whereby a designer can manipulate interior elements to bring a better rhythmic order to space. Matthew Frederick describes our movement in space in this way: "The shapes and qualities of architectural spaces greatly influence human experience and behavior, for we inhabit the spaces of our built environment and not the solid walls, roof, and columns that shape it. Positive spaces are almost always preferred by people for lingering and social interaction. Negative space tends to promote movement rather than dwelling in space" (2007, p. 6).

This relationship of solid and void can be used to create an interplay of light and dark color contrast for rhythmic harmony. In Figure 6.2 the light and dark values create an undulating pattern that ripples from the painted color at the distant wall onto the adjoining surface as a textile. The use of a single hue—orange—suggests a focal point in stark contrast to the remaining interior palette of achromatic values, reinforcing the playful character of this color rhythm. Rhythm is the repetition, recurrence, or sequencing of similar design elements in the built environment, creating a pattern. Rhythm can also be achieved through color contrast or similarity in hue, value, and intensity. The hierarchy we assign to architectural elements with color helps to communicate the activity for a particular space and adds priority or focus. The rhythm of color guides us like a map to understand the functionality of the space and to create

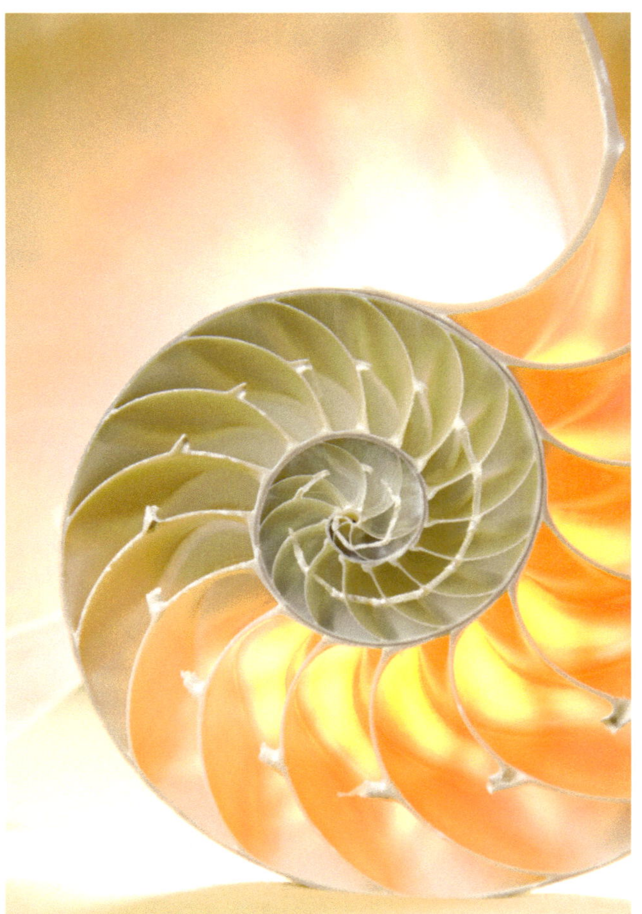

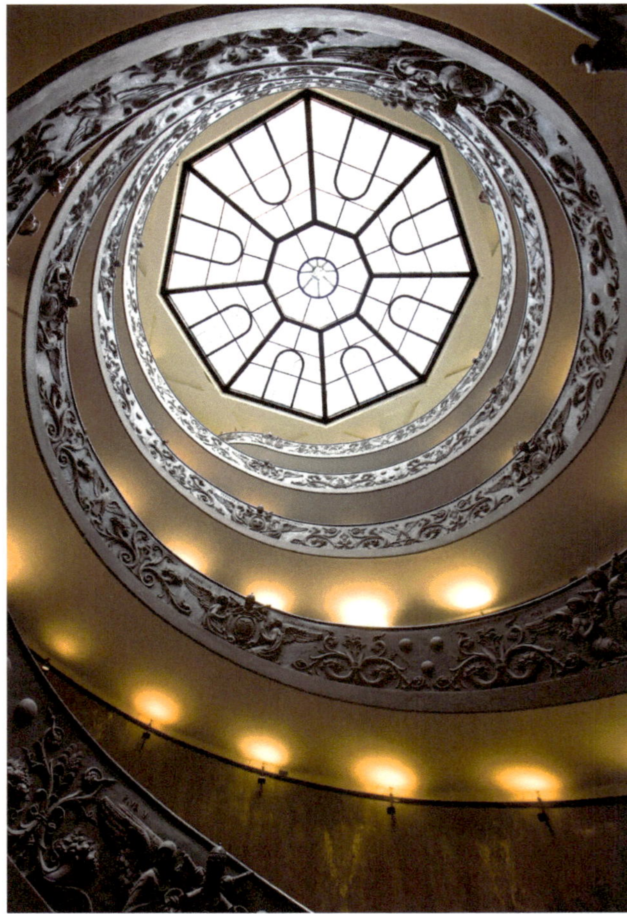

Figure 6.1 (left) Nautilus seashell; (right) Spiral staircase, Vatican Museum, Rome.

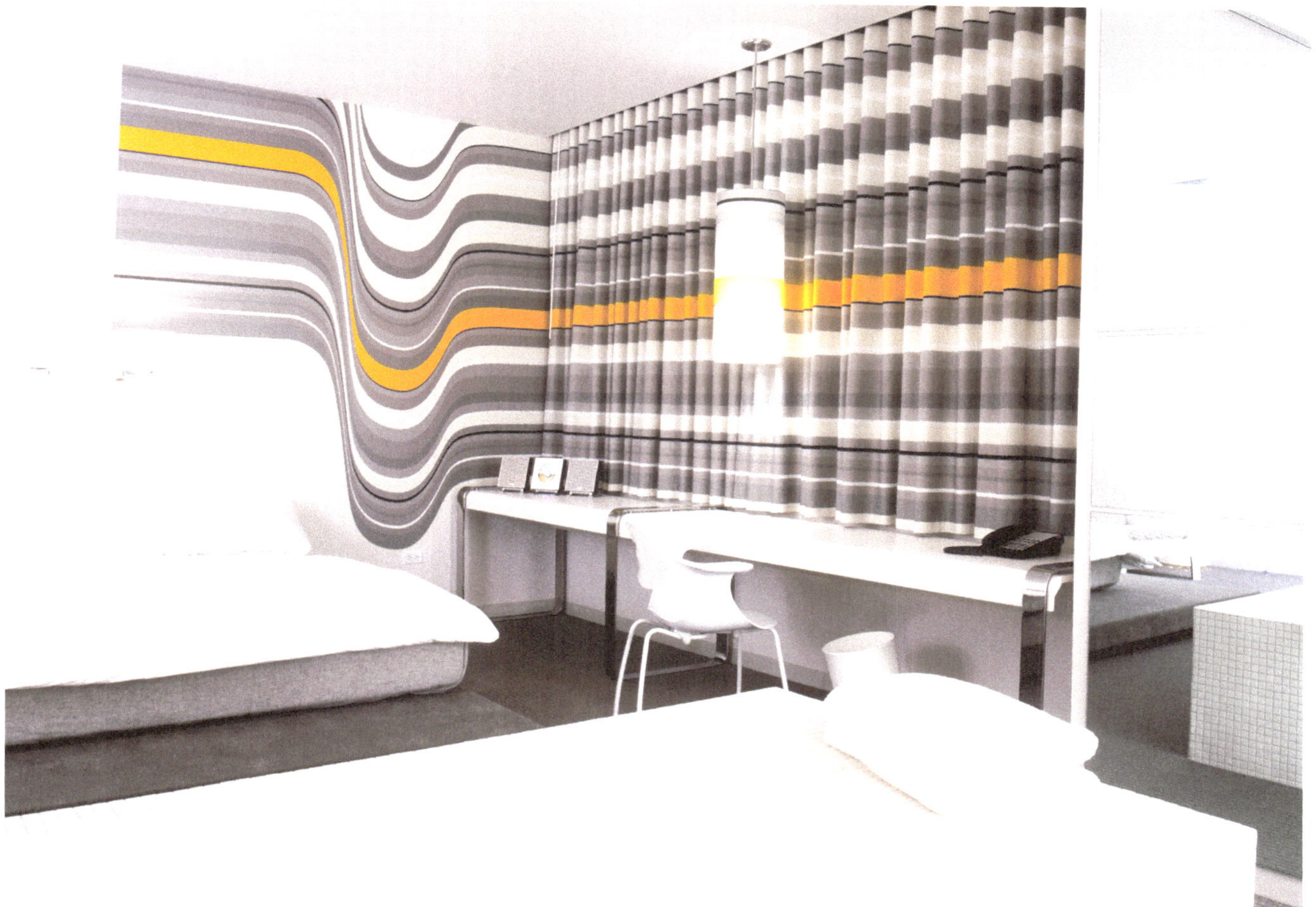

Figure 6.2 Bedroom with striped drapery and mural carries the eye around the space at the Standard Hotel, Los Angeles.

a holistic experience. Arnheim is noted in *The Interior Dimension* as saying that "if humans are to interact with a building functionally there must be visual continuity" (Malnar & Vodvarka, 1992, p. 73). Good continuity of space occurs when the users have an ongoing visual experience of the space. The spatial design of an interior should aim to provide the user a unique experience that entices the senses through sight, color and light, sounds, materials, textures, and innovative use and integration of technology. As a person moves through a space, the use of color and rhythm should guide him or her along the path or intended sequence. There is no beginning or end to a design unless there is the desire for the user to stop and pause to experience items of importance. In this case, you may apply focal points or points of interest such as a sculpture or a directory to aid in orienting users to their position in the interior.

Color and Music

In much the same way a symphony composer balances sound and melodies, where one note combined with many creates chords, one color combined with many creates visual harmony. In the late nineteenth and early twentieth centuries, theorists began to make psychological associations between color and music. Goethe noted the work of J. L. Hoffman, who proposed that musical timbre created by instruments related to certain colors: "yellow for clarinets, red for trumpet, crimson for flutes, ultramarine for violins, and so on" (Gage, 1993, p. 236). The high pitch of the trumpet and flute clearly suggests the strength and brightness of the hue red, whereas the soft, melodic pitch of the violin suggests blues. This example illustrates that, universally, aspects of color are not so far removed from other experiences. When we can draw the connections

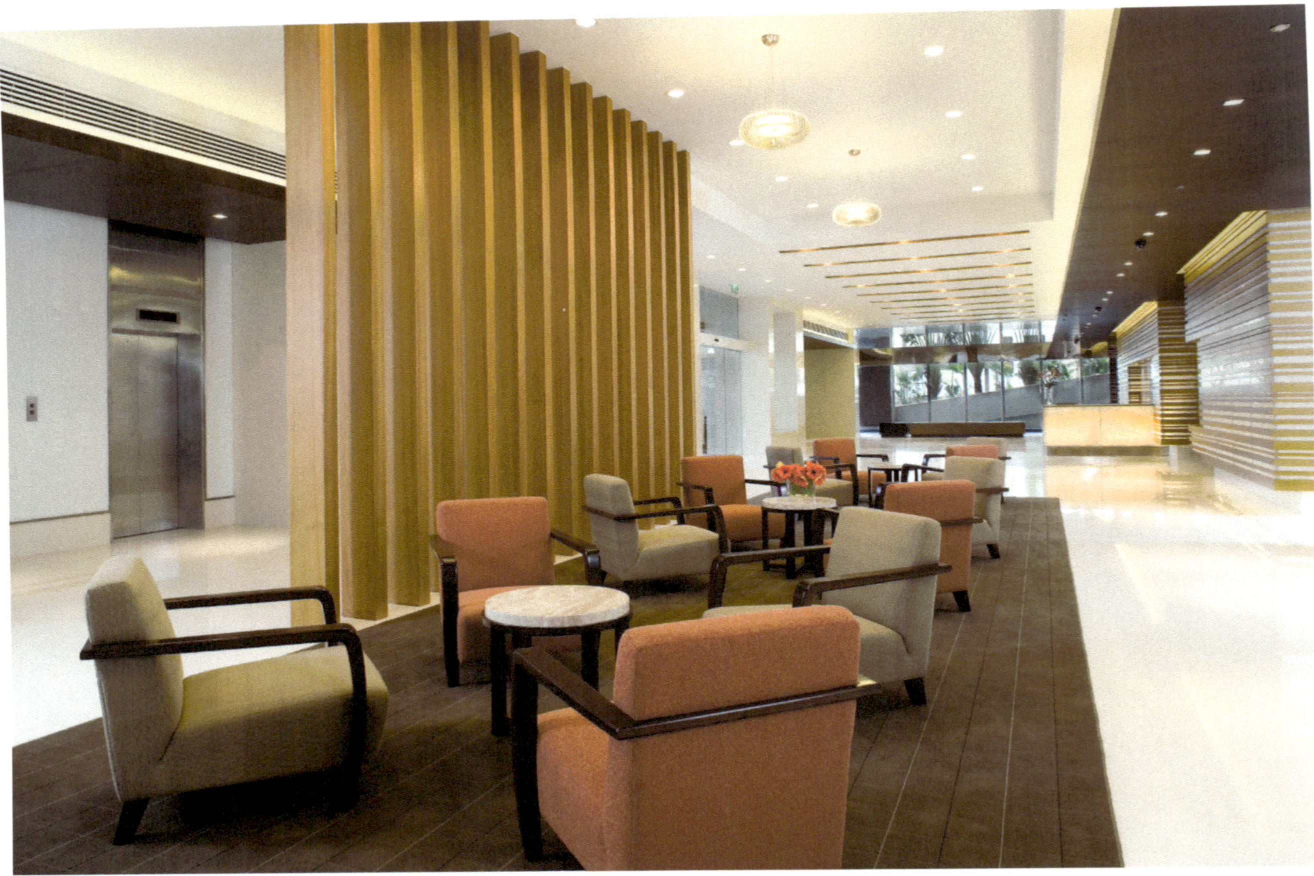

Figure 6.3 Contrasting forms and shapes of horizontal and vertical lines add movement and direction through this lobby waiting area. The large open sitting area is defined with a wall of repeating vertical slats in wood, carrying the eye upward. The dark carpeting grounds the sitting area that is also balanced by the dark finish on the underside of the dropped ceiling spanning over the reception area.

and make analogies, the once-overwhelming use of color can become easier for the aesthetician. As with musical compositions, color can be used to create rhythm and movement. Placement of hues in rhythmic succession helps to visually unify similar or dissimilar elements in space. Whether your color is moving vertically, horizontally, or diagonally, it can be used to maximize the visual impact required for your project. The horizontal and vertical lines contrast with the surrounding neutral finishes in Figure 6.3, greeting you in this space. Contrasting materials emphasize the shapes and forms that direct and move patrons to the reception area in the background.

Nature and Rhythm

Interior designers and architects seek inspiration from many sources. From the jagged lines of mountaintops to the simple curves of a calla lily, organic patterns from nature are all around us. We draw inspiration and examples from nature for interior designs, from simple chairs to ornate light fixtures, using recognizable forms that allow a person to immediately form a connection with the object or interior space being experienced. The circular repetitive forms of a shell, the angles and rhythms of a palm frond, and the radial symmetry in the petals of a flower are examples of natural pattern forms. These patterns exist in every natural form, whether human, animal, or plant. Richard Dubé states that "when a designer chooses a pattern form on the basis of aesthetics, the choice will likely be driven by one or more of the following factors: emotions, scale, texture, or broad applicability" (1997, p. 63).

The Bahá'í Temple in New Delhi is a geometric form that represents a giant lotus flower. This symbol represents the spiritual connection the lotus flower has to the Bahá'í faith. The temple's color reflects the white of the flower, and the natural progression of shape and size adds rhythmic order to the architecture. Nature and color, therefore, can be a metaphor. Using **bio-inspired** color and design creates a personal connection, familiarity, and importance to an object or space that may not have existed otherwise.

Nature and natural objects provide inspiration for design. A designer (or the manufacturers of building products, coatings, and textiles he or she chooses) might try to replicate the exact color of a leaf or color of a sunset seen in the outdoors. An architectural column might be inspired to resemble palm trees. An interior ceiling design that is radiating outward from a focal center may emulate the many concentric circles found in nature—a rippling drop of water, a conch seashell, a bird's nest, and more. Familiar patterns in interior design and architecture may imitate nature: tessellations, floras, spirals, and anything that grows from the ground and appears to blossom. A ceiling detail may be designed to emulate clouds in the sky, offering a layered, open and airy experience to the users of the space. A home library, den or theater may resemble a cave or cocoon, with texture, low contrast of materials, wood finishes and darker colors creating a sense of protection and to envelop the user of the space. The honeycomb of a beehive, the snowflake, the butterfly wing, and many more organic shapes and form can feed the creative imaginations of designers. As a beginning interior designer, collect photos and actual organic samples from nature so that you can work these patterns, shapes, forms, textures and colors into your designs. Challenge your creative work to incorporate more complex biophilic fractal geometry. The goal is to tap into nature to inspire your work, forming an opportunity for your clients to produce symbolic and personal connections to the natural environment.

Mimicking elements in nature helps to build connections with the user of the design. The ocean is an excellent source for colors, textures, and patterns to influence and inform your use of color in design. The interior of the contemporary restaurant in Figure 6.4a illustrates a color palette of warm browns and beige, curvilinear ceiling design, and repetition of a striped pattern reminiscent of a seashell (Figure 6.4b). The spiral pendant by Danish furniture designer and architect Verner Panton, from 1970, is made of chrome-plated plastic suspended by clear nylon strings (Figure 6.4c). The floating and spiraling effect resembles a swimming school of silver-colored sardines (Figure 6.4d).

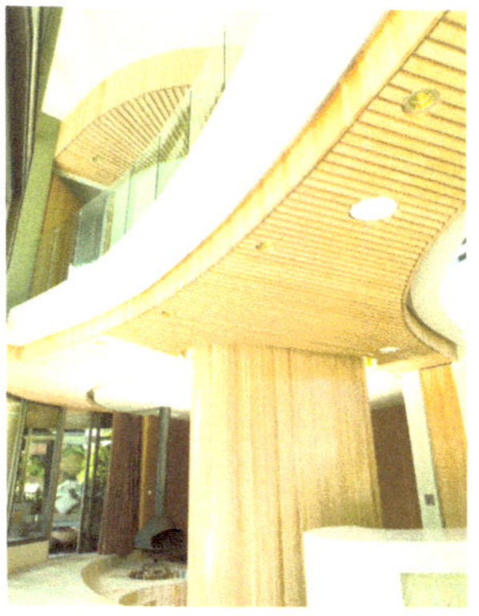

(a) Modern residential interior with natural vertical and horizontal slat wood column and ceiling details, curving and organic lines and forms.

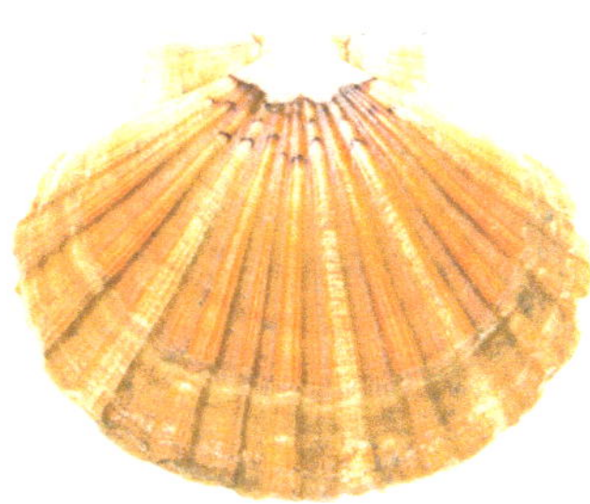

(b) Pecten Jacobaeus shell.

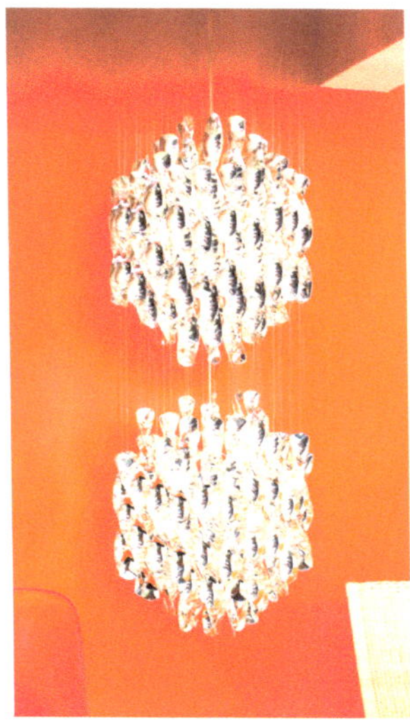

(c) Spiral pendant by Verner Panton, 1969.

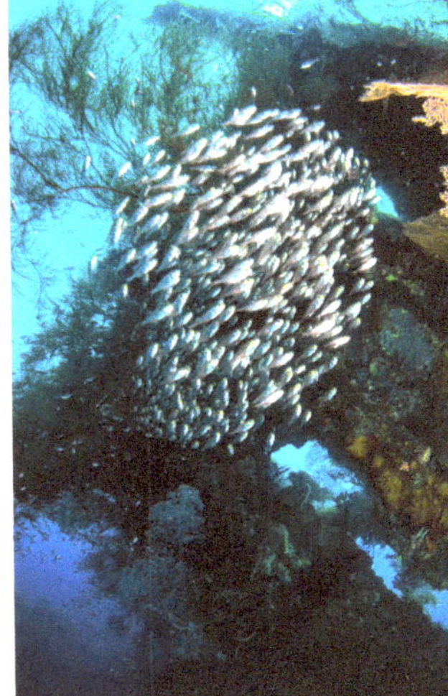

(d) School of sardines.

Figure 6.4 Bio-inspired colors, patterns, materials, and texture

The student biophilic design project in Figure 6.5 is inspired by the coloration of the yellow jacket wasp and its honeycomb-shaped paper nest. The selected materials, color, pattern, shape, and composition work to emulate the natural forms and, in turn, create a unique, functional, and versatile product concept for workplace furnishings.

Noticing color and rhythm in nature can provide an extended source of inspiration for your interior design projects. See Figure 6.6a–f for examples of color in nature and color rhythm expressed through the progression of colors on the natural forms.

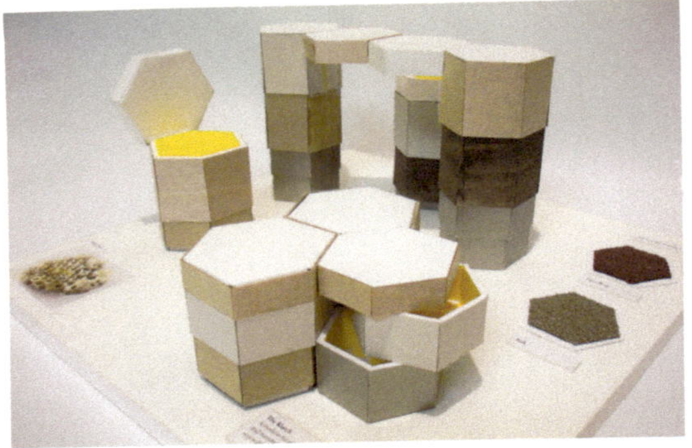

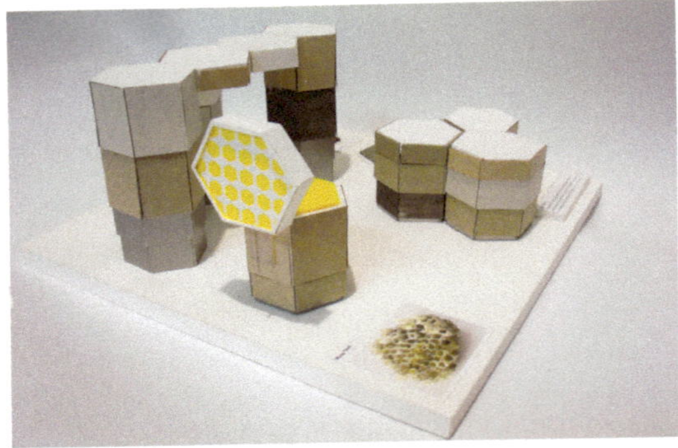

Figure 6.5 "The Klatch" by interior design student Julee Owens, a versatile seating group inspired by a yellow jacket wasp nest. The yellow textile pattern and selection of materials represent the colorations of the wasp and the papery nest material.

(a) Color palette based on a graphic image of cactus in Ixtapa Zihuatanejo, State of Guerrero, Mexico.

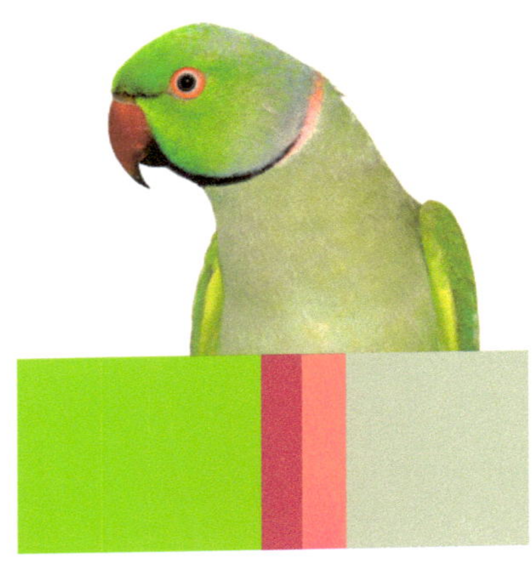

(b) Color palette based on a ring-necked parakeet.

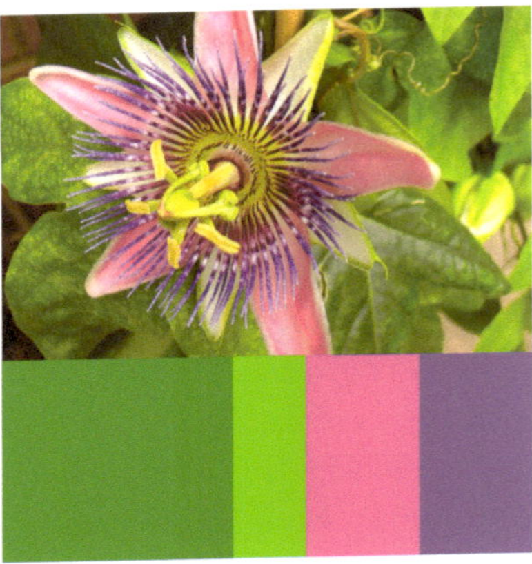

(c) Color palette based on a passionflower vine.

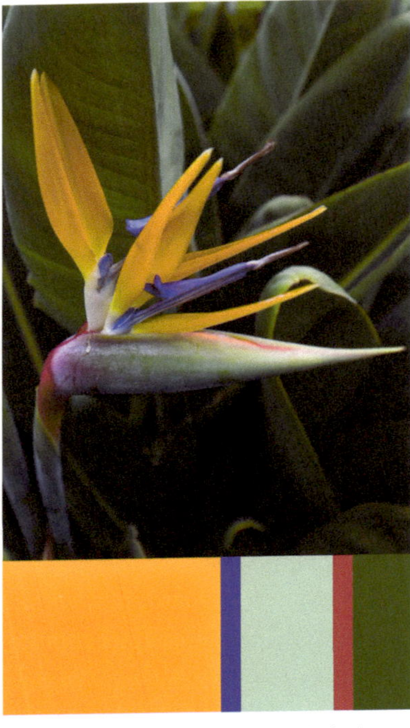

(d) Color palette based on the bird of paradise flower.

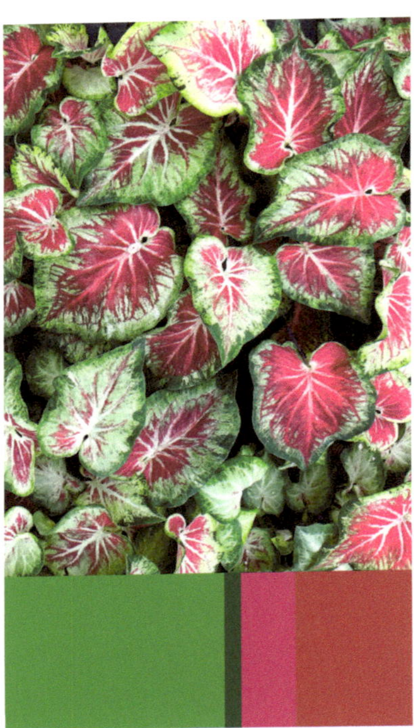

(e) Color palette based on foliage of the caladium plant.

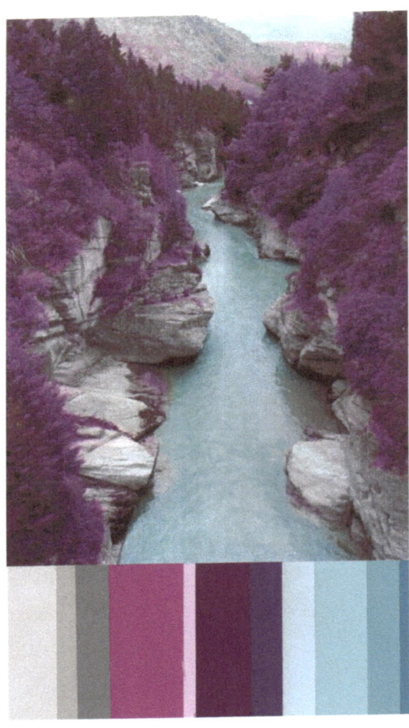

(f) Student example of color palette based on natural color harmonies.

Figure 6.6 Bio-inspired color palettes.

Recognizing organic patterns will help you mimic the shapes and patterns that can be used in your designs. These palettes have been prepared in proportional relationship to the natural form. The proportions indicate the "natural" progression of color that nature can provide you. Being observant of your surroundings will open up a wide range of color patterns in nature and will be an effective tool to help you plan your proportional relationships of color in your design plans.

Types of Rhythm

Rhythm can be created in a number of ways using color and pattern. Five types of rhythm are associated with color: repetition, alternation, progression, continuation, and radiation. The purpose of rhythm is to provide an opportunity to move the viewer through the space, creating moments for emphasizing or downplaying various design elements. Color rhythm primarily evolves through color contrast of high and low saturation achieved through hue sequence, value sequence, or multiple-color sequence. A strong contrast of color will create a dynamic, active, and spatially intense experience. If, on the other hand, we were to reduce the separation of chroma, the space would appear passive and static. These principles apply whether you're working in hue, value, or chroma contrasts. A repeating row of columns or arches, a continuous line of crown molding, and the alternating pattern of colored mosaic tiles are examples of the many ways musical timbre is imitated in our built environment. The analyses of any interior space will uncover the use of at least one if not multiple types of rhythm. Each rhythm type can work independently or in combination with other types to create further visual interest to unify the visual composition.

In Figure 6.7a, the staircase incorporates two rhythmic concepts of progression and repetition highlighted in a vibrant red hue contrasting against the light gray wall and black tile floor. The design for the stair railing, which is painted black, uses line to accentuate the vertical movement of the stair. The grid structure in front of the stair introduces a second repetitive concept with the negative square space and positive rectangular colonnade. The tension created between the foreground and stair is emphasized with the intense, powerful red, as if the stairs are being squeezed between these two forms. This example of rhythm illustrates great contrast of design further supported with color. If we switch the red stair coloring and foreground wall color, the emphasis is reversed and the rhythm is focused more on the lines created by the colonnade (Figure 6.7b). If we remove all color, the two rhythms are weakened (Figure 6.7c). In your design projects, try applying the chosen colors in different locations within various room mockups to see what happens to the overall perception of the space in your design. This is a way to test and further examine if the placement of color in the space achieves both the desired color effect and the desired design solution.

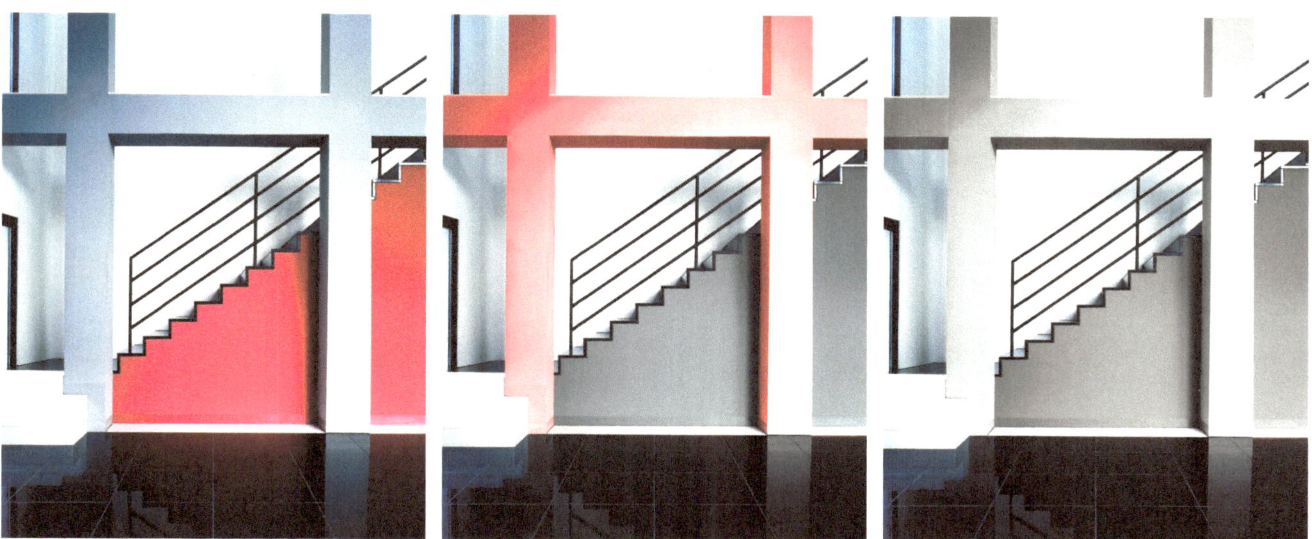

Figure 6.7 (a) The staircase incorporates the rhythmic concepts of progression and repetition, which are emphasized with a vibrant, red hue. (b) Color rhythm emphasis is reversed and placed on the repetitive square design of the colonnade. (c) No single particular rhythm is emphasized with hue or contrast.

As you read further and we discuss each color rhythm type, refer to Figure 6.8. These illustrations provide a simple visual dictionary of the various color rhythms discussed next. Keep in mind that in any color selection processes aiming for rhythm, color saturation, illumination brightness, and surface textures and reflection need to be considered as part of the desired effect. With brighter lighting levels and color saturation, the visual reaction to the color rhythm will be stronger. Dimmer light and muted color may produce a more subtle result.

(a) Color alternation of light and dark contrast. The shape is repeated; however, the use of color contrast shifts the type of rhythm from repetition to alternation.

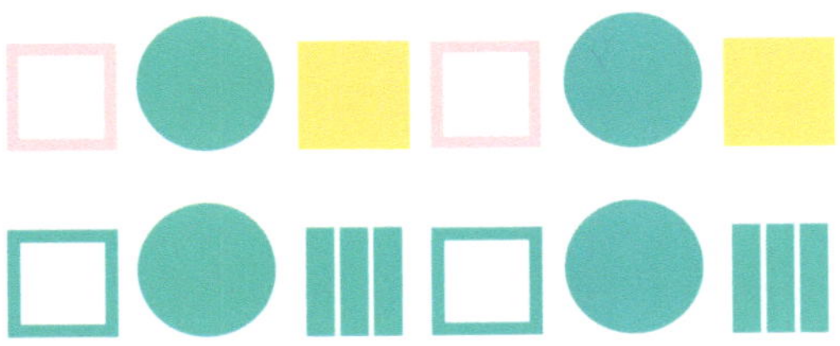

(b) Color continuity, in this example, is achieved by carrying the similar hue throughout the composition to connect dissimilar elements and create a more fluid rhythm.

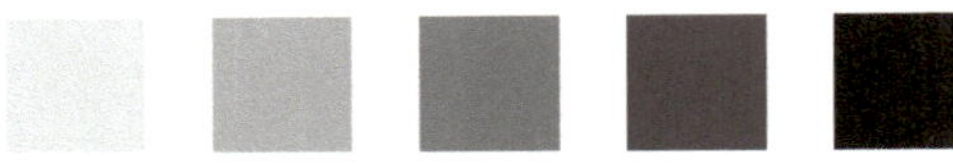

(c) Progression using values from light to dark.

(d) Repetition by similarity in shape and hue.

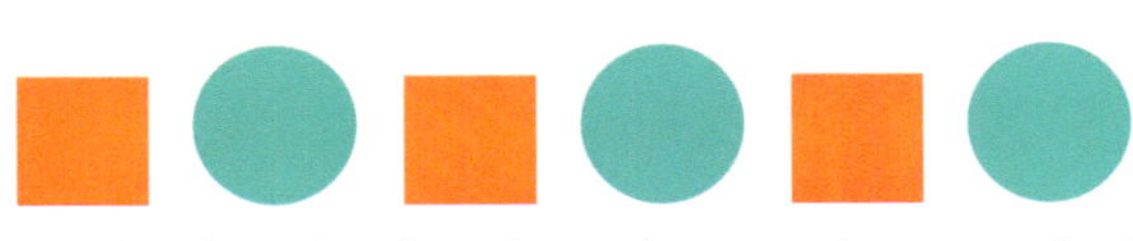

(e) Color alternation through complementary hues, warm/cool contrast, and shape.

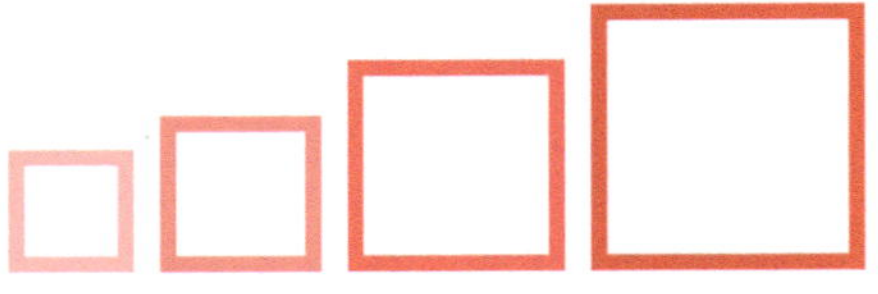

(f) Progression through size and value.

Figure 6.8

Repetition

Repetition is the systematic orderly succession of identical design elements (shape, line, color, form) along a defined path in space. Early twentieth-century American architect Frank Lloyd Wright's Solomon R. Guggenheim Museum, which opened on October 21, 1959 in New York City, uses undulating, curvilinear forms for the sculptural ramp that leads the eye upward and around the interior space. The absence of color emphasizes the design, with natural light penetrating the volume and adding light and dark contrast (Figure 6.9).

Repeating similar elements will create visual unity within an interior space, whereas too much variation could create chaos and confusion. When using a particular color harmony (monochromatic: 1; complementary: 2; triadic/split complementary: 3; or tetradic: 4), the number of hues that form these color harmonies need to be repeated throughout the room to adequately create rhythm and balance. Attention should be paid to

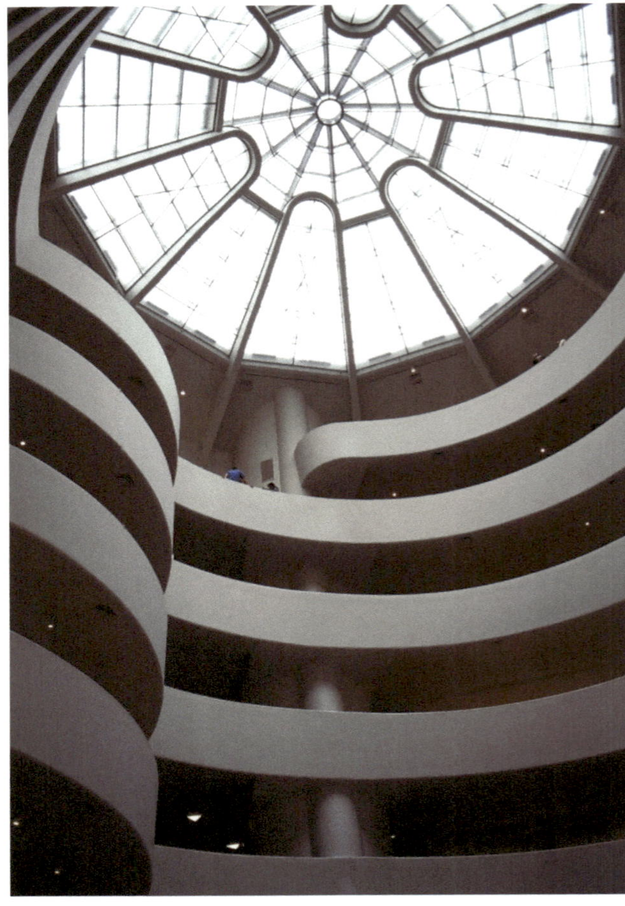

Figure 6.9 The Guggenheim Museum, in New York City, designed by Frank Lloyd Wright.

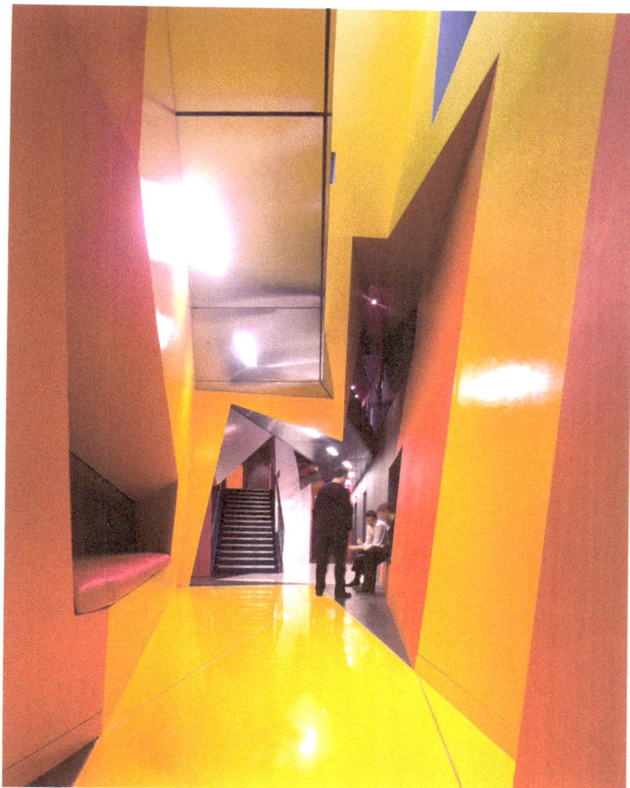

Figure 6.10 Example of "rhythmic turmoil." Birkbeck College–Film Studies, London.

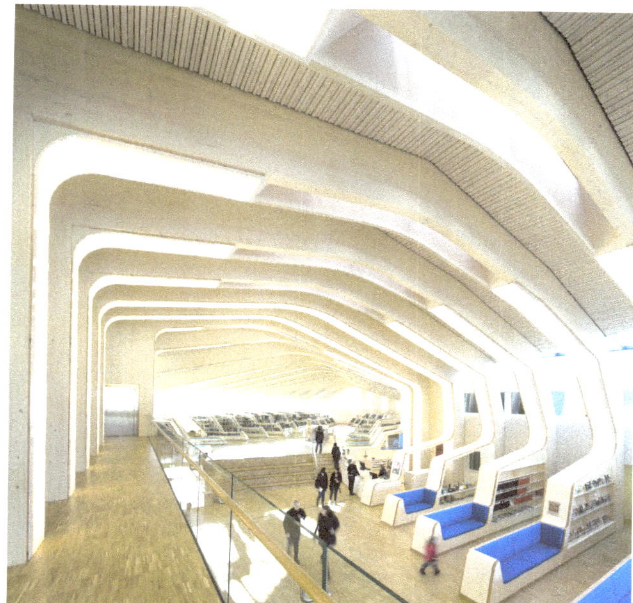

Figure 6.11 Interior of Vennesla Library, Vennesla, Norway, uses inset lighting and material contrast with glue-laminated timber ribs spanning the width of the space to add visual rhythm to the interior ceiling and walls.

variations in value, intensity, and warm versus cool hues. Too many hues assigned within the space will distort the visual rhythm and undermine the effectiveness of other design principles planned for the same space (balance and harmony). Rhythmic order is essential when color is applied to forms, shapes, and the organized structure of the interior environment. The work of an interior designer should support and strengthen the interior structure, not distract from or alter the intended design purpose. This can be minimized by placing color on key design elements or areas of larger proportion to downplay the rhythmic turmoil. Too much visual movement and users of the space may end up disoriented and confused (see Figure 6.10). The eye will need a place to rest. In every project we should seek "to build color rhythms into design as opportunities offer" (Ellinger, 1980, p. 97).

Alternation

Alternation occurs when two design elements are repeated in sequence, as in repetition; however, the difference is that the pattern includes two distinctly different elements (round to square, red to blue) as opposed to one element repeating. Successive, alternating, horizontal bands of color can be used to compress the verticality of space.

In Figure 6.11, the interior is a good example of using alternating structural bands emphasized with light, color, and material to break the vastness of the library. If you were to remove the bands, the result would be a cavernous space that lacked the original movement, which carries the viewer's eye from one side of the space, over the ceiling, and terminates into the integrated reading lounges accented in a solid blue textile. In Figure 6.12, the alternating horizontal bands of light and dark neutral color create both vertical and horizontal movement. If the contrast between the two colors were minimized, the movement would be lessened. The two neutral colors complement each other well, being neither too intense nor overwhelming one another. The contrast or saturation between two hues when the intensity of the two colors is similar is typically noticeable at the edge and transition of two colors, and the resulting experience is a **vibrancy** or perception of movement. This could become overstimulating and thus compromise the type of rhythm applied to a design solution. The example in Figure 6.13 illustrates the vibrancy that could result due to the high contrast of the two opposing complementary hues. In Figure 6.14a, the interior red carpeting is potentially too strong

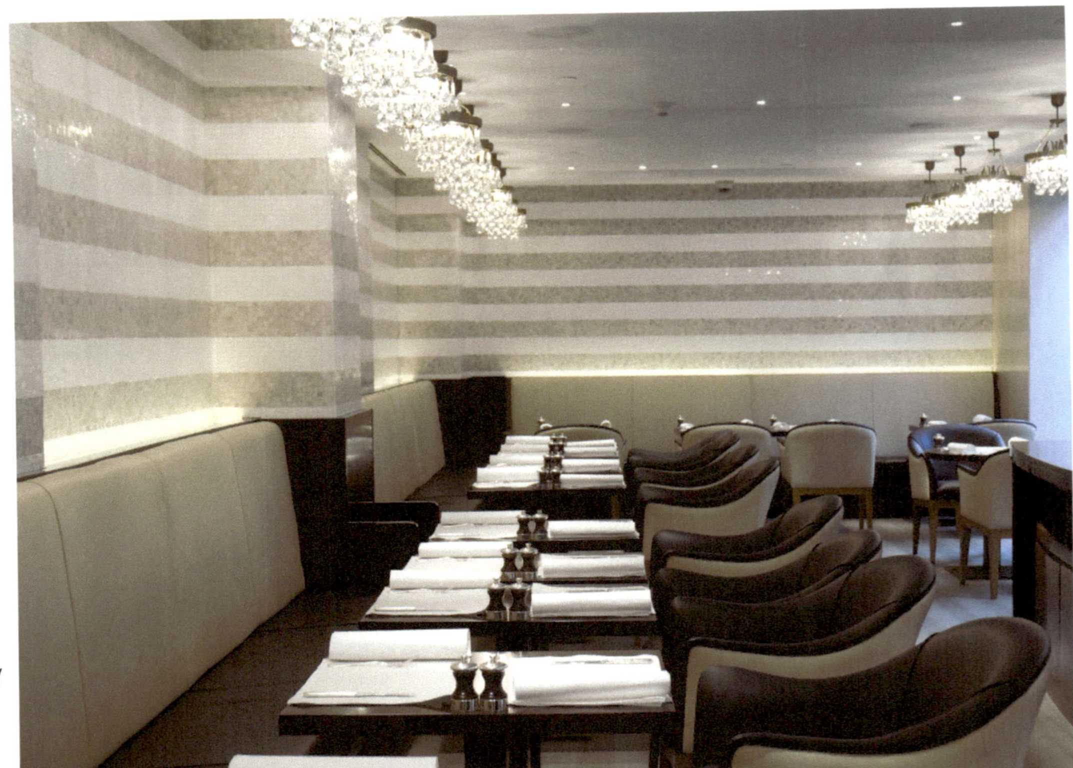

Figure 6.12 Striped wall pattern in a contemporary restaurant accentuates movement both vertically and horizontally around the space.

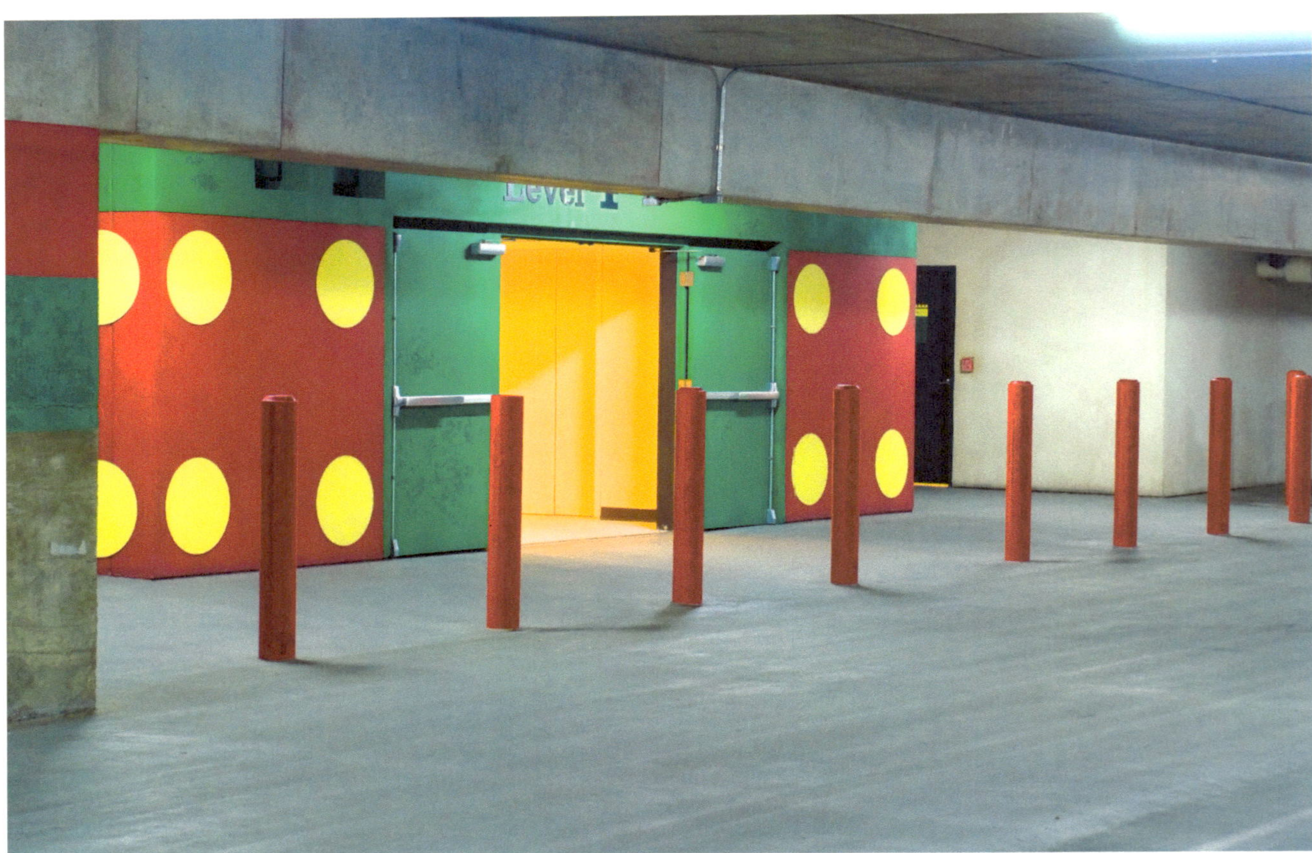

Figure 6.13 Using high-saturated contrasting color creates a strong vibrancy, resulting in an overly visually stimulating entrance from this parking garage.

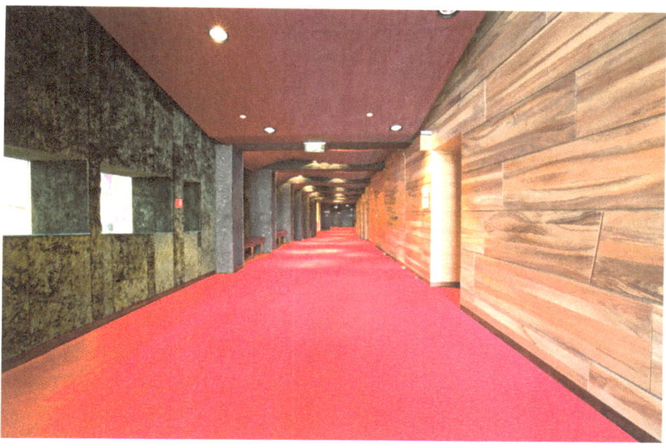

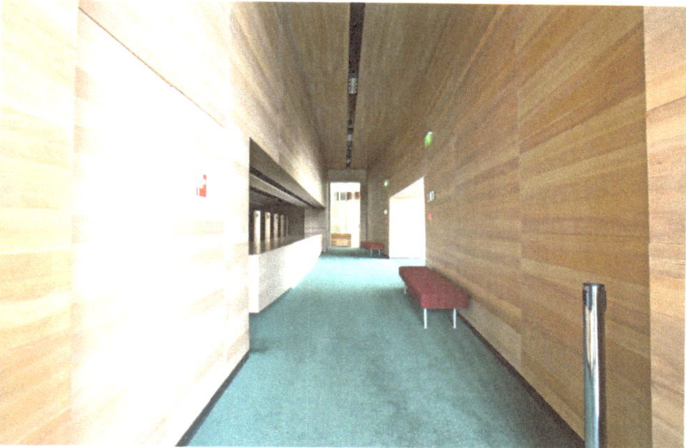

Figure 6.14 (a) Intense red flooring coupled with green marble and heavily patterned wood grain create an overly stimulating interior experience. (b) Subtle color intensity and material pattern result in a more pleasing interior experience.

for this long corridor. The color is repeated on the ceiling above and contrasted with patterns from the green marble along with the wood walls, which overwhelm the space. In contrast, the corridor in Figure 6.14b uses less intense color combined with subtle patterns in the wood walls, creating a more inviting and pleasant space.

Progression

Progression involves the repetition of similar elements with a continuous change (large to small, low to high, narrow to wide, light to dark). Progression or sequencing of color rhythm can open up or close in space, depending on the contrast levels and number of hues used. For instance, when spaces are rather narrow or confined, using color rhythm enables the viewer's eye to move continuously through, giving the perception of widening space. In Figure 6.15, the bands of colored light behind the curved glass block, progressing from warm to cool hues, draw you in and around the space. Because the bands of color run vertically instead of horizontally, your eye moves toward the ceiling of the space, where additional design details are present.

Color rhythm in an interior should be created to gradually move the eye sequentially from one hue to the next or from one design element to the next. Without color and pattern, the lack of rhythm that creates the perception of visual texture can also leave a space dull and uninspiring (Figure 6.16a). When color is introduced with strong geometry applied to the flooring, wall surfaces, and

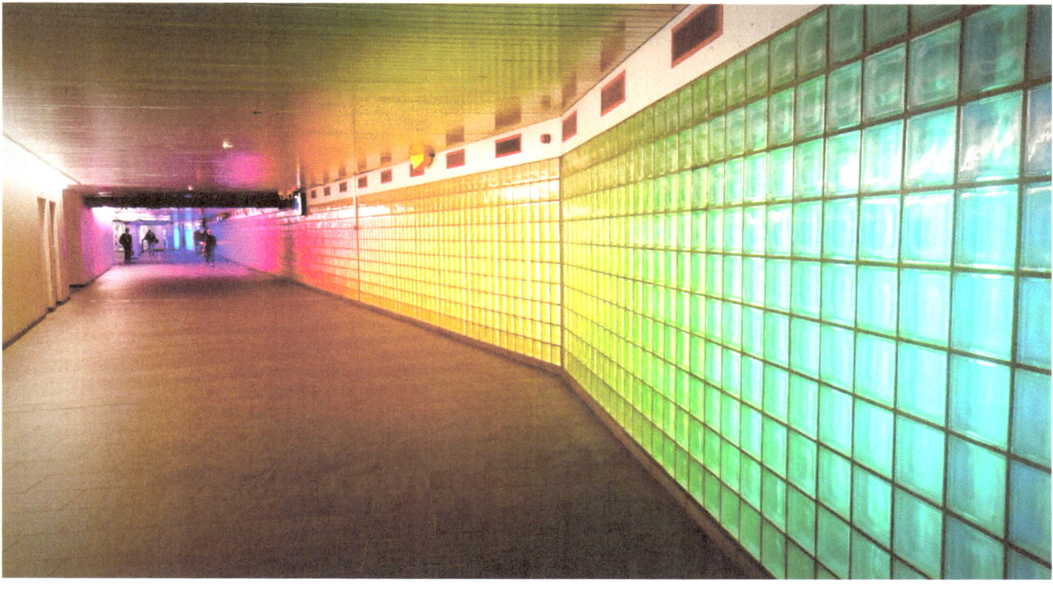

Figure 6.15 Progression of warm- and cool-colored lights filter through the curving glass block wall.

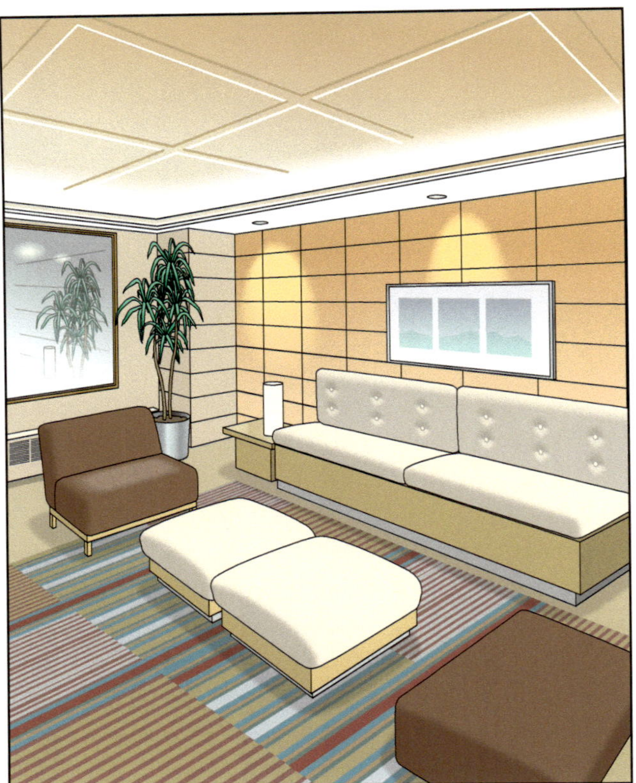

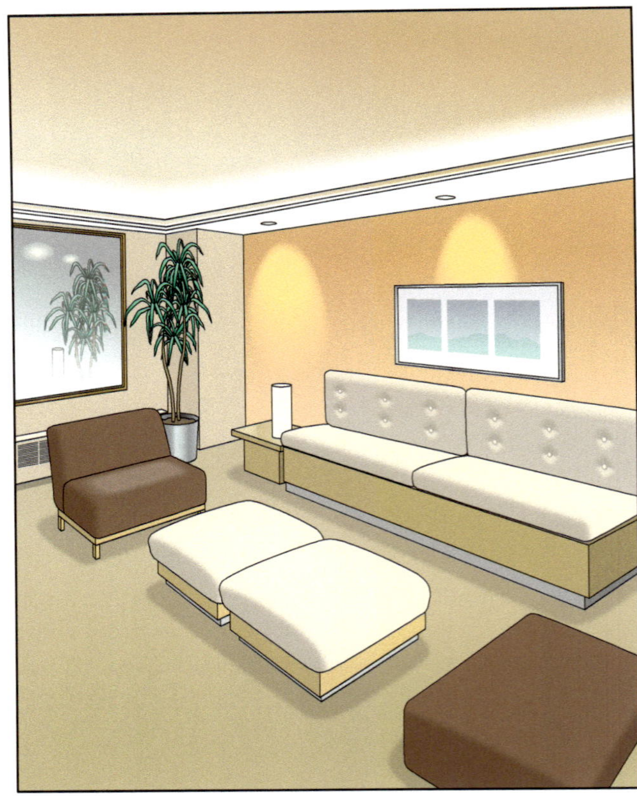

Figure 6.16 (a) With color and pattern missing, this hotel lobby waiting area is absent of rhythm, creating a visually uninteresting space. (b) The addition of color and pattern carries the eye around the lobby space, adding texture and visual interest to the space.

ceiling, we can increase the movement of the eye around the interior and reinforce a clear design concept through color, line, and pattern (Figure 6.16b).

Our goal is to create visual movement that connects all the parts of the whole. When the eye is forced to stop or unable to find a point of interest or repeating pattern, the result will be displeasing to the user of the space. When considering the use of different patterns or colored hues to create visual texture and movement, be cautious of overwhelming the final design.

Continuation or Transition

Color **continuation** refers to the placement of one or more colors throughout an interior to create a continuous movement of the eye through the space. It is the "fluid connection among composition parts" (Stewart, 2002, pp. 3–5). This concept is important for creating a sense of rhythm. Referring back to Figure 4.8b, note that the top example is confusing because of compositional elements that are varied in shape and color. Using color continuity with each shape, the previously unrelated elements now share similarity and allow the eye to easily focus on each element and move continuously through the design. Whether this is done experimenting with a combination of curving, fluid lines or sharp, contrasting shapes, color is ultimately applied to visually animate forms and to bring liveliness to space and place. The rhythm sequence will send visual messages to indicate the mood or emotional movement of the interior, and it will evoke the spatial experience you wish the user to have. If we were to apply cool greens and blues to a series of curvilinear and circular shapes and forms moving through a space, this might be calming and restful. If this were a busy, active, working environment, the experience would contradict the desired outcomes—productivity and vigilance—and workers may become lethargic and less productive. However, applied to a spa or health-care space, the use of color, shape, and rhythm would be appropriate for calming the guests. The key here is to make sure the selected colors, shapes, and sequence of shapes create rhythmic patterns related to one another for maximum effectiveness.

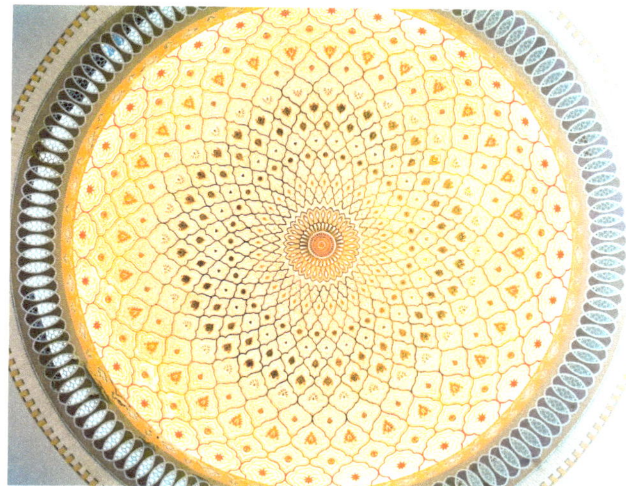

Figure 6.17 Radial pattern supported by complementary colors orange and blue.

Radiation

Radiation traditionally refers to an arrangement of objects in a radial pattern. Color **radiation** uses a concentric *color* arrangement to unify design elements and create visual movement. Figure 6.17 is an example of interior color radiation (notice the natural concentric pattern similar to a sunflower or pineapple). The orange dome over the Qur'an & Manuscripts Gallery at the Islamic Arts Museum Malaysia incorporates a palette of deep oranges and aqua blue to support the rhythmic pattern with complementary contrast. In Figure 6.18a, the orange band of carpet is laid in a radial pattern to accentuate the complementary contrast of the blue accent wall and door color. If the carpet accent color were removed and replaced with the same gray-colored field carpet, the radial pattern would no longer be as evident and supported in the architectural plan in order to move the visitor around the perimeter of the space to the elevator bay, which is also accented in the orange hue (Figures 6.18b and 6.18c).

Color and Line as Rhythm

Color can be used with line to "outline" a space, an effective and easy way to introduce rhythm to an interior that is limited in visual movement. This can be achieved with ceiling molding painted in a contrasting color to the walls, or with more detailed trellis work that provides a grid pattern and alternation of rectangular shapes. The contrast will focus viewers' attention on the use of line as a design element, moving their eyes around the space in which it is applied. Using a contrasting color both horizontally and vertically in the trellis and wall surface will highlight the design and the introduced movement. Adding complexity on a wall also reinforces its presence, in this case, affording users a sense of enhanced privacy,

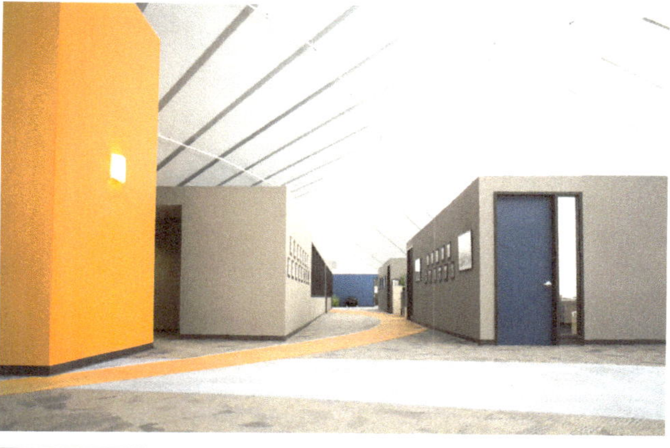

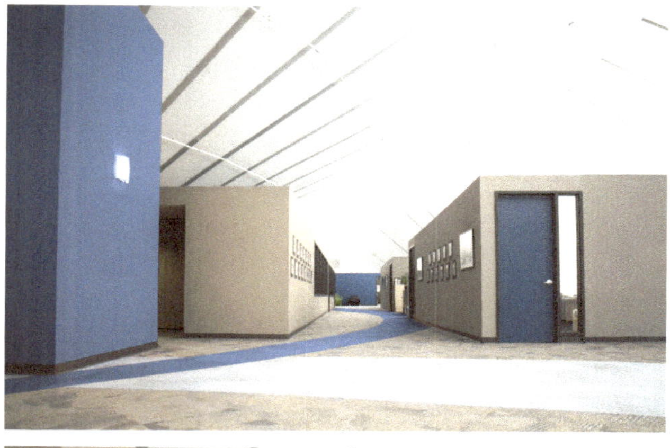

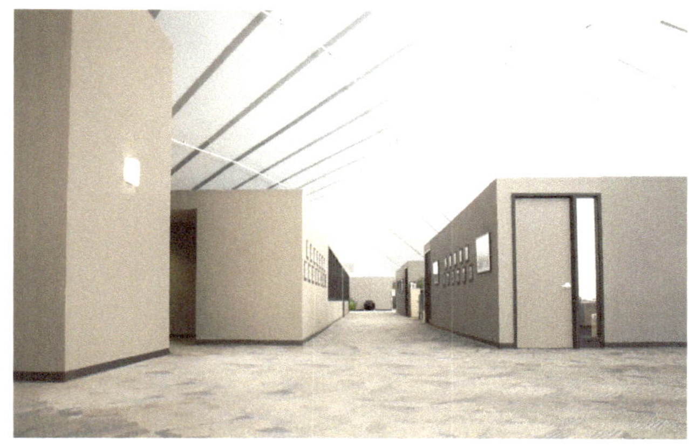

Figure 6.18 (a) The orange hue of the interior flooring, which leads to the elevator bay accented in orange, complements the blue accent color on the walls and doors of this office space, reinforces by contrast the radial pattern of the architecture, and is supported by the interior design. (b) Removal of orange reduces the strength and expression of the rhythm of the space. Harmony and subtle interest are maintained. (c) Elimination of accent colors reduces the movement in the space, visual interest, and wayfinding.

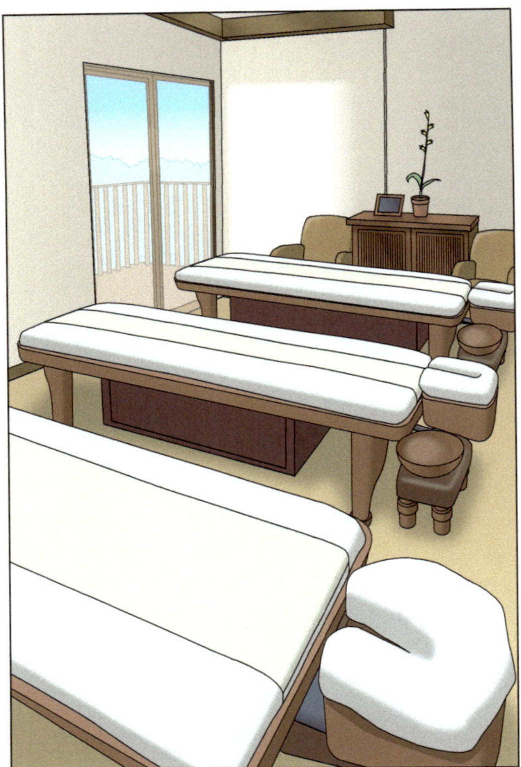
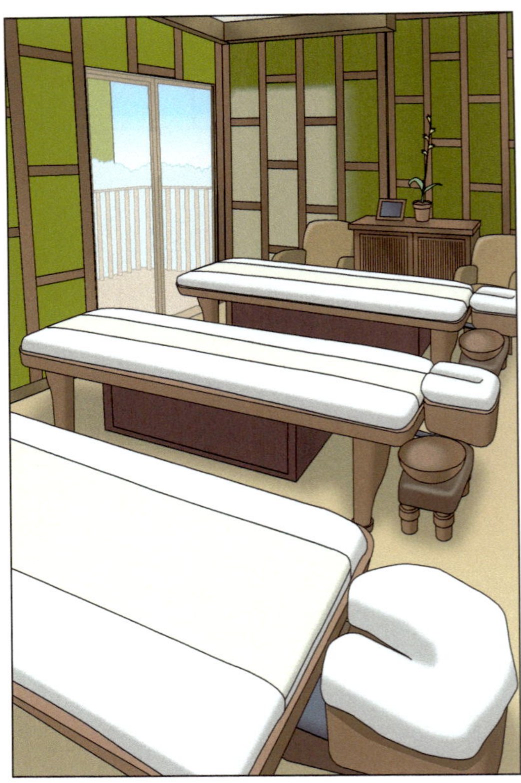

Figure 6.19
(a) Consideration of color and pattern is required if this massage room is to become a space for relaxation and meditation. (b) Using natural greens and the line reminiscent of a wooded forest creates visual interest and movement for this massage room.

which aids their ability to relax. Compare the difference between Figures 6.19a and 6.19b; utilizing the element line with subtle contrasts in earthy green hues and dark wood achieves rhythm and the desired mood for this relaxing massage room.

Final Thoughts on Rhythm and Hue

Color can also be applied to spaces to diminish design elements perceived as inhospitable. We've discussed that strong hues are associated with right angles and straight lines. Applying values of blue, green, and violet would therefore reduce and soften the rigid impression of the design. Awkward design elements, unpleasing interior compositions, and permanent interior architectural features can be minimized by limiting value contrast and avoiding colors high in saturation. This technique is valuable when designers are renovating interior spaces and must contend with certain architectural features in existing buildings or structures that cannot be changed or removed.

Combine the various shapes presented in this chapter and repeat them in any one of multiple methods discussed to create an array of patterns that can be incorporated into your design. Textiles, wall coverings, and carpets are materials that present the opportunity to incorporate various patterns into a design solution. A good rule of thumb when selecting patterns for an interior is to balance the scale with large and small patterns—a mixture of curvilinear or free-flowing designs, contrasted against more geometric designs (you may choose one type or both), that incorporates solid spaces to give the eyes a place to rest. It is your decision which patterns receive the greatest attention based on scale and color contrast. Be cautious of using too much pattern and unrelated color harmonies in your solution. This may introduce visual disorder and can easily overwhelm a space and the user experience (Figure 6.20).

When working color into a rhythmic pattern, consider that interior design, like two-dimensional art, is subjective and speculative. There are principles and elements of design theory when needed, but intuition and creativity must also be supported and valued. With the theories of color rhythm in mind, place hues at regular intervals for an orderly, calm, relaxing environment. Reduce sudden changes in the size and spacing of colored values unless the desired effect is an energetic and vibrant space.

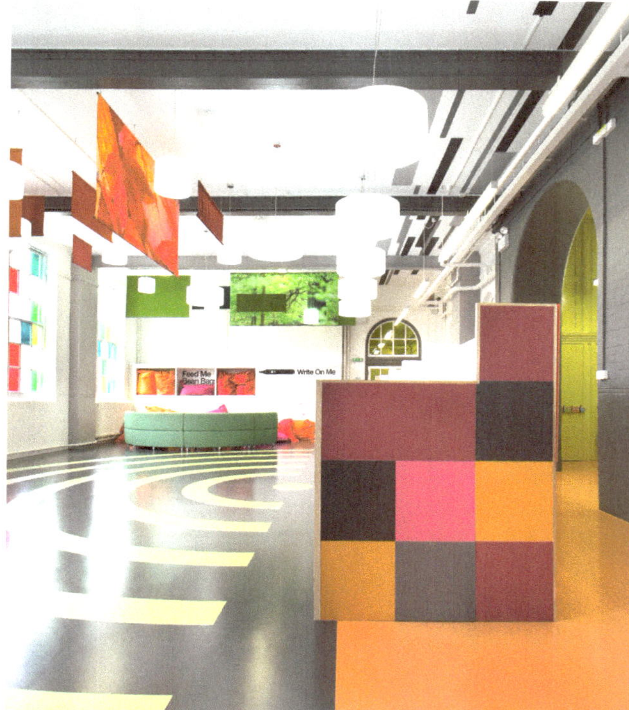

Figure 6.20 Interiors that contain many variations in patterns, shapes, color, and contrast may be disorienting and overwhelm the users experience of the space.

High-contrast colors combined with complex visual patterns and rhythms can diminish a room's apparent spatial volume. The outcome could be claustrophobic, cramped, and unwelcoming. However, a restaurant where people linger in a seated position under low lighting might benefit from high contrasts. In health-care environments, visual contrasts could add anxiety to already stressful situations that bring users to the space. In these cases, consider the length of time a person will be exposed, as this could have an undesirable impact on one's mood and successful use of the space. Here are some tips to remember when using rhythm and hue:

- Highlight important architectural and interior design elements (columns, ceilings, flooring, walls, furnishings, etc.).
- Consider the potential for positive or negative emotions using color perception, as mentioned in Chapter 3.
- Organize the design elements into a compositional whole. Unify with color and saturation.
- Group design elements together, or isolate them completely. Consider similarity in color or color contrast of these elements to support either desired outcome.

REVIEW QUESTIONS

1. Explain the design principle of rhythm.
2. Explain how contrast of color can be used to influence rhythm.
3. Provide an example of bio-inspired design.
4. How can natural forms be used to explore and express color harmony and rhythm?
5. List the five types of rhythm associated with color and explain each.
6. Describe two ways in which color can be used to express alternation.
7. Explain how line and color can be used to impart rhythm in an interior.
8. How can permanent design features that are unwanted be minimized with the use of color?

Vocabulary

Rhythm	vibrancy
bio-inspired	progression
repetition	continuation
alternation	radiation

EXERCISES

1. Using the drawing and shape tools in Microsoft Word, Adobe Illustrator, or colored papers, generate a series of rhythmic patterns using color and shape. Create one for each of the five types of rhythm discussed in the chapter: repetition, alternation, progression or sequencing, continuation or transition, and radiation.
2. Locate any designed object (building, furniture, appliance, electronic device, interior space, light fixture, etc.) whose influence was derived from the natural environment. Find a picture of this natural form and analyze how the shape and color rhythm were used in the design. How does the color support the rhythmic order and impart meaning?
3. Select four to six pictures from design publications of interior spaces that use the different types of rhythms mentioned in the chapter. Analyze what types are used, how they are used, and what effect they have on the space (volume, scale, proportion). In each example, analyze how color plays a role in amplifying or adding to the effect.

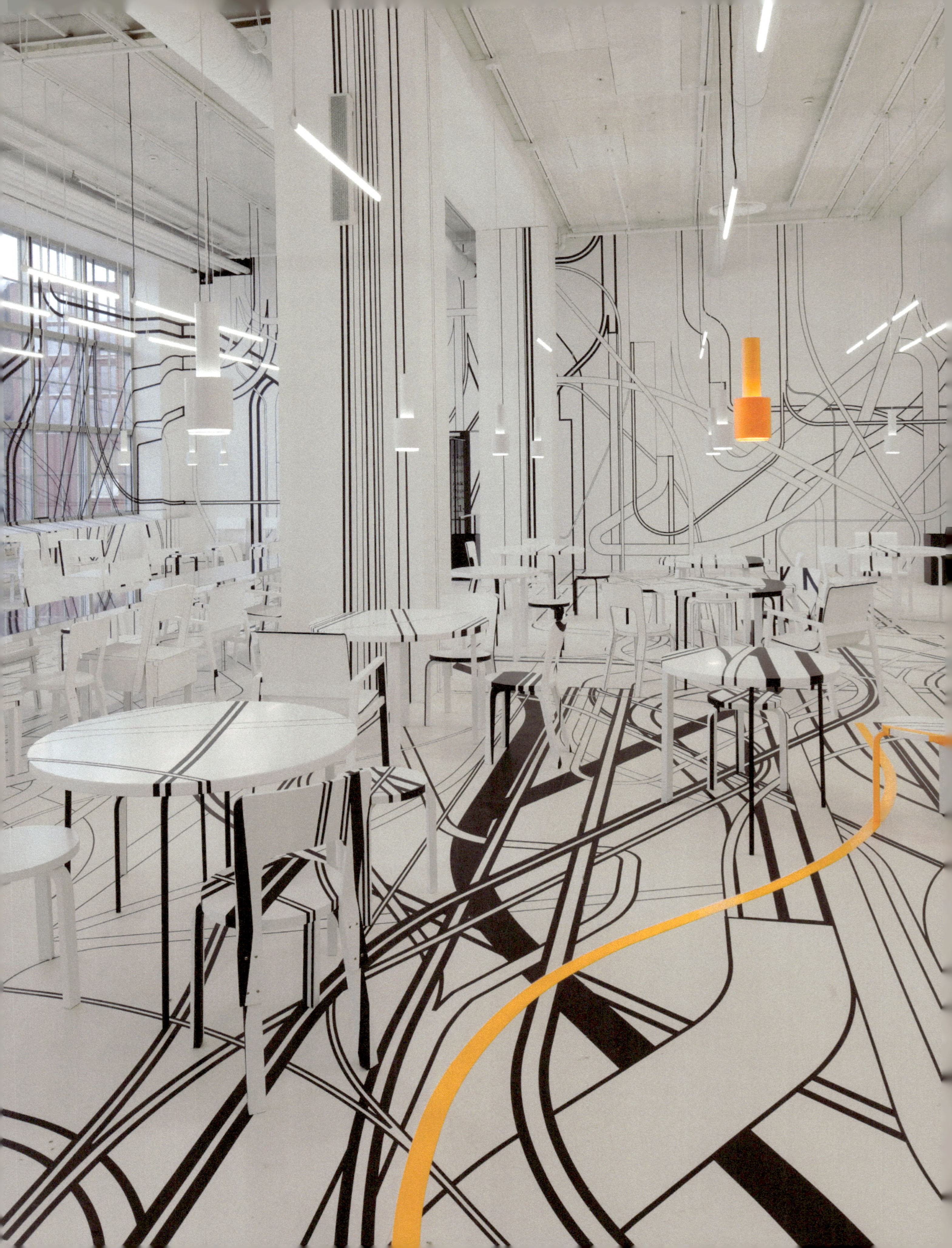

7

color + emphasis

Learning Outcomes

After studying this chapter, you will be able to:

- **Explain how color and contrast can create focal points in a space.**
- **Demonstrate how texture, pattern, value, and color can all be used to create emphasis.**
- **Provide examples of using emphasis for wayfinding, assisting those with memory loss, and adding visual stimuli.**
- **Describe how color as emphasis can attract and hold the attention of its viewer.**
- **Compare and contrast how warm and cool colors—when added to three-dimensional forms—advance certain features, adding to the perceived importance of the object being highlighted.**
- **Recognize when color that is selected and applied to a design feature and is further isolated in the space by contrast can have more visual power than the actual object that is being colored.**
- **Explain why most people see color first, then the object.**

All design principles are important; however, visual emphasis through contrast is essential in helping users find their whereabouts in space. Emphasis is like the lighthouse that guides the boat safely to shore. For the designer, **emphasis** is a tool for creating points of interest not only for aesthetic purposes but also to orient users of the space. I want to impress upon you that the principles of design are critical to functional design. Notice I did not use the overly used term "good design," because no design is either good or bad—only some designs function more efficiently than others in the context of the space they are implemented. If any design principles, elements, and combinations thereof are used less successfully, the overall design will be less impactful and ultimately not satisfy the design concept, resolve the design problem or meet our client's needs.

Enter color—color attracts attention. It is the first thing that a person registers before object recognition is processed. Applying the strength of color to a particular area of a space or design element can bring greater attention to important features within our built environment. Color informs, and emphasis guides the user's attention to deliver an intended message. For example, a hotel plan would optimally draw your attention to its reception desk first. A dark mahogany base against a light beige backdrop is inviting and also conveys comfort and luxury.

Emphasis is an important design principle that is critical to all design disciplines, including interior design, architecture, landscape architecture, mixed media art, and fashion design. Emphasis is the direct method of establishing a point of visual interest. "Emphasis is the stressing of a particular area of focus rather than the presentation of a maze of details of equal importance. When a composition has no emphasis nothing stands out . . . the effective use of emphasis calls attention to important areas" (Bernard, 2016, ¶ 1).

Careful attention should be paid to where the visual emphasis is to be directed. Given physical movement through space, a focal point can be the intended destination. The path along that route is the journey, and once the destination has been reached, what do you intend for the user to experience? With seating, emphasis may be on a fireplace, a showcased piece of artwork (sculpture, painting), or a grouping of furniture. How does the destination affect the total design? Are we redirected away from other critical visual information? How does the focal point support the overall design concept? These are a few important questions to ask when deciding what element in our interior to feature. The task of the designer when using the principle of emphasis is to analyze the interior space to determine what hierarchy of importance the content has. Once this is determined, concepts can be generated that carry out these intended functions and goals. It is too easy for an eager, young designer to select and apply visual importance to too many design features. Use a bit of restraint and limit overemphasizing—no one element should demand 100 percent of the user's attention, or the remaining elements of your design are lost and serve no real purpose. "If you try to emphasize everything, you effectively emphasize nothing" (McNeil, 2007, ¶ 1).

Unlike artwork, which is primarily a static form of visual experience where the work is revealed to us all at once, interiors are experienced on multiple layers and levels. We move through our environments experiencing elements simultaneously. Emphasis, in tandem with rhythm, creates implied movement. The perception of movement is achieved through contrast of value, color, light, material and texture to guide the eye, and person, in a particular direction. In multilevel spaces, our experience is different on each level, as well as in places for repose where one might look over a cantilevered ledge to the people below; in this instance, the bird's-eye view gives the user a sense of spaciousness, ascendency, freedom of choice, and spectatorship. Because of this multisensory experience of space, emphasis has the potential to change and morph. Unlike an object on a wall, we can move around above or below an element. The point to be made is that when using emphasis, consider it from the multiple perspectives the user might possibly be able to see. Each vantage point will create different opportunities for interactive experience. "The aesthetic intent is to uplift the awareness of the viewer" (Zelanski & Fisher, 1995, p. 73).

Emphasis with Contrast

One of the key principles of color use for design is **contrast**. Wong (1997, p. 14) defines contrast as the "visual (characteristics of shape and color), dimensional, or quantitative differences that distinguish one shape, part of a shape, or group of shapes from another shape, another part of the same shape, or another group of shapes." The composition in Figure 7.1a illustrates no real visual distinctions other than different shapes. In this example, no unique shape or color is emphasized. If we alter one shape by adding a color (Figure 7.1b), the hierarchy is established and the rectangle now has visual dominance within the composition.

Contrast can be used to draw attention to the most important elements in the interior environment and can add variety to the overall design. Depending on clients' needs, the scale of the project, or the design type, the interior designer may choose to draw attention to certain elements through the deliberate control of contrast. When used, it features a particular design element as the dominant or focal point. There are a variety of methods for creating visual emphasis through contrast, including isolation, placement, and dominance or focal point.

Artist Shirl Brainard (2003, p. 119) identifies several types of contrast that are applicable to the interior environment:

- Contrast of position or location in relation to other design features (asymmetrically placed).
- Contrast of size to other design features (large/small).
- Contrast of value (light/dark).
- Contrast of color (*hue*: red vs. green; *saturation*: bright vs. dull).
- Contrast of shape and form (a circular form amidst a grouping of rectilinear forms).
- Contrast of textures (soft to hard, smooth to rough, texture to texture).
- Contrast of anomaly, defined as a "deviation from the norm" (Brainard, 2003, p. 119). An example of this technique could be an antique chair positioned within a modern space, where styles contrast, but the single chair draws attention as different from the "norm."

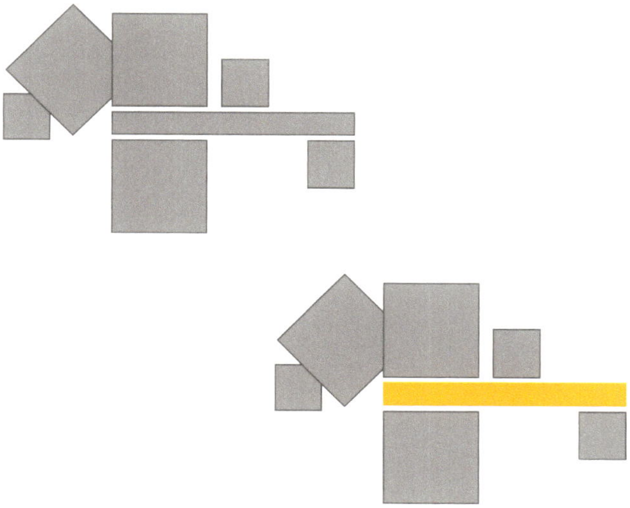

Figure 7.1 (a) Composition with no emphasis. (b) Composition with visual dominance through color assigned to one shape.

Emphasis can be generated with any one of these techniques, and several can be combined to create a more visually interesting point of dominance in your projects. If everything is of equal emphasis, there is no contrast. Early studies conducted on color and aesthetics indicate that "individual choices differed most with respect to hue and that pairs showing strong contrasts were preferred" (Ball, 1965, p. 442).

Color Emphasis through Location and Isolation

By alienating a particular design element from its surroundings, we can increase its visibility and importance. In Figure 7.2, the gradation of yellow on the lower levels changing to green at the upper levels provides a provocative focal point of color contrasting against the vertical aluminum slats of the building's façade. In terms of visual emphasis based on the individual spectral hues, orange has been graded as the color with most visibility, followed by yellow, green, red, and blue (Ball, 1965, p. 445). Depending on the spatial characteristics (large or small volume, abundant or limited light, other hues and materials and their level of lightness or darkness, and proportions), the relative brightness of the individual hues in full saturation will vary in degree of emphasis.

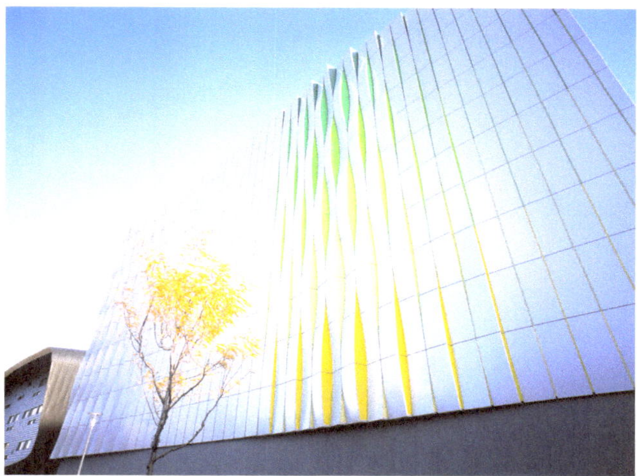

Figure 7.2 Color used strategically to emphasize the vertical shapes of the Research Laboratory at Groningen University, Holland.

This applies more when making color decisions for existing interior conditions and you do not have the flexibility to make changes to the space. On the other hand, consider the apparent shifts in color intensity relative to the features and elements you are designing and the color planned for this particular design feature. In Figure 7.3, the light washing the lobby of this hotel diffuses the intensity of the bold color. The gold scroll pattern in the flooring is intensified in brightness when surrounded by a darker field of color. The metallic finishes used throughout the space take on different intensities as both natural and artificial lighting reflects from their surfaces. In this space, pattern scale, spatial volume, and contrast of color value in the carpet pattern and ceiling details generate the main focal point, which leads the guests towards the reception desk in the background.

Isolating color is an additional way to apply the concept of emphasis. Rather than using a colored material or media to accentuate a particular design feature, you can use colored light from incandescent bulbs, fluorescent tubes, halogens, and floodlights, to name a few, or apply colored gels to the rim of a light fixture to filter a specific color. Using light to lightly wash or graze a wall surface can add a dominant feature at low cost and allow the space to change at the owner's will. In Figure 7.4a, the nighttime interior of this luxury, modern bar and lounge

Figure 7.3 The reception and waiting area at the Burj Al Arab hotel.

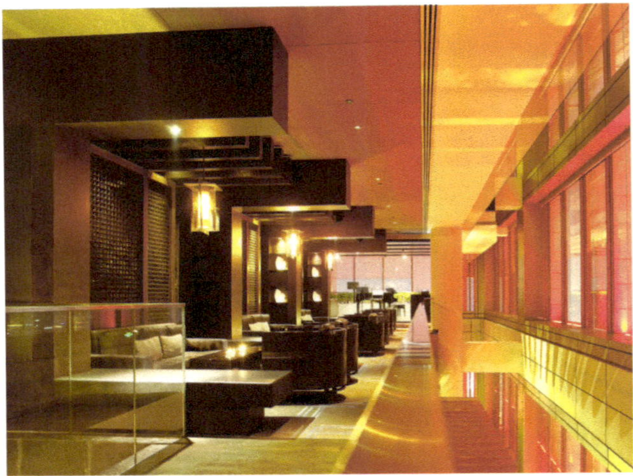

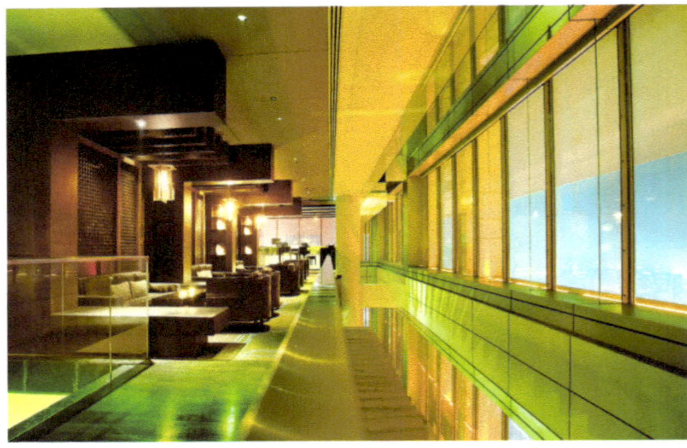

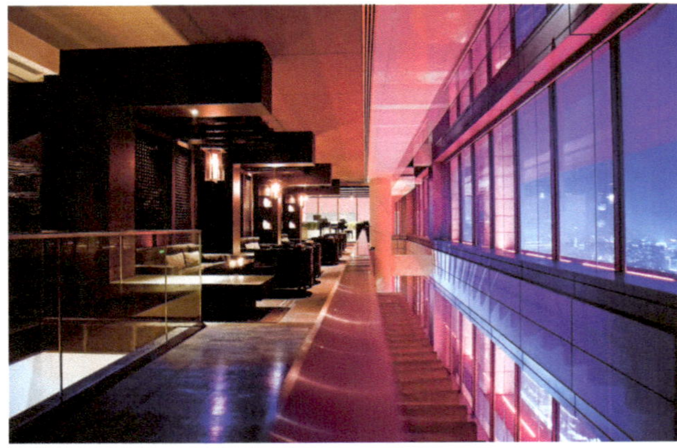

Figure 7.4 Luxury bar and lounge. Nighttime interior with (a) Red-orange light setting; (b) Green and yellow light setting; and (c) Red and blue violet light setting.

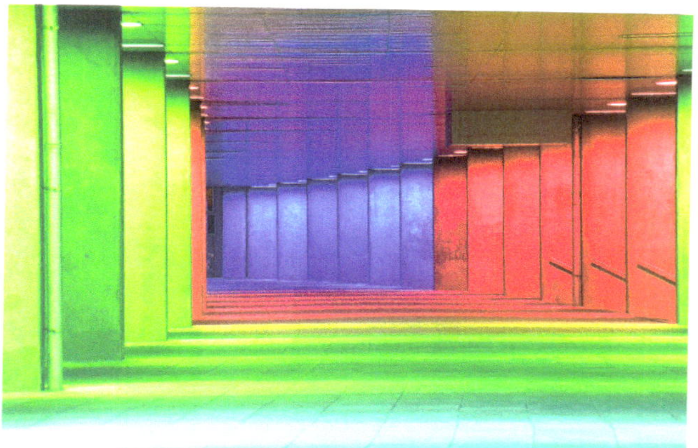

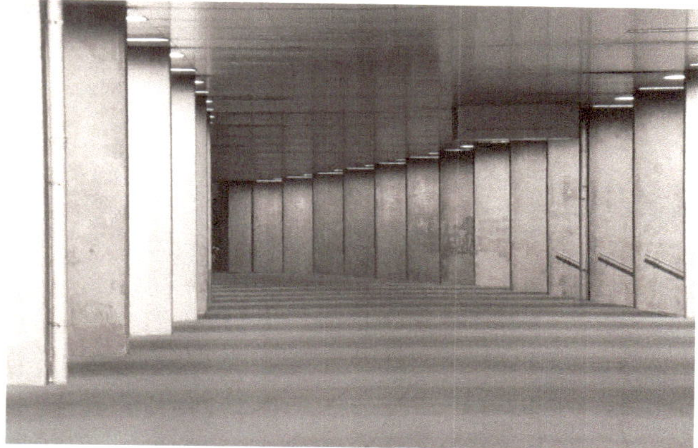

Figure 7.5 (a) Colored light used to draw viewers into as well as accent the space, which is limited in color or texture contrast. (b) In this example, we've removed the colored light to illustrate how the illumination created a much-needed ambiance, visual interest, and sense of direction in the space.

uses colored light to emphasize the architectural features and drive the intimate mood of the space. The light is set against an interior layout with low contrasting materials in an achromatic palette to provide a simple background as the subdominant feature, so the colored light remains the focal point. Additional emphasis is given with a lighting system that slowly changes color to create different experiences from energetic to calming (Figure 7.4b and c). The changing spectrum of light also alters the visual perception of the space, with each color rendition creating a unique experience. Figure 7.5a is another example where the progression of different-colored lights adds direction (rhythm) by drawing the visitor inward. The darker blue compared to the other hues pulls the viewer's attention toward the back of this space. The advancing red hue and light value of green contrast with the darker blue value. If this space lacked a color assignment, the emphasis and visual importance would be removed (Figure 7.5b).

Contrast of Hue and Value

For contrast of hue, select colors that are opposite one another on the color wheel. Using color at full intensity is a very striking method for forming interesting focal points. The colors of lower intensities are more subtle and are enjoyed for secondary elements or general room use. As colors become less intense and lighter, the contrast factor diminishes and contrast for dominance is more difficult to attain. Refer back to Figure 3.9c in Chapter 3 to refresh lessons on contrast levels

In Figure 7.6a, the conference space is dark and drab and lacks the necessary energy and stimulation required for brainstorming, conferencing, and corporate conversations to take place. Additionally, the space lacks "image" or an identifiable feature that a client might relate to the firm. The floor space is broken by the border; the horizontal bars require extension to the room's corners, as well as a higher level of contrast for stimulation. The introduction of a vibrant red-orange draws attention and emphasis to the video conferencing wall, while the surrounding gray slightly neutralizes the hue's effect to provide the eye with areas of rest. The conference table and credenza have been replaced with a cool gray to blend with interior surfaces (Figure 7.6b).

In Figure 7.7, the interior colonnades, in a series of highly saturated spectrum colors, contrast with each other as well as with the opposite window wall. The blue ceiling provides the needed unity; otherwise, the colored columns would be overwhelming and lack connection to the interior space. In this example, the scale allows for the saturated colors. A space on a smaller scale would be consumed by this application of intense color.

Value contrast is probably the easiest of the contrast types. A light/dark contrast of black, gray, or white values can emphasize without the use of chromatic (colored) hues. The residential staircase in Figure 7.8a is an example of value contrasts. The warm, dark, wood finish of the stair treads contrasts against the white walls, cabinetry, and furniture, adding to the visual importance of the design feature. If we were to remove the contrast, the stair no longer would have any added value or importance (Figure 7.8b).

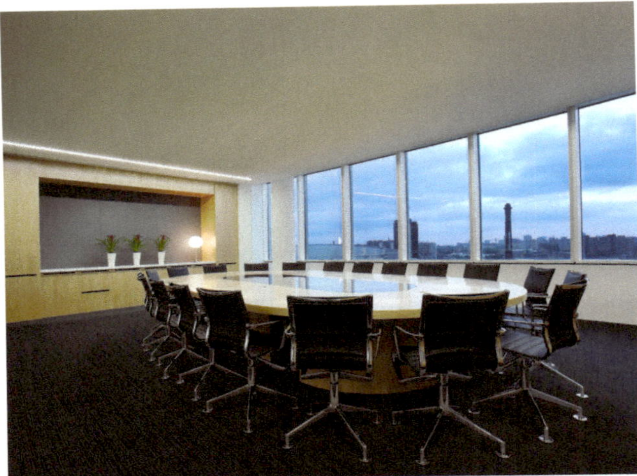

Figure 7.6a Color, materials and style are key elements for branding and marketing a business image. This conference room is absent of architectural detail and interest for potential clients to make an association and connection with the firm through the design of the space. Attracting the staff or client's attention to a particular eye-catching area or feature helps to show what is important in your design.

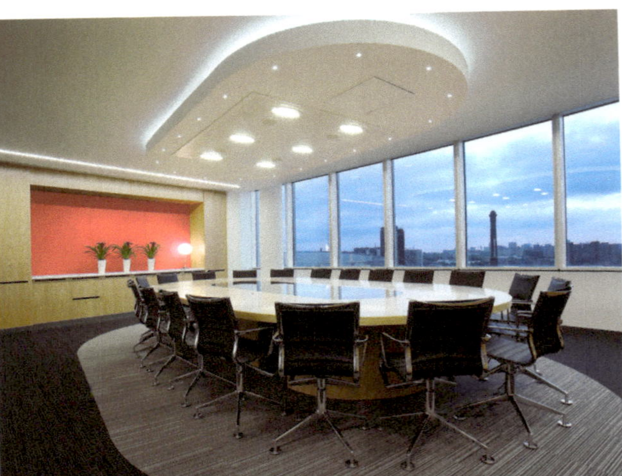

Figure 7.6b The placement of an accent color in the built-in storage wall, contrast in values, and repeating oval forms draws a clear focal point emphasizing the conference furniture within the space. The remaining neutral finishes and furnishings provides necessary balance of the materials and color finishes.

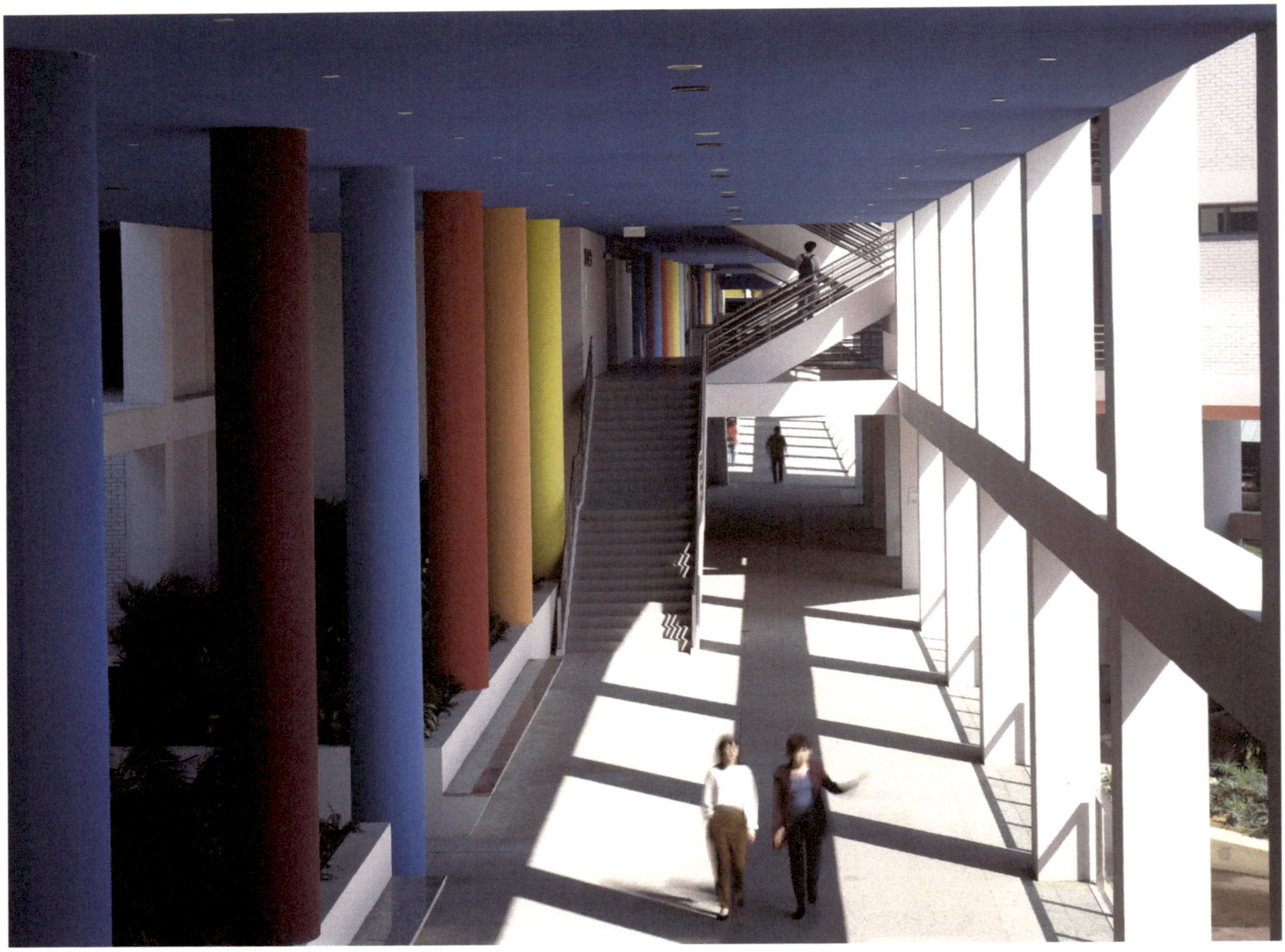

Figure 7.7 Temasek Polytechnic, Singapore, 1991–1995. Architect: James Stirling, Michael Wilford and Associates.

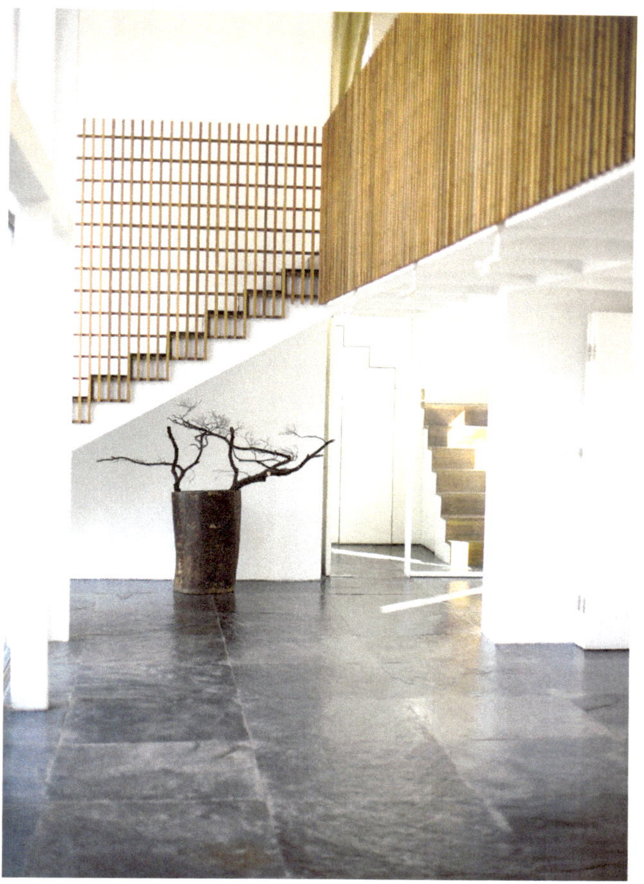

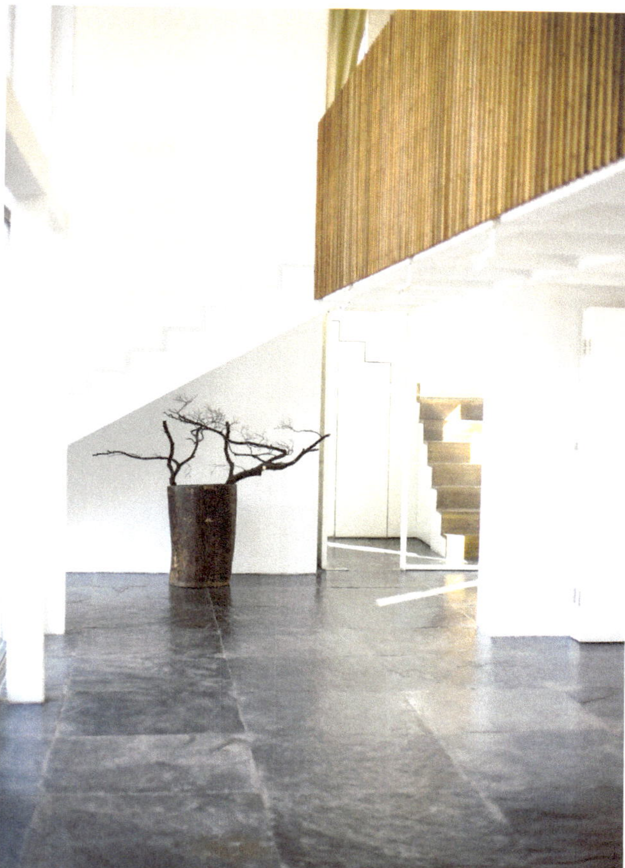

Figure 7.8 (a) Residential corridor using material for color and design contrast to emphasize the stairway. (b) Removal of the color contrast eliminates the stair as a focal point.

Contrast of Design Feature (Shape and Form)

Graphically, emphasis can be established as hierarchy of information when the information is presented in alternative styles. When *reading* a line of *text*, there are several ways emphasis can be given to a word for added importance, including color. This added e m p h a s i s informs the reader that one phrase should be attended to more than another. Too much emphasis and individual elements fight for dominance. In this example, we contrasted various text styles with roman type. In Figure 7.9, the jagged recess in this interior wall is the focal point against a neutral palette that is also using line to direct and lead a person to the staircase in the background, through contrasts of both design feature (shape and form) and color.

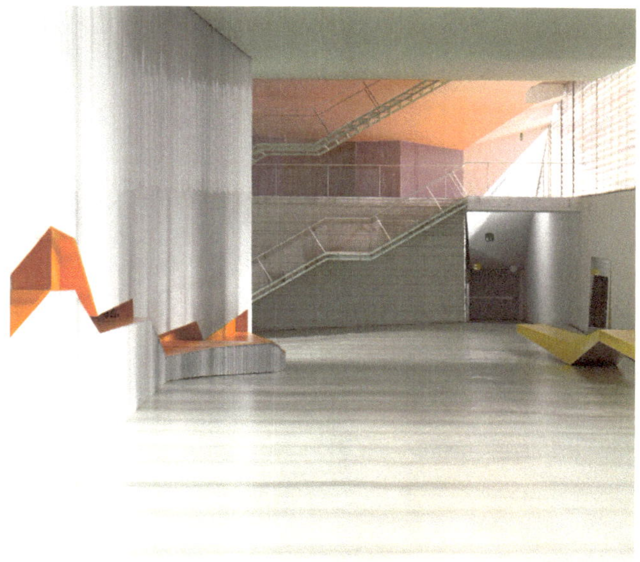

Figure 7.9 Interior view from hallway to a plexiglass staircase, El Batel Conference Centre, Selgascano Architects, Cartagena, Spain, 2011. Notice how the colored plastic membranes creating the windows towards the back filter the natural daylight pouring from the right into the interior and bathes the surrounding neutral wall and ceiling surfaces with reflected color as we discussed in Chapter 2.

Contrast of Texture

Using color and texture contrasts (smooth vs. rough) can add emphasis. The London, England, Serpentine Pavilion

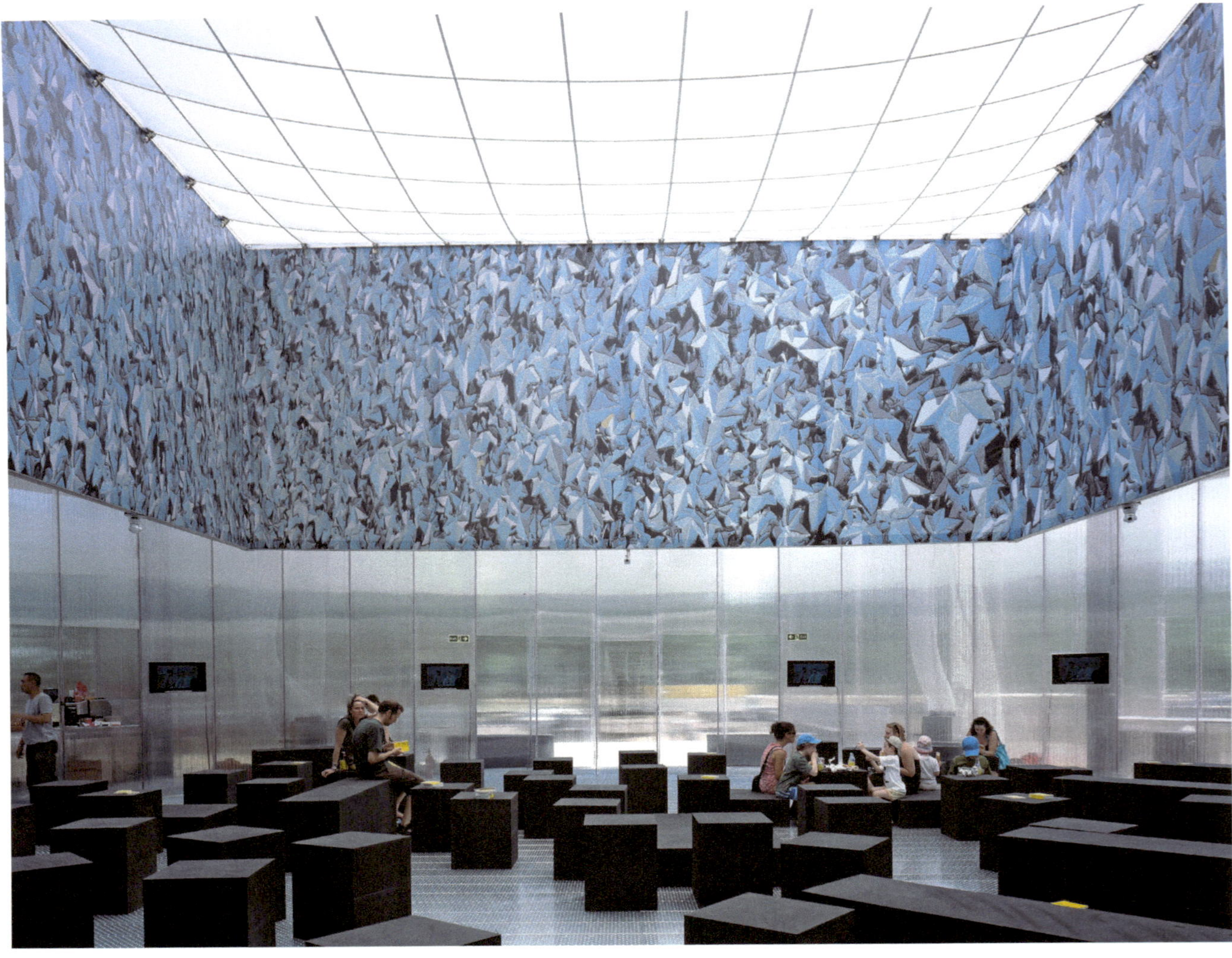

Figure 7.10 Serpentine Pavilion, 2006, London. An inflatable balloon-like cloud canopy illuminates like the sky above the foam block café seating of the pavilion. The ivy panels surrounding the café were a collaborative project between German artist Thomas Demand and Dutch architect Rem Koolhaas. Demand constructed ivy from colored paper and cardboard, which was later photographed and installed as wallpaper art.

(2006) by Dutch architect Rem Koolhaas in Figure 7.10 is a perfect example of mixing color and texture to create a dramatic effect. The textured blue contrasts nicely against an achromatic interior with smooth, slick surfaces.

Emphasis with Color Dominance (Focal Point)

A **focal point** is a *single* design element that receives the greatest visual emphasis in a room. We use focal points to give the eyes a place for rest or contemplation. In terms of wayfinding, visitors to a space will usually be attracted to and walk toward the focal point, which may be an art object, piece of furniture, or functional module such as a reception center. Unlike emphasis, which can have one or multiple elements contrasting, focal points stand out from the crowd. Just as symmetrical balance draws your eyes to the center of a composition or room layout, so does color used with emphasis draw your attention to the color first and the object second.

Focal points can be achieved by using isolation (placement), by highlighting with contrast of shape, size, or color (which differentiates the element from its surroundings), or by implementing directional movement that leads the eye toward the element to be emphasized. This is accomplished using the rhythmic properties discussed in Chapter 6 (progression, repetition) or other combinations of the above to create a focal point.

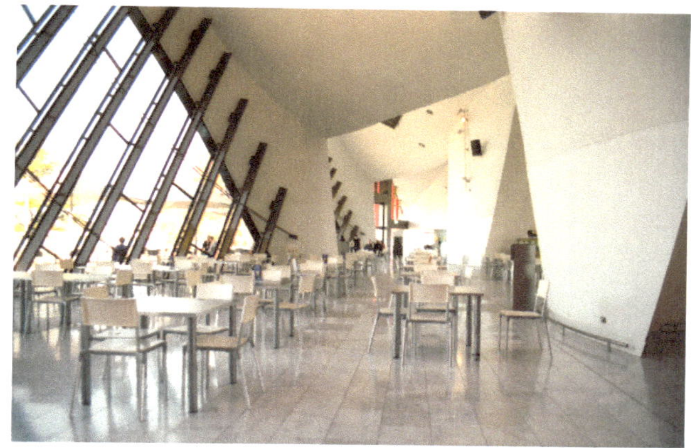
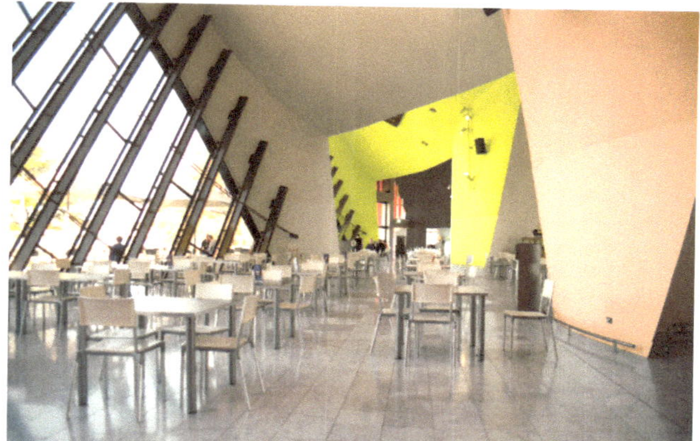

Figure 7.11 (a) International airport concourse with low contrast and color assigned to highlight specific interior architectural surfaces of this amorphous interior. (b) Application of color highlights interior selected surfaces creating contrast and visual interest that draws attention upward through the spatial volume and towards the exit in the background.

Compare the difference between the two color approaches to the interior of an international airport. The original illustration (Figure 7.11a) is an example of deconstructed geometry and sculptural design. The large mass of windows, broken by structural I-beams, frames the view from the interior concourse. Here the view as focal point and an interior in neutral grays yearn for color to highlight specific forms. In Figure 7.11b, a split complementary color plan placed in the foreground, middle ground, and background provides directional movement and focus through the concourse to the space beyond. The violet contrasted with the yellow-orange provides additional emphasis and draws attention to the space beyond. A slight increase in value assigned to the I-beams increases their distinction in the space, and the new hues result in a more comfortable scale and highlighting of specific interior forms.

Dominant color in a color solution can accent the appearance of an item that previously received little visual attention, create visual enhancement in an architectural feature, or add a contrast of visual weight to something of importance (memorabilia, collectibles).

Rengel (2007), when he discusses emphasis, draws a dichotomy between dominance and distinctiveness. Dominance, as he defines it, can be realized by "size, intensity, or interest" (p. 187). Distinctiveness occurs when a focal object or area is noticeably different from its surroundings. In Figure 7.12, the spiral staircase form and textured stone wall in the background are equally balanced. Each form is distinctive from its

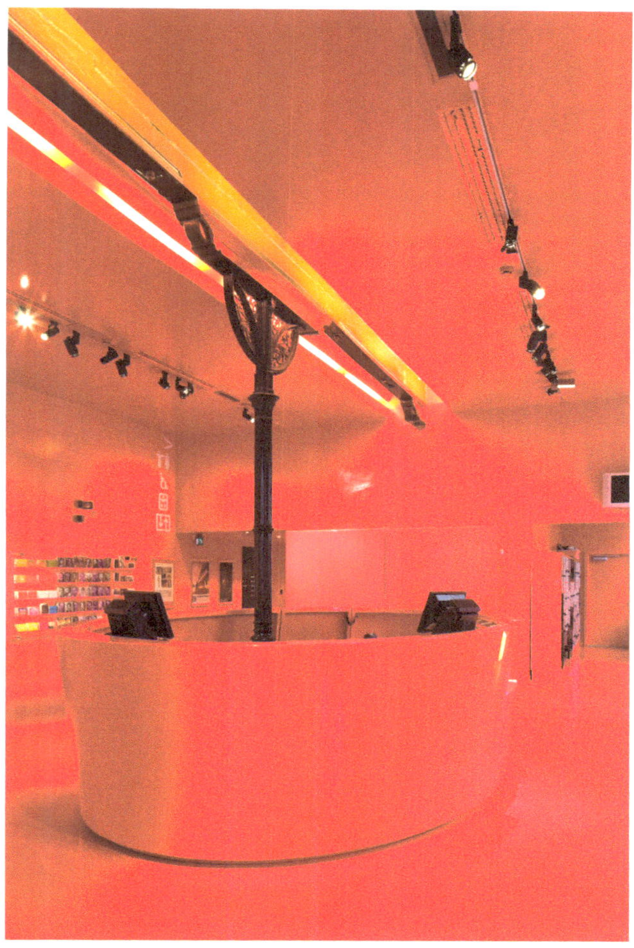

Figure 7.12 The spiral stair is highlighted by contrast of line, form and smooth texture against the darker wall to the right. The scale and mass of the stair is further balanced with the darker, textured stone wall finish. Asprey Courtyard, London. Architecture firm: Foster Partners.

surroundings—the stair with its free-flowing form and the feature wall with a heavy texture; both design features use neutral hues visually highlighted by light and dark contrast of materials.

Contrast of Anomaly

An **anomaly** is an irregular deviation or departure from what one considers to be normal. In interior design, this takes the form of contrasting distinct styles where one becomes the focal point. Figure 7.13 shows a historical space with Corinthian columns, an intricate flooring pattern, iron stair railings, and marble finishes that contribute to the traditional interior architecture. These elements heavily contrast against the sleek, contemporary circular cocktail bar and lounge of the renovated hotel's entry. The modern reception area design contradicts the traditionally styled interior, even though it is set against a similar white and black background—it refuses to blend, and thus becomes a focal point for this hotel lobby.

Color Contrast for Safety and Welfare

Viewers prefer contrast. Viewers need variety and interest among colors in their immediate surroundings. A complete lack of contrast can lead to lack of stimulation or direction, boredom, and difficulty processing visual cues in spaces where activity and alertness are important. These might include workplaces, classrooms, operating rooms, and areas where detailed work on machinery is being performed. Most interior designs require a certain amount of contrast to assist with differentiation between spatial planes and elements. Too much similarity of the components in any design becomes disorienting and limits the functionality of the space.

Especially in larger complex commercial spaces, visual signals are necessary for orientation and recognition of one's location within the interior. "Visual aids that use colors help us quickly and easily orient ourselves in buildings and spaces" (Meerwein, Rodeck, & Mahnke, 2007, p. 71). Color can become a visual map

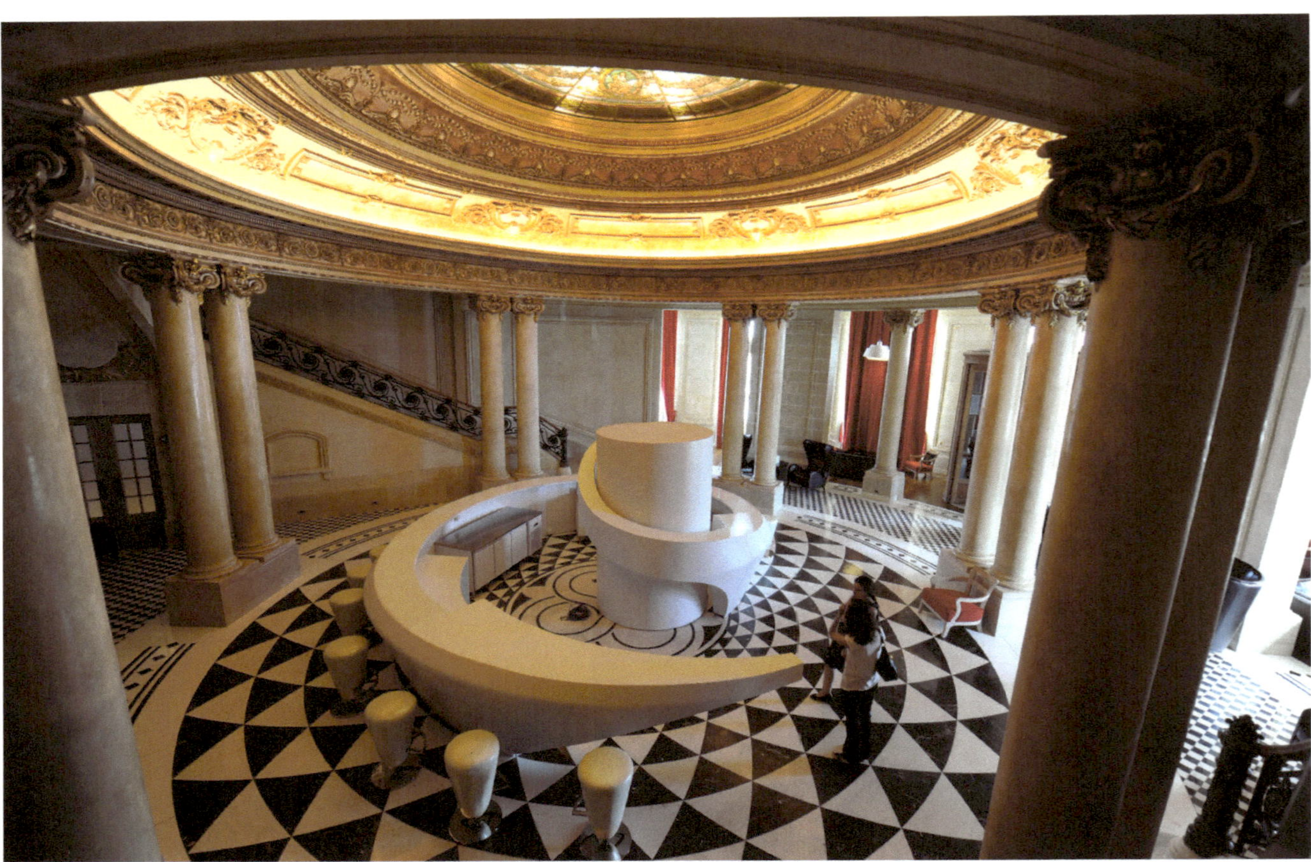

Figure 7.13 A view of the historical, ornate lobby within the newly renovated, and contemporary bar counter with white leather stools centered within the 1921 Restaurant rotunda at Sofitel Montevideo Casino Carrasco and Spa in Montevideo, Uruguay, 2013.

that allows you to recall specific places you have been based on color. Imagine your average American parking garage leading to your average American mega mall. Often patrons are encouraged to memorize their color-coded location, making it easier to return to. This type of design tool can be beneficial to the public at large, as well as to clients with special needs. In the case of patients with Alzheimer's disease, color recognition is a way to offset memory loss and provide a method of recall. A color-coded chest of drawers could help a patient know where to find articles of clothing in a series of drawers that might otherwise be difficult to distinguish in a standard wood-stained cabinet. The furniture piece takes on two functions—a colorful design feature and a functional tool for patients with memory loss.

Color can be used to emphasize the space type. The coloration indicates not only its function but its identity; what one is likely to encounter; and in association, assumptions are made in "revealing the type of people who are and will be visiting this place" (Smith, 2008, p. 317).

The corridors in the Evelina Children's Hospital in London use colors themed to the natural world. The colors and shapes help entertain and distract attention from the fact that this is a hospital for children (Figure 7.14). The playfulness of the colors arranged in the familiar shapes of insects might relax patients and families and add cheer. Each floor is themed, the beach and sea at the bottom levels moving to the sky at the top floor. The color coding provides wayfinding cues to access the interior easily.

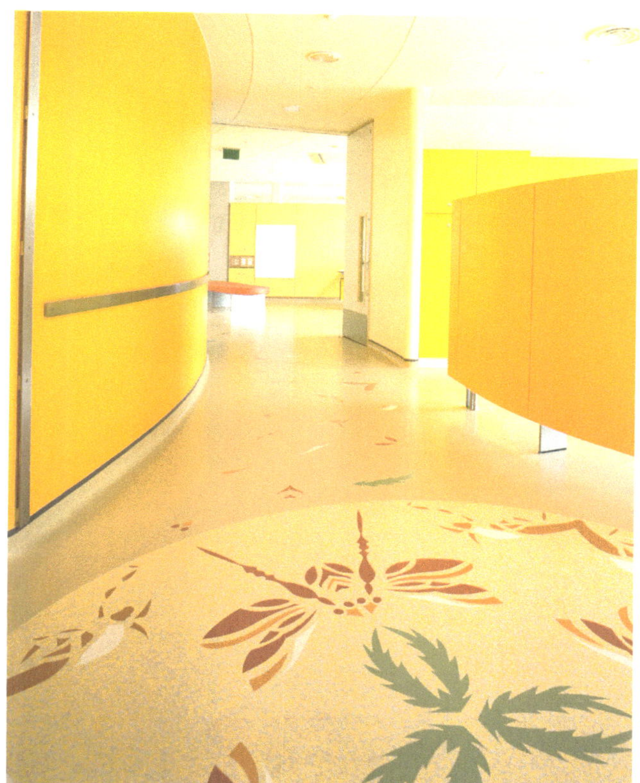

Figure 7.14 A cheerful, colorful, and fun place for care at the Evelina Children's Hospital, London, United Kingdom, Hopkins Architects, 2005, with abstract painting on the floor.

Design Tips

Trying to select what design feature or object to emphasize or make into a focal point in a project can pose a challenge. This is a good conversation to have with your client; the choice of emphasis can be based on a personal object or item the client has a historical connection with. In this case, the interior space should be worked around this object. If you are working on a project from the ground up, the cost of certain elements might dictate what items receive attention. An original Piet Mondrian wouldn't be placed in a location where you're sitting or standing facing away from the painting. In residential design, one of the common issues facing many homeowners is the fight between the flat-screen television and the fireplace. Luckily, advances in entertainment technology have resolved this design dilemma—now, several hidden, recessed, or projected options for television mean a client won't have to compromise space for enjoyment of art objects or furniture. Here are some tips to guide you:

- Use the accent color sparingly; otherwise, it is no longer an accent and might be confused with the dominant color. Cluttered or overly saturated color detracts from meaning.
- Establish a recognizable amount of value or hue contrast for the design feature to generate attention.
- Keep in mind that a contrast of value will receive greater attention than contrast of different hues or saturation. Use the type of contrast that works for your individual project needs; this will vary from project to project. Emphasis can be subtle or extreme.
- Use a warm hue versus cool to increase the dominant effect. Remember, warm hues generally advance; therefore, receding cool colors would have a lesser impact visually.

- Use light to accentuate your dominant feature. Lighting coupled with color can enhance the drama of the focal point with reflection and shadow.
- In some instances, you may wish to downplay a particular design element or change the perception or character of a space. There will be situations where preexisting interior walls, structures, ceiling elements, or mechanicals are not removable and the visual attention they demand becomes a distraction. In other instances, the space may not allow renovation or demolition. In this case, the use of **color-masking** techniques can lend unity to disorganization or visual distraction from the true nature of the space. Color masking involves deceiving the eye using an existing design element with careful placement of color, value, or patterns, which blend interior architectural features into its surroundings (Figure 7.15). A common application involves painting return air vents in the ceiling or walls the same color as their adjacent surroundings to hide and blend them. Interior surfaces covered in a single hue can support masking an undesirable element by blending and reducing emphasis given to a particular design feature. Conversely, using a focal point with additional color or pattern to draw your attention away from the features may be successful. As you study color, observe the many places where designers have used camouflage techniques to mask necessary objects that are not meant to be focal points. Keep in mind that residential clients will have different concerns about cosmetics than commercial clients, and solutions should be tailored to the environment and programmed use of the space.

When working to create emphasis in your design work, the goal is to catch and hold the viewers' attention. Emphasis can be used to accent and isolate an object and, in turn, increase the perceived importance of that design element in the space. Color should be planned from the outset of the design process—and not be an afterthought. When color is considered for emphasis during planning, it is important to understand the various contrast methods that may enhance the emotion, meaning, expression, or psychological impact of the design (Stewart, 2008). A designer must carefully consider all potential symbolism and meanings that users might interpret as they interact with the spaces they inhabit.

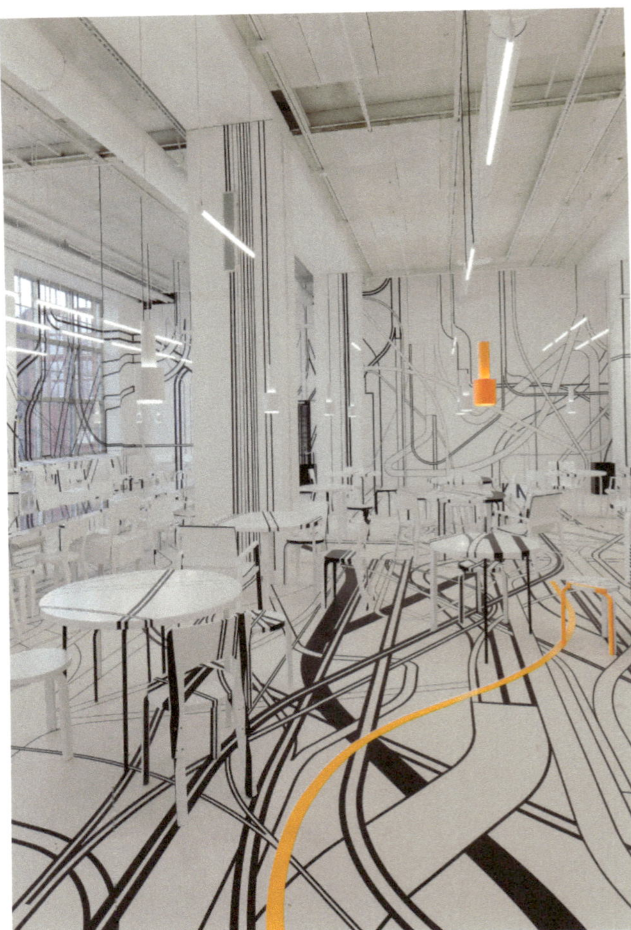

Figure 7.15 Logomo Café in Turku, Finland, a collaboration between German art st Tobias Rehberger and Finnish furniture manufacturer Artek. In this example of color masking, camouflage and optical illusion, an ndustrial space has been transformed with pattern, bold contrast, and color. The use of varying widths of black and white lines attempts to blur the distinction between the existing structural columns and the exposed ceiling. Attention is placed on the floor and furniture relationship, with deliberate placement of the design mirrored on the floor. Glass and mirrored surfaces are used to help carry the design throughout the space. The solitary use of orange color provides the eye momentary relief.

REVIEW QUESTIONS

1. Explain the design principle emphasis.
2. Explain the use of color contrast to achieve emphasis.
3. List and explain the seven types of contrast that are applicable to the interior environment.
4. Explain the concept of color emphasis through location and isolation.

5. Describe contrast of design feature and texture.
6. What is a focal point, and how can this be achieved with color?
7. Explain the concept of contrast by anomaly.
8. How might color be used in an interior to promote safety and welfare for the users of the space?
9. Describe color masking and two techniques for achieving this in an interior.

Vocabulary

Emphasis
contrast
focal point
anomaly
color masking

EXERCISES

1. Locate several magazine photos of interior spaces or architectural exteriors. Describe how dominance and color contrast are used to highlight points of interest in an interior space. Select from several different design types to compare and contrast the strategies that have been used and how they relate to their intended functions.
2. Locate three examples of focal points using color as the main driver for emphasis. Select from across several design disciplines (art, communication design, interior design, architecture).
3. Generate a three-dimensional model of an interior (four walls, a ceiling, and a floor) using foamboard, chipboard, cardboard, or other forms of sturdy artist board, approximately 12 by 10 by 14 inches. Next, create a series of forms (spheres, cubes, cones, organic shapes) out of card stock, museum board, and so on. Using the methods described in this chapter, generate a few spatial studies examining how color emphasis can be applied and manipulated in your model. Use colored media (Color-aid, artist papers, or other colored material) to generate your experiments. Try at least two or three variations. Compare and contrast what works well and what does not work well. Photograph your models.
4. At your school, work, local shopping venue, or community hospital, document ways in which color is used as a communication device to visually inform, direct, and provide orientation and spatial recognition within your surroundings. Pay attention to color patterning on walls, floors, and ceilings, signage, color in art as a communication tool, design features that are emphasized, or color blocking (color-keyed to areas for recognition, such as the *blue room*). How might you use these same strategies in your own work?

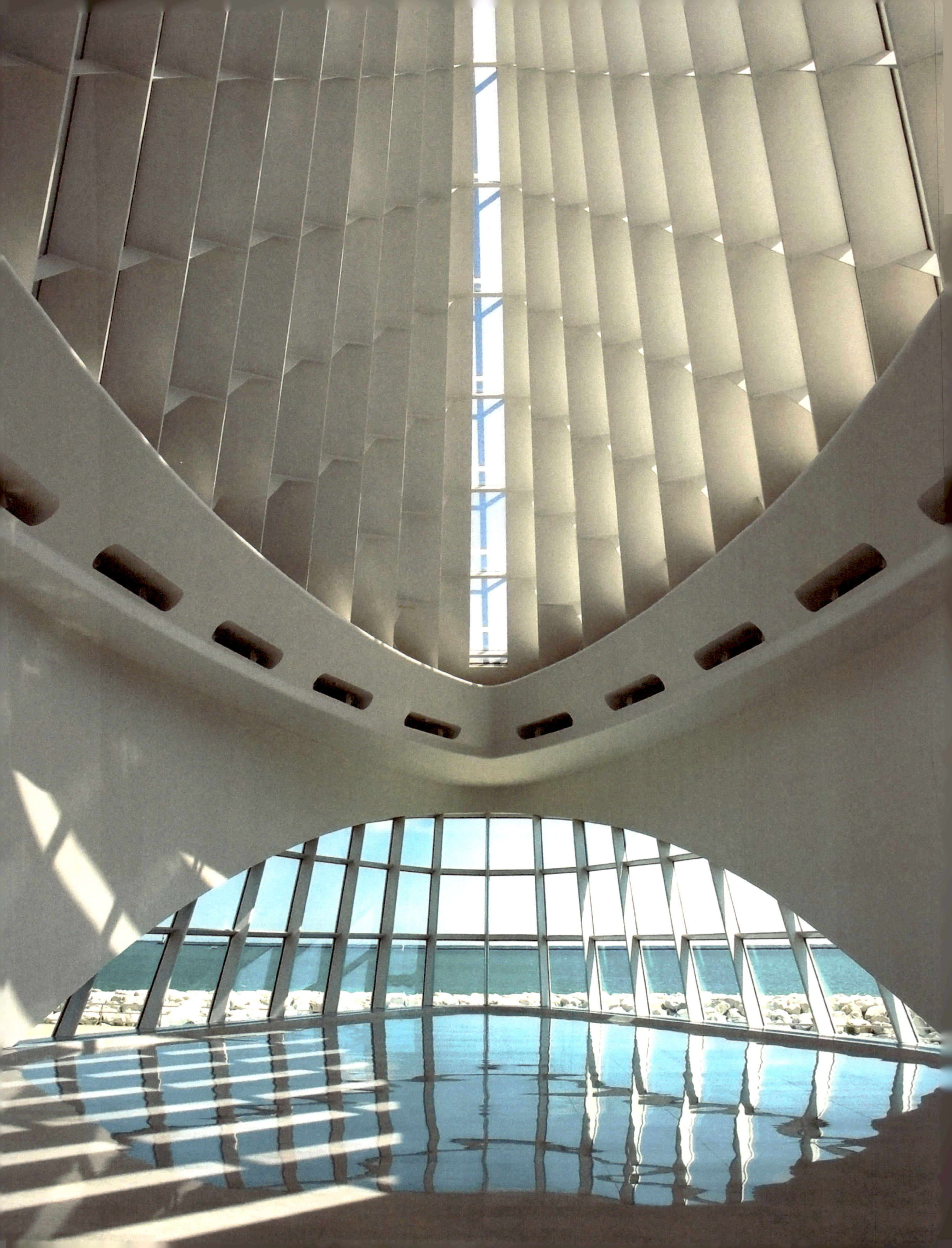

8

color + proportion + scale

Learning Outcomes

After studying this chapter, you will be able to:

- **Establish how proportions of color should be considered in the context of the scale of the space and amount of lighting available.**
- **Compare grid systems based on the golden section, Fibonacci Sequence, Le Modular, or natural forms and explain how each can provide a more accurate method for establishing relative color proportions in the initial planning stages of your design projects.**
- **Give examples of using scale and proportion to enhance and alter the visual perception of our environment.**
- **Explain the difference between scale and proportion.**
- **Recognize examples of natural color forms to establish relative proportions for interior projects.**
- **Demonstrate shape grammar with three-dimensional studies for exploring the color proportions in the built environment.**

Any subjective review of design considers proportion as one of the key elements that we use to seek order in the things around us. The beauty we see in the natural world grows from the divine proportions that help to make sense of everything, a correctness or fitting of parts into a composition pleasing to the eye. **Proportion** is defined as the size relationships between elements (parts) and the visual composition or space (whole). Proportion and scale are much the same, are often confused with one another, and inevitably are used interchangeably. Although they are not exactly synonymous, we cannot discuss one without the other. Proportion and scale are related in that you are using a hierarchy of color information where these proportions are given to each color to create the accent color, followed by subdominant, and finally dominant color, or the color that appears within two-thirds of the space volume. Many times the two terms—proportion and scale—are combined when a designer is describing the relationships between one part of a design and another. **Scale** refers to the size of a shape in relation to a given known—in most cases, the human body and its position within space. Because we use our bodies to make comparisons between various elements and physical activities, our world has been proportioned to accommodate the size and shape of our bodies. Figure 8.1 illustrates the need for human-to-object relationships in your design planning to establish the relative scale of the surroundings. If the human figure were removed, the scale of the interior would be in question, making it difficult to gauge further planning of additional design elements accurately. If our proportions were removed from the equation of design, the idea of function and aesthetics would be altered considerably. In Figure 8.2, the exaggerated proportion of a chair relative to the person sitting would limit the usability of this object; we can make an assessment that the proportions simply do not "feel right" or "look right." However, for a sense of humor or playfulness, exaggerated proportions are applicable in some scenarios. This natural intuition can be beneficial in working proportional color plans.

Color and Proportion

Color palettes can contain between one and five colors. Limiting the number of colors in an interior space is crucial for achieving balance and a unified composition. Too much color can be overwhelming and compromise the intended communication of the design and its function;

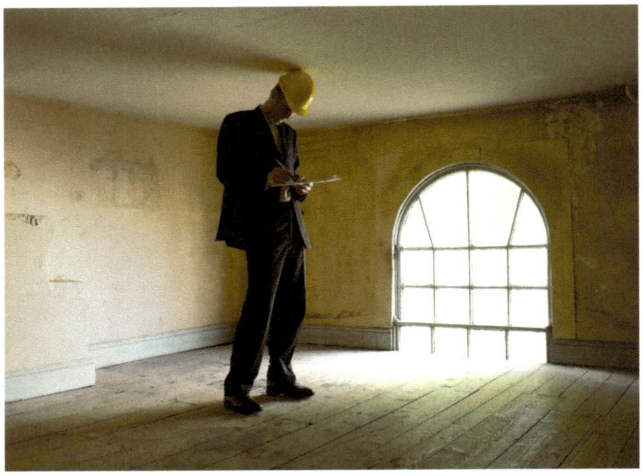

Figure 8.1 The man in this image establishes an estimated height of this room at less than 6 feet tall.

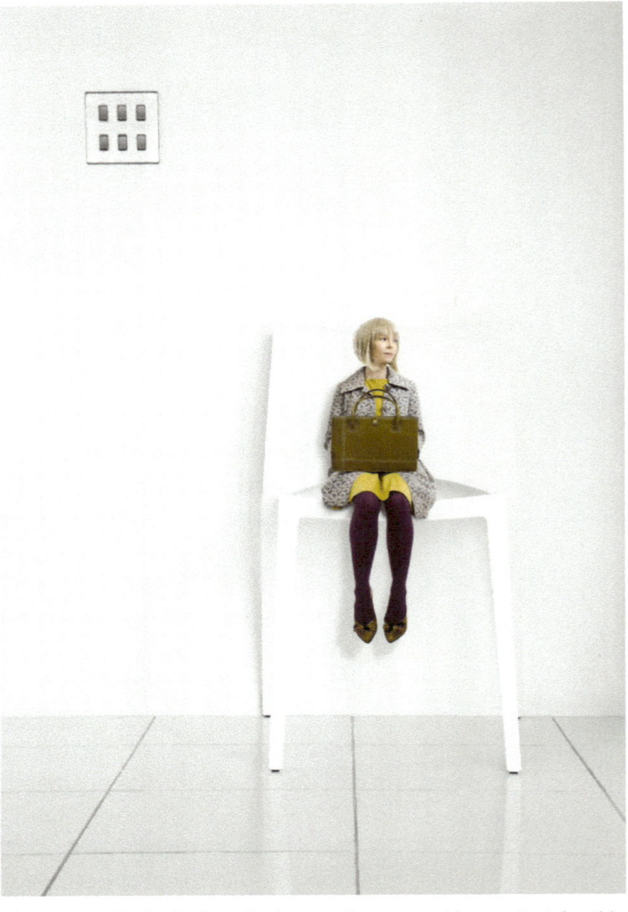

Figure 8.2 The inclusion of a human figure provides context for this chair and floor tiles; the proportions are exaggerated.

conversely, limiting color can elicit negative reactions of boredom, monotony, or general lack of interest in the design. Paint manufacturers use proportions of paint when mixing color to get the desired hue. If the proportion is off, the color will be incorrect. This same principle applies to interiors; if the proportions are off, the desired effect will be compromised.

Through multiple modes of inquiry and experimentation, students will form a deeper understanding and connection to design theory at an earlier stage in their education. The grids provided in Figure 8.3 can be copied and used to generate your color proportions. Base color or dominant color makes up the ground or background of your space. The second and third colors are secondary or subdominant, and the smaller proportions are your accent colors. Another method for establishing proportion is the "rule of thirds", using the dominate color in two-thirds of the space, secondary color in one-third, with accent color reserved for the small elements—décor and art—to draw attention. These proportions can be adjusted to suit the needs of the project. Other variations include 60–30–10 or 70–20–10 each as represented proportions of color dedicated to the areas within the space. Be careful of equal proportions which may remove dominance or focal point.

Assign dominant and subdominant colors with accents for visual contrasts in your color plan. Keep these proportions in mind for a three-color scheme: 60 to 70 percent dominant, 20 to 30 percent subdominant, and 10 to 20 percent accent. Depending on the number of colors in your plan, these percentages may shift slightly. The various proportions of a given color will determine the physical sensation or perception. In Figure 8.4a, the color scheme uses a grid to proportion the five-hue palette. If we relocate the various hues assigned different proportions in the grid, the visual perception of the color relationship, weight, and impact of the scheme changes (see Figure 8.4b). This tool can be valuable in gauging the

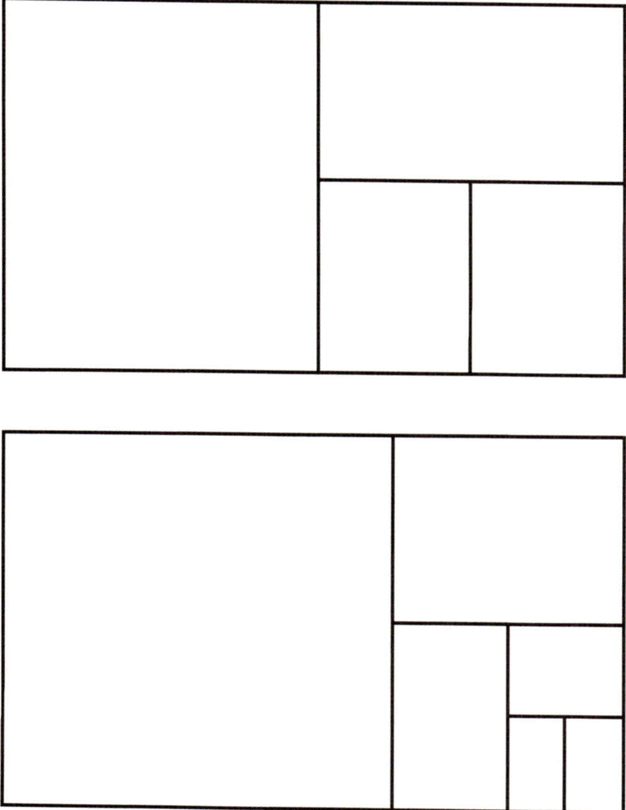

Figure 8.3 Grid proportions using the Fibonacci Sequence. These can be used for initial color planning and comparison of proportions. As you progress in your color studies, this will become natural and automatic.

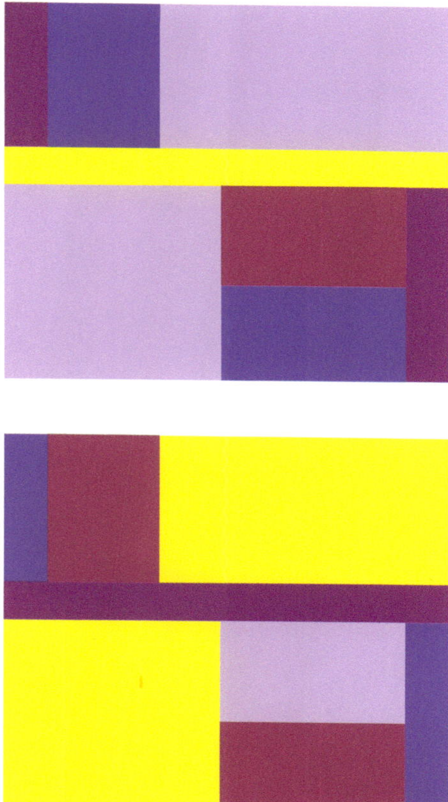

Figure 8.4 (a) Five-color plan arranged to evaluate proportioned color strength and relationship. (b) Color plan illustrating perceptual changes in color language when proportions are reassigned.

overall sensation you are attempting to achieve within your interior space. An intensely bright color will dominate an interior; therefore, it is advantageous to use these hues for smaller areas of your interior and assign less saturated, lighter hues for larger areas of the space. Intense color will naturally draw attention and should be limited or balanced with its complement; avoid having a color overwhelm your design. From previous discussions, we know that the larger the color area, the lighter a color appears, and the smaller the color area, the darker it will appear. When preparing your proportions, these phenomena and the concepts mentioned in Chapter 5 (balance of value, hue, intensity, etc.) ought to be taken into consideration. Many variables are combined when we work with color; this is precisely why every step taken to address all possibilities of color change and manipulation early in the color-planning process is important.

Architect Janet Ford suggests that as we prepare our color proportions, we should keep in mind that "our eyes perceive a visual mix . . . and the mix will differ depending on the proportions of allocated areas" (n.d., ¶ 1). She goes on to identify six key elements to consider for color proportioning:

- The color with the largest proportional area is the dominant color (the ground).
- Smaller areas are subdominant colors.
- Accent colors are those that occupy a relatively small area but offer a contrast because of a variation in hue, intensity, or saturation.
- To create an accent, place small areas of light color on a dark background, or a small area of dark on a light background.
- If large areas of a light hue are used, the whole area will appear light; conversely, if large areas of dark values are used, the whole area appears dark.
- Alternating color by intensity rather than proportion will also change the perceived visual mix of color.

The proportion of color will be relative to other design elements and scaled to fit interior spaces on a

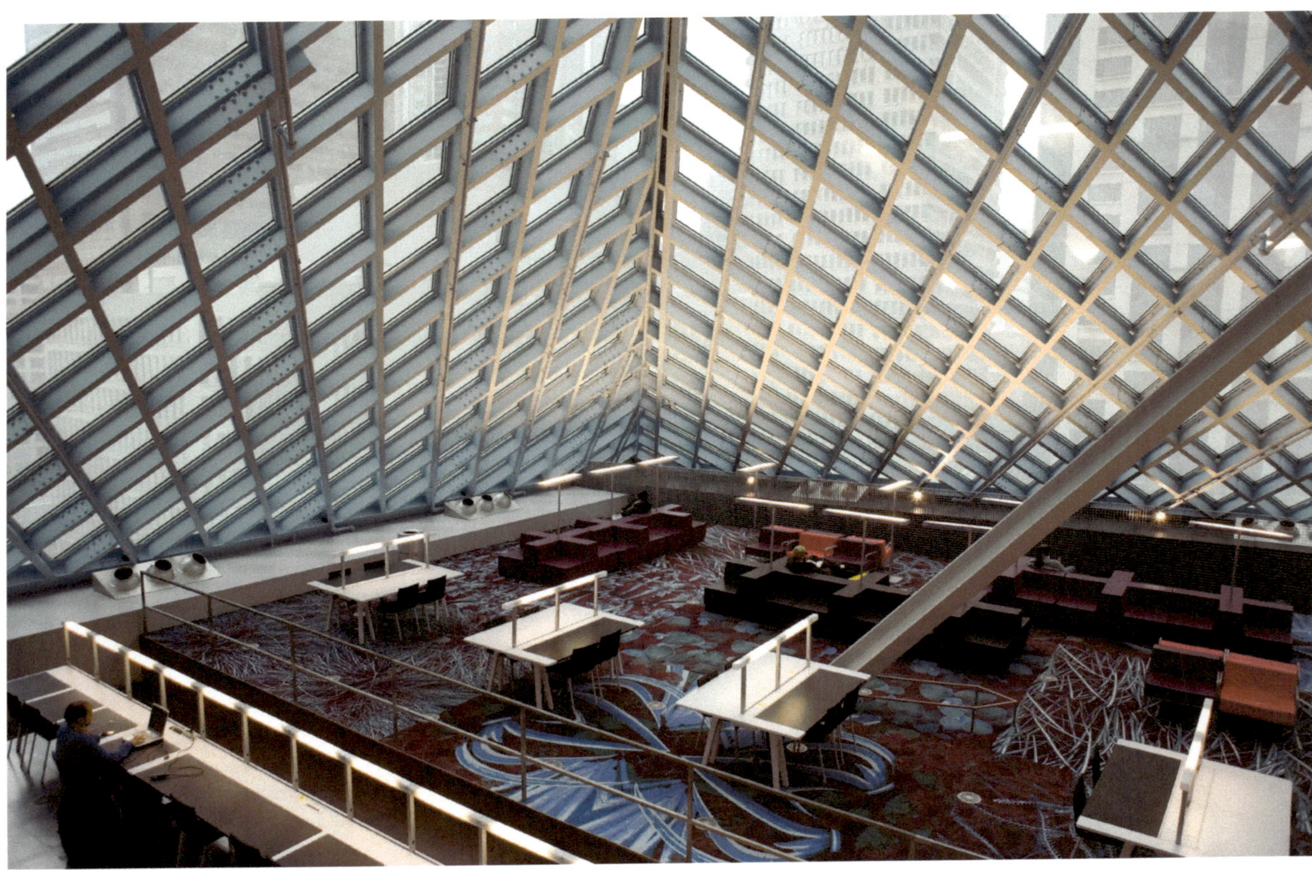

Figure 8.5 The Seattle Central Library designed by architects Rem Koolhaas and Joshua Prince-Ramus. The large-scale carpeted floor pattern balances with the large volume of space. The red accent paint color placed at the base of the diagonal column grounds the structural element, providing a focal point that visually connects the glass roof to the flooring color below.

situation-by-situation basis. Red can be overwhelming as a dominant color in a small space; a larger space with adequate natural light can handle a strong color in large quantities. Color, contrast, and spatial volume work together to create the intended effects for the space's purpose and its users.

The top floor of the Seattle Central Library is saturated in natural light and accentuated with geometric shapes, forming a sculpturally inviting space (see Figure 8.5). The volume is accented with a floral carpet in deep hues of red and blue. The sheer volume of the space is balanced with the exaggerated scale of the dark carpet pattern and geometric glass and steel frame ceiling.

The modern living space in Figure 8.6a is predominantly neutral, with a few touches of color contrasts. In this example, the geometry, volume, and application of horizontal line in the space highlights the interior design, but our attention is not focused on a particular feature because of the limited contrast or color with other design elements in the room. The adage "a small amount of color can go a long way" in an interior space may hold true for most; however, too little, and the color that is used may seem arbitrary and not achieve the desired result. When color is planned, whether the color of the materials or the applied color (paints, wall coverings, textiles, etc.), the resulting character and visual appeal of the design solution will not be distracted from the otherwise arbitrary or decorative placement of color.

There is a desire to assign color to add distinction but also to create a more intimate proportion for the spaces we inhabit. In Figure 8.6b, localized color and contrast has been placed to change our spatial perception of the interior. The added contrast pulls the living space inward, creating a more intimate conversation space as well as adding a dramatic, darker contrast between surfaces and planes. Notice how the placement of color and contrasting features and textures changed the proportion, brightness, and emphasis on design elements of the space compared to the original illustration.

In certain situations, an exaggerated proportion may be needed; in this case, proportion and emphasis are united as a means of drawing attention to a particular design element. Distorting or exaggerating proportions can be used to convey specific meaning or suggest a particular feeling that is to be experienced by the viewer. For example, Figure 8.7 shows Spanish architect Santiago Calatrava's ultra-modern, expansive volume in the Quadracci Pavilion at the Milwaukee Art Museum. The volume is exaggerated, giving the visitors a spatial experience and sensation of endlessness as the interior frames and reflects the lakefront waters beyond. The inspiration of the structure emulates the nearby lake, sailboats, and birds in flight.

Although we are examining the principles of design separately to better understand how to use color in design, all these elements ultimately work together, simultaneously achieving the final result. Only by examining them independently can you see the intricacy of how they work and then be able to execute more successful color and design solutions.

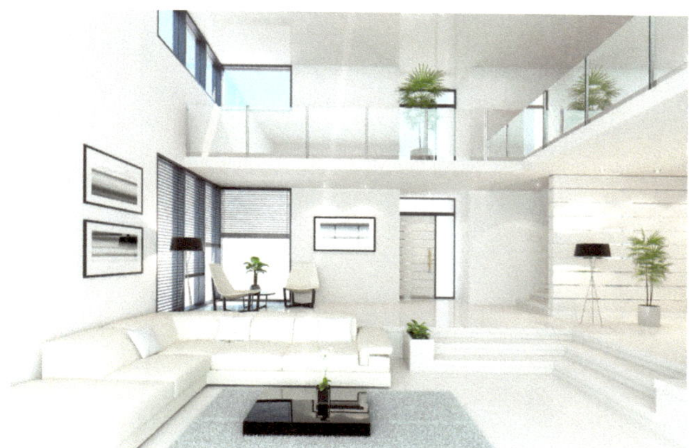

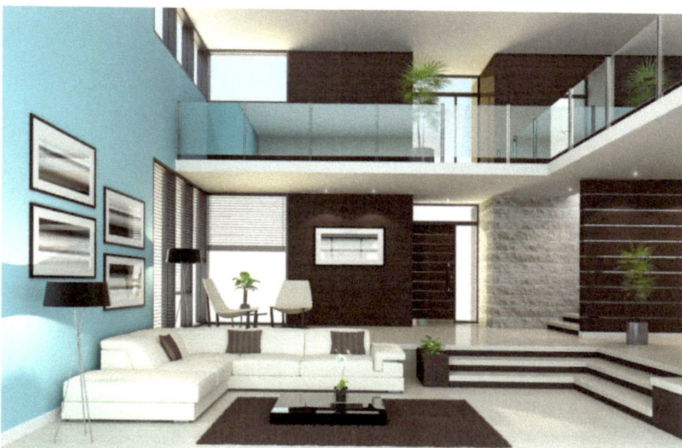

Figure 8.6 (a) Left. Imposing space and volume with limited color, contrast, and interest doesn't help the viewer connect to the spatial features easily and with relatable scale. (b) Right. Recoloration of the vertical and horizontal space with value contrast and color decreases the perception of the room's large scale, also creating unity and a more relatable spatial experience.

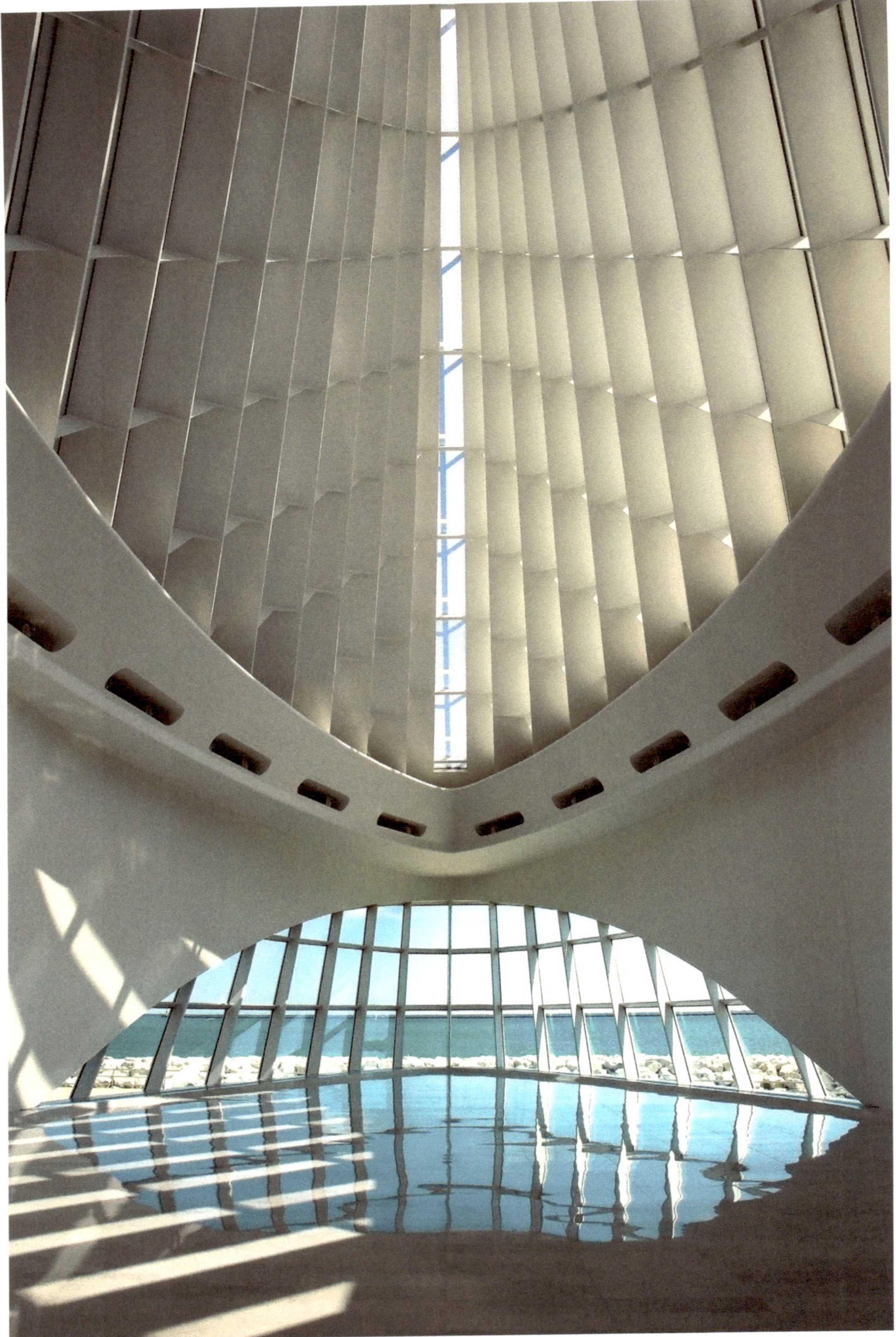

Figure 8.7 Scale and volume are increased in the interior of the Quadracci Pavilion by Santiago Calatrava, Milwaukee Art Museum, with the use of natural light, low contrast, and light-colored materials. The structure contains a moveable, wing-like brise soleil, which reduces heat gain in the building and opens up for a wingspan of 217 feet during the day, folding over the tall, arched structure at night or during inclement weather.

Color and Scale

Whereas proportion is concerned with the relationships of various parts arranged to create an aesthetically pleasing whole, scale is concerned with the relative size of space (large, small, short, tall, narrow, wide). Color can be used to change our visual perception of a space's actual size.

Children live in an adult's world, where large spaces can seem overwhelming and frightening (Figure 8.8a). Color is critical in the classroom to reduce boredom and provide an environment that "improves visual processing, reduces stress, and challenges brain development through visual stimulation/relationships and pattern seeking" (Daggett, Cobble, & Gertel, 2008, p. 1).

In Figure 8.8b, the introduction of a primary color to this classroom setting has the potential to increase students' creativity, imagination, and willingness to learn. The blue horizontal band around the room's perimeter (1) divides the vertical height to a relatable scale for children and (2) grounds and frames the two wooden storage units into the total design. The color also provides the needed dark contrast with the other hues. The darker blue on the bottom third of the space lowers the perception of the ceiling height as an additional measure to make the scale of the space more comfortable for children.

The location of green on the ceiling and yellow on the upper observation balcony reduces the ceiling height and adds visual interest to the spatial volume. The addition of a dark contrasting pattern to the floor divides the space into zones so activity areas can be arranged and identified for the children. This also helps to reduce the perceived scale of the classroom. The design direction for the primary color plan is adding more variety and contrast to the space, therefore reducing the apparent visual scale. Additional texture or pattern was not added in the illustration because the workspaces and shelving ultimately would be filled with books, toys, and games, providing the needed variety and textural effects.

Practical Applications with Color and Perception of Scale

Following are a few tips to keep in mind when working with color and scale:

- Light colors advance, and dark colors recede. Figure 8.10 illustrates this concept. The purple appears to recede into the gray field, whereas the yellow advances toward you. Does the yellow appear to be larger than the purple? In fact, they are the same.
- Use a hue in two to three close values. This will create high contrast and separation of visual elements, resulting in the perception of large space. Recall that Munsell's value scale "trunk" starts at the ground with black and moves upward to white. This principle relates to gravity, where color takes on the property of having perceived weight. When working in space, use this natural order of value—darker values will be placed toward the bottom of the interior (the floor or approximately the bottom one-quarter or one-third of

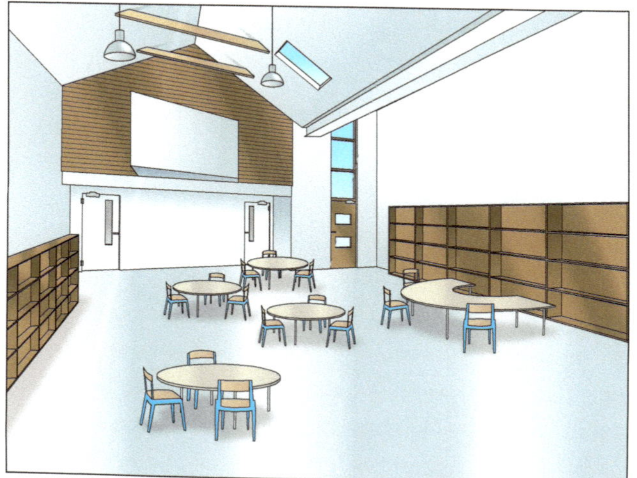

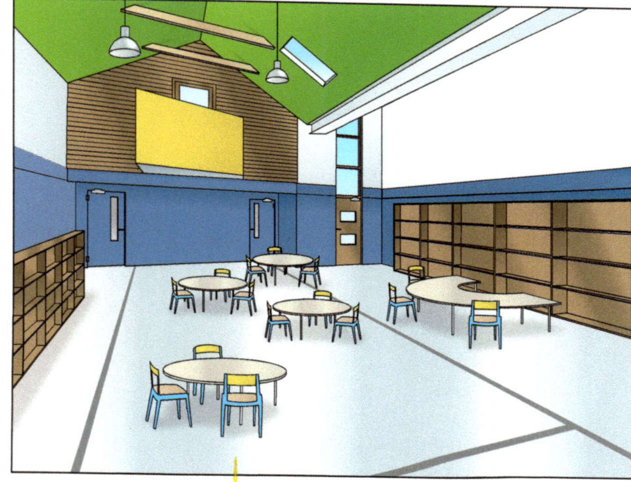

Figure 8.8 (a) Left. This learning environment for young children lacks logical relationships, with its massive volume and scale. (b) Right. Careful color location decreases and breaks up the spatial volume, while introducing contrast and visual interest to keep young learners stimulated.

the space), middle values at the center, and the lightest values at the top. This will create a better sense of balance.

- A room with a dark ceiling and light floor will appear top-heavy and out of balance. Dark values when placed approximately 36 to 42 inches high on a wall will visually slice a room in half. If the ceiling is 8 or 9 feet high, this can be oppressive, whereas, applied to a high ceiling of 10 feet or more, the dark color can make an expansive space appear more intimate.
- Small spaces can be made to appear much larger if similar colors are used throughout, especially if they are keyed to the same floor covering color.
- Dark, strong, or warm colors like red or dark orange will make the wall seem to advance and make the room feel much smaller.
- Cool, dull, or light colors (reduction in chroma or value) will appear to stretch space—to push the wall outward. This can be achieved if the wall, floor, and ceiling colors are keyed to the same color.
- A long corridor will seem shorter if the end wall is painted or covered in a warm color, just as a small space will seem larger if all surfaces are painted the same white or neutral color. Washing the walls with light adds to this perception.
- A low ceiling will seem higher if it is painted a lighter value than the walls and emphasized with the use of crown molding around the perimeter of the room painted the same value as the walls. The crown molding will visually extend the wall, making the room appear taller.
- Large pieces of furniture will look smaller if upholstered in the same color value as the walls. The blending of visual edges diminishes the apparent weight. The same concept applies to darker upholstery against darker-valued walls. To increase the visual weight of a rather small piece of furniture, use opposing value and color contrasts.
- While the concept that warm colors advance and cool colors recede to make a space appear small or large is still fresh in our mind, let's not confuse the use of dark hues with light hues. A dark hue, whether warm or cool, can decrease the apparent size of space, and, conversely, if the hue is light, whether warm or cool, it tends to visually open a space.

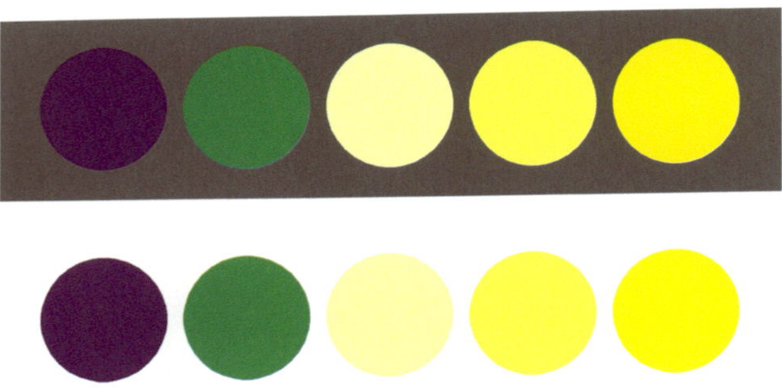

Figure 8.9 Lighter hues appear to advance forward when surrounded by darker color and have the ability to change perceived object and spatial scale and proportion.

Additional Methods for Establishing Proportional Relationships

Relying on intuition can result in good proportional relationships and ultimately adequate color planning. However, there are quantitative measures that can ensure reliable results. "Elements of mass and space have dimensions and, therefore, exist in a mathematical relationship to one another" (Malnar & Vodvarka, 1992, p. 87). Mathematical proportions can be seen in a variety of circumstances—natural forms, the **golden section** (a mathematical formula where an object's width is to its length as its length is to the sum of its length plus width), and the **Fibonacci Sequence** (a series of numbers where each number in the sequence is the sum of the two preceding numbers). We will examine these theories to establish tools for applying color in proportional amounts later in this chapter. Now, the mention of mathematics may sound a bit daunting. The power of grids for solving complex design problems is limitless. This theory for designing space had long been the practice of many architects and designers. Using grids based on proportional ratios will help you achieve precise proportions and harmony in your work.

Artists such as Piet Mondrian, Robert Mangold, Theo van Doesburg, and Diana Ong have all incorporated grid systems into their art. This system is also commonplace in approaching the interior design and layout of a building's partitions, windows, doors, and other architectural details and forms (Figure 8.10). Using the grid method establishes an organizing principle for the interior volume that creates balance, good proportions, and overall

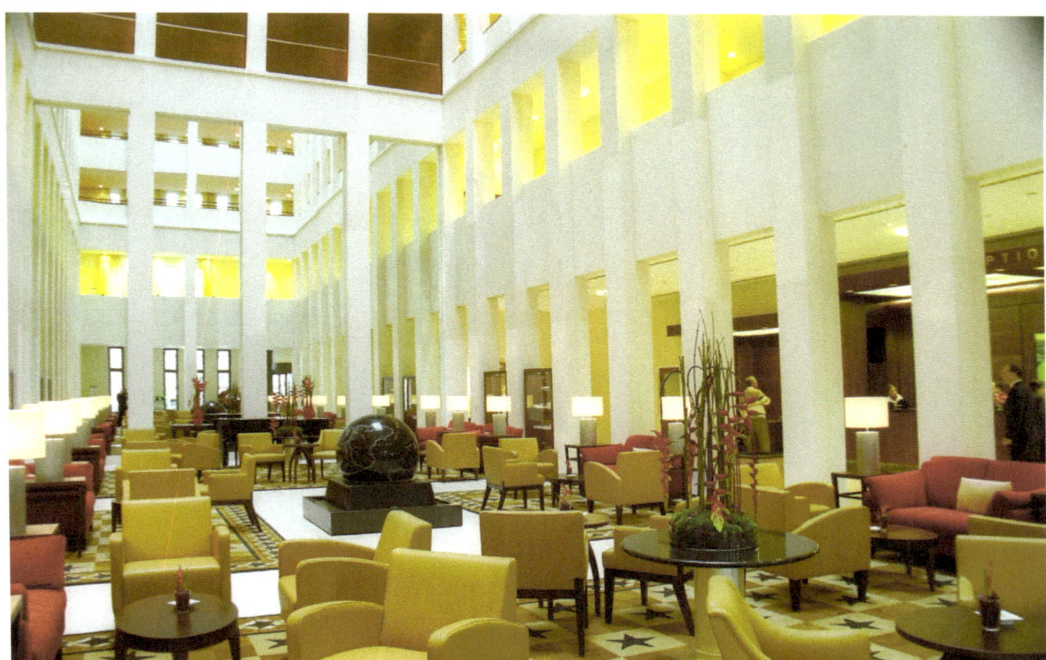

Figure 8.10
This ten-story atrium lobby of the luxury Marriott Hotel in Berlin, Germany, clearly utilizes grids to organize the design. The grid can be seen in the interior architecture as well as the placement of furnishings. The illuminated copper colored panels balance the large volume while simultaneously providing a dramatic focal point.

harmony of the space. Applying a geometric system can be useful in establishing color relationships.

Charles Rennie Mackintosh (1968–1928), a Scottish architect and designer who studied at the Glasgow School of Art, was known for his modern style and innovative work during the Art Nouveau movement. One of his most interesting pieces of work is the House for an Art Lover, Glasgow, Scotland (Figure 8.11). Mackintosh originally designed this house in 1901, but the building was not built until many years later, in 1989–1996. He clearly worked his use of grids into the lighting, details, and furnishing of the home.

Terry Knight expresses color and shape in terms of **color grammar**. Much like shape grammar (the relationships between various geometric shapes, arrangements, and alignments that explore a new design language), "in a color grammar the rules and initial shape are defined in terms of lines, labels and *color regions* . . . in two-dimensional color areas or three-dimensional color volumes" that are assigned to specific regions or color spaces in a particular design (1998, p. 119). The grammar produces a series of divisions of a square or other abstract shapes such as **Froebel blocks**—a series of wooden stacking blocks in various geometric shapes developed by German Frederick Froebel, who created the concept of kindergarten in the nineteenth century—to study color proportions and qualities

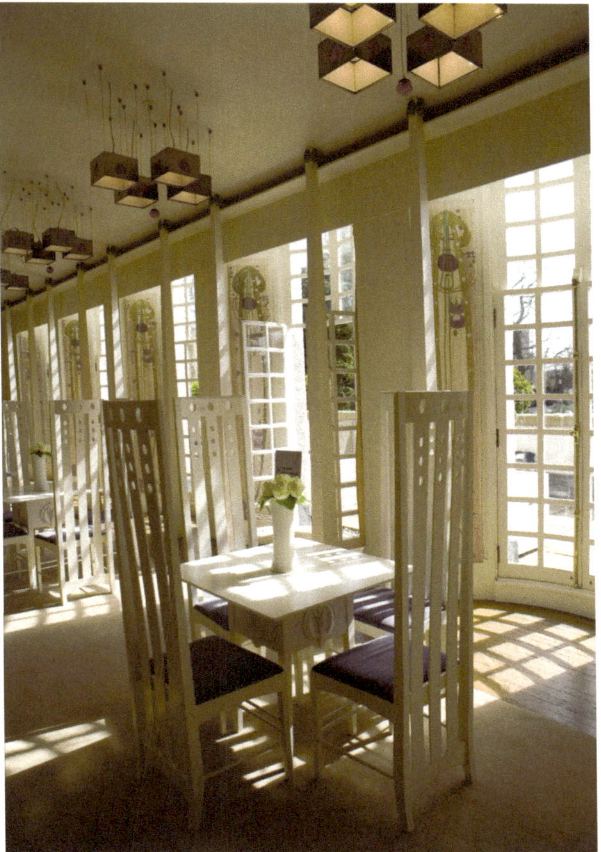

Figure 8.11 Originally designed by Mackintosh for a competition as a country retreat home, the House for an Art Lover was built as a gallery and exhibition space on the grounds of the Bellahouston Art Park in Glasgow, Scotland.

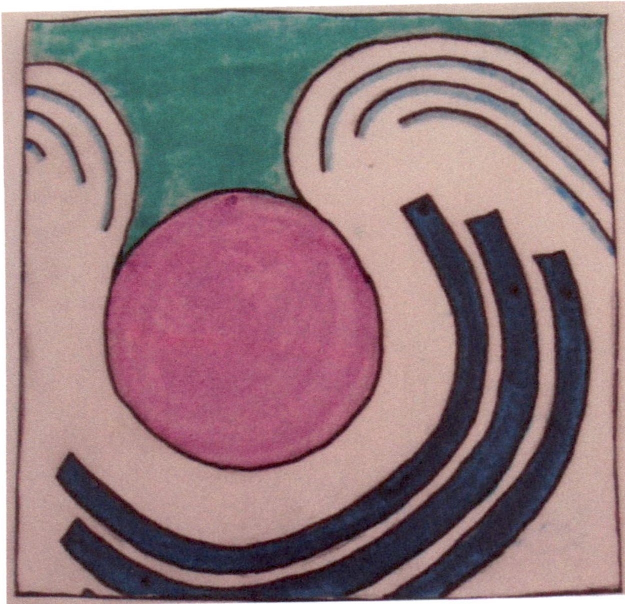

Figure 8.12 Color concept diagram.

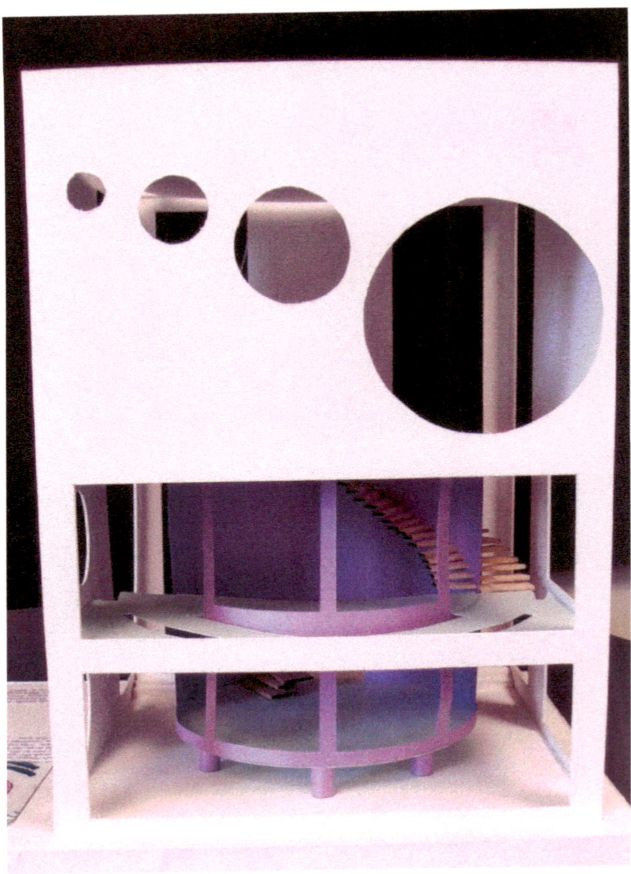

Figure 8.13 Color grammar in a three-dimensional space.

of color that are expressed differently through three-dimensional forms versus two-dimensional shapes. For instance, a rectangular form becomes the "vocabulary," two shapes combine in "spatial relation," and when color is applied on the shape, a "color grammar" is created (p. 122). Multiple color grammars can be joined to create a design. In applying this method, you are able to explore color, space, and shape qualitatively.

In Figure 8.12, student Lindsay Perry has applied the concept of color and shape in a conceptual diagram. This diagram serves as the conceptual foundation and color-proportioning system in a two-dimensional format to later be expanded into a three-dimensional design. This color grammar is one of a series of solutions prepared by the student to explore variations of color and proportional layouts. Once a color/shape grammar has been decided, the student progresses to studying the color proportions and shapes three-dimensionally. Figure 8.13 shows examples of where the color grammar has been applied to a study of vertical path and movement using music and metaphor as the initial determinants for the color grammar. Students apply a limited amount of color as a design feature in order to explore the effects of the color that may not otherwise be seen in a scale model. In this approach, the focus of the learning is evenly distributed between color and design.

In Figure 8.14, the concept of shape and color grammar is applied to an additional three-dimensional conceptual study of color, form, and space. In this example, student Christina Masters was assigned the word "flow" as a concept generator. Using this word, the student generated and developed a series of sketches, schematic designs, and finally model prototypes to explore and evaluate the design process. The result is neither an interior nor an exterior but a study of formal relationship of space and order. This project is one of two beginning studies assigned in a course that predominately involves modeling as the primary tool for exploring space. The exercise requires the use of white museum board, cardboard, or other lightweight medium instead of color to place emphasis on the conceptual design versus materiality and is further restricted to the use of one or two colors integrated with the final design. The intent is to reinforce the individual color connection the student has with the design and how the color is incorporated and supports the final solution. The isolation and added significance of the color in the model make the exercise challenging and require the student to think less decoratively about color application. In this example, a contrast of texture

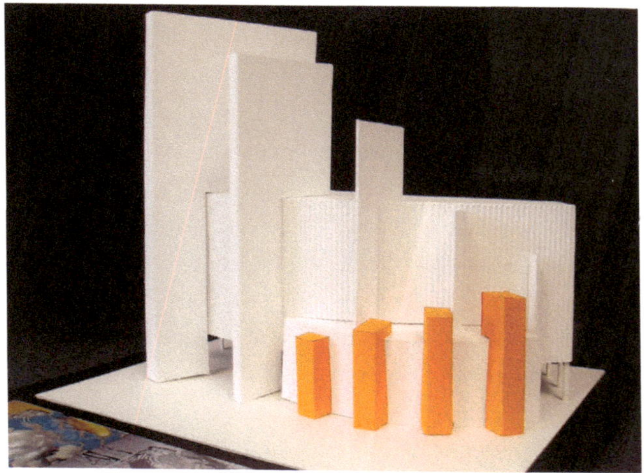

Figure 8.14 Color grammar in a three-dimensional space.

using corrugated cardboard and smooth museum board adds interest. The sweeping motion of the design from left to right and back again moves the eye throughout the design for a complete experience. The strong orange color balances nicely with the larger white rectangular forms. The rear portion of the design was elevated to provide a relief and to add further interest with the juxtaposition of positive and negative space.

A grid provides the reasoning behind your color design decisions. Choosing color irrationally or without any research or serious thought can have consequences in your design solutions. Leave the guesswork out when working with color; there are several systems and processes that will make the task less burdensome and overwhelming. When working from photos of interiors or images used as inspiration for clients, you can present a preset palette that expresses proportion (before the project is executed in paints, fabrics, and materials and a grand investment is made). This method can be used to train your eye to see color percentages and map out placement, while working with colored media to formulate a color palette and assign colors to objects and areas within a room. Try doing this with several photos on your own and see how you do.

The Golden Section

The golden section, also known as the golden mean, the golden rectangle, and the golden ratio, was developed by the ancient Greeks and is the division of a line in two sections, where the ratio between the smallest section and the largest section is identical to the ratio between the largest section and the entire length of the line (AB is to AC as AC is to CB). "The Golden Section determines a proportion between the whole and its two parts, such that the ratio between the smaller and the larger is the same as the larger and the whole" (Malnar & Vodvarka, 1992, p. 89). This system yields a pleasing proportion of structure and space. The golden section is expressed in the illustration known as the golden rectangle in Figure 8.15. The most notable example of the golden section is the Parthenon in Athens, Greece, completed in 438 BC.

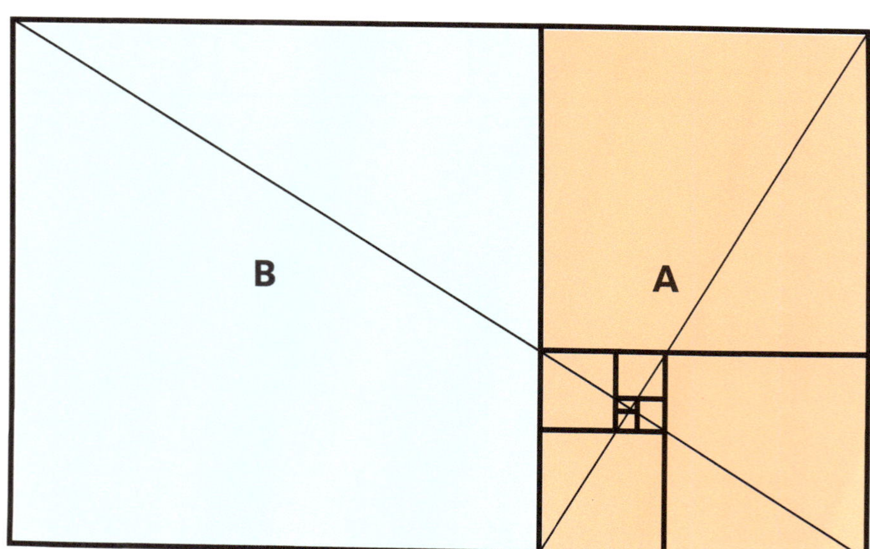

Figure 8.15 The golden rectangle.

Fibonacci Sequence

Leonardo Pisano, more commonly known as Fibonacci, was an Italian mathematician who was born in 1170 and lived during the Renaissance period. He is most known for having discovered the Fibonacci numbers, a sequence of numbers where each successive number is the sum of the two previous numbers (e.g., 1, 1, 2, 3, 5, 8, 13, 21, 34, 55, 89, 144, and so forth). The higher these numbers progress in the sequence and divide into one another, the closer two numbers next to one another mathematically equal the golden section, which is 1.618. Figure 8.16a illustrates a grid using the Fibonacci Sequence. This grid can be used and expanded to accommodate any proportions that can be applied to initial color planning, as shown in Figure 8.16b.

Nature, as mentioned earlier, tends to organize growth patterns into this sequence. The spiral growth of shells follows the golden spiral, and the golden section is naturally evident; therefore, we automatically judge something in nature as aesthetically pleasing or beautiful. Without the proportion control factor, objects would lack visual appeal and unification. Items such as doors, windows, concrete blocks, and common house bricks are examples of "manufactured proportions" that ensure that a system is used to maintain consistency and relationship between various architectural design elements (Ching, 1996, p. 282). When you consider that openings and various other elements in an interior correspond to a proportion system or set of rules, and that architects commonly work with a grid to develop the building shell, it is only logical to consider this same system in your initial color planning. Use these proportions to determine the amount of a color to use. When you identify the formula based on specific laws of proportion, you create a final composition or design that is innately perceived as accurate and sensible. When you choose to work intuitively, the final result may not be as effective. Keep in mind: Color + Proportion = Aesthetic value!

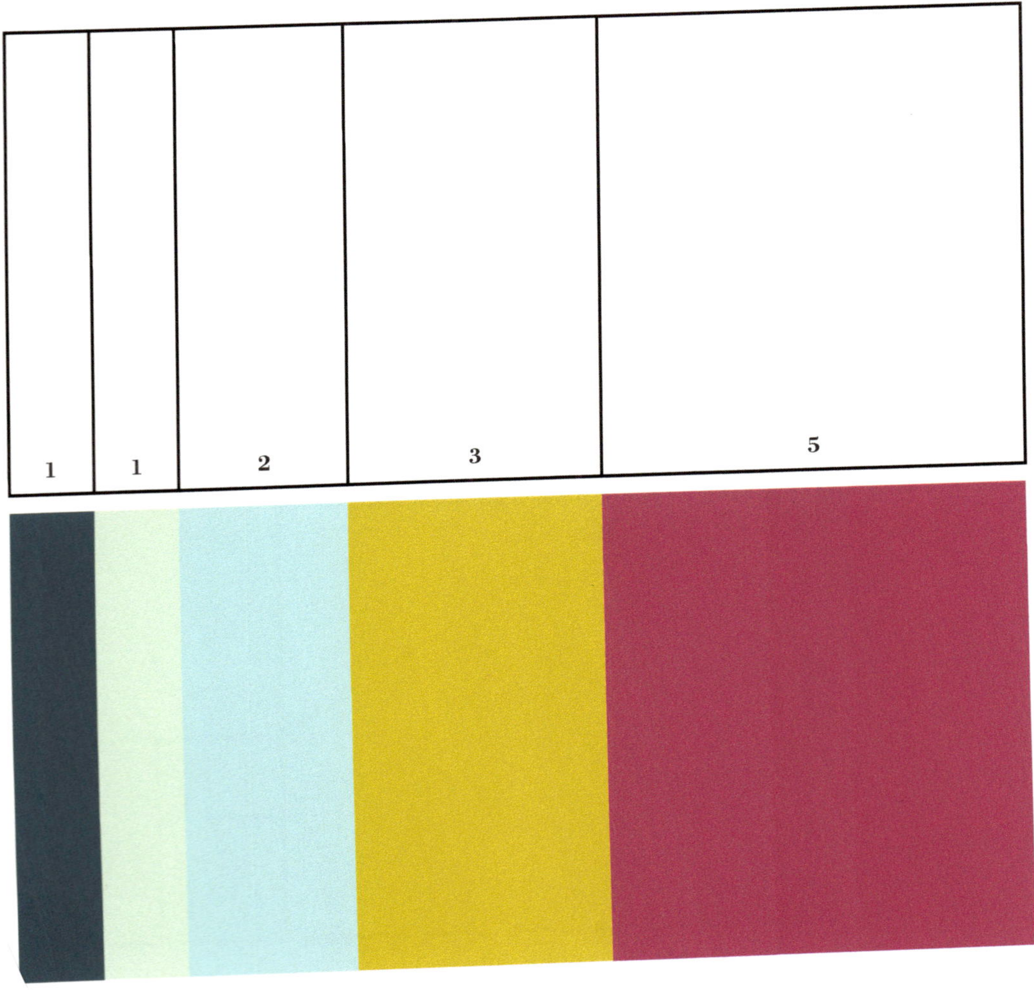

Figure 8.16
(a) Grid proportions using the Fibonacci Sequence.
(b) Color palette using the grid from Figure 8.17a.

Le Modulor

Charles Édouard Jeanneret-Gris, who is better known to the design world as Le Corbusier, was a Swiss-born architect who developed the proportioning system, **Le Modulor**, in 1948. Le Corbusier used the golden ratio and Leonardo da Vinci's Vitruvian man (actually created by Vitruvius) to base his system on the human proportions (Figure 8.17). The Modular Man is approximately 6 feet tall, with a raised-arm height of about 71/2 feet. The height to the navel is 271/2 inches. Corbusier took the various points within the human body (ankle height, knee height, waist height, etc.) and devised a series of intervals to be used as a proportioning device based on the golden section ratio. **Anthropometrics** is the study of the average human body dimensions and measurements. These measurements have been used for establishing many of the standard dimensions of consumer used products and building design elements.

The golden section developed by the Greeks, the Fibonacci Sequence from Italy, and Le Modular from Switzerland illustrate that divine proportions are culturally relative. Modern-day Japan still uses a system based on the traditional tatami mat for residential spaces. The mats are 35.5 by 71 by 2 inches and are configured to produce a proportional space (Figure 8.18). The mats are

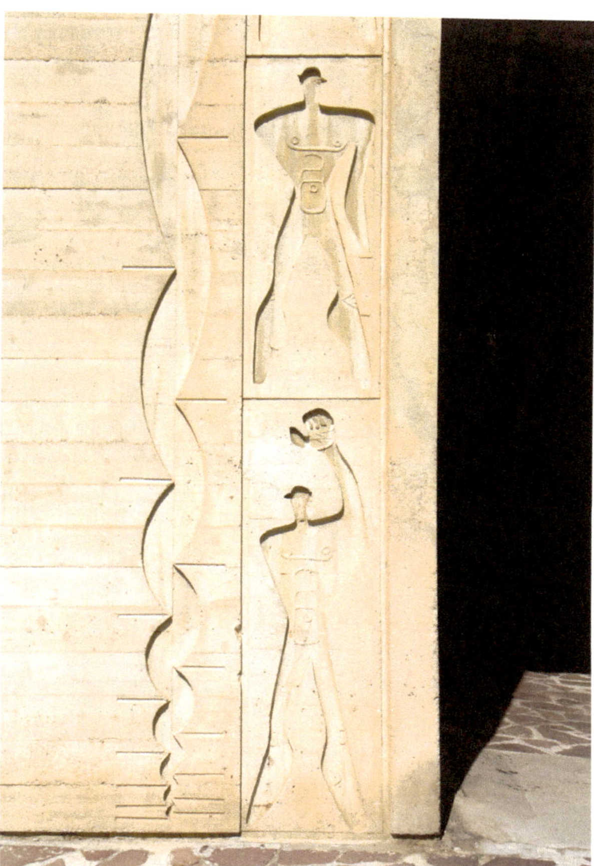

Figure 8.17 Le Modulor: Le Corbusier's Unite d'habitation, Marseille.

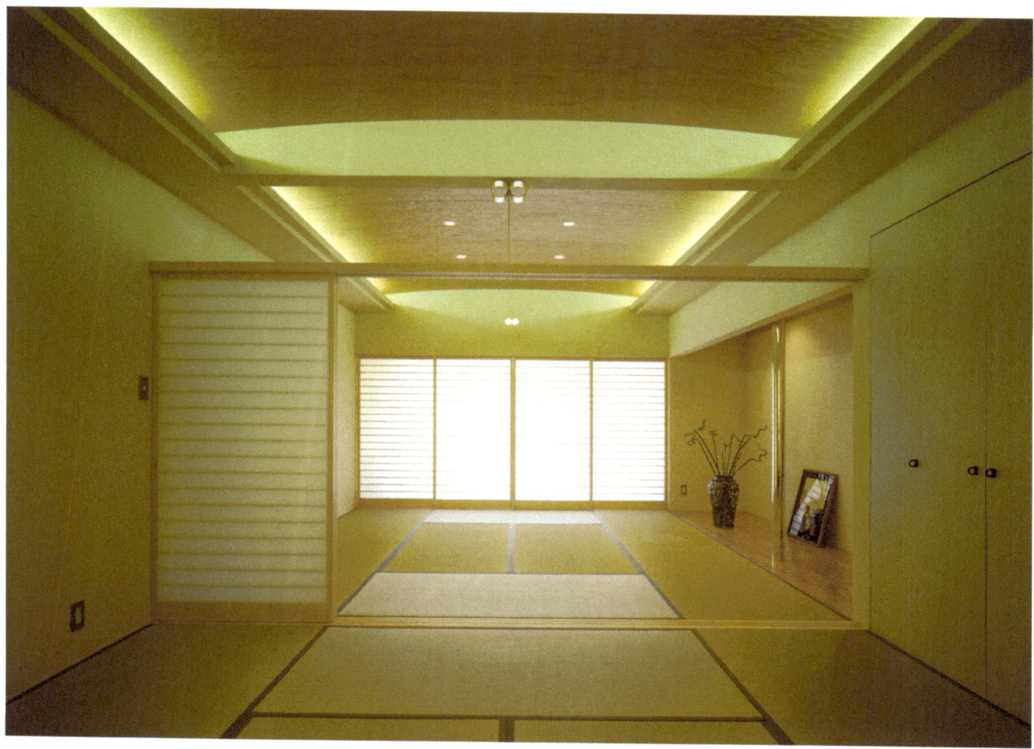

Figure 8.18 Tatami mats in a Japanese home interior in Kurashiki, Japan.

to be laid in an arrangement where no more than three mats meet at one corner.

Tatami size is said to have been determined by the sleeping area of a person. The introduction of the *shoin-zukuri* style expanded the use of tatami as the entire floor covering over wooden planks. Tatami became the unit of measure of room size. Many believe that there is just one size of tatami, approximately 6 feet by 3 feet. In fact, there are now three standard sizes depending on geography. Kyo-to-style tatami are 6.3 feet by 3.1 feet, Nagoya tatami are 6 feet by 3 feet, and Tokyo tatami (Edoma) are 5.8 feet by 2.9 feet. These differences relate to the regional perception of space or lack thereof.

Nature's Proportions

Examine various naturally occurring flora and fauna and you can see proportional evolution and growth in natural materials. A prime example of this occurs in the spiraling growth patterns of a flowering cactus (Figure 8.19a) or pinecone (Figure 8.19b).

The basic components of all design are simple shapes—rectangles, circles, squares, and triangles. Frank Lloyd Wright drew inspiration from the hollyhock flower for his design of the 1921 Hollyhock House in Los Angeles, California (Figure 8.20). His refinement of the natural form into basic geometric shapes illustrates the flexibility of nature in creating new forms. Similarly, if we

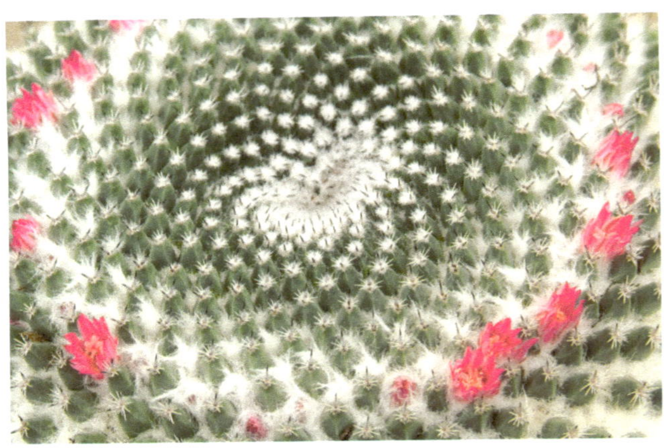

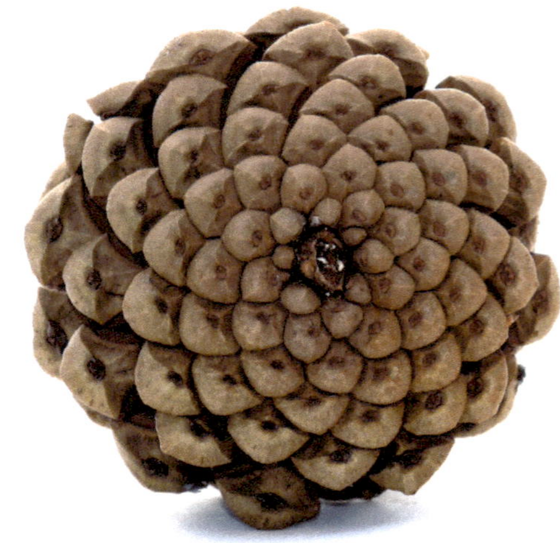

Figure 8.19 (a) Flowering cactus showing proportional growth pattern at Royal Horticultural Society Wisley Garden, Surrey, England. (b) Closeup of pinecone showing proportional growth patterns.

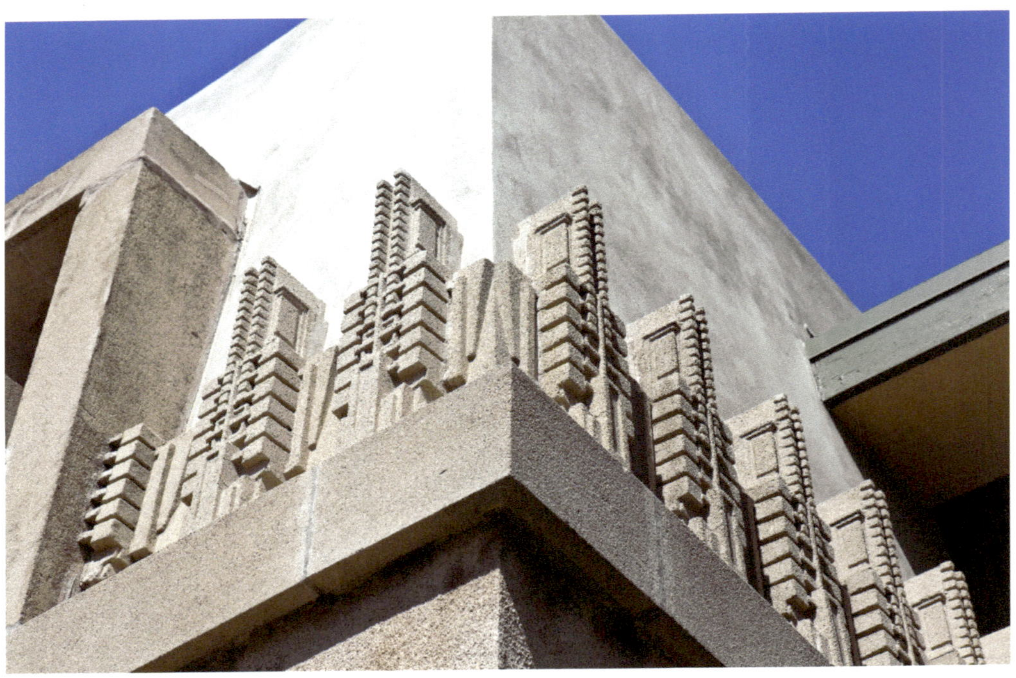

Figure 8.20 The Hollyhock House, Los Angeles, CA, 1919–1921. Detail of block design capturing the appearance of the hollyhock flower.

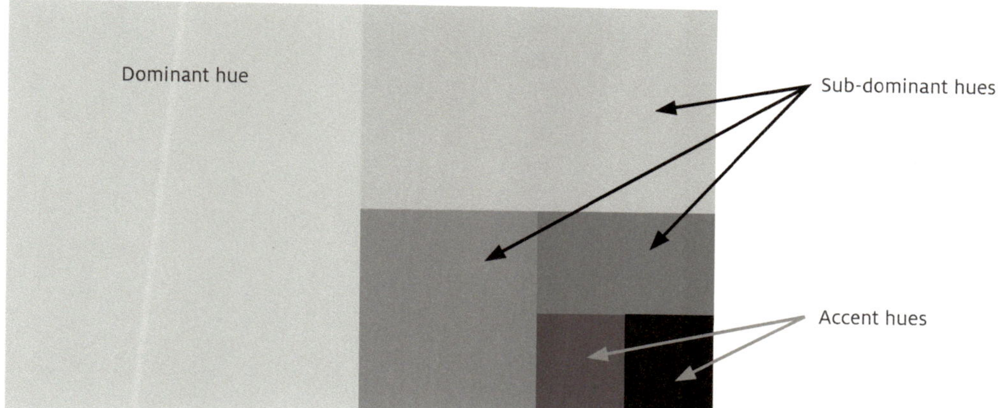

Figure 8.21 Variation of a grid for portioning color values.

break color down into the basics for analysis, then applications have the potential to be much easier and more understandable (Figure 8.21).

The iconic Egg chair designed in 1958 by Arne Jacobsen is an example of the modernistic approach to using simple forms. Jacobsen carved out the desired shape for his chair, creating interplay of positive and negative space while maintaining the simplicity of the original form (Figure 8.22). This same concept is evident in the Ear chair, 1968, by Georges Laporte (Figure 8.23a) and the Tongue chair designed by Pierre Paulin in 1967 (Figure 8.23b). These examples suggest the use of human forms in addition to natural forms for shaping objects into proper proportions.

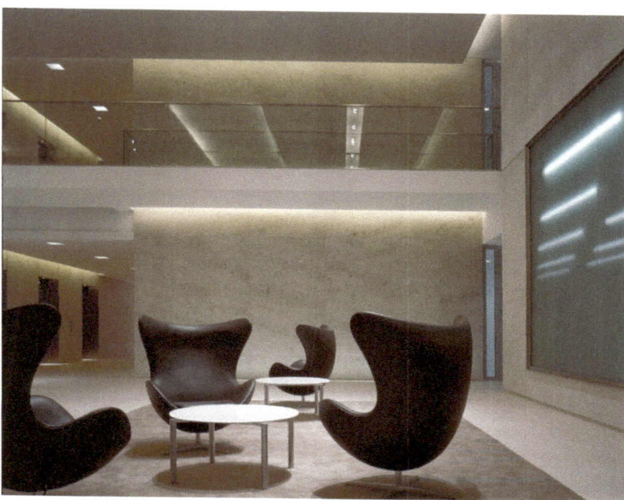

Figure 8.22 Classical Arne Jacobsen Egg chairs in the Belgrave House, London, modern lobby.

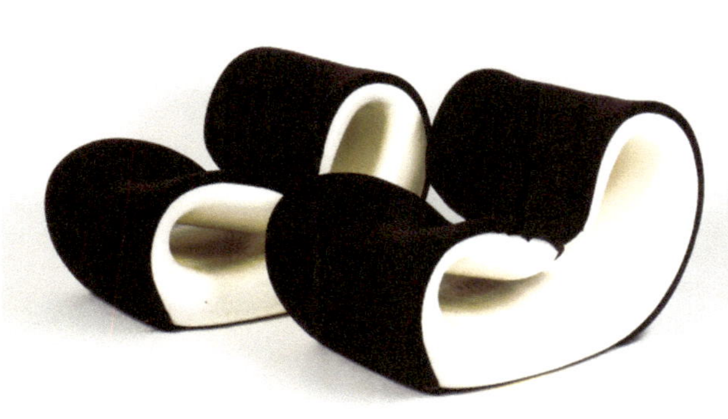

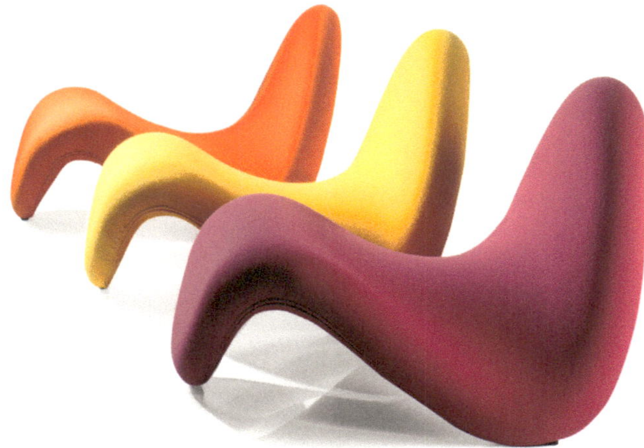

Figure 8.23 (a) Ear chair by Georges Laporte, 1968. High-color contrast between inside and outside forms highlights this chair's design features. (b) Tongue chair by Pierre Paulin, 1967. The whimsical design of this chair is accentuated using bright, saturated hues for the upholstery.

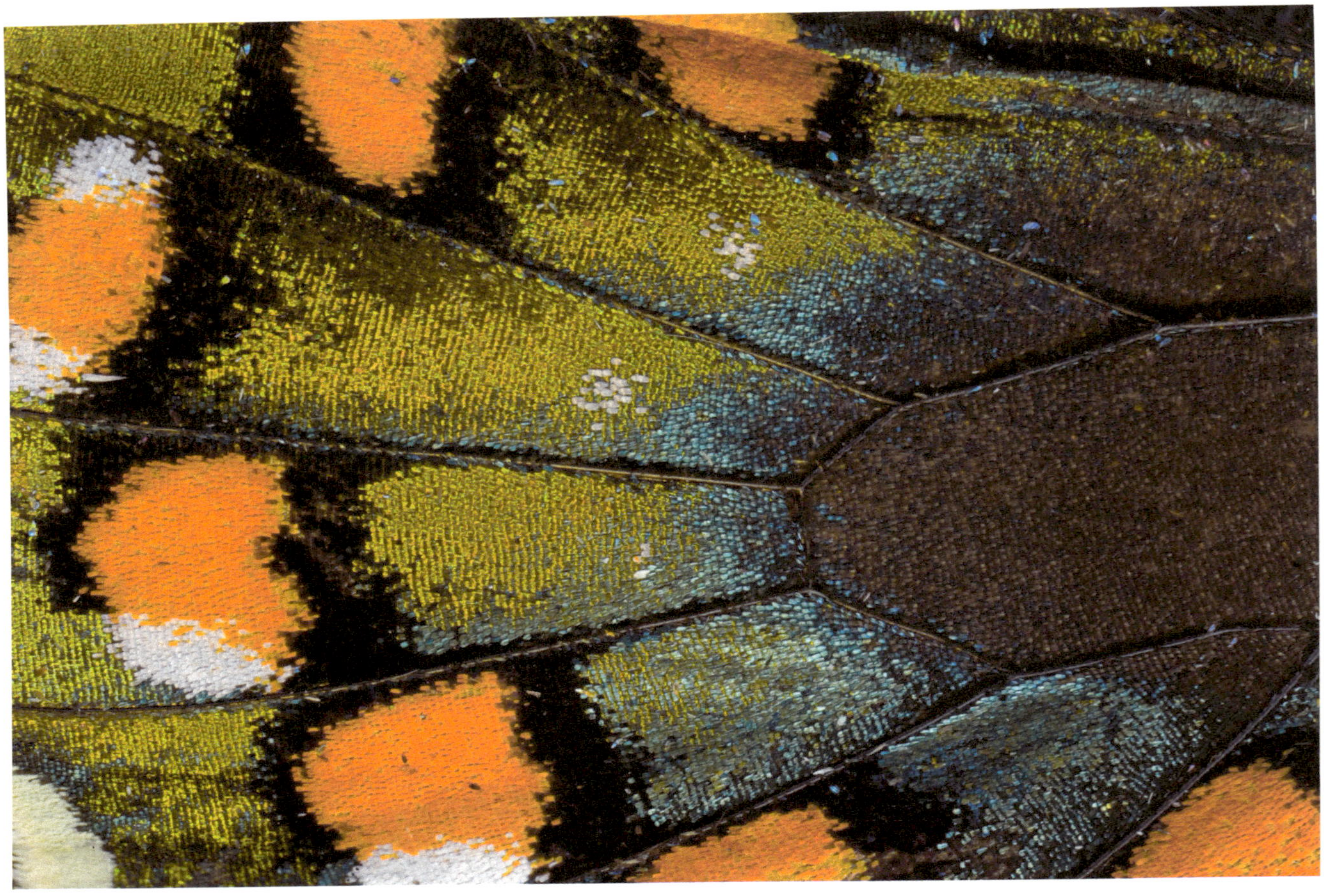

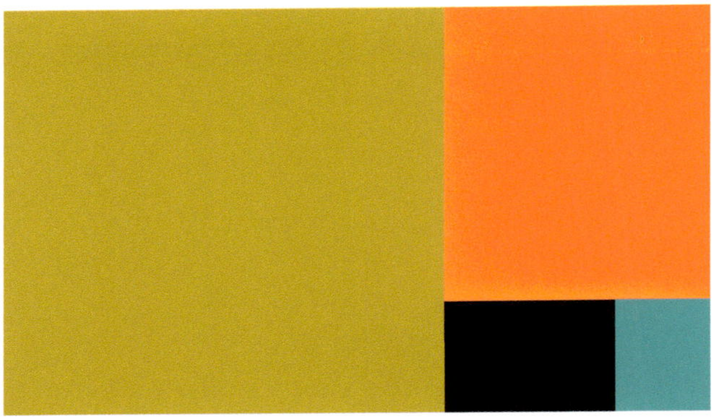

Figure 8.24 (a) Thousands of tiny colored scales create a mosaic pattern on the wing of a Spicebush Swallowtail butterfly. (b) Butterfly wing color proportioned into a palette using the grid format.

Examine the color proportions in this closeup view of a butterfly wing in Figure 8.24a. Immediately you can see the accent (blue), a high-intensity hue in the mix that receives the smallest proportion. This is followed by three other colors with identifiable proportions that we can apply to a grid for comparison, as shown in Figure 8.24b.

Nature informs design. Recall from Chapter 6 that analyzing nature's color assists in establishing good proportional rhythm. These proportions can therefore be broken down into increments using a grid system based on the golden section or Fibonacci Sequence. Using nature as a source for inspiration and creativity allows for your design to develop more fluidly. Students are exposed to alternative forms for exploring design and therefore retain a greater awareness through observation and exploration of uncommon forms and color patterns, tapping into the beauty of nature and its potential to influence color design decisions.

It is only natural that we consider proportion and color. The visible spectrum itself is separated into wavelengths of different proportions and lengths, innately informing us that the basis for color itself is a proportionate measure. Color by proportion seeks a completeness and aesthetic value. When designers communicate color in combination with the principles of design, they create a new design process for exploring the use of colors. In doing so they have opened up an opportunity to express new ideas and design concepts as well as to establish the foundation for future perspectives and creative approaches to interior design. Design is approached using the elements and principles to find the right balance of creativity and function while introducing style and aesthetic value. Don't be afraid to experiment with color. According to Galen Cranz, "The implicit theory is that the design line, proportions, shapes, and decorative motifs of the time crystallize the concerns and aspirations of the day" (2000, p. 11).

REVIEW QUESTIONS

1. Explain the difference between proportion and scale.
2. What are the six elements to consider when proportioning color?
3. Describe the purpose for using a grid system for initial color planning.
4. List three examples of proportioning systems and describe each.
5. Propose four applications with color that can alter the perception of proportion and scale.
6. Who was Leonardo Fibonacci? Explain his contributions to ideas of proportion.
7. Which system was developed based on the proportions of the human body?
8. Give an example of a natural form that illustrates the principles of the golden section and describe its proportional characteristics.

Vocabulary

Proportion
scale
golden section
Fibonacci Sequence
color grammar
Froebel blocks
Le Modular
anthropometrics

EXERCISES

1. Using the proportional systems discussed in the chapter, develop a color composition using one to five colors that vary in value and intensity. Next, develop a second composition that reverses the assigned proportions to see the change that occurs in the perception of the overall scheme. Develop a one to two-paragraph analysis of what occurs with the color reversal. Exchange designs (but not analyses) with a classmate and analyze one another's compositions in one or two paragraphs. Compare your own analyses with the classmate's analyses. Where did your opinions and impressions overlap, and where did they differ?
2. Locate a photo of a quality designed interior from a credible design publication. The photo can be of any type of interior (retail, hospitality, healthcare, residential, office, and more). Using colored papers and the image, develop an abstract collage composition of color proportion based on variations of the color scheme within the photo. Mount your design onto illustration board or other sturdy recyclable artist board. Do not duplicate the shapes or recreate the image. Provide a written analysis of how the collage relates in proportion and scale to the magazine clipping. Document and provide credit to the magazine, page number, and designer (if available) for the photo chosen. The purpose is to emulate (1) the color palette, (2) the proportions, and (3) the essence of the photo.
3. Locate a natural object such as a seashell, leaf, flower, or pinecone, or a photo of a colorful fish, bird, or butterfly. Using any colored media of your choosing, create a composition of colors with proportions the same as those within the natural object. This exercise tests your ability to identify color proportion, and it also tests your ability to correctly select colored media that accurately mirror the colors in the natural object.

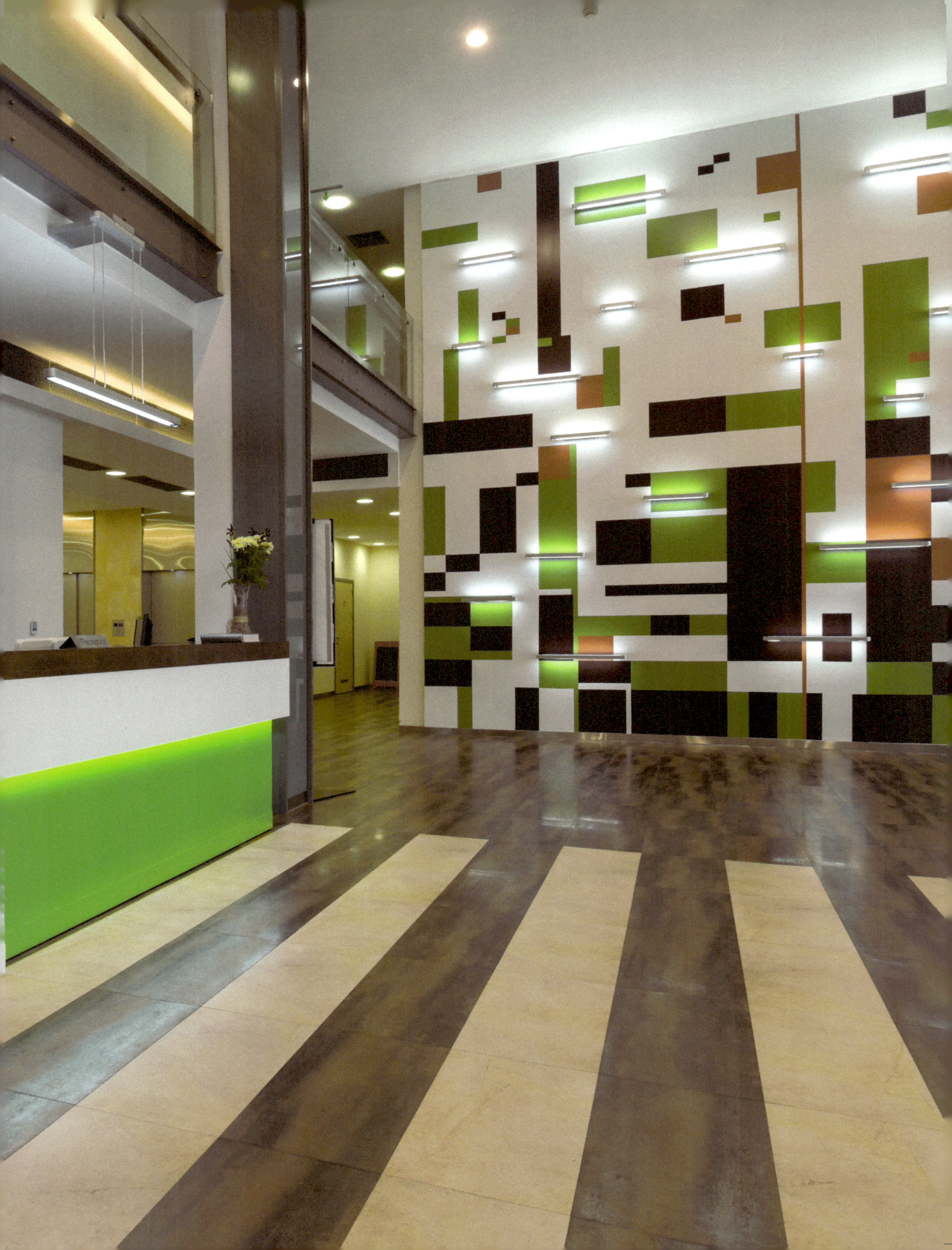

9

color + unity + harmony

Learning Outcomes

After studying this chapter, you will be able to:

- **Discuss how colors that share a common hue will relate and harmonize better than colors that have no common color connection.**
- **Create repetition of color throughout a space to unify the palette and the interior design.**
- **Discuss how a single color can be used to unify two different design elements.**
- **Explain how color gradation of value and intensity can be used to distinguish between two similar design elements.**
- **Create uniform distribution and use of color in a complex interior space to harmonize the visual clutter.**
- **Demonstrate how color harmonies should be planned to accentuate the interior, not overwhelm the space.**

Color is the personality of each design element chosen for an interior. Before we can touch an object, we see it, and in that moment, the color and object communicate. The color combination in any design can attract attention, establish meaning, and provide beauty. **Unity** is defined as the repetition of color to achieve a unified whole. **Harmony** is the result of a perfect balance between individual color relationships. A color harmony can be recognized when our eyes are not overworked when trying to view the applied color solution. If the color combinations result in a pleasing whole where no one color stands out, then you've achieved a color harmony. "Our brains look for elements, and when we recognize them we see a cohesive design rather than unorganized chaos" (Lauer & Pentak, 2007, p. 29).

Unity and harmony of space can be achieved through similarity of color, shape, and form. Color, shape, and form are inseparable design elements. Individually, shape and color may be perceived as being modified in appearance due to their surroundings or by the angle in which they are viewed; separately they are unpredictable, while together they are much stronger. Without unity there is no harmony. Color harmony suggests "that color cannot be separated from one another" and that "form strengthens color and vice versa" (Burchett, 2005, p. 50). For instance, when a round button on a computer is accented with the hue red, the button communicates what the object is, and it is color that allows the eye to discern its purpose: Power OFF. "A literal application of this theory might lead to the conclusion that color produces an essentially emotional experience, whereas shape corresponds to the intellectual control" (Arnheim, 1974, p. 336). A careful balancing of the emotional and visual stimuli will result in unity and harmonizing of interior spaces.

Achieving visual harmony varies with the systems being used. What might look right in the red, yellow, blue (RYB) pigment system may not look the same using the CMYK process system. Therefore, the variation of color harmonies will be dictated by the source. For our purposes, we will use the standard RYB, which is more common among artists and paint manufacturers. The work of most designers will eventually move beyond traditional color harmonies to exploring more dynamic and innovative approaches to color use. Now it is time to learn the basics of color harmonizing and those colors that work well together and those that do not. There is no one ideal way to identify and select harmonious color schemes. Regardless of whether you know anything about color harmony, you can see when a color combination is in **discord**—that is, clashing, unbalanced, disharmonized combination that departs from the natural ordering of color. For instance, a combination of a pale blue paired with a more intense, saturated orange will create a color discord, or when the colors are widely separated from one another on the color wheel. This may be the experience desired for drawing attention and to stand-out from the overall design. The harmonies described ahead will hopefully lead you to explore other variations of color pairings, intensity levels, and values shifts. Today, a wide variety of color palettes are generated in the marketplace and constantly evolve to fill the needs of consumer tastes. As long as theory is used as a general guide and the tendency is suppressed to impart your own subjective and personal attributes to a particular project, the opportunities for creating interesting color palettes are endless. The importance of getting to know your client should not be understated.

Six Elements of Color Harmony

Birren identified six elements of color harmony based on the original research conducted in 1839 by Chevreul. In *Principles of Color* (1969, pp. 34–35); these include harmonies of analogy and harmonies of contrast.

1. "The harmony of scale in which closely related values of a single hue are exhibited together."
2. "The harmony of hues in which analogous colors of similar value are exhibited."
3. "The harmony of a dominant colored light in which an assortment of different hues and values is pervaded as if by a dominant tinted light."
4. "The harmony of contrast of scale in which strongly different values of a single hue are combined."
5. "The harmony of contrast of hues in which related colors are exhibited in strongly different values (and strongly different degrees of purity or chroma)."
6. "The harmony of contrast of colors . . . colors belonging to scales very far asunder"—in other words, colors that are separated or that are farther apart from one another on the color wheel (red and green, blue-green and red-orange). The farther apart hues are located on the color wheel, the higher the contrast. Contrasts

between hues ultimately add visual rhythm and variety to a space. Colors closer together have a softer contrast, while colors farther apart have a harder and stronger visual contrast.

Harmonies of Analogy

Adjacent hues on the color wheel have lesser contrast and will come together in color solutions that are either warm (red, red-orange, yellow-orange) or cool (blue, blue-green, green). A palette could include both warm and cool hues (blue, blue-violet, red-violet). The inclusion of warm and cool hues balances the color harmony.

The closer the hues are placed to one another on the color wheel, the lower the apparent color contrast will be within an interior space. Creating expanded analogous harmonies that incorporate both warm and cool hues—blue-green, green, yellow-green, yellow—will increase the contrast level; however, contrast is still moderate because they are relatively close or adjacent to each other on the color wheel to be considered analogous. The next section features several types of color combinations that designers use for successful color harmony.

Harmonies of Contrast

Color opposites on the color wheel create the most vivid contrasts. These color solutions are used whenever visual impact is required. This color harmony is effective for retail and hospitality spaces associated with activity, excitement, and energy.

The Seven Color Harmonies

Harmony in color is beauty in nature; the color compositions seem natural as if plucked from the ground where no one color battles for dominance nor does one color stand out in the crowd. Harmony is totality, a palette that is seen as one versus many. When your eyes analyze a color palette and you get a sense or feeling that all is correct, your intuition is telling you that the color arrangement is harmonious. For some, this intuitive skill requires refinement; for others, it comes naturally. However, good intuition does not rule out the need to understand the color relationships that theorists have studied and written about for decades.

Harmony in interior spaces can be achieved through similarity of color applied, despite differences that may exist to interior and architectural elements within the environment. The principle of **uniform connectedness** suggests that "elements that are connected by uniform visual properties, such as color, are perceived to be more related than elements that are not connected" (Lidwell, Holden, & Butler, 2003, p. 200). When all the elements and principles of design work in tandem, a natural organization of space occurs. When interior design elements do not share a basic visual language, a recognizable pattern is required to better understand the relationship of the parts to the whole. One way this can be done within your home involves a room setting where you wish to group together a variety of photos (places, people, landscapes, contemporary, traditional) that share no common visual language in one location within an interior space. If you group each of these photos with frames in a similar color and style, the collection will appear to relate, now that they have a common organizational design feature. With this method, you have unified the different photos and created harmony of the collection. Color harmony is critical when you consider that a space can be composed of many different materials (wall covering, paint, carpets, wood, fabrics, and decorative elements) in different quantities. The interior design must relate these interior features using the appropriate color (hue) for the space, the right balance of values (lights and darks) to add depth and articulation of design features, and lastly, chroma (bright and dull) to add drama and visual interest to create personality and purpose for the space in use.

Color perception differs from person to person. Particular color "personalities" come forth as a result of individual differences in hue, value, and saturation levels. Depending on these levels, certain color personalities harmonize well together and others do not. When too many colors are combined with too many variations in value and saturation level, the result can be chaotic and lack unity. On the other extreme, if too much of the same color is used extensively throughout a space, the interior becomes uninteresting. "Variety, on the other hand, when carried to an extreme for the sake of interest, can result in visual chaos . . . it is the careful and artistic tension between order and disorder, between unity and variety that enlivens harmony and creates interest in an interior setting" (Ching & Binggeli, 2005, p. 136).

It is important to understand the difference between a color "harmony" and a color "scheme." A scheme is a plan for a color solution or a selection of colors assembled to create a harmonious color palette. It is when the right selection of hues, values, and saturation emerge and appear to "match" with one another that harmony results. Often what we plan for a space isn't always the best solution. Interior designers are confronted on occasion with color schemes prepared by other sources, oftentimes retailers of fabrics, paints, wall coverings, and so forth. In most of these cases, the schemes are well prepared, and in other times, they need reworking to be effective for your particular design. In the latter, you are seeking a "harmony" for an outcome that works well and is desirable to you and your clients. When we refer to a specific color "harmony"; we are generally speaking to the basic techniques used by color theorists to describe fundamental color harmony from which more complex color schemes will emerge, and the creativity and exploration of color is tested. Here we will discuss the theory for specific harmonies that can be applied when selecting colors for a particular scheme.

There are seven types of color harmonies: monochromatic, complementary, split complementary and double complementary, analogous, triadic and tetradic, multi-hue, and achromatic. In Chapter 2 we defined the basic color harmonies most interior design practitioners utilize in their work. Of these seven types, two are more practically usable and easier to work with: complementary (contrast) and analogous (gradation of hue, not chroma).

Monochromatic

Monochromatic is the easiest harmony to identify and work with. A single hue is selected with variations in tint, tones, and shades to provide variety in the palette (Figure 9.1a). This palette is very simple and easy to recognize partially due to the absence of or limited high contrasts. To prevent this color solution from being monotonous, the use of textures and value contrasts is important in creating visual interest in the space (Figure 9.1b). In addition, without enough visual contrast, the space can be confusing and potentially add to safety concerns if changes in floor and other surface levels are not easily identifiable. In Figure 9.2, the abundant use of the same value of red can be disorienting, and therefore a potential concern

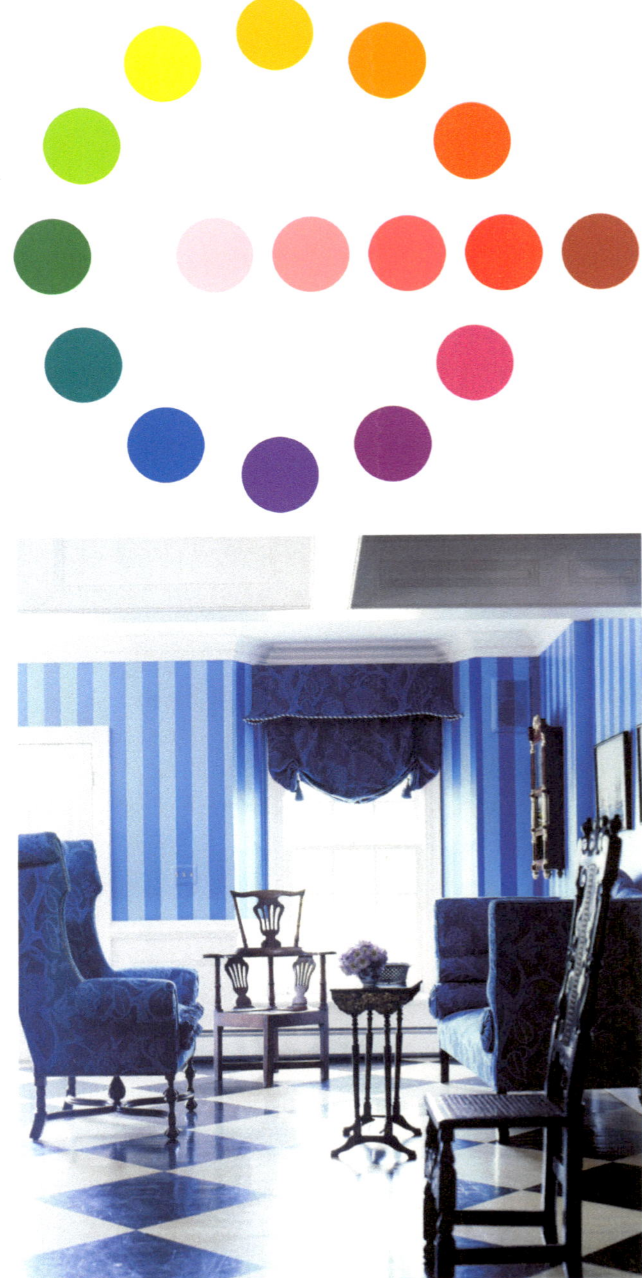

Figure 9.1 (a) Monochromatic red color harmony. (b) Monochromatic blue interior color scheme.

when a person is attempting to navigate the space. This is an example of how color has the potential to influence the behavior of a person, such as feeling anxious or excited, or even safety with someone who has a vision impairment or is sensitive to color and light including older adults who often have difficulty distinguishing between surface level changes. Imagine this in a large-scale commercial

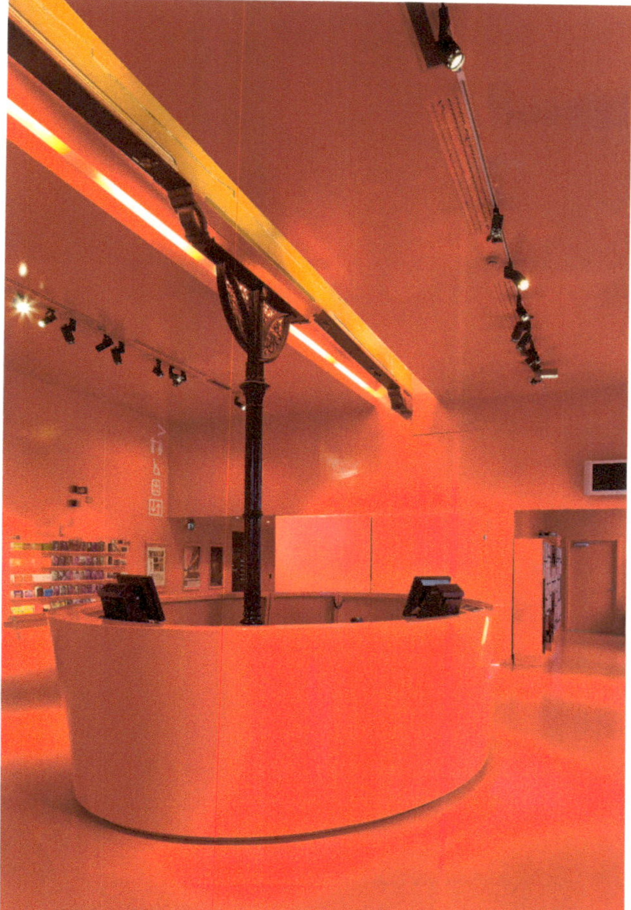

Figure 9.2 Nobel Peace Center, Adjaye Associates, Oslo, Norway, 2005. The foyer with reception desk and shop to one side is blanketed in red, glossy surfaces that decreases the ability to distinguish features. The interior is counterpointed to a connecting space, not shown, that is bathed in green where the two colors symbolize times of peace and war. The afterimage of the color red–green—from the prolonged viewing of the color makes the transition into the adjoining green space less bothersome.

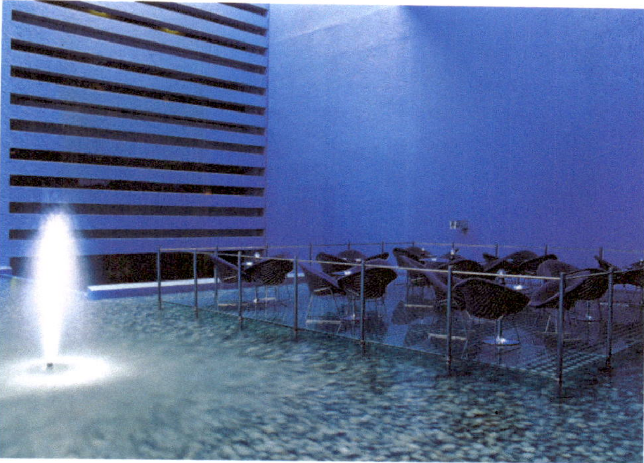

Figure 9.3 The Blue Lounge at the Camino Real Hotel in Mexico City.

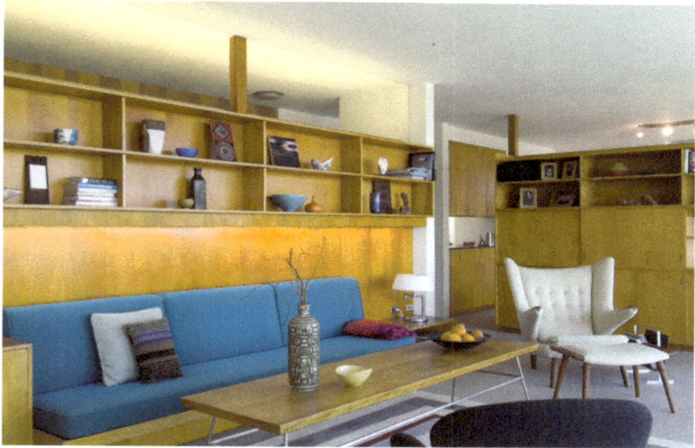

Figure 9.4 Color harmony can be achieved in ways beyond the traditional paint and textiles. Woods, stones, glass, and metals will also contribute to the overall interior palette. The blue textile on the sofa and blue décor, along with the orange coloring of the surrounding oak woodwork, combine to create a complementary blue-orange color harmony.

space versus a small residential space. The outcomes could be harmful without consideration of the possible physiological effects that could occur.

In Figure 9.3, the opposite is true of the monotony theory. This interior of the Blue Lounge at the Camino Real Hotel in Mexico City uses a highly saturated blue that is meant to relax visitors in the lounge area. Sound from the pool of water, horizontal lines of the architectural elements on the far wall, and low color contrast all lead to the desired outcome.

In Figure 9.4, the large gathering space is predominantly one shade of blue; however, the space works for two different reasons: (1) There is a good balance between textural surfaces and contrast of light and dark materials, and (2) the wood finish casts a yellow-orange hue that complements the blue. Materials and textiles all work to create a color harmony.

Complementary

Complementary color palettes (Figure 9.5) are often chosen for their visual interest, their high contrast, and their ability to accent the interior with a dominant hue. These color solutions usually include one cool and one warm hue, which create the vivid contrasts (Figure 9.6a) and high energy associated with complements. Varying

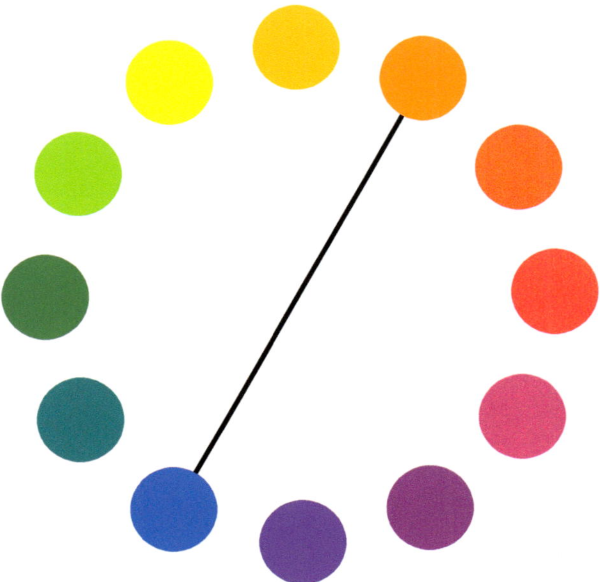

Figure 9.5 Complementary color harmony.

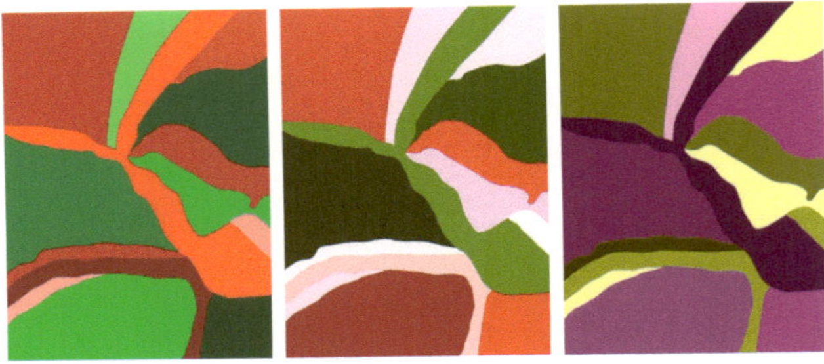

Figure 9.6 (a) Itten's contrast of warm and cool. (b) Itten's contrast of tint and shade. (c) Itten's contrast of complements.

the degree of lightness (tint) and/or darkness (shade) of one of the complementary hues will minimize this effect (Figure 9.6b). Figure 9.6c illustrates a concept of opposing colors overlapping one another to show the brilliance, purity, and contrast level that can be achieved with complementary harmonies. You will notice that in each of these three illustrations, varying the amounts of each color will create a more pleasing harmony. With each color solution, you do not have to have equal amounts of each color. Equal amounts of each color could result in monotony. Light color can balance the dark, and the dark colors could provide visual relief from intense colors. For each of these harmonies, a careful balance of light and dark, high and low saturation is achieved.

Complementary neutralization

Two complementary colors, or colors opposite one another on the color wheel, will combine to form a brown hue as previously illustrated with digital color mixing shown in Chapter 2, Figure 2.27. But it is important to understand the concept of **complementary neutralization**, the result of combining two complementary colors of paint, pigment, dyes, or other colorants together. We might consider neutral, or achromatic color, as black, white, and gray; true neutrals, however, also encompass browns or warm and cool nuances of hues, resulting from mixing two complementary hues together. Similar to the value scale discussed in Chapter 2, a **chromatic scale**—the value of a color from light to dark, or with a complementary color on one end of the scale and the second complement on the other end with the toned neutral in the middle of the gradual shift in color scale—is created when you mix two complementary colors together (red and green; blue and orange, purple and yellow), not neutral or with black, white, and gray. Depending on the amount of complementary color mixed together, the resulting desaturated color

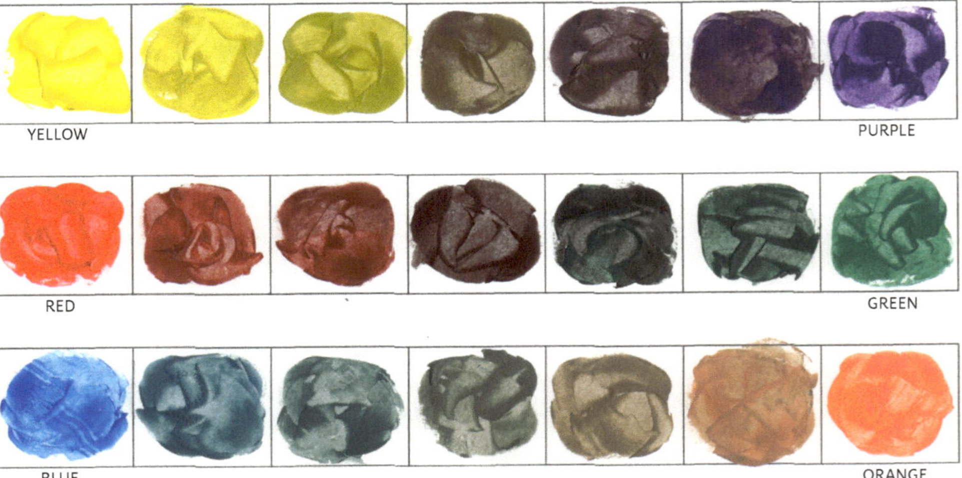

Figure 9.7 Complementary neutralization with pigments, or gradual dulling of color, resulting from the mixture of two complementary colors to create a neutral hue.

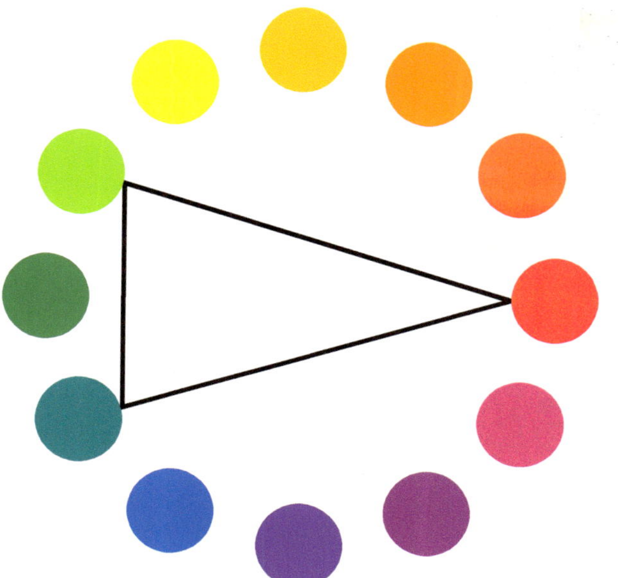

Figure 9.8 Split complementary color harmony.

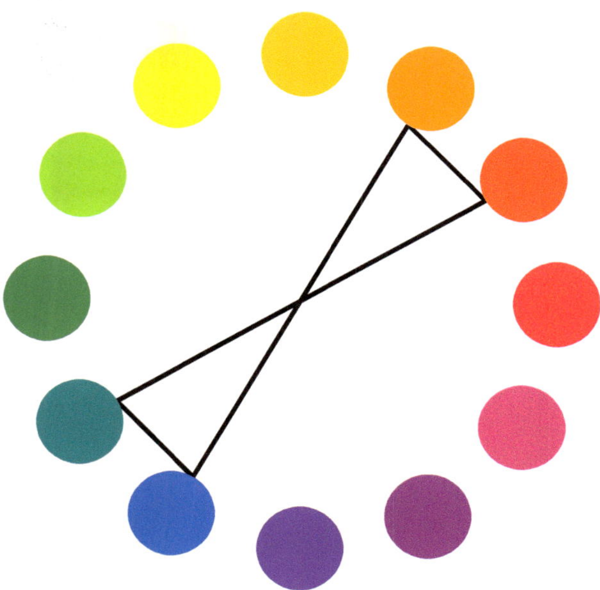

Figure 9.9 Double complementary color harmony.

will gradually produce a warm or cool gray or brown tone (Figure 9.7). The resulting hues are also called toned neutrals since a subtle presence of the parent hues can be seen in the gradual mixtures creating a more dynamic palette. If you want to lighten the resulting neutral, and to increase its value range, the gradual addition of white will expand the palette.

Split Complementary and Double Complementary

Split complements (Figure 9.8) are much the same as complementary; rather than taking the opposite color from the starting hue on the color wheel, you select the two colors on either side of its complement. This **split complementary** harmony has less visual contrast than a direct complement but adds the third color to give you more variety in your color planning. **Double complementary** harmony includes two adjacent hues and their complements (Figure 9.9). As with any color scheme, proportioning is the key to making it successful. Refer to the strategies outlined in Chapter 8.

Analogous

Analogous harmonies, which incorporate between three and five adjacent hues, allow a designer to vary color while still maintaining a recognizable relationship

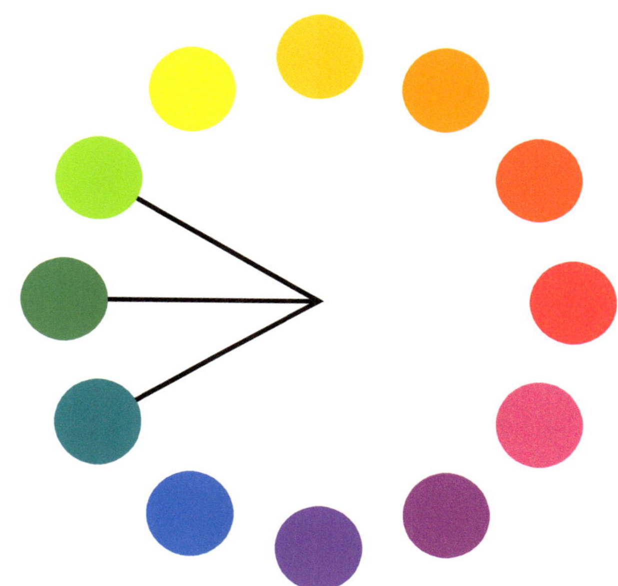

Figure 9.10 Analogous color harmony.

(Figure 9.10). An analogous color solution, with its absence of a strong complement, makes the color palette less startling and more inviting. This color mix might be used in a space where people want to feel calm and relieved of anxiety, or when extended periods of stay may occur, such as in hospital waiting rooms, restaurants for fine dining, living and conversation spaces, and places for rest and sleeping. Choose an analogous color solution that incorporates at least 50 percent of the hues from the

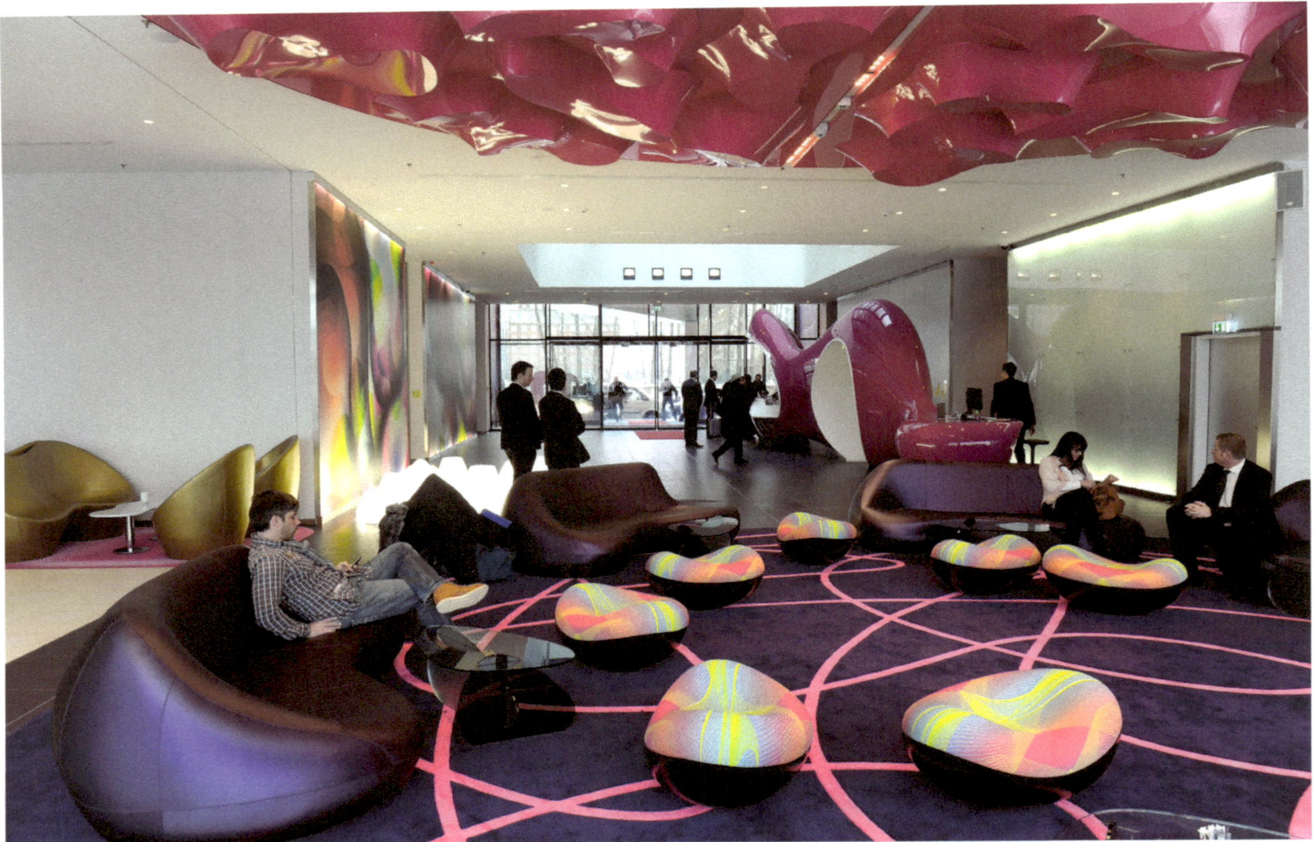

Figure 9.11 The music and lifestyle hotel Nhow designed by Karim Rashid in Berlin, Germany, boasts a vivid use of red, red-violet, and violet hues, forming an analogous color harmony.

cool side of the color wheel. Analogous color harmony will have one parent hue that is repeated in at least two-thirds of the total composition (red, red-orange, orange or blue, blue-green, green). In Figure 9.11, this lounge and bar space illustrates an analogous color palette of blue-violet, violet, red-violet, and red. The predominate use of a blue-violet hue in the carpet and textiles grounds the space and circular seating group. A playful and repeated use of fluid lines, amorphous shapes, vivid colors, contrast of surface textures, and exaggerated scale creates a unified space. Any one of the colors within the analogous harmony can be used as the dominant color, or the colors can be equally distributed in the space; in any situation, analogous color harmonies provide great flexibility.

Triadic and Tetradic

Triadic color harmonies include three colors that are equidistant from one another, and **tetradic** harmonies include four equally spaced colors on the color wheel. Much like the complementary harmony, triadic and tetradic harmonies offer obvious contrast and result in palettes that are predominately warm or cool depending on the location of the color selection within the color wheel (Figure 9.12a and b). With three colors opposing one another and vying for dominance, the triadic harmony should establish one of the hues as the dominant proportion, with the remaining two taking on subdominant roles to be most effective. Figures 9.12a and b are interior examples of triadic and tetradic color harmonies, respectively.

In Figure 9.13a, the triadic harmony of purple, orange, and green has been applied. In this kitchen space, the orange hue is represented in the natural color of the wood cabinetry and bar stool textile, green accents the island, and the dominant purple hue is used for the interior wall surfaces. In Figure 9.13b, the color harmony has been modified to include a tetradic harmony of blue-green (wall color), red-orange (wood tones), red-violet (accent wall color), and yellow-green (barstools). Notice how the darker flooring changes the overall spatial volume and

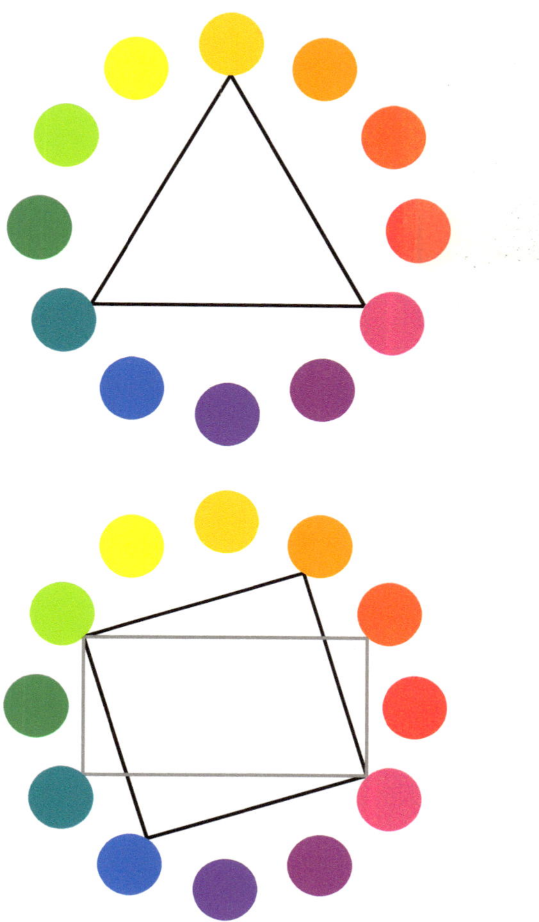

Figure 9.12 (a) Triadic color harmony. (b) Tetradic color harmony.

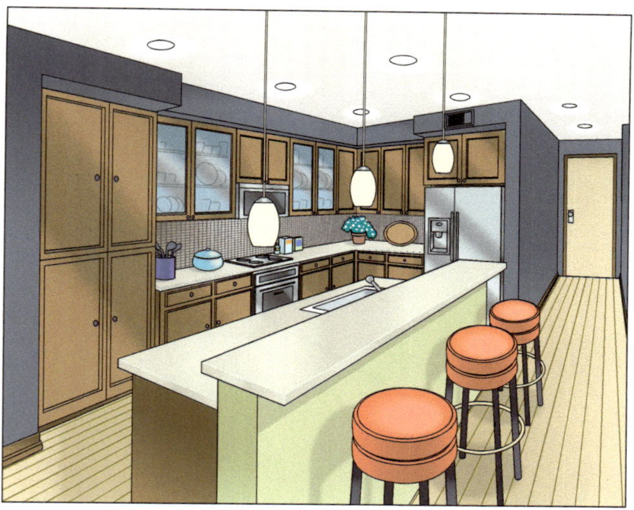

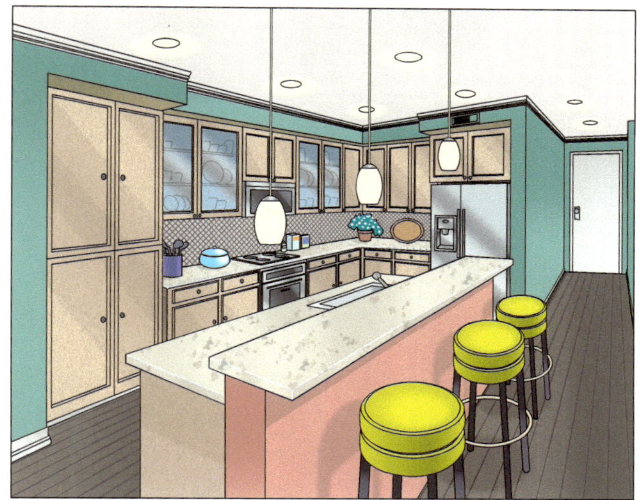

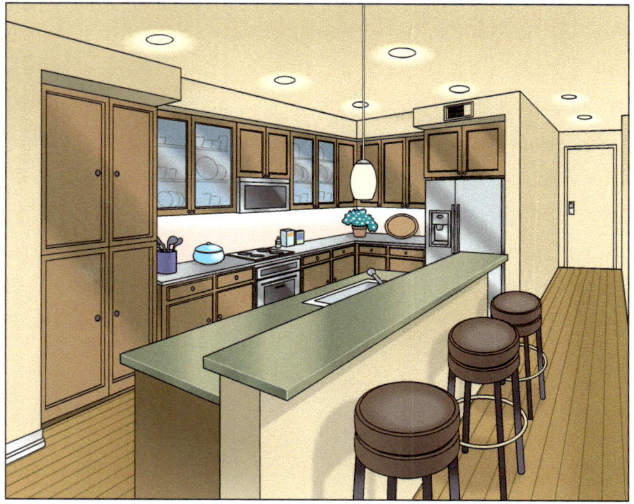

Figure 9.13 (a) Interior example of a triadic color harmony. (b) Interior example of a tetradic color harmony. (c) Original kitchen interior before color harmonies were assigned.

proportions of the space. Establishing dominance and proportions is a key to making this successful. Much like the complementary color harmony, the triadic and tetradic color solutions, being equidistant across the color wheel, create dynamic and attention-grabbing spaces. Figure 9.13c is the original, unchanged kitchen.

Multi-hue

Another harmony to be discussed is the **multi-hue** color solution. This palette appears to suggest that all rules are out—select whatever and however many colors you want. On the contrary, this scheme is the most difficult to use because it is entirely dependent on the proportions of the colors to achieve the right harmony. Two key concepts have to be considered. First, you need to establish a relationship within the palette between all colors—for instance, in the series of blue, blue-green, red-orange, and red. Because of shared hues, they are

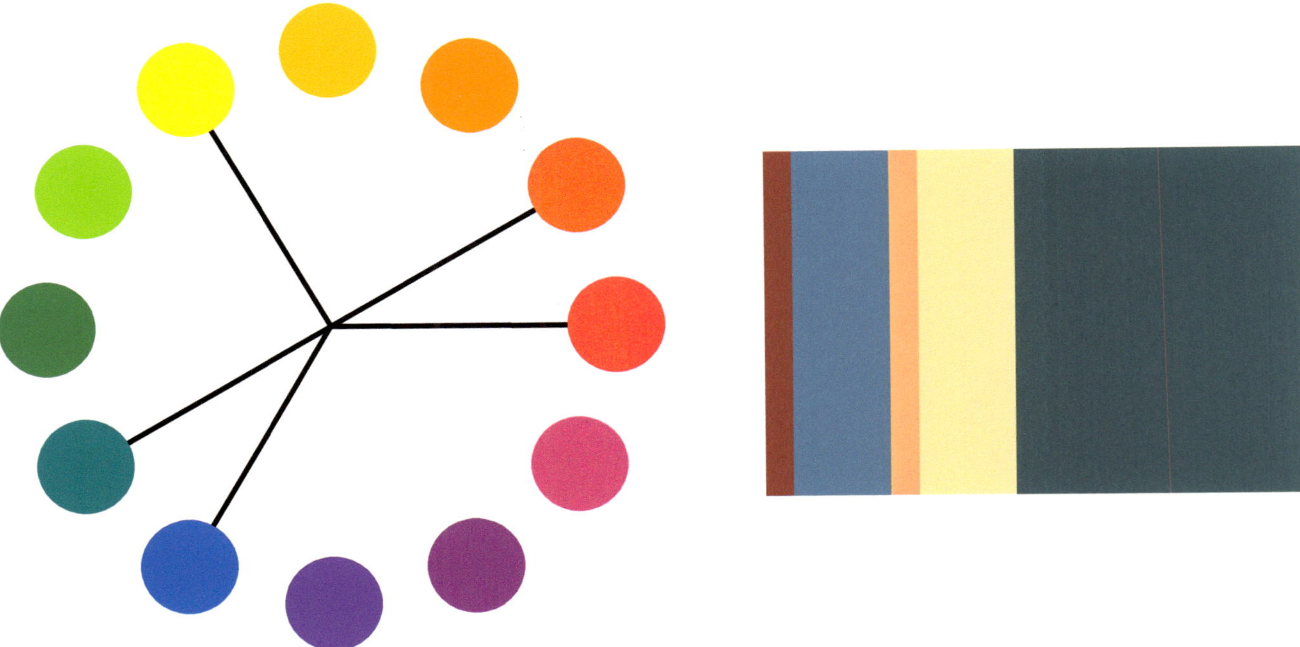

Figure 9.14 Multi-hue color harmony. The saturation levels have been adjusted to harmonize the color palette.

all complementary to one another. You can insert an accent—in this case yellow—and you have a five-part color harmony. Second, you need to properly proportion the colors to balance the mix. A dominant hue will need to be identified that will be the obvious color emphasized within the space. Figure 9.14 illustrates the twelve-step color wheel and the colors proportioned into a multihued color harmony. If you refer back to Figure 7.7, you can see an example of multicolor harmony. The blue painted onto the ceiling is used as the dominant hue to unify the series of painted columns and harmonize the space. Figure 9.15 provides a chart for monochromatic, analogous, triadic, and complementary color harmonies in an expanded color range of all twelve hues in the basic color circle. This can be used when you are making decisions about particular color harmonies in your projects.

Achromatic

Achromatic or color-neutral solutions are popular in many interiors because of their simplicity and focus on natural color, and restful backdrop to other elements in the space. These color palettes are usually based around hues such as gray, ivory, tan, brown, khaki, beige, black, and white. In most cases, such color applications are intended to place focus on the physical characteristics, including texture and pattern, of the interior and materials, rather than color used in the design of the space. Mies van der Rohe's Farnsworth House, designed and built from 1945 to 1951 in Plano, Illinois, is an exemplary use of natural materials and an open plan, with the large, light-glazed area blurring the lines between inside and outside (Figure 9.16). In this setting, the use of colored hues would be out of place. To prevent monotony, add light and dark value contrasts of the neutral scheme, vary the lighting sources between both natural and artificial, and vary the textures to harmonize an achromatic color palette. In Figure 9.17, the green accent color and graphic feature wall add interest and reduce the perceived size of the space for an otherwise neutral material palette of this interior. The interior has been designed with high contrasts of values from light to dark, various visual textures, and a variety of materials (glass, wood, and metals), all harmonizing with clean, simple lines, allowing the color accents to brighten the space and take its place as the focal point. The addition of an accent color is sometimes used in achromatic color solutions to add more visual interest.

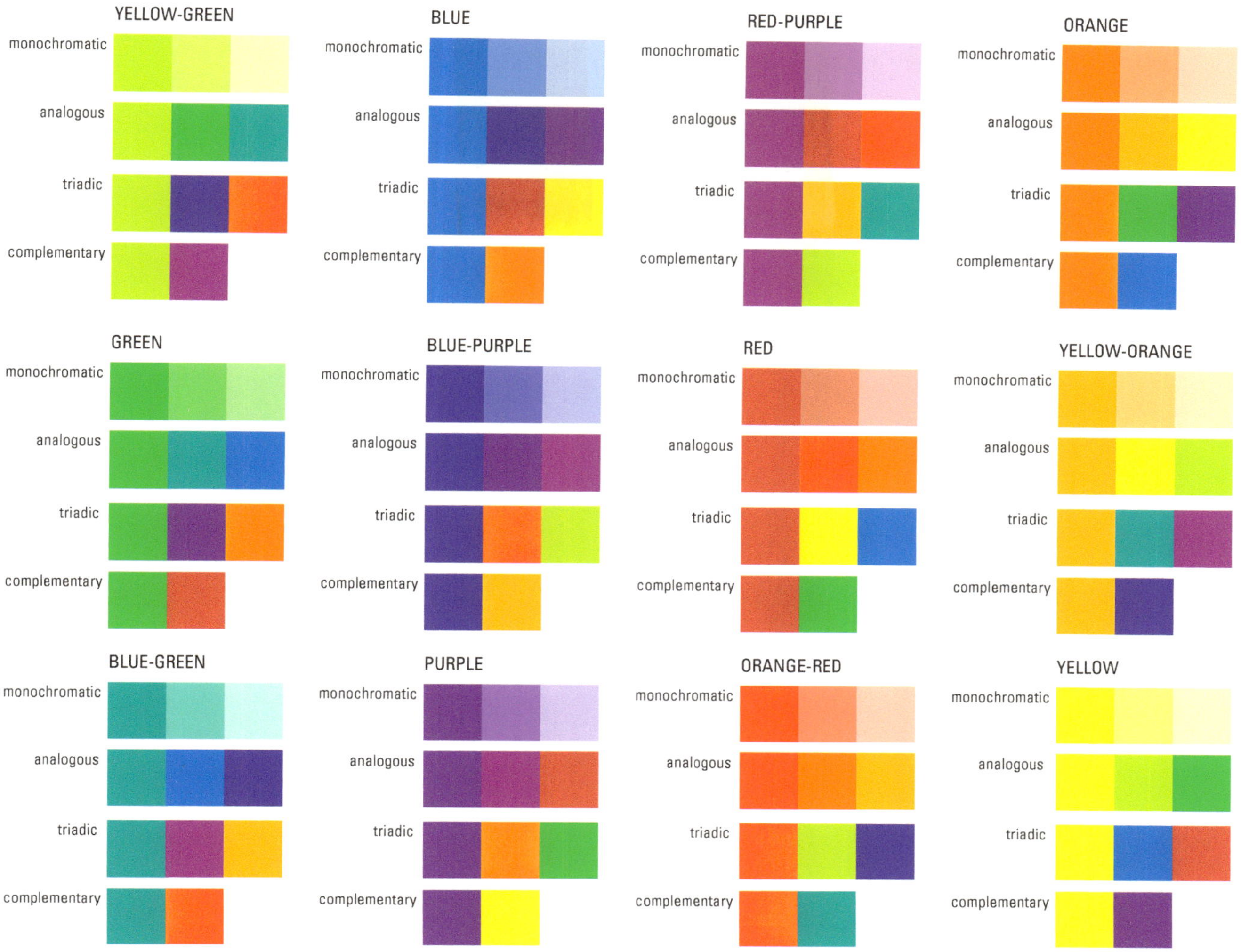

YELLOW-GREEN
monochromatic
analogous
triadic
complementary

BLUE
monochromatic
analogous
triadic
complementary

RED-PURPLE
monochromatic
analogous
triadic
complementary

ORANGE
monochromatic
analogous
triadic
complementary

GREEN
monochromatic
analogous
triadic
complementary

BLUE-PURPLE
monochromatic
analogous
triadic
complementary

RED
monochromatic
analogous
triadic
complementary

YELLOW-ORANGE
monochromatic
analogous
triadic
complementary

BLUE-GREEN
monochromatic
analogous
triadic
complementary

PURPLE
monochromatic
analogous
triadic
complementary

ORANGE-RED
monochromatic
analogous
triadic
complementary

YELLOW
monochromatic
analogous
triadic
complementary

Figure 9.15 Twelve-hue color harmony chart.

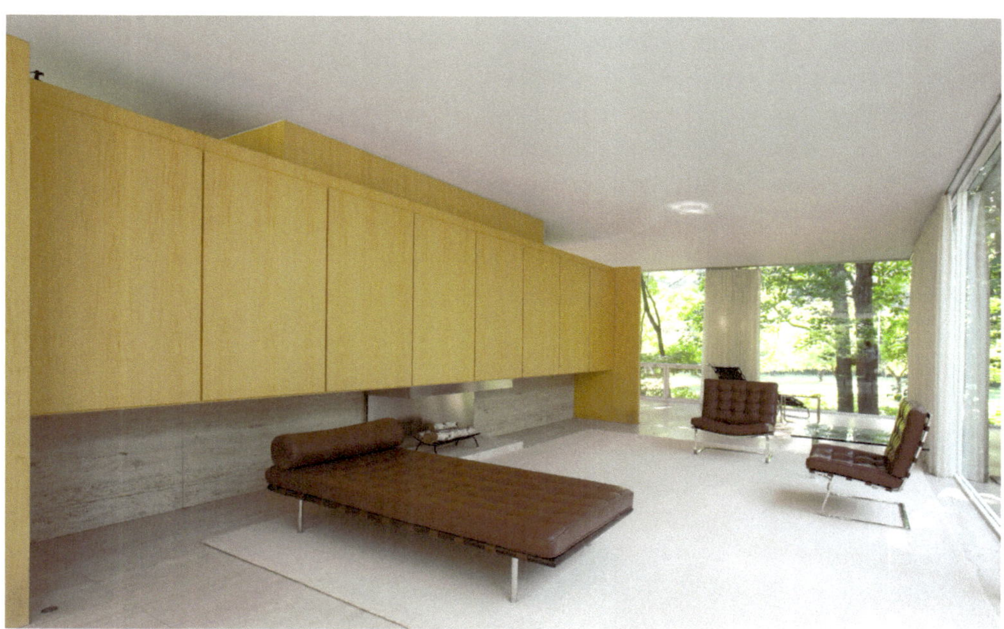

Figure 9.16 Interior living room view with Barcelona daybed in the Farnsworth House.

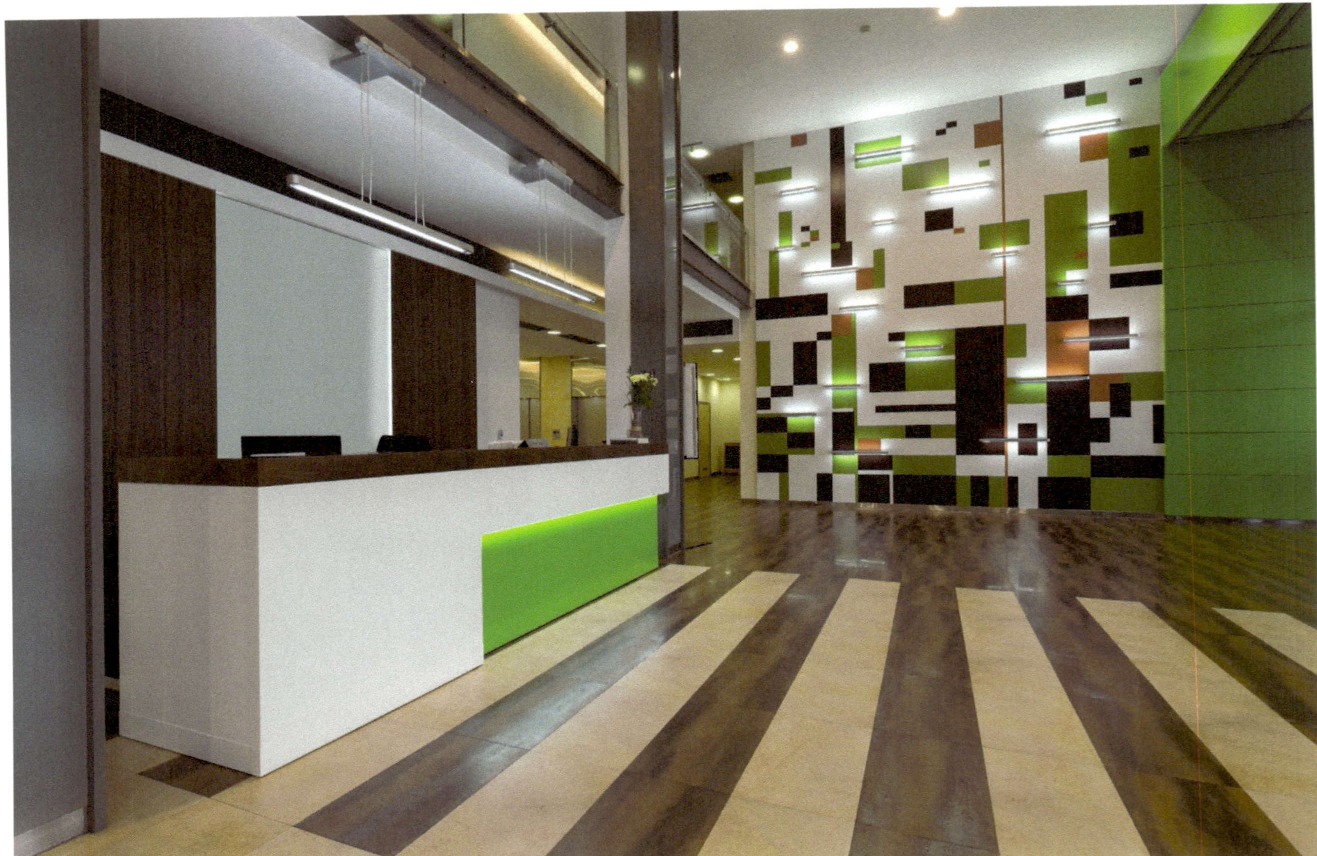

Figure 9.17 The use of green color in the background and integrated into the reception desk contrasts with the otherwise neutral interior. Bold graphics and a single color accent wall become the focal points in this modern space. The repetition and placement of color and material unifies the design solution.

Color, Space, Harmony

The fear of using bright color might be called in Latin "mega-pigmentochromophobia" (Lehndorff, 2002, p. 1E). The tendency and sage advice have historically been to stick with safe, neutral tones that won't make a splash. People who are simply untrained in the methods for applying color principles may suffer from indecision at crucial moments in the planning process—the conceptualization and application of color to a room's design elements. Many a client has lived in spaces with poor color harmonies only never to realize that the source of the problem *was* color.

"Excessive unity is often the pitfall of the beginning designer who, in an effort to keep control over the design, limits the visual palette too much . . . the best design is actually varied and subtly complex; it does not reduce the problem to its simplest terms, yet remains controlled" (Faimon & Weigand, 2004, p. 29). In Figure 9.18a, the interior of this hospital waiting room has been excessively limited in color. In addition, the single hue (blue) has been overused, creating a lifeless interior. Dark and highly saturated deep blue, a cold hue, is often perceived as depressive. Blue in this interior can produce a calming effect, suitable for a hospital waiting space, where anxiety and emotions can run high; however, this particular hue is too brash and not suitable for this particular application. Alone, the subtle use of violet for the guest chairs isn't enough of an analogous shift to circumvent the solemn character of the space. Often we think that cool, calming hues are the only option for relaxing or reducing nervous tension, but it is the use of saturation that can bring about the same results without relying solely on cool or analogous hues. If we (1) introduce an extended palette of colors, (2) reduce the intensity of those hues, and (3) create a contrast of hues, attention is drawn to

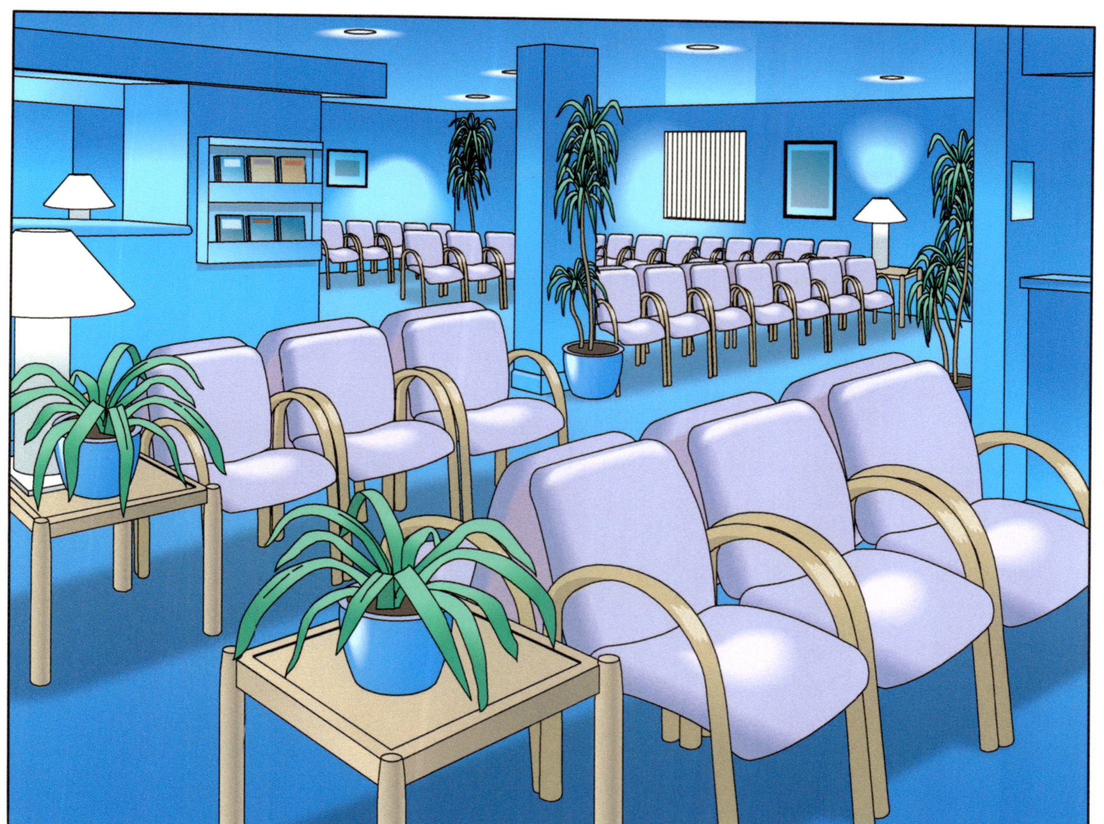

Figure 9.18a
The character of this hospital waiting room can be perceived as solemn and depressing when the wrong hue and intensity are used.

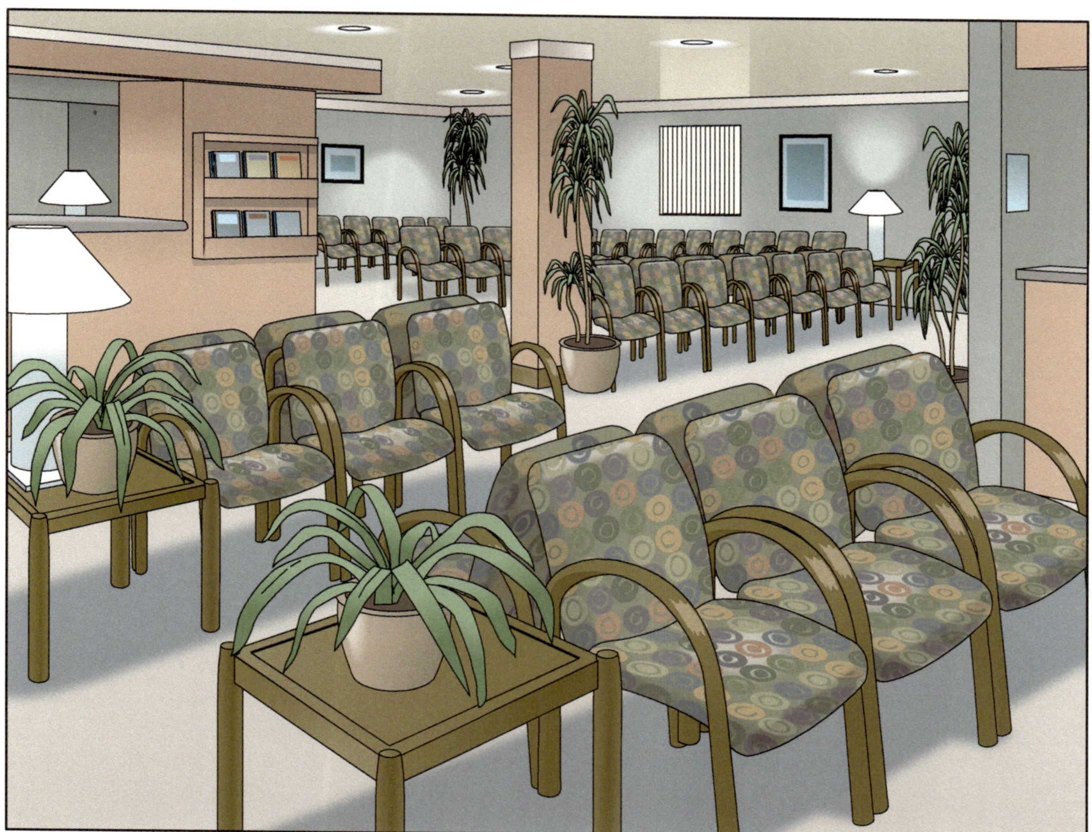

Figure 9.18b
Introducing color harmony, light and dark contrasts, and textile patterns; the interior of this waiting room is transformed into a welcoming and calm space.

architectural details such as moldings, columns, and the nurses' station. These areas "pop" in contrast to the original space and now have more visual interest and still maintain a soft, warm, welcoming space. The contrast between the crown molding and wall serves to introduce rhythm and carry the eye around the room's perimeter without being overwhelming (Figure 9.18b). By introducing contrasting hues (adobe red and sage green) that are lowered in chroma, the color plan is calm and begins to harmonize and unify the furnishings and accessories. Additionally, warm wood tones contrast and balance the finished interior.

When working out various color harmonies, consider the surface background you are using, because this will affect the perceived value of the color and strength of the harmony. We know that no color is isolated and thus colors affect one another. A blue-green hue next to a blue hue will appear greener than when next to a green hue. A white or black background will alter the lightness or darkness of a color; therefore, it is recommended that work be based on a neutral light gray, which will have the least visual impact on the color harmony. Figure 9.19 illustrates this concept. A single palette could look dramatically different with changes in background surface.

Many observational, scientific and theoretical approaches to understanding color harmony have been presented for centuries by artists, interior designers, graphic designers, and architects in an effort to help them make sound color choices. Experimentation in your own space or in design projects for others with the color harmonies presented in this chapter is part of learning and understanding color through trial and error. Natural and artificial light, age, vision, value and intensity are just some of the factors that influence unity and harmony of color.

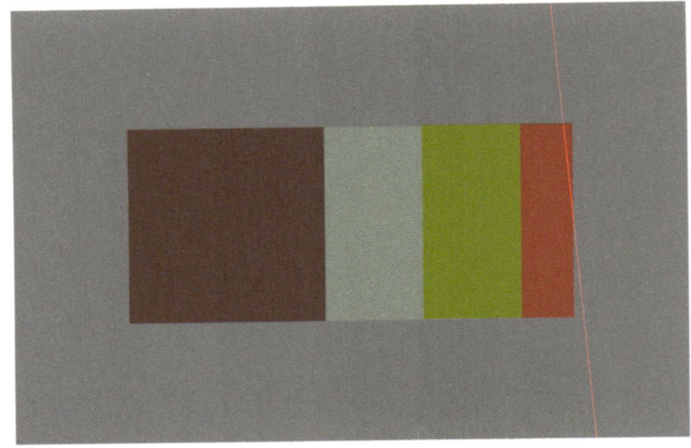

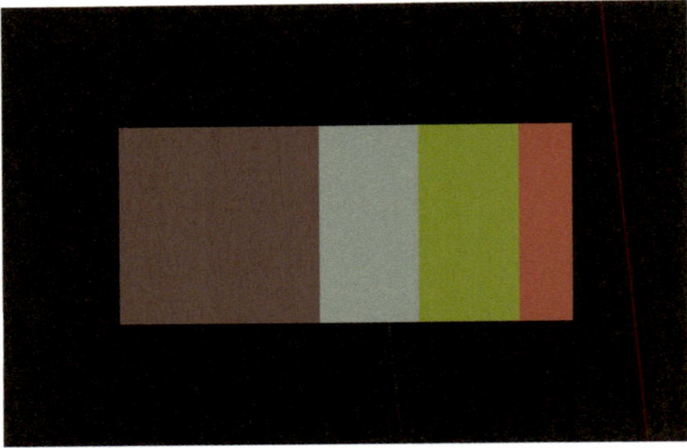

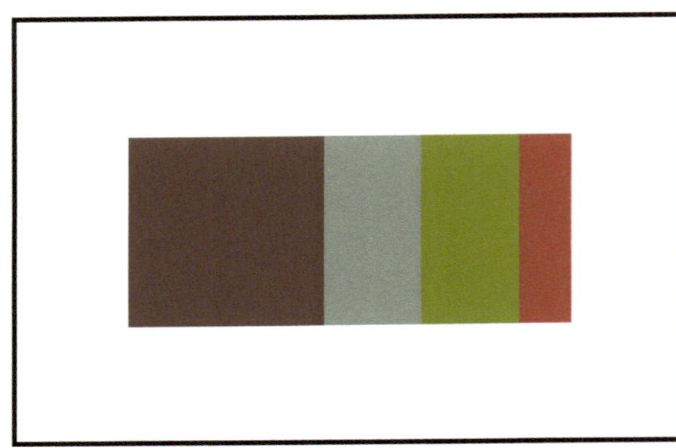

Figure 9.19 Color palettes alter when viewed on different background surfaces—simultaneous contrast.

REVIEW QUESTIONS

1. Explain the principles of unity and harmony.
2. List the six elements of color harmony developed by color theorist Faber Birren.
3. What is the difference between color harmony and color scheme?
4. List the seven major color harmonies and describe each.
5. What two color harmonies are easier to identify and prepare when starting a color plan?
6. Which type of color solutions can be monotonous and need contrast to be visually stimulating?
7. Describe an achromatic color palette.

Vocabulary

Unity
harmony
discord
uniform connectedness
monochromatic
complementary
complementary neutralization
chromatic scale
split complementary
double complementary
analogous
triadic
tetradic
multi-hue

EXERCISES

1. Create a twelve-step color wheel using Color-aid or other forms of colored media. This tool will be used in developing color harmonies. While purchasing a color wheel is an option and less of a time commitment, the act of creating the wheel will teach you about the relationship of various hues and their placement along the wheel.
2. Create a monochromatic color harmony with a minimum of three values.
3. Create two analogous color harmonies (one keyed to red and one keyed to blue).
4. Create three complementary color harmonies (one with each major hue: red, blue, green).
5. Create a split complementary color harmony using violet as your dominant hue.
6. Create a triadic color harmony.
7. Create a tetradic color harmony.
8. Create a multi-hue color harmony, paying attention to proportion and keying it to a dominant hue for unity in the composition. Use a minimum of five hues.
9. Select a piece of art from an art catalog. Use this art to create a color board based on the color harmony in the artwork. Select the interior finish materials such as wall paint, trim, flooring, and four textiles (for sofa, chair, drapery, and accent) to convey the essence of the art.
10. Create a discord harmony using three to four colors. Using the same parent hue for each color chosen in the discord, select three to four new colors, varying only the original color's value or saturation to bring the discord into harmony. Compare the two harmonies, and analyze the steps taken to correct the discord.
11. Practice complementary neutralization color mixing using water-based gouache paints from exercise 4 in Chapter 2. Use white watercolor or other artist paper for the exercise and suitable paint brushes. Have a cup of water nearby to clean your brush as you work. Having more than one brush for each color is also helpful to avoid color contamination between pigments. Next, prepare a range of complementary chromatic value steps for each of your primary and secondary complementary hues by gradually adding the complementary colors to one another as shown in Figure 9.7. Generate at least a five-step chromatic scale and up to ten steps to challenge and improve your skill.

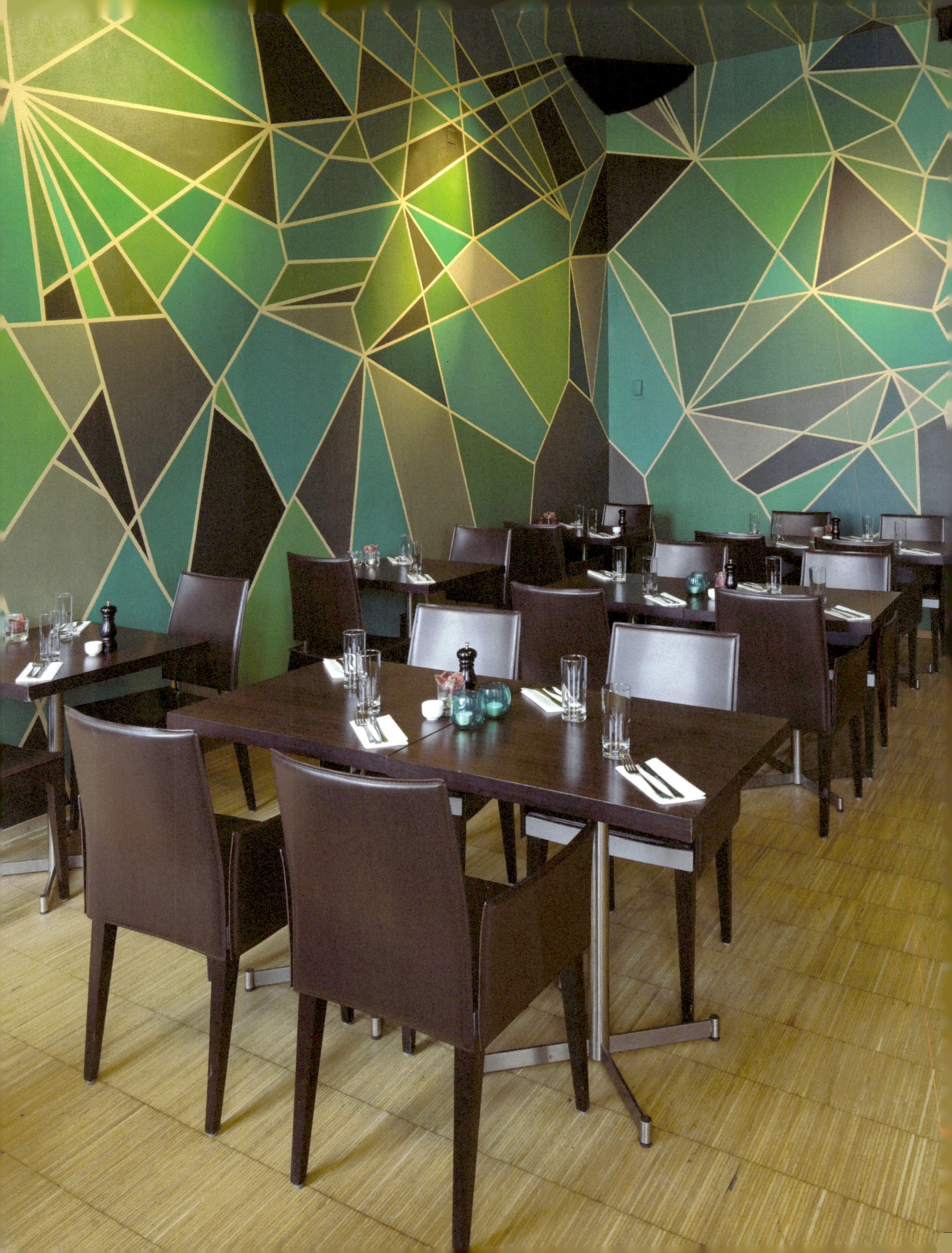

10

color + variety + design elements

Learning Outcomes

After studying this chapter, you will be able to:

- **Describe how the right amount of variety in colors can create or modify an interior.**
- **Change rooms that are too simple or "boxlike" into more visually interesting interiors when one or more elements in the space are treated with color to differentiate those elements from the other design features in the room.**
- **Recognize that impulsive uses of color can provide too much variety that lacks unity and harmony within the space.**
- **Show how colored light and colored translucent materials can add to the visual variety; however, be constantly aware of the amount and type of light source (natural or artificial) that is to be used, and control it.**
- **Recognize that excessive light can add too much visual contrast and upset the color varieties intended.**
- **Arrange color with line, shape, texture, and pattern to add visual stimuli and create a variety of experiences for users of the built environment.**

In order to understand how color can further add interest and excitement to a space, we will look at variety as the remaining principle of design to achieve this end. Variety takes into consideration all the techniques with color we've discussed to this point in the book. It is essential to train one's color judgment, to build confidence in using color, and to learn color use with the right amount of knowledge and information combined with intuition. After reading this book and completing the exercises, you will be able to create many stimulating color solutions for your interior design projects.

"Order without diversity can result in monotony or boredom, diversity without order can produce chaos. . . . A sense of unity with variety is the ideal" (Ching, 1996, p. 320). **Variety** is the principle of design that combinations of one or more different hues, values, shapes, forms, patterns, and textures can create diversity, contrast, and interest in an interior space. Without variety, a space is static, inactive, and monotonous, making the visual composition uninteresting. "Design implies a plan, a conscious intent. When an image becomes too complex, whether by intention or by accident—when too much variety becomes visually chaotic—the image ceases to be designed . . . design implies some amount of control" (Faimon & Weigand, 2004, p. 27). It is simple: Don't decorate. The lack of control shows a lack of skill and will be evident to your clients.

A balance of visual dullness and visual variety is necessary to prevent an overly animated space. Kopacz states in *Color in Three-Dimensional Design* that "an overabundance of complexity may over-stimulate the occupant to the point of stress, evidenced by changes in pulse rate, blood pressure, or breathing" (2004, p. 68).

Early in this book we discussed the power of using a grid to prepare proportional relationships among colors. When seeking to unify a variety of different objects, using a grid is a way to organize a design into a system that allows for the variation of design elements to be viewed as a whole. This method is a great way to organize a personal collection. Often times, clients' spaces are cluttered with a scattering of objects collected from travels or personal collections they've accumulated over the years. At some point, the collection reaches a size that requires one to edit the collection or use a design plan that establishes order using one or two objects as a focal point. The vintage, colored typewriter case collection displayed in Figure 10.1 becomes a focal point on the wall through variety of color, shape, size, and material. The cases are organized into a grid—framed with a black backdrop to contrast—unified into a successful design feature.

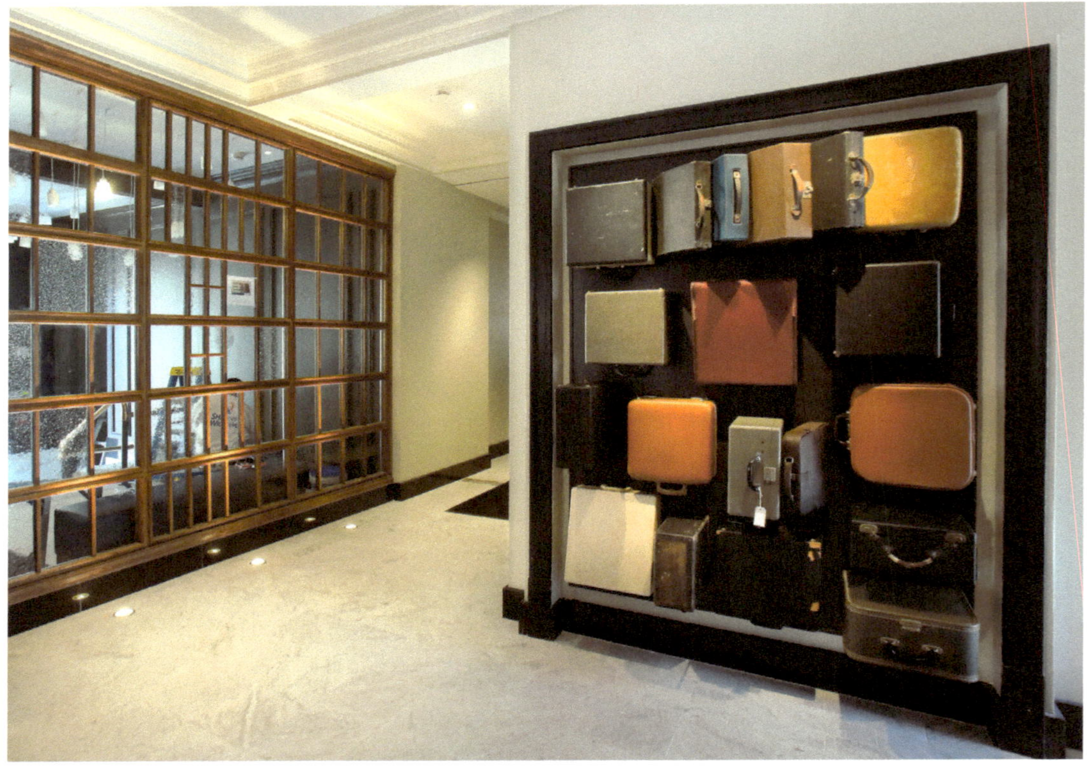

Figure 10.1 Old typewriter cases adorn a wall near the entrance to the Press Hotel in Portland. The window framing at left is designed to recall letterpress boxes that used to hold type used in printing. Developer Jim Brady has branded the history of the *Portland Press Herald* and newspaper journalism throughout the hotel, which is housed in the former Press Herald building.

Variety and Interest

A color scheme can enhance the visual interest of your interior space. Selecting one or more hues from a color wheel and varying the lightness or darkness of the chosen color allows variety and interest to form. As you are selecting hues, keep in mind that values—black, white, and gray (achromatic)—are just as visually active as colored hues (Figure 10.2). Achromatic color schemes need texture, pattern and value contrast to achieve the best results. Use color to reinforce your design, not merely to decorate. If you use color purely for decorative means, the final design could lessen the opportunity for the user of the space to form meaning, a personal connection and the possibility for long-term enjoyment of the solution. The physical design of a particular space—the layout, interior architectural features, lighting design, hardware, and textiles, to name a few elements—should be supported by the colors you mutually agree on with partners, clients, and consultants. Color applied decoratively may not consider the perception it creates of the design, its intended purpose, and the way the user is to respond and interact with the design. For instance, using a dark, dull color at an interior entrance might give the signal "stay away" or "private," thus contradicting the motive to enter through a clear entrance and stay in an inviting space. This color choice could obscure the entrance and hide or distract from the design's purpose. However, an entrance that is dark surrounded with lighter hues within will add interest, stand out, and therefore draw attention and provide "identity and hierarchy" (Ching, 1996, p. 108). To be successful, think about the color and its contexts in the overall design of the space; color as decoration may not guarantee the best intended outcome.

Variety adds the visual break from a design, much like emphasis but in a more complex manner. Variety consists of more than one design element, clustered in a composition sharing similar traits such as size, shape, or pattern. Use color, or similar color values, and saturation to group design elements or concepts and establish correlations within your design. In Figure 10.3, the lobby ceiling in the Bellagio Hotel, Las Vegas, is covered with colored, amoeba-like glass forms by Dale Chihuly. The variety of color adds the drama and interest, while the cluster application is a unified whole.

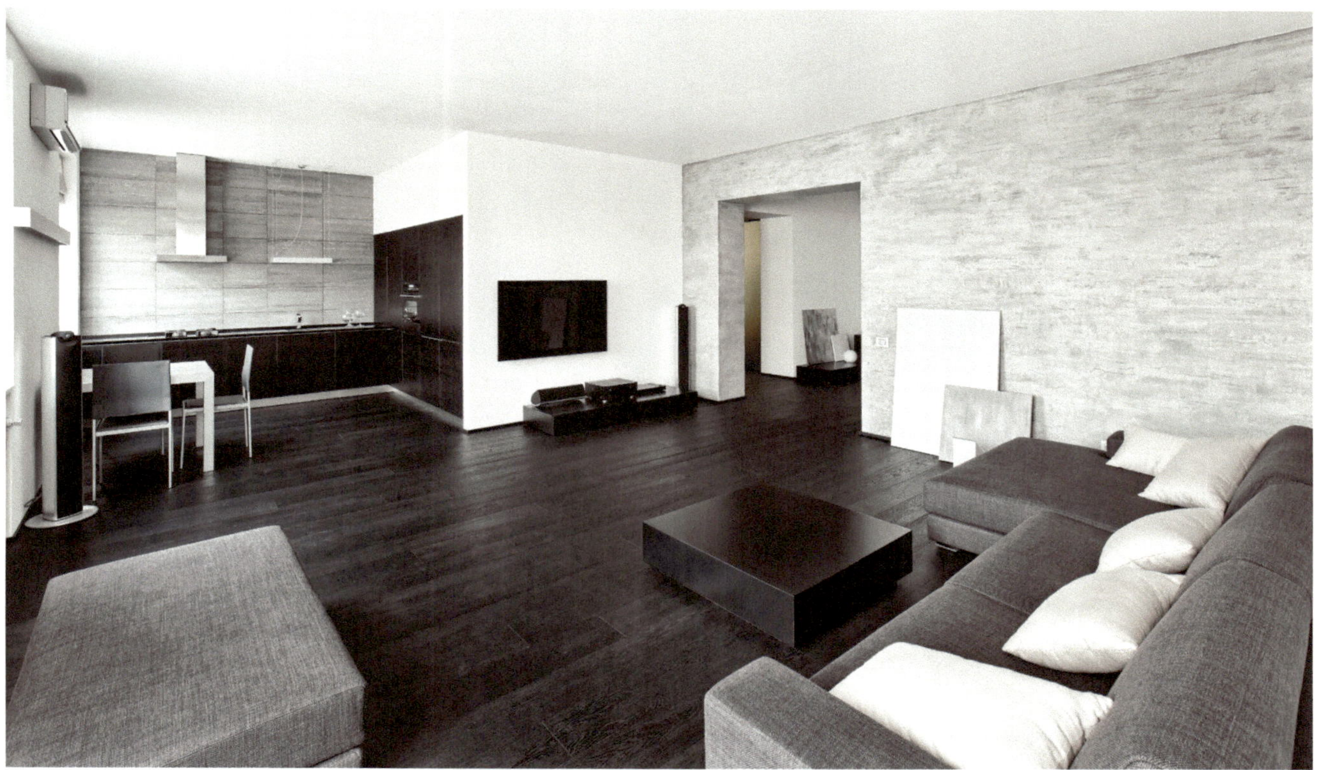

Figure 10.2 A modern living space using achromatic color—black, white, and gray—through contrast of flooring, wall, and furniture materials and finish add visual interest and variety to this minimalistic space.

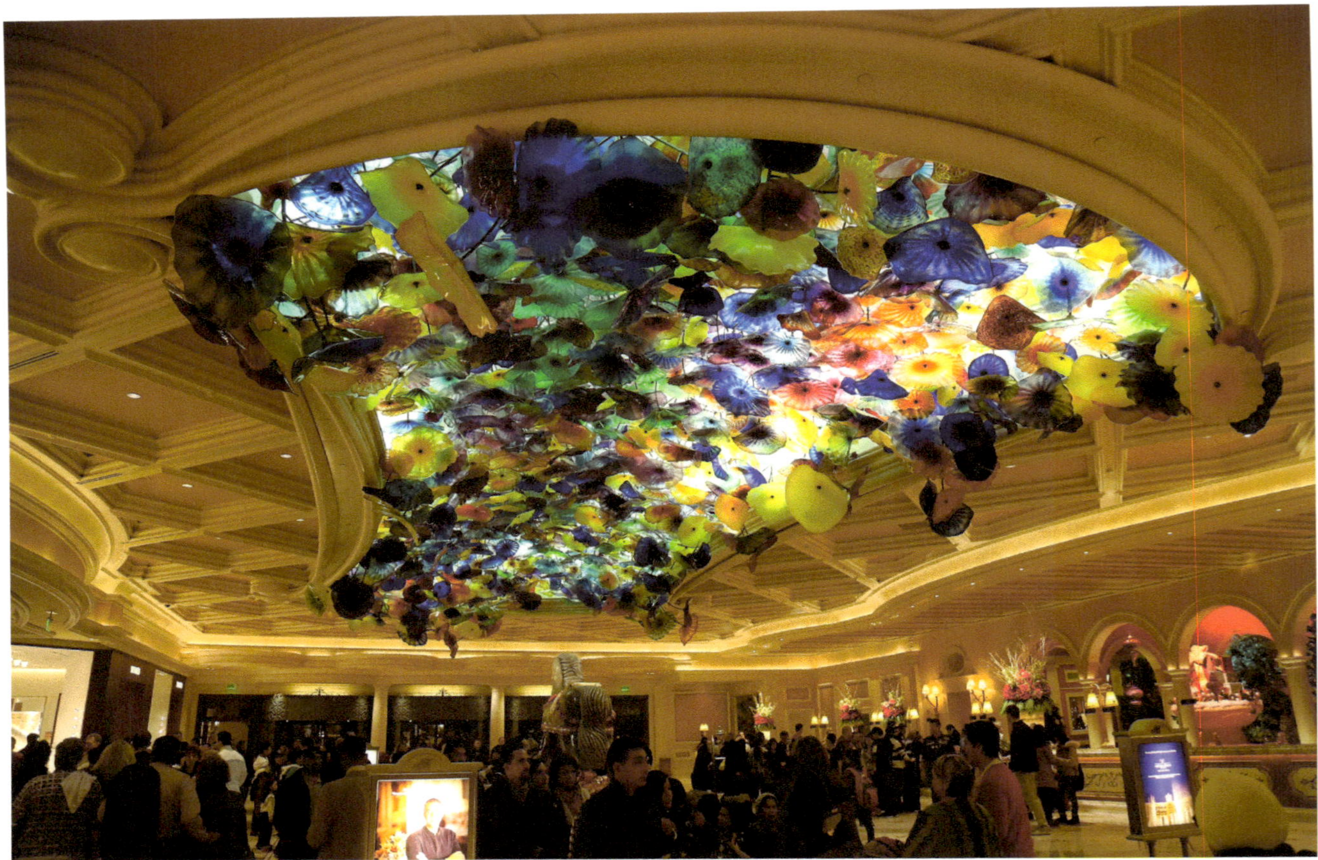

Figure 10.3 Contemporary glass art installation entitled *Fiore di Como* by Dale Chihuly breaks the monotony of a white in the lobby of the Bellagio Hotel and Casino, Las Vegas. The organic sculptural shapes of glass creates variety through contrast in material and design to the traditional coffered ceiling.

Variety introduces a different character to an element for the purpose of creating contrast that in turn creates interest. Unity, as discussed in Chapter 9, limits disorganization and "decorative" novelty, while variety generates contrast and visual interest. The two design principles are interconnected; however, unity and harmony must dominate if the interior space is to work as a whole unit. Unity is achieved when variety is balanced, or the interior space could be less interesting or visually cluttered. Variety occurs through contrast. Contrast in design elements can be a device to hold the attention of the viewer and create a visually stimulating interior. **Contrast**—or the juxtaposition of different forms, lines, or colors in a space "to intensify each element's properties and produce a more dynamic expressiveness"—especially if it is unusual, is often the feature that earns the most attention (Ching, 1996, p. 380). The red lounge in Figure 10.4 contrasts with the neutral palette of materials and finishes in this modern bedroom space. These contrasting design principles help prevent boredom and loss of interest.

Visual differentiation among objects, surfaces, planes, foreground, and background not only aids in communicating your design intent but also adds the visual texture and movement necessary to form unity and harmony. In Figure 10.5a, the dining room needs color variety and definition of spatial elements to clarify and unify the design. Without color and pattern, the space loses the distinction necessary for a user to appreciate the furnishings and define the space for dining. The wall at the end of the dining table can be accented and serve as a design feature. Applying square-shaped mirrors with the negative space painted in the orange hue of the chairs creates needed variety and pattern. The physical dining space is further defined by a wood floor inlay to offset this zone and mimic the ceiling design. This carries the wood finish throughout the interior (Figure 10.5b).

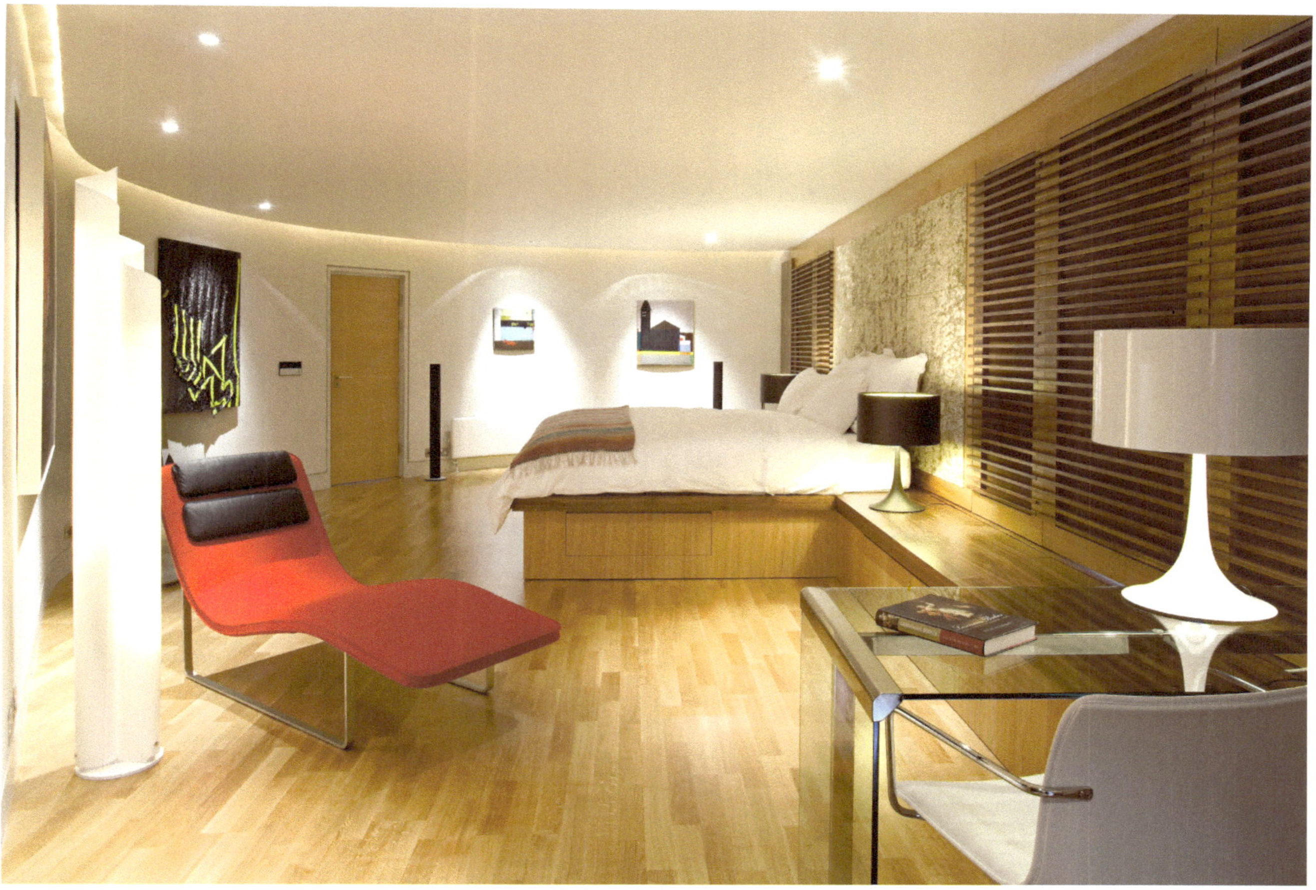

Figure 10.4 Varying scale, shape, color, texture, and pattern accentuates and adds interest in this modern bedroom space.

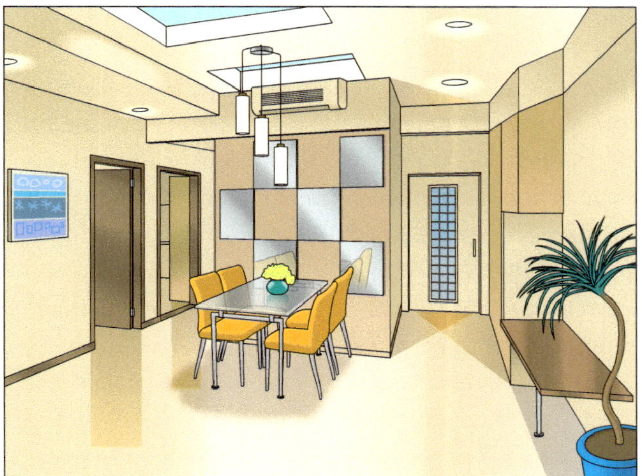

Figure 10.5a This residential dining space requires variety through color and pattern to accentuate the interior and further define the eating area.

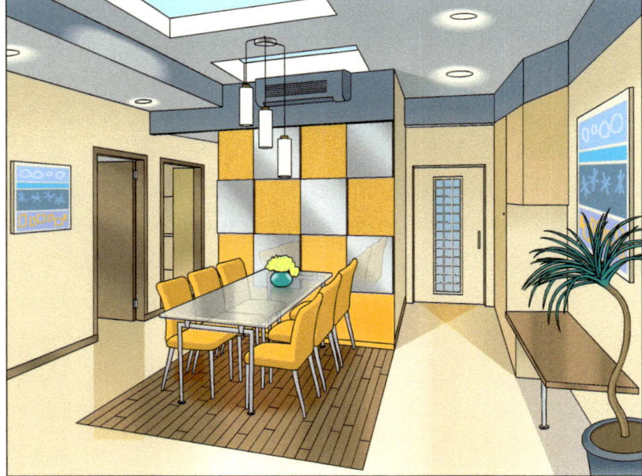

Figure 10.5b A complementary color harmony of blue and orange enlivens this dining space with added elements to define and strengthen the interior design.

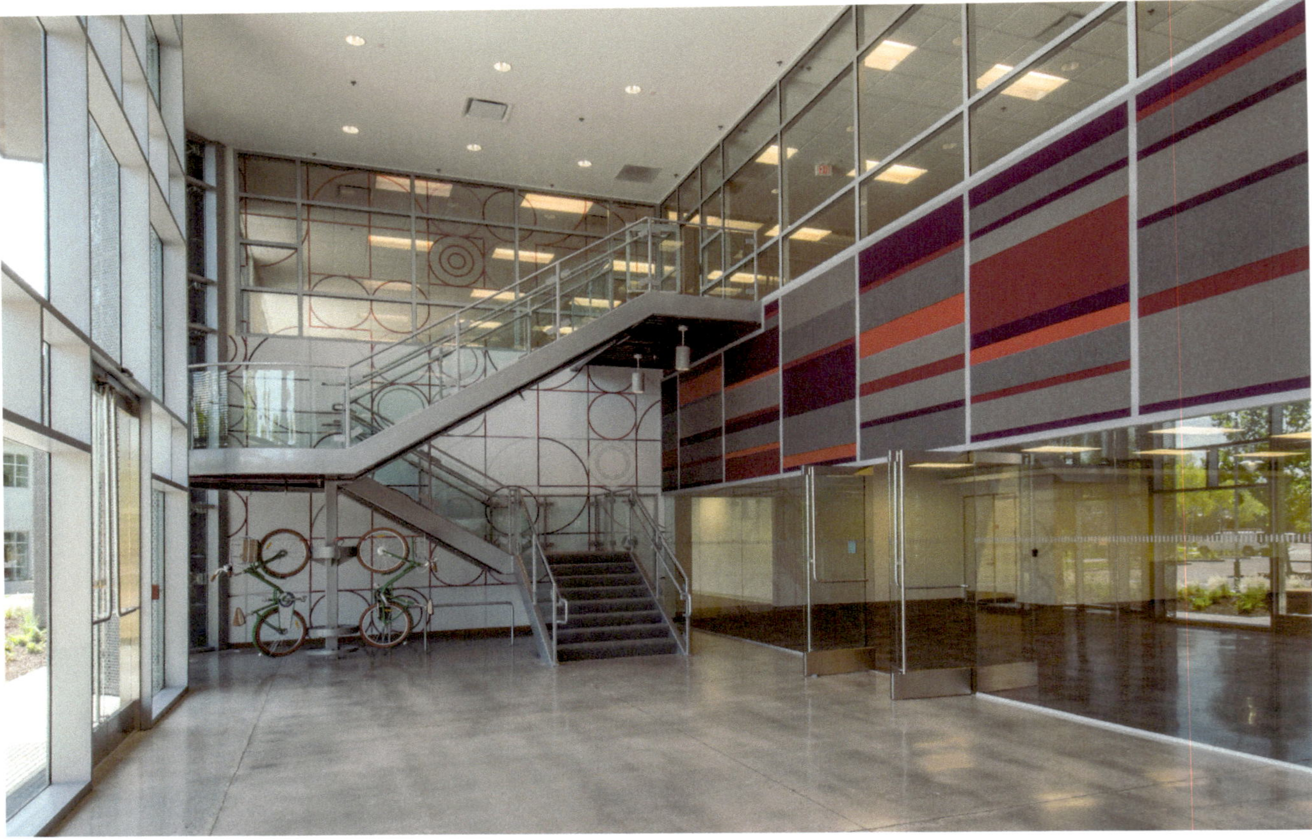

Figure 10.6 Colored circles and squares add variety and interest to an office lobby.

Use color to establish a variety of textures, patterns, and visual expectations from your design plan. Patterns, when used consistently, can unify one or multiple adjoining spaces. Once you have established a color plan, it's imperative you stick to it. If you choose to depart from your design plan and use a different set of color patterns within a single space, do so only to emphasize a particular design element. You can encourage the emphasis by using a hue with a higher saturation level or high-contrast colors to attract attention to major design features in your space. With an open floor plan, the tendency is to change color pattern and hue within separate activity areas. Be cautious not to add variety that will not unify with the other adjoining spaces. When changing hues, stay with similar values and intensities to avoid adding visual clutter. Remember: Less is more. By limiting your use of color, you will maximize its impact on the overall design. In Figure 10.6, the entrance vestibule of this office building uses horizontal lines and geometric shapes in analogous hues to accent the neutral-colored interior finishes. To add contrast and variety, the circles and curves applied to the glass curtain wall in different scales serve as a backdrop to the stair, creating visual texture and interest for a clean, simple, modern space.

At the same time, a colorless space can appear dismal and uninviting. Consider the space in Figure 10.7a. A restaurant is a place of socialization and celebration. Color is key to setting a particular mood and theme for spaces of entertainment. For example, in a fine-dining restaurant, colors may be reduced in intensity and made darker to increase the desire to linger, whereas in a fast-food restaurant, bright colors give the perception of quick service. In the figure, the large window wall provides ample natural light, giving the space the option of being darkened for an intimate dining experience. The curvilinear design elements do not receive importance or separation from other materials through value contrast. The open kitchen concept, a common point of focus in a restaurant, blends in with the surroundings. This spatial composition needs variety through added color contrast that will unify and strengthen the design. Introducing a greater degree of contrasts assigned to key elements (ceiling, rear accent wall, and open kitchen) creates added variety in the restaurant to stimulate patrons' experience

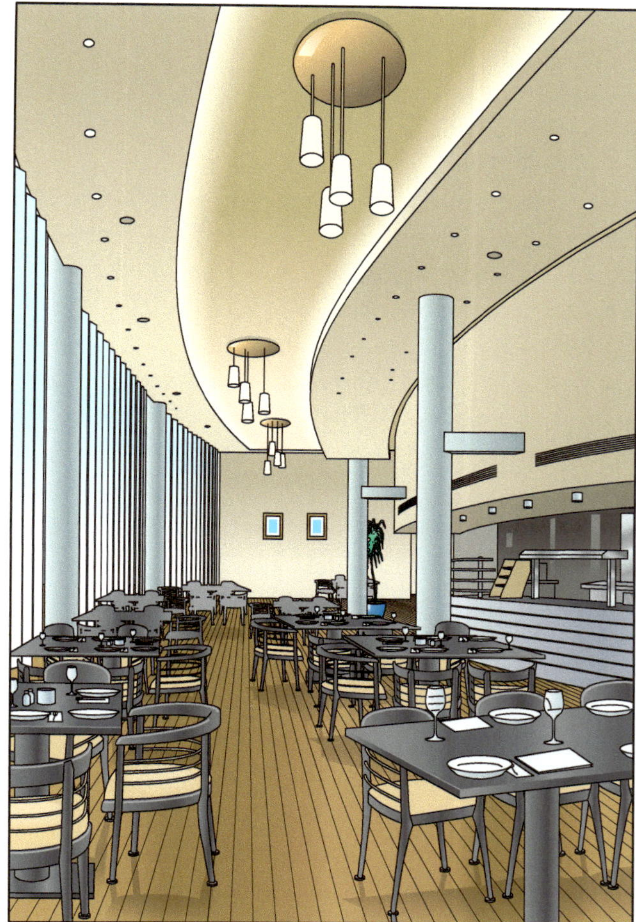

Figure 10.7a The interior of this restaurant space requires key colors to stimulate and introduce the perception of a fine-dining experience.

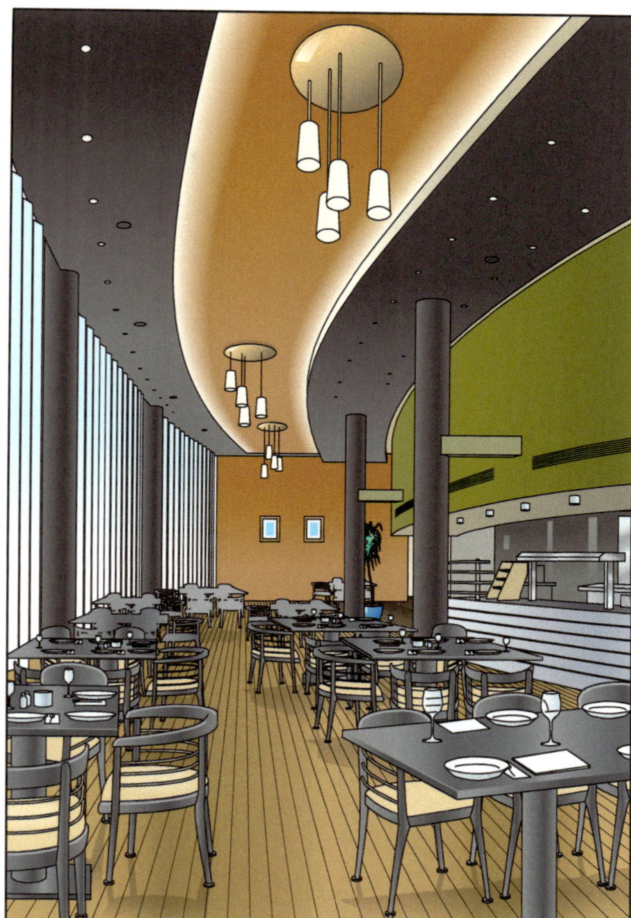

Figure 10.7b Key design elements are highlighted and contrasted with color, adding variety and visual stimulation in this restaurant space.

of place. The changes in Figure 10.7b provide the visual contrast and variety necessary to the layout.

Design planes (columns, walls, and ceilings) can each be enhanced with color to add more variety. No wall has to be painted a single hue, and we know from earlier examples that adding color and pattern increases the arousal and curiosity of the viewers. Figure 10.8 provides examples and methods for simple color application techniques to break the visual monotony of interior columns and walls. Experiment with variations of the technique to achieve different color expressions and outcomes.

Color and the Design Elements

Look for ways you can introduce color and variety into your work. Variety is the principle of design that can catch and keep the interest of users of the space. Naturally, people dislike looking at the same object over and over. Variety of shapes, lines, textures, and patterns breaks up the monotony and gives the viewers an array of visual stimuli.

To this point in our journey on color, we have discussed the theories of design—balance, rhythm, emphasis, proportion, scale, unity, harmony, and variety. These are the rules or guidelines on how to combine, organize, and compose the design as part of our visual experience. Color, which is an element of design, will be discussed with the remaining elements of design, line, shape, form pattern and texture, and time.

Color and Line

Line is the connection between two points in space. A line can create many shapes, define forms, and include icons and symbols, as in the lines that create our stars and

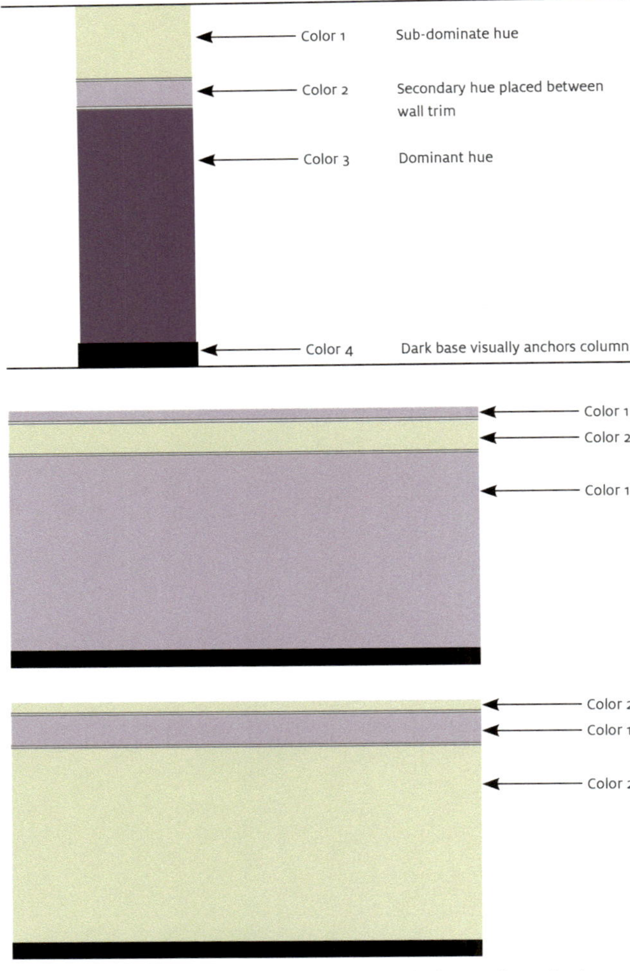

Figure 10.8 (a) Interior column detail. The darkest paint color is placed on the column base; the lower portion of the column receives the dominant, darker violet hue; the secondary, mid-value violet hue is placed between the architectural trim or reveal; and lastly the top portion receives the lightest, neutral subdominant hue. (b) Wall elevation illustrating color locations—Option 1. (c) Wall elevation illustrating color locations—Option 2.

stripes of the American flag. A line can be used to communicate action, like the arrows in a road sign or the yellow lines that indicate a two-way street. The bark of a tree is a series of jagged lines that tells us before we touch it that the texture of the bark is rough. Subtle, layered lines of color gracefully indicate the contour of the horizon at sundown. The way in which lines are utilized and combined with color can determine the effectiveness of an interior space. Without line, no other part of a composition could happen. There are several types of lines: vertical, horizontal, diagonal, curved, jagged, spiral, broken, thick, and thin, to name a few. Let us explore the four commonly used: vertical, horizontal, diagonal, and curved.

Vertical lines symbolize strength and stability, like the columns that support a building. Verticality provides the upward and downward movement, accentuating height and giving rise to expansive interiors or directing the viewer to the ceiling, where further design details may be present. Use vertical lines to emphasize the height and perception of a larger space. The strength and power of vertical lines are reinforced with strong, warm hues of red, orange, and yellow.

Horizontal lines are restful and remind us of a body at rest. Horizontal lines can break vertical surface planes to decrease the height of the space or widen the interior where they are used. Horizontal lines create movement from side to side, reminiscent of the horizon or plateau of a tabletop mountain. Using cool colors with horizontal lines increases the perception and sensation of a space being restful, relaxing, and calm. Horizontal lines lead the eye across an object and emphasize width.

Diagonal lines are dynamic and unusual in that they defy gravity. These lines inspire interest and awe while suggesting quick action and radical movement to the viewer. Diagonal lines are effective in informal design planning where a progressive, imaginative solution is required. They tend to give the illusion of instability and uncertainty, and they imply potential danger, like a steep slope. This perception can be supported with warm hues such as red, yellow, and orange. Purple, coined a "mysterious" color because it is a combination of polar opposites (red and blue), would also serve well in supporting the impressions conveyed by diagonal lines and angled shapes.

Curved lines are soft, gentle, and fluid. They remind us of femininity, clouds, flowers, and nature. The curved line supported by blues and greens reminds us of nature, water, and growth. Soft pastels, pinks, and red-violets will also make a curved line seem graceful, peaceful, and relaxing. Curvilinear lines are organic and peaceful and can be combined with sharp right angles and straight lines for contrast and added emphasis. Curved lines are friendly, not abrupt, as well as inviting and informal. Canadian-American architect Frank Gehry, the master of expressive forms and curved lines, uses color and contrast to emphasize the organic shape of the Marqués de Riscal Hotel located in Elciego, Spain (Figure 10.9). In this example the red-violet accentuates the curve and adds emphasis to the organic shapes used in the architecture.

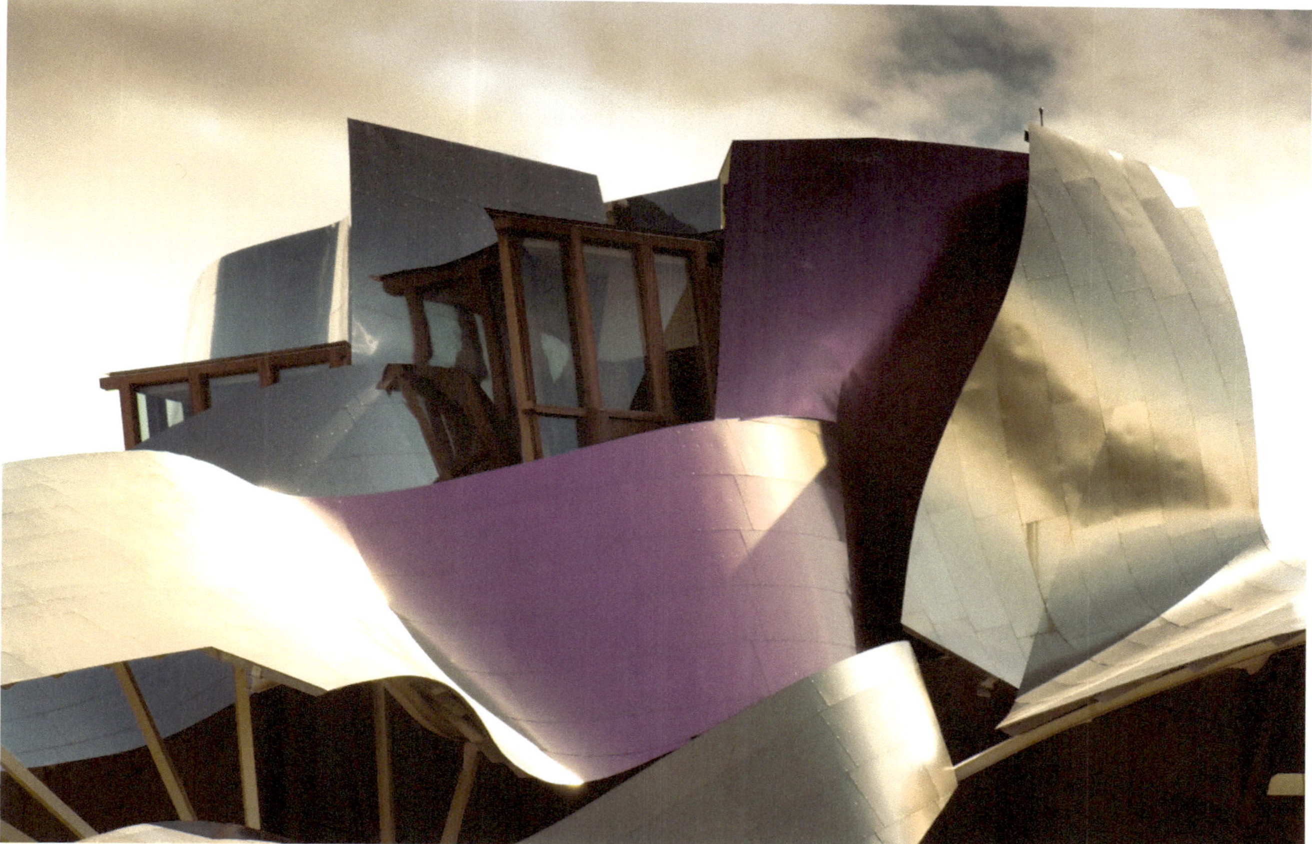

Figure 10.9 The winery of the hotel Marquis de Riscal in Elciego, Basque County, Spain, designed using pink and gold titanium with stainless steel. The purple reflects the color of the wine, the gold the mesh covering the Riscal wine bottles, and the stainless steel the foil that covers the cork. Designed by architect Frank Gehry.

Color and Shape

Shape is the result of one or more lines connecting to form a two-dimensional image such as a square, circle, triangle, hexagon, pentagon, or octagon. Design basics that influence and form the language of all spaces have their roots in the Bauhaus school in Dessau, Germany, started in 1919 by architect Walter Gropius. To identify and provide the viewer with a variety of shapes, textures, and forms reinforced by colors, we can stimulate the senses and create an environment that is visually pleasing to the occupants. The circle represents fluid movement, not something static, and enables the eye to travel around freely. Variation of circle size and concentric circles can add rhythm and movement to your design. We are naturally drawn to differences—they stand out—and a circle offers a calming softness. Using color for contrast offers more visual variety. The café wall in Figure 10.10 uses vertical lines in various widths and colors contrasted against colored circles to add visual drama in the Tate Modern Art Museum, London. The simple furnishings and dark floor balance the intense pattern and color. The selection of color and graphic pattern indicates a modern style. A traditional color palette of dark navy and less intense sage green in combination with a traditional **damask** pattern wouldn't be appropriate because it could misrepresent the intended purpose and identity of the museum. The bold pattern and color in the café generate excitement and energy, thus encouraging conversation, laughter, and enjoyment of friends and family in a welcoming and playful setting.

The square, a combination of vertical and horizontal lines, is stable and secure with its predictable equal sides; however, when rotated to stand on a corner, it seemingly defies gravity, which could add dynamic variety and a dramatic focal point. The square does not occur

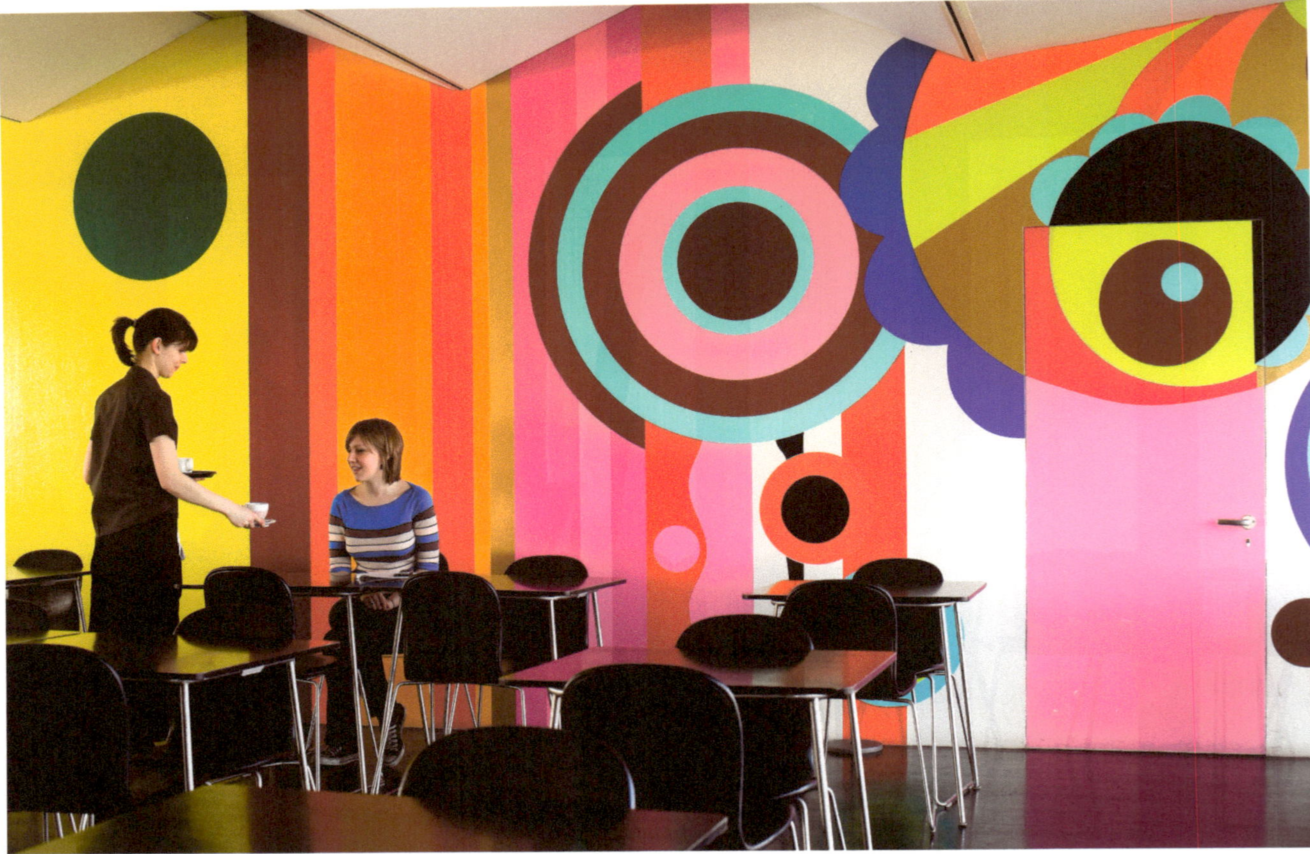

Figure 10.10 The large scale multi-colored graphic creates a unique visual identity of this space in Tate Modern Restaurant, London.

organically in nature, and therefore, as a man-made artifice, it calls attention to the artisan's creativity. Strong, saturated colors are supported with this shape. In Figure 10.11, the long corridor of this contemporary office is broken into smaller segments with bands of orange, which in turn shortens the perceived length of the space. Color applied to the soffit and onto the inlaid carpet border creates a square portal that adds rhythm and a transitional experience for visitors.

The rectangle is also a stable shape, adding more variety with two sides of a different width. This shape is more restful than the square when laid on its long axis and just the opposite when positioned on its short axis, where it resembles support columns and strength. A rectangle is a more visually interesting shape than a square, and a rectangular room provides more opportunities for spatial arrangement because it is slightly more complex.

A triangle suggests stability when at rest on its base, and it leads the eye upward toward the sky. Triangles use the dynamic elements of angles and diagonals to create visual movement and energy. The interest of a triangle can be enhanced by applying the color yellow.

The characteristics of shape and color outlined by Itten can be translated into our interior spaces. When color and shape combine, their meanings are intensified, giving the space a soul and a language that speaks to us.

Color and Form

Form is the perception of weight, volume, and mass of an object. What constitutes an object's three-dimensional quality versus a flat, two-dimensional quality can vary. For instance, a textured surface appears to have a sense of depth due to the way the source of light falls onto the object. The light and dark areas on the surface convey a sense of depth even though the object may be relatively flat or have little mass. When light is cast onto an object and we factor its density—solid versus transparent—the portions of the object receiving light will be illuminated and highlighted while the areas blocked from the light

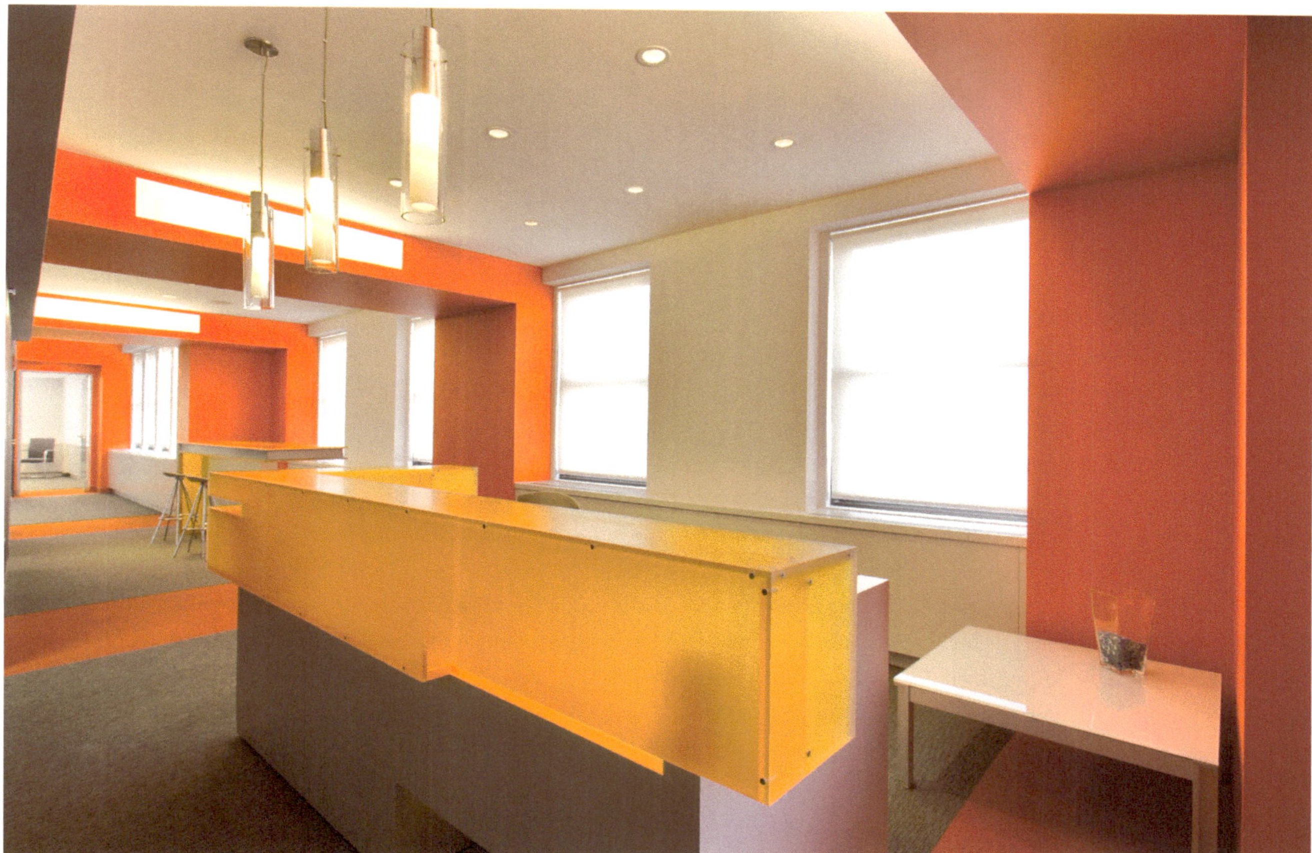

Figure 10.11 In this office example, the reception desk with yellow-orange translucent panels with walls and floor surfaces in orange-colored arcades break up the long corridor in this contemporary interior and create a unique and visually pleasing rhythmic spatial experience for the user. The selection of different surface materials, values and contrast of color, and textures creates a cohesive space.

will produce shade and cast shadow. The brightness of the light, direction of light, and how close the object is to the source of the light will also factor into our perception of form and color. Lower levels of light and light sources placed further away from the object will diminish the object's form and make it less distinguishable. Couple the light source with the color of the object and its surrounding, and we can further emphasize or deemphasize the perception of space, volume, and forms.

Color, color temperature, and value (Chapter 4) can be used to affect how we perceive space and form. Color contrast and temperature help to create form and perception of depth. Recall that the illusion of depth and space is created by the combination of warm colors and light/bright colors (which appear to advance) with cool colors and dark/dull colors (which appear to recede). Contrasts in color also produce the perception of depth. For instance, a dark blue object surrounded by a light-yellow background will move forward, giving the viewer an experience of depth. Reversing the color scenario produces the same effect. Gradation of color value can also be applied to give the illusion of depth and roundness to an object. These color strategies allow the designer to generate the perception of increased space within interiors or produce depth perception in a two-dimensional, flat printed document.

Referring to our discussions on emphasis in Chapter 7, focal points can occur when contrast is produced. Consider the forms and masses within your design and how you wish these forms to be received by the user. This will help you narrow the approach to communicating color relationships. Color application is a layered process and is best approached considering the multiple outcomes simultaneously as you move forward in making final design decisions. Test various effects until you achieve your desired outcome.

Color and Pattern and Texture

Pattern is the repetitive arrangement of shapes and colors in a systematic horizontal, vertical, diagonal, or organic sequence. Color pattern and texture applications are the easiest and quickest methods for adding variety into your projects. Pattern scale, material textures and finishes, and color harmony all work simultaneously to produce visually interesting design. The key, again, is to manage the variation; otherwise, the pieces may not fit to make a unified whole. Figure 10.12a and b illustrate the use of color, pattern, and texture to create variety. Color patterns can also be produced with transmitted light filtered through transparent objects made with materials such as glass or plastic that are cast onto adjoining surfaces. The colored glass panels in Figure 10.13 create a kaleidoscope of colorful patterns on the floor of the Miami Airport. The use of colored glass is an effective way of designing with color; the transparency filters light and allows the color to be enjoyed without the intense saturation of pigment paint that could be visually overwhelming.

Texture is the visual or tactile surface quality and characteristic of a material that results from the way it is constructed, prepared or combined. Texture and surface quality of materials, finishes, and building products in your design can vary greatly. Surfaces can be hard, soft, smooth, rough, dull, or reflective. Physical texture is the actual tactile texture and characteristic of the material surface that can be felt. Texture can also be perceptual, or visually implied by using pattern, repetition, value and contrast to produce the illusion or appearance of texture, such as **faux finishes** which replicate the appearance of other materials when in fact, it is a flat smooth surface. Textures can include naturally rough or smooth surfaces with little reflective properties, or matte finishes, which include materials such as wood and stone, or reflective or translucent surfaces and materials such as high-gloss, semigloss, or **satin finishes**, which include glass, metals, acrylic, or paint finishes.

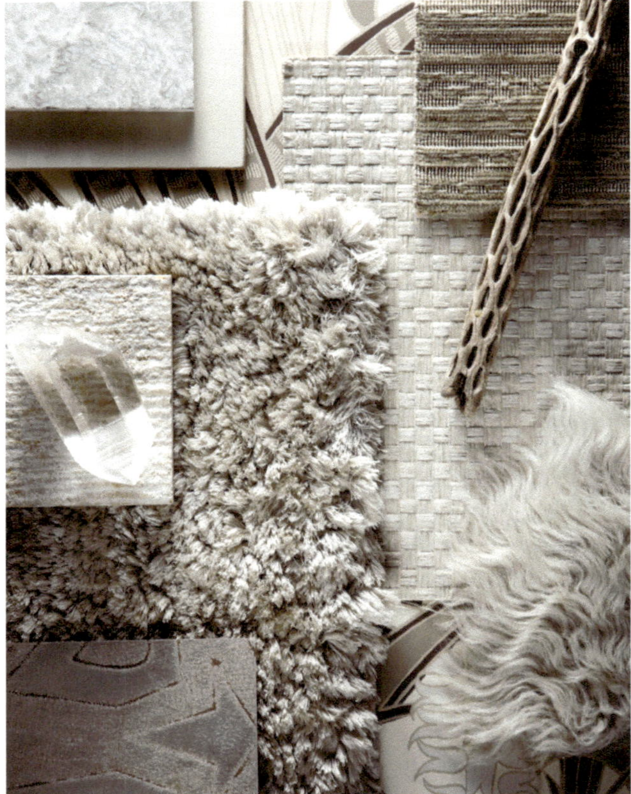

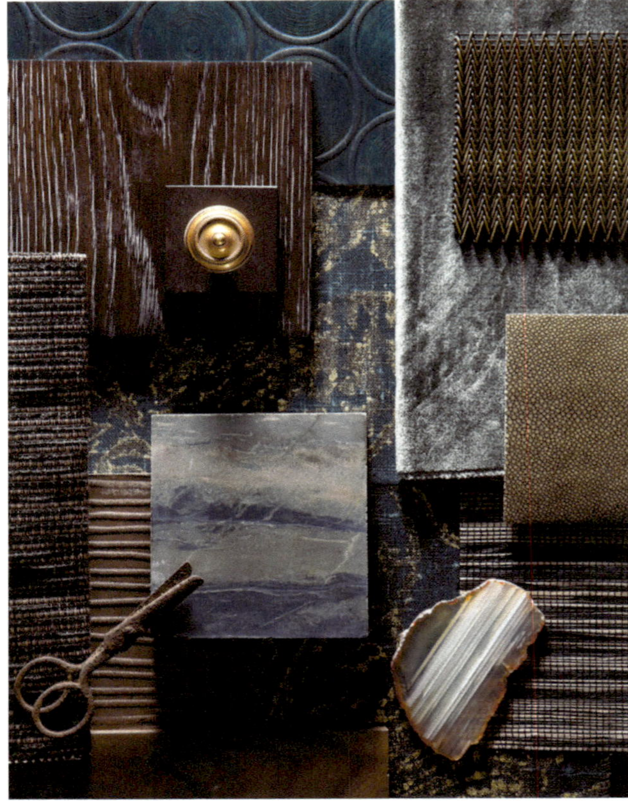

Figure 10.12 Color, pattern, and texture add variety and visual interest in these examples of (a) Left, a neutral color scheme and (b) a monochromatic blue color scheme.

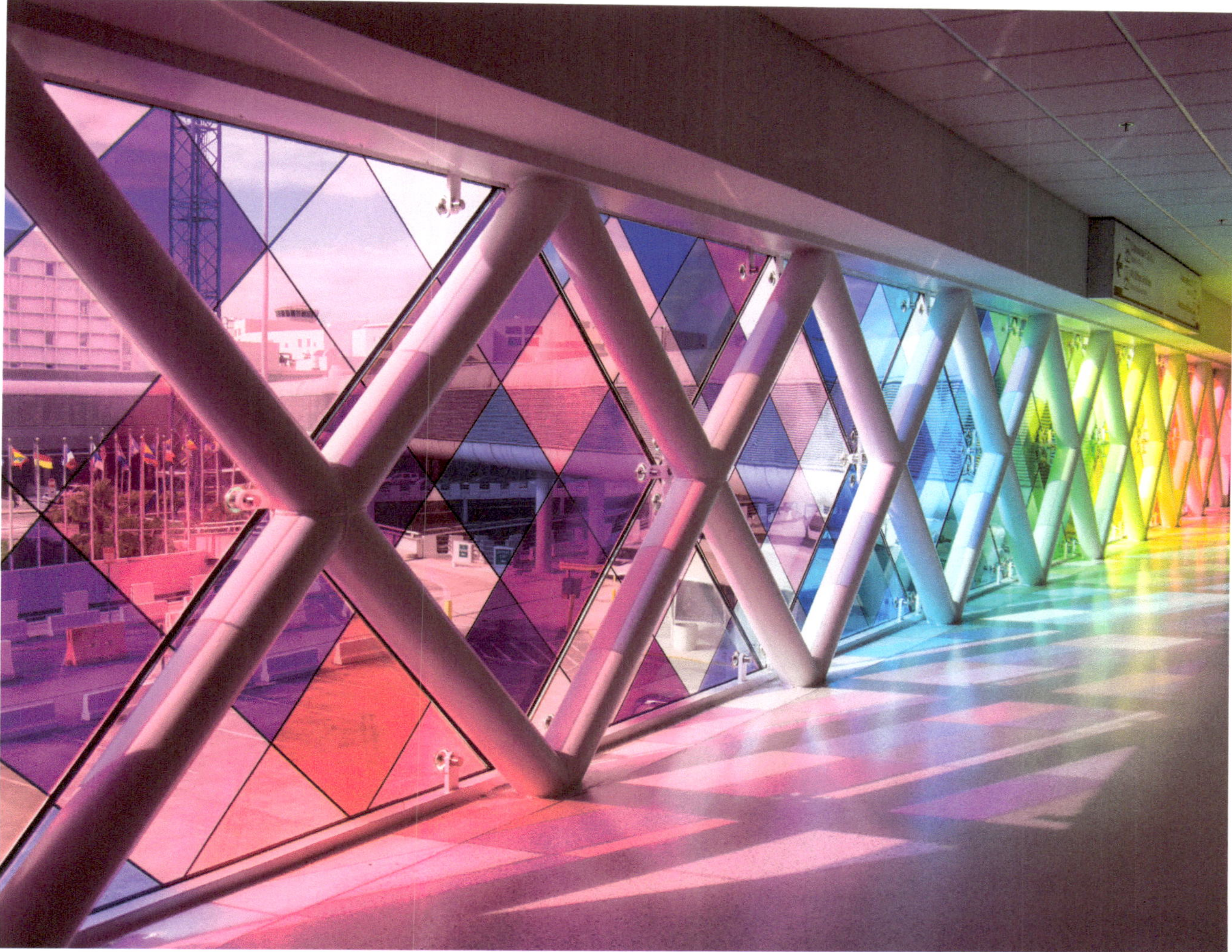

Figure 10.13 Brightly colored interior of Miami Airport, with light falling through colorful Perspex strips, creating multicolored patterns on the floors and walls.

Our hands and fingers are sensitive to texture, collecting information as we run our fingers across a surface. The sensory experience can either calm or stimulate the brain. The emotional experience is attributed to the type of surface texture involved. When we see a smooth surface, such as glass, we might associate quiet, calm, and cool. A rough textured surface might be seen as more exciting and inviting. These surface characteristics can be further reinforced with color and value based upon the associations discussed in Chapter 3—light and cool colors versus dark and warm colors, for instance.

Contrast of surface quality and texture adds richness and depth to your design. Texture creates a visual and visceral connection to our spatial experience. We see our environment first, and touch second to aid us in understanding and distinguishing our surroundings. The texture of various surfaces helps to describe the character of our spatial experience and the arrangements of elements in a design solution (Figure 10.14). Color and texture can be used to draw attention to a design feature, creating a focal point. The level of opacity or transparency of the surface texture can reduce or increase our perception of spatial size. A transparent material involves both the material itself and also what is seen beyond, which now becomes part of the design. The way the transparent material is expressed changes in relation to the color and material seen through it as shown in Figure 10.13.

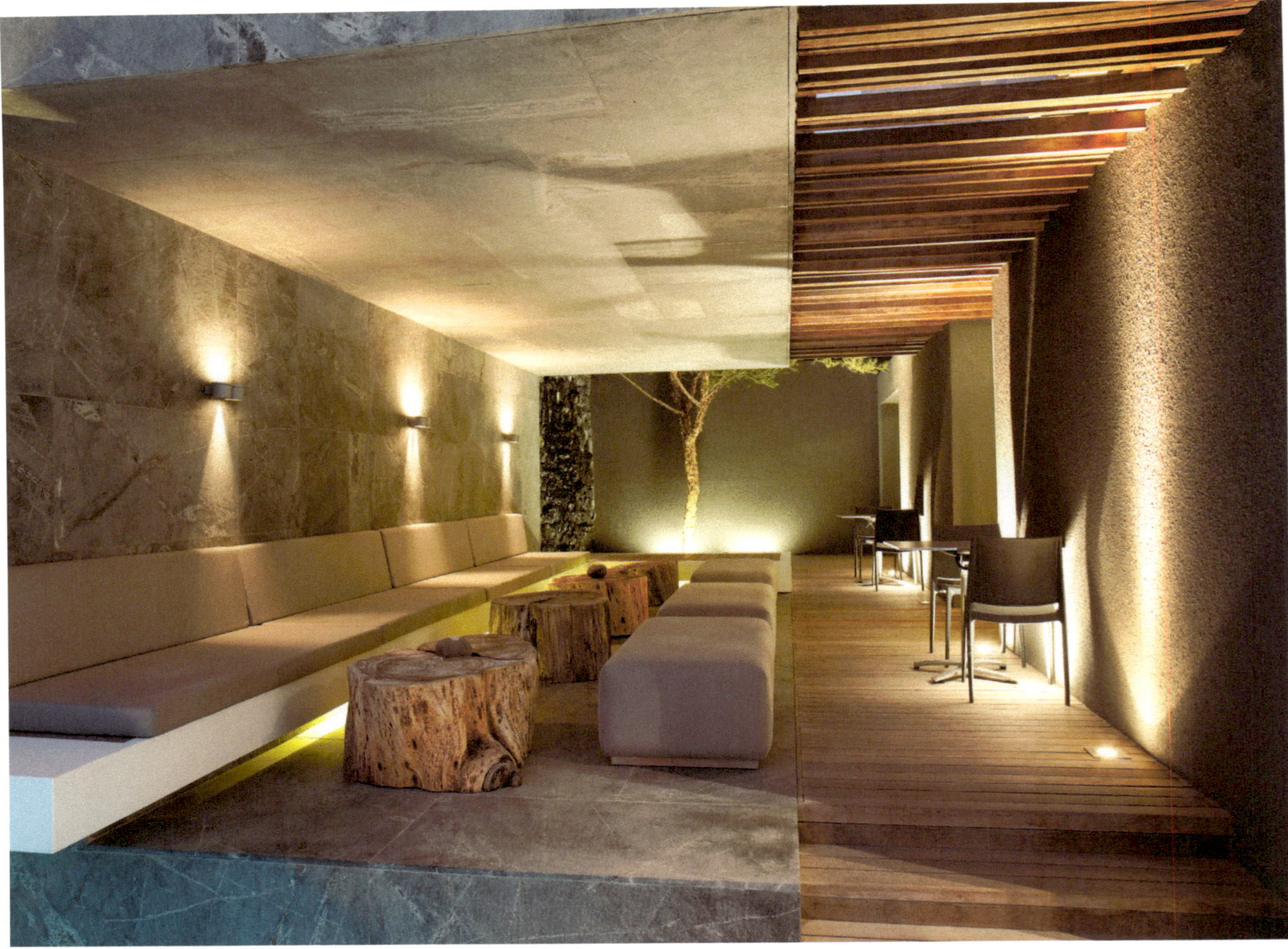

Figure 10.14 This outdoor pool seating area in a luxury apartment community illustrates the use of several natural textures and materials, both visual and tactical. The lighting placement accentuates and enhances the textural quality of the surfaces.

The use of materials and finishes adds to the variety of a design, and well-chosen combinations will give the sensory and visual contrast needed to make the space more interesting. If the textural pattern is uniform in your design, this could be monotonous and uninteresting, and lack stimulation for the user. Vary the scale of texture to balance and add harmony to the solution. If all textures in a space are the same with the exception of one element or feature of a different texture, the distinctive element becomes a point of emphasis to enhance the space. Much in the same way of using a single color without varying the value and contrast is monotonous, if the texture must be uniform, consider color and value changes to help with visual appeal of the design.

We depend on the tactile sensation of feeling textured surfaces within our environment. This kinetic connection is essential and can be experienced when colors of different hues and values are combined to create the illusion of texture, even when no tactile texture is present. The wall covering in Figure 10.15a is an example of color and pattern used to create the visual appearance of texture. In spaces where there is a limited amount of visual stimulation or open design plans with few interior walls to delineate areas or to clearly zone for separate activities, incorporating contrast in the design with shapes, color, and patterns can provide the necessary interest and division of space. The dining space example requires visual contrast of pattern, shape, and dark value to add excitement and a backdrop to the dining space. If we remove the design, we lose the variety and visual texture that the wall color and pattern provide to the space (Figure 10.15b).

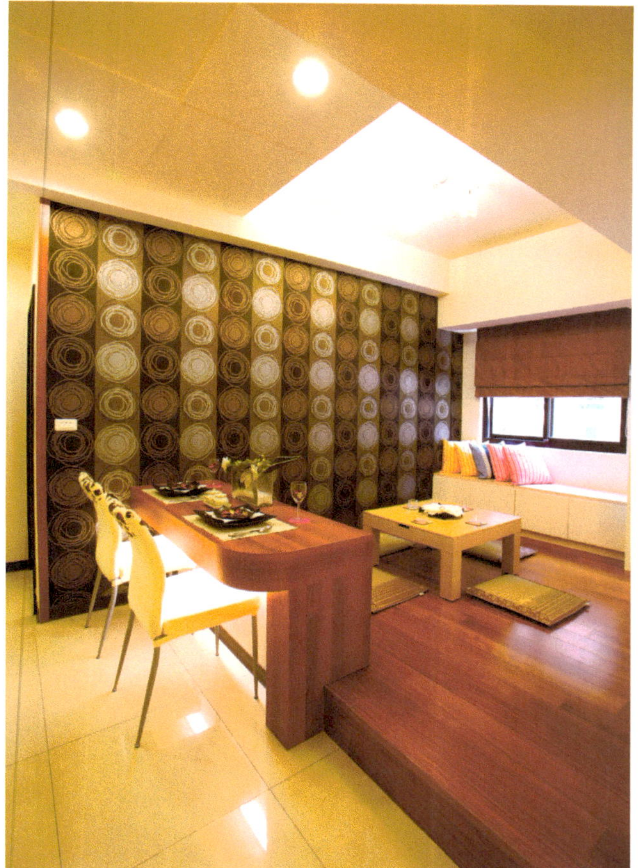

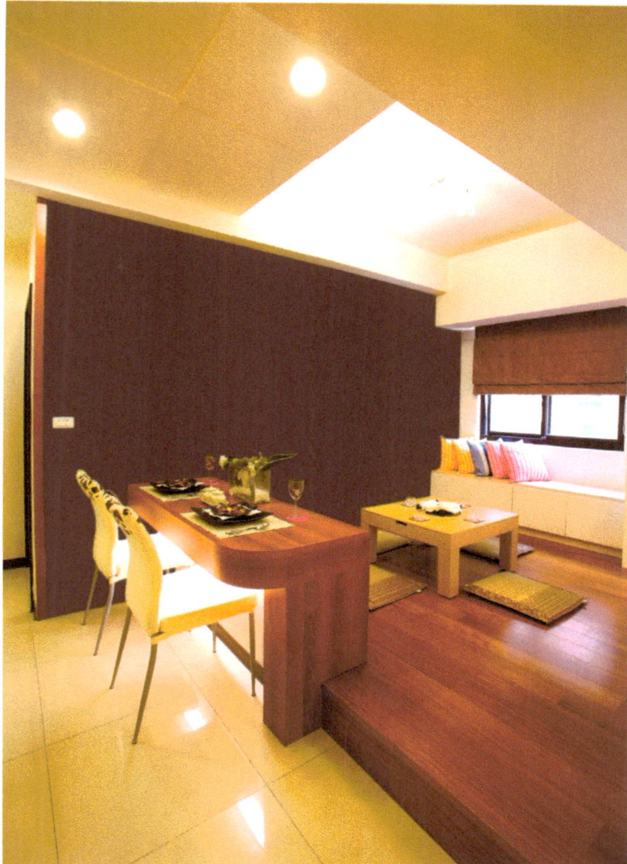

Figure 10.15 (a) Color and pattern create visual texture in this dining space. (b) Removal of the wall covering eliminates the pattern that provided the visual interest.

In Chapter 7, we discussed using color to help mask or hide interior architectural elements that must remain but may not want to be seen or emphasized in your design solution. The texture of materials and their color work together for successful color masking. Lighter colors reflect more light and will highlight flaws in a surface or design more so than darker colors, which reflect less light and reduce the apparent visibility of design flaws. Surface texture and reflection also help to support the masking; heavy texture hides more than a smooth surface, and a flat or **matte** surface will hide more than a reflective, **glossy** surface. Color, contrast, and shape, with the resulting textural quality generated by these elements of design, can create illusions where the transition between vertical and horizontal planes is blurred (Figure 10.16).

Due to varying textures within a designed space, color appearance will vary. It is not the color of the material we see, but the appearance of the color and its surface character (Cler, pg. 183, 2011). This is of particular importance when color matching is needed across materials with different texture or surface reflection—matte versus glossy. Changing the color of the materials may be needed to create the perception of a color pair, or match. The distance of the viewer from the material texture and color will affect the color perception as well. Will the material placement be seen in close proximity to the viewer, or will the material be seen at a distance? The interplay of light on the material surface, shadows, and reflection properties will also alter the perception of the color. In general, the color of a textured surface seen close by the viewer will appear lighter than when seen at a distance. Despite the presence of unpredictable conditions in the environment affecting your design solution, including natural light and differences between individuals or considering the variables related to surface texture and color discussed can help you to overcome potential problems later on.

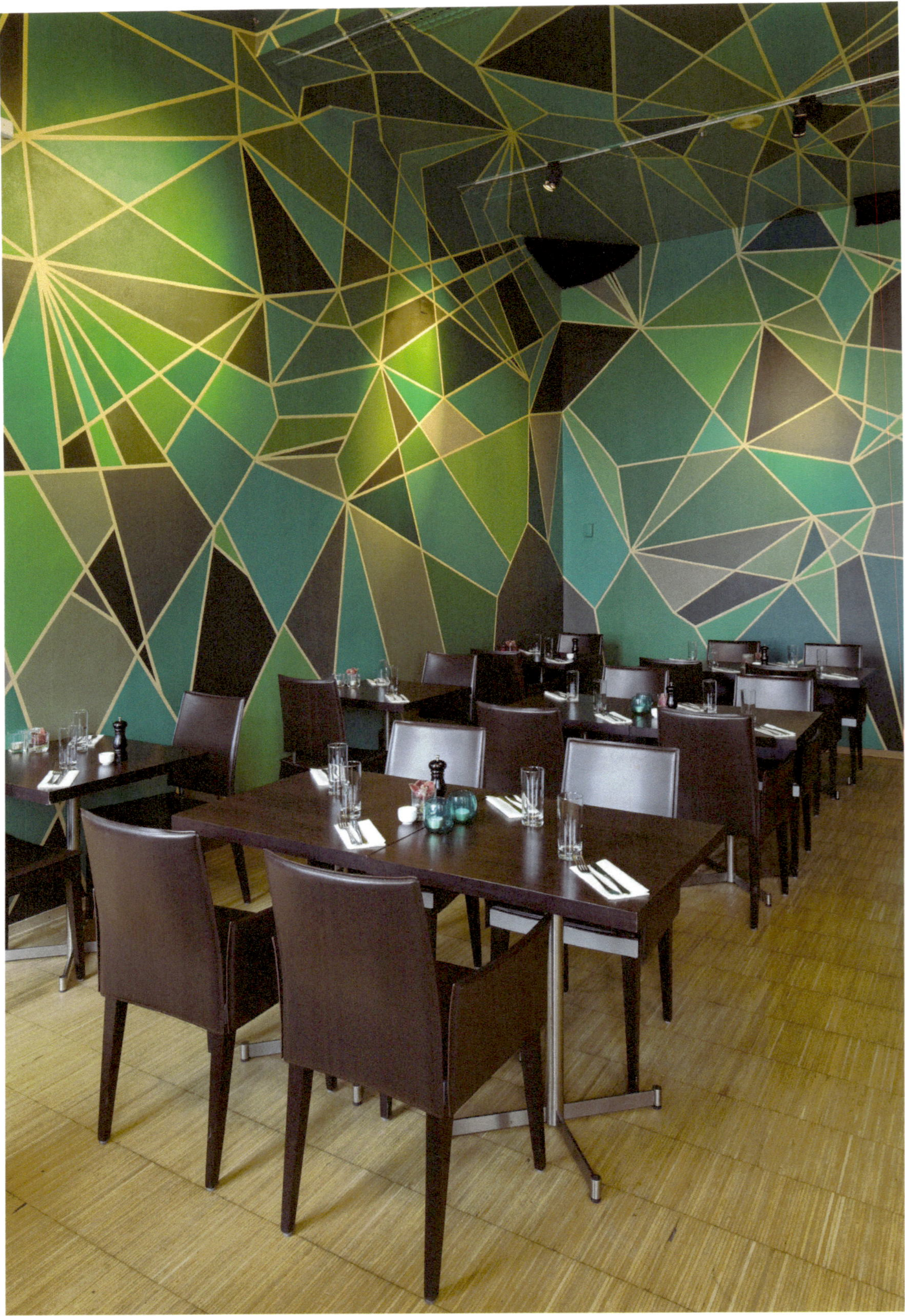

Figure 10.16 Nobel Peace Center by architects Adjaye Associates in Oslo, Norway, 2005. The geometric mural of the restaurant is an interplay of various shapes and colors, forming a pattern than can obscure forms and produce effects that expand our perception of depth—both what is near and what is far.

Color and Time

One aspect of color and design that can be easily overlooked is time. The color of materials will be affected by forces of nature over **time**. Color changes can occur in materials as the result of exposure to weather (rain and sunlight) over a span of several weeks, months, and even years. For instance, as copper ages and is exposed to water, the shiny surface will lose its luster, darken, and even transform into a rich, green patina. Wood that is exposed to water and sunlight will turn to a silver-gray. Dyed textiles that receive too much sun exposure will fade. An example would be a red fabric that will eventually turn to pink with prolonged exposure to sunlight. As previously discussed in Chapter 2, sunlight alters our perception of color throughout the day. The eventual change and shifts in the color of these materials needs examination as part of the intended and final design outcome.

Lastly, we must consider linear time change, or the past and the present of color. Color trends and historical color previously discussed in Chapter 3 influence our selection and preference for specific color. Returning to history to reflect on these cultural and societal influences can be valuable for understanding similar influences on color in the future.

There is a vast array of colored materials available to the designer to craft the interior environment. Various wood types, specialty finishes, plastic laminates, natural stones, porcelain tiles, wall coverings, textiles, metals, and colored glass can all be utilized to enhance our visual experience of space and place. Creating a color plan is an important part of visually communicating your design intention to a client (Figure 10.17). Careful attention needs to be paid to all of the principles of design we have discussed and how color can combine with these materials to accentuate the built environment.

Variety is a powerful element for adding interest, contrasts, and life within an interior space. Using color in your projects is an enjoyable and meaningful experience for both you and your clients. With each new project, you'll continue to learn about color complexities and the ways in which you can use color to give your work personality. Use of color with intention and informed research will ensure a successful color solution.

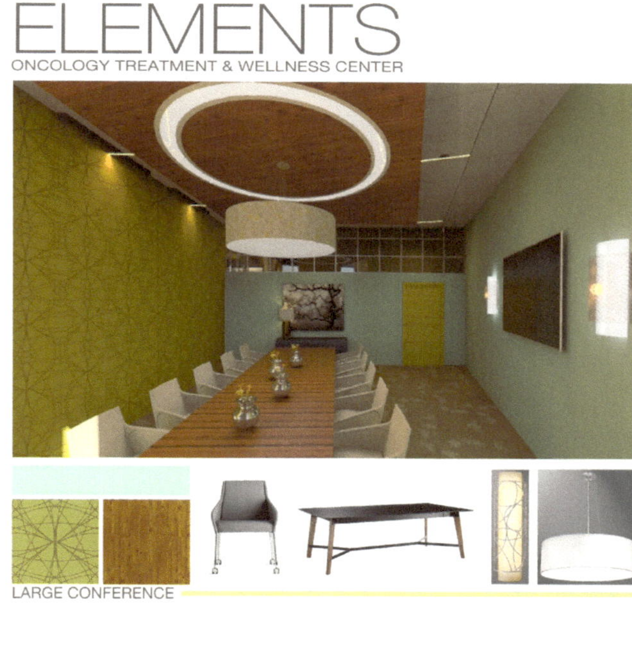

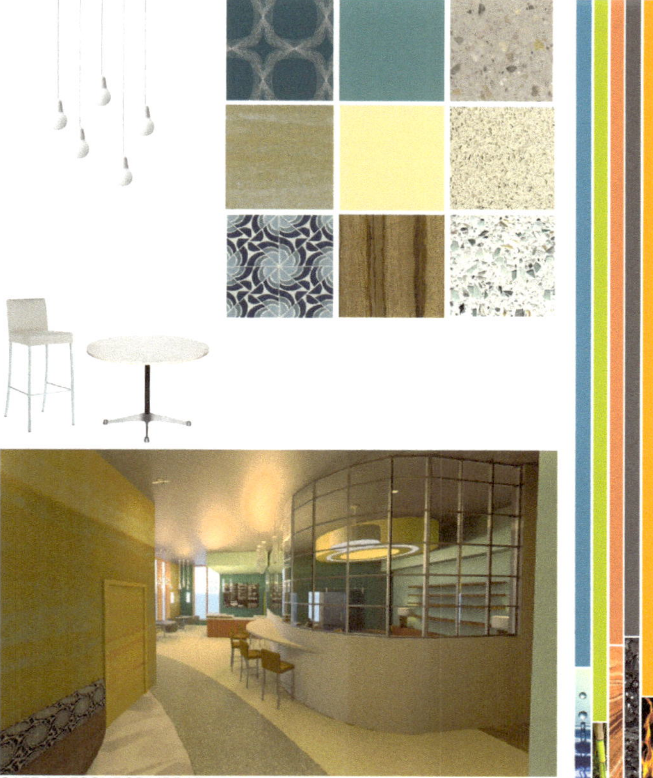

Figure 10.17 Example of a design presentation with digital renderings that includes furniture, finishes, and color for a children's oncology treatment and wellness center.

To experience design is to experience the world and the personal connections that occur in our built environment. Our experiences shape our spaces, and our spaces, in turn, shape us. Color, masterfully coordinated with the principles of balance, rhythm, emphasis, proportion, scale, unity, harmony, and variety, is the designer's most expressive tool.

REVIEW QUESTIONS

1. What is variety, and why is it important to interior space?
2. List the elements of design and explain their purpose and characteristics.
3. Explain how color temperature and value can be used to create the perception of space and depth.
4. Describe the various perceptual characteristics that can be achieved with the application of horizontal, vertical, diagonal, or curved lines.
5. Explain how particular hues can further achieve the perceptual characteristics of the line types listed in the chapter.
6. Explain how matte or satin finishes can add variety to an interior.
7. What two design elements can provide the quickest method for adding variety to a color plan?

Vocabulary

Variety
contrast
line
shape
damask
form
pattern
texture
faux finishes
matte
satin
glossy
time

EXERCISES

1. Is texture, pattern, or contrast more predominant in a color scheme? Select a series of interior images and discuss how each of the elements affects the variety of colored spaces.
2. If there is no pattern in a room, how can texture, contrast, and color intensities create variety? Discuss and give visual examples, from your own portfolio or from magazines and Web sites, to explain the idea.
3. Take a common natural object, and model the object abstractly using color, pattern, and texture. Use the character of the original object to influence the model prototype now redefined into a usable object (e.g., a light fixture, piece of furniture, storage element, or structural feature).

AFTERWORD

In the design profession, we tend to learn the intricacies of our craft in practice. The world is a far different place than the classroom, and you have to be ready at any given moment to quickly adjust, find fast solutions, and work effectively to communicate with your clients. Many of my own color errors occurred in practice, through which I have learned to avoid many of the color design problems that were never presented in academia. Color is a little science, a little art, and a little intuition. Color planning that occurs early in the stages of the design process will strengthen the project and assist with developing both the vision and concept for your design.

Color can't be avoided; it is a sensation—an emotional experience—that necessitates an open mind and freedom to explore the many possibilities with informed direction. Fear is the primary emotion I see from clients when we work with color. Clients have made a decision, and there is a risk that they will hate the color that is placed in their space, not realizing that it is fluid, changeable, and, with paint, the least expensive item to work with. The furnishings and materials, in my professional opinion, should come after the main color palette selections have been made and the client is at ease with those choices. In that regard, the other more expensive items can be selected with less anxiety, and the project will be a great success.

With any project, the goal is to achieve success through planned results with deliberate and informed use of color theory. Working with paint chips or small colored samples is fine in the initial selection process, but these are far from reliable when magnified a thousand times in a space. There are a few ways to make the process easier. First, narrow your selections with a client to the top two or three options to make the decision process less daunting. Then purchase rather inexpensive sample containers of paint that are available from most paint manufacturers, or at the very least, purchase a quart of paint. Use a sheet of white foam-core board (24 inches by 36 inches or 20 inches by 30 inches, depending on the size available at your local art supply store). Using a sponge artist brush, paint the surface of the foamboard in each of the color options. Tack the corners down to prevent bowing and let it dry.

This tool can now be pinned on wall surfaces in various locations of the space to examine under different lighting conditions and in relation to other materials and colors in the room. This same concept can be used for woods, carpets, and fabrics. If you are working with a design professional, inquire about their use of technology to create photorealistic views of the interior space which allows you to see color application completely. A few paint manufacturers now have apps that allow you to take a photo of your space to upload onto their Web site, or you can explore preset room vignettes to change and explore color. The key is this: Take caution on making a final decision on color with small samples since there are many variables that will influence the outcome and color perception—texture, daylight, artificial light, scale, volume, placement in the room, perceived intensity, influence by surrounding color—to name a short few we've referenced in the book.

Socially Responsible Use of Color

Interior designers, more than ever, are encouraged to consider the environmental, health, and wellness impact of their interior design projects. Ecological consciousness should by now be commonplace and therefore evident in our work.

I leave you with a task. Color comes in a variety of materials—paints, metals, wood, plastics, glass, and paper samples, to name a few. As consumers of products and designers who specify, I encourage you with each project to consider the long-term effects of the use of color media on the environment and well-being of those who come into contact with these spaces. Your eco-challenge is to research and use products that are socially responsible. Paint manufactures offer color products that are low in volatile organic compounds (VOCs) and that have minimum impact on the air quality of the interior space. Materials that are recycled or made from post-consumer materials help alleviate detrimental impacts on the environment. Creating healthy buildings extends beyond the structure to the inhabitants, to support healthy people.

Visit the Web site for the United States Green Building Council (http://www.usgbc.org) and Leadership in Energy and Environmental Design (LEED) for more information on design strategies to make your projects green. Additionally, review the Web site for the International WELL Building Institute (http://www.wellcertified.com) and the WELL Building Standard to see how your projects can be designed to support human health and well-being.

APPENDIX
color theory history

The following historical timeline tracks the chronological evolution of color systems, colorants, dyes, and advancements in color science and technology. Portions dated from 1611 to 2003 were adapted from Connie B. D'Imperio, http://www.coloryourcarpet.com.

1611 Finland—The oldest known color system is credited to astronomer, priest, and Neoplatonist Aron Sigfrid Forsius (1569–1637). In his color circle, between the colors black and white, red has been placed on the one side since the classical antiquity, and blue on the other; yellow then comes between white and red, pale yellow between white and yellow, orange between yellow and red.

1613 Belgium—Franciscus Aguilonius (1567–1617) was a Jesuit priest in Brussels when his color diagram appeared in 1613 in a work on optics. It is possibly the oldest system to use the trio of red, yellow, and blue wherein colors are defined within a linear division.

1656 Carman, a transparent magenta lake, replaced dragon's blood and madder lake; none were really permanent.

1659 Holland—Dutch artist Rembrandt (c. 1606–1669) understood the color theory that yellow darkened to brown and red was half yellow, so it too darkened to brown. A problem arises when the brown is darkened with black instead of its opposite color, ultramarine blue.

1672 England—Isaac Newton (1642–1726) devises the first color wheel. His theory "Optics" had the right idea, dividing the prism and bringing it back together again. However, he chooses the wrong colors—magenta and cyan were missing. Magenta doesn't show up in a crystal spectrum. It was 32 years later before his color theory was published.

1700 English vermilion dark is developed, a synthetic similar to the cool dark Chinese vermilion, antimony vermilion, mercuric sulfide vermilion (which will blacken some colors), mercuric iodide vermilion (impermanent), and eosine vermilion (with the fugitive coal-tar dye eosine). Since all are opaque today, cadmium red is a better choice and cheaper. The color is almost the same.

1705 Bister is developed, a transparent yellow-to-brown, duel-tone color made from charred beech wood. It's mainly a water-color pigment.

1724 Prussian blue is developed, a dual-tone transparent color that was getting close to cyan in its transparent undertone. The deep mass color has a black-green quality that produces a "dirty purple"—but nice greens. Heated Prussian blue makes a permanent Prussian brown.

1731 France—Jacques Christopher Le Blon (1667–1742) invents the fundamental three-color palette and demonstrates his system with many dyes;

however, he does not extend his ideas to a properly organized color system.

1755 Germany—Mathematician Johann Tobias Mayer (1723–1762) develops color theory by math, and his selection of triad colors (red, blue, and yellow) created the hexahedral color solid. Two years later, Mayer tried to identify the exact number of colors that the eye is capable of perceiving.

1766 England—The first known use of a color wheel is developed by Moses Harris (1731–1785). This one had red, yellow, and blue, but he included black as the only neutral.

1772 Germany—Astronomer J. Heinrich Lambert (1728–1777) presents the first three-dimensional color system.

1772 Austria—Ignaz Schiffermüller publishes his color circle in Vienna based on four colors: red, blue, green, and yellow.

1775 Germany—Tobias Mayer's color triangle is first published by the Göttinger physicist George Christopher Lichtenberg.

1780 Cobalt blue imitation is developed. Cobalt aluminate blue spinel replaced natural cobalt calcined oxide by 1802, and synthetic cobalt never produced the original color again.

1788 Emerald green is developed, a copper arsenate (and the most poisonous color) that can't be matched by any other element. Also, it turns lead and cadmium to black.

1788 England—Mosas Harris and Gainsborough make an 18-color wheel, again with no cyan or magenta. They also place ultramarine blue opposite orange, a long-lived mistake.

1790 England—A new color wheel is developed, the first made for light instead of pigments. Uses red, green, and blue as primaries and is credited to Movwell of Great Britain.

1800 Artists have a transparent triad palette in tubes for the first time. The three mixed into a neutral dark that could be pushed warm or cool.

1. Transparent duel-toned Indian yellow.
2. Transparent duel-toned madder lake (close to magenta).
3. Prussian blue, an iron-based transparent color close to cyan.

1809 Germany—Philipp Otto Runge's color wheel has white at the top and black on bottom. Also, the colors wrap around the middle of the sphere, and he chooses the wrong primary colors: red, yellow, and blue opaque plus the pigment black for shades.

1810 Germany—Johann Wolfgang von Goethe (1749–1832) makes a double intersecting triangle color wheel—a six-color wheel without magenta or cyan. Blood red was opposite emerald green, instead of cyan.

1810 Germany—The painter Philipp Otto Runge introduces his version of a color-sphere construction after eight years of work with colors.

1826 Permanent alizarin is discovered in natural root madder lake. The purpurin was subtracted with sulfuric acid.

1828 Synthetic ultramarine blue is developed, made from clay, soda, sulfur, coal, and heat.

1839 France—A 12-color wheel is made by chemist Michel Eugène Chevreul (1786–1889). Yellow, red, and blue again, with wrong complements and wrong afterimages. Yellow is not opposite purple, ultramarine blue is not opposite orange, and red is not the complement of green. His complements in "Simultaneous Contrast of Color," as he termed it, made mud. He never completed his solid model, and he was unable to discover a law of color harmony.

1858 Verguin discovers magenta (fuchsine), the second basic dye that, at the time, superseded the use of mauve.

1859 England—Physicist James Clerck Maxwell (1831–1879) publishes his "Theory of Color Vision," which is seen as the origin of colorimetry (quantitative color measurement).

1859 Italy—Magenta is the new name of a rich pink-purple color derived from the bloody location of a battle in Italy—even though magenta is not blood red. It was transparent, but fugitive. Also called solferino.

1860 Germany—Cobalt violet is developed (cobaltous crystalline phosphate, calcined cobalt oxide, and phosphorus oxide). A cool magenta color, it is required to make colors that fall between magenta and cyan, including ultramarine blue and azure (no other element can make this color). It sometimes contains arsenic and darkens (cobaltous oxide arsenate).

1862 Japan—Japanese color wheel is recognized, with five colors: white, yellow, red, ultramarine blue, and black under a new color theory. Yellow came from white and blue from black, with no magenta or cyan. The internal prism spectrum is similar.

1868 Germany—New colors are introduced: manganese violet, (manganese chloride, phosphoric acid, and ammonium carbonate), and a permanent cool magenta.

1868 England—Architect William Benson proposes and publishes his cuboid system, the first of his many color cubes.

1870 New opaque, permanent colors are discovered, including cerulean blue (cobaltous stannate, made from cobalt oxide and tin oxide).

1874 Germany—Wilhelm von Bezold (1837–1907) introduces his color cone, based on red, green, and blue as primaries.

1874 Germany—Wilhelm Wundt (1832–1920), psychologist and philosopher, introduces his color sphere, which has eight basic colors: white and black are placed at the poles, and the equator comprises eight colors, including green, green-blue, blue, violet, purple, red, yellow, and yellow-green. The colors form a circle with gray at its center.

1878 Austria—Physiologist Ewald Hering (1834–1918) theorizes three opposing sets of colors: yellow and ultramarine blue, red and green, and black and white. A different concept in its time, this opposed the purely phenomenal or physical understanding of colors.

1879 United States—American Nicholas Odgen Rood (1831–1902) makes a double cone color model, his "scientific" color circle, which he had constructed on the basis of experiments using rotating discs, a color point being placed precisely opposite its complementary partner. It had white on top and black at the bottom, and red, green, and blue as the triad. Although the development was a major contribution to color, magenta and cyan were still absent.

1881 France—French Artist Seurat (1859–1891) touts "pointillism," the new scientific method, which includes the folly that red is the opposite of green. Although they do vibrate, there is no harmony.

1886 Germany—The first and at the same time the last standard of pigment colors for artists is presented by A. W. Keim, of the German Society for the Promotion of Rational Methods in Painting. The following colors were deemed necessary by selected artists to set up control for the pigments in colors in an attempt to guarantee the colors' characteristics and ingredients:

1. White lead
2. Zinc white
3. Cadmium yellow light and medium, and cadmium orange
4. Indian yellow
5. Naples yellow light and dark
6. Yellow to brown, natural and burnt ocher and sienna
7. Red ocher
8. Iron oxide colors
9. Graphite
10. Alizarin crimson madder lake (a magenta-colored fugitive pigment)
11. Vermilion
12. Umbers
13. Cobalt blue, native and synthetic
14. Ultramarine blue, natural and synthetic
15. Paris-Prussian blue
16. Oxide of chromium, opaque and transparent viridian
17. Green earth
18. Ivory black
19. Vine black

1890 Thomas Young and Von Heimholtz develop the wave theory of light.

1905 United States—American painter Albert Henry Munsell (1858–1918) creates an "eight-color wheel." His wheel was absent cyan, and his color opposites were incorrect. He darkened the colors with black, mixed them with gray, and tinted them with white, and numbered them all. This is still taught today.

1909 Cadmium red is discovered.

1915 United States—Munsell introduces an order of colors—also known as a "color tree" due to its irregular outer profile grouped around a central vertical gray-scale. Munsell constructed his system around a circle with ten segments, arranging its colors at equal distances and selecting them in such a way that opposing pairs would result in an achromatic mixture.

1916 Germany—Wilhelm Ostwald (1853–1932), the Nobel Prize winner for chemistry, compiles his Color Primer. His color circle was actually two cones that meet at the flat circumferences of the top circles. The last color wheel (square) of college record was by Church-Ostwald. It has yellow, red, sea green, and ultramarine blue at the corners.

1923 United States—Introduction of the first color-matching cabinets in which a sample could be matched under a variety of light sources. Prior to this, only daylight, which is very inconsistent, was used to match colors.

1950 United States—ROYGBIV (red, orange, yellow, green, blue, indigo, and violet) is the "seven-color wheel." It is out of order and dispels the unity of opposition—more evidence that the color wheel has been misunderstood by every generation since, in and out of college.

1958 X-rite was founded and provides color forecasting, color measurement, and management for a wide range of industries, including packaging, clothing, electronics, cosmetics, home furnishings, paint, food and beverage, and construction, that supply colored products.

1963 Pantone color matching system (PMS) was developed to provide a standardization for global color identification and communication of color across graphic, architecture, and design industries. In 2007, Pantone was acquired by X-rite.

1990 United States—A new "color theory" is created by Color Your Carpet, Inc. for on-site re-dyeing of textiles, specifically carpets and rugs. The theory is applied to the system's proprietary dyeing process. Much like electronically produced colors, the spectrum is capable of millions of colors. Since carpet fibers (those that are re-dye-able) are actually transparent, and dyes are water-based and therefore transparent as well, the dyes that are in place from the factory can be re-dyed by introducing specially formulated dyes that "bond" with the existing dyes to become a "new color." This was the first true introduction of cyan, magenta, and yellow (not red, yellow, and blue) as the true primaries and the true basis of all colors in transparent color theory.

1992 United States—A new "color wheel" is produced by the Color Wheel Company that is based on CYMK (cyan, yellow, magenta, and black), using thin film plastic and half-tone dpi (dots per square inch) colors. This color wheel is sold to printing, graphics, and textile companies. However, it is very limited in practical use, since only 40,000 colors are possible to display, and in the industries, (as on a computer today), more than 16 million colors are possible (depending on the number of available dye sites) in true transparent color when dyes are the coloring medium.

1995 United States—Daniel Smith prints a "Color Square" using the "LAB" color chart. With white and black being the poles, this system is not for the artists who need to work with true opposition; it's better suited for the photo and printing industries. This model has the opposition colors, yellow and blue, on the top and bottom. Magenta and green are at the sides. A plus-and-minus number system relates the square with these colors as the primaries.

1996 United States—A brilliant new color wheel called the Real Color Wheel is created by Don Jusko. This new theory more truly represents transparent colors and their relationship to each other.

There are 12 to 36 base colors in the Real Color Wheel, which joins the pigment and the light color wheel together as one, and agrees with the nature of your eyes' afterimage.

The main issues with current color wheels, except the Real Color Wheel, which is not yet available to the public, are the lack of defined differences of the following:

1. Opaque colors (paint/pigments—solid mediums)
2. Transparent colors (dyes—liquid mediums)
3. Light colors (sunlight or electronic reproduction of light)

2003 Artist Donald Jusko developed the Real Color Wheel—the only transparent three–primary color wheel consisting of 36 rings of pigment with 360 hues. It is the only color wheel of its kind using color complements for mixing shadows and shade without the use of black pigment.

2009 ICEmaker (Intelligent Color Engine) technology and ICEmaker software reproaches the traditional RGB to CMYK color conversion challenge during printing. The software defines chroma and luminance of a color separately to achieve "color that is stable and vibrant color, and separate color automatically." FineEye Color software approach recalculates color conversions that now accounts for the color of the paper color values during the printing processes for greater accuracy in color translation.

2012 Scientists claim that purple, or magenta, does not exist in the visible light spectrum. Visible color is a product of our brain's interpretation of light. The mixture of red and violet results in our perception of the color magenta, two colors that are on opposite ends of the visible spectrum, but do not connect and theoretically cannot produce this color in the spectrum since it does not have its own wavelength. Visit the following video to learn more about this phenomenon: https://www.youtube.com/watch?v=iPPYGJjKVco.

2015 New eyewear is developed that allows individuals with color blindness to be restored to near normal color vision. The glasses address the common red and green cone color deficiencies that account for the majority of color blindness by capturing the light and adjusting for normal color vision. More information on this new technology can be found at the following URL: www.enchroma.com

2019 E Ink, a leader in electronic ink and ePaper technology, developed the first advanced color ePaper installation using full-color Electronic Paper Display (EPD). The retail point of sale signs can generate over 32,000 colors. The color allows for individual displays branded to specific products and can be changed instantly reducing the need for paper by removing unnecessary waste created from traditional printed paper in-store promotions and displays.

In the FUTURE—Retinal bionic eye prosthesis that grant color vision to the blind and families able to genetically choose the eye and hair color of their unborn child!

GLOSSARY

achromatic: refers to black, white, and gray, each of which is without color.

adaptable design: design that can be easily changed over time to accommodate the anticipated needs of an individual who may have a mobility or physical impairment limiting their function of a space.

additive color: color creation with light vs. pigment by *adding* the primary colors of light red, blue, and green in various combinations and intensities. Adding all colored light produces white light.

aging in place: the ability for a person to remain in their home of choice as they grow older.

alternation: occurs when two design elements are repeated in sequence, as in repetition; however, the difference is the pattern includes two distinctly different elements (round to square, red to blue) rather than one element repeating.

Americans with disabilities act (ADA): a civil rights law enacted in 1990 that prohibits discrimination against people with a disability.

analogous: describing color schemes resulting from two or more colors adjacent to one another on the color wheel, such as blue, blue-green, and green.

anomaly: an irregular deviation or departure from what one considers normal. In interior design, this takes the form of contrasting two distinct styles where one becomes the focal point.

anthropometrics: the study of the average human body dimensions and measurements.

asymmetry: results when elements on either side of an implied axis are equal weight but vary in shape and size.

attention deficit hyperactivity disorder (ADHD): a cognitive impairment identified with symptoms of inattention, hyperactivity and impulsivity that limits the individual's ability to process information or reduced mental focus and functioning, specifically for extended periods of time.

autism spectrum disorder (ASD): a cognitive disorder characterized by impairment in a person's ability to communicate, engage in social interaction, or become unresponsive and withdrawn with fixated patterns in behavior.

balance: refers to the relationship of colored elements as they occupy an implied axis within a space perceived to be equal in visual weight.

Bezold effect: developed by rug maker Wilhelm von Bezold during the nineteenth century, the effect occurs when the largest color area is replaced by a new color, creating a color interaction that changes the overall impression of the design.

bari: a package of garments that is sent by the groom's family to the bride, neatly wrapped and displayed a week before the wedding day.

bio-inspired design: design that emulates the growth patterns, structures, and characteristics of natural occurring organisms (e.g., plants, animals, marine life).

cataracts: a clouding or yellowing condition of the lens of the eye that creates blurred and distorted color vision.

chroma: refers to the purity of a color, completely absent of any white, gray, or black that would lessen its *intensity* or *saturation*, two additional terms acceptable for describing the color strength.

chromatic colors: any hues other than white, gray, and black.

chromatic scale: the degree of lightness or darkness of a single color or sequence of value that occurs when gradually mixing a complementary pair of hues together.

chromotherapy: the practice of using colored light and color in the environment to cure specific illnesses and in general to bring about beneficial healthy effects.

circadian rhythm: a natural biological process that regulates a person's sleep cycle.

color: the visual property of an object that results from light reflecting off the object's surface and being perceived by the eye.

color blindness: a deficiency of color perception resulting in the inability to distinguish one or more colors.

color forecasting: the result of identifying global patterns in the tastes of consumers and the projection of common color preferences for marketing of goods and services.

color grammar: the spatial relationship between various color arrangements and alignments to explore a new design language.

color interaction: illusion that occurs when two or more hues placed next to one another interact and change our visual perception of the colors.

Color Marketing Group: a nonprofit organization that identifies global color trends in the marketplace.

color masking: using color to hide design features through shading, color patterns, or blending to deemphasize their presence within the space.

color rendering index (CRI): indicates the light source's ability to render the true color of an object as it would appear in natural light, using Kelvin to identify the color temperature.

color theory: the study and practice of a set of principles used to understand the logical relationship among color and light in our visual experiences of art and design.

complementary: referring to two colors opposite one another on the color wheel: red/green, blue/orange, and violet/yellow.

complementary neutralization: grayed or brownish color created by the mixture of two complementary hues—red and green, blue and orange, violet and yellow. The intensity of the resulting neutralized color depends on the proportional amount of the two hues mixed together.

cones: the portion of cells within the retina of the eye responsible for seeing in daylight and recognizing color.

continuation: placement of one or more colors throughout an interior to create a continuous movement of the eye through the space.

contrast: opposition in order to show or emphasize differences between two objects; the juxtaposition of different forms, lines, or colors in a space to intensify each element's properties and produce a more dynamic experience, especially if it is unusual, is often the feature that earns the most attention.

damask: in paint and wall covering, a pattern resulting from printing one color in matte and satin finish or in lighter and darker values; in textiles, a reversible pattern that originated in Damascus during medieval times.

Day of the Dead: celebration in Mexico held yearly in October honoring those who have passed.

deuteranopia: color blindness where red and green colors are not as distinguishable.

diffraction: the bending of light around objects to produce light, dark, and/or different colored bands of light.

direct color: the manner of interfacing directly with a particular color source without obstruction.

discord: a loosely organized, disharmonized color combination that departs from the natural ordering of color.

double complementary: includes two adjacent hues and their complements on the color wheel, such as yellow-green, green, red-violet, and red.

emphasis: a tool for creating points of interest not only for aesthetic purposes but also to orient users of the space.

evidence-based design: the process of making decisions about the design of the built environment utilizing credible research to achieve the best possible outcomes.

fad: a short-lived interest by an individual or group of people for the purpose of quick sales that is driven by mass popularity.

faux finish: a painting or printing technique used to generate realistic three-dimensional objects, including plants, wood, stone, marble, and other naturally occurring materials, in two dimensions.

Fawn Lep: a traditional Thai dance known as the *fingernail dance*.

Fibonacci Sequence: a sequence of numbers where each successive number is the sum of the two previous numbers (e.g., 1, 1, 2, 3, 5, 8, 13, 21, 34, 55, 89, 144, etc.).

focal point: the *single* design element receiving the greatest visual emphasis in a room.

form: the perception of weight, volume, and mass of an object.

Froebel blocks: a series of wooden stacking blocks in various geometric shapes developed by German Frederick Froebel, who created the concept of kindergarten in the nineteenth century.

fusuma: traditional Japanese opaque sliding doors or shoji panels made of wood and paper, used to screen rooms for privacy.

glossy/gloss: a high sheen on a material surface; usually reduces the intensity of the color.

golden section: also known as the golden rule, the rectangle, and the golden ratio, developed by the ancient Greeks; the division of a line in two sections, where the ratio between the smallest section and the largest section is identical to the ratio between the largest section and the entire length of the line: a is to b as b is to $a+b$ or (a/b = b/a+b).

harmony: the result of a perfect balance between individual color relationships.

health: the condition of a person being sound in body, mind, or spirit; free from physical disease or pain.

hue: color that is the property of light by which the color of an object is classified and named as red, blue, green, or yellow in reference to the visible spectrum.

indirect color: natural or artificial light bouncing color from one colored surface onto adjoining surfaces so that the original color becomes lighter in intensity.

kalamandi: images common in Baluch rugs: large hexagons filled with stylized patterns including trees.

Kelvin: the unit of measurement for the color temperatures of various light sources.

Le Modular: a measuring system developed by architect Le Corbusier based on the proportions of man.

light emitting diode (LED): a device that emits light when an electric current passes through it to create light without heat.

light reflectance value (LRV): refers to the percentage of light that is reflected from a colored surface back into the interior space, referenced in a range of 0–100.

line: the connection between two points in space.

lux: a unit of measurement in illumination of a surface area by a light source.

matte: a dull, non-reflective surface. This surface texture typically makes colors appear darker.

Mayoun: one of two festivals held during a traditional Pakistani wedding; it celebrates the bride.

medicine wheel: a symbol used to represent health, healing, and harmony among all living things.

Mehendi: one of two festivals held during a traditional Pakistani wedding; it celebrates the groom.

memo sample: a large textile sample that shows the full horizontal and vertical pattern repeats and the color range of the design.

metamerism: the change in perception of a color under different lighting conditions, such as natural daylight in contrast to interior artificial light.

monochromatic: a color scheme based on variations in value and chroma of one particular hue.

multi-hue: a color scheme that is not limited in the number of hues but requires careful proportions to work effectively.

nanometer: the unit of measurement for different colored wavelengths within the visible spectrum.

palette: a range of colors assigned to the design for a particular interior space.

pattern: the repetition and arrangement of shapes and forms.

primary hues: red, yellow, and blue for pigment mixing; red, yellow, and green for light mixing; cyan, magenta, and yellow for printing.

programming: the stage in the design process when you begin the data collection for a project.

progression: involves the repetition of similar elements with a continuous change (large to small, low to high, narrow to wide, light to dark).

proportion: the size relationships between elements (parts) and the visual composition or space (whole).

protanopia: color blindness where only red wavelengths of light are not as visible. Individuals will have difficulty distinguishing between red and green coloring.

pure hue: a color that is void of any white, gray, or black and is at its highest intensity or brightness. These colors are the product of mixing various amounts of primary and secondary colors.

radiation: concentric color arrangement to unify design elements and create visual movement (versus the traditional sense of an arrangement of objects in a radial pattern).

radial balance: balance that is achieved by the equal rotation of design elements around a central axis.

recoloration: an interior or exterior space that has had its color scheme changed.

reflection: the bouncing of one or more colored wavelengths of light off an object, resulting in the color of the object being seen.

refraction: the bending of light that results from its being slowed as it moves from one medium through a denser medium.

repetition: the systematic orderly succession of identical design elements (shape, line, color, form) along a defined path in space.

rhythm: movement or path created by related visual elements, resulting in a constant pattern.

rods: the portion of cells within the retina of the eye responsible for seeing in dim light and recognizing values.

Saltillo: a porous, nonglazed, clay tile handmade in the Mexican city of Saltillo, commonly made in reds, oranges, and yellows.

satin finish: a material with a medium sheen, reflecting less light than a gloss but more than a matte surface.

scale: refers to the size of a shape in relation to a given known; in most cases, the human body and its position within space.

seasonal affective disorder (SDA): a type of depression associated with the changes in the season, often occurring in the fall and winter, due to decreased exposure to daylight.

secondary hues: violet, green, and orange, each made from combining two primary hues.

shade: the result of physically or visually adding varying amounts of black to any pure hue, reducing the color's intensity.

shalwar kameez: loose pajama-like clothing to be worn by the bride during the Mayoun festival, one of two festivals celebrated the week before a traditional Pakistani wedding.

shape: one or more lines connecting to form a two-dimensional image such as a square, circle, or triangle.

sherwani: the traditional white, long coatlike garment embroidered in gold worn by men during the traditional Pakistani wedding.

simultaneous contrast: when any two colors are placed side by side or surrounded by one or the other, resulting in a change in the colors' visual perception. This effect is intensified with complementary colors of high saturation or brightness.

Songkran: a festival in Thailand that celebrates the traditional New Year's Day beginning on April 13 and ending April 15.

space: the combination of the elements and principles of design used to create a three-dimensional inhabitable environment.

Spanish colonial: a mélange of styles with open courtyards, tiled roofs, archways, heavy wooden doors, and plain stucco wall surfaces.

split complementary: color scheme composed of three colors consisting of one main hue plus the two hues each adjacent to its complement (for example, blue, red-orange, and yellow-orange).

subtractive color: pigment color mixing using paint, dyes, colorants, and inks where red, blue, and yellow are commonly identified as the primary colors. The *subtraction* of all color produces white.

symmetry: the arrangement of elements on either side of an implied axis that are equally balanced and of the same shape and form (i.e., *mirror image*).

talking stick: decorated stick used during Native American tribal meetings and storytelling to identify the individual who may speak.

tertiary hues: red-violet, blue-violet, blue-green, yellow-green, yellow-orange, and red-orange, each made by combining a secondary hue with one of the primaries.

tetradic: color schemes composed of four colors equally spaced along the color wheel, such as yellow, red-orange, violet, and blue-green.

texture: the characteristic visual and tactile quality of the surface of a material resulting from the way in which the materials are constructed or combined together.

Theravada Buddhism: the primary religion in Thailand and the more conservative of the two Buddhist traditions.

thermochromatic: the property of an object that changes color due to changes in temperature.

time: the physical qualities of color and materials that change in appearance over the course of time.

tint: the result of physically or visually adding varying amounts of white to any pure hue to reduce the color's intensity.

tone: the result of physically or visually adding varying amounts of gray to any pure hue to reduce the color's intensity.

tritanopia: color blindness where blue and yellow wavelengths of light are not as distinguishable.

trend: a prevailing tendency toward something, or a particular fashionable interest over an extended period of time.

triad/triadic: color schemes composed of three colors equally spaced along the color wheel, such as green, purple, and orange.

uniform connectedness: occurs when two or more design elements are connected by visual properties, such as color, shape, or pattern, and will be perceived as more related than two or more design elements that are not connected with similar visual properties.

unity: the repetition of color to achieve a unified whole.

universal design: the design of buildings, spaces, or objects that make them accessible and useable by all people.

value: refers to the lightness or darkness of a color.

variety: the combination of one or more color elements with shape, form, pattern, and texture to create diversity and contrast in an interior space.

vibrancy: the perception of movement at the boundary between two highly saturated colors, often recognized with complements.

visible spectrum: the portion of colored light within the electromagnetic spectrum that is visible to the human eye.

visitability: design approach to a space that permits users who may use a wheelchair full access to the first floor or ground level of a home or building.

wayfinding: text, symbols, and color cue techniques used to orient and assist in physical awareness of one's place or orientation in space.

well-being: the state of being and feeling happy, healthy, and prosperous.

BIBLIOGRAPHY

Albers, Josef. (1975). *Interaction of color*. London: Yale University Press.

Arditi, Aries. (2016). *Designing for people with partial sight and color deficiencies*. Retrieved from http://li129-107.members.linode.com/accessibility/design/accessible-print-design/effective-color-contrast/.

Arnheim, Rudolf. (1969). *Visual thinking*. Berkeley: University of California Press.

_____. (1972). *Art and visual perception: A psychology of the creative eye*. Berkeley: University of California Press.

_____. (1974). *Art and visual perception*. Berkeley: University of California Press.

Augustin, S. (2009). *Place advantage: applied psychology for interior architecture*. Hoboken, NJ: John Wiley & Sons, Inc.

Ball, Victoria K. (1965). The aesthetics of color: A review of fifty years of experimentation. *Journal of Aesthetics and Art Criticism*, *23*(4), 441–452.

Benz, Ernest, Izutsu, Toshihiko, Portman, Adolf, et al. (1972). *Color symbolism*. Dallas: Spring Publications.

Bernard, Teresa. (2016, April 22). *Principles of good design: Contrast*. Retrieved from http://www.bluemoonwebdesign.com/art-lessons-4.asp.

Binggeli, Corky. (2007). *Interior design: A survey*. Hoboken, NJ: John Wiley & Sons.

Birren, Faber. (1961). *Color psychology and color therapy: A factual study of the influence of color on human life*. New York: University Books.

_____. (1969). *Principles of color: A review of past traditions and modern theories of color harmony*. New York: Van Nostrand Reinhold.

_____. (1992). *The power of color: How it can reduce fatigue, relieve monotony, enhance sexuality, and more*. Secaucus, NJ: Citadel Press.

Biyela, N. (2013). Colour metaphor in Zulu culture: Courtship communication in beads. *American International Journal of Contemporary Research*, *3*(10), 37–41. doi:http://www.aijcrnet.com/journals/Vol_3_No_10_October_2013/6.pdf.

Bonnardel, V., Beniwal, S., Dubey, N., Pande, M. & Bimler, D. (2017). Gender difference in color preference across cultures: An archetypal pattern modulated by a female cultural stereotype. *Color Research & Application*, *43*(2), pp. 209-223.

Bosch, S. J., Cama, R, Edelstein E, Malkin J. (2012). *The Application of Color in Healthcare Settings*. Concord, CA: The Center for Health Design. Retrieved from: https://www.healthdesign.org/system/files/CHD%20Color%20Paper%20FINAL-5.pdf.

Boyce, P.R. (2003). Lighting for the elderly. *Technology and Disability*, *15*, 165–180.

Brainard, Shirl. (2003). *A design manual* (3rd ed.). Upper Saddle River, NJ: Prentice Hall.

Bright, Keith, & Cook, Geoffrey. (2010). *The colour, light and contrast manual*. West Sussex, UK: Wiley-Blackwell.

Brusatin, Manilio. (1991). *A history of color*. Boston: Shambhala Publications.

Burchett, Kenneth E. (2005). *A bibliographical history of the study and use of color from Aristotle to Kandinsky*. New York: Edwin Mellen Press.

Cabarga, L. (2001). *The designer's guide to global color combinations: 750 color formulas in CMYK and RGB from around the world*. Cincinnati, OH: How Design Books.

Caivano, J. L. (2005). *The research on environmental color design: Brief history, current developments, and possible future*. Retrieved from http://www.ad-chroma.com/files/aic_2005_caivano_ecd_history_705_714.pdf.

Card. A., Taylor, E., Piatkowski, M. (2018). *Design for Behavioral and Mental Health: More than just safety*. Concord, CA: The Center for Health Design. Retrieved from: https://www.healthdesign.org/system/files/res_files/Issue%20Brief_Behavioral%20Health_2018_3.pdf.

Carter, R. (1982). Visual search with color. *Journal of Experimental Psychology: Human Perception and Performance*, *8*, 127–136.

Center for Healthcare Design. (2020). *EDAC: Evidence-based design accreditation and certification.* Retrieved from: https://www.healthdesign.org/certification-outreach/edac/about.

Center for Universal Design. (2008). *About UD.* North Caroline State University College of Design. Retrieved from: https://projects.ncsu.edu/ncsu/design/cud/about_ud/about_ud.htm.

Ching, Francis D. K. (1996). *Architecture: Form, space, & order* (2nd ed.). New York: John Wiley & Sons.

Ching, Francis D. K., & Binggeli, Corky. (2005). *Interior design illustrated.* Hoboken, NJ: John Wiley & Sons.

Cho, J. Y., & Lee, E.-J. (2016). Impact of Interior Colors in Retail Store Atmosphere on Consumers' Perceived Store Luxury, Emotions, and Preference. *Clothing and Textiles Research Journal, 35*(1), 33–48.

Clarke, T., & Costall, A. (2008). The emotional connotations of color: A qualitative investigation. *Color Research & Application, 33*(5), 406–410. doi: 10.1002/col.20435.

Cler, M. (2012). Colour appearance in urban chromatic studies. In C.P. Biggam, C.A. Hough, C.J. Kay, and D.R. Simmons (Eds.), *New Directions in Colour Studies.* (pp. 181–189). Amsterdam: John Benjamins.

Cohan, Tony, Takahashi, Masako, & Levick, Melba. (1998). *Mexicolor: The spirit of Mexican design.* San Francisco: Chronicle Books.

Color Matters. (2008). *Drunk tank pink.* Retrieved from http://www.colormatters.com/body_pink.html.

COLOURlovers. (2007). *11 Great color legends.* Retrieved from http://www.colourlovers.com/blog/2007/05/01/11-great-color-legends/print/.

Cranz, Galen. (2000). *The chair: Rethinking culture, body, and design.* New York: W.W. Norton & Company.

Crayola. (2012). *Crayon and color info.* Retrieved from http://www.crayola.co.uk/about-us/crayon-chronology.aspx.

Daggett, Williard R., Cobble, Jeffrey E., & Gertel, Steven J. (2008). *Color in an optimum learning environment.* Retrieved from http://www.sagusinternational.com/downloads/resource_dtails.asp? ID=3&s=6&s2=6&p=6.

Dael, N., Perseguers, M.-N., Marchand, C., Antonietti, J.-P., & Mohr, C. (2016). Put on that colour, it fits your emotion: Colour appropriateness as a function of expressed emotion. *Quarterly Journal of Experimental Psychology*, 69(8), 1619–1630.

Day, J. (2013). *Line color form: The language of art and design.* New York: Allworth Press.

De Bortoli, M., & Maroto, J. (2001). Colours across cultures: Translating colours in interactive marketing communications. Retrieved from http://global propaganda.com/articles/TranslatingColours.pdf.

Dearing, B. & Sangeeta, S. (1996). Photosensitive assessment: a study of color preference, depression and temperament. *Subtle Energies and Energy Medicine*, 7(1), 89–110.

Department of Homeland Security. *Homeland security advisory system.* Retrieved from http://www.dhs.gov/xabout/laws/gc_1214508631313.shtm.

Department of Veteran Affairs-Office of Construction and Facilities Management. (2010, December). *Mental Health Facilities Design Guide.* Retrieved from: https://www.cfm.va.gov/til/dGuide/dgMH.pdf.

D'Imperio, Connie B. (2007). History of color systems. Retrieved from http:// www.coloryourcarpet.com.

Dockstader, F. (1961). *Indian art in America: The arts and crafts of the North American Indian.* Greenwich, CT: New York Graphic Society.

Droste, Magdalena. (2006). *Bauhaus 1919–1933.* Los Angeles: Taschen.

Dubé, Richard L. (1997). *A pattern language: A practical source for landscape design.* New York: Van Nostrand Reinhold.

Edmunds Inc. (2008). *Traffic ticket urban legends: Debunking 10 driving myths that all your friends believe.* Retrieved from http://www.edmunds.com/advice/youngdrivers/articles/125550/article.html.

Edwards, Betty. (2004). *Color: A course in mastering the art of mixing colors.* New York: Tarcher/Penguin Books.

Eiseman, Leatrice. (1998). *Color for your every mood.* Sterling, VA: Capital Books.

_____. (2006). *Color: Messages and meaning.* Gloucester, MA: Hand Books Press.

Elam, Kimberly. (2001). *Geometry in design: Studies in proportion and composition.* New York: Princeton Architectural Press.

Ellinger, Richard G. (1980). *Color structure and design.* New York: Van Nostrand Reinhold.

Faimon, Peg, & Weigand, John. (2004). *The nature of design.* Cincinnati: How Design Books.

Fairchild, M. D. (2005). Human color vision. In *Color appearance models* (2nd ed.). New York: John Wiley & Sons.

Fehrman, Kenneth & Cherie. (2004). *Color: The secret influence.* Upper Saddle River, NJ: Pearson Education.

Feisner, Edith Anderson. (2006). *Color studies* (2nd ed.). New York: Fairchild Publications.

Feldman, Edmund Burke. (1992). *Varieties of visual experience* (4th ed.). Upper Saddle River, NJ: Prentice Hall.

Fetterman, A. K., Liu, T., & Robinson, M. D. (2014). Extending Color Psychology to the Personality Realm: Interpersonal Hostility Varies by Red Preferences and Perceptual Biases. *Journal of Personality, 83*(1), 106–116. doi: 10.1111/jopy.1208.

Flags of the World. *Italy.* Retrieved from http://flagspot.net/flags/it.html.

Ford, Janet Lynn. (n.d.). *Worqx.* Retrieved from www.worqx.com/color/color_proportion.htm.

Frederick, Mathew. (2007). *101 Things I learned in architecture school.* Cambridge, MA: MIT Press.

Froebel Web. (2002). *Johannes Itten 1888–1967.* Retrieved from http://www.froebel web.org/web2018.html.

Gage, John. (1993). *Color and culture: Practice and meaning from antiquity to abstraction.* Berkley: University of California Press.

Gaines, K. S. & Curry, Z. D. (2011). The inclusive classroom: the effective of color on learning and behavior. *Journal of Family & Consumer Sciences Education*, *29*(1), 46–57.

Ghamari, H., and Amor, C. (2016). The role of color in healthcare environments, emergent bodies of evidence-based design approach. *Sociology and Anthropology 4*(11): 1020-1029. doi: 10.12189/sa.2016.041109.

Gibbs, Jenny. (2005). *Interior design: A practical guide*. New York: Harry N. Abrams.

Goldberg, Paul, & Becom, Jeffery. (2003). *Mediterranean color*. New York: Abbeville Press.

Hardy, Paula. (2007). *Lonely Planet Morocco* (7th ed.). Oakland, CA: Lonely Planet Publications.

Health Learning Network. Retrieved from: https://www.psychcongress.com/article/facility-architecture/how-effectively-use-color-treatment-facilities.

Hegde, A. (2011). Effect of light and color on subjective evaluative impressions by the elderly: Implications for creating nurturing and aesthetically pleasing interior environments. *International Journal of Health, Wellness and Society*, *1*(1), 1–11.

Hoisington, A. (2017, August 2). How to effectively use color in treatment facilities. Retrieved from https://www.psychcongress.com/article/facility-architecture/how-effectively-use-color-treatment-facilities.

Holtzschue, Linda. (2006). *Understanding color: An introduction for designers*. Hoboken, NJ: John Wiley & Sons.

Hope, Augustine, & Walch, Margaret. (1990). *The color compendium*. New York: Van Nostrand Reinhold.

Hunt, J. M., Sine, D. M., & McMurray, K. N. (2019). *Behavioral Health Design Guide, Edition 9.0*. Behavioral Health Facility Consulting, LLC. Retrieved from: http://www.bhfcllc.com/wp-content/uploads/2019/06/Design-Guide-8.1-web.pdf.

Itten, Josef. (2001). *The elements of color*. Hoboken, NJ: John Wiley & Sons.

Jefferson, L. (1973). *The decorative arts of Africa*. New York: Viking Press.

Jonauskaite, D., Dael, N., Chèvre, L., Althaus, B., Tremea, A., Charalambides, L. & Mohr, C. (2018). Pink for girls, blue for boys, and blue for both genders: Color preferences in children and adults. *Sex Roles, 80*(9–10), pp. 630–642.

Kelly, Kenneth L., & Judd, Deane B. (1976). *Color: Universal language and dictionary of names*. Washington, DC: National Bureau of Standards.

Kente: A Royal Fabric of Your Heritage. (n.d.). Retrieved from https://www16.corecommerce.com/~primeheritage/uploads/file/KenteStolesHistory.pdf.

Khouw, Natalie. (2007). *The meaning of color for gender*. Retrieved from http://www.colormatters.com/khouw.html.

Kilmer, Rosemary, & Kilmer, W. Otie. (2014). *Designing interiors* (2nd ed.). Hoboken, NJ: John Wiley & Sons.

Kislenko, A. (2004). *Culture and customs of Thailand*. Westport, CT: Greenwood Press.

Knight, Terry W. (1998). Color grammars: The representation of form and color in designs. *Leonardo*, *26*(2), 117–124.

Kobayashi, Shigenobu. (1987). *A book of colors*. Tokyo: Kodansha International.

_____. (1990). *Color image scale*. Tokyo: Kodansha International.

Koenig, Becky. (2007). *Color workbook* (2nd ed.). Upper Saddle River, NJ: Pearson Education.

Kopacz, Jeanne. (2004). *Color in three-dimensional design*. New York: McGraw-Hill.

Kopec, David. *The importance of color in home sales*. Retrieved from http://realtytimes.com/rtapages/20030513_color.htm.

Korkmaz, S., Özer, Ö., Kaya, ?., Kazgan, A., & Atmaca, M. (2016). The correlation between color choices and impulsivity, anxiety and depression. *Electronic Journal of General Medicine*, *13*(3). doi: 10.29333/ejgm/81905.

Krause, J. (2015). *Color for designers: ninety-five things you need to know when choosing and using color for layouts and illustrations*. San Francisco, CA: New Riders, an imprint of Peachpit.

Laframboise, S., & Sherbina, K. (2008). *The Medicine Wheel*. Retrieved from http://www.dancingtoeaglespiritsociety.org/medwheel.php.

Lauer, David A., & Pentak, Stephen. (2007). *Basic design* (6th ed.). Belmont, CA: Wadsworth/Thomas Learning.

Lehndorff, Betsy. (2002, October 5). Living color. *Rocky Mountain News*, p. 1E.

Leland, Nita. (1998). *Exploring color: How to use and control color in your painting*. Cincinnati: North Light Books.

Lidwell, William, Holden, Kristina, & Butler, Jill. (2003). *Universal principles of design*. Beverly, MA: Rockport Publishers.

Machin, Rob. (2005). *Trigger happy*. Retrieved from http://emea.promax.tv/emea/dec_news_1.html.

Mahlangu, E. (2014, October 27). People of South Africa: Ndebele. Retrieved from http://www.sahistory.org.za/article/people-south-africa-ndebele.

Mahnke, Frank H. (1996). *Color, environment, and human response*. New York: John Wiley & Sons.

Mahnke, Frank H., & Rudolf, H. (1987). *Color and light in man-made environments*. New York: Van Nostrand Reinhold Company.

Malnar, Joy Monice, & Vodvarka, Frank. (1992). *The interior dimension: A theoretical approach to enclosed space*. New York: John Wiley & Sons.

Marshall Editions Limited. (1980). *Color*. Los Angeles: Knapp Press.

Mayo Clinic. (2020). *Seasonal affective disorder (SAD)*. Retrieved from: https://www.mayoclinic.org/diseases-conditions/seasonal-affective-disorder/symptoms-causes/syc-20364651.

McCleary, Kathleen. (2002, September 29). Living colors. *USA Weekend*, p. 5.

McNeil, Patrick. (2007). *The design principle: Emphasis*. Retrieved from http://www.designmeltdown.com/chapters/Emphasis/.

Meerwein, Gerhard, Rodeck, Bettina, & Mahnke, Frank H. (2007). *Color: Communication in architectural space*. Base, Switzerland: Birkhäuser Verlag AG.

Morton, Jill. (1997). *A guide to color symbolism*. [Electronic version] Honolulu: Colorcom.

______. (2008). *Color matters for the home*. [Electronic version]. Honolulu: Colorcom.

______. (2004). *Global color clues and taboos*. [Electronic version]. Honolulu: Colorcom.

Munsell, Albert. (1905). *A color notation*. Boston: Geo. H. Ellis Co.

National Alliance on Mental Illness. (2020). *You are NOT alone*. https://www.nami.org/NAMI/media/NAMI-Media/Infographics /NAMI-You-Are-Not-Alone-FINAL.pdf.

National Association of Home Builders–NAHB. (2020). *Aging-in-place remodeling checklist*. Retrieved from: *https://www.nahb .org/Education-and-Events/Education/Designations/Certified -Aging-in-Place-Specialist-CAPS/Additional-Resources /Aging-In-Place-Remodeling-Checklist*.

National Association of Home Builders–NAHB (2002). *Remodeling for today & tomorrow: home modifications resource guide*. NAHB Research Center, Inc.

National Eye Institute. (2015). *Facts about color blindness*. Retrieved from https://nei.nih.gov/health/color_blindness /facts_about.

National Institute of Mental Health-NIMH. (2020). *Seasonal Affective Disorder*. Retrieved from: https://www.nimh.nih.gov /health/topics/seasonal-affective-disorder/index.shtml.

Native American Designs and Colors. (2011). Retrieved from http://indiancommission.state.nv.us/index6c2d.html ?option=com_content&task=view&id=1102&Itemid=27.

Native American Culture. (n.d.). Retrieved from http://indians.org /articles/native-american-cutlure.html.

Nelson, J. (2008). Household alters in contemporary Japan: Rectifying Buddhist "Ancestor Worship" with Home Décor and Consumer Choice. *Japanese Journal of Religious Studies*. doi: 10.18874/jjrs.35.2.2008.305–330

Nielson, Karla J., & Taylor, David A. (2007). *Interiors: An introduction* (4th ed.). New York: McGraw-Hill.

O'Connor, Z. (2011). Colour psychology and colour therapy: caveat emptor. *Color Research and Application 36*(3), 229–234.

Oh, J. H., Yang, S. J., & Do, Y. R. (2014). Healthy, natural, efficient and tunable lighting: four-package white LEDs for optimizing the circadian effect, color quality and vision performance. *Light: Science & Applications*, *3*(2). doi: 10.1038/lsa.2014.22.

Ormiston, Rosalind, & Robinson, Michael. (2007). *Colour source book*. London: Flame Tree Publishing.

Pathak, A. (2012, June). Color code: Interpretations and perceptions of colors in the world. Retrieved from https:// community.qlik.com/servlet/JiveServlet/previewBody /4505-102-3-5272/Color Code_Technical Brief.pdf.

Paron-Wildes, A. J. (2013). *Interior design for autism from childhood to adolescence*. Hoboken, NJ: John Wiley & Sons.

Pile, John. (1997). *Color in interior design*. New York: McGraw-Hill.

Platt, L. S., Bosch, S. J., & Kim, D. (2017). Toward a framework for designing person-centered mental health interiors for veterans. *Journal of Interior Design 42*(2) 27–48.

Paoletti, J. B. (2013). *Pink and blue: Telling the boys from the girls in America*. Indiana University Press.

Rengel, Roberto. (2007). *Shaping interior space* (2nd ed.). New York: Fairchild Publishers.

Robertson, A. R. (1968). Computation of correlated color temperature and distribution temperature. *Journal of the Optical Society of America*, *58*(11), 1528–1968.

Rompilla, Ethel. (2005). *Color for interior design*. New York: Harry N. Abrams.

Routio, Pentti. (2004, March 31). *Theory of design*. Retrieved from http://membres.lycos.fr/routio/122.htm.

Shepley, M. M., & Pasha, S. (2013, July 28). *Design Research and Behavioral Health Facilities*. The Center for Health Design. Retrieved from: https://www.healthdesign.org/sites/.

Silvis, J. (2012, October 11). Interior design use is alleviating depression and anxiety. *Healthcare Design Magazine*. Retrieved from: https://www.healthcaredesignmagazine.com /architecture/interior-design-use-alleviating-depression-and -anxiety/.

Simmons, D.R. (2012). Colour and emotion. In C.P. Biggam, C.A. Hough, C.J. Kay, and D.R. Simmons (Eds.), *New Directions in Colour Studies*. (pp. 395-414). Amsterdam: John Benjamins.

Singh, Satyendra. (2006). Impact of color on marketing. *Journal of Management Decision*, *44*(6), 783–789.

Skorinko, Jeanin L., Kemmer, Suzanne, Hebel, Michelle R., & Lane, David M. (2006). A rose by any other name . . . : Color-naming influences on decision making. *Psychology & Marketing*, *23*(12), 975–993.

Slotkis, Susan J. (2006). *Foundations of interior design*. New York: Fairchild Publications.

Smith, Dianne. (2003). Environmental colouration and/or the design process. *Color Research and Application*, *28*(5), 360–365.

______. (2008). Color-person-environment relationships. *Color Research and Application*, *33*(4) 312–319.

Stewart, Mary. (2008). *Launching the imagination: A comprehensive guide to basic design* (3rd ed.). New York: McGraw-Hill.

Stimpson, Miriam. (1987). *Modern furniture classics*. New York: Watson-Guptill Publications.

Stone, Nancy J., & English, Anthony J. (1998). Task type, posters, and workspace color on mood, satisfaction, and performance. *Journal of Environmental Psychology, 18(2)*, 175–185.

Tantanatewin, W., & Inkarojrit, V. (2016). Effects of color and lighting on retail impression and identity. *Journal of Environmental Psychology*, 46, 197– 205.

Tazawa, Yutaka. (1973). *Japan's cultural history: A perspective*. Japan: Ministry of Foreign Affairs.

Talking Sticks. (2011). Retrieved from http://www.iaismuseum.org/education/teacher-resources/crafts-talking-sticks.pdf.

Think Marketing. (2014, February 17). *How color affects buying behavior*. Retrieved from: https://thinkmarketingmagazine.com/how-color-affects-buying-behavior/.

United States Department of Justice. (2010) ADA Accessibility Guidelines–ADAAG. (2010). Retrieved from: https://www.ada.gov/regs2010/2010ADAStandards/2010ADAstandards.htm.

Uribes, Johanna. (2008). *Color—Does it really affect your mood?* Retrieved from http://www.johannauribes.com/freearticle1.php.

U.S. Census Bureau. (2010). *American Indian and Alaska native tribes in the United States and Puerto Rico: 2010*. Retrieved from http://www.census.gov/population/www/cen2010/cph-t/t-6tables/TABLE%20%281%29.pdf.

Varley, Helen. (Ed.). (1980). *Color*. Los Angeles, CA: Knapp Press.

Verhoeven, J. W. M., Pieterse, M. E., & Pruyn, A. T. H. (2006). Effects of Interior Color on Healthcare Consumers: A 360 degree Photo Simulation Experiment. *Advances in consumer research*, *33*(1), 292–293.

Versa. (n.d.). *Color symbolism by culture*. Retrieved from http://www.versacreative.com/au/vault/inside_design/colour_symbolism.htm.

Wiles, J. L., Leibing, A., Guberman, N., Reeve, J., & Allen, R. E. S. (2011). The Meaning of Aging in Place to Older People. *The Gerontologist*, *52*(3), 357–366. doi: 10.1093/geront/gnr098.

Wong, Wucius. (1997). *Principles of color design*. New York: John Wiley & Sons.

World Flags. (n.d.). *National Flag of Thailand*. Retrieved from http://www.world flags101.com/t/thailand-flag.aspx.

_____. (n.d.). *National Flag of South Africa*. Retrieved from http://www.world flags101.com/s/south-africa-flag.aspx.

World Health Organization (2020). *Mental health: strengthening our response*. Retrieved from: https://www.who.int/en/news-room/fact-sheets/detail/mental-health-strengthening-our-response.

Xerox. (2008). International Color Guide—Mexico, Mexico's Color Palette Is a Mix of Historical Associations and the Environment's Deeply Toned Offerings. Retrieved from http://www.office.xerox.com/small-business/tips/color-guide/mexico/enus.html.

Young, J. M. (2007, August 31). A summary of Color in Healthcare Environments: A Critical Review of the Research Literature. *Healthcare Design Magazine*. doi: https://www.healthcaredesignmagazine.com/architecture/summary-color-healthcare-environments-critical-review-research-literature/.

Zauderer, C., & Ganzer, C. A. (2015). Seasonal affective disorder: An overview. *Mental Health Practice*, *18*(9), 21–24.

Zelanski, Paul, & Fisher, Mary Pat. (1995). *Shaping space: The dynamics of three-dimensional design*. Belmont, CA: Wadsworth/Thomas Learning Publishing.

_____. (1999). *Color*. Upper Saddle River, NJ: Prentice Hall.

Zollinger, Heinrich. (1999). *Color: A multidisciplinary approach*. Weinheim, Germany: Wiley-VCH.

Zulu Beadwork Culture. (n.d.). Retrieved from http://zulubeadculture.weebly.com/symbols-and-meanings.html.

CREDITS

Frontis

Andreas von Einsiedel/The Image Bank Unreleased/Getty Images

Part 1

ferrantraite/E+/Getty Images

Chapter 1

1.1 Maisna | Dreamstime
1.2 Bernardo Martino | Dreamstime
1.3 Debra James | Dreamstime
1.4 Education Images/UIG/Getty Images
1.5 KaraGrubis/Getty Images
1.6 Jordi Angrill/Getty Images
1.7 Brigitte MERLE/Getty Images
1.8 Francoise CAVAZZANA/Gamma-Rapho via Getty Images
1.9 VanReeel/Getty Images
1.10 De Agostini/G. Dagli Orti/Getty Images
1.11a Carlos Sanchez Pereyra/The Image Bank Unreleased/Getty Images
1.11b Education Images/Universal Images Group via Getty Images
1.12 Hemis/Alamy
1.13a ivanastar/E+/Getty Images
1.13b Radius Images/Alamy
1.14 Walter Bibikow/Photolibrary/Getty Images
1.15 Digital Vision/Alamy
1.16 LOOK Photography/Upper Cut Images/Getty Images
1.17 Image Source/Getty images
1.18 Mary Baratto/iStock.com
1.19 lauradibiase/iStock.com
1.20a BUILT Images/Alamy
1.20b Buena Vista Images/Getty Images
1.21 liangpv/DigitalVision Vectors/Getty Images
1.22 commoner28th/iStock.com
1.23 ASIF HASSAN/AFP/Getty Images
1.24a Christine Osborne/CORBIS
1.24b Ocean Photography/Veer Images
1.25 Kypros/Moment/Getty Images
1.26 Sabino Parente Photographer - www.sabinoparente.com/Moment Open/Getty Images
1.27 Education Images/Universal Images Group via Getty Images
1.28 Kelly Cheng Travel Photography/Moment/Getty Images
1.29 Image Source/Getty Images
1.30 Cliff Parnell/Getty Images
1.31 Walter Bibikow/Getty Images
1.32 Education Images/Univeral Images Group/Getty Images
1.33 Bruno PEROUSSE/Gamma-Rapho via Getty Images
1.34 Buena Vista Images/Getty Images
1.35 DE AGOSTINI PICTURE LIBRARY/Getty Images
1.36 John Esperanza/Alamy
1.37 Zhang Peng/LightRocket via Getty Images
1.38 Image Source/Getty images
1.39 Kypros/Moment/Getty Images
1.40 Noppawat Tom Charoensinphon/Getty Images
1.41 Atid Kiattisaksiri/LightRocket via Getty Images
1.42 DeAgostini/Getty Images

Chapter 2

2.1 Fairchild Books
2.2 Encyclopaedia Britannica/UIG Via Getty Images
2.3 View Pictures/UIG via Getty Images
2.4 Ron Reed
2.5 Fairchild Books/Rendered by Yelena Safronova
2.7 JordiRamisa/E+/Getty Images
2.8 Peter Hermes Furian/Shutterstock.com
2.9 petrroudny/iStock.com
2.10 petrroudny/iStock.com
2.11 Artur Debat/Moment/Getty Images
2.12 gualtiero boffi/Shutterstock.com
2.13 modigia/Shutterstock.com
2.14 Jim Long/Fairchild Books
2.15 Imagenav/Getty Images
2.17 brightstars/Getty Images
2.21 Brad Barket/Getty Images
2.22 PeterHermesFurian/iStock.com

2.23 National Color Systems
2.25b serts/E+/Getty Images
2.26b Anthony Weller/View Pictures/Universal Images Group via Getty Images
2.27b Hufton+Crow/View Pictures/Universal Images Group via Getty Images
2.28b sesteven/Getty Images

Chapter 3

3.2 SSPL/Getty Images
3.3a Suzanna Ruby/FOAP/Getty Images
3.3b DeAgostini/Getty Images
3.3c Adam Jones/Getty Images
3.4 View Pictures/Universal Images Group via Getty Images
3.5 Courtesy of student Kelly Geister, El Centro College
3.6a View Pictures/UIG via Getty Images
3.6b De Agostini / G. Dagli Orti / Getty Images
3.8 Pieter Estersohn/Corbis Documentar/Getty Images
3.9 Eric Robert/Sygma/Sygma via Getty Images
3.10 Janet Lynn Ford
3.16 Alex Segre /Alamy
3.17 Alex Segre /Alamy
3.18 Westend61/Getty Images
3.19 anastasiia agafonova/Shutterstock.com
3.20a Courtesy of Charli Winston, Chuck Reed, Kathleen Shelton, and Kameron Thomas, El Centro College
3.20b Courtesy of Ryan Young, Vita Palmeri, and Bamma King, El Centro College
3.20c Courtesy of Jessie Dodd, Kristen Dow, and Lee Francis, El Centro College

Chapter 4

4.1 Nagel Photography/Shutterstock.com
4.2 Jeff Gritchen/Digital First Media/Orange County Register via Getty Images
4.3 View Pictures/Universal Images Group via Getty Images
4.4 Monkey Business Images/Shutterstock.com
4.5 Carruthers, H.R., Morris, J., Tarrier, N. et al. The Manchester Color Wheel: development of a novel way of identifying color choice and its validation in healthy, anxious and depressed individuals. BMC Med Res Methodol 10, 12 (2010). https://doi.org/10.1186/1471-2288-10-12
4.6 Elliot Kaufman/The Image Bank/Getty Images
4.7a HAFIZULLAHYATIM/Shutterstock.com
4.7b HAFIZULLAHYATIM/Shutterstock.com
4.8 kocakayaali/iStock
4.10 Irina Kuznetsova/Getty Images
4.11 kowalska-art/Getty Images
4.12 Fairchild Books/Rendered by Yelena Safronova
4.13 View Pictures/Universal Images Group via Getty Images
4.14 Fairchild Books/Rendered by Yelena Safronova
4.15 KeskiHeikkila/Shutterstock.com
4.16 View Pictures/Universal Images Group via Getty Images

Part 2

ferrantraite/E+/Getty Images

Chapter 5

5.1 Anthony Weller/View Pictures/Universal Images Group via Getty Images
5.2 View Pictures/Universal Images Group via Getty Images
5.6a–b Fairchild Books/Rendered by Steven Stankiewicz
5.12 piovesempre/Getty Images
5.14a–b Fairchild Books/Rendered by Steven Stankiewicz and Yelena Safronova
5.15a Craig Cozart/Getty Images
5.15b Craig Cozart/Getty Images/Image edited by Yelena Safronova
5.16 Ranplett/Getty Images
5.17 Gregory Rec/Portland Press Herald via Getty Images
5.18 Olaser/Getty Images
5.19 David H. Lewis/Getty Images
5.23 View Pictures/UIG via Getty Images

Chapter 6

6.1a Tooga/Getty Images
6.1b Renee Morris/Alamy
6.2 Tim Street-Porter/Beateworks/Corbis
6.3 ShutterWorx/Getty Images
6.4a Robert Daly/OJO Images/Getty Images
6.4b Julichka/Getty Images
6.4c Kenneth Johansson/Corbis Images
6.4d atese/Getty Images
6.5 Courtesy of student Julee Owens, University of North Texas
6.6a1 Pierre Arsenault/Alamy
6.6b1 imagebroker/Alamy
6.6c1 Miss Gracie B/Alamy
6.6d1 Luis Davilla/Getty Images
6.6 e1 David Q. Cavagnaro/Getty Images
6.6f Courtesy of student Candace Dolan, Allied ASID, Texas State University
6.7 Fancy/Veer/Corbis
6.8a–f Fairchild Books
6.9 DeAgostini/Getty Images
6.10 View Pictures/UIG via Getty Images
6.11 View Pictures/UIG via Getty Images
6.12 penguenstok/Getty Images
6.13 weberfoto/Alamy
6.14a–b Ferenc Szelepcsenyi/Alamy
6.15 Cleopatra Gomez/EyeEm/Getty Images
6.16a–b Fairchild Books/Rendered by Steven Stankiewicz
6.17 Bare Essence Photography/Alamy
6.18a–c Hero Images/Getty Images
6.19a–b Fairchild Books/Rendered by Steven Stankiewicz
6.20 View Pictures/UIG via Getty Images

Chapter 7

7.1a–b Fairchild Books
7.2 Dutchy/Getty images
7.3 Education Images/Universal Images Group via Getty Images
7.4a–b Nikada/Getty Images
7.5a–b Iconotec/Alamy
7.6a–b View Pictures/Universal Images Group via Getty Images
7.7 Arcaid/UIG via Getty Images
7.8a–b Floresco Productions/Corbis
7.9 View Pictures/Universal Images Group via Getty Images
7.10 View Pictures/Universal Images Group via Getty Images
7.11a–b Van Vendi/Alamy
7.12 View Pictures/Universal Images Group via Getty Images
7.13 MIGUEL ROJO/AFP/Getty Images
7.14 View Pictures/Universal Images Group via Getty Images
7.15 View Pictures/Universal Images Group via Getty Images

Chapter 8

8.1 Alan Thornton/Getty Images
8.2 Andrew Bret Wallis/Getty Images
8.5 Ramin Talaie/Corbis via Getty Image
8.6a–b tulcarion/E+/Getty Images
8.7 Chuck Eckert/Alamy
8.8a–b Fairchild Books/Rendered by Steven Stankiewicz
8.10 Schraps/ullstein bild/Getty Images
8.11 Maurice ROUGEMONT/Gamma-Rapho via Getty Images
8.12 Courtesy of Lindsay Perry, University of North Texas
8.13 Courtesy of Lindsay Perry, University of North Texas
8.14 Courtesy of Christina Masters
8.17 Jack Hobhouse/Alamy
8.18 Akira Kaede/Getty Images
8.19a Marion Smith/Alamy
8.19b SamCastro/iStock.com
8.20 trekandshoot | Dreamstime.com
8.22 View Pictures/UIG via Getty Images
8.23a Photo © Christie's Images / Bridgeman Images
8.23b Artifort
8.24a Darrell Gulin/Getty Images

Chapter 9

9.1b Pieter Esterso/Corbis Documentary/Getty Images
9.2 View Pictures/UIG via Getty Image
9.3 Franz-Marc Frei/The Image Bank/Getty Images
9.4 Fotosearch/Getty Images
9.6 Images courtesy of http://www.worqx.com © Janet Lynn Ford, 1998
9.7 ColorWheelArtist.com/ShirleyWilliamsArt.com
9.11 dpa picture alliance archive/Alamy
9.13 Fairchild Books/Rendered by Steven Stankiewicz and Yelena Safronova
9.15 Image provided courtesy of Claritas Consortium design group, Portland, Oregon, www.claritasconsortium.com.
9.16 Carol M. Highsmith/Buyenlarge/Getty Images
9.17 33523studio/Shutterstock.com
9.18a Fairchild Books/Rendered by Steven Stankiewicz
9.18b Fairchild Books/Rendered by Steven Stankiewicz and Yelena Safronova

Chapter 10

10.1 Gregory Rec/Portland Press Herald via Getty Images
10.2 HamsterMan/Shutterstock.com
10.3 David Livingston/Getty Images
10.4 Andrew Twort/Alamy
10.5 Fairchild Books/Rendered by Steven Stankiewicz
10.6 alacatr/iStock.com
10.7 Fairchild Books/Rendered by Steven Stankiewicz
10.9 Artur Debat/Getty Images
10.10 Hemis/Alamy
10.11 Tom Sibley/Corbis Documentary/Getty Images
10.12 Shana Novak/The Image Bank/Getty Images
10.13 oneinchpunch/Shutterstock.com
10.14 Clerkenwell/Getty Images
10.15 Imagemore Co., Ltd./Corbis
10.16 View Pictures/Universal Images Group via Getty Images
10.17 Courtesy Hailey Harrison, Texas State University

Any uncredited illustrations are by Fairchild Books.

INDEX

Note: Page numbers with f indicate figures; those with t indicate tables.

A

Aalto, Alvar, 63
achromatic, 43
achromatic color harmony, 166
adaptable design, 86
additive color, 31, 31f
Adjaye Associates, 57f, 161f, 188f
adults, color guidelines for older, 85–86
aging eye, 85
aging in place, 85
Albers, Josef, 39, 98
  color interactions, 61f
  Homage to Square, 40f
alternation, 117, 118–19f, 119
Alzheimer's disease, 135
Americans with Disabilities Act (ADA), 87, 87f
analogous, 43
  color harmony, 163–64, 163–64f
analogy, harmonies of, 159
anomaly, 134, 134f
anthropometrics, 151
anxiety, 77–80
Arnheim, Rudolph, 51
Art Deco style, 63
The Art of Color (Itten), 40
asymmetry, 98, 98f
attention deficit hyperactivity disorder (ADHD), 74–75, 80
autism spectrum disorder (ASD), 75, 80–81, 81f

B

bad design, *xv*
balance. *See also* color balance
  defined, *xvi*t, 94
  radial, 94, 95f
  symmetry and, 94
Baluch rugs, 12, 13f
bari, 12
Barragán, Luis, 8
beads, African culture, 16, 16f
Behavioral Health and Design Guide, 77, 82
Berber carpets, 14, 14f
Bezold effect, 62, 62f
Bighorn Medicine Wheel (Wyoming), 4–5, 5f
bio-inspired, 113, 113–14f
Birren, Faber, 41, 54, 158
Black Mountain College, 39
Brady, Jim, 174f
Breuer, Marcel, 63
Buddhism, 17, 18, 20

C

Calatrava, Santiago, 143, 144f
cataracts, 85
Chihuly, Dale, 175, 176f
China, color symbolism in, 21, 22t
chroma, 39
  3-D environment and, 104, 105f
chromatic, 43
chromatic scale, 162
chromotherapy, 82
circadian rhythm, 82
color
  aging in place, 85
  associations, 51–52, 60f
  association to moods and health, 75t
  defined, *xvi*t
  forecasting, 66–67
  history of, 63–64, 65f, 66
  influence of, 63–69
  myths and biases, 53–54, 55–56t
  perceptions, 51–52
  perceptual properties and associations, 55–56t
  personal choice, *xvii*
  responses, 52–53
  socially responsible use of, 192
  space and, 56–60
  for special populations, 85–86
  trends, 66–67
  vision and, 82–85
Color-aid®, 42
color and design elements, 179–90
  form and, 182–83
  line and, 179–80, 181f
  pattern and texture, 184–87, 184–88f
  shape and, 181–82, 182–83f
  time, 189f, 189–90
color associations, 51–52
color balance, 94–107
  balance defined, 94
  defined, 96
  hue, 98–99, 98–99f
  intensity contrast, 99–100, 100f
  overview of, 94
  size of color area, 100f, 100–101

types of, 96–101
value contrast as, 96–98, 97f, 98f
within 3-D environment, 101f, 101–7
color blindness, 83–85, 84f
The Color Compendium (Hope and Walch), 67
color concept diagram, 148f
color consumerism, 68–69
color contrasts, 61f, 61–63
Bezold effect, 62, 62f
guidelines for older adults, 85–86, 86f
perception tips and techniques, 63
signage design, 87f
simultaneous contrast, 61, 61f
color design process, *xiv*, *xv*, 50f, 50–51
color forecasting, 66–67
color grammar, 147, 148f, 149f
color harmonies/harmony, 158, 159–71
achromatic, 166
analogous, 163–64, 163–64f
color, space and, 168, 169f, 170
complementary, 161–62, 162f, 177f
complementary neutralization, 162f, 162–63
double complementary, 163, 163f
monochromatic, 160f, 160–61
multi-hue, 165–66, 166f
six elements of, 158–59
split complementary, 163, 163f
tetradic, 164–65, 165f
triadic, 164–65, 165f
twelve-hue chart, 167f
color interaction, 100
Color in Three-Dimensional Design (Kopacz), 174
Color in Vision (Birren), 41
color language, 43–45, 43–46f
Color Marketing Group, 66, 68
color-masking, 136, 136f
color myths and biases, 53–54, 55–56t
A Color Notation (Munsell), 39
Color of the Year, Pantone, 66, 67f
color perception, 51–52
natural/artificial light and, 33f, 36f, 36–37
quiz, 70t
color preferences, 70t
color psychology, 1
color rendering index (CRI), 33
color responses, 52–53
color symbolism, 3, 4
cross-cultural, 21, 22t
Native American tribes, 5–6, 7f
in United States, 4
color systems, 37–43, 38t
Albers and, 39, 40f, 42
Birren and, 41
Color-aid®, 42
digital color media, 42–43
historical development of, 37, 38t
Itten and, 40, 40f
Munsell and, 39, 39f
Natural Color System® (NCS®), 41f, 41–42
Newton and, 37, 38f
Pantone® and, 42
color theory, 25–46
additive color, 31, 31f, 83f
color language, 43–45, 43–46f
color mixing, 31, 31–32f
color rendering index (CRI) and, 33
color systems and, 37–43, 38t
defined, 26
history of, 193–97
Kelvin and, 32, 33, 34f
LED (light emitting diode), 32
light and, 26–37, 26–27f
light reflectance value and, 37, 37f
metamerism, 32
natural/artificial light and, 33f, 36f, 36–37
properties of light, 29–31
subtractive color, 31–32, 31–32f
complementary, 43, 43f, 46f
color harmony, 161–62, 162f, 177f
complementary neutralization, 162f, 162–63
complements, hue balance, 98–99, 98–99f
cones, 83, 83f
continuation, 120
contrast
defined, 126, 176
harmonies of, 159
value, 96–98, 97–98f
contrast, emphasis with, 126–35
anomaly and, 134, 134f
color dominance and, 132–34, 133f
design feature, 131, 131f
focal point and, 132–34, 133f
hue and value, 129, 130–31f
for safety and welfare, 134–35, 135f
texture and, 131–32, 132f
through location and isolation, 127–29, 127–29f
Cranz, Galen, 155
culture and color, 3–23
in China, 21, 22t
in Egypt, 21, 22t
in India, 21, 22t
in Ireland, 21, 22t
in Italy, 10–11
in Japan, 17–19
in Korea, 21, 22t
in Mexico, 7–10
in Morocco, 13–15
in Native America, 4–6
in Pakistan, 12, 13f
in South Africa, 15–17
in Thailand, 20–21

D

damask, 181
da Vinci, Leonardo, 10, 151
Day of the Dead, 10
Department of Homeland Security, 52
depression, 77–80
design. *See also* color and design elements
contrast of, 131, 131f
principles and elements of, *xv*, *xvii*, 91
design for access
adaptable design, 86
Americans with Disabilities Act (ADA), 87, 87f
color and, 86–88
universal design, 87–88
wayfinding, 87, 87f
deuteranopia, 84, 84f
diffraction, 29, 30f
digital color media, 42–43
direct color, 29
discord, defined, 158
double complementary color harmony, 163, 163f
Dubé, Richard, 112

E

Egypt, color symbolism in, 21, 22t
electromagnetic spectrum, light, 27, 27f
The Elements of Color (Itten), 40
emphasis, 126–37. *See also* contrast, emphasis with
color and, 127–29
defined, *xvii*, 126
design tips, 135–36
focal point and, 132–34, 133f
with contrast, 126–35
evidence-based design, 74

F

fad, 67
faux finishes, 184
Fawn Lep, 21, 21f

Fibonacci Sequence, 141f, 146, 150, 150f, 154
fingernail dance, 21, 21f
focal point, emphasis with, 132–34, 133f
Ford, Janet, 142
forecasting, color, 66–67
form
  color and, 182–83
  defined, *xvi*t
Frederick, Matthew, 110
Froebel, Frederick, 147
Froebel blocks, 147
functional color, 54
fusuma, 18, 18f

G

Geffrye Museum, 64f, 65f
Gehry, Frank, 180, 181f
Gerritsen, Frans, 45
glossary, 198–201
glossy, 187
Goethe, Johann Wolfgang von, 45, 111
Golden Age of Hollywood, 63
golden rectangle, 149f
golden section, 146, 149, 154
good design, *xv*
Google SketchUp, 63
Gorman, Carolyn, 54
Gropius, Walter, 39, 181

H

harmony. *See also* color harmonies/harmony
  color, space and, 168, 169f, 170
  defined, *xvi*t, 158
health
  anxiety and depression, 77–80
  attention deficit hyperactivity disorder (ADHD), 74–75, 80
  autism spectrum disorder (ASD), 75, 80–81, 81f
  color and, 74–81
  color and light therapy, 82
  defined, 75
  International WELL Building Institute (IWBI), 81
  mental health and well-being, 74–75, 76–77f, 77
  relationship and association of color to moods and, 75t
  seasonal affective disorder (SAD), 82
history of color, 63–64, 64–65f, 66
Hoffman, J. L., 111
Hope, Augustine, 67
horizontal/vertical space, 3-D environment and, 101–2, 102–3f
hue, 39
  color balance, 98–99, 98–99f
  contrast of value and, 129, 130–31f
  rhythm and, 122–23
human eye, cones and rods, 83, 83f

I

India, color symbolism in, 21, 22t
indirect color, 29
intensity contrast, 99–100, 100f
Interaction of Color (Albers), 39, 98
interest, variety and, 175–76, 177f, 178–79, 179f
The Interior Dimension (Arnheim), 111
International WELL Building Institute (IWBI), 81, 192
Ireland, color symbolism in, 21, 22t
Italy
  culture and color in, 10–11
  flag of, 10, 10f
Itten, Johannes, 40, 58
  color contrasts, 61f
  color star by, 40f

J

Jacobsen, Arne, 153, 153f
Japan
  culture and color, 17–19, 17–19f
  flag of, 19, 19f
Jeanneret-Gris, Charles Édouard, 151

K

kalamandi, 12
Kelvin, 32, 33, 34f
Kente cloth, 17, 17f
Knight, Terry, 147
Koolhaas, Rem, 132, 132f, 142f
Korea, color symbolism in, 21, 22t

L

Laporte, Georges, 153, 153f
Latin America, culture and color, 7, 7f
Leadership in Energy and Environmental Design (LEED), 192
Le Corbusier, 63, 151, 151f
LED (light emitting diode), 32
Legorreta, Ricardo, 8, 9f
Le Modulor, 151f, 151–52
light. *See also* color theory
  color theory, 26–37
  electromagnetic spectrum, 27, 27f
  nanometers, 27, 27t
  natural/artificial, 33f, 36f, 36–37
  properties of, 29–31
  reflection and, 29, 30f
  refraction and, 29, 30f
  visible spectrum of color, 26f
  wavelengths of visible, 27t
light reflectance value, 37, 37f
light therapy, color and, 82
line
  color and, 179–80, 181f
  color and, as rhythm, 121–22, 122f
  defined, *xvi*t
location and isolation, emphasis through, 127–29, 127–29f
lux, 82

M

machine age, 63
Mackintosh, Charles Rennie, 147, 147f
Manchester Color Wheel, 78, 78f, 79
Mangold, Robert, 146
Masters, Christina, 148
matte, 187
Mayoun, 12
medicine wheel, 4
  Bighorn Medicine Wheel (Wyoming), 4–5, 5f
  hand-crafted Native American, 5f
Mehendi, 12
memo samples, 34
Memphis Group, 64
mental health, well-being and, 74–75, 76–77f, 77
Mental Health Facilities Design Guide, 75
metamerism, 32
Mexico
  color and culture in, 7f, 7–10, 9–10f
  Day of the Dead, 10
  flag of, 8, 8f
  Spanish colonial interiors and, 8, 8f
  Talavera tiles, 7f, 8, 9f
Michelangelo, 10
mind, concept of, 81
Mondrian, Piet, 135, 146
monochromatic, 44
  color harmony, 160f, 160–61
Morocco
  culture and color, 13–15, 14–15f
  flag of, 13, 14f
multi-hue color harmony, 165–66, 166f
multiple-color overload, 105–7, 106f
Munsell, Albert H., 39, 78
  color space, 39f
  color tree system, 39f
  value scale, 96, 97f, 145
Museum of the Home, 64–65f
music, color and, 111–12
myths and biases, color, 53–54, 55–56t

N

nanometers, 27, 27t
National Alliance on Mental Illness (NAMI), 74
National Association for Home Builders Research Center, 86
National Association of Psychiatric Health Systems, 77
Native America
  color symbolism, 5–6, 7f
  medicine wheel, 4, 5f
Natural Color System® (NCS®), 41f, 41–42
natural light, color and light therapy, 82
nature
  proportion and, 150, 152–54f, 152–55
  rhythm and, 112–13, 113–14f, 115
Navajo blanket, 6, 7f
Navajo Indian Gourd Dance, 6f
Newton, Isaac, 37
  color wheel, 38f
  refracted colors, 38f

O

Ong, Diana, 146
Opticks (Newton), 37
Ostwald, Wilhelm, 45
Owens, Julee, 114f

P

Pakistan
  culture and color, 12, 13f
  flag of, 12, 12f
  kalamandi and, 12, 13f
  marriage in, 12, 13f
palette, 58, 59f, 67f
  bio-inspired, 113, 113–14f
  color, and nature, 113, 114f
  color trends and forecasting, 66–67, 67f
  complementary, 161–62, 162f
  Fibonacci Sequence, 150f
  history of color, 63–64, 66, 67f
  in Mexican architecture, design, and arts, 8, 9f
  of Moroccan culture, 14–15, 15f
  multiple-color overload, 105–7, 106f
  natural light and, 36–37
  single-color overload, 104–5, 106f
Panton, Verner, 113, 113f
Pantone®, 42
  color of the year, 66, 67f
pattern
  color and, 184–87, 184–88f
  defined, *xvit*, 184
  element of design, 184–87, 184–88f
Paulin, Pierre, 153, 153f
perception, visual, of color, 57
Perry, Lindsay, 148
Pisano, Leonardo, 150
primary hues, 43, 46f
Prince-Ramus, Joshua, 142f
Principles of Color (Birren), 158
programming, 50
progression, 115f, 119–20, 119–20f
proportion
  color and, 140–43
  color and scale, 145–46
  defined, *xvit*, 140
  Fibonacci Sequence, 146, 150, 150f
  golden section, 146, 149
  Le Modulor and, 151–52
  nature and, 150, 152–54f, 152–55
protanopia, 84, 84f
PTSD (post-traumatic stress disorder), 79
pure hue, 43, 43f

R

radial balance, 94, 95f
radiation, 121, 121f
Rainbow Nation, 15
Raphael, 10
recoloration, 58, 58f
red, yellow, blue (RYB) pigment system, 158
reflection, 29, 30f
refraction, 29, 30f
Rehberger, Tobias, 136f
repetition, 115–17f, 116–17
rhythm
  alternation and, 117, 118–19f, 119
  color and line as, 121–22
  color and music, 111–12
  continuation or transition, 120
  defined, *xvit*, 110
  hue and, 122–23
  nature and, 112–13, 113–14f, 115
  progression and, 115f, 119–20, 119–20f
  radiation, 121, 121f
  repetition and, 115–17f, 116–17
  types of, 115–22, 116f
  vibrancy, 117, 118f
rods, 83, 83f
Routio, Pentti, *xiv*

S

sacred hoop, 4–5, 5f
safety and welfare, 134–35, 135f
Saltillo, 8
satin finishes, 184
scale
  color and, 145–46
  defined, *xvit*, 140
  perception of, 145–46
scheme, 160
seasonal affective disorder (SAD), 82
secondary hues, 43, 46f
shade, 43, 43f
shalwar kameez, 12
shape, 60f
  color and, 181–82, 182–83f
  defined, *xvit*
sherwani, 12
simultaneous contrast, 61, 61f
single-color overload, 104–5, 106f
Smith, Dianne, 50
Songkran, 21, 21f
South Africa
  beads in culture, 16, 16f
  culture and color, 15–17, 16–17f
  flag of, 15, 15f
space, 56
  color, harmony and, 168, 169f, 170
  color and, 56–60
  defined, *xvit*
Spanish colonial interiors, Mexico, 8, 8f
split complementary, 44, 44f
  color harmony, 163, 163f
subtractive color, 31–32, 31–32f
symmetry, 94

T

Talavera, 7f, 8, 9f
talking feather, 6, 6f
talking stick, 6
tatami mats, 151f, 151–52
tertiary hues, 43
tetradic, 44, 46f
tetradic color harmonies, 164–65, 165f
texture
  color and, 184–87, 184–88f
  contrast of, 131–32, 132f
  defined, *xvit*, 184
Thailand
  culture and color, 20–21, 20–21f
  Fawn Lep in, 21, 21f
  flag of, 20, 20f
  Songkran festival in, 21, 21f
  Theravada Buddhism in, 20
Theravada Buddhism, 20
thermochromatic, 68
3-D environment
  chroma/value factor, 104, 105f
  color balance within, 101f, 101–7
  multiple-color overload, 105–7, 106f

3-D environment *(continued)*
single-color overload, 104–5, 106f
vertical/horizontal space and, 101–2, 102–3f
time
color and, 189f, 189–90
definition, *xvi*t
tint, 43, 43f
tone, 43, 43f
trends, color, 66–67
triadic, 44, 45f
triadic color harmonies, 164–65, 165f
tritanopia, 84, 84f

U
uniform connectedness, 159
United States Green Building Council, 192
unity, *xvi*t, 158
universal design, 87–88

V
value, 39
value contrast
color balance, 96–98, 97–98f
hue and, 129, 130–31f
Munsell value scale and, 96, 97f, 145
one color like two principle, 98
van der Rohe, Mies, 63, 166
van Doesberg, Theo, 146
variety in design, 174. *See also* color and design elements
color and, 179–90
defined, 174
definition, *xvi*t
interest and, 175–76, 177f, 178–79, 179f
vertical/horizontal space, 3-D environment and, 101–2, 102f, 103f
vibrancy, 117, 118f
visible spectrum, 26f, 27
vision
aging eye and, 85
color and, 82–85
color blindness, 83–85
cones, 83, 83f
human eye and, 83, 83f
rods, 83, 83f
visitability, 87
von Bezold, Wilhelm, 62

W
Walch, Margaret, 67
wayfinding, 87, 87f
weather satellite, 52f
welfare and safety, 134–35, 135f
well-being
defined, 75
mental health and, 74–75, 76–77f, 77
World Health Organization, 75
Wright, Frank Lloyd, 63, 116, 116f, 152

Y
Yale University School of Art, 39

Z
Zulu beadwork, 16, 16f

Made in the USA
Columbia, SC
03 September 2020